T0315489

Software Quality

About IEEE Computer Society

IEEE Computer Society is the world's leading computing membership organization and the trusted information and career-development source for a global workforce of technology leaders including: professors, researchers, software engineers, IT professionals, employers, and students. The unmatched source for technology information, inspiration, and collaboration, the IEEE Computer Society is the source that computing professionals trust to provide high-quality, state-of-the-art information on an on-demand basis. The Computer Society provides a wide range of forums for top minds to come together, including technical conferences, publications, and a comprehensive digital library, unique training webinars, professional training, and the TechLeader Training Partner Program to help organizations increase their staff's technical knowledge and expertise, as well as the personalized information tool myComputer. To find out more about the community for technology leaders, visit http://www.computer.org.

IEEE/Wiley Partnership

The IEEE Computer Society and Wiley partnership allows the CS Press authored book program to produce a number of exciting new titles in areas of computer science, computing, and networking with a special focus on software engineering. IEEE Computer Society members continue to receive a 15% discount on these titles when purchased through Wiley or at wiley.com/ieeecs.

To submit questions about the program or send proposals, please contact Mary Hatcher, Editor, Wiley-IEEE Press: Email: mhatcher@wiley.com, Telephone: 201-748-6903, John Wiley & Sons, Inc., 111 River Street, Hoboken, NJ 07030-5774.

Software Quality
Concepts and Practice

Daniel Galin

WILEY

Registered Office

John Wiley & Sons, Inc., 111 River Street, Hoboken, NJ 07030, USA

Editorial Office

111 River Street, Hoboken, NJ 07030, USA

For details of our global editorial offices, customer services, and more information about Wiley products visit us at www.wiley.com.

Wiley also publishes its books in a variety of electronic formats and by print-on-demand. Some content that appears in standard print versions of this book may not be available in other formats.

Library of Congress Cataloging-in-Publication Data

Names: Galin, Daniel, author.
Title: Software quality : concepts and practice / by Daniel Galin.
Description: Hoboken, NJ : John Wiley & Sons, 2017. | Includes
   bibliographical references and index. |
Identifiers: LCCN 2017039554 (print) | LCCN 2017044698 (ebook) | ISBN
   9781119134503 (pdf) | ISBN 9781119134510 (epub) | ISBN 9781119134497
   (cloth)
Subjects: LCSH: Computer software–Quality control.
Classification: LCC QA76.76.Q35 (ebook) | LCC QA76.76.Q35 G35 2017 (print) |
   DDC 005.3028/7–dc23
LC record available at https://lccn.loc.gov/2017039554

Cover Design: Wiley
Cover Images: (Codes) © Degui Adil/EyeEm/Gettyimages; (Three Checks) © NuStock/Gettyimages

Set in 10/12pt TimesLTStd-Roman by Thomson Digital, Noida, India

10   9   8   7   6   5   4   3   2   1

To my beloved family,
Amira, Michal, Yoav, Guy and Maayan.
I love all of them.

Contents

19. IMPROVEMENT PROCESSES – CORRECTIVE AND PREVENTIVE ACTIONS   **404**

20. SOFTWARE PROCESS ASSURANCE ACTIVITIES FOR EXTERNAL PARTICIPANTS   **421**

21. SOFTWARE PROCESS QUALITY METRICS   **448**

Preface

The following software "glitches" seem very real:

- Thousands of the US students in numerous cities around the United States had just taken their examination. Tired and excited, they pressed the submit button only to find that their answers could not be uploaded with the software (purchased specifically for this purpose). As expected, the anger, utter frustration, and disappointment of the students turned into a flood of lawsuits against the exam software company.

- More than 24 inmates from a US jail were wrongly released, among them were prisoners jailed for violent crimes. The faulty release was caused by the erroneous release of documents that were produced by a new software system recently implemented to manage the institute's records. According to the spokesman of the county jail, the mistake was due to glitches in the software, which caused the misprocessing of a number of input documents. The early detection of the software failure prevented a much higher number of faulty inmate releases.

- A software failure in an income tax collection system caused millions of citizens to use the wrong tax code in the income tax site program. This mistake caused many people to pay less than required, and many to pay more than required. Unfortunately, it took a whole year to identify the failure. Naturally, the inevitable happened, and the income tax department now faces innumerable filings for tax returns. Only when these return procedures have concluded, will the income tax department be able to estimate the total damage caused by the software failure.

The above are just a sample of glitches that happen every day. These software failures have the potential to cause substantial damages. Every single one of them could have been eliminated, or practically eliminated, if only the software project teams would have performed appropriate software quality assurance processes, and SQA professionals would have carried out properly the required process coordination, follow-up, and evaluation tasks. These software quality assurance processes, and many more, are the contents of my book *Software Quality: Concepts and Practice*.

The book structure

The book is structured in six parts that follow the IEEE Std. 730:2014 outline:

Part I: Introduction – Presents definitions and topics associated with software quality.

Part II: SQA Process Implementation Activities –Dedicated to software quality assurance activities of the SQA function, and includes establishing the SQA processes in the organization, planning the SQA activities, and the application of software quality costs.

Part III: Product Assurance Activities for Conformance – Deals with evaluation and product quality measurement.

Part IV: Process Assurance Activities for Conformance – Discusses process quality evaluation and measurement, process improvements, and also the assessment of staff skills and knowledge and the required training.

Part V: Additional Tools and Methods Supporting Software Quality – Presents configuration management, CASE tools, and the topic of templates and checklists – all of significant contribution to achieve software quality requirements.

Part VI: Appendices – Presents basic software quality and software engineering topics associated with SQA: software engineering and SQA standards and models and project progress control. This part also includes a review of software development methodologies and processes, and their quality assurance activities.

Unique features of this book

The following key features of this book are of special importance:

a. **A broad view of SQA.** The book delves extensively into the SQA subject matter and covers issues much beyond the classic boundaries of custom-made software development by large established software houses. It dedicates significant attention to issues related to in-house software development, subcontractors, suppliers of readymade software, and other external participants in the software development process, and also covers small software projects.

b. **An up-to-date wide range coverage of SQA and SQA-related topics.** The book provides comprehensive coverage on a wide range of SQA and SQA-related subjects, and includes topics that are rarely discussed in SQA texts. These include procedures and work instructions, tools and supporting techniques such as templates and checklists, documentation control, staff certification, and cost of software quality.

c. **A comprehensive discussion of new technology and methodology topics.** The text covers extensively the current SQA topics, and discusses the impact of new software development methodologies, computerized SQA tools, and international SQA standards.

d. **A thorough presentation of the SQA function.** and its tasks Establishes the SQA processes, planning, coordinating, follow-up, reviewing and evaluation of SQA processes performed by software process teams and others.

e. **Special emphasis on the SQA plan and project plan topics.** The processes of preparing and updating the plans and their implementation are discussed in detail.

f. **Special attention is given to SQA implementation issues.**

g. Throughout the book a focus is placed on implementation issues in specialized chapter sections, examples, implementation tips and topics for discussion. **Consistent structure in each chapter:**

   A mini case study at the beginning followed by subject matter that includes examples, summary, selected bibliography, review questions, and topics for discussion – the book is tailor-made for semester classes in software engineering programs, and should prove to be very useful as a textbook for many different courses.

h. **An Instructor's Guide**

The author's former book on SQA

The author's former book *Software Quality Assurance: From Theory to Implementation*, (Addison-Wesley, 2004) had a wide readership and was also adopted as a textbook for a variety of courses in numerous faculties at higher education institutes and professional training and hi-tech upskill courses around the world.

The current book differs from the previous (2004) book mainly in the following ways:

- The book's topics themselves and their coverage have been updated according to technological and methodological developments.
- New topics have been added to the already wide variety of subjects covered by the 2004 book.
- The subject of SQA function has received substantially more attention, and the book provides a thorough presentation of the SQA function and its tasks.
- The structure of the book now follows the IEEE Std. 730: 2014 outline.
- The readability of the book has been improved, notably by the many mini cases that open the chapters.

The book's audience

The book is intended to address challenges faced by a wide audience interested in software quality assurance. The five main audience types are as follows:

- University and college students
- Software engineering practitioners, naturally involved in quality issues of software development and maintenance
- Practitioners of software quality assurance
- Vocational training course – students and lecturers
- Managers of software development departments, project managers, and others

Special interest groups of readers

- **Readers interested in the ISO 9000-3 Standard.**
- **Readers interested in the ASQ Certified software quality engineers (CSQE) body of knowledge.**
- Readers interested in the QAI (Quality Assurance Institute) CSQA CBOK (Certified Software Quality Analyst common body of knowledge).

Readers of both interest groups will find comprehensive discussions on both topics throughout the book.

The Instructor's Guide

An Instructor's Guide that includes PowerPoint presentations for each of the book's chapters has been prepared by the author.

The guide is available to instructors who have adopted the book for a course. It can be obtained by sending an email to ieeeproposals@wiley.com.

Acknowledgments

I would like to take this opportunity to express my heartfelt gratitude to all those who helped me write this book. This book has benefited from practical experience gained from consulting projects, and greatly from interactions with students throughout numerous sessions and courses. I have not listed all the names here, albeit I am grateful to each and every one of them.

I owe many thanks to my reviewers for their important comments that contributed greatly to this book.

Special thanks to Ms. Mary Hatcher, Editor at Wiley-IEEE Press for her cooperation, guidance, and valuable advice throughout the writing and publishing process. I would also like to express my appreciation and thanks to Victoria Bradshaw, Vishnu Narayanan, and Melissa Yanuzzi at Wiley, as well as Abhishek Sarkari at Thomson Digital typesetter, responsible for production of this book.

I wish to express my appreciation to Lisa Harel, who edited my drafts with devotion and contributed substantially to their readability and accuracy.

Finally, I wish to express my gratitude to my family: my wife, Amira Galin, who is a constant source of inspiration, has always encouraged scientific thinking and is a role model, and my daughter, Michal, and my son, Yoav, for their continuous support, important comments on the book's drafts, and for always believing.

About the Author

Dr. Daniel Galin received his BSc in Industrial and Management Engineering, and his MSc and DSc in Operations Research from the Faculty of Industrial Engineering and Management, the Technion – Israel Institute of Technology, Haifa, Israel.

He acquired his expertise in SQA through many years of consulting, teaching, and writing in the field. His courses include software quality assurance, analysis and design of information systems, and strategic information systems. Dr. Galin has been a member of staff at the faculty of the Lander Institute in Jerusalem and the Ruppin Academic Center, where he headed the Information Systems Studies.

Dr. Galin published a book entitled *Software Quality Assurance: From Theory to Implementation* (Addison-Wesley, 2004), and an earlier book on the same topic, coauthored with Dr. Z. Bluvband, entitled *Software Quality Assurance,* (Opus, 1995 – in Hebrew). Many of his papers have been published in English language professional journals. Dr. Galin has also authored additional books in Hebrew, which were published by Israel's leading publishers.

Guides for Special Groups of Readers

Among the readers interested in software quality assurance, one can distinguish two **special groups:**

- Readers interested in the ASQ (American Society for Quality) CSQE BOK E (Certified Software Quality Engineer body of knowledge).
- Readers interested in the QAI (Quality Assurance Institute) CSQA CBOK (Certified Software Quality Analyst common body of knowledge).

Guide to the ASQ's CSQE body of knowledge

Almost all the elements of the CSQE (Certified Software Quality Engineer) body of knowledge, as outlined in ASQ (American Society for Quality), are available in the book. The following table directs the reader to the relevant chapters and sections.

CSQE BOK 2016 Table

CSQE BOK chapter		CSQE BOK subject	Book reference
I. General knowledge	A	Benefits of software quality engineering	Section 1.1, Chapter 18
	B	Ethical and legal compliance	—
	C	Standards and models	Appendices A and B
	D	Leadership skills	Chapter 4
	E	Team skills	Chapter 23
II. Software quality management	A	Quality management system	Sections 6.1, 7.4, 20.3, and 20.5, Chapter 11
	B	Methodologies	Chapters 9, 13, and 19
	C	Audits	Sections 6.2, 12.4, and 15.5
III. System and software engineering	A	Lifecycle and process models	Appendices .D.1, D.3, and D.5
	B	System architecture	—
	C	Requirement engineering	Chapter 2
	D	Requirement management	Chapter 22
	E	Software analysis, design and development	Chapter 2, Appendix D
	F	Maintenance management	Chapter 15

(continued)

(Continued)

CSQE BOK chapter		CSQE BOK subject	Book reference
IV. Project management	A	Planning, scheduling, and deployment	Sections 7.4–7.6
	B	Tracking and controlling	Section 6.2, Appendix C
	C	Risk management	Section 7.4
V. Software metrics and analysis	A	Process and product measurement	Chapters 16 and 21
	B	Analysis and reporting techniques	—
VI. Software verification and validation	A	Theory	Chapters 12 and 14
	B	Test planning and design	Chapter 14, Section 20.5 and 20.6
	C	Reviews and inspections	Chapter 13
	D	Test execution documents	Sections 14.7 and 14.8
VII. Software configuration management	A	Configuration infrastructure	Section 25.3
	B	Configuration identification	Section 25.2
	C	Configuration control and status accounting	Section 25.6
	D	Configuration audits	Section 25.9
	E	Product release and distribution	Sections 25.3, 25.7, and 25.8

Guide to the QAI's CSQA common body of knowledge

Almost all the elements of the CSQA (Certified Software Quality Analyst) common body of knowledge, as outlined in the QAI (Quality Assurance Institute), are available in the book. The following table directs the reader to the relevant chapters and sections.

CSQA CBOK 2012 Table

CSQA CBOK chapter		CSQA CBOK subject	Book reference
SC1. Quality principles and conceptions	1.1	Vocabulary of quality	Section1.1
	1.2	The different views of quality	Section 1.1, Chapter 2
	1.3	Quality concepts and practices	Section 1.3,
	1.4	Quality control and quality assurance	Section 1.6
	1.5.	Quality pioneers approach to quality	—

(*Continued*)

CSQA CBOK chapter		CSQA CBOK subject	Book reference
SC2. Quality leadership	2.1	Leadership concepts	Section 6.2
	2.2	Quality management infrastructure	Chapter 4
	2.3	Quality environment	Section 3.3
SC3. Quality baseline	3.1	Quality baseline concepts	Section 25.2
	3.2	Methods used for establishing baselines	Section 25.3
	3.3	Models and assessment fundamentals	Appendices B.5 and B.6
	3.4	Industry quality models	Appendices A and B
SC4. Quality assurance	4.1	Establishing a function to promote and manage quality	Sections 3.3, 4.5, Chapter 6
	4.2	Quality tools	Appendix C
	4.3	Process deployment	—
	4.4	Internal auditing and quality assurance	Appendix C.5
SC5. Quality planning	5.1	Planning concepts	Sections 7.2 and 7.4
	5.2	Integrating business and quality planning	—
	5.3	Prerequisites to quality planning	Section 7.3
	5.4	The planning to mature IT work processes	Section 7.4, Appendices B.5.3 and B.6.3
SC6. Define, build, implement, and improve work processes	6.1	Process management concepts	Section 18.1
	6.2	Process management processes	—
SC7. Quality control practices	7.1	Testing concepts	Section 14.1
	7.2	Developing testing methodologies	Section 14.3
	7.3	Verification and validation methods	Sections 14.5 and 14.6
	7.4	Software change control	Chapter 22
	7.5	Defect management	Section 21.3

(*continued*)

(Continued)

CSQA CBOK chapter	CSQA CBOK subject		Book reference
SC8. Metrics and measurements	8.1	Measurement concepts	Section 16.2.1
	8.2	Measurement in software	Chapters 16 and 21
	8.3	Variation and process capability	Appendices B.5.2 and B.6.3
	8.4	Risk management	Section 7.3, Appendix C.3
	8.5	Implementing and measurement program	Section 16.2.4 and 21.7
SC9. Internal control and security	9.1	Principles and concepts of internal control	Section 6.1
	9.2	Risk and internal control models	—
	9.3	Building internal controls	Chapter 6
	9.4	Building adequate security	—
SC10. Outsourcing, COTS, and contracting quality	10.1	Quality and outside software	Sections 20.3 and 20.4
	10.2	Selecting COTS software	Sections 20.5 and 20.6
	10.3	Selecting software developed by outside organizations	Section 20.5.1
	10.4	Contracting for software developed by outside organizations	Sections 20.5.1 and 20.6.1
	10.5	Operating for software developed by outside organizations	Section 20.3 and 20.6.2

Part I

Introduction

The opening part of the book presents definitions and background subjects related to software quality:

- SQA – definitions and concepts (Chapter 1)
- Software quality factors (attributes) (Chapter 2)
- SQA challenges (Chapter 3)
- Organization for assuring software quality (Chapter 4)
- An additional chapter, Chapter 5, presents "the world of SQA", an overview of the book.

Chapter 1

SQA – Definitions and Concepts

1.1 Software quality and software quality assurance – definitions

We shall Start by delving into our target topic of software quality and discuss the following basic definitions:

- Software quality
- Software quality assurance (SQA)
- Software quality assurance – an expanded definition
- The objectives of SQA activities

The definition of software quality is shown in Frame 1.1.

Frame 1.1: Software quality – a definition

Source: IEEE Std. 730-2014 (IEEE, 2014)

Software quality is
The degree to which a software product meets established requirements; however, quality depends upon the degree to which established requirements accurately represent stakeholder needs, wants, and expectations.

Two aspects of software quality are presented in the above definition: one is meeting the requirements, while the other is generating customer/stakeholder satisfaction. A high quality software product is expected to meet all written development requirements – whether defined fully before the development began, or later in the course of the development process – and to meet the relevant regulations and professional conventions. Quality is also achieved through fulfillment of stakeholder needs and wants.

Software Quality: Concepts and Practice, First Edition. Daniel Galin.
© 2018 the IEEE Computer Society, Inc. Published 2018 by John Wiley & Sons, Inc.

Software quality assurance – definition

One of the most commonly used definitions of SQA is proposed by the IEEE, cited in Frame 1.2.

Frame 1.2: Software quality assurance – a definition

Source: IEEE Std. 730-2014

Software quality assurance is
A set of activities that define and assess the adequacy of software process to provide evidence that establishes confidence that the software processes are appropriate for and produce software products of suitable quality for their intended processes. A key attribute of SQA is the objectivity of the SQA function with respect to the project. The SQA function may also be organizationally independent of the project, that is, free from technical, managerial, and financial pressures from the project.

This definition may be characterized by the following:

- Plan and implement systematically. SQA is based on the planning and implementation of a series of activities that are integrated into all stages of the software development process. These activities are performed in order to substantiate the client's confidence that the software product will meet all the technical requirements.
- Refer to the software development products keeping the specified technical requirements and suitability for stake holder's intended use. However, it does not include quality of the operation services.
- Refer to the technical appropriateness of the development process. However, important attributes of the development process, namely schedule and budget keeping, are not included. It is noteworthy that:
  a. The appropriateness of project schedule and budget is a major issue in SQA as can be seen by requirement for performing contract reviews and project planning.
  b. The major part of project progress control procedures, given to the issues of schedule and budget.
  c. The close relationships that exist between software product quality, project schedule, and project budget, where schedule and budget failures result, almost always, in unavoidable software quality failure.

An extended SQA definition was created considering the importance of the quality of the software operation and the important effect of schedule and budget keeping on the software quality product.

The resulting expanded SQA definition is shown in Frame 1.3.

Frame 1.3: Software quality assurance – an expanded definition

Software quality assurance
A set of activities that define and assess the adequacy of software process to provide evidence that establishes confidence that the software processes are appropriate for producing software products of suitable quality, for their intended processes, or for their intended operation services and fulfils the requirements of schedule and budget keeping

The objectives of SQA activities

The objectives of SQA activities refer to the functional and managerial aspects of software development and software maintenance. These objectives are listed in Frame 1.4.

Frame 1.4: The objectives of SQA activities

The objectives of SQA activities are
• Ensuring an acceptable level of confidence that the software product and software operation services will conform to functional technical requirements and be suitable quality for its intended use. • According to the extended SQA definition – ensuring an acceptable level of confidence that the software development and software operation process will conform to scheduling and budgetary requirements. • Initiating and managing activities to improve and increase the efficiency of software development, software operation, and SQA activities. These activities yield improvements to the prospects' achieving of functional and managerial requirements while reducing costs.

The other sections of the chapter deal with the following issues:

- What is a software product?
- The principles of SQA
- Software errors, faults, and failures
- The causes of software errors
- Software quality assurance versus software quality control (SQC)
- Software quality engineering and software engineering

1.2 What is a software product?

Intuitively, when we think about software, we imagine an accumulation of programming language instructions and statements, usually referred to as "code."

However, when referring to a professional software product, "code" by itself is not sufficient. Software products need to undergo defect corrections, and other maintenance services, which typically include user instruction, corrections, adaptations, and improvements of the software product during their life cycle. Accordingly, software products also comprise components, required to ensure operational success of the services provided by the product. The ISO/IEC/IEEE definition shown in Frame 1.5 lists these components.

Frame 1.5: Software product definition

Source: ISO/IEC/IEEE Std. 90003:2014 (ISO/IEC/IEEE, 2014)

Software product is
Set of computer programs, procedures, and possibly associated documentation and data.

The software product components are:

Computer programs "the code". The computer programs activate the computer system to perform the required applications. The computer programs include several types of code, such as source code, executable code, test code, and so on.

Procedures. Procedures define the order and schedule within which the software or project programs are performed, the method for handling common malfunctioning of software products, and so on.

Documentation. The purpose of the documentation is to instruct or support new software product version developers, maintenance staff, and end users of the software product. It includes the various design reports, test reports, and user and software manuals, and so on.

Data necessary for operating the software system. The required data include lists of codes and parameters, and also standard test data. The purpose of the standard test data is to ascertain that no undesirable changes in the code or software data have occurred during bug corrections and other software maintenance activities, and to support the detection of causes for any malfunctioning.

To summarize the above discussion, the definition of a software product is presented in Frame 1.6.

Frame 1.6: Software product definition

Software product is
A collection of components necessary to ensure proper operation, and efficient maintenance during its life cycle. The components include (1) computer programs ("code"), (2) documentation, (3) data necessary for its operation and maintenance (including standard test), and (4) procedures.

It should be noted that software quality assurance refers to the quality of all components of the software product, namely, the code, documentation, necessary operating and standard test data, and procedures. Moreover, the composition of software product components varies significantly according to the software development tools and methodology.

1.3 The principles of SQA

Source: after ISO 9000:2000 (ISO, 2000)

The following principles guide organizations in their process to ensure the software quality of their software products and services satisfies the needs and wants of stakeholders.

- **Customer focus.** Organizations depend on their customers, and thus need to understand their current and future needs, fulfill their requirements, and achieve their satisfaction.
- **Leadership.** An organization's leaders should create an internal environment in which employees are involved in achieving the quality targets.
- **Involvement of people-employees.** The involvement of employees at all levels enables benefiting from their capabilities to promote software quality issues.
- **Process approach.** Managing activities and resources as processes results in their improved efficiency.
- **System approach to management.** Process management achieves higher effectiveness and efficiency through identification, analysis, and understanding of interrelated processes.
- **Continual improvement.** Continual combined improvement of quality and processes' effectiveness and efficiency performance are a permanent objective of the organization.
- **Factual approach of decision-making.** Decisions should be based on data and information.
- **Mutually beneficial supplier relationships.** Understanding that an organization's supplier relationships based on mutual benefits contributes to improved performance of the organization with regard to quality, efficiency, and effectiveness.

1.4 Software errors, faults, and failures

To better understand the essence of software errors, faults, and failures, let us take a look at the performance of a deployed software system, as perceived by customers.

Example: The Simplex HR is a software system that has been on the market for 7 years. Its software package currently serves about 1200 customers.

One of the staff from the Simplex HR Support Centre reported a number of quotes from typical customer complaints:

1. "We have been using the Simplex HR software in our Human Resources Department for about four years, and have never experienced a software failure. We have recommended the Simplex HR to our colleagues."

2. Immediately following this positive testimony, the same employee complained that he could not prepare a simple monthly report.

3. "I started to use the Simplex HR two months ago; we have experienced so many failures that we are considering replacing the Simplex-HR software package."

4. "We have been using the software package for almost five years, and were very satisfied with its performance, until recently. During the last few months, we suddenly found ourselves having to contend with several severe failures."

Is such a variation in user experience relating to failures possible for the very same software package?

Can a software package that successfully served an organization for a long period of time "suddenly" change its nature (quality) and be full of bugs?

The answer to both these questions is YES, and the reason for this is rooted in the very characteristics of software errors.

The origin of software failures lies in a *software error* made by a software designer or programmer. An error may refer to a grammatical error in one or more of the code lines, or a logical error in carrying out one or more of the specification requirements.

A *software fault* is a software error that causes improper functioning of the software in a specific application, and in rare cases, of the software in general. However, not all software errors become software faults. In many other cases, erroneous code lines will not affect the functionality of the software (software faults are not caused). It should be noted that in some software fault cases, the fault is corrected or "neutralized" by subsequent code lines.

Naturally, our interest lies mainly in *software failures* that disrupt the use of the software. A software failure is a result of a software fault, hence our next question.

Do all software faults inevitably cause software failures? Not necessarily: A software fault becomes a software failure only when it is "activated" – that is when the software user tries to apply the specific, faulty application. In many cases, a software fault is in fact never activated. This is either due to the user's lack of interest in the specific application, or to the fact that the combination of conditions necessary to activate the software fault never occurs. The following two examples demonstrate the software fault – software failure relationships.

Example 1 The Simplex HR software package

Let us return to the Simplex HR software package mentioned above.
The software package includes the following fault:

1. Overtime compensation – This function was defined to allow two levels of daily overtime, where the user can specify the details and compensation per each level. For instance, the first 2 hours' overtime (level 1) should be paid at a rate that is 25% more than the regular hourly rates, while each following additional hour (level 2) should be paid at a rate that is 50% more than the regular hourly rates.

   The programmer's mistake caused the following fault: In cases when two levels of overtime were reported, the higher compensation was paid for overtime hours reported for both the levels.

Let us now examine the software failures experienced by two of Simplex HR users:

a. **A chain of pharmacies**

   Overtime pay – The policy of the chain was to implement overtime for no more **than 2 hours on top. The first level of overtime compensation was defined at 3** hours.

   Thanks to its policy, the chain did not experience software failures relating to the overtime features?

b. **A regional school**

   Overtime pay – The school has lately introduced the Simplex HR software package to support the management of its teacher staff. Cases of overtime happen quite frequently, and are due to the replacement of teachers on sick leave, personal leave of absence, and so on. The teachers' compensation was 30% above their hourly regular rate for the first 2 hours (level 1), and 75% above their hourly rate per each additional hour overtime (level 2). The failure related to overtime calculations was evident from the first salary calculations. Teachers who worked relatively long hours' overtime (over 2 hours per time) in the past months were both astonished and delighted to discover significantly higher overtime compensation than anticipated.

It should be noted that once software failures are identified, Simplex HR maintenance team is expected to correct them.

Example 2 The "Meteoro-X" meteorological equipment firmware

Meteoro-X is a computerized recording and transmission equipment unit designed for meteorological stations that perform temperature and precipitation measurements. The Meteoro-X is also equipped with three wind vanes for wind velocity measurements. Meteorological measurements are defined to be transmitted every 5 minutes to a meteorological center.

"Meteoro-X" firmware (software embedded in the product) includes the following software fault:

Temperature threshold – The safety control specifications require shutting down the equipment if its temperature rises above 50 degrees centigrade.

The programmer error that resulted in a software fault – he registered the threshold as 150 degrees centigrade. This fault could only be noted, and consequently cause damage, when the equipment was subjected to temperatures measuring higher than 50 degrees.

Let us now examine the failure experienced by some of the Meteoro-X users:

a. Meteorological authorities of a southern European country

Temperature threshold – The Meteoro-X performed with no failures for about 3 years, due to the fact that temperatures higher than 50 degrees centigrade had not been recorded. It was only in the month of August of the fourth year when temperatures reached 57 degrees centigrade that an equipment disaster in one of the meteorological stations occurred.

b. North European Meteorological Board

Temperature threshold – The Meteoro-X had no failures due to the fact that temperatures higher than 50 degrees centigrade were not recorded.

A review of the specification document and the relevant code modules revealed the causes of the software faults, and enabled their correction.

These examples clearly demonstrate that at some time during the software service, some software faults will become software failures. Other software faults, and in some cases even a major portion of them, will remain hidden, invisible to software users, only to be activated when specific conditions are in place.

Figure 1.1 illustrates the relationships between software errors, faults, and failures; of the 17 software errors yielded in the development process, 8 become

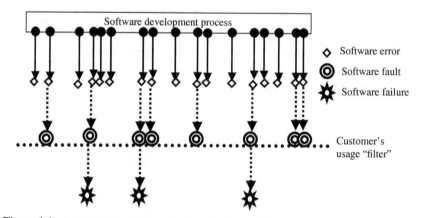

Figure 1.1   Software errors, software faults, and software failures

software faults, while only 3 of these faults become software failures. The customer's software usage characteristics determine which software applications are used, and thereby which faults become failures. In other words, the characteristics serve as a "failure filter."

1.5 The causes of software errors

As software errors are the cause of poor software quality, it is important to investigate their causes, in order to prevent them. It should be noted that these errors are all human errors, made by system analysts, programmers, software testers, documentation experts, managers, and sometimes clients and their representatives. Even in rare cases where software errors may be caused by the development environment: interpreters, wizards, automatic software generators, and so on, it is reasonable to claim that these too are human errors, as someone is responsible for the failure of the development. The causes of software errors can be classified according to the stages of the software development process in which they occur. A classification of error causes into nine classes is presented:

a. Faulty definition of requirements

A faulty definition of a requirement, usually prepared by the client, is one of the main causes of software errors. The most common errors of this type are:
- Erroneous definition of requirements
- Lack of essential requirements
- Incomplete requirements definition

For instance, one of the requirements of a municipality's local tax software system refers to discounts granted to various segments of the population: senior citizens, parents of large families, and so on. Unfortunately, a discount granted to students was not included in the requirements document.
- Inclusion of unnecessary requirements, functions that are not expected to be applied.

b. Client–developer communication failures

Misunderstandings resulting from defective client–developer communication are additional causes for errors that prevail in the early stages of the development process:
- Misunderstanding of the client's instructions in the requirement document.
- Misunderstanding of the client's requirement changes presented to the developer in written form or verbally during the development period.
- Misunderstanding of the client's responses to design issues presented by the developer.
- Lack of attention to client messages relating to requirement changes, and client responses to questions raised by the developer.

c. Deliberate deviations from software requirements

In several circumstances, developers may deliberately deviate from the documented requirements – an action that often causes software errors. The most common situations of deliberate deviations are:

- Developer reuses software modules from previous project without sufficient analysis of the changes and adaptations needed to correctly fulfill all relevant customer requirements.
- Developer decides to omit part of the required functions in an attempt to better handle time or budget pressures.
- Developer-initiated improvements to the software introduced without managerial or client approval. Improvements of this type frequently disregard project requirements deemed minor by the developer. Such "minor" requirements when ignored create changes that may eventually cause software errors.

d. Logical design errors

Software errors can enter the system when professionals designing the system; system architects, software engineers, system analysts, and so on formulate the software requirements into design definitions. Typical logical errors include:

- Definitions that represent software requirements by means of erroneous algorithms.
- Process definitions that contain sequencing errors.

    Example: The software requirements for a firm's debt collection system define a debt collection process that includes the following requirement: Once a client, after receiving three successive notification letters, does not pay his debt; the client details are to be reported to the Sales Department Manager, who will decide whether to proceed to the next stage, which is referral of the client to the Legal Department. The system analyst defined the process incorrectly by stating that if no receipt of payment is noted after sending three successive letters, the client personal and debt details will be included on a list of clients delivered to the Legal Department. The logical error was caused by the analyst's erroneous omission of the Sales Department phase from the debt collection process.

- Erroneous definition of boundary conditions.

    Example: The client requirements stated that a special discount will be granted to customers who make more than three purchase transactions in the same month. The analyst erroneously defined the software process to state that the discount would be granted to those who make three or more transactions in the same year.

- Omission of required software system states.

    Example: Real-time computerized apparatus is required to respond in a specific way to a combination of temperatures and pressures. The analyst did not define the required response when the temperature is over 120 degrees centigrade, and the pressure between 6 and 8 atmospheres.

- Omission of definitions concerning reactions to illegal operation of the software system.

    Example: A computerized theatre ticketing system operated by the customer has no human operator interface. The software system is required to limit sales to 10 tickets per customer. Accordingly, any request for the purchase of more than 10 tickets is "illegal." In the design, the analyst included a message stating that sales are limited to 10 tickets per customer, but did not define the system response to cases when customers (who might not have properly understood the message) key in a number higher than 10. When performing this illegal request, a system "crash" may be expected, as no computerized response was defined for this illegal operation.

e. Coding errors

A wide range of reasons cause programmers to make coding errors. These include misunderstanding the design documentation, linguistic errors in programming languages, errors in the application of CASE and other development tools, errors in data selection, and so on.

f. Noncompliance with documentation and coding instructions

Almost every development unit has its own documentation and coding standards that define the content, order and format of the documents, and code developed by team members. For this purpose, the unit develops and publicizes templates and coding instructions. Members of the development team or unit are required to comply with these directions.

As it may be assumed that errors of noncompliance with instructions do not usually become software faults, one may ask why cases of noncompliance with these instructions should be considered as software errors. Even if the quality of the "noncomplying" software is acceptable, difficulties will inevitably be presented when trying to understand it. In other words, future handling of this software (by development and/or maintenance teams) is expected to substantially increase the rate of errors in the following situations:

- Team members, who need to coordinate their own code with code modules developed by "noncomplying" team members, can be expected to encounter more difficulties than usual when trying to understand the software.
- Individuals replacing the "noncomplying" team member (who retired or was promoted) will find it difficult to fully understand the "noncomplying" code.

- The design review team will find it more difficult to study a design document prepared by a "noncomplying" team, and as a result will probably misunderstand part of the design details.
- The test team will find it more difficult to test the "noncomplying" module; consequently, their effectiveness is expected to be decreased, leaving more errors undetected. Moreover, team members required to correct the detected errors can be expected to encounter greater difficulties when doing so. They may leave some errors only partially corrected, and even introduce new errors as a result of their incomplete grasp of the other team member's work.
- Maintenance teams required to contend with "bugs" detected by users, and to change or add to the existing software will face extra difficulties when trying to understand the "noncomplying" software and its documentation. This is expected to result in an excessive number of errors, along with increased maintenance expenditures.

g. **Shortcomings of the testing process**

Shortcomings of the testing process affect the error rate by leaving a greater number of errors undetected or uncorrected. These shortcomings result from:

- Incomplete test plans failing to test all or some parts of the software, application functions, and operational states of the system.
- Failure to document and report detected errors and faults.
- Failure to promptly correct detected software faults, as a result of inappropriate indications of the reasons for the fault.
- Incomplete testing of software error corrections
- Incomplete corrections of detected errors due to negligence or time pressures.

h. **User interface and procedure errors**

User interfaces direct users in areas such as the performance of input and output activities, and data collection and processing. Procedures direct users with respect to the sequence of activities required at each step of the process. Procedures are of special importance in complex software systems, where processing is conducted in several steps, each of which may feed a variety of types of data and enable examination of intermediate results. User interface and procedure errors may cause processing failures even in cases of error-free design and coding. The following example presents a procedure error.

Example

"Eiffel," a construction material store, has decided to grant a 5% discount to major customers, who are billed monthly. The discount is offered to customers whose total net purchases in the store in the preceding 12 months exceeded $1 million. The discount is effective for the last

Table 1.1 "Eiffel" billing procedures – correct and incorrect discount procedures

Correct procedure	Incorrect procedure
At the beginning of each month, Eiffel's information processing department:	At the end of each month, Eiffel's information processing department:
1. Calculates the cumulative purchases for the last 12 months (A) and the cumulative returns for the last 12 months (B) for each of its major customers. 2. Calculates the net cumulative purchases ($A-B$) for each major customer for the last 12 months in the store. 3. For major customers, whose ($A-B$) > $1 million and $B/(A-B)$ <10%, calculate 5% discount on their last month's account.	1. Calculates the cumulative purchases for the last 12 months (A) and the cumulative returns for the last 12 months (B) for each of its major customers. 2. For major customers, whose A > $1 million, and ($B/A$) <10%, calculate 5% discount on their last month's account.

month's account. Furthermore, the management decided to withdraw the discount from customers who returned goods valued in excess of 10% of their net purchases during the last 12 months.

Table 1.1 presents a comparison of correct and incorrect procedures regarding application of the discount.

It is clear that under the incorrect procedure, customers, whose net purchases ($A-B$) are equal or below $1 million and/or their percentage of returned goods ($B/A-B$) is equal or exceeds 10%, may be mistakenly found to be eligible for the 5% discount

i. **Documentation errors**

The documentation errors of concern to the development and maintenance teams are those found in the design, software manuals, documents, and in the documentation integrated into the body of the software. These errors can cause additional errors in further stages of development and during the maintenance period.

Another type of documentation errors that affect mainly users are errors in the user manuals and in the "help" displays incorporated in the software. Typical errors of this type are:

• Omission of software functions.

• Errors in the explanations and instructions given to users, resulting in "dead ends" or incorrect applications.

• Listings of nonexisting software functions, usually functions planned in the early stages of development but later dropped, but also functions that were active in previous versions of the software but cancelled in the current version.

Frame 1.7 summarizes the causes of software errors.

Frame 1.7: The nine causes of software errors

The nine causes of software errors are:
a. Faulty requirements definition
b. Client–developer communication failures
c. Deliberate deviations from software requirements
d. Logical design errors
e. Coding errors
f. Noncompliance with documentation and coding instructions
g. Shortcomings of the testing process
h. User interface and procedure errors
i. Documentation errors
Additional approaches to classification of software defects and their causes are presented by Ko and Myers (2005) and Thung et al. (2012).

1.6 Software quality assurance versus software quality control

Two terms are constantly repeated within the context of software quality: "software quality control" and "software quality assurance." Are they synonymous? How are they related?

Definitions of software quality assurance are already presented in Frames 1.2 and 1.3. In order to compare the two terms, definitions for SQC are presented in Frame 1.8.

Frame 1.8: Software quality control – the IEEE definitions
Source: IEEE Std. 610.12-1990 (IEEE, 1990)

Software quality control is
1. A set of activities designed to evaluate the quality of a developed or manufactured product. Contrast with software quality assurance.
2. The process of verifying one's own work or that of coworker.

SQA and SQC represent two distinct concepts.

Software quality control relates to the activities needed to evaluate the quality of a final software product, with the main objective of withholding any product that does not qualify. In contrast, the main objective of **software quality assurance** is to minimize the cost of ensuring the quality of a software product with a variety of infrastructure activities and additional activities performed throughout the software development and maintenance processes/stages. These activities are aimed at preventing the causes of errors, and at detecting and correcting errors that may have occurred at the earliest possible stage, thus bringing the quality of the software product to an acceptable level. As a result, quality assurance activities reduce substantially the probability that software products will not qualify and, at the same time, in most cases, reduce the costs of ensuring quality.

In summary,

1. SQC and SQA activities serve different objectives.

2. SQC activities are only a part of the total range of SQA activities.

1.7 Software quality engineering and software engineering

The definition of **software engineering**, according to the IEEE, is presented in Frame 1.9.

Frame 1.9: Software engineering – the IEEE definition

Source: IEEE Std. 610.12-1990

Software engineering is
The application of a systematic, disciplined, quantifiable approach to the development, operation, and maintenance of software, that is, the application of engineering to software.

The characteristics of **software engineering**, especially those of the systematic, disciplined, and quantitative approach at its core, make it a good infrastructure for achieving effective and efficient software development and maintenance objectives. The methodologies and tools applied by software engineering determine the process of transforming a software requirement document into a software product, and also include the performance of quality assurance activities. **Software quality engineering** employs the development of quality assurance methodologies, procedures, and tools together with methods for follow-up of quality assurance activities performed by software development and maintenance teams.

Software quality engineering and software engineering have a great number of topics in common. Albeit the two groups view these topics from different standpoints – respective to their profession, their shared knowledge and cooperation are the basis for successful software development.

An indication of the extent of shared topics may be perceived when comparing the software engineering body of knowledge (SWEBOK) (Bourque and Fairley, 2014) and the certified software quality engineer body of knowledge (CSQEBOK) (ASQ, 2016). A detailed discussion of an earlier version of the CSQEBOK was compiled by Westfall (2009).

Summary

1. **Definitions of software, software quality, and software quality assurance**

   Software, from the SQA perspective, is the combination of computer programs ("code"), procedures, documentation, and data necessary for operating the software system. The combination of all four components is needed to ensure the quality of the development process, as well to ensure quality during extended maintenance periods.

   Software quality, according to Pressman's definition, is the degree of conformance to specific functional requirements, specified software quality standards, and Good Software Engineering Practices (GSEP).

   Software quality assurance. This book adopts an expanded definition of the widely accepted IEEE definition of software quality assurance. Accordingly, software quality assurance is the systematically planned set of actions necessary to provide adequate confidence that a software development, or maintenance process, conforms to established functional technical requirements, and also to the managerial requirements of keeping to schedule and operating within budget.

2. **The distinction between software errors, software faults, and software failures**

   Software errors are sections of the code that are partially or totally incorrect as a result of a grammatical, logical, or other type of mistake made by a system analyst, programmer, or other member of the software development team.

   Software faults are software errors that cause the incorrect functioning of the software during one of its specific applications.

   Software faults become **software failures** only when they are "activated," that is, when a user tries to apply the specific software section that is faulty. Thus, the root of any software failure is a software error.

3. **The various causes of software errors**

There are nine causes of software errors: (1) faulty requirements definition, (2) client–developer communication failures, (3) deliberate deviations from software requirements, (4) logical design errors, (5) coding errors, (6) noncompliance with documentation or coding instructions, (7) shortcomings of the testing process, (8) procedure errors, and (9) documentation errors. It should be emphasized that all errors are human errors, and are made by system analysts, programmers, software testers, documentation experts, and even clients and their representatives.

4. **The objectives of software quality assurance activities**

The objectives of SQA activities for software development and maintenance are:

1. Ensuring, with acceptable levels of confidence, conformance to functional technical requirements.
2. Ensuring, with acceptable levels of confidence, conformance to managerial requirements of scheduling and budgets.
3. Initiating and managing activities for the improvement and greater efficiency of software development and SQA activities.

5. **The differences between software quality assurance and software quality control**

Software quality control is a set of activities carried out with the main objective of withholding software products from delivery to the client if they do not qualify. In contrast, the objective of software quality assurance is to minimize the costs of software quality by introducing a variety of infrastructure activities and other activities throughout the development and maintenance processes. These activities are performed in all stages of development to eliminate causes of errors, and detect and correct errors in the early stages of software development. As a result, quality assurance substantially reduces the rate of nonqualifying products.

6. **The relationship between software quality assurance and software engineering**

Software engineering is the application of a systematic, disciplined, quantifiable approach to the development, operation, and maintenance of software.

Software quality assurance practices are intertwined with the software engineering process in several ways: (1) SQA considerations affect the choice of software development tools and procedures. (2) SQA activities, such as design reviews and software tests, are incorporated in the software development activities. (3) SQA participation in the development of the software development infrastructure of procedures, staff training, configuration management, and so on.

Selected bibliography

ASQ (2016) *The Certified Software Quality Engineering Body of Knowledge (CSQE BoK)*, American Society for Quality.

Bourque P. and Fairley R. (Eds.) (2014) *Guide to the Software Engineering Body of Knowledge SWEBOK*, Ver. 3.0, IEEE and IEEE Computer Society Press, Piscataway, NJ.

IEEE (1990) *IEEE Std. 610.12-1990-IEEE Standard Glossary of Software Engineering Terminology*, Corrected Edition, in IEEE, *IEEE Standards Collection*, The Institute of Electrical and Electronics Engineering, New York.

IEEE (2014) *IEEE Std. 730-2014 Software Quality Assurance*, The IEEE Computer Society, IEEE, New York.

ISO (2000) *ISO Std. 9000:2000 – Quality Management Systems – Fundamental and Vocabulary*, International Organization for Standardization (ISO), Geneva, Switzerland.

ISO/IEC/IEEE (2014) *ISO/IEC 90003:2014 – Software Engineering – Guidelines for the Application of ISO 9001:2008 to Computer Software*, International Organization for Standardization (ISO), Geneva, Switzerland.

Ko, A. J. and Myers, B. A. (2005) *A framework and methodology for studying the causes of software errors in programming systems*, Journal of Visual Languages and Computing, Vol. **16**, pp. 41–84.

Thung F., Lo, D., Jiang, L. (2012) *Automatic defect categorization, in* Proceedings of the 19th Working Conference on Reverse Engineering, pp. 205–214.

Westfall L. (2009) *The Certified Software Quality Engineer Handbook*, ASQ Quality Press, Milwaukee, WI.

Review questions

1.1 A software product comprises four main components.

   a. List the four components of a software system.

   b. How does the quality of each component contribute to the quality of the developed software?

   c. How does the quality of each component contribute to the quality of the software maintenance?

1.2 Refer to the following terms: software error, software fault, and software failure.

   a. Define the terms.

   b. Explain the differences between these undesirable software issues.

   c. Suggest a case where in a software package serving 300 clients, a new software failure ("bug") appears for the first time 6 years after the software package was first sold to the public.

1.3 Consider the principles of SQA

    a. Explain in your own words the importance of the 6th principle.

    b. How can the implementation of the 8th principle contribute to the quality of software product?

1.4 a. List and briefly describe the various causes of software errors.

    b. Classify the causes of errors according to the group/s responsible for the error – the client staff, the system analysts, the programmers, the testing staff – or is the responsibility a shared one, belonging to more than one group?

1.5 What are the differences between the IEEE definition of SQA and the expanded definition discussed in this book?

1.6 According to the IEEE definition of SQC, SQC is in contrast with SQA.

    a. In what respect does SQC vary from SQA?

    b. In what way can SQC be considered part of SQA?

Topics for discussion

1.1 A programmer claims that as only a small proportion of software errors turn into software failures, it is unnecessary to make substantial investments in the prevention and elimination of software errors.

    a. Do you agree with this view?

    b. Discuss the outcome of accepting this view.

1.2 George Wise is an exceptional programmer. Testing his software modules reveals very few errors, much less than the team's average. He is very rarely late in completing a task. George always finds original ways to solve programming challenges, and uses an original, individual version of the coding style. He dislikes preparing the required documentation, and rarely does so according to the team's templates.

    A day after completing a challenging task, on time, he was called to the office of the department's chief software engineer. Instead of being praised for his accomplishments (as he expected), he was warned by the company's chief software engineer that he would be fired, unless he began to fully comply with the team's coding and documentation instructions.

    a. Do you agree with the position taken by the department's chief software engineer?

    b. If you agree, could you suggest why his/her position was so decisive?

    c. Explain how George's behavior could cause software errors.

1.3 The claim, according to the expanded definition of SQA, that a development team should invest its efforts equally for complying with project requirements as they invest in keeping project schedule and budget supports client satisfaction.

    a. Do you agree with this claim?

    b. If yes, provide arguments to substantiate your position.

1.4 Five reasons for shortcomings of the testing process are mentioned in Section 1.5.

    a. Explain these five reasons in your own words.

    b. Could you suggest circumstances of a testing process which could cause these shortcomings?

Chapter 2

Software Quality Factors (Attributes)

2.1 Complaints from the City Computer Club members – an introductory mini case

The City Computer Club was established by municipal corporations and public services' IT department managers. The discussion topic of club meeting was implementation experiences of members in their organizations.

Below is a transcription of part of the meeting.

- "Our new sales information system seems okay. The invoices and inventory records are correct, the discounts granted to our clients follow our very complicated discount policy precisely, **but** our new sales information system frequently fails. Recently, it has been failing at least twice a day, and each time for at least twenty minutes. Yesterday, it took an hour and half for us to get back to work . . . Just imagine how embarrassing this is to store managers . . . and Softbest, the software house that developed our computerized sales system, does not accept responsibility . . . ."

- "Just a year ago, we launched our successful new product – RD-1, a police radar detector. The RD-1 firmware embedded in the product seemed to be the reason for its success. **But,** when we began planning the development of the European version of the product, RD-E1, we found out that the RD-1 firmware had only been partially documented, and the code, mostly written with no adherence to the company's work instructions. Consequently, the development department had to develop a new firmware, as almost no parts of the RD-1 design and programming could be reused."

- "Believe it or not, our software package for schoolteachers "Blackboard", launched just three months ago, is already installed in 187 schools. The development team just returned from a week in Hawaii - their vacation

Software Quality: Concepts and Practice, First Edition. Daniel Galin.
© 2018 the IEEE Computer Society, Inc. Published 2018 by John Wiley & Sons, Inc.

bonus. **But** we have suddenly started to receive daily complaints from the "Blackboard" maintenance team. They claim that the lack of failure detection features in the software, in addition to the poor programmer's manual, have caused them to invest more time to deal with bugs and minor software changes, than that agreed upon in the purchasing contracts with clients."

- "The new version of our loan contract software is really accurate. We have already processed 1,200 customer requests, and checked each of the output contracts - no errors were found. **But** we did face a severe unexpected problem – training a new staff member to use this software takes about three weeks. This is a real problem in customer departments suffering from high employee turnover...The project team claims that as they were not required to include software user training as a requirement to be considered during the software development period, an additional two to three months of work will be required to solve the problem."

There are a number of characteristics common to all these "**but**s":

- The software projects satisfactorily fulfilled the basic requirements to perform the correct calculations (correct inventory figures, correct average class scores, correct loan interests, etc.).

  Apparently the software packages successfully fulfilled the **correctness** requirements.

- The software projects suffered from poor performance in important areas such as software maintenance, software reliability, software reuse, and user training.

  Apparently, the software packages fail to fulfill the **maintainability**, **training usability**, **reliability,** and **reusability** requirements.

- The common cause, for poor performance of the software projects developed in these areas, was a lack in essential parts of the project requirements. These parts should have been designated to cover important aspects of software functionality.

2.2 The need for comprehensive software quality requirements

The examples already shown represent difficulties faced by users, developers, and maintenance staff. All of which could have been avoided if the relevant requirement had been included in the requirement document. This leads us to understand the imperative need for a comprehensive requirements set that covers all attributes of software and aspects of its use needed throughout the software life cycle. Software products that fulfill such a comprehensive requirements set, including aspects of usability, reusability, maintainability, and so forth, are expected to achieve increased user satisfaction, and higher efficiency of development and maintenance teams. In other words, such a requirements set will ensure the improvement of software performance records and user satisfaction.

When analyzing typical examples of software quality requirements, one cannot but note their multidimensional nature. The great variety of attributes/characteristics of software quality defined in software requirement documents can be classified into content groups; these groups are also termed **software quality factors.** We expect the team responsible for defining the requirements of a software system to examine the needs and to define specific requirements that belong to each software quality factor. Software requirement documents are expected to differ in the degree of emphasis placed on various quality factors, hence the differences between software projects and the expectation that not all factors are universally included in all requirement documents.

This chapter is, therefore, dedicated to the review of the wide spectrum of software quality factors that represent aspects of software use that may be operative throughout the life cycle of software systems. Over the last four decades, groups of these software quality factors have been presented in several software quality models. Several criteria (subfactors/subcharacteristics) for each of these factors have been suggested. These criteria/subfactors are expected to be measurable, and to support the reviewing, testing, and quality measurement of software products with respect to these factors.

The following sections deal with:

- McCall's classic model for software quality factors
- The ISO/IEC 25010 model and other alternative models of software quality factors
- Software compliance with quality factors.

2.3 McCall's classic model for software quality factors

Several models of software quality factors and their classification to factor categories have been suggested over the years. The classic model of software quality factors, suggested by McCall, consists of 11 factors (McCall et al. 1977). The McCall factor model, despite decades of "maturation," continues to provide a practical, up-to-date method for classifying software quality requirements. Subsequent alternative models and factors, additional to McCall's factors, will be discussed later in this chapter.

McCall's factor model classifies all software requirements into 11 software quality factors. The 11 factors are grouped into three categories: product operation, product revision, and product transition. McCall's software quality model is presented in Frame 2.1

Frame 2.1: McCall's software quality factors model

McCall's software quality factors model	
Product operation factors:	Correctness Reliability Efficiency Integrity Usability
Product revision factors:	Maintainability Flexibility Testability
Product transition factors:	Portability Reusability Interoperability

McCall's model and its categories are illustrated in McCall's model of software quality factors tree (see Figure 2.1).

The next three sections are dedicated to a detailed description of the software quality factors included in each of McCall's categories.

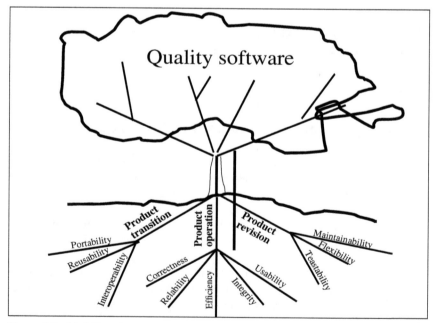

Figure 2.1   McCall's software quality factor model tree

2.3.1 McCall's product operation software quality factors

According to McCall's model, five software quality factors are included in the product operation category, all of which deal with requirements that directly affect the daily operation of the software. These factors are:

Correctness

Correctness requirements are related to the outputs of software systems, such as a query display of a customer's balance in the sales accounting information system or the air supply as a function of temperature specified by the firmware of an industrial control unit. A specification is required for each output (system function). This output specification is usually multidimensional; some common dimensions are:

- The required accuracy of the output. This may be adversely affected by inaccurate data or inaccurate calculations. For example, the probability of nonaccurate inventory information, containing one or more mistakes, will not exceed 1%.
- The required completeness of the output information. This may be adversely affected by incomplete data. For example, the probability of missing data from a club member's record: the number of his cellular phone or home address will not exceed 1%.
- The required up-to-datedness of information (defined according to the frequency of data updating). In other words, the up-to-datedness defines the time between the event and its recording and actual usage by the software system. For example, it is required that information regarding club member payments be up dated within one working day (with probability 99.5%).
- The required response time, defined as the time needed to obtain the requested information, or as the requested reaction time of the firmware installed in a computerized apparatus. Two examples: (1) Response time for queries regarding the inventory item will be on average less than 2 seconds; (2) The reaction time to open a valve for a cooling agent flow, when the liquid temperature rises above 90 degrees centigrade, will be less than 10 seconds.
- The standards for coding and documenting the software system.

Reliability

Reliability requirements deal with failures to provide service. They determine the maximum allowed software system failure rate, the maximum allowed percentage of a software system's downtime, and the maximum allowed recovery times. The requirements can refer to the entire system or to one or more of its separate functions.

Examples

1. The failure frequency of a heart-monitoring unit operating in a hospital's intensive care ward is required to be less than one in 20 years. Its heart attack detection function is required to have a failure rate of less than one per 100 years.

2. One requirement of the new software system to be installed in the main branch of the Independence Bank, which operates 120 branches, is that on average, it will not fail more than 1 time per 12 months during the bank's office hours. In addition, the probability that the off-time (time needed for repair and recovery of all the bank's services) be more than 10 minutes is required to be less than 0.5%.

Efficiency

Efficiency requirements deal with the hardware resources needed to perform all the functions of the software system in conformance with all other requirements. The main hardware resources to be considered are the computer's processing capabilities (measured in Million Instructions Per Second (MIPS), megahertz – million cycles per second, etc.), its data storage capability in terms of memory and disk capacity (measured in gigabytes (GBs), terabytes (TBs), etc.), and the data communication capability of the communication lines (usually measured in megabits per second (MBPSs), and gigabits per second (GBPSs). These will all be applied to a developed software system or the firmware.

Another type of efficiency requirement deals with the time lapse between recharging the system's portable units such as information system units located in portable computers and meteorological units placed outdoors.

Examples

1. A chain of stores is considering two alternative bids for a software system. Both bids consist of placing the same type of computers in the chain's headquarters and its branches. The bids differ solely in the storage volume: 2 TB per branch computer, and 20 TB in the head office computer (Bid A), 1 TB per branch computer and 10 GB in the head office computer (Bid B). There is also a difference in the number of communication lines required: Bid A comprises three communication lines of 28.8 MBPS between each branch and the head office, whereas Bid B is based on two communication lines of the same capacity between each branch and the head office. In this case, it is evident that Bid B is more efficient than Bid A because fewer hardware resources are required.

2. An outdoor meteorological unit. The system performs measurements once per hour, logs the results, and transmits the results once a day to the meteorological center by means of wireless communication. The unit is equipped with a 1,000 milliampere hour cell, which is capable of supplying the power requirements of the unit for at least 30 days. An alternative meteorological unit of higher efficiency is able to cope with all the requirements with a 500 milliampere unit.

Integrity

Integrity requirements deal with the software system security, that is, requirements to prevent unauthorized access, to distinguish between the majority of personnel only allowed to see the information (read only permit), and a limited group who will be allowed to add and change data (write permit), and so forth. Integrity requirements are defined to cope with risks of "nonfriendly" unauthorized attempts to damage the software system and its performance.

Example
    The Engineering Department of a local municipality operates a geographic information system (GIS). The department is planning to allow citizens access to its GIS files through the Internet. The software requirements include: the possibility to view and copy information, but not to make changes to maps of the citizens' own assets, and neither to those of any other asset in the municipality area ("read only" permit). Access will be denied to plans in progress, and to those maps defined by the department head as having "limited access."

Usability

Usability requirements deal with the scope of staff resources needed to train a new employee and to operate the software system. The usability requirements relate to the (a) operation usability, the productivity of the user, that is, the average number of transactions performed per hour, and (b) training usability, the average time spent training a new employee.

Example
    The software usability requirements for the new help desk system initiated by a home appliance manufacturing company lists the following specification requirements: (1) A staff member should be able to handle at least 60 service calls a day. (2) Training a new employee will take no more than 2 days (16 training hours), at the end of which the trainee will be able to handle 45 service calls a day.

2.3.2 Product revision software quality factors

According to the McCall model of software quality factors, three quality factors comprise the product revision category. These factors deal with those requirements that affect the complete range of software maintenance activities: corrective maintenance (correction of software faults and failures), adaptive maintenance (adapting the current software to additional circumstances and customers without changing the software), and perfective maintenance (enhancement and improvement of existing software with new applications with respect to relevant developments of products, services, and new government regulations and their impact etc.). These factors are:

Maintainability

Maintainability requirements determine the efforts needed by users and maintenance personnel to identify the reasons of a software failure, to correct the failure, and to verify the success of the correction. This factor's requirements refer to the modular structure of software, the internal program documentation, and the programmer's manual, among other items.

Example
    Typical maintainability requirements: (a) The size of a software module will not exceed 30 statements. (b) The programming will adhere to the company coding standards and guidelines.

Flexibility

The flexibility factor deals with the capabilities and efforts required to support adaptive maintenance activities. These capabilities include the resources (i.e., in man-days) required to adapt a software package to a variety of customers, with a variating extent of activities, and a different range of products, but of the same trade. No software changes are needed in these cases as the package is planned for flexibility. This factor's requirements also support perfective maintenance activities, such as changes and additions to the software in order to improve its service, and to adapt it to changes in the firm's technical or commercial environment.

Example
    Teacher Support Software (TSS) is a software product that deals with the documentation of student achievements, calculation of final grades, printing of term grade statements, and automatic printing of warning letters to parents of failing pupils. The software specifications included the following flexibility requirements: the software should be suitable for teachers of all subjects and school levels (elementary, middle, and high school). Another flexibility requirement: nonprofessionals should be able to use TSS to create new types of reports according to the schoolmaster's requirements and/or demands of the city's department of education.

Testability

Testability requirements deal with the testing process of a software system, as well as with its operation. Testability requirements for the ease of testing are related to special features in the programs that help the tester, for instance by providing predefined intermediate results and log files. Testability requirements related to software operation include automatic diagnostics performed by the software system prior to operating the system, to find out whether all components of the software system are in working order and to obtain a report on the detected faults. Another type of these requirements deals with automatic diagnostic checks to be applied by the maintenance technicians to detect the causes of software failures.

Example
    An industrial computerized control unit is programmed to calculate various measures of the production status, report the performance level of the machinery, and operate a warning signal in predefined situations. One testability requirement demanded was to develop a set of standard test data, including the expected correct reactions of the system in each case. This standard test data is to be run every morning before production begins, to verify that the computerized unit responds properly.

2.3.3 Product transition software quality factors

According to McCall, three quality factors are included in the product transition category, a category that pertains to the adaptation of software to other environments, and its interaction with other software systems.

Portability

Portability requirements relate to the adaptation of a software system to other environments consisting of different hardware, different operating systems, and so forth. These requirements make it possible to widen the market for the software product and enable using the same basic software in diverse situations: in different hardware and operating systems.

Example
    A software package designed and programmed to operate in a Windows 2007 environment is required to allow a low cost transfer to Linux environments.

Reusability

Reusability requirements deal with "two-directional" requirements. One direction is the use of a software module, or an entire application, taken from an existing software product in a new software project currently being developed.

The existing software module or entire application may be software former developed by the organization, or open source software, or purchased software. The other direction relates to a requirement to develop modules or a group of modules, or even an entire project, in a way to enable their reuse in future projects. Reused software is expected to be tested by its developers, and already corrected according to failures experienced by former users. In other words, it is assumed that most of the software faults have already been detected by quality assurance activities performed by the original software developers, and any failures identified by users of the software, corrected accordingly. Thus, the reuse of software is expected to save development resources, shorten the development schedule, and provide higher quality software modules.

Example

A software development unit has been required to develop a software system for the operation and control of a hotel swimming pool serving hotel guests and members of a pool club. Although the management did not define reusability requirements, the unit's team leader, after analyzing the information processing requirements of the hotel's spa, decided to add the following reusability requirement: A list of the software modules for the pool project should be designed and programmed in a way that will allow its reuse in the spa's future software system planned to be developed next year. These modules include:

- The entrance checks of membership cards module
- The club members visit recording module
- The pool's restaurant billing module
- The processing of membership renewal payments

Interoperability

Interoperability requirements focus on creating interfaces with other software systems or equipment firmware (for example, the firmware of the production machinery and testing equipment interfaces with the production control software). Interoperability requirements sometimes specify the name(s) of the software or firmware to which an interface is required. They may also specify the accepted standard output structure in a specific industry or application area.

Example

The firmware of a medical laboratory's equipment is required to process its results (output) according to a standard data structure that can then serve as the input for a number of standard medical laboratory information systems. Another interoperability requirement at the same lab: the laboratory information system is required to interface with a medical clinic information system, in order to transmit patients' test results automatically to the physician's clinic.

2.4   The ISO/IEC 25010 model and other alternative models of software quality factors

Several software quality factor models, alternatives to the classic McCall's model, have been developed during the last four decades. Some of these models are Boehm's model (Boehm et al., 1978), FURPS model (first proposed by Grady and Caswell, 1987), Evans and Marciniak's model (Evans and Marciniak, 1987), Deutsch and Willis's model (Deutsch and Willis, 1988), Dromey's model (Dromey, 1995), GEOQUAMO model (developed by Georgiadou, 2003), ISO/IEC 25010:2011 (ISO/IEC, 2011), and AOSQUAMO model (2012) proposed by Kumar (2012).

2.4.1   The ISO/IEC 25010 model

The ISO/IEC 25010:2011 model is of significant importance. It was developed by a joint ISO/IEC international professional team. The ISO/IEC 25010:2011 product quality model is composed of eight factors, and shows a substantial similarity to McCall's model, as four out of its eight factors are included in McCall's model. The factors (characteristics) that compose the ISO/IEC 25010 quality model are presented in Frame 2.2.

Frame 2.2: The ISO/IEC 25010 quality model

Source: The ISO/IEC 25010:2011

The ISO/IEC 25010 quality model
• Functional suitability
• Performance efficiency
• Compatibility
• Usability
• Reliability
• Security
• Maintainability
• Portability

The ISO/IEC 25010:2011 standard replaced the ISO/IEC IS 9126-1:2001 (ISO/IEC, 2001) Software engineering - Product quality – Part 1: Quality model. The ISO/IEC 9126 standard and its three technical reports were used as a basis for the development of software metrics for COTS components (Carvallo and Franch, 2006), e-Government services (Quirchmayr et al., 2007), and for other specific areas.

The next paragraphs include descriptions of the software quality factors of the ISO/IEC 25010:2011 (not included in McCall's model).

Functional suitability

Functional suitability is the capability to fulfill the functions needed by the customer, stated or implied (not necessarily the specified requirement). It covers a wide variety of aspects of software use, including the accurate and complete production of needed results. A significant similarity exists between the functionality factor and the correctness, integrity and interoperability factors of McCall's model.

Performance efficiency

Performance. Software performance efficiency relates to the amount of hardware resources required to fulfill the software system tasks. The lower the amount of hardware resources, the higher the performance. A significant similarity exists between the performance factor and the efficiency factor of McCall's model.

Compatibility

Compatibility refers to the capability of a software system or component to (a) exchange information with other software systems or components and (b) perform other system required functions, sharing its hardware system and software environment

Security

Security relates to the capability of a system product to protect the software system, data stores, and information produced from the reading, modification, or destruction by unauthorized persons or systems. To accomplish this, the system controls access to it through levels of authorization to persons and software products, and denies unauthorized ones. A significant similarity exists between the security factor and the integrity factor described in McCall's model.

2.4.2 Alternative software quality models

A great variety of software quality factors were presented in the alternative quality models. While including part of the software quality factors of McCall's and the ISO/IEC 25010:2011 models, the alternative models also suggest additional factors. A total of 14 additional factors were proposed by these alternative models. Most of these factors are shared by two or more of the alternative models. It should be noted that some of the additional factors overlap factors of McCall's model, as well as each other. The list of additional factors is presented in alphabetical order in Frame 2.3

Frame 2.3: Software quality factors of alternative quality models
(For factors not included in McCall's and ISO/IEC 25010:2011 product quality models.)

Additional software quality factors Additional to McCall's factors	
1	Effectiveness
2	Evolvability
3	Expandability
4	Extensibility
5	Human Engineering
6	Manageability
7	Modifiability
8	Productivity
9	Safety
10	Satisfaction
11	Supportability
12	Survivability
13	Understandability
14	Verifiability

The additional factors are explained and described as follows:

Effectiveness. Effectiveness relates to successful completion of tasks, including schedule and error frequency considerations.

Evolvability. Evolvability refers to efforts required to fulfill future requirements for software system changes, and to adapt the system to technological developments and changes in the operational environment. A significant similarity exists between the evolvability factor and McCall's flexibility factor.

Expandability. Expandability requirements refer to the future efforts required to serve larger populations, improve service, or add new applications, in order to improve system performance. The majority of these requirements are covered by the evolvability quality requirement, as well as by McCall's flexibility factor.

Extensibility. Extensibility refers to efforts required to fulfill future requirements to enhance the software product to meet new requirements, resulting from economic and technological developments. A significant similarity exists between the evolvability factor and McCall's flexibility factor.

Human Engineering. The human engineering factor deals with the "man–machine" user interface with the application or software, the ease to understand and work with the application, the ease to perform any communication involved with working with the application.

Manageability. Manageability requirements refer to the administrative tools that support software modification during the software development and maintenance periods, such as configuration management, software change procedures, and the like.

Example

"Chemilog" is a software system that automatically logs the flow of chemicals into various containers to allow managing the liquid inventory, and for later analysis of the efficiency of production units. The development of "Chemilog's" new versions and releases are required to be documented and monitored by a configuration management application.

Modifiability. Modifiability refers to the efforts that will be needed to modify the software product according to specific requirements of customers. Significant similarity exists between the modifiability factor and McCall's flexibility factor.

Productivity. Productivity relates to the rate at which the software product performs tasks. This factor is the basis for development of quantitative metrics for the operational productivity of the software product. A relationship exists between the productivity factor and the usability factor of McCall's model.

Example

A supermarket management is considering replacing their point of sale equipment and so conducted trials as follows. The trials were based on the point of sale processing of a standard supermarket trolley with a variety of 30 different products. The results from a full day's trial with the proposed equipment averaged 9.2 and 8.3 trolleys per hour for offers A and B, respectively. As the difference in price was negligible, the supermarket management chose offer A based on its higher productivity.

Safety. Safety requirements are designed to eliminate conditions that may be hazardous to equipment and equipment operators, as a result of errors in process control software. These errors can result in inappropriate reactions to dangerous situations, or to the failure to provide alarm signals when the dangerous conditions, specified to be detected by the software, arise.

Example

In a chemical plant, a computerized system controls the flow of acid according to pressure and temperature changes occurring during production. The safety requirements refer to the system's computerized reactions, such as closing and opening valves in dangerous situations, and also specify the types of alarms needed per case.

Satisfaction. Satisfaction refers to user (and customer) perception of the extent the software product meets user expectations in relation to the requirements. The degree of the complete provision of all specified requirements has substantial impact on the level of user satisfaction.

Supportability. Supportability refers to the ease of performing install tasks and various maintenance tasks of error corrections, the adaption of the software product to specific customer needs, and modification of the product according to changing market requirements.

Survivability. Survivability requirements refer to the continuity of service. They define the minimum time allowed between system failures, and the maximum time permitted for recovery of service – two factors that pertain to service continuity. Although these requirements may relate to all types of service failures, they are especially geared toward failures of essential functions or services. A significant similarity exists between the survivability factor and the reliability factor described in McCall's model.

Example

Taya National Lottery Inc. operates a national lottery held once a week. About 2,400,000 to 4,000,000 bets are placed weekly. 250,000 to 350,000 bets are placed in the hour preceding the lottery draw. The computerized lottery system, serves customers at thousands of betting stations by recording their bets. Any failure of the computerized lottery system or its wide communication system, especially during the last hour before the draw, is expected to cause colossal losses to Taya. The new lottery software and communication system (that connects all the betting machines to the central computer) is required to operate without any communication failure for at least 24 months.

Taya added the following survivability requirement to its high reliability requirements: the probability that unrecoverable damage to the betting files will occur in case of any communication system failure is to be less than one in a million communication failures.

Understandability. Understandability refers to the user's capability to find out how to use the software for particular tasks, and to grasp the conditions of use. It relates to the user interface design, the user manual, and the online help instructions. Another type of understandability requirements relate to the use of software comments and program documentation. It is accepted that conformity to design and company coding guideline instructions ensures good understandability by both developers and maintenance staff.

Verifiability. Verifiability requirements define design and programming features that enable efficient verification of the design and programming. Most verifiability requirements refer to modularity, simplicity, and adherence to documentation and programming guidelines. A significant similarity exists between the verifiability factor and McCall's testability factor.

2.5   Software compliance with quality factors

The software quality models call for implementation – for the evaluation of the quality of software development and maintenance processes, and of software products. In other words, we would like to find out the extent to which the software development and maintenance processes comply with the requirements of the various quality factors to be examined in design reviews, software inspections, software tests, and evaluated by software quality metrics. In efforts to do so, we face the gap between the factors defined as general attributes, and explicit review questions, requiring quantitative measurement.

A way to bridge this gap is by adding explanatory criteria (subfactors) for each of the factors. As a result, each of the software quality factors is represented

Table 2.1   McCall's model factors and criteria (subfactors)

Software quality factors	Criteria (subfactors)	Software quality factors	Criteria (subfactors)
Correctness	Accuracy	**Flexibility**	Modularity
	Completeness		Generality
	Up-to-datedness		Simplicity
	Availability (response time)		Self-descriptiveness
Reliability	System and application reliability	**Testability**	Simplicity
			Failure maintenance testability
	Failure recovery		
	Hardware failure recovery		Traceability
Efficiency	Efficiency of processing	**Portability**	Software system independence
	Efficiency of storage		
	Efficiency of communication	**Reusability**	Modularity
	Efficiency of power usage (for portable units)		Self-descriptiveness
			Modularity
Integrity	Access control		Coding and documentation guidelines compliance (consistency)
	Access audit		
Usability	Operability		
	Learning and training ability		Software system and application independence
Maintainability	Simplicity		Self-descriptiveness
	Modularity		Generality
	Self-descriptiveness		Simplicity
	Coding and documentation guidelines compliance (consistency)	**Interoperability**	Commonality
			System compatibility
			Software system independence
			Modularity

by several quality criteria. The criteria (subfactors) are quantitative and qualitative criteria, where preference is given to the quantitative ones. These quantitative measurable criteria are believed to help formulate the specification of software requirements, the definition of review questions, the preparing of test plans, and the development of software metrics. These measurable criteria enable examining the degree of compliance of a software project to the factors for which the criteria were defined. Many authors investigated the software models and proposed criteria for their factors. To mention but a few: Evans and Marciniak (1987), Sharma et al. (2012), Al-Qutaish (2010), and Kumar (2012). The importance of measurable criteria, the methods used to measure them, their planning and implementation, and more about software measures are discussed by Fenton and Bieman (2015).

Table 2.1 presents a selection of criteria (subfactors) for McCall's factors.

Table 2.2 presents the criteria (subfactors) for ISO/IEC 25010:2011 product quality models.

Table 2.3 Presents criteria for factors of alternative quality models, not included in McCall's and ISO/IEC 25010:2011 product quality models.

Table 2.2 ISO/IEC 25010 product quality model factors and criteria (subfactors)

Software quality factors	Criteria (subfactors)	Software quality factors	Criteria (subfactors)
Functional suitability	Functional completeness	**Security**	Confidentiality
	Functional correctness		Integrity
	Functional appropriateness		Nonrepudiation
Performance efficiency	Time behavior		Accountability
	Resource utilization		Authenticity
	Capacity	**Maintainability**	Modularity
Compatibility	Coexistence		Reusability
	Interoperability		Analyzability
Usability	Appropriateness recognizability		Modifiability
			Testability
	Learnability	**Portability**	Adaptability
	User error protection		Installability
	User interface aesthetics		Replaceability
	Accessibility		
Reliability	Maturity		
	Availability		
	Fault tolerance		
	Recoverability		

Source: – ISO/IEC Std. 25010:2011

Table 2.3   Factors and criteria of Alternative quality models (**For factors not included in McCall/s and ISO/IEC 25010 quality models**)

Software quality factors	Criteria (subfactors)	Software quality factors	Criteria (subfactors)
Effectiveness	Production plan compliance	**Productivity**	Operability
	Production schedule compliance		Resource efficiency
		Safety	Avoidance of hazardous operating situations
	Low failure rate	**Safety**	Unsafe conditions alarm reliability
Evolvability	Modularity		
	Generality	**Satisfaction**	User perception of requirements fulfillment
	Simplicity		User perception of performance
Expandability	Self-descriptiveness		
	Extensibility		
	Modularity	**Supportability**	Installability
	Generality		Maintainability
	Simplicity		Modifiability
	Self-descriptiveness	**Survivability**	System reliability
Extensibility	Modularity		Application reliability
	Generality		Computational failure recovery
	Simplicity		
	Self-descriptiveness	**Understandability**	Self-descriptiveness
Human Engineering	Man–machine interface		Hardware failure recovery
	Understandability		Simplicity
Manageability	Completeness and ease of support provided to infrastructure services for software modifications in the development process		Modularity
			Coding and documentation guidelines compliance (consistency)
	Completeness and ease of support provided to infrastructure services for software modifications in maintenance activities	**Verifiability**	Coding and documentation guidelines compliance (consistency)
			Documentation accessibility
			Traceability
Modifiability	Modularity		Modularity
	Generality		
	Simplicity		
	Self-descriptiveness		

As you have probably noticed, several criteria (subfactors) relate to more than one factor. This reflects the fact that several criteria contribute to successful compliance in more than one factor. It also reflects the extensive overlapping, and the many similarities of software quality factors.

Summary

1. The need for comprehensive requirements documents

Many cases of low customer satisfaction are situations where software projects have satisfactorily fulfilled the basic requirements of correctness, but suffer from poor performance in other important areas such as maintenance, reliability, software reuse, or training. One of the main causes for these lapses is the lack of defined requirements pertaining to these aspects of software functionally. Therefore, a comprehensive definition of requirements to cover all aspects of software use throughout all stages of the software life cycle is crucial.

Software quality models define the broad spectrum of quality factors that relate to software quality requirements. We expect that those individuals who define software quality requirements refer to each factor and, accordingly, examine the need to incorporate the respective requirements in their requirement specification documents.

2. The structure (categories and factors) of McCall's classic factor model

McCall's factor model classifies all software requirements into 11 software quality factors. These 11 factors are grouped into three categories: product operation, product revision, and product transition, as follows:

Product operation factors:	Correctness
	Reliability
	Efficiency
	Integrity
	Usability
Product revision factors:	Maintainability
	Flexibility
	Testability
Product transition factors:	Portability
	Reusability
	Interoperability

3. Quality factors of the ISO/IEC 25010:2011 model

The ISO/IEC 25010:2011 model was developed by a joint ISO/IEC international professional team and is of significant importance. The model includes the eight following factors, while four of them were already included in McCall's model.

- Functional suitability
- Performance efficiency
- Compatibility

- Usability
- Reliability
- Security
- Maintainability
- Portability

4. **The additional factors suggested by alternative factor models**

    Several software quality models, alternatives to McCall's 1976 classic software quality model and to the ISO/IEC 25010:2011 software quality models, have been presented since the late seventies. These alternative models propose 14 additional software quality factors, several of which show similarities to McCall's factors and also overlap each other.

5. **Software compliance with quality factors**

    The gap between the general character of software quality factors, and the explicit nature of software specification requirements causes difficulties when implementing software quality models in software development processes. A set of explanatory criteria for each factor is believed to bridge the gap, and help customers and software developers specify quality requirements, define review questions, prepare test plans, and develop software quality metrics. As a result, the criteria help to examine the degree software projects comply with the software quality factors.

Selected bibliography

Al-Qutaish R. E. (2010) *quality models in software engineering literature: an analytical and comparative study, Journal of American Science*, Vol. **6**, No. 3, pp. 166–175.

Boehm B. W., Brown J. R., Caspar H., Lipow M., MacLeod G., and Merritt M. (1978) *Characteristics of Software Quality*, North Holland Publishing, Amsterdam, The Netherlands.

Carvallo J. P. and Franch X. (2006) Extending the ISO/IEC 9126-1 quality model with non-technical factors for COTS components selection, in *Proceedings of the 2006 International ACM Workshop on Software Quality (WoSC)*.

Deutsch M. S. and Willis R. R. (1988) *Software Quality Engineering: A Total Technical & Management Approach*, Prentice-Hall, Englewood Cliffs, NJ, Chapter 3.

Dromey R. G. (1995) *A Model for Software Product Quality, IEEE Transactions on Software Engineering*, Vol. **21**, pp. 146–162.

Evans M. W. and Marciniak J. J. (1987) *Software Quality Assurance and Management*, John Wiley & Sons, New York, Chapters 7 and 8.

Fenton, N. E. and Bieman J. (2015) *Software Metrics – A Rigorous and Practical Approach*, 3rd Edition, CRC Press, Boca Raton, FL.

Georgiadou E. (2003) *A generic, multilayered, customisable, software quality model, International Journal of Cybernetics*, Vol. **11**, No. 4, pp. 313–323.

Grady R.H and Coswell D. L. (1987) *Software Metrics – Establishing a Company-wide Program*, Prentice Hall.

ISO/IEC (2001) *ISO/IEC IS 9126-1 Software Engineering: Product Quality – Part 1: Quality Model*, ISO, Geneva, Switzerland.

ISO/IEC (2001) *ISO/IEC 25010:2011 Systems and Software Engineering: Systems and Software*, ISO, Geneva, Switzerland.

Kumar P. (2012) *Aspect-oriented software quality model: the AOSQ model, Advanced Computing: An International Journal (ACIJ)*, Vol. **3**, No. 2, pp. 105–118.

McCall, J., Richards P., and Walters G. (1977) *Factors in Software Quality, Volume 1, Concepts and Definitions of Software Quality*, Vol. **1**, No. 3, Rome Air Development Center Air Force Systems Command, Griffiss Air Force Base, NY. Nov. 1977.

Quirchmayr G., Funilkul S., and Chutimaskul W. (2007) A quality model of e-government services based on the ISO/IEC 9126 standard, in *The Proceedings of International Legal Informatics Symposium, (IRIS)*, pp. 45–53.

Sharma A. H., Kalia A., and Singh H. (2012) *An analysis of optimum software quality factors, IOSR Journal of Engineering*, Vol. **2**, No. 4, pp. 663–669.

Review questions

2.1 a. What are the three factor categories belonging to McCall's factor model?

  b. Which factors are included in each of the categories?

2.2 The software requirement specification document for the tender for the development of "Super-lab," a software system for managing a hospital laboratory, consists of chapter headings that are in accordance with the required quality factors. In the following table, you will find sections from the mentioned requirements document.

For each section, fill in the name of the McCall's factor that best fits the requirement (choose only one factor per requirements section).

No.	Section taken from the software requirement document	The quality factor
1	The probability that the "Super-lab" software system will be found in a state of failure during peak hours (9 am to 4 pm) is required to be below 0.5%.	_____
2	The "Super-lab" software system will enable the direct transfer of laboratory results to those files of hospitalized patients managed by the "MD-File" software package.	_____
3	The "Super-lab" software system will include a module that prepares a detailed report of the patient's laboratory test results during the current hospitalization. The time required to obtain this printed report will be less than 60 seconds.	_____
4	The "Super-lab" software to be developed for hospital laboratory use may be adapted later for private laboratory use.	_____
5	The training of a laboratory technician, requiring no more than 3 days, will enable the technician to reach level C of "Super-lab" operator. This means that the trainee will be able to manage the reception of 20 patients per hour.	_____
6	The "Super-lab" software system will record details of users logging in. In addition, the system will report attempts by unauthorized persons to obtain medical information from the laboratory test results database. Reports will include detailed information about unauthorized attempts to access the database of "Super lab".	_____

7   The "Super-lab" subsystem that deals with billing patients _____
    for their tests may eventually be used as a subsystem in the
    "Physiotherapy Centre" software package.

8   The "Super-lab" software system will process the monthly _____
    reports of the hospital departments' management, the
    hospital management, and the hospital controller, in
    accordance with Appendix D of the development contract
    (not attached).

9   The software system should be able to serve 12 work stations _____
    and 8 automatic testing machines with a single model AS20
    server; and a CS25 communication server that will be able to
    serve 25 communication lines. The hardware system should
    conform to all availability requirements as listed in
    Appendix D.

10 The "Super-lab" software package developed for the Linux _____
    operating system should be compatible with applications in
    the Windows NT environment.

2.3 The ISO/IEC 25010:2011 model includes eight different factors.

a. List the factors included in the ISI/IEC model.

b. Discuss the similarity of the ISO/IEC model with McCall's model.

2.4 South cottage Inc. is a manufacturer of washing machines and dishwashers. The requirements document for the new control unit includes the following specifications:

a. The firmware should be suitable for all six variations of the following year's washing machines models.

b. The water level control module of the washing machine should be suitable for use for the dishwasher model planned to be released in 2 years' time.

    a. To which of McCall's factors do the above requirements belong?

    b. Explain your answer.

2.5 Some people claim that testability and verifiability are actually different terms for the same factor.

a. Do you agree?

b. If not, explain your reasoning.

Topics for discussion

2.1 Four "but" complaints reflecting items missing from the requirement documents are mentioned in Section 2.3.1.

a. To which McCall factors do the missing requirements belong?

b. Can you suggest software quality requirements that could fill the gap?

2.2 Some professionals claim that increased software usability necessarily involves decreased efficiency. Others claim that no dependence between software efficiency and usability exists.

a. Do you agree with the first or second group?

b. Discuss your answer.

Chapter 3

The Software Quality Challenges

3.1 Introduction

A basic question often asked is "Do we need a specialized quality assurance methodology for software products?" In other words, Why don't we use the general quality assurance tools and methodologies applied successfully in the food and metal industries, as in many others? The answer rests in the unique character of software, the software development process, and its maintenance. Thus, we are inevitably faced with a need for unique quality assurance tools and methodologies for software development and maintenance.

The other topic of the chapter deals with "the software development, maintenance, and SQA environment" – the combination of legal, managerial, social, and technological requirements that need to be fulfilled with the software development, maintenance, and SQA activities. The need to cope with the unique difficulties of assuring software quality in the software development, maintenance, and SQA environment is the very challenges of software development, maintenance, and SQA.

This chapter deals with two basic topics:

1. The uniqueness of software quality assurance in relation to the characteristics of software products and their development process.

2. Software development, maintenance, and the SQA environment.

3.2 The uniqueness of software quality assurance

"What is so special about software quality that it needs separate warranty documents, and a specialized ISO 9000 standard all of its own?" I was asked by my students at the beginning of a software quality assurance course.

I shall, as I did then, before I address to approach the fundamental issue of the uniqueness of software quality assurance, I shall begin with two typical examples.

First – **warranty document comparison**

Typical limited warranty documents of household or industrial devices, and in our case – computer printers, state the following:

> The Manufacturer warranty commences on the date of purchase of the original retail customer for a period of one year. Should the product become defective within the warranty period, the Manufacturer will repair or replace it at no charge, provided it is delivered at the customer's expense to an authorized service facility.

In comparison, a typical limited warranty document of a software product is actually a disclaimer rather than a guarantee document, and states that the following:

> Although the Manufacturer has tested the software and reviewed the documentation of the software, the Manufacturer makes no warranty or representation, either expressed or implied, with respect to this software or documentation, its quality, performance, merchantability, or fitness for a particular purpose. As a result, this software and documentation are licensed 'AS IS,' and the licensee is assuming the entire risk as to its quality and performance.
>
> The Manufacturer warranty commences on the date of purchase of the original retail customer for a period of one year. Should the product become defective within the warranty period, the Manufacturer will repair or replace it at no charge, provided it is delivered at the customer's expense to an authorized service facility.

The most striking difference relates to the situation of product failure. For the printer it says, "Should the product become defective within the warranty period, the Manufacturer will repair or replace it at no charge." However, for the software package it says, "The Manufacturer makes no warranty or representation, either expressed or implied, with respect to this software or documentation, its quality, performance, merchantability, or fitness for a particular purpose. As a result, this software and documentation are licensed 'AS IS.'" The basic meaning is that while the printer manufacturer is sure about the quality of his product, the software package manufacturer is not sure about the quality of his product. In other words, he is not sure the software he sells is free of bugs. This difference actually reflects the fact that in spite of investing vast resources to assure the quality of the software package, total software quality ("no bugs") could not be achieved.

Second – **Standards for general use versus specialized standard**.

ISO/IEC 9000 is a "family" of standards that includes several standards, which are updated once every few years. The three current standards of the "family" are:

- ISO/IEC 9000:2015 – Quality management systems – Fundamentals and vocabulary.

- ISO/IEC 9001:2015 – Quality management systems – Requirements.
- ISO/IEC 9000:2015 – Quality management systems – Managing for the sustained success of an organization (continuous improvement).

These standards serve almost every industry. However, a special ISO 9000 family member has been developed for the software industry, namely:

- The ISO/IEC 90003:2014 standard – Software engineering – Guidelines for the application of ISO 9001:2008 to computer software.

A great part of the requirements included in the ISO/IEC 90003 standard are not included in the other ISO/IEC standards, for instance:

- Documentation requirements
- Quality planning
- Design and development planning
- Customer-related requirements
- Customer communications during development requirements

The above two examples may serve as indicators for the uniqueness of software quality assurance. Now, let us investigate the three root causes for the challenging uniqueness of software quality assurance.

- **Software is complex**. Software complexity may be measured by the number of software modes of operation. This number reaches many thousands, frequently millions, and sometimes even more. The task of ensuring the correct operation for each of the multitude modes of operation is actually impossible – a fact reflected in the software "limited warranty" document. While on the other hand, the number of operation possibilities for hardware products is substantially lower, making it possible to test and verify the correctness of each operation mode.
- **Software lacks visibility**. Defects in software products (whether stored on a disk-on-key, computer hard disc, or elsewhere) are invisible and intangible, just as any missing parts of a software package or from a software file are. A predefined process of displaying the software listings on screen or in print is required to enable the identification of software defects, or missing software parts. While in the case of industrial products, it is most likely that a defective or missing part will be identified by the production line team. Imagine the case of a missing door, or a wrong car headlamp on a car on an assembly line.
- **Few opportunities to identify defects**. Software defects may only be identified in the *software product development phase*. In this phase, designers and programmers develop software products, while staff members and SQA function staff review and test the software to detect defects.

When examining industrial products, for example, cars, a wide range of opportunities *to identify defects are evident.* These opportunities transpire over three phases: the *car model prototype development phase*, the *car production planning phase*, and finally the *manufacturing phase*. In the *car model prototype development phase*, designers design a new model and construct a prototype, while the staff member and the quality assurance (QA) function perform verification with the design requirements documentation and test the prototype to detect defects. This phase corresponds to the *software product development phase*.

During the *car production planning phase*, the production process is planned, tools are designed and prepared, and a tailored production line is devised and built. This phase thus provides additional opportunities to review, inspect, and test the product, while defects, that may have "escaped" reviews and tests conducted during the *car model prototype development phase*, may be revealed. Defects detected during the car production planning phase processes can usually be corrected by performing changes to the product design, components, or production tools. This phase is very limited in software products, and deals almost only with the publication of software manuals (prepared in the *software product development phase*), and planning the software product files packaging on CDs, or other media. These limited activities include practically no SQA activities, or in other words, are unable to contribute to the software product's quality. This situation applies to all software products, whether their number of copies is small, as in custom-made software, or large, as in software packages sold to the general public.

In the *car manufacturing phase*, defects are identified by the assembly line staff, and also identified at a later stage, when QA procedures are applied to detect failures in each of the manufactured cars. Defects detected in a car during this phase can usually be repaired by replacing faulty parts, and only in extreme cases is a car declared unfit for sale. When compared with the manufacturing of a car, the release of a software product is limited to automatic electronic copying of software product files to the chosen media, and printing software manuals. Consequently, there are no expectations for detecting software defects in this phase.

To summarize, while SQA activities are practically limited to the development phase only, industrial products benefit from QA activities performed throughout three phases: development, production planning, and manufacturing phases. Moreover, QA activities for industrial products are conducted by three independent teams, a fact that significantly contributes to the effectiveness of defect identification.

It should be noted that a significant number of products in advanced machinery, as well as in household machines, include embedded software components (usually termed "firmware") that are integrated into the product. These software components (the firmware) share the very same characteristics of software products discussed herein, and so it follows that the comparison shown above should actually be of software products versus nonsoftware components of industrial products.

The unique characteristics of software quality assurance versus the characteristics of industrial products are shown in Frame 3.1.

Frame 3.1: The uniqueness of software quality assurance

The ununiqueness of software quality assurance
Software's high complexity versus substantially lower complexity of industrial products
Software's lack of visibility versus visibility of industrial products   **Software's few opportunities to identify defects**: product development phase only for software versus product development, production planning, development, and manufacturing phases of industrial products.

Its great complexity and invisibility, as well as the few available opportunities to identify defects, makes the development of SQA methodology and its successful implementation extremely challenging.

3.3 Software development, maintenance, and SQA environment

Software serves multifarious purposes, and is developed by many individuals and organizations in many different environments. Our discussion deals with software development maintained by commercial bodies: by software houses or software development and maintenance units (teams, departments, etc.) of both small and large industrial, financial, and other organizations.

Software development and maintenance is performed under a series of legal, managerial, social, and technological requirements. These requirements may be defined as the "software development, maintenance, and SQA environment." Whoever participates in software development and quality assurance activities is required to cope and deal with these environment requirements.

The main characteristics of the software development, maintenance, and SQA environment are:

1. **Contractual conditions of software development, maintenance, and SQA activities**

   The commitments and conditions between the software developer–maintainer and the customer are defined in the contract. The contract affects the activities of software development that include, in addition to development, the delivery, installation, and running-in activities, and the maintenance activities include software operation and the three types of maintenance activities. All these need to cope with:

- Defined list of project functional requirements
- Development and maintenance project budget
- Project schedule
- Professional license or academic qualification requirements of project team leader and team members

It is expected that an internal software development project be managed in environment conditions similar to those specified in the project contract conditions, and according to an approved development plan serving as part of the "internal contract." The familiar situations prevailing in internal projects, where no formal contracts and less "binding" customer–supplier relationships are in place, often lead to unsuccessful projects, which are over-budget, completed late, and whose functional requirements are only partially met.

2. Subjection to customer–supplier relationship

All software development and SQA activities throughout the process are overseen by the customer, and therefore it is of great importance that the project team continuously maintains a cooperative working relationship with the customer. This cooperation is vital to accomplish the following activities: obtaining information required for the development process from customer, discussing customer's request for changes with customer, discussing customer comments regarding project issues, and obtaining customer approval for work performed, and for changes initiated by the development team. Environmental and contractual conditions similar to those of customer projects also need to exist in internal projects, between the software development team and representatives of the department who initiated and ordered the project.

3. The need for teamwork

Three factors usually motivate the establishment of a project team, rather than assigning the whole project to just one professional:

- Schedule requirements. The project workload to be performed requires the participation of more than one person if the project is to be completed on time.
- The need for a range of professional specializations in order to carry out the project.
- The objective to benefit from professional mutual support and review for the enhancement of project quality.

4. The need for cooperation and coordination with other internal development teams

The carrying out of projects, especially larger projects, by more than one team is a very common event in the software industry and cooperation and coordination may be required with the following:

- Other software development team in the same organization.
- Hardware development teams in the same organization. This is usually the case when the software development task is part of a hardware manufacturer development project.

5. **The need for cooperation and coordination with external participants in the software development project**

   The carrying out of projects, especially large-scale projects, requires, in many cases, participation of one or more external organizations with whom the development team is required to coordinate and cooperate:

   - Software and hardware suppliers
   - Subcontractors and outsourcing development teams
   - Development teams of partners performing the project
   - Customer's development teams – in cases that the customer participates in project

   An outline of cooperation and coordination between the internal and external environment, as seen from the perspective of a development team ("Our software development team"), is shown in Figure 3.1. The team is part of a hardware–software product development effort. The relationships of our software development team with the hardware

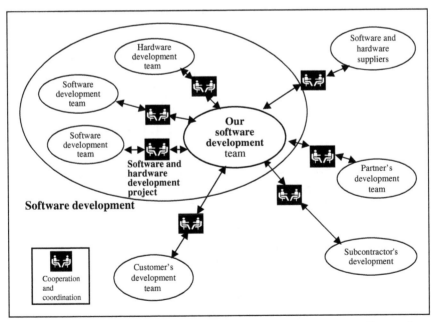

Figure 3.1 Cooperation and coordination scheme for software development team of large-scale software project

development teams and the rest of the product development teams are represented by one relationship with the hardware development team. For reasons of simplicity, the figure does not show the professional relationships with the system engineers and project management.

6. The required product interfaces with other software systems.

Today, most software systems include interfaces with other software packages. These interfaces allow data in electronic form to flow between the software systems.

The main types of interfaces are:

• Input interfaces, where other software systems transmit data to your software system.
• Output interfaces, where your software system transmits processed data to other software systems.
• Input and output interfaces to a software system, as in medical and laboratory control systems.

Typical input and output interfaces to other software packages may be seen in salary processing software packages. An example is shown in Figure 3.2.

Let's examine Figure 3.2. First, let us look at the input interfaces of the salary processing package. In order to calculate salaries, the employee attendance information is required. This data is captured by the time clocks placed at the entrance to the office building, and later processed by the attendance control software system. An additional input

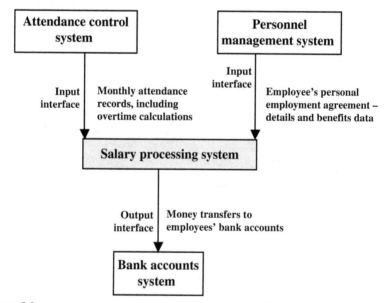

Figure 3.2   A salary software system – example of software interfaces

interface transmits data from the personnel information system, namely, employee salary details including payable benefits, as agreed upon in the employment agreement and employee bank account details. Once a month, the input information from these two software systems is electronically transmitted to the salary processing system. These data transmissions represent two input interfaces for the salary processing software system, and at the same time they represent output interfaces of the attendance control system and the personnel software system. Let's now examine an output interface of the system. One of the outputs of the salary processing system is the list of "net" salaries (after deduction of income tax and other items) payable to the employees. The list of net salary payments and the employee bank account details are electronically transmitted to the bank. This transmission represents an output interface for the salary processing system, and an input interface for the bank's accounts system.

7. **The need to continue carrying out a software project despite team member changes**

It is common practice for team members to leave during the software project period, whether owing to a promotion, an employer switch, a transfer to another city, and so on. It is the team leader's responsibility to replace the departing team member with either another company employee, or a newly recruited employee. Regardless of how much time and effort need to be invested in training the new team member, "the show must go on," and the original project contract schedule remains unchanged. It should be noted that the software project includes the development phases as well and the delivery, installation, and the running-in phases. The same rule holds when a team leader leaves a team; however, in this case it is management's task to replace the team leader promptly.

8. **The need to maintain software systems for extended periods**

Customers who develop or purchase a software system expect to continue utilizing it for a long time, usually for 5–10 years. During the service period, the need for maintenance will eventually arise. In most cases, the developer is required to supply these services directly. In cases when the software was developed in-house, internal customers share the same expectation regarding software maintenance of their software system.

In most cases, it is the environmental characteristics that create the need for intensive and continuous managerial efforts. These efforts are invested in parallel to the professional efforts required in order to ensure project quality, or in other words, to ensure the project's success.

A summary of the main characteristics of the SQA environment is shown in Frame 3.2.

Frame 3.2: Software development, maintenance, and SQA environment

The main characteristics of the SQA environment
1. Contractual conditions of software development, maintenance, and SQA activities
2. Subjection to customer–supplier relationship
3. The need for teamwork
4. The need for cooperation and coordination with other internal development teams
5. The need for cooperation and coordination with external participants in the project
6. The required product interfaces with other software systems
7. The need to continue carrying out a software project despite team member changes
8. The need to maintain software systems for extended periods

Implementation tip
The existing familiar terms between the internal customer and the internal supplier frequently create "nonbinding contract projects." These projects, supported by the notion that it "would save time," usually take the same course; no existing requirement documents (or at best a one pager consisting of a short vague definition of the "functional expectations") and no budget or schedule commitments are in place. These widespread conditions for in-house projects are undesirable for both parties – both sides are inevitably unsatisfied. The customer will find his functional expectations to be only partially fulfilled correctly, while the developer will have wasted substantial resources developing undesired functionalities. A reasonable level of formality is expected to be beneficial to budget and schedule management, to the successful fulfillment of project requirements as well as contributing to reducing wasted resources by software developers. For a discussion on internal customers – internal supplier relationships and the pitfalls involved – see Sec. 8.6.

A significant amount of software, as well as firmware development, is not carried out under formal contracts or formal customer–supplier relationships, as mentioned in the first two SQA environment characteristics. This situation usually relates to software or firmware developed in-house for internal use. The informal relationship – between the marketing department, that initiates and defines the requirements of a new product, and the respective in-house software development department – may be likened to a relationship under a nonbinding contract, or that of a less "binding" customer–supplier relationship. Typically, for these situations, there is no documentation requirements, no commitment for budget and schedule, and no regular coordination meetings between the developing department and the customer department. In these conditions, an unsuccessful project – over-budget, late completion (if at all), and partial requirements met – is almost inevitable. Accordingly, many managers claim that the more the relationship resembles a formal (vendor–customer) relationship, the greater the prospects are for the project to reach a successful conclusion.

Summary

1. **The uniqueness of software quality assurance**. The fundamental differences between software products (including firmware) and other industrial products, namely, higher product complexity, the invisibility of software, and the contrasting fewer opportunities to detect defects. These differences create substantial challenges for SQA methodologies and tools required to meet these extremely difficult challenges and produce quality software products.

2. **The environments in which SQA methods need to be employed**. The SQA methods and tools discussed in this book are specially aimed at the needs of professional software development and maintenance, and activities required to contend with legal, managerial, social, and technological conditions – in other words the SQA environment. The method and tools to be applied in professional software development and maintenance are subject to these environmental characteristics, namely:
   - Contract conditions defining functional requirements, budget, schedule, and, in many cases, also team qualifications.
   - The need to maintain customer–supplier relationships required for consultations with the customer, customer approvals, and more.
   - The need to implement teamwork.
   - The need for cooperation and coordination with other internal software and hardware development teams.
   - The need for cooperation and coordination with external participants in the software development project, namely, suppliers, subcontractors, outsourcing teams, partner teams, and, in many cases, also customer development teams participating in project.
   - The need for interfaces with other software systems.
   - The need to continue carrying out a project during and after team members changes.
   - The need to conduct maintenance activities for the software system for several years.

   These characteristics demand that intensive and continuous managerial efforts be expended in parallel to the professional efforts invested to ensure project quality or, in other words, to ensure project success.

These environmental characteristics also apply to the internal development of software and firmware.

Review questions

3.1 There are three major differences between software products and other industrial products.

a. Identify and describe the differences.

b. Discuss the ways in which these differences affect SQA.

3.2 It is claimed that no significant SQA activities are expected to take place during the production planning and manufacturing phases of software products.

a. Discuss this claim.

b. Compare the required production planning and manufacturing for a new refrigerator model, with the production planning and manufacturing efforts required for the new release of a software product.

3.3 Eight issues characterize the professional software development and maintenance environment.

a. Identify and describe these characteristics.

b. Which of these environmental characteristics require managerial efforts for executing software development and maintenance projects?

List the characteristics, and explain why such efforts are needed.

Topics for discussion

3.1 It is assumed that educational systems prepare students to cope with real-life conditions.

Examine the environmental requirements of a final software development project at your college, and determine which of the higher education requirements could be considered preparatory to professional life situations, as discussed above.

3.2 Which of the eight environmental characteristics of software development and maintenance become severe when large-scale projects are to be carried out?

3.3 The interfaces of a salary processing system are exhibited in Figure 3.2.

a. **List the main benefits of applying computerized interfaces instead of** transferring printouts.

b. Give two additional examples where input interfaces are employed.

c. Give two additional examples where output interfaces are employed.

d. Suggest additional situations where the use of input and output interfaces is not applied but could be recommended.

3.4 It is clear that a software development project executed by a software house for a specific customer is carried out under content and schedule obligations, and that an existing customer–supplier relationship also needs to be maintained.

    a. Discuss how contractual commitments and customer–supplier relationships are expected to exist? Be maintained? In cases when the software product is developed in-house, and is to be sold to the public as a software package.

    b. Discuss how contractual commitments and customer–supplier relationships are expected to exist when software is developed for in-house usage, as in the case when a software development department develops an inventory program for the company's warehouses.

    c. Some managers claim that the closer contractual commitments and customer–supplier relationships are to formal ones; the greater the prospects are for an in-house project to be successful. Discuss whether implementing customer–supplier relationships in the situations mentioned in (1) and (2) above is beneficial to the company, or an unnecessary burden to the development team.

Chapter 4

Organization for Assuring Software Quality

4.1 Introduction

Who initiates, activates, operates, and controls all those components of the software quality assurance described briefly in Chapter 5 and discussed throughout this book? Who is responsible for all the activities needed to run an effective and efficient SQA system? Partial answers to these questions are sprinkled throughout the chapters of the book's first part.

In this chapter, we take an integrated look at the quality assurance organization. We focus on mangers of the various levels, from top management to development, and maintenance team leaders. All of them carry out tasks related to software quality assurance, namely, defining the quality assurance policy, performing quality assurance activities, and managing and following-up the performance. The tasks of planning SQA activities, developing SQA tools, initiating, consulting, supporting, and professionally overviewing the performance of quality assurance activities are carried out by the SQA function/unit.

For the purposes of our discussion, we refer to three levels of management found in many software development organizations and to the SQA function:

- **Top management level**, including the organization's general manager and its chief executive officers (CEOs).
- **Department managers level**, including managers of software development, maintenance, and software testing departments.
- **Project managers and team leaders** of development projects and maintenance services.
- **The SQA function and its associated players in the SQA system.** Many SQA activities are performed by the SQA unit and its associated actors associated with the SQA unit.

Software Quality: Concepts and Practice, First Edition. Daniel Galin.
© 2018 the IEEE Computer Society, Inc. Published 2018 by John Wiley & Sons, Inc.

Many quality assurance managerial tasks are shared by managers of more than one level, with each manager taking on the responsibilities suitable to his or her level of authority and expertise.

ISO/IEC 90003:2014 (ISO, 2014) software engineering standard dedicates its Chapter 5 to management responsibility, defining the standard requirements regarding management commitments, customer focus, planning, management's responsibility, authority and communication, and the performance of management reviews. Additional aspects of software management are presented by Berki et al. (2004) and Gill (2005).

4.2   Top management's quality assurance activities

Among its responsibilities, top management is committed to software quality management requirements, as summarized in Frame 4.1.

Frame 4.1:   Top management's commitment to software quality management requirements

Source: After ISO/IEC 90003:2015 (ISO/IEC 9001:2008)

Top management's commitment to software quality management system requirements
1. Communicate the importance of software product and services meeting customer and regulatory requirements to employees at all levels.
2. Establish a software quality policy and ensure that quality objectives related to the company's software products and software maintenance services are established and accomplished consistently.
3. Ensure that quality objectives are established for the organization's SQA system and that they are accomplished.
4. Ensure availability of the resources required for performing software quality assurance activities.
5. Conduct periodical management reviews.

The following are the three main tools available to top management for fulfillment of its responsibilities:

- Establish and update the organization's software quality policy.
- Assign one of the executives to be responsible for software quality issues (e.g., Vice President of SQA)
- Conduct regular *management reviews* of performance with respect to software quality issues.

The next three sections deal with these tools.

4.2.1 Software quality policy

The organization's software quality policy, defined by top management, though very general in its contents and their statement, should communicate the following, as presented in Frame 4.2:

Frame 4.2: Quality policy as defined by top managements.

Source: After ISO/IEC 90003:2015 (ISO/IEC 9001:2008)

Quality policy as defined by top managements
The quality policy: • Conforms to the organization's goals and purpose. • Establishes continuous improvement of the organization's quality and productivity, and the effectiveness of software quality assurance systems. • Establishes commitment to conform to project requirements and ensure customers satisfaction. • Establishes and states need for review of the software quality assurance objectives. • Is reviewed and updated to ensure its continuous suitability. • Is communicated and understood at all levels of the organization.

An example of a software quality policy – formulated by (the fictional) Bridge Quality Software (BQS) Ltd. – is presented in Frame 4.3.

The organization's software quality policy, as might be anticipated, is stated in general terms. So, it is quite common to find that one organization's software quality policy declaration can be easily transferred to another organization "as is" or with only minor changes.

4.2.2 The executive in charge of software quality

The following may be classified as the responsibilities of the executive in charge of software quality issues:

1. Responsibility for defining the quality policy to be adopted by top management and policy reviews.
2. Establish the system's SQA objectives for the coming year.
3. Responsibility for preparation of an annual SQA activities program and budget.
4. Determine the scope of subcontractor services and software purchases planned for the coming year.

Frame 4.3: Bridge Quality Software (BQS) Ltd. – Software Quality Policy.

Bridge Quality Software (BQS) Ltd.

Software Quality Policy

The Company's quality goal

The principal goal of Lion Quality Software is to provide software products and software maintenance services that fully comply with customer requirements and expectations, at the scheduled time and according to the agreed-upon budget.

The Company's quality policy

The quality policy adopted by LQS supports this by:

1. Assigning maximum priority to customer satisfaction by promptly fulfilling requirements, expectations, requests, and complaints.

2. Involving employees in determination of quality objectives and commitment to their achievement.

3. Performing development and maintenance tasks correctly the first time around and minimizing the need for rework and correction.

4. Ensuring the high and adequate professional and managerial level of its employees, a value maintained by offering incentives and encouragement to the employees to achieve professional excellence.

5. Performing quality assurance activities throughout the software life cycle to ensure the achievement of the required quality objectives.

6. Applying its quality assurance standards to subcontractors and suppliers. Only those who qualify will be incorporated in the Company's development projects and maintenance services.

7. Aiming at continuous improvement of development and maintenance productivity as well as SQA effectiveness and efficiency.

8. Allocating all the organizational, physical, and professional resources necessary to realize software quality assurance objectives.

Lionel Johnson

L. T. Johnson, President

Marcel Talbot

M. Talbot, General Manager

Industrial Park, CA, February 12, 2016

5. Preparing development plans for human and other resources for the coming year, including adoption of new technologies, methodologies, and standards.

6. Overall control of implementation of the annual SQA regular activities program and planned SQA system development projects and their compliance with SQA procedures and standards.

7. Presentation of the annual activities program and budget for top management approval.

8. Presentation and advocacy of SQA issues to executive management, and conducting of the management review sessions.

4.2.3 Management review

Management review is the name given to the periodic meeting dedicated to quality issues. The meeting is convened to allow executives to obtain an overview of their organization's software quality issues. Management review meetings tend to be scheduled from several times a year to at least twice a year.

A *management review report*, prepared by the SQA unit, sets the stage for the discussions by providing items that appear on the meeting's agenda. A sample of typical items reviewed in management reviews is presented in Frame 4.4.

Frame 4.4: Typical items included in management review reports.

Source: After ISO/IEC 90003:2015 (ISO/IEC 9001:2008)

Typical items included in management review reports
1. Follow-up of approved actions and unsolved identified risks discussed in the previous management review meeting.
2. Periodic performance records, including quality metrics.
3. Customer satisfaction feedback.
4. Follow-up of SQA annual regular activity program and SQA projects.
5. Summary of special quality events related to customers, suppliers, subcontractors, and so on.
6. Review of significant findings of internal and external quality audits, as well as special quality events related to customers, suppliers, subcontractors, and so on.
7. Status of previous preventive and corrective action tasks.
8. Identification of new major changes that could affect software quality and became software quality risks.
9. Recommendations for improvements to be introduced in the software quality management system (e.g., development of new SQA components, purchase of tools, invitation of consultant) to be submitted for final approval.

Objectives of management reviews

The main objectives of management reviews are to assess the SQA system's compliance with the organization's quality policy, that is, to:

- Assess achievement of the quality objectives set for the organization's software quality management system.
- Assess the compliance of the SQA system with the organization's quality policy.
- Initiate updates and improvements of the software quality management system and its objectives.
- Initiate improvement of software product and software operation services to better fulfill customer requirements and improve customer satisfaction.
- Outline directions for remedying major SQA deficiencies and software quality management problems.
- Allocate additional resources to the software quality management system, if required.

Decisions made during management reviews are expected to guide and direct the operation of the software quality management system for the subsequent period ending at the next review.

4.3 Department managers with direct responsibilities for quality

This section only refers to department managers who are directly responsible for software quality, namely, the managers of software development, software maintenance, and software testing departments (henceforth referred to as "department managers"). The department managers carry responsibilities for the quality of software development projects and maintenance services performed by the department steams and the operation of infrastructure services. The SQA unit supports the department managers in performing their quality assurance tasks.

The departments' management quality assurance responsibilities include responsibilities for quality activities related to the department and infrastructure services (*department level responsibilities*), and those related to quality issues of particular software projects and maintenance services (*project level responsibilities*).

The department-related responsibilities include infrastructure operation and SQA activities related to the department itself:

1. Preparation of the department's annual SQA activities program and budget.
2. Preparation of the department's SQA systems development plans.
3. Control of implementation of the department's annual SQA activities program and development projects.

4. Presentation of the department's SQA issues to the executive in charge of software quality.

5. Development and updating of procedures and programming conventions.

6. Ensure that quality objectives for the organization's SQA system are established and that they are accomplished.

7. Control of compliance to quality assurance procedures, related software development, and maintenance processes, and to infrastructure services, including CAB, SCM, and CCA bodies.

8. Initiate planning and implementation of changes necessary to adapt the SQA system to changes related to the organization's customers, competition, and technology.

9. Initiate and promote software reuse in the department's projects.

Project-related responsibilities vary according to the organization's procedures and distribution of authority; they usually involve:

1. Detailed follow-up of contract review results and proposal approvals.

2. Follow-up of implementation of planned review activities; approval of project documents and project phase completion.

3. Follow-up of software tests and test results; approval of project's software products.

4. Follow-up of progress of software development projects: schedules, budget, and project's risks. Advice and support project managers to resolve project difficulties.

5. Follow-up of quality of maintenance services provision.

6. Approval of large software change orders and significant deviations from project specifications.

4.3.1   The SQA system-related responsibilities of department management

These responsibilities relate to department-level SQA tasks:

1. Preparation of the department's annual SQA activities program.

2. Preparation of the department's SQA system development plans.

3. Control performance of the department's annual SQA activities program and development projects.

4. Presentation of the department's SQA issues to top management, in coordination with the executive in charge of software quality.

5. Development and updating of procedures and programming conventions.
6. Ensure quality objectives are established and accomplished.
7. Control of compliance to quality assurance procedures, to related software development and maintenance and to infrastructure services.

4.4 Project management responsibilities for quality

Most project management responsibilities are defined in procedures and work instructions; the project manager is the person in charge of making sure that all the team members comply with the said procedures and instructions. His tasks include professional hands-on and managerial tasks, particularly:

Professional hands-on tasks

1. Preparation of project and quality plans and their updates.
2. Participation in joint customer–supplier committees.
3. Close professional follow-up regarding the implemented solutions and method, and professional support when needed.
4. Close follow-up of project team staffing, including attending to recruitment, training, and instruction.

Management tasks

Project managers address the follow-up issues:

1. Progress control of project schedule, budget, and project risk handling.
2. Performance of review activities and the consequent corrections, including participating in reviews.
3. Software development and maintenance unit performance with respect to development, integration, and system test activities as well as corrections and regression tests.
4. Performance of acceptance tests.
5. Software installation in customer sites and the running-in of the software system by the customer.
6. SQA training and instruction of project team members.
7. Schedules and resources allocated to project activities (many interventions to correct deviations).

8. Customer requests and satisfaction.

9. Evolving project development risks, application of solutions, and control of results (implementation of the risk management process – see Appendix 7.A).

The SQA system-related tasks required **of** project managers

1. Preparation of project and quality plans and their updates.

2. Participation in joint customer–supplier committee.

3. Close professional follow-up regarding the implemented solutions and method, and professional support when needed.

4. Review of project's teams' staffing, including recruitment and training.

4.5 The SQA unit and its associated players in the SQA system

4.5.1 The SQA system

In the previous sections we discussed the contributions made by management levels as an involved party in the *software quality assurance framework*. In the following sections we present the SQA unit and its associated players (The SQA system).

The SQA system major party is the SQA function/team. Additional players in the SQA system also include, beside the SQA unit professionals, interested practitioners found among the software development and maintenance staff. These SQA interested people contribute to the SQA system in the following formats:

- SQA trustees
- SQA committee members
- SQA forum members

The SQA system includes the SQA unit and the associated players are presented in Figure 4.1.

4.5.2 The SQA unit

The structure of an SQA unit varies according to the type, and of course, size of the organization. As it is impossible to describe all the optional arrangements, this section presents a model whose structure and task distribution are readily adaptable to the characteristics and procedures characterizing the internal environment of a major share of organizations.

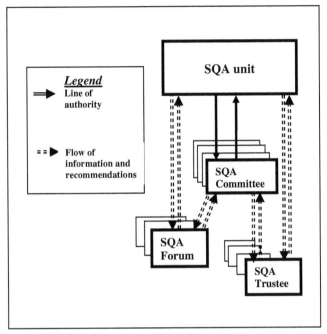

Figure 4.1 The SQA system

The proposed model of an SQA unit presented here is based on IEEE Std. 730-2014. The SQA unit is composed of three areas as follows:

- SQA area 1: SQA process implementation activities
- SQA area 2: The product assurance activities for conformance
- SQA area 3: The process assurance activities for conformance

The proposed model is shown in Figure 4.2.
The tasks of the SQA areas are described in the next sections.

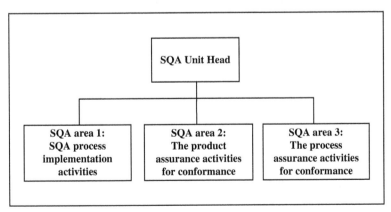

Figure 4.2 Proposed model for an SQA Unit's organizational structure

4.5.3   Tasks of SQA area 1: SQA process implementation activities

The SQA tasks performed by the SQA process implementation activities of the SQA area may be classified into five groups:

a. Establishing SQA processes and their coordination with the software development processes

b. SQA plan and project plan

c. Preproject process – contract review

d. Cost of software quality

e. SQA records and documentation control

The tasks descriptions follow.

a. Establishing SQA processes and their coordination with the software development processes
- Supporting the establishment, updating, and implementation of the organizational quality policy.
- Supporting the establishment, method, and responsibility for their performance of the SQA processes.
- Coordinating and collaborating for performing the SQA activities with the software process activities.

b. SQA plan and project plan
- Preparing a comprehensive SQA plan (SQAP) that includes the SQA activities and responsibility for their performance, including the evaluation of software product risks.
- Updating the SQAP
- Following-up of the implementation of the SQAP, and periodically reporting the status of performance to the project managers and the organization quality management.
- Identifying noncompliance of SQAP activities with expected outcomes and reporting to project managers and the organization quality management.
- Following-up of project changes, and if needed, updating the SQA respectively.

c. Preproject process – contract review
- Supporting the organization to carry out contract reviews.

d. Cost of software quality
- Evaluating the costs of software quality according to the findings of the SQAP activities conducted.

e. SQA records and documentation control
- Documenting the findings of SQAP activities to provide the required performance evidence.

- Implementing documentation control to avoid record changes and securing the records.
- Supplying specific records, as specified in the project contract, to stakeholders.

4.5.4 Tasks of SQA area 2: product assurance activities for conformance

SQA tasks performed by product assurance activities for conformance of the SQA area may be classified into three groups:

a. Evaluation of products for conformance

b. Assuring software operation services quality conformance

c. Software product quality metrics

The tasks descriptions follow.

a. Evaluation of products for conformance
- Identifying the contract requirements for the project plans
- Evaluating project plans for conformance to contract requirements, regarding required established processes and consistency.
- Documenting noncompliance of project plans with plans required by contract.
- Identifying the established requirements relating to the software products and their documentation, and evaluating the product and its documentation conformance with the requirements.
- Identifying the criteria for the software product acceptance, evaluating the product's conformance to the acceptance criteria, by applying reviews, audits, tests, and so on.

b. Assuring quality conformance of software operation services
- Identifying the contract requirements for customer support services.
- Evaluating the customer support services for consistency with contract requirements.
- Documenting noncompliance of customer support services with the contract requirements.
- Performing regular measurements of the level of customer support services and their conformance to the service plans.

c. Software product quality metrics
- Allocating standards and procedures used by the project or organization.
- Analyzing the proposed product metrics for consistency with the standards and procedures adopted by the project or organization, and verifying that they represent the product quality.

- Analyzing product measurement procedures for compliance with expectations, and in cases of gaps, suggesting process improvements to close them.
- Evaluating the effectiveness of the suggested improvements by subsequent measurements of the software product.
- Analyzing product measurement procedures to determine whether they satisfy measurements required by contract, and project's processes and plans.
- Applying process measurements for all subcontractors' products.

4.5.5 Tasks of SQA area 3: process assurance activities for conformance

The SQA tasks performed by the process assurance activities for conformance SQA area may be classified into six groups:

a. Evaluation of processes for conformance

b. Evaluation of environment for conformance

c. Improvement processes – corrective and preventive actions

d. Software process assurance activities for subcontractors

e. Software process quality metrics

f. Staff skills and knowledge – training and certification

The tasks descriptions follow.

a. Evaluation of processes for conformance
- Evaluating the appropriateness of the software life cycle processes selected by the project team in respect to applicable process requirements and product risks.
- Evaluating project plans and the selected software lifecycle processes for appropriateness to meet the contract requirements.
- Auditing software development activities for consistency with software life cycle processes and project plans.
- Applying process evaluations for subcontractors' software life cycle processes.

b. Evaluation of environment for conformance
- Evaluating the software engineering environment for conformance to the relevant contract requirements.
- Evaluating the software engineering libraries and test environment for conformance to the contract and project plans.

c. Improvement processes – corrective and preventive actions
- Evaluating the SQA processes result for nonconformance and suggesting improvement processes within the scope of the corrective and preventive activities of the organization.

- Supporting the corrective and preventive actions in evaluation process records and developing improvement proposals.
- Performing follow-up process measurements to examine the effectiveness of the suggested improvements.
- Supporting the project team in resolution of development process problems.

d. Software process assurance activities for subcontractors
- Identifying process requirements from subcontractors as defined in the contracts with subcontractor.
- Evaluating the subcontractors' processes for conformance to the contract

e. Software process quality metrics
- Allocating standards and procedures used by the project or organization.
- Analyzing the proposed process metrics for consistency with the standards and procedures adopted by the project and the organization and seeing whether they conform to the project's processes and plans.
- Analyzing process measurement procedures to determine whether they satisfy measurements required by the contract and the project's processes and plans.
- Reviewing process measurement to find out whether the SQA function's required measurements are conducted.
- Applying product measurements for all subcontractors' products.

f. Staff skills and knowledge – training and certification
- Identifying gaps between the required skills and professional knowledge for carrying out a project, and the current skills and knowledge of the project staff in place.
- Evaluate the capability of the existing organization's training activities to close the skills and professional gap.
- Verify whether new team members are examined for their skill and professional knowledge and are trained to cover skill and knowledge gaps.
- Review training activities regularly for completeness and effectiveness.

4.6 The associated players in the SQA system

A major part of the SQA system is the SQA function/team. Additional players in the SQA system include interested practitioners found among the software development and maintenance staff. These people with an interest in SQA contribute to the SQA system in the following formats:

- SQA trustees
- SQA committee members
- SQA forum members

4.6.1   SQA trustees and their tasks

SQA trustees are staff members who, being strongly interested in software quality, volunteer part of their time to promoting quality. They are frequently instructed by the SQA unit on new and updated subjects of interest. As SQA "agents", trustees are expected to provide the internal support necessary to successfully implement SQA components.

Trustee tasks vary substantially among organizations. Tasks may be unit related and/or organization related, and include some or all of the following activities:

Unit-related tasks

- Support their colleagues' attempts to solve difficulties arising in the implementation of software quality procedures and work instructions.
- Help their unit manager to perform his or her SQA tasks (e.g., preparation of a project's work instructions, collection of data for calculating SQA metrics).
- Promote compliance and monitor implementation of SQA procedures and work instructions by colleagues.
- Report substantial and systematic noncompliance events to the SQA unit.
- Report severe software quality failures to the SQA unit.

Organization-related tasks

- Initiate changes and updates of **organization-wide** SQA procedures and work instructions.
- Initiate organization-wide improvements of development and maintenance processes and applications to the CAB for solutions to recurrent failures observed.
- Identify organization-wide SQA training needs and propose an appropriate training or instruction program to be carried out by the SQA unit.

The major part of the SQA system is the SQA function/team. Additional players in the SQA system also include, beside the SQA unit professionals, interested practitioners found among the software development and maintenance staff. These SQA interested people contribute to the SQA system in the following formats:

- SQA trustees
- SQA committee members
- SQA forum members

4.6.2   SQA committees and their tasks

SQA committees can be either permanent or ad hoc. The subjects dealt with authority granted, as well as division of tasks between permanent and ad hoc committees, vary considerably among organizations.

Permanent committees commonly deal with SCC (software change control), CA (corrective actions), procedures, methods, development tools, and quality metrics.

Ad hoc committees commonly deal with specific cases, such as updates of a specific procedure, analysis and solution of a software failure, elaboration of software metrics for a targeted process or product, and updates of data collection methods for a specific issue.

Permanent SQA committees are integral parts of the SQA organizational framework; their tasks and scope of operation are usually defined in the organization's SQA procedures. In contrast, ad hoc committees are established on a short-term, per-problem basis, with members nominated by the executive responsible for software quality issues, the head of the SQA Unit and the head of SQA ad hoc committee. In some cases, permanent SQA committees may initiate the formation of an ad hoc committee and follow its findings.

4.6.3 SQA forums – tasks and methods of operation

SQA forums are informal components of the SQA organizational framework; they are established by volunteers and display some features of a community. The forums operate rather freely, as are not subject to any standard requirements or procedures. A forum's subjects, activities, and participants vary from one organization to another and reflect, more than anything else, the individuals belonging to the organization's software quality community, who are eager to create a meeting place for the exchange of SQA experiences and ideas. An organization generally benefits from the activities of its SQA forums, which can function independently or in some kind of cooperative relationship.

Members of an SQA forum usually define its scope and mode of operation, which can be limited or broad in scope. The forum can meet regularly or sporadically, and can define its preferred means of communication (Internet, Intranet, electronic mail, etc.).

SQA forums typically focus on:

- SQA procedures' improvement and implementation
- Quality metrics
- Corrective actions – analysis of failure and success cases
- Quality system issues – development and implementation of new tools
- Quality line management problems – daily operational software quality problems brought before it by quality managers from every level

Participation in SQA forums may be closed (e.g., limited to quality line managers) or open to all. Members of an open forum may include:

- SQA unit members
- SQA trustees

- Software development and maintenance staff
- SQA and software engineering consultants/experts
- Customer representatives

Forum publications. Forums also maintain the option of publication. Publications can range from newsletters to members, periodic reviews of SQA issues, reports of professional task force, or special forum committees. In addition to describing and analyzing a quality issue, the publications may include recommendations for corrective actions. The forum also decides upon a distribution list, and whether it will remain limited to its members or extended to other members of the organization.

An example of a forum operating for several years in a well-known software house was the "Template Forum". Four team leaders, two of whom had a reputation for being outstanding report writers, established the forum, whose sole objective was to prepare a set of templates for the 11 teams working within the framework of the Software Development Department. On average, the forum membership comprised 8–11 members, but membership never exceeded 15. During the Forum's 3 years of activity, about 20 different templates were issued, most of which were also updated at least once during this period. The templates were publicized in the Department's data communication network and were defined as the Department's standard in the space of about a year. The Forum discontinued its activities after two of its initiators left the firm. Several attempts by the SQA unit to renew the Forum's activities failed in the absence of a staff member to drive its reactivation.

Summary

1. **The managers participating in a typical quality assurance organizational framework**

    The managers participating in the SQA framework are of the three organization levels:
    - **Top management executives:** Especially the executive directly in charge of software quality assurance.
    - **Department managers:** Managers of the software development, software maintenance, and software testing departments.
    - **Project managers:** Managers of software development and software maintenance projects.

2. **The top management responsibilities regarding software quality**

    Top management is responsible to:
    1. Communicate the importance of software product and services meeting customer and regulatory requirements to employees at all levels.
    2. Establish the software quality policy and ensure that quality objectives related to the company's software products and software maintenance services are established and accomplished consistently.

3. Ensure that quality objectives are established for the organization's SQA system and that they are accomplished.
4. Ensure availability of the resources required for performing software quality assurance activities.
5. Conduct periodical management reviews.

3. The software system-related responsibilities of the executive in charge of software quality issues

The SQA tasks of the executive in charge include:

- Responsibility for preparation of an SQA annual activities program and budget for final approval by top management.
- Responsibility for preparation of SQA development plans to respond to changes in the organization's internal and external environments.
- Overall control of implementation of the annual SQA regular activities program and SQA development projects.
- Presentation and advocate SQA issues to the organization's executive management and conduct management reviews.

4. The description of the main objectives of management reviews

Management reviews are instruments that enable the organization's executives to:

- Assess the compliance of the SQA system with the organization's quality policy.
- Assess the achievement of quality objectives.
- Initiate changes and improvements of the software quality management system.
- Initiate improvement of software products and software operation services to better fulfill customer requirements and improve customer satisfaction.
- Outline directions for the solution of major deficiencies and problems in the organization's software quality management system.
- Allocate additional resources for software quality activities when necessary.

5. The SQA system-related responsibilities of department management

These responsibilities relate to department-level SQA tasks:

- Preparation of the department's annual SQA activities program.
- Preparation of the department's SQA system development plans.
- Control performance of the department's annual SQA activities program and development projects.
- Presentation of the department's SQA issues to top management, in coordination with the executive in charge of software quality.
- Development and updating of procedures and programming conventions.
- Ensure quality objectives are established and accomplished.
- Control of compliance to quality assurance procedures, to related software development and maintenance, and to infrastructure services.

6. The SQA system-related responsibilities required of project managers

- Preparation of project and quality plans and their updates.
- Participation in joint customer–supplier committee.
- Close professional follow-up regarding the implemented solutions and method, and professional support when needed.
- Review of project's teams' staffing, including recruitment and training.

7. The Tasks of SQA area 1: SQA process implementation activities

The SQA area tasks may be classified into five groups:

- **a.** Establishing SQA processes and their coordination with the software development processes
- **b.** SQA plan and project plan
- **c.** Preproject process – contract review
- **d.** Cost of software quality
- **e.** SQA records and documentation control

8. The tasks of SQA area 2: product assurance activities for conformance

The SQA area tasks may be classified into three groups:

- **a.** Evaluation of products for conformance
- **b.** Assuring software operation services quality conformance
- **c.** Software product quality metrics

9. The tasks of SQA area 3: process assurance activities for conformance

The SQA tasks performed by the process assurance activities for conformance SQA area may be classified into six groups:

- **a.** Evaluation of processes for conformance
- **b.** Evaluation of environment for conformance
- **c.** Improvement processes – corrective and preventive actions
- **d.** Software process assurance activities for subcontractors
- **e.** Software process quality metrics
- **f.** Staff skills and knowledge – training and certification

10. The tasks of SQA trustees

SQA trustees are involved in unit-related tasks and organization-related tasks, which vary considerably among organizations.

- **Typical unit-related tasks:** Support other unit/team members in solving difficulties in the implementation of software quality procedures, help their unit manager in performing his SQA tasks, and report the SQA unit on substantial and systematic noncompliance situations and severe software quality failures.
- **Typical organization-related tasks:** Initiation of changes and updates of SQA procedures, initiation of organization-wide improvements of development and maintenance processes and applications to the CAB, identification of SQA training needs, and preparation of proposals for appropriate training and/or instruction programs.

11. The comparison of SQA committee types

SQA committees may be permanent or ad hoc. The subjects, membership criteria, and authority of permanent SQA committees are usually defined by SQA procedures. Ad hoc committees are established and their task definitions are initiated by various bodies, according to circumstances and current needs. Members of ad hoc committees are chosen mainly for their professionalism and authority. One may expect great variation among the ad hoc committees nominated for the same task by different initiators at different times.

12. SQA forum characteristics: scope and participants

SQA forums are informal components of the SQA organizational framework. They are established, operated, and developed freely.

Scope of SQA forums: limited or broad. Forum subjects, activities, and participants vary by organization and typically relate to SQA procedure improvements and implementation, quality metrics, development of software engineering tools, and implementation of new tools.

Participation in SQA forums may be closed or open. Participants of open SQA forums can include SQA unit members, SQA trustees, members of software development and maintenance teams, customer representatives, and software engineering consultants.

Selected bibliography

Berki E., Georgiadou E., and Holcombe M. (2004) Requirements engineering and process modeling in software quality management – towards a generic process metamodel, *Software Quality Journal*, Vol. 12, No. 3, pp. 265–283.

Gill N. S. (2005) Factors affecting effective software quality management revisited, *ACM SIGSOFT Software Engineering Notes*, Vol. 30, No. 2, pp. 1–4.

ISO (2014) *ISO/IEC 90003:2014 Software Engineering – Guidelines for the Application of TSO 9001: 2008 to Computer Software*, International Organization for Standardization, Geneva, Switzerland.

Review questions

4.1 The top management contributes to software quality by employing three main managerial tools.

    a. List the tools applied by top management to achieve the software quality objectives.

    b. Describe each tool in your own words and explain how it affects software quality.

4.2 Refer to the software quality policy document presented in Frame 4.2.

   a. List the policy clauses and explain their meaning in your own words.

   b. Explain how each policy clause contributes to the achievement of the Company's quality goals.

4.3 Refer to the BQS Ltd. software quality policy document presented in Frame 4.3.

   a. Examine each clause of the policy document and identify the SQA components directly referred to in the clauses.

   b. Examine the document and identify those components of the SQA system indirectly addressed by the policy document.

   c. List the SQA components not referred to at all.

4.4 The executive in charge of software quality issues is responsible for the preparation of the annual SQA activities program and budget.

   a. Describe in your own words the activities the executive has to perform to prepare the mentioned program and budget.

   b. Refer to Chapter 19 and describe the participation of the heads of the SQA unit and subunits in the preparation of the program and budget.

4.5 The executive in charge of software quality issues is responsible for overall control of the performance of SQA activities.

   a. List the types of SQA activities under the executive's responsibility.

   b. Describe in your own words the activities the executive has to perform to control the SQA activities listed in (a).

4.6 Nine typical items contained in a management review report are mentioned in Frame 4.4.

   a. List at least five of these items.

   b. Suggest possible decisions that can be taken, based on the items listed in (a).

4.7 The responsibilities of department management may be classified into department-related responsibilities, project-related responsibilities, and SQA system-related responsibilities.

   • List the SQA system-related responsibilities and explain in your own words the objective of each task.

4.8 The responsibilities of project management may be classified into professional hands-on tasks and management tasks and SQA system-related tasks.

   • List the project manager's SQA system-related tasks and explain the objective of each task in your own words.

4.9 The organizational structure of an SQA unit according to a model presented in Figure 4.1 includes three area units that deal with SQA activities.

   a. List the three area units.

   b. Describe in your own words the tasks performed by each area unit.

4.10 According to a model presented in Figure 4.1, the organizational structure of an SQA unit includes two area units that deal with SQA development and maintenance.

   a. List the two subunits.

   b. Describe in your own words the tasks performed by each subunit.

4.11 It has become customary in recent years for subcontractors to perform parts of software developing projects.

   a. Describe the tasks of the SQA function/unit involved in SQA issues relating to subcontractors.

   b. Discuss the importance of the SQA functions involved with the work of subcontractors.

4.12 Discuss the contribution to software quality of associated players in the SQA system.

Topics for discussion

4.1 It is commonly agreed that "SQA objectives are achieved through the cooperation and integrated activities of all players involved in the quality assurance organizational framework."

   a. Define in your own words who should be considered a player in a quality assurance organizational framework, and provide a list of typical players. Refer also to the SQA unit and its associated players in the SQA system.

   b. Explain the unique contribution of each player to the SQA system.

4.2 The organization's software quality policy should conform to the organization's purposes and goals.

   a. List three or more organization goals, and suggest examples, where an organization's software quality policy conforms to the organization's purpose and goals.

   b. Suggest at least one example where an organization's software quality policy does not conform to the organization's purpose and goals.

4.3 "Alpha Software" was a medium-sized software house specializing in telecom real-time software, and employing about 180 professionals. As no executive volunteered for the position of "executive in charge of software quality", the general manager of "Alpha Software" did not insist on nominating an executive to this position. Moreover, he did not assign any great importance to issue a quality policy document, as he claimed, "the Company is anyway committed to quality"; hence, there was no need for any written document. This situation continued for about two years without any critical failures.

   a. Suggest what unnoticed and undesired events may have resulted from this position.

   b. Suggest what an executive in charge of software quality, in addition to an adequate and updated policy document, could contribute to company product quality.

4.4 Computerized SQA information systems are already available in most organizations. The objective of the SQA tasks related to the information system is to make the SQA system more effective and efficient.

   a. Describe in your own words the SQA tasks related to the SQA information system.

   b. Improvements of the SQA information systems are expected to contribute to reduction of failure rates and quality costs. If you agree, give two or three examples of such reductions.

   c. Suggest types of information services to be provided by an SQA Intranet site, and list the advantages of the SQA system of Intranet-based systems over the classic paper-based systems.

4.5 SQA trustees are expected to be SQA agents in their teams/units and provide the internal support for successful implementation of SQA components.

   a. Explain how SQA trustees complement the formal activities performed by SQA units and unit managers.

   b. Evaluate the contributions of SQA trustees to software quality.

4.6 The permanent Software Metrics Committee of Venus Software has identified a significantly high failure rate in two software quality metrics for the new version 6.1 of its popular "Customer-Venus" software package, to be released in the next month. The package is used by about 2,500 consumer clubs all around the country. The Product Development Committee (permanent committee) decided to establish an ad hoc committee to contend with the failures.

   a. Suggest a list of tasks for the ad hoc committee.

   b. Suggest who should be nominated to the ad hoc committee and who should head it.

   c. List the assumptions on which you based your answers to (a) and (b).

4.7 SQA forum activities are conducted entirely informally: For instance, participants may join and leave the forum whenever they wish and they may undertake or refuse to perform tasks of interest to the forum. Accordingly, some SQA experts tend to consider forums to be worthless.

   a. Do you agree with this opinion? If not, list your arguments.

   b. In what ways can an organization promote and encourage SQA forum activities?

Chapter 5

The SQA World – An Overview

Today's software quality assurance (SQA) world comprises a great variety of components, belonging to six distinct areas – all of which are discussed in this book.

Just before we dive into the details of SQA processes, activities, and tasks, we will take a short tour to the SQA process areas in the world of software quality assurance. I hope the "guided tour" will help you plan your reading of this book, and especially strengthen your will to read it.

We start our tour with a visit to the introductory area, where we will be examining several basic issues.

5.1 First area: introductory topics (Part I of the book)

The following issues will be presented in the area:

- SQA – definitions and concepts
- Software quality factors (attributes)
- SQA challenges
- Organization for assuring software quality

5.1.1 SQA – definitions and concepts (Chapter 1)

A combination of two rivaling classic definitions for software quality is presented in the IEEE's definition of software quality: (a) Software quality is the degree to which a software system meets specified requirements, and (b) it is also the degree to which a software system fulfils customer or user needs and expectations.

Software Quality: Concepts and Practice, First Edition. Daniel Galin.
© 2018 the IEEE Computer Society, Inc. Published 2018 by John Wiley & Sons, Inc.

Software quality assurance is defined as an "Asset of activities that define and assess the adequacy of a software process to provide evidence that establishes confidence that the software processes are appropriate for, and produce, software products of suitable quality for their intended purposes."

The discussion on quality issues naturally continues with the causes of software errors. Nine main causes are listed; beginning with faulty requirements definitions and client–developer communication failures, and ending with documentation errors – all of which are human errors.

5.1.2   Software quality factors (attributes) (Chapter 2)

There is a great variety of attributes that characterize software quality: They are also termed software quality factors. McCall classifies these factors into three classes:

a. Product operation factors (correctness, reliability, efficiency, integrity, and usability)

b. Product revision factors (maintainability, flexibility, and testability)

c. Product transition factors (portability, reusability, and interoperability)

Several other factor modes have been developed over the years, with high or medium levels of similarity to McCall's model.

5.1.3   SQA challenges (Chapter 3)

The first SQA challenge is the need to manage the unique quality assurance difficulties stemming from the high complexity of software products, their lack of visibility, and, finally, the fewer opportunities in which errors may be identified, compared with products from other industries.

The second SQA challenge is the need to manage development, operation, and environment characteristics: First – contract conditions, including functional requirements, schedule and budget, and the customer–supplier relationship. Second – the need to maintain teamwork and the team's cooperation and coordination with other internal and external teams. Third – the required product interfaces with other software systems. Fourth – the need to continue the project despite team member changes, and later to maintain the software system, often for many years.

5.1.4   Organization for assuring software quality

The organization's organs that contribute to a product's quality are many. I have chosen to focus on those who mostly affect software quality: management levels (top management, department managements, and project/team management staff), and the SQA function/unit.

The following are the management level's quality assurance responsibilities:

- Establish and update the organization's software quality policy.
- Assign one of the executives to be responsible for software quality issues (e.g., Vice President of SQA).
- Conduct regular *management reviews* of performance with respect to software quality issues.

The departments' management quality assurance responsibilities include responsibilities for quality activities related to the department and infrastructure services, and those related to quality issues of particular software projects and maintenance services.

Most project management responsibilities are defined in procedures and work instructions; the project manager is the person in charge of making sure that all team members comply with the said procedures and instructions. His tasks include professional hands-on and managerial tasks.

The SQA unit's activities may be classified into three areas: SQA process implementation activities, product assurance activities for conformance, and process assurance activities for conformance.

The SQA unit is supported by the unit's "associates": SQA trustees, SQA committee members, and SQA forum members, these may all contribute substantially to the unit's quality achievements.

We have now completed our visit to the introductory area, after examining the basics of software quality and software quality assurance, and shall proceed to the second area.

5.2 Second area: SQA process implementation activities (Part II of the book)

SQA process implementation is the strategic infrastructure development of policy, processes, and SQA roles that, when applied by the organization to software projects, enable producing software products of the required level of quality.

The following issues will be presented in the second area:

- Establishing SQA processes and their coordination with related software processes
- SQA plan (SQAP) and project plan
- Preproject process – contract review
- Cost of software quality

- The effectiveness and cost of a verification and validating plan (V&V) plan – the SQA model
- SQA records and documentation control

5.2.1 Establishing SQA processes and their coordination with related software processes (Chapter 6)

SQA processes and their related procedures serve as SQA infrastructure. These SQA processes and their related procedures are designed so that when implemented in a software development project, they enable the developers to fulfill the established requirements.

The SQA processes to be defined and developed include the following:

- Define the organization quality policy.
- Establish the organization's SQA processes.
- Allocate tasks to those responsible for SQA processes.
- Define the management's follow-up tool/method.
- Develop a follow-up and review method for the SQA function.

In order to realize the intended benefits from the SQA processes, their performance needs to be coordinated with the relevant software processes. The coordination ensures that the SQA processes are performed in the appropriate stage of the software process, and so contribute to the achievement of the required level of software product quality.

5.2.2 SQA plan and project plan (Chapter 7)

The SQAP deals with the activities and tasks the SQA function is required to carry out over the next year, and enables estimating resources required to perform the SQAP. The planners of the resource estimates refer to the professional knowledge and experience requirements of the various activities and tasks, and classify the staff requirement accordingly. In this way, the SQA function may be appropriately staffed to carry out the SQAP in the coming year.

The project plan deals with the activities and tasks to be performed by the project team throughout the project's life cycle, namely, during the development and operation stages. Probably two of the most important elements of the project plan are the activities schedule and the resource estimates for each activity.

The two plans are tightly connected, and need to be coordinated. A great part of the SQAP activities has to be coordinated with the relevant project plan activities.

5.2.3 Preproject process – contract review (Chapter 8)

Contract review is a process where SQA function, by reviewing the project proposal and the contract draft, can assist in forming a successful contract. It is natural for an SQA function to be involved in contract review as from the viewpoint of SQA, a bad contract – usually characterized by loosely defined requirements, and unrealistic budgets and schedule – is expected to yield low-quality software.

The contract review process begins with a reviewing the proposal draft, and later, in the second stage, the contract draft is reviewed.

The role of the SQA function in carrying out contract reviews is major, due to the knowledge and experience.

5.2.4 Cost of software quality (Chapter 9)

The following are the objectives of application of cost of software quality measurements:

- Control organization-initiated costs to prevent and detect software errors.
- Evaluate financial damages of software failures as a basis for revising the SQA budget.
- Evaluate plans to increase/decrease SQA activities, or to invest in new/updated SQA infrastructure.

The classic quality cost model differentiates between controlled costs (prevention costs and appraisal costs) and software failure costs (internal failure costs and external failure costs).

The chapter also presents an extended software quality cost model that adds managerial quality costs to those included in the classic model.

Application of a cost of software quality system requires:

- Definition of a cost of software quality model and a standardized list of cost items – specifically for the organization, department, team, or project.
- Definition of a method of data collection.
- Application of a cost of software quality system, including thorough follow-up.
- Actions to be taken in response to the findings produced.

5.2.5 The effectiveness and cost of a V&V plan – the SQA model (Chapter 10)

The SQA model is an effective tool to provide project planners with estimates of the effectiveness of a V&V plan. Such a tool enables comparing alternative programs by supplying the expected percentage of errors to be removed in each screening stage, when applying a given V&V plan, and also the expected costs of performing the plan. This method of estimating could also be useful for the SQA function when evaluating project plans.

The model deals with two quantitative aspects of a V&V plan consisting of several defect detection activities. The plan itself is to be integrated within a project's development process:

a. The V&V plan's total effectiveness in removing project defects.

b. The V&V plan's total costs of removal of project defects.

An application of the model for comparing a standard V&V plan with a comprehensive V&V plan is presented in this chapter.

5.2.6   SQA records and documentation control (Chapter 11)

During the software life cycle many types of documents are created. Some of the documents are required immediately for the continuation of the development, while others may become vital for software quality assurance over the life cycle of the system. Documents displaying these characteristics and treated according to special procedures are:

Controlled documents. Documents produced during the development and operation of software systems, which are immediately necessary for software processes, or during the life cycle of the system for software quality assurance.

Quality records. Quality records are controlled documents aimed mainly to provide evidence that the development and maintenance processes performed were in compliance with requirements.

The following are the implementation of documentation control:

a. Definition of the list of the controlled document types.

b. Design and development of controlled documents.

c. Document production and their regular use.

d. Updating (maintaining) the controlled documents list.

Leaving the second SQA area, we shall now approach the third area, which is dedicated to software product quality issues.

5.3 Third area: product assurance activities for conformance (Part III of the book)

This area is dedicated to the product software quality assurance activities, and discusses the following issues:

- The SQA activities aimed at evaluating the conformance of software products and related documentation to contract requirements and relevant regulations and conventions.
- The review methods applied for evaluating documents, reports, and performance records.
- The testing methods used to verify and validate software code files.
- Assuring software operation services quality conformance.
- The software product quality measurement techniques.
- Procedures and work instructions and their development and usage.

5.3.1 Evaluation of products for conformance (Chapter 12)

A substantial part of the SQA function's efforts is devoted to evaluating the products of the software processes. These are produced during the software development life cycle (SDLC), and include software and any relevant documentation. Software products include software packages/systems and software services, while the relevant documentation includes various development and operation reports, such as design reports, test reports, and periodical customer services reports.

The evaluation for conformance subjects include:

- Project plans
- Project software products
- Project products for acceptability by the customer
- Project operation phase products
- Software product evaluation by measurements

5.3.2 Reviews (Chapter 13)

A review is defined as a process for evaluating a documented software project product, in which a group of professionals and stakeholders raise comments regarding the contents of a document presented to them beforehand.

The following are the direct objectives of a review:

- To detect analysis, design, and other documentation, functional, logical, and implementation errors.

- To identify changes, deviations, and omissions with respect to the original specifications and approved changes.
- To locate those deviations from templates, style procedures, and conventions, which are expected to cause difficulties to development and maintenance teams.
- To identify new risks that are likely to affect completion of the project.
- To approve, in formal reviews, the analysis, design, or other respective development stage of the product, and allow the team to progress to the next development phase.

The following review methods are common:

- Formal design reviews
- Peer reviews – inspections and walkthroughs

In general, the knowledge that an analysis, design, or other development product will be reviewed stimulates the development team to do their best work. This represents a further contribution of reviews to the improved product quality.

5.3.3   Software testing (Chapter 14)

Software testing is an activity in which a **system or component** is **executed under specified conditions**, the results are observed or recorded, and evaluation is made of some aspect of the system or component.

The following are the direct objectives of software testing:

- To identify and reveal as many errors as possible in the tested software.
- To bring the tested software to an acceptable level of quality, after correction of the identified errors and retesting.
- To perform the required tests efficiently and effectively, and within the budgetary and scheduling limitations.
- To establish with a degree of confidence that the software package is ready for delivery (or installment at customer premises).

It is recommended that the software testing program be incremental and include unit tests and integration tests, rather than to only be based on final "big bang" system tests. Software testing programs are constructed from a variety of tests: some manual and some automated. All tests have to be designed, planned, and approved according to development procedures. The advantages and disadvantages of automated testing are discussed in the text.

Another issue presented is the choice between black box and white box testing. A major factor in test planning is the size of the test case file. Line coverage instead of path coverage enables reducing the test case file in white box testing. For black box testing, the equivalent class method is offered to minimize the test case file. Review activities for the programming phase are discussed as complementary to software testing. Automated testing with its advantages and disadvantages is also discussed in the text.

5.3.4 Assuring software operation services quality conformance (Chapter 15)

The main part of the software life cycle is the operation phase, which usually lasts for 5–10 years, although cases of software being operational for 15 years, and even longer, are not rare. What makes one software package capable of reaching "old age" with satisfied users, while another package, serving an almost identical population, "perishes young?" The main factor responsible for a long-term service success is the quality of operation services, namely, the user support and maintenance services. Estimates of the percentage of resources invested in operation phase services throughout its life cycle range from 50 to 75% of the total invested software system resources.

User support services may be classified into two kinds:

User support services through the phone. This kind of service frequently applies remote intervention in the user's computer to solve the problem.

Onsite user support service. This kind of service is only used when support through the phone is inapplicable. Usually this kind of service is critical situation.

In part of the users support calls, the solution requires corrective maintenance service.

Software maintenance services include the following three components, all essential for successful maintenance:

- **Corrective maintenance** – user support services and software corrections.
- **Adaptive maintenance** – adapts the software package to changes in new customer requirements, changing environmental conditions, and the like.
- **Functionality improvement maintenance** – combines (1) **perfective maintenance** of new functions added to the software to enhance performance; (2) **preventive maintenance** – activities that improve software package reliability, enabling easier and more efficient maintainability.

5.3.5 Software product quality metrics (Chapter 16)

Software product metrics are a quantitative representation of software products or intermediate product's attributes, as experienced by the user when applying the software trying to adapt it or change it, such as size, effectiveness, productivity, and reliability.

The product metrics are classified into two classes:

1. Software product size metrics

2. Software attributes metrics

A measure of software product size is needed mainly: (a) to estimate the required development resources at the stage of preparing a proposal for a software project or planning and scheduling its process of development, and (b) for use in other metrics when comparing the performance proportionally to the software project size, for example, in metrics of productivity, quality (defects rates), and so on.

Two approaches for software size metrics are offered:

a. KLOC (thousands of lines of code). This metric represents metrics based on the physical completed size of software, such as the number of lines of code.

b. Function points (FPs). This metric represents the result of applying a measure from the group of functional size measurement (FSM) methods. These estimating methods are based on the functionality specified by the software project requirements. More specifically, the FSM concept requires counting items such as inputs and outputs of software systems.

Software product attribute metrics relate to attributes like software functionality, software reliability, software usability, and software efficiency. The chapter presents examples of metrics for each of the software attributes.

5.3.6 Procedures and work instructions (Chapter 17)

Application of the organization's accumulated know-how, experience and expertise.

SQA procedures and work instructions aim at:

• Performance of tasks, processes, or activities in the most effective and efficient way without deviating from quality requirements.

• Effective and efficient communication between the different teams involved in the development and maintenance of software systems. Uniformity in performance, achieved by conformity with procedures and work instructions, reduces misunderstandings that lead to software errors.

• Simplified coordination between tasks and activities performed by the various bodies of the organization. Better coordination translates into fewer errors.

Procedures supply all the details needed to carry out a task according to the prescribed method for fulfilling the task's function. Professionally developed and maintained SQA procedures conform to an organization's quality policy, and also tend to conform to international or national SQA standards. **Work instructions** deal with the application of procedures, and are adapted to the requirements of a specific project team, customer, or other relevant party.

Procedures need to be updated from time to time. The motivation to update existing procedures is based, among other reasons, on the following:

External changes

- Technological changes in development tools, hardware, communication equipment, and so on
- Changes in legal requirements
- Changes in the organization's areas of activity

After being impressed by the software product quality issues, we shall move on to the next area, which is dedicated to software process quality issues.

5.4 Fourth area: process assurance activities for conformance (Part IV of the book)

This area is dedicated to the process quality assurance activities and presents the following issues:

- The SQA activities aimed at evaluating the conformance of software processes and related documentation to contract requirements and relevant regulations and conventions.
- The process improvements processes and the services of corrective and preventive actions (CAPAs).
- The activities applied for assuring the quality of software processes to be performed by subcontractors and other external participants.
- The process quality measurement techniques.
- The software change control (SCC) process.
- The issues related to the assessment of staff skills and knowledge, conducting training and certification of staff members.

5.4.1 Evaluation of processes and development environment for conformance (Chapter 18)

This chapter is dedicated to activities performed to evaluate process assurance and development environment for conformance to requirements, standards, regulations, and conventions. "Process requirements specify the processes the project will use to produce the project outcomes. The software engineering environment provides assistance to the programmer through a workstation equipped with compilers, program database systems, an interactive debugger, and other development tools."

The test environment enables performing efficient testing by local computing when adequate capacity exists or with cloud computing technology.

The evaluation process to be performed by the SQA function includes the following activities:

1. Identify the life cycle processes required by the contract requirements, regulations, and conventions.

2. Review planned life cycle processes for their conformance to the relevant established process requirements.

3. Review processes being performed for their conformance to the relevant established process requirements. The review should yield lists of nonconformities.

The evaluation of software development and test environments include the following activities:

1. Evaluate the software development environment planned to be used, and that which is actually used by the project team for conformance to contract requirements and conventions.

2. Evaluate the software and application libraries and software development tools used by the project team for conformance to contract requirements and planned libraries.

3. Evaluate the test environment for conformance to contract requirements and planned environment.

   All evaluation activities are followed by lists of nonconformities to be corrected.

5.4.2   Improvement processes – corrective and preventive actions (Chapter 19)

Continual improvement, in other words, ongoing improvement of overall performance, is also a basic principle of software quality assurance. The issues involved in successful implementation of this principle by CAPAs are discussed in this chapter.

   Corrective action is a regularly applied feedback organizational process that initiates and performs actions to eliminate causes of nonconformities (software faults).

   Preventive action is a regularly applied feedback organizational process that initiates and performs actions to prevent the occurrence of potential nonconformities (software faults).

The corrective and preventive actions process includes:

- Information collection
- Analysis of information
- Development of solutions and improved methods
- Implementation of improved methods
- Follow-up of CAPA activities – implementation and outcome

5.4.3 Software process assurance activities for external participants (Chapter 20)

The organization that undertakes to carry out the development contract (the "supplier") is very often not the only participants in a development project. This is especially true for large-scale projects, which frequently include external participants. The four external participant types are classified into two main groups: external performers (subcontractors and the customer, as a participant in performing the project) and readymade software suppliers (COTS software and reused software modules and open-source software).

The main risks with external participants:

- Delays in completion of the project
- Low quality of project parts developed by external participants
- Communication problems with subcontractors
- Loss of control over project parts
- Future maintenance difficulties
- Termination of work on contracted activities due to the subcontractor going out of business

The main risks with readymade software:

- Difficulties in integrating readymade software
- Difficulties in correcting faults revealed in readymade software
- Future maintenance difficulties

QA activities applied to subcontractor's participation in a software development project:

- Reviewing the requirements document and subcontractor contract
- Evaluation of selection process regarding external\performers
- Review of the external performers' project plans and development processes
- Establishment of project coordination and joint control committee

- Participation in external participants' design reviews and software testing
- Formulation of external performers' procedures
- Certification of external performers' team leaders and members
- Regular follow-up of progress reports of external performers' development activities

QA tools applied to usage of readymade software in a software development project:

- Requiring document reviews
- Performing appropriate selection process
  - The system requirements
  - The readymade software product characteristics
  - The provider's characteristics
  - Estimates of efforts required for readymade component's integration
- Requirement changes to adapt to readymade software features
- Peer reviews and testing readymade package or component
- Knowledge management of components integrated in the software system
- Preparing specialized procedures

5.4.4   Software process quality metrics (Chapter 21)

Software process metrics are a quantitative representation of software processes, as encountered by developers and maintainers throughout the software life cycle, such as prerelease defects, percent of modified code lines, and density of detected defects.

The software process metrics are classified into four classes:

1. Software development process quality metrics
2. Software operation process quality metrics
3. Software maintenance process quality metrics
4. Management process quality metrics

Many examples of software process quality metrics may be found in this chapter.

5.4.5   Software change control processes (Chapter 22)

The software development process is inevitably characterized by a constant flow of change requests, mainly from customers. The need to cope with software changes throughout the software life cycle is one of the more important and onerous tasks of the software development and maintenance teams. Moreover, performing changes – usually under time constraints – is one of the processes more susceptible to software errors.

The process of examining change requests, selecting which should be rejected and which should be approved, along with scheduling of the implementation of approved changes is the SCC process. The SCC function in the development organization performs the following tasks:

a. Examination of requested or suggested changes.

b. Approval of implementation of only those changes that are worthy and necessary, while all remaining are rejected.

c. Scheduling of the implementation of each of the approved changes.

d. Follow-up of the approved changes.

Software change requests (SCRs) initiatives may relate to one or more of the following:

- A need to correct a software error.
- A need to adapt the software to changes in the operations of a customer's business or organization missions.
- A need to adapt the software to a new customer's needs.
- A need to adapt the software to changes in general business and market changes.
- A proposal to update and improve the software product, to achieve higher customer satisfaction (in custom-made projects), or to affect the marketability of the software (in COTS software).
- A need to adapt the software to budget and schedule constraints.

The chapter details the processes involved in software changes.

5.4.6 Staff skills and knowledge – training and certification (Chapter 23)

Successful team performance is based on the staff possessing adequate skills and knowledge. Also, it goes without saying that keeping staff abreast of the latest professional advancements available is the key to achieving quality in development and maintenance. Moreover, it is generally accepted that regular professional training, retraining, and updating are mandatory, if the gap between required and current professional knowledge is to be maintained as narrow as possible.

Position certification (hereinafter "certification") is conducted for staff members assigned to key positions, and is a way of achieving conformance of a candidate's skill and knowledge to a specific position's skill and knowledge requirements. It may be conducted for software development and maintenance positions. Certification may be considered as another complementary tool for ensuring suitable professional skill and knowledge of team members.

The operation of successful training demands that the following activities be regularly performed:

- Determine needs for professional training and updating needs for filling any knowledge gaps for the software development staff.
- Plan training and upskill programs for the software development staff.
- Conduct training programs for the software development staff.
- Perform follow-up on training activities and new knowledge acquired by trainees.

The following activities are required for the certification process:

- Define positions requiring certification
- Plan certification programs for the selected positions
- Deliver certification programs
- Perform certification follow-up

The chapter discusses in detail the training and certification processes.

After completing our visit to the area of process assurance activities, we shall now advance to the next area that presents three additional tools and methods that support the software quality assurance efforts of the development teams.

5.5   Fifth area: additional tools and methods supporting software quality (Part V of the book)

In this area the following are the three additional tools and methods that support development teams in their efforts to ensure the quality of their software processes and software products quality:

- Templates and checklists
- Configuration management
- CASE tools and IDEs – their impact on software quality

5.5.1   Templates and checklists (Chapter 24)

Software development and maintenance processes involve the production and use of a multitude of documents. Two simple SQA tools, templates and checklists, could support the preparation of documents. In addition to timesavings, these tools improve the quality of reports including their structures (contributed by templates), and also provide better preparation for debate on reports by improving them according to checklists and by preparing responses to the checklist topics.

The usage of templates is quite advantageous to development teams and to review teams.

For development teams, using templates:

- **Facilitates the process of preparing documents** by saving the time and energy required to create the document's structure.
- **Means that documents prepared by developers are more complete** as all the subjects to be included in the document have already been defined.
- **Provides for easier integration of new team members** through familiarity. The document's standard structure, prepared according to templates that may be known to the new member from previous work.

For DR Committee members, template use:

- **Facilitates review of documents** by eliminating the need to study a document's structure and confirm its completeness – if the document is based on the appropriate template.

For software maintenance teams, template use:

- **Enables easier location of the information** required for performing maintenance tasks.

Checklists are used:

- By developers prior to completing a document to ensure that all required topics have been included and discussed properly.
- By developers prior to performing an activity (e.g., installing a software package at the customer site) and to ensure the completeness of preparations.
- By DR committee members for verifying that a document complies with content topics requirements.
- By DR committee members to verify the correct order of topics in the review sessions discussions.

The advantages of using templates to the development teams:

- **Help developers carry out self-checks of documents or software code** prior to formal design reviews, inspections, or testing
- **Assist developers in their preparations for tasks** such as installation of software at customer sites or performance of quality audits at subcontractors' sites.

The advantages of using templates to the review teams:

- **Ensure completeness of document reviews by review team members** as all relevant review topics appear on the list.
- **Facilitate improved efficiency of review sessions** as the subjects and their order of discussion are defined and well known in advance.

5.5.2 Configuration management (Chapter 25)

The need to cope with software versions throughout the software life cycle is one of the more important tasks of software development and maintenance teams. The software quality support function to perform this task is software configuration management (SCM).

The SCM tasks include:

- Systematic storage of identified versions of software configuration items and other approved items.
- Release of SCI and software configuration versions.
- Provision of information services based on recovery of stored data.
- Verification of compliance to CM procedures.

The SCM serves versions of four classes, as follows:

- Design documents
- Software code
- Data files including files of test cases and test scripts
- Software development tools

5.5.3 CASE tools and IDEs – their impact on software quality (Chapter 26)

CASE tools are computerized software development tools that support the software developer and maintenance staff by increasing the efficiency and effectiveness of the processes, and reducing the resources required and reducing defects generated when supporting the performance of one or more phases of the software life cycle.

The contribution of CASE tools to the software project:

- Substantial savings in software development resources
- Shorter time to market
- Reduced generation of defects
- Increased automatic identification of defects and their correction during development
- Greater reuse due to increased standardization of software components and programs and improved search of potential COTS components and software
- Substantial savings in maintenance teams' resources
- Improved project scheduling and control of project performance

CASE tools may be classified into three groups:

The classic CASE tools group includes the well-established computerized software development support tools (such as interactive debuggers, compilers, configuration management services, and project progress control systems).

The IDE CASE tools group includes CASE tools based on the integration of several classic CASE tools into a common work environment, providing a substantial improvement on the efficiency and effectiveness of software development.

The Real CASE tools group includes new tools that support the developer during several consecutive project development phases; it is customary to distinguish between *upper* CASE tools that support the analysis and design phases, *lower* CASE.

After being introduced to additional tools and methods supporting software quality, we shall move on to the last area to be visited.

5.6 Sixth area: Appendices (Part VI of the book)

The appendices in this book present basic software quality and software engineering topics that are very much related to SQA:

- Software development and quality assurance process standards
- Quality management standards and models
- Project progress control
- From SDLC to Agile – processes and quality assurance activities

5.6.1 Software development and quality assurance process standards (Appendix A)

The use of standard is a vital part of engineering as software and software quality engineering. The main benefits gained by using project development process standards are:

- The ability to apply the most professional software development and maintenance methodologies available.
- Better mutual understanding and coordination among teams, especially between development and maintenance teams.
- Better cooperation between the software developer and external participants in the project.
- Better understanding and cooperation between suppliers and customers, based on incorporation of accepted standards within the contract.

Software process standards focus on methodologies for carrying out software development and maintenance projects, and assure their quality, that is, on "how" a software project is to be implemented. These standards define steps to be taken, design documentation requirements, the contents of design documents, and so on. Naturally, due to their characteristics, many standards in this class can serve as software engineering and SQA textbooks versa.

The chapter presents three important software engineering and software quality assurance international standards:

- IEEE Std. 730-2014 – Software quality assurance
- ISO/IEC/IEEE 12207:2008 – Systems and software engineering – Software life cycle processes
- IEEE Std. 1012-2012 – Systems and software verification and validation

5.6.2 Software quality management standards and models (Appendix B)

Quality management standards and models focus on the organization's SQA system, infrastructure, and requirements while leaving the choice of methods and tools to the organization. By complying with quality management standards, organizations can constantly ensure that their software products achieve an acceptable level of quality.

These standards may be classified into two classes:

- Certifying standards enable the software quality assurance to be examined by a professional body to determine its quality level. When the quality level is established as satisfactory, the developing organization is certified.
- Assessment standards enable the developing organization to assess its professional level and plan any necessary improvements.

The following are the aims of certification standards:

- To enable a software development organization to demonstrate consistent ability to ensure that its software products or maintenance services comply with acceptable quality requirements. This is achieved through certification granted by an external body.
- To serve as an agreed-upon basis for customer and supplier evaluation of the supplier's quality management system. This may be accomplished with a quality audit of the supplier's quality management system conducted by the customer. The audit will be based on the certification standard's requirements.
- To support the software development organization's efforts to improve quality management system performance.

The following are the aims of assessment standards:

- To serve software development and maintenance organizations as a tool for self-assessment of their ability to carry out software development projects.
- To serve as a tool for improvement of development and maintenance processes. The standard indicates directions for process improvements.
- To help purchasing organizations determine the capabilities of potential suppliers.
- To guide training of assessor by delineating qualifications and training program curricula.

The chapter includes a detailed discussion of the following standards and models:

- ISO/IEC 90003: 2014 – Software engineering – Guidelines for the application of ISO 9001:2008 to computer software, for Services
- Capability Maturity CMMI: 2010 – CMMI for acquisition for development and for services (3 models)
- ISO/IEC 15504:2011-2015 – Information technology – Process assessment

5.6.3 Project progress control (Appendix C)

Months of project delay and budget overruns exceeding 10% and sometimes up to 30% and even more over project estimations, typical of too many software development projects, are "red flags" for software project management. Unfortunately, these events are usually coupled with the low quality of software projects – a natural reaction of the developers to schedule and budget issues. This chapter is dedicated to methods and procedures that ensure timely performance in a software project, verifying schedule and budget keeping.

The main components of project progress control are:

- Control of risk management activities
- Project schedule control
- Project resource control
- Project budget control

Special cases of project progress control are internal projects and projects performed by external participants.

Project progress control of internal projects, such as projects undertaken for other departments, excludes, by definition, the option of external customers. These projects thus tend to be assigned a lower management priority. The inadequate attention awarded is often accompanied by inappropriate or lax follow-up on the part of the internal customer. Similar tendencies are observed in the earlier preproject stage, inappropriate contract reviews (if any at all), and project development plans. Significant delays in project completion time, together with overrun project budgets, are typical results of these situations.

It is expected that loose development contracts of internal projects, if exist, will also result in a lower quality of project software products. The SQA function is required to manage these risks by meticulous reviews and follow-up activities.

Project progress control of projects performed by external projects includes subcontractors, suppliers of COTS software, open-source software and reused software modules, and, in some cases, the customer himself. The more sizeable and complex the project, the greater the likelihood that external participants will be required, and the larger the portion of work allocated to them. Management turns to external participants for a number of reasons, ranging from economic to technical to personnel-related interests. The agreements entered into by the external participants in a project have become so intricate that communication and coordination have become problematic for the project team as well as for management. In response, more significant efforts are called for in order to achieve acceptable levels of control. Hence, project progress control of external participants must focus mainly on the project's schedule and the risks identified in planned project activities.

It is much more difficult to perform reviews and follow-up quality issues (SQA tasks) on the work and responsibilities of external participants than that of the developer's software project teams. These difficulties result from coordination and cooperation issues, typical to external participants. Coordination and cooperation of contract requirements, as well as an appropriate choice of external participants, are ways to overcome these difficulties.

5.6.4   From SDLC to Agile – processes and quality assurance activities (Appendix D)

This chapter is dedicated to the various software development models in current use, putting emphasis on the way that quality assurance activities are integrated into the development process. Furthermore, the way the customer's team is involved in the quality assurance process is also discussed.

Seven models of the software development process are discussed in this chapter:

- Classical software development models
  - The SDLC model
  - The prototyping model
  - The spiral model
- The object-oriented methodology
- The incremental delivery model
- The staged models
- The Agile methodology models

The models presented here are not merely alternatives, but could represent a complementary ways of software development, or refer to different development contexts.

At the end of our SQA tour I believe that participants of the tour have understood the key for SQA success – application of a great variety of processes and activities on the one hand and a strong need for cooperation and coordination of all parties involved in the efforts to produce software of the required quality on the other.

5.7 The SQA Hall of Fame

We have reached the end of our tour, but just before departing you are invited to visit the SQA Hall of Fame (Figure 5.1):

- The pillars are in honor of the SQA processes and methodologies.
- The base structure units are in honor of the tools and methods that support software quality.

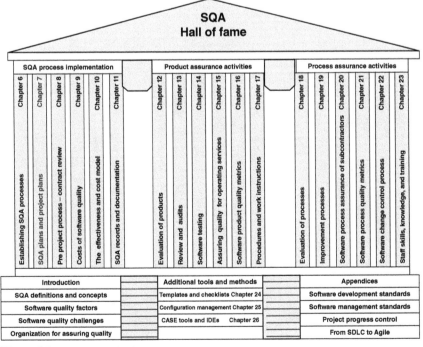

Figure 5.1 The SQA Hall of Fame

Part II

SQA Process Implementation Activities

The SQA processes are classified into three areas:

1. **SQA process implementation,** which is the strategic infrastructure and development of policy, processes and SQA roles that, when applied by the organization and software projects, will enable to produce software products of the required level of quality.

2. Product quality assurance related to the evaluation of software products for their compliance with project requirements.

3. Process quality assurance related to the verification of software project compliance with established processes and procedures. Additional processes evaluate the effectiveness and efficiency of the established processes, and list improvement suggestions.

This part of the book is dedicated to the first area, SQA process implementation. The following issues will be presented:

- Establishing SQA processes and their coordination with related software processes (Chapter 6)

Software Quality: Concepts and Practice, First Edition. Daniel Galin.
© 2018 the IEEE Computer Society, Inc. Published 2018 by John Wiley & Sons, Inc.

- SQA plan and project plan (Chapter 7)
- Preproject process – contract review (Chapter 8)
- Cost of software quality (Chapter 9)
- The effectiveness and cost of a V&V plan – the SQA model (Chapter 10)
- SQA records and documentation control (Chapter 11).

Chapter 6

Establishing SQA Processes and Their Coordination with Relevant Software Processes

6.1 Establishing SQA processes

The established SQA processes are intended to serve as infrastructure for the performance of SQA processes in the organization's software project, and as a basis for software quality management by the organization. These infrastructure development activities are of a strategic nature for the organization. The SQA processes to be defined and developed include the following:

- Defining the organization's quality policy.
- Establishing the organization's SQA processes.
- Defining tasks to those responsible for SQA processes.
- Defining the management's follow-up tool/method.
- Developing a follow-up and review method for the SQA function.

All these SQA processes have to be defined and developed independently from the organization's software projects. In new organizations, these infrastructure processes are intended to be completed before software contacts are signed.

The role of the SQA function in the establishment of the organization's SQA processes is to initiate and support the development. The SQA processes discussed here follow the IEEE Std. 730-2014 (IEEE, 2014).

A discussion of SQA processes follows.

a. **Defining the organization quality policy**

   The definition and development of the organization's quality policy will include the roles and responsibilities of SQA in the organization, and the

Software Quality: Concepts and Practice, First Edition. Daniel Galin.
© 2018 the IEEE Computer Society, Inc. Published 2018 by John Wiley & Sons, Inc.

obligatory status of SQA processes to be performed in the organization's software projects. The quality policy will also define the roles and responsibilities of the SQA function.

b. **Establishing the organization's SQA processes**
The organization's SQA processes should be defined and developed for all the SQA processes required for achieving adequate quality of software products and services. The development effort of the SQA processes should include development of the related procedures. It is expected that the SQA function will take a major part in carrying out the tasks of the SQA process development due to the team's professional knowledge and experience.

c. **Defining tasks to those responsible for SQA processes**
Performing the SQA processes requires defining tasks and responsibilities to persons in the software project teams, and to persons in the organization's software quality management. These persons will be responsible for the execution of the SQA processes.

d. **Defining the management's overseeing tool/method**
It is crucial that management has the whole picture of the SQA performance of the organization. A method for reporting to management about SQA processes performance and the outcomes of reviews and tests should be developed. The management's software quality performance information will be shared with the SQA function. An additional tool for providing management with a periodic review of the SQA performance is the "management review."

e. **Developing a follow-up and review method for the SQA function**
The data collected about the quality performance of software projects, including problems, enables the SQA function to identify process improvement opportunities and to plan their implementation.

6.2 Coordinating SQA processes with related software processes

The need to coordinate SQA processes with relevant software processes
A great part of SQA processes are evaluation activities, namely, verification, validation review, and audit activities. The performance of the SQA processes should be integrated in the software project schedule. The efficient performance of SQA processes requires close coordination between the SQA function and the organization management and project managers.

The required coordination to be performed by the SQA function includes:

• Coordination during the stage when the software quality assurance plan (SQAP) is being prepared. This coordination is required in order to plan correctly the schedule, resources, and budget of the SQA function.

- Coordination with the organization regarding the performance of SQA processes the management is responsible to carry out. Results of these coordination efforts are reflected in the SQAP.
- Coordination between the SQA function and project managers along the project performance.

The benefits of coordination

The following are the benefits of coordinating the SQA processes with project's software processes:

- The coordination ensures that the SQA processes are performed in the appropriate stage of the software process and so contribute to the achievement of the required level of software product quality.
- Resource savings for the SQA function by eliminating task redundancies and duplicate tasks.
- Less disagreements when evaluating performance and nonconformance results reported by the SQA function, as findings are based on common evaluation tasks.

Summary

1. **The SQA processes that should be established**

    The SQA function initiates and supports the establishment of SQA processes that will serve as infrastructure of SQA in the organization:
    - Defining the organization quality policy.
    - Establishing the organization's SQA processes.
    - Defining tasks to those responsible for SQA processes.
    - Defining the management's follow-up tool/method. Developing a follow-up and review method for the SQA function

2. **The benefits of coordinating SQA processes with relevant software processes**

    The following are the benefits of coordinating the SQA processes with software processes:
    - The coordination ensures that the SQA processes be performed at the appropriate stage of the software process, and so will contribute to the achievement of the required level of software product quality.
    - Saving resources for the SQA function by eliminating task redundancies and duplicate tasks.
    - Less disagreements when evaluating performance and nonconformance results reported by the SQA function, as findings are based on common evaluation tasks.

Selected bibliography

IEEE (2014) *IEEE Std. 730-2014 Software Quality Assurance*, The IEEE Computer Society, IEEE, New York.

Review questions

6.1 The head of an SQA function insists that all required SQA processes be established.

    a. List the required SQA processes.

    b. Explain the importance of each of the SQA processes.

6.2 The SQA function is investing efforts to coordinate SQA processes with relevant software processes.

    • List the benefits of the coordination.

Topics for discussion

6.1 The organization is directed to establish the SQA processes prior to contracting the execution of software development projects.

    a. Should the established SQA processes be considered "infrastructure of the organization's SQA?" Discuss this issue.

    b. Why should SQA processes be established prior to carrying out software development projects?

    c. Explain the contribution of each of the SQA processes to the SQA system.

6.2 "The coordination process is a continuous process, which requires the SQAP to be updated frequently due to the flow of software process changes", claims a head of an SQA team.

    a. Do you agree with this claim? List your arguments.

    b. Can you suggest three different situations resulting in software process changes.

Chapter 7

SQA Plan and Project Plan

7.1 Introduction

Planning ahead is always the key to success, this also applies to preparing SQA plans and project plans. The chapter is dedicated to SQA plans and project plans – their preparation process and contents.

The SQA plan (SQAP) deals with the activities and tasks the SQA function is required to carry out over the next year, and enables estimating resources required to perform the SQAP. The planners of the resource estimates refer to the professional knowledge and experience requirements of the various activities and tasks, and classify the staff requirement accordingly. In this way, the SQA function may be appropriately staffed to carry out the SQAP in the coming year.

The project plan deals with the activities and tasks to be performed by the project team throughout the project's life cycle, namely, during the development and operation stages. Probably, two of the most important elements of the project plan are the activities schedule and the resource estimates for each activity.

The two plans are tightly connected, and need to be coordinated. A great part of the SQAP activities has to be coordinated with the relevant project plan activities. In other words, each project plan needs to be coordinated with the relevant part/s of the SQAP. Moreover, the coordination continues in the execution stage, when both plans are updated according to project progress and change requests are performed.

Sections 7.2 and 7.3 present the process of preparing an SQAP and its contents. Sections 7.4 and 7.6 present the process of preparing a project plan. Section 7.5 presents a mini case that illustrates the importance of an updated project plan. Section 7.7 is dedicated to the special cases of project plans for small projects and internal projects.

IEEE Std. 730-2014 dedicates Sec. 6.33 and Annex C to SQA planning. ISO/IEC/IEEE Std. 12207 Sec. 6.3.1 deals with project planning, while ISO/IEC Std. 90003 Sec. 5.4.2 discusses quality management system planning; assuring the quality of software projects.

Software Quality: Concepts and Practice, First Edition. Daniel Galin.
© 2018 the IEEE Computer Society, Inc. Published 2018 by John Wiley & Sons, Inc.

7.2 The process of preparing an SQA plan

The SQAP is a comprehensive plan that directs the work of the SQA function for a year. It is updated during the year according to the changing and new circumstances.

The process of preparing an SQAP described here is based to a great extent on IEEE Std. 730-2014 (IEEE, 2014).

The activities required to prepare an SQAP include:

1. Determining the relevant SQAP outline elements, while considering the needs of each stakeholder in every project performed. This task is accomplished through direct discussions with the stakeholders.

2. Preparing the software quality assurance plan (SQAP) according to the standard required elements, considering the stakeholder needs. Special attention is given to project risks.

3. Finalizing the SQAP according to that agreed with the project managers.

4. Identifying and analyzing product risks in the various projects; risks to users of the software products. Furthermore, it is required to identify activities aimed at reducing or eliminating these risks, enabling to determine the expected success of handling these product risks.

5. Estimating the SQA function resources required for performing the SQAP: size of function team, schedule of planned activities, skill and knowledge required, and equipment required.

6. Defining measurements (metrics) to evaluate software quality and for the performance of the SQA function. These metrics should enable assessing the level of achieving the organization and project objectives.

The following are included in the SQAP updating activities:

1. Follow-up the SQA function's activities and project progress and perform SQAP revisions required.

2. Follow-up the changes performed by projects and perform necessary adaptations to the SQAP.

3. Prepare periodic or on-demand status reports regarding the progress and findings of the SQAP, and present the information to the organization's quality management and project management.

7.3 The SQAP elements

A comprehensive outline of the SQAP elements is presented in IEEE Std. 730-2014 (IEEE, 2014). The SQAP activities presented here are based upon this standard. The activity elements are classified into three groups:

- SQA process implementation activity elements

- Product assurance activity elements
- Process assurance activity elements

The contents of each plan section is presented, and includes general content that applies to all projects, and specific content that applies to a specific software project.

7.3.1 SQA process implementation activity elements

a. Activities for correcting management deficiencies related to quality issues

The following are examples of management deficiencies related to quality issues planned to be corrected by the SQA function over the next year:

- Inadequate management quality policy: Inadequate organization for monitoring SQA software process activities.
- Inadequate activities for establishing a corrective and preventive function in the organization.
- Inadequate resources, trained persons, and equipment available to the SQA function.
- Inappropriate levels of independence of the SQA function in terms of management and financing.

b. Software product risks to users

This section presents a project list, where for each project an evaluation of software product risks has to be performed by the SQA function. These include determination of the risk characteristics, and the method in which to handle the product risks.

c. Development equipment and tools of software projects

This section presents a list of projects, where for each project a list of equipment and tools will be determined, based on an analysis of the nature and contract technical requirements of the project. Following preparation of these lists, the training needs for the project team will be specified. This activity is expected to also yield training needs for the staff in organization general. The evaluation of the equipment and tool lists prepared by project managers will be performed by the SQA function over the next year.

d. Standards, practices, and conventions for software projects

This section refers to the activity that will evaluate lists of standards, practices, and conventions – applicable to all software projects.

It also refers to analysis of activities to evaluate specific lists of standards, practices, and conventions – applicable to each of the software projects.

e. Resources and schedule estimates for the SQA function

This section presents resource and schedule estimates for the SQA function activities planned for the next year. The estimates should be based on the following information derived from the project requirements: staff days, skills and experience, equipment, project activities, type of professional expertise, and schedules. The estimations are quantified as follows:

The total SQA function resources include:

- Calculations of the general workload for every week of the project.
- Calculations of the weekly workload for each of the professional groups.
- Calculations of the weekly load for each type of equipment required.

7.3.2 Product assurance activity elements

a. Conformance evaluation of project plans

This section lists the SQA function's conformance evaluation tasks of the project plan tasks, and includes the following examples:

- Preparing list of project plans to be evaluated for their conformance with contracts, standards, regulations, and conventions.
- Preparing list of plans for processes of software support, software reuse, and other processes to be evaluated for their conformance with contract, standards, regulations, and conventions.
- Preparing list of plans for configuration management and documentation to be evaluated for their conformance with requirement documents, standards, regulations, and conventions.

b. Conformance evaluation of products

This section lists the evaluations of software development products for their conformance to requirements, standards, and conventions. These evaluations are carried by the SQA function and relate to software development products such as design reports, verification and validation, and test and integration reports.

c. Evaluation of product for acceptability

This section lists evaluation of the required confidence level of a software project product (including product documentation) to be acceptable by the acquirer that is required to be carried out by the SQA function over the next year. The evaluation needs to refer, among other subjects, to the criteria for acceptance, the software installation strategy, and maintenance procedures.

d. Conformance evaluation of product maintenance plan

This section lists evaluation of conformance of maintenance plans with contract requirements, regulations, standards, and conventions that have to be carried out over the next year.

e. Measurement plans for products

This section lists the measurement plans and required data collection for software products to be prepared by the SQA function over the next year. The product measurement plans relate to product risks and the organization's quality goals, and include data collection.

7.3.3 Process assurance activity elements

a. Conformance evaluation of life cycle processes

This section deals with the evaluation tasks of life cycle processes, models, and procedures to be performed by the SQA function over the next year, and include:
- Evaluation of adequacy of the processes definitions, maintenance, and improvements.
- Evaluation of adequacy of the responsibility and authority defined to perform the life cycle processes.
- Evaluation of adequacy of process improvement implementation.
- Evaluation of adequacy of configuration management implementation.

b. Conformance evaluation of environment

This section deals with the evaluation of the adequacy of the environment of development, test, and support services to be performed by the SQA function over the next year. The environments to be evaluated for their conformance to project needs, as well as to software engineering practices and relevant contract requirements, include work stations, development tools, testing laboratories, and software libraries.

c. Conformance evaluation of subcontractors' participation in project implementation

This section presents the SQA function evaluation tasks aimed to determine the adequacy of the precontract activities and activities included in the contract for reviewing the subcontractor's capabilities to appropriately perform their part of the project.

d. Measurement of development, testing, and operation processes

This section lists the measurement plans and required data collection for software life cycle processes to be prepared by the SQA function over the next year. The process measurement plans relate to product risks and the organization's quality goals, and include data collection.

e. Assessment of staff skills and knowledge requirements and resulting training needs

This section deals with the evaluation of skills and knowledge required from project staff, identification of deficiencies, and the training program expected to solve these deficiencies.

The list of SQA plan activity elements is presented in Frame 7.1.

Frame 7.1: SQA plan activity elements

SQA plan activity elements

SQA process implementation activity elements

a. Plans activities for correcting management's deficiencies related to quality issues
b. Software product risks to users
c. Development equipment and tools of software projects
d. Standards, practices, and conventions of software projects
e. Resources' and schedules' estimates for the SQA function

Product assurance activity elements

a. Evaluation of project plans for conformance
b. Evaluation of products for conformance
c. Evaluation of products for acceptability
d. Evaluation of product maintenance plan for conformance
e. Measurement plans for products

Process assurance activity elements

a. Evaluation of life cycle processes for conformance
b. Evaluation of environment for conformance
c. Evaluation of subcontractors' participation in project implementation for conformance
d. Measurement of development, testing, and operation processes
e. Assessment of staff skill and knowledge requirements and the resulting training needs

7.4   The process of preparing a project plan

The project plan is a comprehensive document that serves the software project throughout the project life time; the development and operation stages. The project plan that contains software development and quality element, comprises a "development plan" and a "quality plan".

The project plan objectives

The objectives of project plans are presented in Frame 7.2.

Frame 7.2: The objectives of project plans

The objectives of project plans
1. Ensure the successful and timely performance of a project complying with contract requirements, standards, procedures, and conventions.   2. Ensure the quality of the project products.   3. Provide management with the data required for efficient and effective project control.

The process of preparing a project plan

The project manager is usually the person responsible for preparing the project plan – which is expected to be completed and reviewed before the project implementation begins. The process of preparing a project plan requires the following phases:

- Data collection phase, which includes the study of qualified manpower availability for the project, appropriate development tools, possible development risks, and method for their elimination or at least their mitigation. Consultation with other project managers and experts completes the data collection phase.
- Project plan compilation phase
- Project plan reviews
- Project plan updates are usually unavoidable; as change requests originated by the acquirer and methodological and other changes initiated by the project team are very common.

There is a tendency to use the project proposal material as a basis for preparing the project plan, as both documents share many elements. This practice should be implemented carefully as parts of the proposal data may be invalid due to circumstances changing during the period between preparing the proposal and the time the contract was signed.

The project plan is a major subject of Sections 7.1 and 7.3 of ISO/IEC 90003-2014 (ISO/IEC, 2014) and Section 6.3.1 of ISO/IEC/IEEE Std. 12207-2008 (ISO/IEC/IEEE, 2008). The project plan is also an important element in the Integrated Capability Maturity Model (ICMM).

The next section presents a min case that illustrates the importance of a properly planned project plan.

7.5 Jack thanks his department manager – a mini case

Jack Bora, an experienced project manager, has been appointed to manage the Pagoda project, a sizable project for automating a textile manufacturing plant. As is often the case in the software industry, due to an earlier obligation he could only begin organizing and executing the project 5 weeks after the scheduled project start. Naturally, he was under serious time pressure from the very first day. As he was a member of the proposal team and participated in most of the meetings held with the customer's representatives, he was confident that he knew everything that was required to do the job, and could even save himself the tiring task of preparing a project plan. He intended to use the proposal itself and the working papers as the project's development and quality plans. His reliance on these materials was based on the fact that he knew that the proposal and all its estimates, including the schedule, staff requirements, list of deliverables, software products, and list of development risks had all been thoroughly reviewed by the contract review team, and also amended accordingly.

The first month of the Pagoda project was by now progressing well with no notable events. Then, one morning Jack was urgently called into the department manager's office. The development department manager did not waste a minute, and demanded that Jack immediately prepare new full project development plans ("development plan") and project quality plans ("quality plan"). When Jack tried to claim that there was no need for a project plan, as he had all the proposal team materials: working papers, including the project plan, resource estimates, list of project risks, and more. The department manager cut him short saying "I still insist you prepare entirely new project development and quality plans and complete them before the end of next week." After a few moments of silence, he continued "By the way, don't forget that a period of seven months elapsed between the proposal preparation and the signing of the contract. Such a period is a hell of time for changes in our trade. . . ."

So, without actually agreeing regarding the need for development plans, Jack began carrying out "the manager's task." He reexamined the proposal materials and thoroughly updated them.

The new plans were more comprehensive than the approved proposal, especially with respect to schedules, resource estimates, and development risk evaluations, and included additional subjects, which were not covered in the original proposal. The effort invested in preparing the development and quality plans proved to be beneficial:

- He found out that the 5-week delay in the project start necessitates him to change the work sequence of the project to enable finishing on time. This change created a need for an additional team on the project.

- He soon discovered that two of the proposed team leaders would not be available at the newly scheduled dates, due to assignments recently allocated. Another team leader would be needed for the newly created team, so he would now need to locate and recruit three team leaders. ("Lucky I am to discover the team leader shortage, at a time when there is still a good chance to find a suitable candidate," he thought).

- BG Software Consultants, the consulting company that had agreed to provide professional support in a highly specialized and crucial area, had suffered heavy losses and had consequently gone bankrupt 3 months earlier.

- Jerry Fox, the company's expert for the database chosen by the customer, had resigned a month ago.
- The human resource department notified Jack that only three out of the five programmers scheduled on the fourth to sixth month of the project could now be assigned for the project.

When he finally brought the development and quality plans to the department manager, he opened saying "I should have brought a bottle of wine to thank you for making me prepare updated plans. You have no doubt saved me a lot of inevitable problems managing the project."

7.6 The elements of the project plan

A comprehensive outline of project plan elements is presented in ISO/IEC 90003-2014 (ISO/IEC, 2014) and ISO/IEC/IEEE Std. 12207-2008 (IEEE, 2008). The presentation here is based upon these standards. The elements are classified into two groups:

- Development plan elements
- Quality plan elements

7.6.1 Development plan elements

The following elements comprise a development plan.

a. Project products

A development plan includes the following products:
- Designing the documents from each activity, indicating those items to be delivered to the customer (deliverables)
- Software products of each activity, specifying installation sites
- Development process mapping
- Development resources estimation

b. Control methods

The project manager and the department management control project implementation by defining the monitoring practices to be applied: progress report and coordinating meetings and so on.

A comprehensive discussion of project control methods is found in the chapter dedicated to project progress control.

c. Mapping the development process

Mapping of the development process involves preparing detailed definitions of each of the project's activities. These descriptions include definitions of inputs and outputs, and the specific activities planned.

Activity descriptions include:

a. **An estimate of the activity's duration.** These estimates are highly dependent on the size of the team that performs the activity.

b. **The logical sequence** in which each activity is to be performed, including a description of each activity's dependence on previously completed activities.

Implementation tip

In some development plans, quality assurance activities exist throughout the process, but without time allocated for their performance or the subsequent removal of defects. Someone probably assumed that a late afternoon meeting would be sufficient for performing the quality assurance activities and subsequent corrections.

As nothing may be achieved without time, the almost guaranteed result is delay, caused by the "unexpectedly" long duration of the quality assurance process.

Hence, the time allocated for quality assurance activities and defect correction work that follows should be examined. SQA activities, such as design reviews and software tests, should be included among the scheduled project activities. The same applies to the design and code correction activities. Failing to schedule these activities can cause unanticipated delays in the initiation of subsequent activities.

Several methods are available for scheduling and graphically presenting the development process. One of the most commonly used methods is the Gantt chart, which displays the various activities by horizontal bars, whose lengths are proportional to activity duration. The bars represent the activities themselves, and are placed vertically according to their planned initiation and conclusion. Several computerized tools can prepare Gantt charts in addition to producing lists of activities according to their required start and conclusion times, and so forth.

More advanced scheduling methodologies, such as CPM and PERT, both of which belong to the category of critical path analysis, take sequence dependencies into account, in addition to the duration of activities. They enable calculating the earliest and latest acceptable start times for each activity. The difference between start times determines the activity scheduling flexibility. Special attention is awarded to those activities lacking scheduling flexibility (which explains their being called "critical path" activities), and whose tardy completion could delay the conclusion of the entire project.

Several software packages, used in conjunction with these methodologies, support the planning, reporting, and follow-up of project timetables. An example of a software package of this type is *Microsoft Project*. For a more detailed discussion of scheduling, refer to the literature dealing with project management.

d. Estimating development resources

For each project activity, the type of professional resources required and the estimated quantity are determined as follows:

- Internal (developer) staff and their professional skills
- External (subcontractor) staff and their professional skills

The development resources data, when combined with the mapping of the development activities enables:

- To calculate the general workload for every week of the project
- To calculate the weekly workload for each of the professional groups

e. Project staff organization

The organization plan includes:

- Organizational structure: Definition of project teams, their professional area and tasks, including support by subcontractor teams and suppliers.
- Professional requirements for each team: Professional certification, experience in a specific programming language or development tool, experience with a specific software product and type, and so forth.
- Number of team members required for each period of time, according to the activities scheduled. It is expected that teams will commence their activities at different times, and that their team size may vary from one period to the next, depending on the planned activities.
- Names of team leaders and, if possible, names of team members. Difficulties are expected to arise with respect to the project assignment of team leaders and their current assignments. Therefore, staff names are required to help recruit replacement team leaders and keep track of their availability.

Implementation tip

The long-term availability of project staff should be carefully examined. Lags in completing former assignments may result in delays in joining the project team, which increase the risk of failing to meet project milestones. In addition, staff "evaporation" caused by resignations and/or promotions, phenomena that are particularly frequent in the software industry, can cause project staff shortages. Therefore, follow-up of staff availability should be done periodically to avoid "surprises." Early warning of unforeseen staff shortages makes it easier to resolve this problem.

- Training tasks for new recruitments and current staff to get the necessary knowledge of new development tools.

f. Project interfaces

Project interfaces include:

- Interfaces with existing software packages (software interface)
- Interfaces with existing firmware of instrumentation and equipment (hardware interface)

- Interfaces with other software and/or hardware development teams who are working on the same system or project, applying cooperation and coordination links, including suppliers, subcontractors, and partners (teams interface).

g. Project risks
1. Types of project risks
Two types were defined
- Product risk
- Development risks

Product risks
A product risk is a state where the software product may cause damage to the developer and/or to the user of the software. Special efforts should be given by the developer to identify such risks and to eliminate or at least to mitigate them.

Classes of product risks

Physical product risks

Product risks of medical equipment, aerospace equipment, and military equipment are typical physical risks caused when the software embedded product in these types of equipment fails.

Safety product risks

Car safety equipment and household fire safety equipment risks are typical physical risks caused when the software embedded product in these types of equipment fails.

Financial product risks

Typical financial damages are caused when management information systems of financial organizations fail to operate or produce erroneous information.

Development risks
Development risk is a state of a development task or environment, which, if ignored, will increase the likelihood of project failure.

Classes of development risks
The development risks may be classified as follows:

Requirement risks

- Developer failed to fully understand the requirements.
- Excessive change requests will require major redesign or recoding efforts substantially more than the estimates.
- Addition of unnecessary (not required) features, causing a waste of development resources and also schedule delays.

Team member risks

- The assigned team members unexpectedly find tasks above their professional capabilities.
- The assigned team members are inexperienced in the use of the planned development tools.
- Assigned team members are not available for performing planned activities due to former project completion delays.
- Assigned team members have resigned or were promoted, causing a shortage of team members.
- Excessive rate of defects, due to low professional skills of the team.
- Poor system performance regarding response times of real-time systems and information systems.

Organizational risks

- Financial difficulties cause reduction of project budget.
- Difficulties in recruiting staff with the required skills.
- The likelihood that suppliers of specialized hardware or software subcontractors will not fulfill their obligations on schedule.
- Required training on new development tools is not available in the organization.

Development methodology and tools risks

- Code generator or development tool cannot fulfill the required tasks or is not efficient.
- Planned case tool is not adequate for the planned task.
- Chosen methodology proves to be inadequate.
- Poor quality of purchased COTS software and software products developed by subcontractors.

Estimation risks

- The development resources required were underestimated.
- Project schedule was underestimated.
- The software reuse possibilities were overestimated.

2. Development risk management process

The risk management process includes the following activities: risk identification, risk evaluation, planning of risk management actions (RMAs), implementation of RMAs, and monitoring implementation of the risk management plan.

Similar planning activities (although not to the same degree of thoroughness) are part of the proposal draft preparation process and reviewed in the proposal draft review.

The respective planning activities include:

- **Identification of software risk items**

The main tool supporting the identification of SRIs is checklists that specify the team, project, and customer situations that are likely to cause software risks.

Identification of software risk items should begin at the start of the project (preproject stage) and be repeated periodically throughout the project until its completion.

- **Evaluation of the identified SRIs**

Evaluation of the identified SRIs is concerned mainly with:

- Estimating the probability that a software risk will materialize if no RMA is taken (Prob(materialize))
- Estimating damages in case an SRI does materialize (Est(damage))

One common method used to prioritize SRIs is by calculating their expected damage, where:

$$\text{Expected damage} = \text{Est(damage)} \times \text{Prob(materialize)}.$$

- **Planning RMAs**

It is incumbent upon the software risk team to consider alternative ways to resolve the identified SRIs. RMAs include a range of internal, subcontractor, and customer actions.

Table A7.1 provides a list of possible RMAs and their contribution to the prevention or resolution of SRIs.

In preparing the recommended list of RMAs, the planning team should consider:

- The priority assigned to the SRI.
- The expected results of a planned RMA (complete or partial resolution).
- The costs and organizational efforts required for implementation of the RMA.

Implementation tip

In planning RMAs, one should be aware that:

- Some RMAs can prevent, identify, or resolve SRIs of various types.
- Some SRIs can be treated by several RMAs.
- The efficiency of an RMA varies significantly with different projects and different environments.

- **Implementation of RMAs**

  Implementation of a risk management plan requires that the staff members be assigned as personally responsible for each RMA and its implementation schedule.
- **Monitoring implementation of the risk management plan**

  Systematic, periodical activities are required to monitor implementation of the risk management plan. The aim of the monitoring activities is to:

- Determine the efficiency of the RMAs.
- Plan new RMAs for unsuccessful implementation.
- Update the risk evaluation by considering newly identified SRIs.

The process of software risk management is illustrated in Figure 7.1.

The growing importance of software risk management is described in the spiral model for software development. To cope with risks, a special phase of risk assessment is assigned to every cycle of the spiral model. (More information about the spiral model is provided in another chapter.)

The IEEE Std. 1540:2001 (IEEE, 2001) is dedicated to risk management. The subject of product risks is presented in IEEE Std. 730-2014 (IEEE, 2014).

Various aspects of risk management are presented by Sulaman et al. (2013), Lobato et al. (2012), Pekar et al. (2015), Raz and Hillson (2005), Elzamly and Hussin (2015), and Nelson et al. (2008).

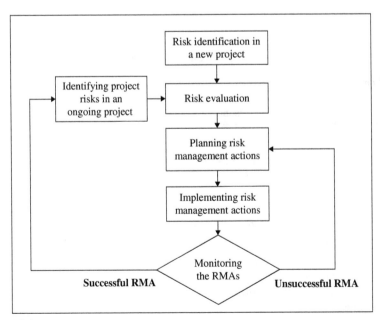

Figure 7.1 The risk management process

h. Project milestones

Project milestones are events of importance in the development process, that is, the completion of the design phase. For each milestone, the completed project products (documents or code) and scheduled times are to be defined.

i. Project cost estimation

Project costs include human resources costs, subcontractor costs, costs of purchased software, and costs of additional resources; such as travel costs and equipment costs. The costs of internal and external (subcontractors) human resources may be calculated according to the prepared resource estimates. The list of planned COTS software products could serve for preparing the purchase budget.

Estimates of project costs that have been prepared by the proposal team could support the project cost estimation, while each cost component should be reviewed thoroughly, and updated according to the updated resource estimates, contracts negotiated with subcontractors and suppliers, and so forth. For instance, part of the project originally planned to be carried out by internal development teams now needs to be performed by a subcontractor, due to the unavailability of an internal team. A change of this nature usually involves a substantial budget change.

j. Project methodology and development tools

The methodology and development tools have to be applied for each phase of the project.

Implementation tip

When evaluating the suitability of the proposed project methodology and development tools, one should also take into account the professional experience of the staff, including the subcontractors' personnel – even though temporary.

---

k. Software development standards and procedures

A list of the software development standards, procedures, and work instructions to be applied in the project. In some cases, software development standards and procedures are determined by the customer as part of the requirements stated in the project contract.

l. Required development facilities

Required development facilities include: hardware, laboratories, software and hardware development tools, office space, and other items. For each facility, the period required for its use should be indicated and scheduled.

m. Documentation control

   The planner is required to define the list of the project's controlled documents and quality records. In addition, a work instruction for the project's documentation control should be prepared.

n. Security including virus protection

   The planner is required to define security controls related to the project documents, code in process, and software products. Special work instructions might be required in certain projects.

The elements comprising a development plan are listed in Frame 7.3.

Frame 7.3: The elements comprising a development plan

Source: Based on ISO/IEC 90003-2014 and ISO/IEC/IEEE Std. 12207-2008.

The elements comprising a development plan
a. Project products
b. Control methods
c. Mapping the development process
d. Estimating development resources
e. Project staff organization
f. Project interfaces
g. Project risks
h. Project milestones
i. Project cost estimates
j. Project methodology and development tools
k. Software development standards and procedures
l. Required development facilities
m. Documentation control
n. Security including virus protection

Development plan approval

Development plan review and approval is to be completed according to the review procedures applied within the organization.

7.6.2   Elements of the quality plan

Depending on the project, all or some of the following elements, presented in Frame 7.4, comprise the elements of a project quality plan:

a. Quality goals

The term "quality goals" refers to the developed software system's substantive quality requirements. "Quantitative measures are usually preferred to qualitative measures when choosing quality goals because they provide the developer with more objective assessments of software performance during the development process and system testing. However, one type of goal is not totally equivalent to the other." The possible replacement of qualitative with quantitative measures is illustrated in the following example.

Example:

Quality goals have to be determined for a help desk system (HDS) that is planned to serve an electrical appliance manufacturer. The HDS is intended to operate 100 hours per week. The software quality assurance team was requested to prepare a list of quantitative quality goals appropriate for the following qualitative requirements:

HDS qualitative requirement	Related quantitative quality goal
The HDS should be very reliable	HDS availability should exceed 99.9% (HDS down time should not exceed 5 minutes per month).
The HDS should operate continuously	In cases of HDS failure, the system's recovery time should not exceed 10 minutes in 99% of cases of failure.
The HDS should be highly efficient	An HDS operator should be able to handle at least 100 customer calls per 8-hour shift.
The HDS should be very responsive to customers	Waiting time for an operator response should not exceed 30 seconds in 99% of the calls. Achievement of this goal depends on the combination of software features, and the number of work stations installed and operated.

The quality goals should reflect the major acceptance criteria indicated in the customer's requirement document (i.e., the RFP document). As such, quality goals serve as measures of the successful achievement of the customer's quality requirements.

b. Procedures and work instructions

The relevant procedures and work instructions should be defined, according to the combined quality assurance and development considerations.

c. **Criteria for ending each project stage**

A criterion for ending each of the development stages, accepted by the customer and developer, is essential for the regular flow of development process. It requires:

- The body that applies the criterion, that is, the design review team, the head of the testing department.
- Defining the criteria, that is, no major design defect that requires redesigning of a system feature was identified; the number of identified code defects in a regression test run is one or less. Quantitative criteria are preferred to qualitative ones.

d. **Project life cycle SQA activities**

Planned review activities

The quality plan should provide a complete listing of all planned review activities: design reviews (DRs), design inspections, code inspections, and so on, with the following determined for each activity:

- The scope of the review activity
- The type of the review activity
- The schedule of review activities (as defined by the mapping of the development activities)
- The specific procedures to be applied
- The party(ies) responsible for carrying out the review activity

Planned software tests

The quality plan should provide a complete list of planned software tests, with the following designated for each test:

- The unit, integration, system test, and acceptance tests to be performed
- The type of testing activities to be carried out, including specification of automated software tests to be applied
- The planned test schedule (as defined by the mapping of activities of the project process)
- The specific procedures to be applied
- The party(ies) responsible for carrying out the test

Planned acceptance tests for externally developed software

A complete list of the acceptance tests planned for externally developed software should be included in the quality plan. Elements to be included are: (a) purchased software, (b) software developed by subcontractors, and (c) customer-supplied software. The acceptance tests for externally developed software should be parallel to those used for internally developed software tests.

e. **Configuration management tools and procedures**

The quality plan should specify configuration management tools and procedures, including the timing of baseline version releases.

f. Monitoring measurement activities

The planners should define software quality metrics for quality, productivity, schedule keeping, and so forth. The responsibility for performing the measurements and for the monitoring of measurements should be determined.

g. Person(s) responsible for approving project outputs

The person(s) authorized to approve each of the project products, documents, and code files, especially the deliverable items, should be determined.

h. Training in usage of new development tools

The need to apply new development tools for a given development activity creates a training requirement. Timing the training schedule before the relevant development activity begins is crucial. The planner should find out which of the scheduled development teams needs training

i. Change management

The change management procedures to be applied throughout the project should be defined and agreed with the customer.

The required software quality plan elements are listed in Frame 7.4.

Frame 7.4: Elements of a software quality plan

Source: Based on ISO/IEC 90003-2014

Elements of a software quality plan
a. Quality goals
b. Procedures and work instructions
c. Criteria for ending each project stage
d. Project life cycle SQA activities
e. Configuration management tools and procedures
f. Monitoring measurement activities
g. Person(s) responsible for approving project outputs
h. Training in use of new development tools
i. Change management

7.7 Project plans for small projects and for internal projects

It is quite natural for project leaders to try to evade the "hassle" of preparing the development and quality plans (and the other surrounding reviews and plan approvals). This behavior reflects the tendency to avoid "bureaucracy" and the sweeping control that customers may attempt to exercise. This tendency is especially common in two specific situations: small projects and internal projects.

The argument for preparing plans for such projects is discussed in the following two sections.

7.7.1 Development and quality plans for small projects

- Does a project scheduled for only 40 working days, to be performed by one professional and completed within 12 weeks, justify the investment of several man-days in order to prepare full-scale development and quality plans?
- Does a project to be implemented by three professionals with a total investment of 30 man-days and duration of 5 weeks require full-scale plans?

It should be clear that the development and quality plan procedures applicable to large projects cannot be automatically applied to small projects. For these projects, special procedures are needed. These procedures determine how to treat the project in question with respect to the plans:

a. Cases/situations where neither development nor quality plans are required, for example, projects requiring 15 man-days or less.

b. Cases/situations where the decision to prepare the plans is left to the project leader's discretion, for example, projects that require less than 50 man-days, with no significant software risk items identified.

c. A small and complicated project that has to be completed within 30 days, with a heavy penalty for not completing on time. In this case, partial planning that includes, at least the following, is needed: project mapping of development activities, cost estimates based on resources estimates, and a list of identified project risks including ways to manage them.

A list of elements recommended for inclusion in development and quality plans for small projects is shown in Frame 7.5.

Frame 7.5: Recommended elements of development and quality plans for small projects

---

Recommended elements of development and quality plans for small projects

Recommended development plan for small projects:

- Project products, indicating "deliverables"
- Project milestones
- Development risks
- Estimates of project costs

Recommended quality plan for small projects:

- Quality goals

Several advantages to "planned" small projects over "unplanned" projects can be identified, even for the less extensive plans:

  a. A more comprehensive and thorough understanding of tasks is attained.

  b. Greater responsibility for meeting obligations may be assigned to project commitments.

  c. Better understanding with respect to the requirements and schedule may be reached between the developer and the customer.

  d. It becomes easier for management and customers to share control of the project and to identify unexpected delays early on.

7.7.2   Development plans and quality plans for internal projects

Internal projects are those projects intended for use by other departments in the organization or by the entire organization, as well as projects dealing with software package development for the software market. The common denominator to all these project types is that no external body participates "as customer" in their development. Internal projects can be of a very large scale. Yet even in these cases, there is a tendency to avoid preparing adequate development and quality plans. The following example illustrates the negative consequences of an "unplanned" internal project.

Example:
The marketing department of Toyware Ltd., a new computer game manufacturer, had planned to hit the market with "Super-Monster V," the firm's new, advanced computer game, during the upcoming Christmas season. The software development department of Toyware claimed that work on the game should commence immediately in order to complete the project on time. Therefore, preparation of a full proposal, along with the subsequent preparation of a project plan, was overlooked. The development department estimated the project budget at $240,000, which was transferred to the department. According to the marketing schedule, system tests were to be completed no later than October 1, so as to allow the development department to manufacture the first batch of the toy packages before November 1.

   The project moved forward with no special difficulties, but as the project progressed, it became evident that there might be a delay. Only at the end of September it became obvious that a three-month delay could not be avoided. The promotional and advertising activities that had taken place before September 30, thus became worthless. The project was finally completed at the end of February. The project's cost overrun was significant – actual costs exceeded $385,000 – but most painful was the company's lost opportunity to exploit the

Christmas market, and damaged reputation from advertising a product which was not available. Last week, the company management decided to avoid any future internal computer game development projects.

This example makes it clear that preparing full-scale development and quality plans for internal projects can be highly beneficial to both sides of internal projects.

The benefits of full scale project plan for an internal project.

Software development departments can enjoy the following advantages of plan preparation:

a. Avoiding budget overruns. This is of special importance when the profit center system is applied.

b. Avoiding damage to other projects caused by delays in releasing professionals occupied in an internal project.

c. Avoiding loss of market status (developer's reputation in the COTS software market) caused by delayed completion of new software products – already advertised – or new versions of current products.

d. Avoiding loss of market status, especially regarding the developer's reputation, caused by delayed completion of external projects triggered by late completion of internal projects.

Internal "customers" can enjoy the following advantages:

a. Smaller deviations from planned completion dates and smaller budget overruns.

b. Better control over the development process, including earlier identification of possible delays that enables the "internal customer" earlier search for, and resolution of, the internal customer's department difficulties caused by the delay.

c. Fewer internal delay damages

The organization can enjoy these advantages:

a. Reduced risk of market loss (i.e., opportunity window) due to late arrival of COTS software product.

b. Reduced risk of being sued for late supply of "custom" software systems; hence, reduced penalties for noncompliance with contract demands.

c. Reduced risk of impairing the firm's reputation as a reliable software developer.

Summary

1. **The SQA process implementation elements of SQA plans**
   The elements are:
   - Plan's activities for correcting management's deficiencies related to quality issues.
   - Software product risks to users
   - Development equipment and tools of software projects
   - Standards, practices, and conventions for software projects
   - Resource and schedule estimates for the SQA function

2. **The product assurance elements of SQA plans**
   The elements are:
   - Conformance evaluation of project plans
   - Conformance evaluation of products
   - Evaluate product for acceptability
   - Conformance evaluation of product maintenance plan
   - Measurement plans for products

3. **The objectives of project plans**
   The plans' objectives are to provide the adequate basis to:
   - Ensure the successful and timely performance of a project that complies with contract requirements, standards, procedures, and conventions
   - Ensure the quality of project products
   - Provide management with data needed for efficient and effective project control

4. **The elements of a development plan**
   Fourteen types of elements constitute a development plan:
   1. Project products
   2. Control methods
   3. Project staff organization
   4. Project interfaces
   5. Development risks
   6. Mapping of development process
   7. Estimating development resources
   8. Project milestones
   9. Project cost estimates
   10. Project methodology and development tools
   11. Software development standards and procedures
   12. Development facilities
   13. Required documentation control
   14. Security including virus protection

5. **The elements of a quality plan**
   Nine elements constitute a quality plan:
   1. Quality goals
   2. Procedures and work instructions

3. Criteria for ending each project stage
4. Project life cycle SQA activities
5. Configuration management tools and procedures
6. Monitoring measurement activities
7. Person(s) responsible for approving project outputs
8. Training on usage of new development tools
9. Change management

6. **The major project risk classes**

Project risks may be classified as follows:
- Product riks
- Development risks
  a. Product risks classification is as follows:
    - Physical roduc risks
    - Safety product risks
    - Financial product risks
  b. Devlopment risks classification is as follows:
    - Requirement risks
    - Team members risks
    - Organizational risks
    - Development methodology and tool risks
    - Estimation risks

7. **The process of software risk management**

Risk management includes planning, implementation, and monitoring activities. The pertinent activities are identification and evaluation of SRIs, planning RMAs to resolve the SRIs, implementation of RMAs, and monitoring the implementation of RMAs.

8. **The benefits of preparing development and quality plans for small projects**

For small development projects (less than 15 man-days), preparation of development and quality plans is usually optional. However, one should consider the substantial advantages gained by the plan's developer. The main advantages of plan preparation are improvements in the developer's understanding of the tasks, and his greater commitment to complete the project as planned. In addition, the plan documents contribute to a better understanding between the developer and the customer, and easier and more effective project control.

9. **The benefits of preparing project plans for internal projects**

It is recommended that internal projects, undertaken on behalf of other departments and for development of COTS software packages geared toward the market, be treated as "regular projects." This implies that full-scale development and quality plans are to be prepared. Benefits of the plans include:

a. The development department may avoid budget overrun incurred by unrealistic schedules and budgets, as well as consequent damage to other projects and to the developer's reputation.

    b. The internal "customer" may enjoy reduced risk of late project completion and budget overruns, in addition to improved project control and coordination with the developer.

    c. The developer's firm will enjoy reduced risk of budget overruns, reduced risk of late entry into the COTS software product market, and reduced risk of a decline in its reputation resulting from late supply.

Selected bibliography

Elzamly A. and Hussin B. (2015) *Classification and identification of risk management techniques for mitigating risks with factor analysis technique in software risk management, Review of Computer Engineering Research*, Vol. 2, No. 2, pp. 22–38.

IEEE (2001) *IEEE Std. 1540–2001 - IEEE Standard for Software Life Cycle Processes - Risk Management*, IEEE standards collection, The Institute of Electrical and Electronics Engineers, New York, NY.

IEEE (2014) *IEEE Std. 730–2014 Software Quality Assurance*, The IEEE Computer Society, IEEE, New York.

ISO/IEC (2014) *ISO/IEC 90003:2014 Software Engineering – Guidelines for the Application of ISO 9001: 2008 to Computer Software*, International Organization for Standardization (ISO), Geneva, Switzerland.

Jones, C. (2014) *Applied Software Measurement: Global Analysis of Productivity and Quality*, 3rd Edition, McGraw-Hill, New York, NY.

Lobato L.L., do Como Machado I., da Mota Silveira Neto P.A., and de Almeida E.S. (2012) Risk management in software engineering: a scoping study, in *16th International Conference on Education & Assessment in Software Engineering (EASE'12)*, Ciudad Real, Spain, May 2012, pp. 243–252.

Nelson C. R., Tyran G., and de Lascurain L. (2008) Explicit risk management in Agile processes, in *Proceedings of the 9th International Conference XP2008, Limerick, Ireland*, June 2008, pp. 190–201.

Pekar V., Felderer M., Breu R., Nickl F., Roßik C., and Schwarcz F. (2015) *Integrating a lightweight risk assessment approach into an industrial development process, Lecture Notes in Business Information Processing*, Vol. 238, pp. 186–198.

Raz T. and Hillson D. (2005) *A comparative review of risk management standards, Risk management International Journal*, Vol. 7, No. 4, pp. 53–66.

Sulaman S. M., Weyns K., and Host M. (2013) A review of research in risk analysis methods for IT systems, EASE'13, *The 17th International Conference on Evaluation and Assessment in Software Engineering*, pp. 86–96.

Review questions

7.1 Explain how the activities of the SQA function directly affect the quality of a software project?

7.2 One of the product assurance elements is measurement plans for products.

    a. Can you suggest a management information system (MIS) product and offer three metrics for the product?

    b. Can you suggest an embedded software product and offer three metrics for the product?

7.3 Evaluation of subcontractor participation in project implementation for conformance is one of the process assurance activities.

  a. At what stage of the software project should this evaluation activity be performed?

  b. Which activities could be carried out to correct negative environment results related to laboratory equipment?

7.4 Significant similarities exist between the proposal draft review and the project plan.

  a. Compare these documents with reference to the subjects reviewed.

  b. Compare these documents and explain the need and purpose of preparing the individual documents.

7.5 Project plans have three objectives.

  a. Can you list the objectives?

  b. Suggest ways in which each objective contributes to the successful and timely completion of the project.

7.6 Development process mapping is one of the most important elements of the development plan.

  a. List possible phases of the development process.

  b. List possible inputs and outputs for each of the phases suggested in (1).

7.7 Some system analysts claim that requirements relating to part of the software quality factors (see Chapter 3) should not be considered when preparing a software development plan.

  a. Do you agree with this claim? If you agree, list the software quality factors that should not be considered.

  b. If you don't agree –present your arguments

7.8 The project's organization is an important element of the development plan.

  a. List the components of the organization element.

  b. Why is it necessary to mention team members by name? Isn't it sufficient to list the number of team members by their expertise as required for each phase of the project?

7.9 Only 4 out of the 14 elements of a development plan, and only 1 out of 9 of the quality plan elements are considered obligatory for small projects.

  a. Do you agree with this statement? If yes – list your main arguments.

  b. If you do not agree with this statement, present your improved list and explain your choices.

7.10 "Preparing full-scale development and quality plans for internal projects can be highly beneficial to both sides of the internal project" (quoted from Sec. 7.7.2).

  a. Explain the benefits for the developer.

  b. Explain the benefits for internal customers.

Topics for discussion

7.1 What is the difference between SQA process assurance activities and product assurance activities?

7.2 IEEE Std. 730 includes product assurance process activities and process assurance activities. What is the special contribution of process assurance activities to the SQA process?

7.3 One of the elements of the process assurance elements is evaluation of subcontractor participation in project implementation for conformance.

    a. In which way can a subcontractor affect the quality of the project part which he is responsible for?

    b. Can you suggest ways in which to reduce or eliminate each of the risks mentioned in (1).

7.4 "As long as the proposal was properly prepared and approved, following an adequate contract review, there is no justification for redoing all this work. Its resource estimates, schedule and risk items may serve as the project plan elementss . . ." Claims like this are often voiced.

    a. Do you agree with this claim? If not – list your arguments against the claim.

    b. Suggest situations when it is clear that the proposal and its materials can serve as development and quality plans.

    c. Suggest situations when it is clear that the proposal and its materials cannot serve as development and quality plans.

7.5 Martin Adams, an experienced project leader at David's Software Ltd., a medium-sized software house, has been appointed project leader for development of an advanced help desk software system for a leading home appliance maintenance service. This is the 12th help desk system developed by his department in the past three years.

    The current project is somewhat special with respect to its schedule. The contract with the customer was signed 6 days after submitting the proposal, and the development team is scheduled to begin working at full capacity, with 8 team members just 10 days following signing of the contract. The contract offers a significant early completion bonus for each week under 26 weeks, but determines high late completion penalties for each week over 30 weeks.

    In a meeting with his superior, Adams claims that the comprehensive proposal documentation "as is," which has been thoroughly checked by the contract review team, should serve as the project's development and quality plans. His superior does not agree with him and demands that he immediately prepare comprehensive project and quality plans, according to company procedures.

    a. Do you agree with Adams? If yes – list the arguments that support his claim.

    b. Do you agree with his superior? If yes – list the arguments that support the superior's claim.

    c. Considering the circumstances of the project, what, in your opinion, should be done in this case.

    d. Comparing the circumstances described here to those of the mini case anecdote presented in Sec. 7.3, are there any justifications for different recommendations?

Appendix 7A   Risk management activities and measures

Various activities and measures (usually termed "risk management actions" or RMAs) that can be taken. The objectives of the RMAs are to:

- prevent software risks,
- achieve early identification of software risk items (SRIs), and
- resolve software risk items (SRIs).

These risk management actions can be grouped into the following classes:

- Internal risk management actions applied within the software developing organization.
- Subcontracting risk management actions dealing with the relationship between the software developer and his subcontractors and suppliers.
- Customer risk management actions dealing with the relationship between the software developer and the customer.

Table A7.1 presents commonly recommended risk management actions (RMAs) and their contributions

Table A7.1   Commonly recommended risk management actions (RMAs) and their contributions

Class of RMA contribution	Item No.	Software risk management action (RMA)
Internal RMA		
Preventive	1	Application of detailed and thorough analysis to requirements and estimated schedules, resources, and costs.
	2	Efficient project organization, adequate staff, and team size
	3	Personnel training with new and current development tools
	4	Arranging for, and training replacements to, take over in case of turnover and unanticipated workloads.
	5	Ensure user participation in the development process.
	6	Apply efficient change control (change requests screening).
	7	Perform, at the earliest, trials of new methodologies and development tools.
	8	Apply intensive software quality assurance activities, such as inspections, design reviews, unit tests, integration tests, system tests, and acceptance tests.

(continued)

Table A7.1 (*Continued*)

Class of RMA contribution	Item No.	Software risk management action (RMA)
Early identification of SRI	9	Progress control of development activities, including resources used and schedule keeping.
	10	Early testing of system performance, including load and availability testing.
	11	Periodical verification of timely availability of company professionals currently occupied with other projects.
Resolution of SRI	12	Arranging for participation of professional staff members with knowledge and experience with SRIs.
	13	Scheduling SRI-related activities as early as possible to provide leeway in case of difficulties.
	14	Prototyping SRI-related modules or project applications.
	15	**Preparing scenarios for complicated SRI-related modules or project applications.**
	16	Simulating SRI-related modules or project applications.
Subcontracting RMA		
Preventive	1	Preparing comprehensive and thorough contracts with subcontractors and suppliers, including contract reviews.
Early identification of SRI	2	Participating in internal progress control and software quality assurance activities of subcontractors planned to participate in the contract.
Resolution of SRI	3	Arranging "loans" of professionals with specialized knowledge and experience – should the need arise.
	4	Hiring consultants to support the team in the absence of sufficient know-how and experience.
	5	Hiring subcontractors to solve staff shortage difficulties.
Customer RMA		
Preventive	1	Perform contract review to ensure formulating comprehensive and thorough contracts with customers.
Resolution of SRI	2	Negotiating with the customer to change requirements regarding risky parts of the project.
	3	Negotiating with the customer to change schedules regarding risky parts of the project.

Chapter 8

Preproject Process – Contract Review

8.1 The CFV project completion celebration – an introductory mini case

A happy gathering of the Carnegie Fruit and Vegetables (CFV) project team at a popular downtown restaurant took place to celebrate the successful completion of a 10-month project for CTV, a produce wholesaler. The new information system registers product receipts from growers, processes customer orders, produces shipment documents for customers (greengrocers and supermarkets), bills customers, and calculates payments to be made to the growers.

The team was especially proud that the project was on schedule, and especially jubilant as earlier that morning, each member had received a nice bonus for completing the project on time.

The third speaker, the software company's Vice President of Finance, altered the pleasant atmosphere by mentioning that this *very successful* project had actually lost about $90,000. During his remarks, he praised the planners for their accurate estimates of resources needed for the analysis and design phase, and for the plans for the broad reuse of software from other systems that were, this time, completely realized. "The only phase where our estimates failed was one of the project's final phases, customer training, when the customer's staff is instructed on how to use the new information system. It now appears that no one had read the relevant RFP (requirement for proposal) section carefully enough. This section stated in a rather innocuous manner that the personnel in all CFV branches where the software was to be installed would be instructed in its use by the software supplier." After a short pause he continued dryly, "Nobody tried to find out how many branches our customer operates before signing the contract. Nobody mentioned that CFV operates 19 branches – 6 of them overseas!"

Software Quality: Concepts and Practice, First Edition. Daniel Galin.
© 2018 the IEEE Computer Society, Inc. Published 2018 by John Wiley & Sons, Inc.

He continued: "We tried to renegotiate the installation and instruction budget items with the customer after completing these activities, but he insisted on sticking to the original contract." Although no names were mentioned, it was clear that the VP blamed the sales negotiating team for the loss.

Similar losses, and in many cases much heavier ones, stem from sloppily drafted proposals or poorly understood contracts.

8.2 Introduction

The above mini case demonstrates the devastating results of a contract not thoroughly examined by the supplier, causing substantial losses to the supplier and at least inconveniences to the acquirer, due to delays of project completion.

A bad contract is always undesirable. Contract review is a process where SQA function, by reviewing the project proposal and the contract draft, can assist in forming a successful contract. It is natural for an SQA function to be involved in contract review as from the viewpoint of SQA, a bad contract – usually characterized by loosely defined requirements, and unrealistic budgets and schedule – is expected to yield low-quality software. In most improper contract cases, due to schedule and budget shortage, management exerts pressure: "save time" and "cut development resources." The unavoidable results are lower than acceptable software quality. In other words, unrealistic low budget and schedule estimates and professional commitments lead to high rates of low-quality projects and even software failures. In the other case, those of over-budgeted proposals, it is most likely that the tender is lost and the proposal is rejected.

The contract review process begins with a reviewing the proposal draft, and later, in the second stage, the contract draft is reviewed. "Contract review" covers both activities. This chapter presents the issues of contract reviews from the point of view of the supplier (the developer).

Contract review objectives

The objectives of contract review are presented in Frame 8.1.

Frame 8.1: Contract review objectives

Contract review objectives
• To reveal and document pitfalls in the software project proposal draft that reduces the probability of such undesirable contract situations.
• To reveal and document pitfalls in the software project contract draft that reduces the probability of such undesirable contract situation.

The factors affecting the extent of a contract review

The most important factors determining the extent of the contract review efforts required are:

- **Magnitude of project**, usually measured in man-month resources.
- **Technical complexity of project**
- **Degree of staff acquaintance and experience with project area**.
- **Organizational complexity of project** – The greater the number of organizations involved (i.e., partners, subcontractors, and customers) taking part in the project, the greater the required contract review efforts.

Accordingly, contract reviews for "small" projects will be carried out even by one reviewer, who will focus on few subjects and invest little time in his review. Also, in very simple and "easy" proposed projects, no contract review is required

The role of the SQA function in contract reviews

The role of the SQA function is major in carrying out contract reviews (including initiating and organizing, participating in the contract review teams). In cases when SQA function teams are small or require support from experts in the proposal field, non-SQA function persons are requested to join the contract review team.

Performing a contract review is a requirement of the IEEE Std. 730-2014 (IEEE, 2014) and the ISO/IEC 90003:2014 standard (ISO, 2014), which dedicate section to these issues.

The next sections are dedicated to the following:

- The contract review process and its stages
- Contract review evaluation subjects
- Implementation of a contract review
- Contract reviews for internal projects

A wide range of review topics that correspond to evaluating the proposal draft ad the contract draft are presented in appendices to this chapter.

8.3 The contract review process and its stages

Several situations can lead a software company (the supplier) to sign a contract with a customer. The most common are:

1. Winning a tender.
2. Submission of a proposal according to a customer's RFP.

3. Winning an unsolicited proposal of an internal request or order from another department in the organization.

One might argue that while a contract in cases of the first two events would be in place, a contract would rarely be found in cases of the third event. In this event, a "contract-substitute" or understanding is prepared. This kind of document is based on general requirements specification (prepared by the internal "customer"), and vague obligations relating to the budget and schedule (prepared by the developer). In this way, a kind of joint project committee exists with a "contract" that requires more contract reviews than contracts in the other circumstances.

Implementation tip

Internal projects tend, in many cases, to become informal. The friendly relationships between the software development department and the ordering department, that is, the software marketing department, yield undefined requirements by the customer department, and a vague definition of schedule and budget by the development department. The expected "flow" of a project of this kind regularly includes dissatisfaction expressed by the customer: "Our needs are entirely different than those you have assumed," or "You promised us the software would be ready by the beginning of September, and you are already three months late." or "You told us that 40–50 working days would be required – now you mention that 90 working days were invested." Typical complaints from the developer: "You totally confused the whole department with new requirements every week," or "You never answered our designer questions on time. In most cases it took you more than a week to respond." Consequently, a great many of such projects are never completed, while in the rest of the cases, the projects are not such a big success. And, to add to it all, the software development and marketing departments are no longer friends...

It is clear that a great majority of internal project disasters of this kind could have been avoided, if the participants had taken care to prepare an adequate requirement specification, a proper schedule and budget estimates, and if regular joint project follow-up activities were ensured...in other words – if a kind of a contract had existed between the internal parties.

The contract review process is conducted in two stages:

- **Stage One – Review of the proposal draft** (proposal draft review). This stage reviews the final proposal draft and the proposal's foundations: customer's requirement documents, customer additional details to, and explanations regarding, the requirements, cost and resource estimates, existing contracts or contract drafts with partners and subcontractors.

- **Stage Two – Review of contract draft** (contract draft review). This stage reviews the contract draft on the basis of the proposal and the understandings (including changes) reached during the contract negotiation sessions.

The review process can begin once the relevant draft document (proposal draft or contract draft) has been completed. The individuals who perform the review thoroughly examine each draft while referring to a comprehensive range of review subjects. After the completion of a review stage, the necessary changes, additions, and corrections are introduced by the proposal team (following the proposal draft review), and by the legal department (following the contract draft review).

The combined work of the proposal team and the contract review team in preparing a proposal till it turns into a signed contract is presented in Figure 8.1.

After the completion of a review stage, the necessary changes, additions, and corrections are introduced by the proposal team (following the proposal

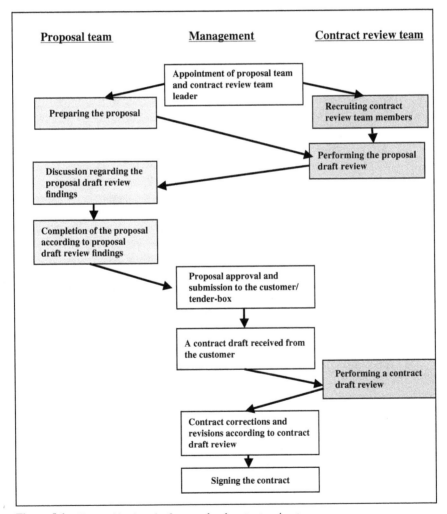

Figure 8.1   The combined work of proposal and contract review teams

draft review) and by the legal department (following the contract draft review).

8.4 Contract review evaluation subjects

As can be expected, the two contract review stages have different evaluation subjects, which are detailed in the following sections.

8.4.1 Proposal draft review evaluation subjects

The objective of the proposal draft review is to make sure that the following activities were satisfactorily carried out by the proposal team:

   a. *Have customer requirements been clarified and documented?* RFP documents and similar technical documents can be too general and imprecise for the project's purposes. As a result, additional details should be obtained from the customer. Clarifications of vague requirements and their updates should be recorded in a separate document that is approved by both the customer and the software developer.

   b. *Have alternative approaches for carrying out the project been examined?* Often, promising and suitable alternatives to execute a project have not been adequately reviewed (if at all) by the proposal team. This stipulation refers especially to alternatives encompassing software reuse, incorporation of COTS software and partnerships, or subcontracting with firms that have specialized knowledge or staff that can qualify for meeting the proposal's terms.

   c. *Have formal aspects of the relationship between the customer and the software developer been specified?* The proposal should define formalities that include: (1) customer – development communication and interface channels, (2) project deliverables and acceptance criteria, (3) formal phase approval process, (4) customer design and test follow-up method, and (5) customer change request procedure.

   d. *Have development risks been identified?* Development risks, such as insufficient professional know-how regarding the project's professional area or the use of required development tools, need to be identified and resolved. For a comprehensive description of identified software risk items and methods for risk management actions, see Appendix 8.A.

   e. *Have project resources and schedule been adequately estimated?* Resource estimations refer to professional staff and development facilities, as well as the project's budget. These include subcontractor fees. Scheduling estimates should take into account the schedule requirements of all parties participating in the project.

Implementation tip
In some situations, a supplier deliberately offers a *below*-cost proposal, after considering factors such as future sales potential. In these cases, when the proposal has to be based on realistic schedule estimates, and budget and professional capabilities, the loss incurred is considered a calculated loss, not a project failure.

f. *Has developer's capacity with respect to the project been verified?* This examination should consider professional competence as well as the availability of the required team members and development facilities during the scheduled time.

g. *Has customer's capacity to fulfill his commitments been verified?* This examination refers to the customer's financial and organizational capacities, such as personnel recruitment and training, installation of the required hardware, and upgrading of its communications equipment.

h. *Have partner and subcontractor participation conditions been defined?* These conditions cover quality assurance issues, payment schedules, distribution of project income/profits, and cooperation between project management and teams.

i. *Have definition and protection of proprietary rights been identified?* This factor is of vital importance in cases where reused software is integrated into a new package or when rights for future reuse of the current software need to be decided. This item also refers to the use of proprietary files of data crucial for operating the system and security measures.

The objectives of a proposal draft review are summarized in Frame 8.2.

Frame 8.2: Proposal draft review – evaluation topics

The nine proposal draft review evaluation topics
To evaluate the following activities carried out by the proposal team:
a. Have customer requirements been clarified and documented?
b. Have alternative approaches for carrying out the project been examined?
c. Have formal aspects of the relationship between the customer and the software developer been specified?
d. Have development risks been identified?
e. Have project resources and schedule been adequately estimated?
f. Has developer's capacity with respect to the project been verified?
g. Has customer's capacity to fulfill his commitments been verified?
h. Have partner and subcontractor participation conditions been defined?
i. Have definition and protection of proprietary rights been identified?

8.4.2 Contract draft review evaluation subjects

The objectives of the contract draft review are to make sure that the following activities have been performed satisfactorily:

a. **Are there unclarified issues in the contract draft?**

b. **Have all the understandings reached subsequent to the proposal been correctly documented?** All understandings reached between the customer and the developer are to be fully and correctly documented in the contract and its appendices. These understandings are meant to resolve all unclarified issues and differences between the customer and the developer that have been revealed so far.

c. **Have "new" changes, additions, or omissions been entered into the contract draft.** No changes, additions, or omissions that have not been discussed and agreed upon should be introduced into the contract draft. All changes, whether intentional or not, may result in additional, substantial, and unanticipated commitments on the part of the developer.

The objectives of a contract draft review are summarized in Frame 8.3.

Frame 8.3: Contract draft review – evaluation subjects

The three contract draft review evaluation subjects
To evaluate the following issues of the contact draft: a. **Are there unclarified issues in the contract draft?**   b. **Have all the understandings reached subsequent to the proposal been correctly documented?**   c. **Have "new" changes, additions, or omissions been entered into the contract draft?**

Checklists for contract review evaluations are usually useful tools in helping review teams organize their work, and adequately cover the relevant topics. It is clear that while part of the topics on these lists may be irrelevant for some projects, even a comprehensive checklist may exclude some important topics relevant to a given project proposal. It is the task of the contract review team, and especially of its leader, to determine the list of relevant topics pertinent to the specific project proposal.

Lists of contract review topics, classified according to contract review evaluation subjects, are presented in the appendices to this chapter:

Appendix 8.A: Proposal draft review – topics checklist

Appendix 8.B: Contract draft review – topics checklist

8.5 Implementation of a contract review

This section refers to the following subjects:

- Who performs the contract review?
- Implementation of a contract review for a major proposal.

8.5.1 Who performs the contract review?

In order to ensure the review is effective, it should be performed by independent persons, in other words, by members of the proposal team. It may be conducted by various individuals, as listed here:

- Members of the SQA function.
- Leader of software projects of similar complexity and magnitude.
- Senior professional staff members, experienced in projects similar to the proposed project.
- Outside professional experts, experienced in projects similar to the proposed project. Usually, outside experts are called in for major proposals (see the next section). Outside experts may also be called in for contract reviews in small software development organizations that lack an adequate number of contract review team members in their staff.

8.5.2 Implementation of a contract review for a major proposal

Major proposals are for projects characterized by at least a number of the following: very large scale, very high technical complexity, new professional area for company, and high organizational complexity (realized by great number of organizations participating in project, that is, partners, subcontractors, and customers). Implementation of a contract review process for a major project usually requires investing many working hours, and thus may incur substantial organizational difficulties. Some avenues for overcoming these difficulties are suggested here. The following are a review of the factors that introduce difficulties to the smooth completion of a contract review.

The difficulties of carrying out contract reviews for major proposals

It is unequivocal that contract reviews are an excellent means of reducing the risks for major project failures. However, several inherent difficulties in performing these reviews exist, especially when major projects are at hand.

- *Time pressures.* The proposal draft reviews are usually performed when the tender proposal team is under considerable time pressure. As a result, the review needs to be completed in a too short time, within a few days. This does not allow for a proper review and subsequent proposal corrections.

- *The potential contract review team members are very busy.* The potential members of the contract review team are often senior staff members and experts, who are usually committed to performing their regular tasks at the very time the review is to be conducted. Freeing professional staff can therefore be a significant, if not impossible, logistical problem. It should be mentioned that performing a major proposal review requires substantial time.

Recommended avenues for implementing major contract reviews

The careful planning of contract reviews is required for its successful completion. As should be clear by now, this holds doubly for major contract review. It is recommended that the following steps be taken to facilitate the review process.

- **The earlier the beginning** of the proposal preparation, the better. It is expected that sufficient time will be set aside for a proper proposal draft review.
- **The contract review should be scheduled.** Contract review activities should be included in the proposal preparation process, leaving sufficient time for a contract review and the ensuing corrections.
- **A team should carry out the contract review, not a single reviewer.** Teamwork makes it possible to distribute the workload among the team members so that each member of the contract review team can find sufficient time to do his share (which may include preparing a written report that summarizes his or her findings and recommendations).
- **A contract review team leader should be appointed at the earliest time.** It is important that the responsibility for organizing, managing, and controlling the contract review activities, especially recruiting members, is performed by the contract review team leader. Activities of the team leader include:
  - Recruitment of the team members
  - Distribution of review tasks among the team members
  - Coordination between the review and proposal teams.
  - Coordination and follow-up of activities, especially compliance with the schedule
  - Summarization of the findings and participation in discussions regarding the review findings with the proposal team

---

Implementation tip

As contract reviews may impose a substantial workload and additional pressures on the proposal team, thought should be given to when it may be appropriate to avoid conducting a contract reviews. Such situations may be cases of small-scale projects, or small- to medium-scale cost-plus projects, and medium-sized projects that repeat projects executed in the past. Contract review procedures should therefore define those types of projects for which a contract review is not obligatory.

For other defined types of "simple" projects, it is recommended that authority be given to a senior professional of the software development department to make the decision as to whether to perform the review for a given project.

8.6 Contract reviews for internal projects

A substantial number, if not the majority, of software projects are internal projects –"in-house" projects – carried out by one unit of an organization for another unit of the same organization. In such cases, the software development unit is the supplier/developer, while the other unit may be considered the customer. Typical internal projects and their in-house customers are listed in Table 8.1.

Frequently, internal software development projects are not based on what could be considered a complete customer–supplier relationship. In many cases, these projects are based on general understandings, with good will playing an

Table 8.1 Typical internal projects and in-house customers

Type of internal project	The *in-house* customers	Project examples
1. Administrative or operative software	Administration and operating units	1. Sales and inventory systems 2. Financial resource management systems 3. Human resource management systems 4. The organization's intranet site
2. Software packages developed to be sold to the public as "carry off-the-shelf" packages	Software marketing department	1. Computer games 2. Internet shop generator 3. Educational software 4. Word processors 5. Sales and inventory management software packages
3. Firmware to be embedded in the company products	Electronic and mechanical product development departments	1. Electronic hospital instrumentation firmware 2. Household amusement equipment and machinery firmware 3. Advanced toys firmware

important role in the relationship between the two units. It follows that the developing unit will only perform a "super quick" contract review, or not perform one at all.

Unfortunately, loose relationships are usually characterized by insufficient examination of the project requirements, its schedule, resources, and development risks. As a result, the following problems are likely to arise:

1. Inadequate definition of project requirements
2. Poor estimates of required resources
3. Poor scheduling
4. Inadequate awareness of development risks

As this list indicates, we can easily conclude that in-house projects performed for internal customers are more prone to failure than outside contracted projects. The potential disadvantages of the loose relationships typical of internal projects are shown in Table 8.2.

It may be concluded that customer–supplier relationship and contract review that proves to be fruitful for external projects should be applied to internal projects as well. The chances of avoiding the abovementioned

Table 8.2   Disadvantages of "loose relationships" internal projects

Subject	Disadvantages to the internal customer	Disadvantages to the internal developer
1. Inadequate definition of project requirements	• Implementation deviates from the needed applications • Low satisfaction	• Higher than average change requirements • Wasted resources due to introduction of avoidable changes
2. Poor required resource estimates and unrealistic commitments	• Unrealistic expectations about project applicability	• Substantial deviations from development budget • Friction between units induced by requirements for budget additions
3. Poor schedule	• Missing scheduled dates for start of new products distribution	• Development activities are under time pressure and tend to be of low quality • Late project completion causes delays in freeing staff for their next project
4. Inadequate awareness of development risks	• Customer unprepared for project risks and their consequences	• Tardy initiation of efforts to overcome difficulties

potential problems could be improved considerably by implementing procedures that define:

- Well-defined requirement specification by the internal customer.
- An adequate proposal for the internal project, based on applying a proper proposal and contract review team process.
- An adequate agreement between the internal customer and the internal supplier/developer.

Summary

1. **The two contract review stages**
   - **Proposal draft review:** This stage reviews the final proposal draft and documents on which it is based.
   - **Contract draft review:** This stage reviews the contract draft on the basis of the proposal and the understandings reached during the customer–supplier negotiations prior to signing the contract.

2. **The objectives of contract review**
   The objectives of the proposal draft review and the contract draft review are:
   - To reveal and document pitfalls in the software project proposal draft that reduces the probability of such undesirable contract situations.
   - To reveal and document pitfalls in the software project contract draft that reduces the probability of such undesirable contract situation.

3. **The factors affecting the extent of the contract review.** The efforts to be expended on the contract review depend on the factors characterizing the project. The most important factors are the project magnitude and complexity, the staff's acquaintance and experience with the project area, and the project organization complexity.

4. **The difficulties in performing a major contract review**
   The main difficulties are the time pressures and the need to recruit contract review team members, senior professionals of the department who are usually heavily loaded with performing and controlling their team's projects, and thus find it difficult to invest time in contract reviews.

5. **The recommended avenues for implementing a major contract review.** To conduct a proper major contract review, one should abide by the following guidelines:
   - The contract review should be part of the proposal preparation schedule.
   - The contract review should be carried out by a team.
   - A contract review leader should be appointed at the earliest time to allow recruitment of team members

6. **The importance of carrying out a contract review for internal projects.** The loose relationships maintained between the internal customer and the internal developer increase the probability of project failure. It is likely that the budget and schedule will not be kept, and the customer's expected applications will only partially be fulfilled. These undesired results can be avoided by adequate procedures and by applying the same guidelines used for external project contract reviews.

Selected bibliography

IEEE (2014) *IEEE Std. 730-2014 Software Quality Assurance*, IEEE, New York.
ISO (2014) *ISO/IEC 90003:2014 Software Engineering – Guidelines for the Application of TSO 9001: 2008 to Computer Software*, International Organization for Standardization, Geneva, Switzerland.

Review questions

8.1 The KFV case is described at the beginning of this chapter. From the vice president's short speech, it can be understood that the proposal preparation was conducted as follows: (a) a negotiating team was appointed by the management, (b) a proposal was prepared by the negotiating team, (c) management approved the proposal before it was presented to the customer, and (d) management signed the contract.

a. Can you suggest steps that would reduce the possible losses caused by a faulty contract?

b. Which relevant contract review evaluation subjects, listed in Appendices 8.A and 8.B, could have revealed the contract faults described in the KFV case.

8.2 List the various aspects involved with the examination of the customer's capabilities.

8.3 One of the objectives of a contract review is to examine development risks.

a. List the most common types of development risks.

b. What proposal team activities are required regarding each of the revealed development risks?

8.4 The extent of a contract review depends on the project's characteristics.

a. Describe an imaginary project that requires an intensive and comprehensive contract review.

b. Describe an imaginary project where a small-scale contract review would be adequate.

8.5 Performing a contract review raises many difficulties.

a. List the "built-in" difficulties when carrying out a large-scale contract review.

b. List the steps that should be taken to make a large-scale contract review feasible.

8.6 List the issues involved with estimating the resources required for a project that should be considered by the contract review team.

8.7 List the supplier's capability issues that should be considered by the contract review team.

8.8 List the partner and subcontractor participation issues that should be considered by the contract review team.

Topics for discussion

8.1 MJS, Mount Jackson Systems, Ltd. signed a contract to develop a comprehensive customer relations management (CRM) system for a large food preparation corporation. In order to fulfill the project requirements, MJS employed three subcontractors. MJS's experience with the subcontractors turned out to be troublesome, especially with regard to keeping schedules, rates of software faults of all kinds, and the number of interface faults with system parts developed by other participants in the project.

The head of the software quality assurance unit stated that had his unit carried out the contract review procedure, most of the described problems could have been averted.

a. What contract review topics are relevant to this case?

b. What process would you recommend when applying a contract review in this case?

8.2 An SQA professional claims: "I find all the reasons given for a proposal draft review to be justified. I also believe that a review contributes to the quality of the proposal, especially in regards to clarifying and precisely defining requirements, and in preparing more realistic estimates, among other issues. However, once the proposal has been presented to the customer, there is no need for a contract draft review. The task of reviewing the final negotiation results and the final version of the contract should be left to the legal department and to management."

a. Do you agree with the above statement? List your arguments.

b. In which situations is a contract draft review not necessary?

c. In which situations is a contract draft review absolutely necessary?

8.3 Many organizations do not apply their contract review procedures to internal projects even though they perform comprehensive contract reviews for all their external projects.

a. List arguments that support this approach.

b. List arguments that oppose this approach.

c. Suggest types of internal projects where omission of a contract review could result in severe damages to the organization (mention the main components of damages listed for each project type).

8.4 One of the objectives of a contract review is to examine the customer's capability to fulfill his commitments. Accordingly, a comprehensive list of contract review topics is suggested in Appendix 8.A. Some managers believe that as the supplier can sue the customer in those cases when he does not fulfill his commitments, there is no justification to invest resources in reviewing the customer's capabilities.

a. Do you agree with these managers?

b. If you disagree, list your arguments in favor of a comprehensive examination of the customer's capabilities.

c. Can you describe a real or imaginary situation where a customer's capability failures *could* create substantial direct and indirect damages to a software developer (the supplier)?

8.5 A contract draft review of a properly prepared contract document is expected to yield no negative findings. Still, in reality, discrepancies in contracts do appear frequently.

a. List real cases and common situations where such discrepancies could be expected.

b. In what situations are discrepancies in the contract draft expected to be least likely?

8.6 The examination of alternatives is one of the major tasks for a proposal team, especially for tender proposals. However, in many cases, important alternatives are omitted or neglected by the proposal team.

a. List real cases and common situations where negligence to define and examine important alternatives can be expected.

b. In what situations are these types of discrepancies least likely to occur?

8.7 National Software Providers Ltd is very interested in the newly developing area of Business Intelligence (BI) for electronic commerce firms. As the company is very keen to gain experience in this area, it was especially interested in winning a tender issued by one of the leading cosmetics manufacturers. The proposal team estimated that in order to win the contract, their proposal should not exceed the sum of $650,000. Accordingly, their quotation was $647,000. As all the team members were aware that the cost of the company's inexperienced development department to complete the project would substantially exceed this sum, they decided that there was little use in investing efforts to estimate the actual costs of the project.

a. Do you agree with the team's decision not to estimate the project's costs?

b. If you disagree, what are your arguments in favor of estimating the costs?

8.8 Consider the case of a custom-made software package developed by a supplier according to the unique RFP (request for proposal) specifications of the customer.

a. What proprietary issues are expected in such a project?

b. Which security issues related to the proprietary rights listed in your answer to (1) should be examined?

8.9 Contract review topics include a variety of financial issues.

a. Why should an SQA activity, such as a contract review, be so heavily involved in financial issues?

   b. Is it likely that an SQA unit member be able to review the financial issues? Who do you believe should conduct the review, and how should the review be organized?

8.10 A contract review can be performed by "insiders" (members of the organization's staff members) or by "outsiders."

   a. What are the advantages and disadvantages of employing outsiders, compared with insiders, for a proposal draft review?

   b. What are the advantages and disadvantages of employing outsiders, compared with insiders, for a contract draft review?

8.11 A medium-size firm submits 5–10 proposals per month, 10–20% of which eventually evolve into development contracts. The company takes care to perform a thorough proposal draft review for each of the proposals.

   a. Do the proposal draft reviews performed for each of the individual projects guarantee that the company will be capable of carrying out all the proposals that eventually evolve into development contracts? List your arguments.

   b. If your answer to (1) is negative, what measures should be taken to reduce the risk of not being able to perform a contract?

Appendix 8.A: Proposal draft review

Checklist for a proposal draft review is presented in Table 8.A.1.

Table 8.A.1   Proposal draft review – topics checklist

Proposal draft review objective	Proposal draft review topics to be verified
1. Customer requirements have been clarified and documented	The following should be defined: 1. The functional requirements 2. The customer's operating environment (hardware platform, data communication system, operating system, etc.). 3. The required interfaces with other software packages and instrument firmware. 4. The performance requirements, including workloads as defined by the number of users and the characteristics of use. 5. The system reliability. 6. The system's usability, as realized in the required training time for an operator to achieve the required productivity. 7. The total training and instruction effort to be carried out by the supplier, including number of trainees and instructed staff, locations, and duration.

(continued)

Table 8.A.1 (*Continued*)

Proposal draft review objective	Proposal draft review topics to be verified
	8. The number of software installations to be performed by the supplier, including locations. 9. The warranty period, extent of supplier liability, and method of providing support. 10. Proposals for maintenance service provision extending beyond the warranty period and its conditions. 11. Completion of all tender requirements relating to the project team, certification and other documents, and so on.
2. Alternative approaches to carrying out the project have been examined	The following should be defined: 1. Integrating reused and purchased COTS software, including reused and purchased functions and costs. 2. Partners, including partnership agreements. 3. Customer's undertaking to perform certain project tasks in-house. 4. Subcontractors, including proposed firms and cooperation understandings. 5. Adequate comparison of alternatives.
3. Formal aspects of the relationship between the customer and the software developer have been specified	The following should be defined: 1. A coordination and joint control committee, including its procedures. 2. The list of documentation that has to be delivered. 3. The customer responsibilities regarding provision of development facilities, data, and answers to the team's inquiries. 4. Indication of the required phase approval by the customer and the approval procedure. 5. Customer participation (extent and procedures) in progress reviews, design reviews, and testing. 6. Procedures for handling customer change requests during development and maintenance stages, including method of costing introduction of changes. 7. Criteria for project completion, method of approval, and acceptance. 8. Procedures for handling customer complaints and problems detected after acceptance, including nonconformity to specifications detected after the warranty period.

Table 8.A.1 (*Continued*)

Proposal draft review objective	Proposal draft review topics to be verified
	9. Conditions for granting bonuses for earlier project completion and penalties for delays.
	10. Conditions to be complied with, including financial arrangements, if part of, or the entire project is cancelled or temporarily halted upon the customer's request.
	11. Service provision conditions during warranty period.
	12. Software maintenance services and conditions, including customer's obligation to update his version of the software as per supplier demands.
4. Identification of development risks	The following should be defined:
	1. Risks regarding software modules or parts that require acquisition of new professional capabilities and solution methods.
	2. Risks regarding the possibility of not obtaining purchased hardware and software components according to schedule, and the suggested risk management plan.
5. Adequate estimation of resources and schedule	The examination of the following subjects will refer, among other sources, to the proposal team's working papers of project program schedule and resources required.
	1. Man-days required for each project phase and their cost. Do the estimates include spare resources to cover any required corrections following design reviews, tests, and so on?
	2. Do the estimates of man-days include the required work to prepare the required documentation, especially documentation to be delivered to the customer?
	3. Are the manpower resources sufficient to fulfill warranty obligations and their cost?
	4. Does the project schedule include time required for reviews, tests, and so on, and making the required corrections?
6. Examination of developer's capacity to perform the project	The following should be defined:
	1. Suitability and availability of proposed team leaders.
	2. Availability of specialized staff (on schedule and in the required numbers).

(*continued*)

Table 8.A.1 (*Continued*)

Proposal draft review objective	Proposal draft review topics to be verified
	3. Availability of computer resources and other development (including testing) facilities (according to quantities and schedule as per project contract). 4. Ability to cope with the customer requirements regarding the use of special development tools or software development standards. 5. Warranty and long-term software maintenance service obligations.
7. Examination of customer's capacity to fulfill his commitments	The following should be examined: 1. Financial capability, including contract payments and payments for additional internal investments. 2. Supply of all development facilities and data. 3. Responses to staff queries as they arise. 4. Recruitment and training of new and existing staff required for operating the new software system. 5. Capacity to complete all task commitments on time and at the requisite quality.
8. Definition of partner and sub-contractor participation conditions	The examination of the following subjects will refer, among other sources, to the proposal team's working papers related to partners, subcontractors, and purchases: 1. Allocation of responsibility for completion of tasks by the partners, subcontractors, or customer, including schedule and method of coordination. 2. Allocation of payments, including bonuses and penalties, among partners. 3. Subcontractor payment schedule, including bonuses and penalties, and the relevant conditions. 4. Quality assurance of work performed by subcontractors, partners, and the customer, including participation in SQA activities (e.g., quality planning, reviews, tests).
9. Definition and protection of software proprietary rights	The following should be defined: 1. Securing proprietary rights to software purchased from other parties. 2. Securing proprietary rights to data files purchased from other parties. 3. Securing proprietary rights to future reuse of software developed in custom-made projects by the developer and his subcontractors, while in regular use by the customer.

Appendix 8.B: Contract draft review

Topics checklist for contract draft review is presented in Table 8.B.1.

Table 8.B.1   Contract draft review – topics checklist

Review objective	Contract draft review topics to be verified
1. No unclarified issues remain in the contract draft	1. Supplier's obligations as defined in the contract draft and its appendices. 2. Customer's obligations as defined in the contract draft and its appendices.
2. All understandings reached subsequent to the proposal are correctly documented	1. Understandings about the *project's* functional requirements. 2. Understandings about financial issues, including payment schedule, bonuses, penalties, and so on. 3. Understandings about the customer's obligations. 4. Understandings about partner and subcontractor obligations, including the supplier's agreements with external parties.

3. No "new" changes, additions, or omissions have been entered into the contract draft	1. The contract draft is complete; no contract section or appendix is missing.
	2. No changes, omissions and additions have been entered into the agreed-upon document:
	  a. No changes, omissions and additions regarding the financial issues have been entered.
	  b. No changes, omissions and additions regarding the project schedule have been entered.
	  c. No changes, omissions and additions regarding the customer's and partners' obligations have been entered.

Chapter 9

Cost of Software Quality

9.1 This time the budget was approved – an introductory mini case

Mary Janus, head of the SQA team, felt very disappointed when for the third time the general manager rejected her investment plan for installing the Java Solver package in the software development department.

The proposed package included proved capabilities for the automatic detection of 92% of Java program errors, and the automatic correction of 85% of them. The quality observed in the trial results of the proposed package was astonishing. It was as good as that measured in manual corrections, and in a great many cases was even better. A document that presented these facts, together with a proposal for installing four workstations (four licenses) in the department amounting to the sum of $48,000 a year, was submitted to the GM, from which Mary and her team were all expecting a positive decision. In actual fact, this document was an improved version of one submitted just 4 months earlier.

It seems that disappointment may sometimes lead to success in rather creative ways. Mary's disappointment lead her to want to convince the GM again, but this time by presenting calculations of the contribution margin of the proposed investment.

Mary now began her "research" project, and first identified the following:

1. The software development department employs 10 Java programmers and 10 Java testers. The cost of an employee is $13,000 per month on average.

2. Department statistics revealed that six of the Java programmers produce new Java code, while the other four dedicate their time to correcting the Java statements according to testing results.

3. The Java programs produced by the programmers are expected to be processed on four Java Solver workstations by two testers (trained by

Software Quality: Concepts and Practice, First Edition. Daniel Galin.
© 2018 the IEEE Computer Society, Inc. Published 2018 by John Wiley & Sons, Inc.

Java Solver staff). The annual cost of four Java Solver licenses is $48,000.

4. The 2-week training course for the Java Solver costs $2,500 per trainee. The cost of employment of a Java Solver trainee during the course is $6,500. It is suggested that four staff are trained to ensure availability of trained staff at all times.

5. It is expected that three Java testers will be employed to complete the testing following the Java Solver automatic testing and corrections.

6. It is expected, according to the trial carried out by the SQA team on the operation of the Java Solver, which two Java programmers could tend to all the manual corrections needed including checking of the automatic corrections.

7. To sum-up, after implementation of the Java Solver project, the Java programmer team will consist of eight programmers (instead of the currently employed 10), while only five Java testers will be needed (instead of the currently employed 10).

In light of the above, the following estimated expenses and subsequent savings were identified:

Cost of four Java Solver licenses	$48,000 per year
Cost of Java Solver training courses (for four)	$10,000
Cost of employing trainees during the course (for four)	$26,000
Savings from Java team reduction (by seven)	$91,000 per year

The expected annual savings are calculated as follows:

For the first year of application

1. Cost of employing seven Java testers	$91,000
2. Cost of training four staff	−$10,000
3. Cost of employing four trainees during the course	−$26,000
4. Cost of four Java Solver licenses	−$48,000
5. **Net savings for the first year of application**	**$7,000**

For the second and subsequent years of application

6. Cost of seven employing seven Java testers	$91,000
7. Cost of four Java Solver licenses	−$48,000
8. **Net savings for the second and subsequent years of application**	**$43,000**

Mary was filled with new hope for getting the "Java Solver"' project approved when she submitted a short memo presenting the above economic facts to the GM. A few days later, Mary was invited to the GM's office for an urgent meeting.

The GM opened the meeting, "We, the deputy of finance and I, read your proposal very carefully." He stopped his speech for a moment, razing Mary's tension, and continued, "We found it to be an excellent investment proposal and approved it immediately." Leaving no time for Mary to react, the GM closed the meeting saying, "Your current proposal deals with the appraisal cost and internal failure cost. I would like your next proposal to be dedicated to the prevention cost."

More and more time management – whether of commercial companies or public organizations – requires economic evaluation of their quality assurance systems. Accordingly, it is becoming more and more likely that proposals for the development of new quality assurance tools, or for investments to improve and expand the operation of existing systems, will be examined through an "economic" microscope. Thus, it is becoming obligatory for QA units to demonstrate the potential profitability for every request made for substantial funds (required for system infrastructure or operating cost).

9.2   Objectives of cost of software quality measurement

Frame 9.1 presents the main objectives to be achieved by application of cost of software quality metrics.

Frame 9.1: Cost of software quality measurement – objectives

Application of cost of software quality metrics enables management to achieve economic control over SQA activities and outcomes. The specific objectives are:

- Control organization-initiated costs to prevent and detect software errors.
- Evaluate financial damages of software failures as a basis for revising the SQA budget.
- Evaluate plans to increase/decrease SQA activities, or to invest in new/updated SQA infrastructure.

Managerial control over the cost of software quality (CoSQ) is achieved by a comparison of actual performance figures with:

- Prevention and appraisal activities budget
- Previous year's failure cost

- Previous project's total quality cost (control cost and failure cost)
- Other department's quality cost (control cost and failure cost)

The following relations may add important indications of the success of an SQA plan:

- Percentage of cost of software quality out of total software development cost.
- Percentage of software failure cost out of total software development cost.
- Percentage of cost of software quality out of total software maintenance cost.
- Percentage of cost of software quality out of total sales of software products and software maintenance.

It is the CoSQ indicators that stress the importance of SQA. For example, the first indicator quite often reaches the level of 50% of the total cost of a software product. Application of SQA tools, which could potentially reduce the CoSQ from 50 to 30%, would contribute substantially to the financial performance of the software house.

We claim that *cost of software quality* – the financial assessment of software quality development and maintenance – is just another class of software quality metrics, where financial values are used as the measuring tool. However, while quality metrics and costs of quality both support management control and decision-making, *cost of quality* is a metric that displays a unique characteristic. Application of common financial measures enables managements to obtain the type of general overview of all software quality assurance activities unavailable with any other metrics.

The unique features of the CoSQ discussed in this chapter reflect the special characteristics of SQA, characteristics that are absent from quality assurance in the manufacturing industry (see Section 2.1).

The cost of software development has been the subject of many research projects, books, and articles in the last two decades. Nevertheless, publications dedicated to the cost of software quality are relatively rare (e.g., Karg, 2009; Karg et al., 2011).

The importance of quality cost data is considered to be used to improve the organization's processes, as discussed in Sec. 4.7 of IEEE Std. 730-2014 (IEEE, 2014).

Section 9.3 discusses the classic model of the cost of software quality, which applies the general costs of the quality model to the software industry. An additional model proposed by the author, the *extended cost of software quality model*, is presented in Section 9.5 as an alternative that more effectively captures features specific to the software industry. Section 9.4 presents industry figures for the scope of the cost of software quality. The concluding part of the chapter deals with the application of a CoSQ system (Section 9.6), and the problems raised in the application of cost of software quality measurements (Section 9.7).

9.3 The classic model of cost of software quality

The classic quality cost model, developed in the early 1950s by Feigenbaum and others, provides a methodology for classifying the costs associated with product quality assurance from a financial point of view. The model was developed to suit quality settings in manufacturing organizations, and has since been widely implemented. The model was adopted for the software industry, and has become the cost of software quality – CoSQ model.

The model classifies quality costs into two general classes.

Costs of control relate to costs controlled by the software developer and includes the following subclasses:

- **Prevention costs** include investments in quality infrastructure and quality activities targeted to reduce software errors. These activities are not directed to a specific project or system, but are general to the organization.
- **Appraisal costs** include the cost of activities performed for a specific project or software system for the purpose of detecting software errors that need to be corrected.

Costs of failure of control relate to costs of correcting failures that occurred due to unsuccessful prevention activities. The model further subdivides these costs into two subclasses.

- **Internal failure costs** include costs of correcting errors, and relate to errors detected by design reviews (DRs), software tests, and acceptance tests (carried out by the customer), which were corrected before the software was installed at customers' sites.
- **External failure costs** include all costs of correcting failures detected by customers or maintenance teams after the software system has been installed at customer sites.

The classic model of the cost of software quality is presented in Figure 9.1. In the next sections, the subclasses of the model are reviewed.

9.3.1 Prevention costs

Prevention costs include investments in establishing, updating, and improving a software quality infrastructure, as well as for performing the regular activities required for its operation. A significant share of the activities performed by the SQA team is preventive in nature, as reflected in the SQA budget.

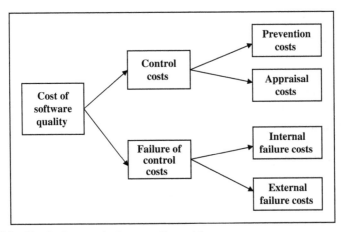

Figure 9.1 The classic costs of software quality model.

Typical preventive costs include:

a. Investments in development of new or improved SQA infrastructure components or regular updating of these components:
- Procedures and work instructions
- Support devices: templates, checklists, and so on
- Software configuration management system
- Software quality metrics
- Cost of software quality measurements

b. Regular implementation of SQA preventive activities:
- Instruction of new employees on SQA topics and procedures related to their positions
- Instruction of employees in new and updated SQA topics and procedures
- Certification of employees for specific positions
- Analysis of errors and additional data and the subsequent performing of corrective and preventive actions
- Consultations on SQA issues provided to team leaders and others

c. Control of the SQA system through performance of:
- Internal quality audits
- External quality audits by customers and SQA system certification organizations.
- Management quality reviews

9.3.2 Appraisal costs

Appraisal costs are devoted to the detection of software errors in specific projects or software systems.

Typical appraisal costs cover:

a. Reviews:
- Formal DRs
- Peer reviews (inspections and walkthroughs)
- Expert reviews

b. Cost of software testing:
- Unit tests
- Integration tests
- Software system tests
- Acceptance tests (participation in tests carried out by customer)

c. Costs of assuring the quality of work performed by external participants, primarily by means of design reviews and software testing. External participants may include:
- Subcontractors
- COTS software systems suppliers and reusable software modules
- The customer (as a project participant)

9.3.3 Internal failure cost

Internal failure costs are those incurred through correcting errors that were detected through design reviews, software tests, and acceptance tests performed before the software was installed at customer sites. In other words, internal failure costs represent the cost of error correction subsequent to formal examinations of the software during its development. It should be noted that corrections and changes resulting from team leader checks or other team-initiated reviews are generally not considered internal failure costs as they are an integral part of the design and coding processes, and as such conducted informally.

Typical costs of internal failures:

- Cost of redesign or reprogramming subsequent to design review and test findings (cost of rework).
- Cost of design corrections subsequent to design reviews and test findings.
- Cost of correcting programs following test findings.
- Cost of repeated design reviews and retesting (regression tests). Notably, although the costs of regular design reviews and software tests are considered appraisal costs, costs from repeated design reviews or software tests directly resulting from poor design and inferior code quality are considered internal failure costs.
- *Domino effect damages*: Delayed software projects, besides their incurred failure costs, may cause damages to other projects performed by other teams, due to the transfer of team members to enforce other projects under pressure. Also, the delayed completion of a project can cause staff

problems in other projects that are relying on staff released from the delayed project. In other words, should a delay materialize, we can expect a *domino effect* obstructing the progress of several other company projects and inducing considerable internal as well as external failure costs.

9.3.4 External failure costs

External failure costs entail the costs of correcting failures detected by customers or maintenance teams after a software system has been installed at a customer site.

These costs may be further classified into "overt" external failure costs and "hidden" external failure costs.

In most cases, the extent of hidden costs is much greater than that of overt costs. This gap is mainly caused by the difficulty in estimating hidden external failure costs in comparison to overt external failure costs, which are readily recorded or estimated. In addition, the estimates obtained are frequently disputed among the professionals involved. As a result, hidden external failure cost estimation is rarely undertaken. Therefore, we will use the term *external failure costs* to refer exclusively to "overt" failure costs.

Typical "overt" external failure costs cover:

- Resolution of customer complaints during the warranty period. In most cases, this may be done over the phone or through data communication. It involves a review of the complaint and transmission of resolution instructions. In most cases, complaints result from a failure of the "help" function or the guidelines found in the instruction manual.

- Correction of software bugs detected during regular operation. Corrections involving code modifications (including tests of the corrected software) followed by its installation are often performed at the customer's site.

- Correction of software failures after the warranty period is over, even if the correction is not covered by the warranty.

- Damages paid to customers in case of a severe software failure detected during regular operation.

- Damages paid to customers in the event of project completion delays.

- Reimbursement of customer's purchase costs, including handling, in case of total dissatisfaction (relates to COTS software packages as well as to custom-made software).

- Insurance against customer claims in case of a severe software failure. In cases when the developer insures against customer claims, the insurance expenses replace damage costs, as the insurance company pays customer damage claims.

- *Domino effect external failure costs*, which mainly include delay penalties and low-quality damages paid to customers.

> ### *Implementation tip*
>
> **Unaccounted exterior failure costs**
>
> In many cases, the developer has a clear interest in "reducing" the external failure costs. He may achieve this by substituting what should have been damage payments with compensation to the customer in the form of unaccounted "arrangements" by one or more of the following methods:
>
> - Forgoing the final project payment.
> - Failing to charge for software changes requested by the customer.
> - Failing to charge for the provision of HD services (beyond warranty period).
> - Granting of discount for future purchase of software products.
>
> The dollar values of such arrangements are not shown in the company's bookkeeping, and thus not included in the external failure costs.

The listed items reflect only "overt" external failure costs, which are directly incurred by software failures detected and recorded during regular operation of the software. In many cases, these costs only represent a small portion of the full range of external failure costs. The greater portion of external failure costs – "hidden" costs – reflect the resulting indirect damages to a software development organization.

Typical examples of "hidden" external failure costs:

- Damages from reduced sales to customers with products suffering from high rates of software failures.

- Severe decline in sales resulting from the firm's damaged reputation.

- Increased investment in sales promotions to counter damaged reputation, caused by past software failures.

- Diminished prospects of winning a tender due to damaged reputation.

- The need to underprice proposals to prevent competitors from winning tenders.

9.4   The scope of the cost of software quality – industry figures

The scope of the CoSQ as part of the overall software product costs is probably one of the most accurate indicators for management, when considering investments in software quality. Several studies of the correlation between the organization's SQA level and the relative part of the CoSQ in the total development costs have been published.

Modeling of CoSQ and the extent of CoSQ as part of the costs of the software product are the subject of several papers, including Daughtrey (2013),

Table 9.1 CoSQ according to CMM levels

	CMM level				
	1	2	3	4	5
Total CoSQ (%)	**60**	**57**	**51**	**36**	**21**
Prevention cost (%)	2	2	4	7	12
Appraisal cost (%)	4	10	12	11	4
Internal failure cost (%)	22	25	25	15	5
External failure cost (%)	32	20	10	3	2

Source: Knox (1993).

Table 9.2 CoSQ for five American and European projects – averages

Software development projects	American	European
Number of projects	2	3
Total CoSQ (%)	57.5	67.7
Prevention cost (%)	13.5	8.7
Appraisal cost (%)	16	26.3
Internal and external failure cost (%)	28	32.7

Source: Laporte et al. (2012).

Jones (2011), Laporte et al. (2012), Krasner (1998), Galin and Avrahami (2007), and Galin (2004).

The CoSQ results for organizations implementing CMM methodology enable us to compare organizations with various SQA levels, as the CMM ranks organizations into five levels according to their software quality achievements (for CMM and CMMI methodologies, see Chapter 26). The results of Knox (1993) show that at the lowest SQA level (CMM level 1), CoSQ reaches 60% of the software product costs, at CMM level 3 it is reduced to 51%, and at the highest CMM level (level 5), it only reaches the low percentage of 21%.

Knox's detailed results for all CMM levels, and for the four components of CoSQ according to the classic model, are presented in Table 9.1 as quality costs defined by the classic model.

More recent results regarding the scope of CoSQ are provided by Laporte et al. (2012) for American and European software development projects, and are presented in Table 9.2.

9.5 An extended model for cost of software quality

Analysis of the software quality costs defined by the classic model reveals that several costs of substantial magnitude are excluded. These costs are either unique to the software industry or negligible factor in other industries. For example, typical software quality failure costs include:

- Damages paid to customers in compensation for late completion of a project due to unrealistic scheduling.
- Damages paid to customers in compensation for late completion of a project as a result of failure to recruit sufficient staff.

The element common to these two failures is that they are not the result of any particular action or lack of professionalism of the development team; they are actually outcomes of managerial failure.

Further observations find activities by management to prevent or reduce quality:

- Contract reviews (proposal draft review and contract draft review). The cost of these reviews is usually negligible for contracts in the manufacturing industries. However, in the software industry, considerable professional work is required to assure that a project proposal is based on sound estimates and comprehensive evaluations of the proposed project. The significant difference in required resources results from the nature of the product, and the production process covered by the contract. While a typical contract in the manufacturing industry deals with repeated manufacturing of catalog-listed products, a typical contract in the software industry deals with development of a new, unique software system (see Chapter 3).
- Preparation of software development and quality plans. Significant resources are required to prepare these plans as they are not comparable to any management activities in other industries. The main benefits of the plans are the early detection of risks of staffing shortages and expected lack of professional expertise for specified project activities.
- Thorough appropriate progress control of the software project. While production control carried out in the manufacturing industry is a repetitive task that can, in most cases, be performed automatically by machines, software development progress control supervises task design and coding activities and is performed the first time by the development team.

The important effect of management on the cost of software quality is reflected in the title of a book by Flowers: *Software Failure: Management Failure* (Flowers, 1996). In his book, Flowers describes and analyzes several colossal software project failures; he concludes by discussing the root of the critical managerial failures and suggests ways to prevent or reduce the failures.

The *extended cost of software quality model*, as proposed by the author of this book, extends the classic model to include management's "contribution" to the total cost of software quality. According to the extended CoSQ model, shown in Figure 9.2, the costs are classified into two groups:

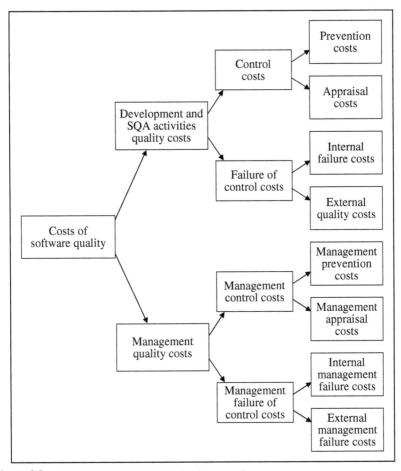

Figure 9.2   The extended model for cost of software quality.

- Quality costs of development and SQA activities defined according to the classic CoSQ model
- Management quality costs

The management quality costs are classified into two general classes.

1. **Management control costs** relate to costs that are controlled by the management and include two subclasses as follows:
   - **Management prevention costs** include preproject activities designed to detect erroneous proposal parts and prepare appropriate plans for project performance.
   - **Management appraisal costs** include the costs of activities to control the performance of a specific project.

2. **Management failure of control costs** relates to costs of correcting failures that occurred due to unsuccessful prevention activities. The model further subdivides these costs into two subclasses.
   - **Internal management failure extra costs** caused by management failures in the project preparations, staff recruitment, and so on.
   - **External management failure costs** include additional error repairs at customer sites, and damages paid to customers due to customer-detected product faults resulting from management commitments and failures. A great part of these subclass costs are considered external costs of a development team according to the classic CoSQ model.

The extended cost of software quality model is shown in Figure 9.2.

In the next sections, the subclasses of the management quality costs are reviewed.

9.5.1 Managerial prevention costs

Managerial preventions costs are associated with activities performed to prevent managerial failures or reduce prospects of their occurrence. These activities are required to be performed before work commences on the project and are the responsibility of management. Several of these activities are discussed in previous chapters related to various SQA frameworks.

Typical managerial preparation and control costs include:

- Cost of carrying out contract reviews (proposal draft and contract draft reviews) – see Chapter 8

- Cost of preparing project plans, including quality plans and their review – see Chapter 7.

- Cost of carrying out contract review of subcontractors proposals for performing parts of projects.

9.5.2 Managerial appraisal costs

Managerial preparations and control costs are associated with activities performed to prevent managerial failures or reduce prospects of their occurrence. Several of these activities are discussed in previous chapters related to various SQA frameworks.

Typical managerial preparation and control costs include:

- Cost of periodic updating of project and quality plans.

- Cost of performing regular progress control of internal software development efforts – see Appendix C.

- Cost of performing regular progress control of the contribution of external participants to the project – see Chapter 20.

9.5.3   Managerial internal failure costs

Managerial internal failure costs may be incurred throughout the entire course of software development. They are most likely to materialize in connection with failed attempts to identify project risks, failed estimate regarding the appropriate project schedule and budget as well as detect in a timely fashion those deviations and problems that necessitate management intervention.

Typical internal managerial failure costs include:

- Unplanned costs for professional and other resources, resulting from underestimation of resources on which submitted proposals are based.
- Additional staff costs paid to outsourcing companies, recruited under the pressure of last-minute situations.
- Additional staff costs of "internal recruitment" made at the last minute, as available staff, as opposed to the most suited, were recruited.
- *Internal managerial domino effect damages*: Damages to other company projects caused by failing management activities or decisions.

9.5.4   Managerial external failure costs

Naturally, most managerial external failure costs incurred after completion of software development and system installation.

These costs are most likely to emerge in connection with failed attempts to detect project risks, failed estimates of the appropriate project schedule and budget, as well as detect in a timely fashion those deviations and problems that demand management intervention.

Typical external managerial failure costs include:

- Damages paid to customers as compensation for late completion of the project, a result of the unrealistic schedule presented in the company's proposal.
- Damages paid to customers as compensation for late completion of a project, resulting from management's failure to recruit appropriate team members.
- *External managerial domino effect damages*: Damages to other company projects caused by failing management activities or decisions.

9.6   Application of a cost of software quality system

In order to apply a cost of software quality system in an organization, the following are required:

- Definition of a cost of software quality model and array of cost items specifically for the organization, department, team, or project.

- Definition of a method of data collection.
- Application of a cost of software quality system, including thorough follow-up.
- Actions to be taken in response to the findings produced.

9.6.1   Definition of the organization's CoSQ items

In the first stage of applying a CoSQ model, the organization should choose its preferred type of cost model – classic or extended. Whichever model is selected, its effectiveness is determined to a great degree by the suitability for the organization of the cost items designed to be measured for the model. In other words, these model items, defined specifically for the organization, are considered relevant to the organization's activities and budget expenditures. Each item should belong to one of the subclasses comprising the cost model.

Example:
The SQA unit of the information systems department of a commercial company adopted the classic model as its cost of software quality model. A member of the unit prepared a draft list of 13 potential CoSQ items to be classified by the head of the SQA unit for compiling the department's first annual CoSQ report. The head of the SQA unit classified the items. He rejected three items, claiming they were costs of software development, rather than CoSQ. The classification results are presented in Table 9.3.

Implementation tip

The software development and maintenance departments should agree upon the structure of the CoSQ model and the related CoSQ items. It is preferable to omit those items over which agreement is difficult to reach, even at the expense of reduced coverage of quality costs.

Some CoSQ items may be shared by several departments or projects. In such cases, the rules determining allocation of costs should be as simple as possible and agreed to by all the relevant parties.

Updates and changes to the quality cost items can be expected. These are based on analyses of the cost of software quality reports as well as on changes in the organization's structure and environment.

9.6.2   Planning the method for costs data collection

The method of costs data collection is a key factor (although regularly underestimated) in the success or failure of the CoSQ system.

Once the list of software quality cost items has been finalized, a method for collecting the relevant data should be determined. One of the major questions

Table 9.3   Classification of potential CoSQ items – an example

Cost item	CoSQ subclass
1. Employment of head of SQA unit	50% prevention cost; 50% appraisal cost
2. Verification of compliance with SQA procedures instructions by SQA team member (employment cost)	Prevention cost
3. Payment to an outsourcing company for preparation of project documentation	Not CoSQ (cost of development)
4. Participation in internal and external SQA audits by development and maintenance teams	Prevention cost
5. First series of tests performed by testing team (time spent in tests)	Appraisal cost
6. Regression tests performed by testing team (time spent in tests)	Internal failure cost
7. Correction of errors identified by the testing team (time spent in corrections (seconds))	Internal failure cost
8. Correction by maintenance team of software failures identified by customer (time spent, and traveling costs to customer site)	External failure cost
9. Team member code checking by development team leader	Not CoSQ (cost of development)
10. Regular visits by unit's SQA consultant (standard monthly fee)	Prevention cost
11. Participation in external failure inquiries by unit's SQA consultant (special invoices)	External failure cost
12. Special security software for the customer relations software system	Not CoSQ (cost of development)
13. Costs of SQA journals, and participation in SQA seminars	Prevention cost

raised at this stage is whether to develop an independent system for collecting data or rely on the existing management information system (MIS). After adaptations, the MIS is usually capable of serving the requirements of data collection for the selected cost model. For instance, its human resource costing system can record working hours invested in quality issues. Relatively simple changes to ledger categories enable the accounting system to record the costs of external services and purchases for the SQA system, as well as damages paid to customers. In general, using existing MIS is preferable to introducing new systems, mainly for the following reasons:

- Expected cost savings by running a working data collection system instead of introducing an independent system.
- Avoidance of disagreements over interpretation of the data provided by the MIS versus the data provided by the independent system; typical

when operating an independent data collection system. Disagreements of this type reduce the reliability of the software quality cost results.

Planning independent CoSQ data collection activities should apply the following considerations:

- Ease of regular reporting and data collection, especially when development team members are required to report.
- The possible bias of data while reporting. The reporting method should reduce as much as possible this potential biased reporting, which could bias the results of CoSQ periodical reports.

9.6.3 Implementation of the planned CoSQ system

Like any other new procedure, implementation of a new cost of software quality system involves:

- Assigning responsibility for reporting and collection of quality cost data.
- Instruction of the team in the logic and procedures of the new system.
- Follow-up:
  - Support for solving implementation problems and providing supplementary information when needed.
  - Identifying cases of partial or total lack of reporting and verifying regular reporting.
  - Identification of cases of clear biased reporting and verifying proper future reporting.
- Processing the collected CoSQ data:
  - Review of data collected, its proper classification, and recording.
  - Review of completeness and accuracy of the CoSQ reports by their comparison with records produced by the general MIS system and previous cost and activity records. This task requires special efforts during the initial implementation period.
- Updating and revising cost item definitions together with the reporting and collecting methods, based on feedback.

9.6.4 Actions taken in response to the model's findings

Most of the actions taken in response to the model's findings – that is, the results obtained after analysis of the CoSQ reports based on comparisons with previous periods, with other units, and so on. In practice, the analysis and subsequent actions taken are rooted in the application of the *cost of software quality balance* concept. According to this concept, an increase in control costs is expected to yield a decrease in failure of control costs and vice versa; a decrease in control

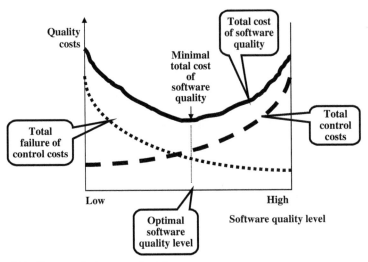

Figure 9.3 The cost of software quality balance concept.

costs is expected to lead to an increase in failure of control costs. Moreover, the effect of changes in control costs is expected to vary according to the desired software quality level. This relationship is expected to yield an optimal total cost of software quality, a minimal total cost achievable at a specified quality level – the optimal software quality level. Figure 9.3 shows a graphic illustration of the cost of software quality balance concept as shown by the control costs and costs and failure of control costs for the different software quality levels.

Management is usually interested in minimal total quality cost, rather than the control or failure of control cost components. Therefore, managers tend to focus on the optimal quality level, and apply this concept when budgeting the annual SQA activity plan as well as when budgeting a project.

Examples of typical decisions taken in the wake of cost of software quality analysis and their expected results are shown in Table 9.4:

In addition to the actions taken by management, additional actions may be initiated by the Corrective Action Board, which bases its analysis of the accumulated cost of quality, quality metrics on different data not considered by management. A comprehensive discussion of such CAB actions is found in Chapter 16.

9.7 Problems in application of CoSQ measurements

Application of a CoSQ model is generally accompanied by problems to be overcome, whatever the industry is. These impinge upon the accuracy and completeness of quality cost data caused by:

- Inaccurate and/or incomplete identification and classification of quality costs.

Table 9.4   Cost of software quality analysis – typical actions and expected results

No.	Actions	Expected results
1	Improvement of software manual and help instructions	Reduction of external failure costs
2	Increased investment of resources in contract review	Reduction of managerial internal and external failure costs
3	Reduction in instruction activities yielding no significant improvement	Reduction of prevention costs with no increase in failure costs
4	Increased investment in training inspection team members and team leaders	Reduction of internal and external failure costs
5	Adoption of more intensive project progress control procedures	Reduction of internal and external managerial failure costs
6	Construction of certified subcontractor list allowed to participate in company projects	Reduction of failure costs, especially of external failure costs
7	Introduction of automated software tests to replace manual testing without a substantial increase in testing costs	Reduction of internal and external failure costs

- Negligent reporting by team members and others.
- Biased reporting of software costs, especially of "censored" internal and external costs.
- Biased recording of external failure costs, due to indirect if not "camouflaged" compensation of customers for failures (e.g., discounted future services, delivery of free services, and so on), whose implications are not recorded as external failure costs.

The abovementioned general quality assurance problems do arise within the context of the software industry, but there are others as well, unique to the software industry. We shall focus on problems faced when recording management prevention and control costs and managerial failure costs as these items significantly affect the validity and comprehensiveness of the total cost of software quality, especially when the extended cost of software quality model is applied.

Problems arising when collecting data on managerial prevention and appraisal costs:

- Contract review and progress control activities are performed in many cases in a "part-time mode," and in addition they are subdivided into several disconnected activities of short duration. The reporting of time invested in these activities is usually inaccurate and often neglected.
- Many of the participants in these activities are senior staff members and are not required to report their time.
- The nature of follow-up activities requiring few hours, and in many cases even less than an hour, makes them difficult to report accurately.

Table 9.5   Causes for deviation from schedule and incurred quality cost

Cause for deviation from schedule	Class of quality costs
1. Changes performed according to customer request, including agreed delays in scheduled completion	Internal quality cost will be effective for delays beyond the agreed delay
2. Customer-delayed installation of communication and other hardware, and/or delays in its staff recruitment and training	No internal failure cost, customer responsibility for failure costs
3. Poor performance by development team, requiring extensive rework and corrections of software detected after software was installed at customer site	External failure cost
4. Project proposal based on unrealistic schedules and budgets	Managerial internal failure cost
5. Late or inadequate recruitment of staff or reliance on company professionals, whose release from other projects does not meet project needs	Managerial internal failure cost

Problems encountered in collection of data on managerial failure costs, especially schedule failures costs:

• Determination of responsibility for schedule failures.

These costs may be assigned to the customer (in cases when the customer caused a delay that resulted in additional developer costs), who is required to compensate the developer, the development team (delay damages are considered an external failure cost), or management (delays caused by management failure to recruit the required staff may result in damages considered as a managerial failure cost). Schedule failure costs are frequently deliberated for lengthy periods because their direct causes or the specific contributions of each participant to the initial failures are difficult to pinpoint. Following are examples of typical causes for delays and the associated quality costs in Table 9.5:

• Late payment of customer's overt compensation. At the time of these compensations it is too late for effective application of the lessons learned.

Summary

1. The objectives of cost of software quality measurements

The objectives of cost of software quality measurements relate to management interventions on the basis of economic data:

• To control the costs associated with error prevention (prior to occurrence) and detection of errors (once they occur).

- To evaluate the extent of financial damages from software failures, and prevention and appraisal costs as a basis for revising and updating the SQA budget.
- To facilitate financial evaluation of planned increases/decreases in SQA activities or investment in new or updated SQA infrastructure, based on past economic performance.

2. **Comparison of the classic software quality cost model with the extended model**

   The classic model for quality costs (Feigenbaum and others, early 1950s) presents a general concept that classifies manufacturing quality costs into two classes: **costs of control** (prevention costs and appraisal costs) – costs controlled by the organization and expended to prevent and detect failures with the purpose of reducing total failures to an acceptable level; **costs of failure of control** (internal failure costs and external failure costs) – costs of failures, regarded as consequences, caused by failures to prevent and detect software errors.

   The extended model expands the scope of the classic model by introducing costs related to management's contribution to project success and failure. According to the extended CoSQ model, the costs are classified into two groups:
- Development and SQA activities quality costs, defined according to the classic CoSQ model.
- Management quality costs. The subclasses of the management quality costs group are: management prevention costs, management appraisal costs, internal management failure costs, and external management failure costs. These subclasses belong to the management control costs and management failure costs classes.

3. **The justification for the formulation of the extended CoSQ model**

   The need for the extended CoSQ model, unique to the software industry, is justified by its inclusion of managerial quality costs. While managerial control costs and managerial failure costs, as a proportion of quality costs, are usually negligible in manufacturing, they may be quite considerable in the development of software. The extent of losses (failure costs) incurred by management's erroneous actions and decisions or its failure to act on time can be colossal. Also, as preparations and progress control involve great efforts, associated costs are very high. This situation stems from the special characteristics of the software industry as described in Chapter 1.

4. **The implementation process of a cost of software quality system**

   Implementation of a cost of software quality system in an organization requires:
- Definition of the organization's CoSQ model including the specific cost items.

- Planning of the cost data collection method.
- Implementation of the planned CoSQ system, including follow-up procedures.
- Taking action on the basis of the cost model's findings.

5. **The general and unique problems involved in implementing a CoSQ software quality system**

   Implementation of such a system for software is generally confronted by problems similar to those encountered in other industries. The general quality assurance difficulties that affect accuracy and completeness of quality cost data are:
   - Inaccurate and incomplete identification and classification of quality costs.
   - Negligent reporting.
   - Human tendency for biased reporting, especially of internal and external costs.
   - Biased external failure cost records due to indirect if not "camouflaged" compensation of customers that is not officially recorded as an external failure cost.

   Besides these general difficulties, unique difficulties typical to the software industry include:
   - Segmentation of contract review and progress control activities into several short and disconnected activities, which interfere with accurate reporting of time invested.
   - Many senior staff members are not required to report time.

   Typical difficulties in collecting managerial failure costs data, especially regarding schedules:
   - Difficulties in determining the responsibility for schedule failures: the customer, the development team, or the management.
   - Late payment of customer's overt compensation. At the time these compensations are too late for effective application of lessons learned.

Selected bibliography

Daughtrey T. (2013) Software quality costs, *Software Quality Professional*, Vol. 15, No. 2, pp. 4–15.
Flowers S. (1996) *Software Failure: Management Failure*, John Wiley & Sons, Inc, Chichester, NY.
Galin D. (2004) Towards an inclusive model for the costs of software quality, *Software Quality Professional*, Vol. 6, No. 4, pp. 25–31.
Galin, D. and Avrahami M. (2007) Benefits of a higher quality level of the software process: two organizations compared, *Software Quality Professional*, Vol. 9, No. 4, pp. 27–35.
IEEE (2014) *IEEE Std. 730-2014 Software Quality Assurance*, The IEEE Computer Society, IEEE, New York.
Jones C. (2011) Software quality and software costs, *Software Quality Professional*, Vol. 13, No. 3, pp. 24–30.

Karg L. M. (2009) Conformance quality and failure costs in the software industry: An empirical analysis of open source software, in *International Conference on Industrial Engineering and Engineering Management, Hong Kong*, December 2009, pp. 1386–1390.

Karg L. M., Grottke M., and Beckhaus A. (2011) A systematic literature review of software quality cost research, *Journal of Systems and Software*, Vol. 84, No. 3, pp. 415–427.

Knox S. T. (1993) Modeling the cost of software quality, *Digital Technical Journal*, Vol. 5, No. 4, pp. 9–15.

Krasner H. (1998) Using the cost of quality approach for software, *CrossTalk – The Journal of Defense Software Engineering*, Vol. 11, No. 11, pp. 6–11.

Laporte C. Y., Berrhouma N., Doucet M., and Palza-Vargas E. (2012) Measuring the costs of software quality of a large software project at Bombardier Transportation – a case study, *Software Quality Professional*, Vol. 14, No. 3, pp. 14–31.

Review questions

9.1 Section 9.3 presents the classic CoSQ model. It classifies quality costs into four subclasses: prevention costs, appraisal costs, internal failure costs, and external failure costs.

a. Explain in your own words the main characteristics of each subclass of costs and indicate the differences between them.

b. Suggest three items for each subclass.

9.2 Both the classic and the extended software quality models assign costs to two main classes: costs of control and costs of failure of control.

a. Explain in your own words the nature of each class.

b. What would you consider to be the idea guiding this classification and what do you consider the managerial aspects to be?

9.3 Section 9.5 presents the extended CoSQ model.

a. Explain the difference between the classic and extended models in your own words.

b. Justify the formulation of a special extended cost of quality model for software. Base your arguments on a comparison of the characteristics of the software development project environment with those of industrial manufacturing companies.

9.4 The annual report issued by Leonard Software Inc. includes several expenditure items, listed in the table below.

Indicate the subclass of cost of software quality to which each of the following expenditures belongs: PC = prevention costs, AC = appraisal costs, IFC = internal failure costs, EFC = external failure costs, MPC = management prevention costs, MAC = management appraisal costs, IMFC = internal management failure costs, and EMFC = external management failure costs. In cases where an expenditure item is not a software quality cost, mark "X" in the "nonsoftware quality cost" column.

Leonard Software Inc.: expenditure

No.	Expenditure item	Subclass of software quality cost	Nonsoftware quality cost
1	Working hours spent installing software at customer's site in Singapore	_____	_____
2	Waiving of customer's debt as agreed to in compromise following software failures detected in the installed software	_____	_____
3	Payment for Dr. Jacobs's participation in a design review	_____	_____
4	Payments made to "King SQA Consultants" for preparing the new version of the software quality procedures	_____	_____
5	Repair of a color printer	_____	_____
6	Working hours spent participating in monthly meetings of the Coordination and Control Committee headed by the Department Manager	_____	_____
7	Travel to Switzerland to examine advanced software testing system proposed to company	_____	_____
8	Purchase of barcode sticker software package to be integrated in the inventory management software system.	_____	_____
9	Working hours spent correcting errors listed in a design review report.	_____	_____
10	Customer's compensation for delay in schedule resulting from the company's inability to recruit sufficient professional manpower for the development team.	_____	_____
11	Working hours spent by the Chief Software Engineer and Martin Fountain, Senior Project Manager, in examining the schedule estimates for the "Top Assets" tender.	_____	_____
12	Working hours spent in preparation of an updated version of Leonard Software's *C Programming Instructions.*	_____	_____
13	Working hours spent by programmer (John) in correcting program bugs detected by his team leader in their weekly meeting.	_____	_____

9.5 The company's last year's annual CoSQ were as follows:

	Cost of software quality class	Previous year's annual costs in thousands $
Development and SQA activities quality costs	Prevention costs	$1,238
	Appraisal costs	$3,450
	Internal failure costs	$4,238
	External failure costs	$2,890
Management quality costs	Management prevention costs	$225
	Management appraisal costs	$127
	Internal management failure costs	$1,840
	External Management failure costs	$4,650
Development costs (design and coding)		$12,876

The software quality assurance manager has proposed a dramatic change in Leonard Software's software quality expenditures policy. It is expected to reduce failure costs by the following significant percentages: internal failure costs – 10%, external failure costs – 25%, and managerial internal and external failure costs – at least 25%.

The SQA manager's proposal involves increasing expenditures as follows: prevention costs $400,000, appraisal costs $700,000, managerial prevention costs $580,000, and management appraisal costs $220,000.

Management commented about the proposed extravagant expenditures required for the proposed SQA progress project. Management requested that you evaluate the SQA manager's proposal.

a. Examine the proposal and calculate its results from a financial aspect.

b. Explain in your own words, how this dramatic program's additional funds should be utilized in order to bring about the expected reduction in failure costs.

c. Can you list any hidden costs of failure that have not been mentioned in the program, but which are expected to be reduced as a result of implementing the proposal?

d. Assuming the scope of development activities for next year will be similar to that of last year, will the proposed project reduce the percentage of CoSQ in the total costs of software products? Present your calculations.

Topics for discussion

9.1 A good part if not the majority of external failure costs are "hidden" costs.

a. List examples of hidden failure costs. For each example, indicate the type of software development organization and situation for which these failure costs could become extremely high.

b. Explain the difficulties faced in estimating the extent of failure costs for each of the examples mentioned in (a).

9.2 Xrider, a leading software house, employs 500 professionals distributed among five departments, each of which works on 20–30 software development projects simultaneously. The company's new classic CoSQ system has successfully completed its second year of operation. The report on the annual cost of software quality presents data on departments and teams as follows; for each department and team: preventive costs, appraisal costs, internal failure costs, external failure costs, department's software development budget, and team's software development budget.

a. Suggest a systematic method, based on the compiled data, for comparing the system's capabilities.

b. Discuss the limitations of some or all of the comparisons suggested in (a) and propose checks to be carried out to prevent reaching erroneous conclusions based on questionable comparisons.

9.3 The SQA unit of AB Dynamics has summarized its "7 years of success" in a colorful brochure. One of the brochure's tables presents the unit's SQA achievements by summarizing the cost of software quality over the period in the following manner:

AB Dynamics: Cost of software quality and annual sales (2010–2016)

	Cost of software quality in thousands $					
Year	Prevention costs	Appraisal costs	Internal failure costs	External failure costs	Total cost of software quality	Total annual sales in millions $
A	B	C	D	E	F	G
2010	380	2,200	930	1,820	5,330	38
2011	680	2,270	760	1,140	4,850	43
2012	840	2,320	500	880	4,540	49
2013	1,200	2,020	490	700	4,410	56
2014	1,110	2,080	420	640	4,250	58
2015	1,170	2,080	400	510	4,160	66
2016	1,330	2,120	410	450	4,310	76

a. Analyze the data in the above table regarding the progressively higher efficiency and effectiveness achieved by the SQA system during the period 1996–2002.

b. Draw a diagram depicting the cost of software quality balance by quality level (see Figure 9.3), based on the data in the above table. For this purpose, assume:

Quality cost to be the cost of quality per $1 million of sales (calculated by applying the following formula: F/G).

Software quality level is assumed to be inversely proportional to the percentage of external failure costs out of annual sales (calculated by applying the following formula: $G/(1.7 \times E)$. The 1.7 factor is used to make the 2016 quality level equal to 100. The lower the percentage of external failure costs, the higher the quality level.

  c. Analyze the data in the diagram drawn in (b) according to the cost of software quality balance concept.

9.4 The classic cost of software quality model employs – unchanged – the general quality cost model applied in manufacturing industries.

  a. Compare the characteristics of prevention costs for software development with a manufacturing industry (e.g., wood products industry, metal products industry).

  b. Compare the characteristics of appraisal costs for software development with a manufacturing industry.

  c. Compare the characteristics of internal failure costs for software development with a manufacturing industry.

  d. Compare the characteristics of external failure costs for software development with a manufacturing industry.

Chapter 10

The Effectiveness and Cost of a V&V Plan – The SQA Model

The SQA model is an effective tool to provide project planners with estimates of the effectiveness of a verification and validating plan (V&V plan). Such a tool enables comparing alternative programs by supplying the expected percentage of errors to be removed in each screening stage, when applying a given V&V plan, and also the expected costs of performing the plan. This method of estimating could also be useful for the SQA function when evaluating project plans.

The model deals with two quantitative aspects of a V&V plan consisting of several defect detection activities. The plan itself is to be integrated within a project's development process:

a. The V&V plan's total effectiveness in removing project defects.

b. The V&V plan's total costs of removal of project defects.

Section 10.1 describes the data required for applying the model.

10.1 The data required for the SQA model

Application of the model is based on three types of data:

a. Defect origin distribution

Defect origins (the phase in which defects were introduced) are distributed throughout the development process, from the project initiation to its completion. Surveys conducted by major software developers, such as IBM and TRW, and summarized by Jones (2008) (Chapters 3 and 5), reveal patterns of defect origin distribution. It may be assumed that this pattern has not changed substantially in recent years. A characteristic

Software Quality: Concepts and Practice, First Edition. Daniel Galin.
© 2018 the IEEE Computer Society, Inc. Published 2018 by John Wiley & Sons, Inc.

Table 10.1 A characteristic distribution of software defect origins

No.	Software development phase	Average percentage of defects originating in phase
1	Requirements specification	20%
2	Design	35%
3	Coding (unit coding – 25%, integration – 10%)	35%
4	Documentation	10%

distribution of software defect origins, based on Jones (2008), is shown in Table 10.1.

b. Defect removal effectiveness

It is assumed that any quality assurance activity filters (screens) a certain percentage of existing defects. It should be noted that in most cases, the percentage of removed defects is somewhat lower than the percentage of detected defects. This is due to the fact that some corrections (about 10% according to Jones (2008)) are ineffective or inadequate (bad fixes). The remaining defects, those undetected and uncorrected, are passed on to successive development phases. The next quality assurance activity applied is designated for a combination of defects: those remaining after previous quality assurance activities, together with "new" defects created in the current development phase. The rates of typical average defect filtering effectiveness for the various quality assurance activities, by development phase, based on Jones (2008) (Chapter 3), Jones (2011), and Pressman and Maxim (2015) (Chapter 20), are listed in Table 10.2.

c. Cost of defect removal

Data collected about development project costs show that the cost of removal of detected defects varies by development phase, while costs rise substantially as the development process proceeds. For example, removal of a design defect detected in the design phase may require an investment of one working day; removal of the same defect during the acceptance tests may require 16 working days. Several surveys, summarized by Pressman and Maxim (2015) (Chapter 19), estimate the relative costs of correcting errors at each development phase. The representative average of relative defect removal costs according to the defect origination and removal phases, based on Pressman and Maxim (2015) (Chapter 19), are shown in Table 10.3.

It should be noted that the data in Tables 10.1–10.3 is based on findings from projects developed according to SDLC sequential processes, and might not represent projects developed according to an incremental delivery model or to an agile methodology. In order to achieve more accurate estimates, an organization

Table 10.2 Average filtering (defect removal) effectiveness by quality assurance activities

No.	Quality assurance activity	Average defect filtering effectiveness rate
1	Requirements specification review	70%
2	Design inspection	55%
3	DR	50%
4	DR after design inspection	30%
5	Code inspection	65%
6	Unit test	60%
7	Unit test after code inspection	35%
8	Integration test	50%
9	Documentation review	50%
10	System tests/acceptance tests	50%

Table 10.3 Representative average relative defect-removal costs

		Average relative defect removal cost (cost units)				
		Defect origination phase				
No.	Defect removal phase	Req	Des	Uni	Int	Doc
1	Requirements review	1				
2	Design inspection	3.3	1			
3	Design review	3.3	1			
4	Code inspection	7	2.1	1		
5	Unit testing	7	2.1	1		
6	Integration testing	18	5.5	2.6	1	
7	Documentation review	18	5.5	2.6	1	1
8	System testing/Acceptance testing	52	16	7.4	2.9	2.9
9	Operation by customer	103	31	15	5.7	5.7

The defect origination phases are: Req = requirement specification, Des = design, Uni = unit testing, Int = integration tests, Doc = documentation.

plan to implement the model should collect relevant performance data, and calculate the local values for these tables.

10.2 The SQA model

The model is based on the following assumptions:

- The development process is linear and sequential, following the Waterfall Model.

- A number of "new" defects are introduced in each development phase. For their distributions, see Table 10.1. It is assumed that no "new" defects are introduced in the phases of system tests and acceptance tests.

- Review and test software quality assurance activities serve as filters, removing a percentage of the incoming defects, and letting the rest pass on to the next development phase. For example, if the number of incoming defects is 30, and the filtering efficiency is 60%, then 18 defects will be removed, while 12 defects will remain and be passed on to be detected by the next quality assurance activity. Typical filtering effectiveness rates for the various quality assurance activities are shown in Table 10.2.

- The filtering efficiency is the same for every defect, irrespective of its origination phase.

- At each phase, the incoming defects are the sum of defects not removed by the former quality assurance activity, together with the "new" defects introduced (created) in the current development phase.

- The average cost of defect removal at the phase it originated is the same for all phases – one cost unit.

- The cost of defect removal is calculated for each quality assurance activity by multiplying the number of defects removed by the relative cost of removing a defect (according to its originating and removal phases – see Table 10.3).

- The remaining defects, not detected by the set of software quality assurance tools, are unfortunately passed on to the customer, and will also be detected by the customer. In these circumstances, removal of defects detected by the customer entails the heaviest of defect removal costs.

In the model, each of the quality assurance activities is represented by a filter unit, as shown in Figure 10.1.

	Ddoc	Dint	Duni	Ddes	Dreq	Total		
Incoming defects (IDef)				35	6	41		20.5
Passed defects (PDef)				17.5	3	20.5	%FE=50	
Removed defects (RDef)				17.5	3	20.5		
Relative defect removal cost (RDRC)				1	3.3	TRC	27.4 cost units (cu)	

Figure 10.1   A filter unit for defect-removal effectiveness and cost – filtering of DR (where the SQA process does not include design inspection).

The filter unit shown in Figure 10.1 presents the filtering process by the DR (design review) activity, where the filtering effectiveness is 50%. Six defects are passed from the former development phase (the requirement review phase), while 35 defects are due to the failures from the design phase process, and introduced into the filter. As the filtering effectiveness of this phase is 50%, the total number of undetected defects passed to the next phase (code review of unit testing) is 20.5, while 20.5 defects are removed in this SQA activity. The resources invested in defect removal during the design phase amount to 27.4 cost units (cu), where removal of defects passed from the requirement phase require 3.3 cost units (cu) for each defect. (The calculation is as follows $17.5 \times 1 + 3 \times 3.3 = 27.4$).

The defects introduced into the filter unit (their values shown in Table 10.3) are:

- Dreq = Defects originated in the requirement phase
- Ddes = Defects originated in the design phase
- Duni = Defects originated in the unit testing phase
- Dint = Defects originated in the integration testing phase
- Ddoc = Defects originated in the documentation phase

The model presents the following quantities:

- POD = Phase originated defects (from Table 10.1)
- IDef = Incoming defects from current development phase and former SQA activities
- PDef = Passed defects to next quality assurance activity
- Rdef = Removed defects in current quality assurance activity
- %FE = % of filtering effectiveness (also termed % screening effectiveness) shown in Table 10.2
- RDRC = Relative defect removal cost (from Table 10.3)
- TRC = Total removal cost of current filtering activity
- cu = cost units

The first illustration of the model applies to a standard quality assurance plan that is composed of six quality assurance activities (six filters) that are implemented internally by the developer. This standard plan does not include design inspection and code inspection. An additional SQA activity, for removing the remaining software defects, is performed for defects detected by the customer during regular operation of the software product. It is assumed that the customer reveals all the remaining defects during regular operation of the software system.

A process-oriented illustration of the standard quality assurance plan model is provided in Figure 10.2.

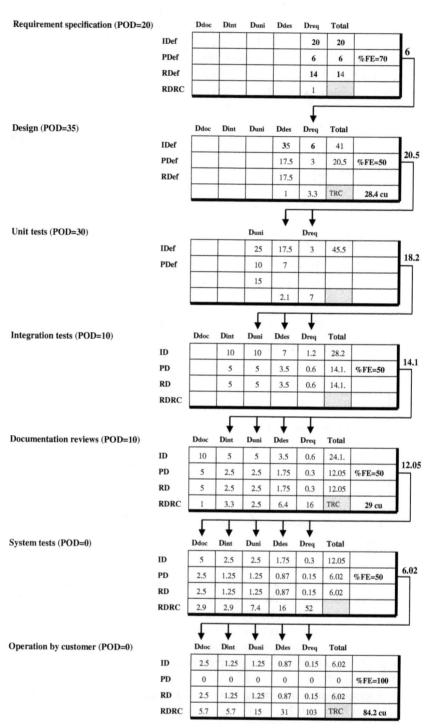

Figure 10.2 Defect removal effectiveness and cost – the standard V&V plan model of the process of removal of 100 defects.

10.3 Application of the SQA model for comparing V&V plans

This section presents a comparison of two V&V plans:

- A standard V&V plan – presented in Figure 10.2
- A comprehensive V&V plan presented in Figure 10.3.

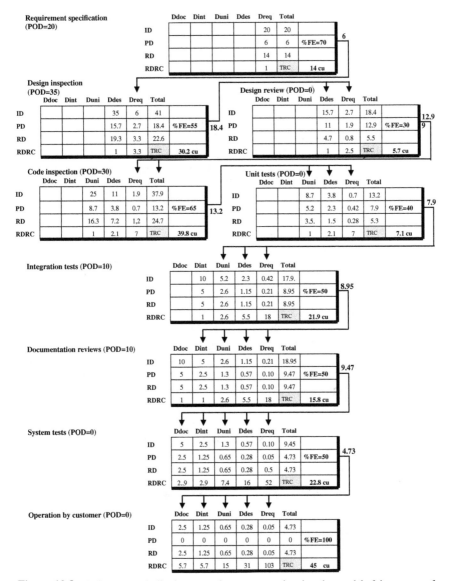

Figure 10.3 Defect removal effectiveness and cost – comprehensive plan model of the process of correction of 100 defects.

Table 10.4   Defect removal effectiveness for quality assurance plans

Quality assurance activity	Defects removal effectiveness for standard V&V plan	Defects removal effectiveness for comprehensive V&V plan
Specification requirement review	70%	70%
Design inspection	—	55%
Design review	50%	30%
Code inspection	—	65%
Unit test	60%	40%
Integration tests	50%	60%
Documentation review	50%	60%
System test	50%	60%
Operation phase detection	100%	100%

The second illustration of the model in Figure 10.3 applies to a comprehensive V&V plan composed of eight quality assurance activities (eight filters), including design inspection and code inspection, implemented internally by the developer. The defect removal effectiveness of design inspection and code inspection are 55 and 65%, respectively. It is assumed that the inspections, by reducing the outcoming "stream" of defects, reduce the defect removal presented in design reviews and found in unit tests to 30 and 40%, respectively. The comparative defect removal activities of the standard and comprehensive V&V plans are presented in Table 10.4.

Figure 10.3 provides a process-oriented illustration of the comprehensive plan model.

A comparison of the percent of defects removed and the cost of removal for each SQA activity of both V&V plans are shown in Table 10.5

Both examples present a detailed flow of calculations according to the process of defect removal effectiveness and cost.

In addition, the examples enable us to examine the SQA defect removal approach that claims: "The more you invest in quality assurance in the earlier stages of the software development process, the higher the total effectiveness of defect removal is, and the lower the total defect removal costs are." Let us further study the comparison between the plans:

A comparison of the outcomes of the standard software quality plan versus the comprehensive plan is instructive. The comparison results are shown in Table 10.6.

The contributions of the additional SQA activities are:

- Reduced percentage of remaining defects passed to customer (operation) by 22%
- Reduced costs of defect removal during the development process by 25%
- Reduced costs involved in defect removal when software product is in regular operation by 47%
- Reduced total cost of defect removal by 32%

Table 10.5   Comparison of standard and comprehensive V&V plans

No.	Quality assurance activity	Standard plan		Comprehensive plan	
		Removed defects in %	Cost of removing defects (cu)	Removed defects in % (cu)	Cost of removing defects (cu)
1	Requirements review	14.0	14.0	14.0	14.0
2	Design inspection	—	—	22.6	30.2
3	Design review	20.5	28.4	5.5	5.7
4	Code inspection	—	—	24.7	39.8
5	Unit test code	27.3	49.7	5.3	7.1
6	Integration test	14.1	48.1	8.95	21.9
7	Documentation review	12.1	29.0	9.47	15.8
8	System test	6.0	41.9	4.73	22.8
	Total for internal quality assurance activities	**94.0**	**210.1**	**95.3**	**157.3**
	Defects detected during operation	6.0	84.2	4.7	45.0
	Total	**100.0**	**295.3**	**100.0**	**202.3**

Table 10.6   A comparison of the effectiveness of the standard and comprehensive plans

	The standard V&V plan	The comprehensive V&V plan
Number of SQA activities during the development process	6	8
SQA activities during regular operation	1	1
Additional SQA activities		**1.** Design inspection **2.** Unit code review
% Defects removed in the requirements and design development phases	34.5%	42.1%
% Defects removed in the coding and testing phases	59.5%	53.2%
The defect removal effectiveness of the V&V plan	94%	95.3%
Defects passed on to the customer (to maintenance)	6%	4.7%
Total SQA costs of defect removal costs during the development process (internal costs)	**210.1 cu**	**157.3 cu**
Defect removal cost during operation	84.2	45 cu
Total defect removal cost	**295.3**	**202.3**

It should be noted that the defect filtering model could be adapted to a wide range of V&V plans developed according to various software development models and methodologies.

Several models for estimating the effectiveness of V&V plans are available, some use the terms "defect containment" or "phase containment" for estimating defect removal achievements – I will mention three of these. A model, similar to the SQA model described here, is presented by Hallowell (2002). The mode enables estimating the percentage of errors detected, the work invested in error detection (person-months), and the percentage of software costs used for fixing defects. The model is comprised of four development stages: requirements, design, coding, and testing. Hallowell illustrates the application of the model by comparing SDLC with an Agile case. The results show that the Agile case is superiority, as expected. A second model, presented by Hedstorm and Watson (1995), is probabilistic considering the defects input in the five stages of the development process according to the Poisson distribution. The model enables predicting the percentage of screened defects for each development stage. The model, defined as a software predictive engine, for which a US patent application was filed in October 1996. Another model dealing with the cumulative effects of several quality assurance activities, is discussed by Pressman and Maxim (2015) (Chapter 20).

Summary

1. **A model for SQA defect removal effectiveness and cost**
     The model deals with two quantitative aspects of a V&V plan designed for a specific project:
   a. Total effectiveness of defect removal plan
   b. Total cost of defect removal plan
     The model is based on three types of data:
   - The distribution of the defects according to their originating phase
   - The defect removal effectiveness according to the type of SQA activity and development phase
   - The cost of defect removal according to the originating development phase and the phase from which it was removed

2. **Possible uses for the model**
     The model enables calculating estimates for defect removal effectiveness, and costs of proposals in regards to the structure of V&V plans, for example:
   - Addition or elimination of a quality assurance activity from a given plan
   - Utilization of the model thus enables comparison of SQA policies/ strategies and activity plans

Selected bibliography

Hedstorm J. R. and Watson D. A. Product defect predictive engine, U. S. Patent 6477471, (2002).

Hallowell D. L. (2002) *Exploring defect containment metrics in Agile*. Available at http//www. Isixsigma.com/methdology/mentrics/exploring-defect-containment-metrics-agile.

Jones C. (2008) *Applied Software Measurement: Global Analysis of Productivity and Quality*, 3rd Edition, McGraw-Hill, New York.

Jones C. (2011) Software quality and software costs, *Software Quality Professional*, Vol. 13, No. 3, pp. 24–30.

Pressman R. S. and Maxim B. R. (2015) *Software Engineering: A Practitioner's Approach: European Adaptation*, 8th Edition, McGraw-Hill, New York.

Review questions

10.1 The chapter lists input data to the SQA model in Tables 10.1–10.3.

  a. Is it possible that the data in these tables suits two of the department projects, but definitely does not suit the third project? Explain your reply.

  b. Provide three examples for situations where the above situation exists?

10.2 Referring to the model for software defect removal effectiveness and costs.

  a. What assumptions rest at the foundations of the model?

  b. Which three of the model's data components are based on published survey results?

Topics for discussion

10.1 Due to time and budget constraints, a project leader has decided to introduce "an economy plan" that limits the quality assurance activities to a standard design review – as required by the contract with the customer (50% filter), and comprehensive system tests (60% filter). Considering the model's contribution to defect-removal efficiency and costs:

  a. What are the expected savings, if any, in resources invested for defect removal during the development process compared to the standard quality assurance plan?

  b. What are the expected effects of the "economy plan" on customer satisfaction? Support your answer with a quantitative comparison to the standard plan.

  c. Compare the overall results of the "economy plan" to the results of the standard and comprehensive plans

  d. Based on your answer to (3), can you suggest some general rules about selecting the preferred quality assurance plan?

10.2 Compare the results of topics for Topics for discussion 10.1 and the results for the comprehensive V&V plan.

  a. Does the comparison of the above results support the belief that investing in verification processes in the early stages of a project reduces the total costs of the SQA activities?

  b. Explain in your own words the findings of (1).

Chapter 11

SQA Records and Documentation Control

11.1 Jeff's troubles – an introductory mini-case

Jeff, head of the legal department, was obviously furious when he entered the office of Roberto, the Software Development Department Manager. Ignoring preliminaries, he walked in and announced: "You cannot imagine the difficulties I'm having collecting evidence to support our case in the Margaret Gardens claim. Jerry managed the development project at the time, and mentioned a lot of documents that were supposed to support our case. But, some of the key documents were carelessly written, while others simply don't exist. Even though the project was completed only six months ago, so many important documents are already unavailable or simply poorly written:

- Minutes of joint meetings that were held with the customer to discuss our proposal prior to contract signing – during which some major changes were agreed to – were discarded, or shredded two months ago.

- A software change request form submitted by Margaret Gardens last August is available but, unbelievably, unsigned. The requested change was implemented during the development process just eleven months ago; however, the respective SCO (software change order) along with the test report for the completed change, are missing.

- According to Margaret Garden's change requests, the original requirement specification document was revised twice. I managed to locate these important documents, but while the original document was written according to procedures, the other two revision documents are of "free structure," making a comparison of the versions virtually impossible.

- Some of the major claims relate to software design, but only one of three design review sessions attended by customer representatives was properly documented. Another review session report, located in the unit's filing system, wasn't signed by customer representatives. The third report was "just" missing.

Software Quality: Concepts and Practice, First Edition. Daniel Galin.
© 2018 the IEEE Computer Society, Inc. Published 2018 by John Wiley & Sons, Inc.

- Lastly, the summary report from tests that Margaret Gardens participated in, and which were issued by the joint testing committee, is missing. The secretary of the Testing Unit believes that the document is in the possession of Ted James, who left us three months ago and moved to Indiana."

When Jeff had left, Roberto called Martin, his deputy, into the office. "Jeff just left after voicing some serious complaints about our department documents. As you I'm sure remember, similar complaints have frequently been heard from our development and maintenance team leaders. Please prepare a proposal, including the necessary procedures, to deal with the use of templates and checklists, as well as documentation control, and let's do our best to finally solve these documentation issues."

11.2 Introduction

During the software life cycle many types of documents are created. Some of the documents are required immediately for the continuation of the development, while others may become vital for software quality assurance over the life cycle of the system. Documents displaying these characteristics and treated according to special procedures are:

Controlled documents. Documents produced during the development and operation of software systems, which are immediately necessary for software processes, or during the life cycle of the system for software quality assurance. Documentation control ensures the availability and quality of these documents in terms of completeness and accuracy.

Quality records. Quality records are controlled documents mainly aimed to provide evidence that the development and maintenance processes performed were in compliance with requirements, and that the software quality system is operating fully and effectively.

Controlled document and quality records are defined in Frame 11.1.

Frame 11.1: Controlled document and quality record – definitions

Controlled document – definition
A document that is currently necessary or that may become vital for the development and maintenance of software systems, as well as for the management of current and future relationships with the customer.

Quality record – definition
A quality record is a special type of controlled document. It is a customer-targeted record of document that may be required to demonstrate full compliance with customer requirements and effective operation of the software quality assurance system throughout the development and maintenance processes.

There are various types of controlled documents, and cover all stages of the software systems life cycle. Frame 11.2 presents an overview of the types of documents that may be categorized as controlled documents. An examination of the document list reveals that a good number of the controlled documents may be classified as quality records.

Frame 11.2: Typical controlled documents (including quality records)

Typical controlled documents (including quality records)

Preproject documents

1. Contract review report
2. Contract negotiation meeting minutes
3. Software development contract
4. Software maintenance contract
5. Software development subcontracting contract
6. Software development plan

Project life cycle documents

1. System requirements document
2. Software requirements document
3. Preliminary design document
4. Critical design document
5. Database description
6. Software test plan
7. Design review report
8. Follow-up records of design review action items
9. Software test procedure
10. Software test report
11. Software user manuals
12. Software maintenance manuals
13. Software installation plan
14. Version description document
15. Software change requests
16. Software change orders
17. Software maintenance requests
18. Maintenance services reports
19. Records of subcontractor evaluations

SQA infrastructure documents

1. SQA procedures
2. Template library
3. SQA forms library
4. CAB meetings minutes

Software quality management documents

1. Progress reports
2. Software metrics reports

SQA system audit documents

1. Management review report
2. Minutes of management review meeting
3. Internal quality audit report
4. External SQA certification audit report

Customer documents

1. Software project tender documents
2. Customer software change requests

Software development and quality standards deal with documentation issues. ISO/IEC Std. 90003:2014 (ISO/IEC, 2014) dedicates a number of its software engineering guidelines (Section 4.2) to documentation requirements, and the control of documentation processes and of record conformity to requirement records. ISO/IEC/IEEE Std. 12207-4008 dedicates Sec. 7.2.1 to software documentation maintenance processes. IEEE Std. 730-2014 (IEEE, 2014) deals separately with control of documents and control of records.

The following sections deal with

- The objectives of documentation control processes.
- The implementation of documentation control.

11.3 Objectives of documentation control processes

The main objectives of documentation control processes are presented in Frame 11.3.

Frame 11.3: The objectives of documentation control processes

The objectives of documentation control processes
- To ensure the quality of the document. - To ensure its technical completeness and compliance with document structure procedures and instructions (use of templates, proper approval process, etc.). - To ensure the future availability of documents that may be required for (a) the continuation of the development process, (b) software system maintenance, (c) further development of a software product being in its operational stage, or (d) responses to a customer's (tentative) future complaints. - To support the investigation of software failure causes and to assign responsibility as part of corrective and other actions.

11.4 The implementation of documentation control

The purpose of documentation control is to verify that the various stakeholders of the software process fulfill the various documentation requirements of the stakeholders of the software process. Documentation control processes, as defined by documentation control procedures, should regulate the handling of controlled documents from their creation to their disposal.

The implementation of documentation control includes the following processes as presented in Frame 11.4 .

Frame 11.4: The implementation of documentation control

Source: Based on ISO/IEC Std. 90003-2014 and ISO/IEC/IEEE Std. 12207-2008 (ISO/IEC, 2008)

Implementation processes of documentation control
a. Definition of the list of the controlled document types
b. Design and development of controlled documents
c. Document production and their regular use
d. Updating (maintaining) the controlled documents list

A description of the implementation processes of documentation control follows:

a. Definition of the list of the controlled document types

The key to managing documentation control is the controlled document types (including quality records) list. Proper construction of the list is based on the establishment of an authority to implement the concept, whether embodied in a person or a committee. Specifically, this authority is responsible for deciding which document type should be categorized as a controlled document and which controlled document types classified as quality records.

Most controlled document types are documents created internally by the organization itself. Nonetheless, a substantial number of external document types, such as contract documents and minutes of joint committee meetings, also fall into this category. Furthermore, it should also be noted that many of the controlled documents listed in Frame 11.2 are products of SQA processes.

Implementation Tip
The use of subcontractors in the development, and in some cases maintenance, of software systems is the source of various documentation control procedures to be applied with subcontractors. These procedures should ensure that subcontractor documents – such as design documents – comply with the contractor's documentation procedures. Communication difficulties as well as negligence often result in subcontractor's partial compliance. Damage caused by such lapses may become apparent months, or even years later, when a vital document is missing, or discovered to provide inadequate or only partial information. Prevention of such situations can be achieved with appropriate contract clauses as well as through continuous follow-up of subcontractor compliance with documentation requirements.

b. Design and development of controlled documents

The documentation requirements involved in the creation of a new document or the revision of an existing document focus on completeness, improved readability, and availability. The following requirements are realized in the documents':

• Structure
• Identification method
• Orientation and reference information

The document's **structure** may be free or defined by a template. Templates and their contribution to software quality are discussed in Section 24.2.

An identification method is devised to provide each document version and revision a unique identity. The method usually entails notation of (a) the software system or product name or number, (b) the document (type) code, and (c) the version and revision number. The method can vary depending on the type of document.

The document's **orientation and reference information** may also be required. Orientation and reference information support future access of required documents by supplying information about the content of the document and its suitability to the needs of the future user. Depending on the document type, a greater or smaller portion of the following items is commonly required:

• The document author(s)
• Date of completion
• Person(s) who approved the document, including position
• Date of approval
• Signatures of the author(s) and person(s) who approved it
• Descriptions of the changes introduced in the new release
• List of former versions and revisions
• Circulation list
• Confidentiality restrictions

The relevant documentation procedures and work instructions pertain to paper as well as electronic documents (e.g., e-mail and Intranet applications).

Document approval. Certain documents require approval, while others may be exempt from the associated review. For those documents requiring approval, the relevant procedures indicate: (a) The position of the person(s) authorized to approve per each type of document, such as department head or a formal design review (FDR) committee. (b) The details of the process implemented, where the approval process usually requires an appropriate review process.

Implementation tip

Observation of the approval process frequently reveals instances of rubber stamping, that is, situations where the process does not contribute to the document's quality due to the absence of a thorough document review. Some claim that formal approval actually reduces the document's quality because the authors know that the person(s) authorized to approve the document do not actually conduct any review, and so they do not have to double check the document before handing it in for approval. By the very act of approval, the person(s) who approve it become directly responsible for its quality. Accordingly, two options may be considered: (a) exemption of document types from approval, meaning that full responsibility is returned to the author, or (b) implementation of an approval process that assures thorough review of the document. In other words, the implied solution to rubber-stamping is either performing the approval process properly or eliminating it.

---

c. Controlled document production and their regular use

This process includes the following activities:
- Controlled document production
- Controlled document storage
- Retrieval of controlled documents and their circulation
- Control document security, including document disposal

Production of controlled documents including its identification details and the adequate orientation and reference information.

Document storage requirements apply to (1) the number of copies to be stored, (2) the unit responsible for storage of each copy, and (3) the storage medium. Storage in electronic media is usually much more efficient and economical than storage on paper. Yet, paper originals of certain documents are still stored in compliance with legal stipulations. In these cases, an image processing copy is stored in addition to the paper original.

Retrieval of documents and their circulation. The requirements refer to: (1) efficient and accurate retrieval of copies, in full compliance with security restrictions, and (2) instructions for circulating a new document on time to the designated recipients. Procedures should apply to the circulation of paper documents as well as the use of e-mail, Intranet, and Internet.

The storage and retrieval tasks of code versions and revisions and other software development products are included among the organization's software configuration management tasks, and performed with a variety of software configuration management tools. Yet, special efforts are still needed to coordinate documentation procedures with those of software configuration management.

Document security, including document disposal requirements, (1) provides restricted access to document types, (2) prevents unauthorized changes to stored documents, (3) provides back-up for stored paper as well electronic files, and (4) determines the storage period. At the end of a specified storage period, documents may be discarded or removed to a lower standard of storage, a shift that usually reduces availability. While paper files are prone to fire and flood damage, modern electronic storage is subject to electronic risks. The planned method for back-up storage reflects the level of these risks and the relative importance of the documents.

d. Updating (maintaining) the controlled documents list

Analyzing follow-up findings of actual use of controlled and no-controlled documents, and initiating the required updates, changes, removals, and additions to the controlled documents list.

Naturally, documentation control procedures vary among organizations according to the nature of their customers, software products, and maintenance services and their structure and size, among other characteristics if relates to the scope of the services. Software developers of large-scale "custom-made" software projects usually require quite different lists of controlled documents than do COTS software packages. In other words, one organization's procedures might be totally inadequate for another one.

Summary

1. The objectives of documentation control activities

The following are the main objectives of managing controlled documents:

- To ensure the quality of the document through its approval.
- To ensure the document's technical completeness, compliance with document structure and usage instructions.
- To ensure future availability of documents that may be required for maintenance, further development of the software system, or responses to customer complaints.
- To support investigation of software failure causes and to assign responsibility as part of corrective and other actions.

2. The processes involved in establishment and maintenance of documentation control

The processes are as follows:

- Deciding which document types are to be categorized as controlled documents and which controlled document types are to be classified as quality records.
- Defining the controlled documents' format, identification details, and their orientation and reference information.
- Producing the documents, and their storage and retrieval as required.
- Analyzing follow-up findings and initiating the required updates, changes, removals, and additions to the controlled documents list.

Selected bibliography

IEEE (2014) *IEEE Std. 730-2014 Software Quality Assurance*, The IEEE Computer Society, IEEE, New York.

ISO/IEC (2008) *ISO/IEC/IEEE Std. 12207-2008 – Systems and Software Engineering – Software Life Cycle Processes*, International Organization for Standardization, Geneva, Switzerland.

ISO/IEC (2014) *ISO/IEC 90003:2014 Software Engineering – Guidelines for the Application of TSO 9001: 2008 to Computer Software*, International Organization for Standardization, Geneva, Switzerland.

Review questions

11.1 The following documents are listed in Frame 11.2:

- Software development contract
- Design review report
- Software metrics report

a. Which of the above documents do you believe should be defined as quality record and why?

b. Suggest an imaginary situation that illustrates the importance of controlling a document belonging to each of the types you specified.

11.2 Choose six of the document types listed in Frame 11.2 (one from each group).

a. Which of the above document types do you believe should be defined as controlled documents? List your arguments.

b. Which of the document types you defined as controlled documents do you believe should also be classified as quality records? List your arguments.

11.3 List the objectives of documentation control processes

11.4 Section 11.4 discusses the procedure 4 component that manages the controlled documents list.

a. Describe in your own words the tasks (activities) to be performed by the authority appointed to implement documentation control and discuss their importance.

b. Explain the contribution of controlled documents and quality records to software quality assurance.

11.5 It has been said that documentation procedures are the main tool for implementing the objectives of documentation control.

a. Explain in your own words the issues addressed by these procedures.

b. Discuss how each of the procedural issues mentioned in (a) contributes to achieving the objectives of documentation control while indicating the associated objectives.

Topics for discussion

11.1 The five examples presented in the mini-case (Section 11.1) deal with documentation control failure in a software development company.

a. Examine each of the examples and determine the type of failure present – a controlled document failure or a quality record failure? Explain your answer.

b. For each of the above examples, describe the lapse in implementation of documentation control procedures that caused the failure.

11.2 Section 11.4 discusses the tasks (activities) to be performed in order to provide an updated controlled documents list, and the responsibilities of the appointed authority that carries out the tasks.

a. Explain the need for such an authority and why local solutions proposed by unit leaders, department managers, and so on are to be rejected.

b. Who do you think should be appointed as the authority? Refer to specific organizational positions and explain their suitability for the assignment.

11.3 Paper-based storage systems can be used alongside electronic systems to serve an organization's documentation control requirements.

• Compare the two storage technologies and list the advantages and disadvantages of each one when performing the various tasks required by the documentation control procedure.

Part III

Product Assurance Activities for Conformance

This part of the book is dedicated to the product software quality assurance activities of the SQA function, and includes six chapters:

- Chapter 12 deals with SQA activities aimed at evaluating the conformance of software products and related documentation to contract requirements and relevant regulations and conventions.

The following chapters describe methods applied to evaluate the conformance of documents and software products:

- Chapter 13 is dedicated to review methods applied for evaluating documents, reports, and performance records.
- Chapter 14 is dedicated to testing methods used to verify and validate software code files.
- Chapter 15 is dedicated to assuring software operation services quality conformance.
- Chapter 16 is dedicated to software product quality measurement techniques.
- The last chapter of this part of the book, Chapter 17, presents procedures and work instructions and their creation and usage.

Software Quality: Concepts and Practice, First Edition. Daniel Galin.
© 2018 the IEEE Computer Society, Inc. Published 2018 by John Wiley & Sons, Inc.

Chapter 12

Evaluation of Products for Conformance

12.1 Introduction

A substantial part of the SQA function's efforts is devoted to evaluating the products of the software processes. These are produced during the software development life cycle (SDLC), and include software and any relevant documentation. Software products include software packages/systems and software services, while the relevant documentation includes various development and operation reports, such as design reports, test reports, and periodical customer services reports.

The different types of software product evaluation activities are presented in Frame 12.1.

Frame 12.1: The types of software product evaluation activities

The types of software product evaluation activities
• Evaluation of project plans for their conformance with contract requirements, relevant regulations, and conventions. • Evaluation of project products, including life cycle support services, for their conformance with the contract, relevant regulations, and conventions. • Evaluation of project products for their acceptability by the customer. • Evaluation of project products by measurement.

Product requirement definition is presented in Frame 12.2.

Frame 12.2: Product requirement definition

Source: IEEE Std. 730-2014 (IEEE, 2014)

Process requirement definition
"Product requirements specify the functions the product is mandated to perform the attributes that the product is mandated to possess. These attributes include performance attributes that specify how well the product should perform. Product requirements, also called system requirements, can be allocated to software or nonsoftware aspects of the product. Product requirements are derived from and are response to stakeholder requirements."

The SQA function performs the evaluations using the documentation of SQA activities performed by the project team and the organization, and by participating in the project team quality activities, like reviews and software tests.

The next sections are dedicated to:

- The evaluation of project plans for conformance.
- The evaluation of project's software products for conformance.
- The evaluation of a project products for acceptability by the customer.
- The evaluation of project's operation phase products for conformance.
- The evaluation of a software product by measurements.

The methods employed for product evaluation are discussed in Chapter 13 (reviews) and Chapter 14 (software testing).

Chapter 15 is dedicated to assuring quality conformance of software operation services.

Chapter 16 is dedicated to product quality measurement techniques.

Chapter 17 presents procedures and work instructions and their creation and usage.

This chapter is based on IEEE Std. 730-2014.

12.2   The evaluation of project plans for conformance

The objective

The objective of the SQA function is to evaluate the project plans for conformance with the project contract. In other words, to verify that the contract requirements are fully covered in the plans. The evaluation should be concluded with a list of nonconformity findings to be corrected by the project team.

The evaluation process

The evaluation process to be performed by the SQA function includes the following:

1. Identify the required plans in the contract document.

2. Evaluate the plan items for conformance with contract requirements, and relevant regulations and conventions. The evaluation will yield lists of nonconformities:
   - Contract requirements not covered by the plans.
   - Contract requirements incorrectly defined in the plans.
   - Plan items not required by contract, relevant regulations, or conventions.

3. Evaluate the plans for consistency and list items that are not consistent.

4. Reevaluate the plans for conformance with contract requirements after the plans have been corrected.

12.3 The evaluation of project's software products for conformance

The objective

The objective of the SQA function is to evaluate the degree of conformance of a project's development products with the project contract and relevant regulations and conventions. The evaluation should be concluded with a list of nonconformities to be corrected by the project team.

The evaluation process

The evaluation process to be performed by the SQA function includes the following:

1. Identify project development products and related documentation, as listed in the project contract.

2. Evaluate the project's products, software and related documents for conformance with contract requirements and relevant regulations and conventions. Evaluation of the software shall be performed mainly by examining review reports and test results and participating in reviews and tests. The evaluation will yield lists of nonconformities:
   - Contract requirements not implemented in the software or related documentation.
   - Contract requirements incorrectly implemented in the software or related documentation.
   - Relevant regulations and conventions not implemented or implemented incorrectly in the software or related documentation.
   - Software applications included in the software products, but not a contract requirement.

3. Reevaluate the software and related documentation for conformance with contract requirements after the software and documentation have been corrected.

12.4   Evaluation of project products for acceptability by the customer

Success of the software product delivery stage, including the related documentation package, depends on the product quality achieved by the development team, in other words, on the degree the contract requirements and the acquirer documented expectations have been fulfilled. The role of the SQA function in product delivery preparations is of importance.

The objective

The objective of the SQA function is to evaluate the degree of confidence that the project's development or operation products fulfill the contract requirements and relevant regulations and conventions and are accepted by the acquirers. The evaluation is required to perform product quality measurement and list nonconformities to be corrected by the project team.

The evaluation process

The evaluation process to be performed by the SQA function includes the following:

1. Derive criteria for acceptance of the software product and the related documentation from the contract, project documentation, SQA reports, joint project committee minutes, and so on.

2. Evaluate the degree to which the project products, software and related documents successfully fulfill the acceptance criteria, and conform to contract requirements and relevant regulations and conventions. The evaluation of the software shall be performed mainly by reviews, audits, and testing. The evaluation will yield lists of criteria not fulfilled by the software or by the related documentation.

3. Reevaluate the software and related documentation for fulfillment of acceptance criteria after the software and documentation have been corrected.

12.5   The evaluation of project's operation phase products for conformance

The objective

The objective of the SQA function is to evaluate the degree of conformance of products from a project's operation phase with the project contract and relevant regulations and conventions. The evaluation should be concluded with a list of nonconformities to be corrected by the project team.

The evaluation process

The evaluation process to be performed by the SQA function includes the following:

1. Identify products from the project operation phase and related documentation, as listed in the project contract.
2. Evaluate the project's operation phase products and related documents for conformance with contract requirements and relevant regulations and conventions. Evaluation of the user support and maintenance services shall be performed mainly by examining software operation service performance reports and direct observation of services. The evaluation will yield lists of nonconformities:
   - Contract requirements for software operation services not implemented.
   - Contract requirements incorrectly implemented or not conforming to required levels of service.
   - Software operation services not conforming to relevant regulations and conventions.
   - Software operation services provided that were not included in the contract requirements.

For more about on assuring the quality conformance of software operation services, see Chapter 15.

12.6 The evaluation of software product by measurements

Quantitative criteria of software products provided by software product metrics are very important tool for evaluation. These metrics, in many cases, are part of standards and procedures: general, organizational, or specific procedures developed for a software projector and its services operation.

Product measurement is discussed in several software engineering standards, one of these is ISO/IEC (2001–2004) ISO/IEC Std. 9126-2001 Software engineering – Product quality – Parts 1–4 (ISO/IEC, 2001, 2002, 2003, 2004).

Objective

To develop and implement software product metrics for evaluating software product quality and the degree, they fulfill the requirements.

The required processes

Software product measurements to be performed by the SQA function include the following activities:

1. Defining a set of product metrics according to relevant general and project specific procedures, where each metric represents correctly a product

Table 12.1 Examples of product metrics

Metrics code	Metrics name	Calculation formula
PHWTET	Percentage of HD calls exceeding target waiting time	$PHWTET = \dfrac{NHYCET}{NHYC}$
HDE	HD efficiency	$HDE = \dfrac{HDYH}{NHYC}$
SFDL	Software system failure density per KLOC	$SFDL = \dfrac{NYF}{KLOC}$

HD, help desk (user support center); NHYCET, the number of calls per year exceeding HD target waiting time; NHYC, the number of HD calls during a year of service; HDYH, total annual working hours invested by the HD servicing the software system; NYF, the number of software failures detected during a year of maintenance service; KLOC, a thousand lines of code.

quality attribute: for example, the response time of the software program to a specific query.

2. Implementation of the metrics that may result in a list of gaps between the results of measurements and the expected quality result. In regard to our former example, measured average response time is 18 seconds, while expected quality result is 5 seconds.

3. Development of software or hardware improvements to close the gaps.

4. Reapply the measurements and determine the effectiveness of the improvements.

5. Activities 3 and 4 may be repeated till measurement results are satisfactory.

Examples of product metrics are presented in Table 12.1.

More about software metrics and specifically about product measurements for evaluation of software product conformance may be found in a chapter dedicated to the subject – Chapter 16.

Summary

1. The types of software product evaluation activities

The types are:

1. Evaluation of project plans for their conformance with the contract requirements, relevant regulations, and conventions.

2. Evaluation of project products including life cycle support services, for their conformance with the contract, relevant regulations, and conventions.

3. Evaluation of project products for their acceptability by the customer.

4. Evaluation of project products by measurement.

2. **The evaluation process of project's development and operation products for conformance**

The evaluation process to be performed by the SQA function includes the following:

1. Identify project development and operation products and the related documentation, as listed in the project contract.

2. Evaluate the project's products and related documents for conformance with contract requirements and relevant regulations and conventions. The evaluation will yield lists of nonconformities.

3. Reevaluate the software and related documentation for conformance with contract requirements after the software has been corrected.

3. **The process of software product evaluation by measurements**

Software product measurements to be performed by the SQA function include the following activities:

1. Defining a set of product metrics according to relevant general and project-specific procedures, where each metric represents correctly a product quality attribute.

2. Implementation of the metrics that result in a list of gaps between the results of measurements and the expected quality result. Development of software or hardware improvements to close the gaps.

3. Redo the measurements and determine the effectiveness of improvements.

4. Activities 3 and 4 may be repeated till measurement results are satisfactory.

Selected bibliography

IEEE (2014) *IEEE Std. 730-2014 Software Quality Assurance*, The IEEE Computer Society, IEEE, New York.

ISO/IEC (2001) *ISO/IEC Std. 9126-2001 Software Engineering – Product Quality – Part 1: Quality Model*, ISO, Geneva, Switzerland.

ISO/IEC (2002) *ISO/IEC Std. 9126-2003 Software Engineering – Product Quality – Part 2: External Metrics*, ISO, Geneva, Switzerland.

ISO/IEC (2003) *ISO/IEC Std. 9126-2003 Software Engineering – Product Quality – Part 3: Internal Metrics*, ISO, Geneva, Switzerland.

ISO/IEC (2004) *ISO/IEC Std. 9126-2004 Software Engineering – Product Quality – Part 4: Quality in Use Metrics*, ISO, Geneva, Switzerland.

Review Questions

12.1 Four types of evaluation of software project products conformance are listed in Frame 12.1.

a. Explain in your own words the purpose of each type of evaluation.

b. Explain the differences between the types of evaluations.

12.2 The evaluation of the conformance of project plans with the contract yields three lists of nonconformities (see Section 12.2).

    a. List in your own words the contents of each of the lists.

    b. Explain the importance of the third list.

12.3 The evaluation of project product conformance requires evaluating software products and the related documentation.

    a. Explain why evaluation of the software product alone (the product directly serving the user) is not sufficient?

    b. Provide at least two situations where missing documentation or documentation not evaluated could cause difficulties in the development process and in the maintenance of the software product.

12.4 Being quantitative, project product metrics are considered more important than qualitative criteria.

    a. Explain in your own words the special importance of product metrics.

    b. Suggest two metrics for a software package for POS (point of sale).

Topics for discussion

12.1 The IEEE Std. 70-2014 requires conformance evaluations for project plans and also for project products and related documentation.

    a. Some claim that the evaluation of project products and related documentation are sufficient – do you agree?

    b. List your arguments for your reply to (a).

12.2 An SQA practitioner claims that the evaluation of project products for their acceptability by the customer should be the only evaluation activity for conformance, as it assures that the project software product and related documentation are accepted by the customer to his full satisfaction.

    a. Do you agree with the practitioner?

    b. List your arguments for your reply to (a).

    c. Could you explain the special contribution of the first two evaluation types in Frame 12.1 to the software project.

12.3 "The evaluation of project products, including life cycle support services, for their conformance with the contract, relevant regulations and conventions, ensures that all contract requirements have been fulfilled and that acceptability by the customer is ensured. Thus, the evaluation of project products for their acceptability by the customer is redundant."

    a. Do you agree with the above quote?

    b. If you disagree, explain in your own words the necessity of the evaluation of project products for their acceptability by the customer.

12.4 Describe the cooperation that is required between the SQA function and the project team for performing the evaluation of project products, including life cycle support services, for their conformance with the contract, relevant regulations, and conventions.

Chapter 13

Reviews

13.1 Introduction

A common product of the software development process, especially in its analysis and design phases, is a document, in which progress of development work performed is recorded. The system analyst or designer who prepares the document reviews it repeatedly in order to detect any possible errors that might have been introduced. In addition, development team leaders are also expected to examine this document and its details to reveal any remaining errors before granting their approval. However, it is clear that as these professionals were involved in actually producing the document, they are unlikely to detect some of their own errors, irrespective of the extent and number of reviews they conduct. Therefore, only others – such as peers, superiors, experts, and customer representatives – who have different experience and points of view and are not directly involved in creating the document, are capable of detecting errors unnoticed by the development team. A review is probably the best method to detect existing errors that remained undetected in a software project document.

As defined by Frame 13.1, a review process is:

Frame 13.1: Review – a definition

Review – a definition
A process for evaluating a documented software project product in which a group of professionals and stakeholders raise comments regarding the contents of a document presented to them beforehand. The reviewers may have the authority to approve the contents of the document, and also to approve the project advancing to the next stage.

Design reviews and other reviews are organized by the project teams and the development departments.

Software Quality: Concepts and Practice, First Edition. Daniel Galin.
© 2018 the IEEE Computer Society, Inc. Published 2018 by John Wiley & Sons, Inc.

The role of the SQA function in reviews

The role of the SQA function is supportive and may include organizing reviews and improving their efficiency and effectiveness. SQA function team members may participate in reviews, as part of the SQA activities of evaluating software products conformance.

There are several objectives that motivate reviews. The review's direct objectives deal with the current project, whereas its indirect objectives are more general in nature, and deal with the contribution of the review to appropriately advance team members' professional development, and the improvement of the development methodologies applied by the organization.

The main review objectives are presented in Frame 13.2.

Frame 13.2: Review objectives

Review objectives
Direct objectives   • To detect analysis, design, and other document functional, logical, and implementation errors.   • To identify changes, deviations, and omissions with respect to the original specifications and approved changes.   • To locate those deviations from templates, style procedures, and conventions, which are expected to cause difficulties to development and maintenance teams.   • To identify new risks that are likely to affect completion of the project.   • In formal reviews – to approve the analysis, design, or other respective development stage of the product, and allow the team to progress to the next development phase.   *Indirect objectives*   • To provide an informal meeting place for the exchange of professional knowledge about development methods, tools, and techniques.   • To record analysis and design errors that will serve as a basis for future corrective actions to be implemented among other development teams. (For more about corrective actions, see Chapter 16).

The various review methods differ in the emphasis attributed to the different objectives. The "filtering out" of errors achieved in the different review techniques depends to a great extent on the optimization of the review procedure. An improved "filtering out" of errors is achieved by the selection of an appropriate review team member and a professional review team leader, who knows how to lead the review session efficiently and effectively.

As the documents are products of the project's initial phases, reviews acquire special importance in the SQA process, as they provide early detection and prevent passing analysis and design errors "downstream," to stages where error detection and correction are much more intricate, cumbersome, and therefore also costly.

Several methodologies can be implemented when reviewing documents. In this chapter, the following review methods will be discussed:

• Formal design reviews (Section 13.3)

• Peer reviews – inspections and walkthroughs (Section 13.4)

• Expert opinions (Section 13.5)

Reviews are not activities to be conducted haphazardly. Procedural order and teamwork lie at the heart of formal design reviews, inspections, and walkthroughs. Each participant is expected to focus on his or her area of responsibility or specialization when making comments. At each review session, the mutually agreed-upon remarks are recorded. The subsequent list of items should include full details of defect location and description, documented in a way that will later enable their full retrieval by the development team. In order to ensure fruitful review sessions, a coordinator is required to supervise the discussion and keep it on track.

In general, the knowledge that an analysis, design, or other development product will be reviewed stimulates the development team to do their best work. This represents a further contribution of reviews to the improved product quality.

The review activities are frequently termed "static software quality assurance techniques," and should be distinguished from "dynamic software quality assurance techniques," which relate to testing that involves running the software.

It should be noted that inspections and walkthroughs are also widely successfully used to detect defects in the coding phase, where the appropriate document reviewed is the code printout.

In general, the knowledge that an analysis, design, or other development product will be reviewed stimulates the development team to do their best work. This represents a further contribution of reviews to the improved product quality.

Before studying the various review methodologies, let us examine the mini case presented in Section 13.2.

13.2 The happy design review – an introductory mini case

John Harris, head of IT unit A, was feeling anxious. The DR of a major project was due to begin in less than an hour, and he knew that the project wasn't going that well, to say the least. The lack of success was due to serious team problems, including staff shortage, and the fact that the team leader had to be replaced right at the beginning of the design phase. On top of everything else, he was sure that failing this DR would affect his chances of promotion, and wondered whether his plan would work.

The DR team showed up on time, nine men and four women, head of the IT department, and several customer representatives, but most were senior employees from IT unit B. The project lead's presentation started on time, and colored slides one after another were shown. The presenter was very polite and answered all the audience questions. It was just after the presentation had being going on for 70 minutes, and more audience questions were being answered in length by the presenter, that John began to feel relieved. It was clear to him that most of the participants had not read the project design report, and it was at this moment that John applied the second stage of his plan – a rich coffee break with the best cakes and cookies in town. Everybody seemed happy with the break and the "goodies." The coffee break was now over, and the presentation was in full swing again. After another 45 minutes, the presenter completed his presentation – in sync with John's special sign.

John stood up, and called on the audience to present their comments. Hesitatingly, three participants raised some basic issues, which the team leader easily addressed in length. Another two questions raised dealt with administrative aspects of the project. Then, about three hours into the whole session, the IT department manager stood up, thanked the team leader for his presentation and detailed answers, and announced that due to other obligations, he would need to leave. The rest of the audience expressed their need to leave too, thanked John for his hospitality and 10 minutes later, all participants had left.

John was really happy. His plan had worked perfectly. No worthy comment was raised, and nobody uncovered any of the many deficiencies of the project. John's assumption that once the DR team grew, nobody would bother to read the design report as they would rely on others to read it, was correct. The other part of the plan, the lengthy presentation, was successful in that it left practically no time for comments and discussion.

To sum it up – John's plan was a success – the DR totally failed to produce any worthy comments from the audience. In other words, the DR was totally worthless as a review, but was a big success in regard to the personal interests of John Harris.

13.3 Formal design reviews (DRS)

Formal design reviews, also called "design reviews", "DRs," and "formal technical reviews" (FTR), differ from all other review methods as they are the only type of review that is a requisite for approving the development product. Without this approval, the development team cannot continue to the next phase of development. Formal design reviews may be conducted at any development milestone requiring completion of a document, whether the document is a requirement specification or an installation plan. A list of common formal design reviews is presented in Frame 13.3.

Frame 13.3: Some common formal design reviews

DPR	Development Plan Review
SRSR	Software Requirement Specification Review
PDR	Preliminary Design Review
DDR	Detailed Design Review
DBDR	Data Base Design Review
TPR	Test Plan Review
STPR	Software Test Procedure Review
VDR	Version Description Review
OMR	Operator Manual Review
SMR	Support Manual Review
TRR	Test Readiness Review
PRR	Product Release Review
IPR	Installation Plan Review

Our discussion of formal design reviews focus on:

- The DR participants
- The DR preparations
- The DR session
- The recommended post-DR activities

13.3.1 Participants in a DR

All DRs are conducted by a review leader and review team. The choice of appropriate participants is of special importance because of their authority to approve or disapprove the development product.

The review leader

As the appointment of an appropriate review leader is a major factor in the DR's success, candidates should possess certain characteristics:

- Knowledge and experience in the development of projects of the type reviewed.
- Preliminary acquaintance with the current project is not necessary.
- Seniority at a level similar to that of the project leader, if not higher.
- Existing good relationships with the project leader and his team.
- Of an independent position, external to the project team.

Thus, appropriate candidates for review team leadership include the development department manager, chief software engineer, a different project's leader, the software quality assurance unit head, in certain circumstances, and the customer's chief software engineer. Appointment of the review leader is expected to be performed by a person of higher seniority than the project leader.

Implementation tip

In some cases, the project leader is appointed as the FDR leader, the main justification for this decision being his/her superior knowledge of the project material. In most cases, this choice proves to be professionally undesirable. A project leader who serves as the review team leader tends, whether intentionally or not, to limit the scope of the review and avoid insightful and constructive criticism, and his review team members also tend to be chosen accordingly. Appointments of this type usually undermine the purpose for the review, and only delay confronting problems to a later time, making issues more sensitive, and more costly to correct.

Small development departments and small software houses typically have substantial difficulties finding an appropriate in-house candidate to lead the review team. One possible solution to this predicament is the appointment of an external consultant.

The review team

The entire review team should be selected from among the senior members of the project team, together with appropriate senior professionals assigned to other projects and departments, customer/user representatives, and in some cases software development consultants. It is desirable that nonproject staff make up the majority of the review team.

An important issue often neglected is the size of the review team. A review team of 3–5 members is expected to be an efficient team, given that the proper diversity of experience and approaches among the participants is assured. An excessively large team tends to create coordination problems, wastes review session time, and decreases the overall level of the review.

Implementation tip

Sometimes, due to circumstances, we may feel obligated to honor 8–10 seniors from the customer organization by appointing them to the review team. The greater difficulty to coordinate the review session seems to be the least of the problems in cases of a larger review team; the most negative result of an excessively large team tends to be the substantial decrease in the level of review preparation, namely, in not reading the document to be reviewed, and subsequently no comments or proposals for corrections are prepared.

Thus, creating an excessively large team, the larger the better, is a "wonderful" tool for the organizer of the DR to avoid a real review.

13.3.2   The DR preparations

DR infrastructure

- Develop checklists for typical reviewed documents, or at least for the most common ones.
- Train senior professionals to serve as review leaders and DR team members.
- Periodically analyze the effectiveness of past DRs in regard to defect detection to improve the DR methodology.

DR schedule

Schedule DRs as part of the project activity plan, and allocate the needed resources as an integral part of the software development organization's standard operating procedures.

The DR contents

In most cases, participants in a DR are required to review a document (the entire document). In cases of large volumes or complex documents, which no review session can effectively cover, the review leader may consider splitting the review material into two or more parts. In some cases, usually due to time pressure, it could be decided to review only part of a document, the more critical part or the part expected to be "richer" in defects. A decision regarding additional reviews may depend on the number and type of defects found in the document reviewed.

There are three main review participant groups – the review leader, the review team, and the development team – while each group is required to focus on distinct aspects of the preparations:

Review leader preparations

The main tasks of the review leader in the preparation stage are:

- To appoint team members
- To schedule review sessions
- To distribute the document to be reviewed among the team members (hard copy, electronic file, etc.)

It is of utmost importance that the review session be scheduled shortly after the design document has been distributed to the review team members. Timely sessions prevent an unreasonable length of time from elapsing before the project team can commence to the next development phase, and thus reduce the risk of going off schedule.

Review team preparations

Team members are expected to review the review document and list their comments prior to the review session. In cases where the documents are of a substantial size, the review leader may ease the load by assigning each team member with only parts in the documents.

An important tool for ensuring the review's completeness is the checklist. In addition to the general design review checklist, checklists dedicated to the more typical development documents are available, and can be constructed when necessary. Checklists contribute to the DR's effectiveness by reminding the reviewer of all the primary and secondary issues requiring attention. For a comprehensive discussion of checklists, see Chapter 24

Development team preparations

As the review session approaches, the team's main obligation is to prepare a short presentation of the design document. Assuming that the review team members have read the design document thoroughly and are now familiar with the project outlines, the presentation should focus on the main professional issues awaiting approval rather than (wasting time) on a general description of the project.

Implementation tip

One of the most common techniques used by project leaders to avoid professional criticism and undermine review effectiveness is the comprehensive presentation of the design document. This type of presentation "excels" in the abundant time it consumes. It exhausts the review team and leaves little time, if any, for discussion. All experienced review leaders know how to handle this phenomenon.

In cases when the project leader serves as the review leader, one can observe especially potent tactics aimed at stymieing an effective review: appointment of a large review team combined with a comprehensive and long presentation.

13.3.3   The DR session

The review leader's experience in leading discussions and sticking to the agenda is the key to a successful DR session. A typical DR session agenda includes:

a. A short presentation of the design document.

b. Comments made by members of the review team.

c. Verification and validation of each of the comments discussed to determine the required action items (corrections, changes and additions) that the project team has to perform. A team member assigned as a scribe is responsible to document each action item that relates to the required corrections, changes, and additions.

d. Decisions about the design product (document), which determine the project's progress. These decisions can take three different forms:

• *Full approval:* Enables immediate continuation to the next phase of the project. On occasion, full approval may be accompanied by requests for minor corrections to be performed by the project team.

• *Partial approval:* Approval of immediate continuation to the next phase for some parts of the project, with major action items (corrections, changes, and additions) required for the remainder of the project. Continuation to the next phase of these remaining parts will be permitted only after satisfactory completion of the action items. Approval may be given by a member of the review team assigned to review the completed action items, by the whole review team in a special review session, or by any other forum the review leader considers appropriate.

• *Denial of approval:* Requires repeating the DR. This decision is applied in cases of multiple major defects – particularly critical defects.

13.3.4   Postreview activities

Apart from the DR report, the DR team or a representative is required to follow up completion of the corrections and to examine the corrected sections.

The DR report. One of the review leader's responsibilities is to issue the DR report immediately after the review session. Early distribution of the DR report enables the development team to perform the corrections earlier and minimize delays to the project schedule.

The report's major sections contain:

• A summary of the review discussions.

• The decision regarding continuation of the project.

• A full list of required action items – corrections, changes, and additions that the project team has to perform. For each action item, the anticipated completion date and project team member responsible are listed.

• The name(s) of the review team member(s) assigned to follow up completion of corrections.

The form shown in Appendix 13.A presents the data items that need to be documented for an inclusive DR report.

The follow-up process. The person appointed to follow up the corrections, in many cases the review leader him/herself, is required to determine whether each action item has been satisfactorily accomplished as a condition for allowing the project to progress to the next phase. The follow-up should be fully documented to enable future clarification of the corrections, if and when necessary.

Implementation tip

Unfortunately, parts of, or even the entire DR report are often worthless, whether because of an inadequately prepared review team or because of the intentional evasion of a thorough review. It is fairly easy to identify such cases from the characteristics of the review report: general short inspection summary, lack of inspection discussion details, and few and minor action items.

Several authors listed guidelines for a successful DR, focusing on preparations for a DR, and the conducting of a DR session. Additional guidelines refer to the infrastructure needed to support a successful DR. Most of these guidelines also apply to inspection and walkthrough sessions. Frame 13.4 presents the guidelines for a successful DR session.

Frame 13.4: Guidelines for a successful DR session

The design review session guidelines

- Discuss professional issues in a constructive way, while refraining from personalizing them. This helps to keep the discussion free of unnecessary tension.

- Deal with stupid comments in the same way you treat other comments, and do not even hint about the value of these comments.

- Keep to the review agenda. Drifting from the planned agenda will only serve to take away from the effectiveness of the review.

- Focus on detection of defects by verifying and validating participant comments. Refrain from discussing possible solutions for the detected defects in order to save time and avoid digressing from the agenda.

- In cases of disagreement about the significance of an error, it is good practice to end the discussion and move the issue to another forum.

- Properly document the discussions, especially details of action items agreed upon by the DR team.

- The duration of a review session should not exceed 2 hours.

13.4 Peer reviews

Two peer review methods, inspections and walkthroughs, are discussed in this section. The major difference between formal design reviews and peer review methods is rooted in the level of authority of the participants. While most participants in DRs hold superior positions to the project leader, participants in peer reviews are, as expected, the project leader's equals, members of the leader's department and other units. The other major difference lies in the degree of authority and objective of each review method. Formal design reviews are authorized to approve the design document so that work on the next stage of the project may begin. This authority is not granted to the peer reviews, whose main objectives lie in detecting errors and deviations from standards.

The level of formality differentiates a walkthrough from an inspection. While the members of an inspection team are required to prepare for the inspection session, walkthrough participants are not requested to make any meaningful preparations. Another difference relates to the findings. While walkthroughs are limited to comments on the document reviewed, the findings of inspections are incorporated into the efforts invested to improve development methods through corrective action processes. Inspections, as opposed to walkthroughs, are therefore considered to be more significant contributors to the general level of SQA.

An inspection is usually based on a comprehensive infrastructure, including:

- Inspection checklists periodically updated and developed for each type of design document, coding language, and tools. A positive contribution of checklists to code inspection was found (Hatton, 2008).
- Typical defect frequency tables based on past findings to direct inspectors to potential "defect concentration areas."
- Training of competent professionals in inspection process issues. This process makes it possible for them to serve as inspection leaders (moderators) or inspection team members. The trained employees serve as a reservoir of professional inspectors available for future projects.
- Periodic analysis of the effectiveness of past inspections to improve the inspection methodology.

Design and code inspections are procedural models and were initially described and formulated by Fagan (1976, 1986). More about inspections can be found in Horta, (2014); Mishra and Mishra, (2009); Parnas and Lawford, (2003); Pressman and Maxim, (2015) and Sommerville, (2015). Regarding walkthroughs, Yourdon (1979) provides a thorough discussion of the related principles and processes.

The inspection and walkthrough processes described here are the more commonly employed versions of these methods. Organizations often modify these methods with adaptations that represent their "local culture." These adaptations are characterized by the development, SQA units, software products developed, team structure, composition, and the likes. It should be noted that in response to this variability, especially common in walkthrough procedures, differences between the two methods are easily blurred. Due to this state of affairs, some specialists view walkthroughs as a type of inspection, and vice versa.

Today, with the development of computerized design tools, including CASE tools, on the one hand, and the widely used COTS software packages and open source software, on the other hand, some professionals tend to diminish the value of manual reviews such as inspections and walkthroughs. Nevertheless, past software surveys as well as recent empirical research findings provide us with much convincing evidence that peer reviews are highly efficient and effective methods.

The debate over which method is preferred has yet to be resolved, with proponents of each arguing for the superiority of their favored approach. However, as far as the development of improved new versions of the method, research empirical, and theoretical studies goes, it seems that inspections are far ahead of walkthroughs.

In the last decade, many efforts were invested in the development of automatic code inspection methods, also called "automatic static analysis." It is the inspection checklists that lead to the development of algorithms for identifying errors in code. This subject is discussed in length in Chapter 24.

Our discussion of peer review methods will therefore focus on:

- Participants in peer reviews
- Requisite preparations for peer reviews
- The peer review session
- Postpeer review activities
- Peer review efficiency
- Peer review coverage

With minor adaptations, the principles and processes of design peer reviews are successfully applied to code peer reviews.

13.4.1 Participants of peer reviews

The optimal peer review team is composed of three to five participants. In certain cases, the addition of one to three participants is acceptable. All participants should be peers of the software system designer author. A major factor contributing to the success of a peer review is the group's "blend" (which is a differentiating factor between inspections and walkthroughs).

A recommended peer review team includes:

- A review leader
- The author
- Specialized professionals

Inspection participants

The review leader (moderator)   Candidates for this position must:

- Be well-versed in the development of projects of the current type, and familiar with its technologies. Preliminary acquaintance with the current project is not necessary.
- Maintain good relationships with the author and the development team.

- Come from outside the project team.
- Display proven experience in coordination and leadership of professional meetings.
- Having undergone training as a moderator is also required – for inspections.

The author   The author is, with no exception, a participant in each type of peer review.

Specialized professionals   The recommended professionals are:

- *A designer:* The system analyst responsible for analysis and design of the software system reviewed.
- *A coder or implementer:* A professional, who is thoroughly acquainted with coding tasks, preferably the leader of the designated coding team. This inspector is expected to contribute his/her expertise to the detection of defects that could lead to coding errors and subsequent software implementation difficulties.
- *A tester:* This experienced professional, preferably the leader of the assigned testing team, focuses on identification of design errors usually detected during the testing phase.

Walkthrough participants

The review leader (coordinator)   Candidates for the coordinator position should have traits similar to those of the inspection moderator.

The author   The author is, with no exception, a participant. In many cases he serves as the coordinator.

Specialized professionals   The recommended professionals are:

- *A standards enforcer:* This team member, who specializes in development standards and procedures, is assigned the task of locating deviations from the standards and procedures. Errors of this type substantially affect the team's long-term effectiveness; primarily, as they cause extra difficulties for new members joining the development team, and will later reduce the effectiveness of the team responsible to maintain the system.
- *A maintenance expert:* The maintenance expert is called upon to focus on maintainability, flexibility, and testability issues (see Chapter 2), and to detect design defects capable of impeding the correction of bugs or the performance of future changes. Another area requiring his/her expertise is documentation, whose completeness and correctness are vital for any maintenance activity.
- *A user representative:* Participation of an internal (when the customer belongs to the same firm) or external user representative in the

walkthrough team contributes to the review's validity, as he/she examines the software system from the point of view of the user/consumer, rather than the designer/supplier. In cases where a "real" user is not available, as is the case in the development of a COTS software package, a team member may take on this role, and focus on validity issues by comparing the original requirements with the actual design.

13.4.2 Preparations for a peer review session

The review leader and team members are to assiduously complete their preparation, while the type of review determines the scope.

Peer review leader's preparations for the review session

The main tasks of the review leader, inspection moderator, and walkthrough coordinator are similar and are as follows:

- To determine, together with the author, which sections of the design document are to be reviewed. Such sections may include:
  - The most difficult and complex sections.
  - The most critical sections, where any defect can cause severe damage to the program application, and thus to the user.
  - The sections prone to defects.
- To select the team members.
- To schedule the peer review sessions. It is advisable to limit a review session to 2 hours; therefore, several review sessions should be scheduled (up to two sessions a day) when the review task is sizable. It is important to schedule the sessions shortly after the pertinent design document sections are ready for inspection. Moreover, for the process to unfold smoothly, the inspection's review leader should schedule an overview meeting for his team.
- To distribute the document to the team members prior to the review session.

Peer review team's preparations for the review session

The preparations required of an inspection team member are quite thorough, while those required of a walkthrough team member are more concise.

Inspection team preparations

Inspection team members are expected to read the document sections to be reviewed, and list their comments before the inspection session begins. The purpose of this advance preparation is to guarantee the session's effectiveness. Team members will also be asked to participate in an overview meeting. At this meeting, the author provides the inspection team members with the necessary relevant background for reviewing the selected document sections: the project in general, the logic, processes, outputs, inputs, and interfaces. In cases where the participants are already well acquainted with the material, an overview meeting may be waived.

An important tool supporting the inspector's review is a checklist. In well-established development departments, one can find specialized checklists dedicated to the more common types of development documents (see Chapter 24).

Walkthrough team preparations

Prior to the walkthrough session, team members briefly read the material in order to obtain a general overview of the sections to be reviewed, and the project and its environment. Participants lacking preliminary knowledge of the project and its substantive area will need far more preparation time. In most organizations employing walkthroughs, team participants are not required to prepare their comments in advance.

13.4.3   The peer review session

Team session assignments

Conducting a review session naturally requires assignment of specific tasks to the team members. Two of these task assignments are for the presenter of the document, and the scribe, who documents the discussions.

- *The presenter:* During inspection sessions, the presenter of the document is chosen by the moderator; usually, the presenter is not the document author. In many cases, the software coder serves as the presenter because he/she is the team member likely to best understand the design logic and its implications for coding. Some experts claim that an author's assignment as presenter may affect team members' judgment; and they therefore argue that the choice of a "neutral" presenter is preferred.

    For most walkthrough sessions, it is the author, the professional most acquainted with the document, who is chosen to present the document to the team.

- *The scribe:* The team leader will often – but not always – serve as the scribe for the session, and record the noted defects to be corrected by the development team. This task is more than procedural; it requires thorough professional understanding of the issues discussed.

The review session

A typical peer review session takes the following form:

After the presenter's short overview of the document and the parts to be read, he/she reads a section of the document and adds, if needed, a brief

Table 13.1   Classification of design errors by severity

Severity level	Description
5 – Critical	**1.** Prevents performance of essential capabilities of health, airborne, and military equipment
	2. Jeopardizes safety, security of critical activities
4	**1.** Adversely affects the performance of equipment, when no alternative way to overcome the situation is known
	2. Adversely affects the performance of scheduling, monitoring, and managing activities in a way that risks and harms the organization, when no alternative way to overcome the situation is known
3	**1.** Adversely affects the performance of equipment, when an alternative way to overcome the situation is known
	2. Adversely affects the performance of scheduling, monitoring, and managing activities in a way that risks and harms the organization, when an alternative way to overcome the situation is known
2	**1.** Causes difficulties or inconvenience to equipment operators in applying the equipment but does not affect the performance of its essential capabilities
	2. Causes difficulties or inconvenience to software system users in applying the software but does not affect the performance of its essential software capabilities
1 – Minor	**1.** All other minor effects to software or firmware

explanation of the issues involved in his/her own words. As the session progresses, the participants either deliver their comments to the document, or address their reactions to comments from other participants. The discussion should be confined to the identification of errors, which means that it should not deal with tentative solutions. During the inspection session, a substantial part of the comments are preprepared, ready before reading begins. Concerning the length of the inspection and walkthrough sessions, the same rules apply as to DRs: sessions should not exceed 2 hours, or be scheduled more than twice daily.

During the session, the scribe should document each noted defect by location in the document and description, type and character (incorrect, missing, or unnecessary parts). The inspection session scribe will add the estimated severity level of each defect, a factor to be used in the statistical analysis of defects found, and formulation of preventive and corrective actions. A typical five-scale severity classification of design errors is presented in Table 13.1.

Session documentation

The documentation produced at the end of an inspection session is much more comprehensive than that of a walkthrough session. Two documents are to be produced and distributed among the session participants following an inspection session.

Inspection session documentation

Two documents are to be produced following an inspection session and subsequently distributed among the session participants:

a. Inspection session findings report. This report is produced by the scribe, and should be completed and distributed immediately following the session's closing. Its main purpose is to ensure the full documentation of identified errors for correction and follow-up. An example of such a report is provided in Appendix 13.B.

b. Inspection session summary report. This report is to be compiled by the inspection leader shortly following the session or series of sessions dealing with the same document. A typical report of this type summarizes the inspection findings and resources invested in the inspection; it presents basic quality and efficiency metrics. The report serves mainly as input for analysis aimed at inspection process improvement, and corrective actions that go beyond the specific document or project. An example of an inspection session summary report appears in Appendix 13.C.

At the end of a session or series of walkthrough sessions, copies of the defects documentation – the "walkthrough session findings report" – should be handed to the development team and the session participants.

13.4.4 Postpeer review activities

A fundamental element differentiating between the two peer review methods discussed here is the postpeer review.

The inspection process, contrary to the walkthrough, does not end with a review session or the distribution of reports. Postinspection activities are conducted to attest to:

- The prompt, effective correction and reworking of all errors by the designer/author and his team, as approved by the inspection leader (or another team member) in the course of the assigned follow-up activities.

- Transmission of the inspection reports to the internal Corrective Action Board (CAB) for analysis. This action initiates the corrective and preventive actions that will reduce future defects and improve productivity (see Chapter 19).

A comparison participants and process elements of the peer review methods is presented in Figure 13.1.

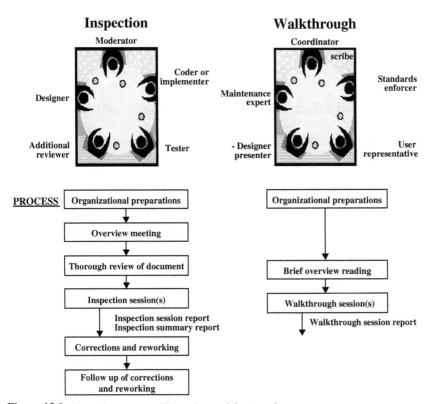

Figure 13.1 Inspection versus walkthrough – participants and processes

13.4.5 Versions of the inspection process

Several proposals for changes in the original pattern of inspection developed by Fagan have been presented during the past decades. One of these proposals suggests a pair inspection, justified by improved individual productivity. Another proposal suggests "active inspection" by directing the team to focus on a series of parts of the document and inspect each of them, instead of inspecting the entire document line by line. In an additional proposed method, the "N-fold inspection method," several independent teams are to inspect the same document. This method is expected to increase the percentage of detected errors. Experiment results show 35% defect detection for a single team, compared to a quite disappointing 78% detection for nine inspection teams.

Still, another process proposal, the "phased inspection," is based on a series of single inspections, each dedicated to a specific aspect of the document. A team session follows the individual inspections, in which the individual findings are presented and discussed to create the final inspection report. Another process-oriented proposal suggests eliminating the team meeting or replacing it with a limited meeting with only two or three team members. According to this proposal, the inspection is individual and the team meeting replaced with correspondence. The proposal is justified by research results that found that only 10 percent of defects are detected during team meetings. A comprehensive survey of software inspection developments is presented by Aurum et al. (2002).

13.4.6   The effectiveness and efficiency of peer reviews

Peer reviews, especially inspections, are widely used. Inspections are also part of the integrated product development process of CMMI. But, how many software developers use peer reviews, particularly software inspections? Very few survey results are available. In a 2002 survey of European software professionals (Ciolkowski et al., 2003), it was found that 40% of the respondents regularly implement inspections for requirement and design documents and for 30% of the code reviews.

The issue of defect detection effectiveness and the efficiency of apt peer review methods, in comparison to other SQA defect detection methods, is constantly being debated. Some of the more common metrics applied to estimate the effectiveness and efficiency of peer reviews suggested in the literature are:

- Peer review effectiveness (the defects detected by peer reviews as a percentage of total defects detected by the developer).
- Peer review detection efficiency (average number of hours invested per defect detected).
- Peer review defect detection density (average number of defects detected per page of the design document/per KLOC).

The literature provides rather meager findings regarding inspection effectiveness and efficiency. Fagan (Fagan, 1986) reported defect removal effectiveness as over 60%. Other publications report higher effectiveness of code inspection: IBM – 83%, AT&T – 92% (O'Neill, 2008). In this regard, one should mention the Cleanroom software development methodology that relies entirely on inspection processes for defect removal. This incremental delivery methodology applies an advanced inspection process and reaches almost 100% effectiveness through inspections.

The effectiveness and efficiency performance of six inspection projects are presented by Nair et al. (2011). The reported effectiveness results are substantially lower than those of Fagan and other authors already mentioned. The wide range of effectiveness results might be explained (partly) by the reported large differences in team size and experience, and project size. The effectiveness and efficiency results are shown in Table 13.2.

Earlier results are presented by Dobbins (1998), who quotes Madachy's findings from an analysis of the design and code inspections conducted on the Litton project, which summarize a large number of inspections. Madachy's findings regarding the efficiency metric already cited are presented in Table 13.3.

Table 13.2 The effectiveness and efficiency results according to Nair et al. 2011

Type of documents	Inspection effectiveness			Inspection efficiency		
	Average effectiveness (%)	Maximal effectiveness (%)	Minimal effectiveness (%)	Average efficiency (worked hours/defect)	Maximal efficiency (worked hours/defect)	Minimal efficiency (worked hours/defect)
Requirement analysis	**43**	50	29	**1.38**	0.32	2.80
Design	**46**	52	40	**3.64**	0.64	8.18
Code inspection	**45**	56	21	**4.76**	3.14	7.86

Table 13.3 The Litton project's inspection efficiency

The type of document	No. of inspections	Total number of defects	No. of major defects	Inspection resources invested (work-hours)	Inspection detection efficiency (work-hour/ defect)	Inspection detection efficiency (work-hour/ major defect)
					Inspection efficiency metrics	
Design inspections						
Requirements description	21	1243	89	328	0.26	3.69
Requirements analysis	32	2165	117	769	0.36	6.57
High-level design	41	2398	197	1097	0.46	5.57
Test procedures	18	1495	121	457	0.31	3.78
Code inspections						
Code review (276422 LOC)	150	7165	772	4612	0.64	5.97

In his paper, Dobbins also quotes Don O'Neill's National Software Quality Experiment, conducted in 1992 in 27 inspection labs in the United States. A total of 90,925 source code lines were code inspected in this experiment. The experiment's results for the inspections conducted:

- Total number of defects detected -   1849
- Number of major defects detected -   242
- Total inspection time (hours) -   380

Dobbins (1998) enables us to present comparable results for the National Software Quality Experiment and the Litton project: (1) Code inspection defect detection efficiency (work-hours defect) and (2) Code inspection defect detection density (number of defects detected per KLOC of software code).

Code inspection defect detection efficiency

	The National Quality Experiment	The Litton project
Defect detection efficiency (work-hours/defect)	0.2	0.66
Major defect detection efficiency (work-hours/major defect)	1.57	5.97

Code inspection defect detection density

	The National Quality Experiment	The Litton project
Total defect detection density (defects per KLOC[a])	20.3	25.9
Major defects detection density (defects per KLOC[a])	2.66	2.80

[a] KLOC = 1000 lines of code

The empirical results shown here present a wide range of results, some are practically incomparable. A possible partial explanation may be the variety of team sizes and project sizes and characteristics.

13.4.7 Peer review coverage

In a substantial number of organizations, which do not rely heavily or entirely on peer reviews, only a small percentage of documents and total volume of code ever undergo peer review. Coverage of about 10–20% of document pages still represents a significant contribution to the total defect detection, as the factor that determines the contribution of peer reviews to the total quality is not the percentage of pages covered, but the actual selection of those pages. More importantly, with the increased usage of reused software, the number of document pages and code lines demanding inspection is obviously declining.

Frame 13.5 lists those document sections that are recommended for inclusion in a peer review, as well as those that may be readily omitted.

Frame 13.5: Sections recommended to be included in, or omitted from, peer reviews

Sections recommended for inclusion	Sections recommended for omission
1. Sections of complicated logic	1. "Straightforward" sections (without complicated logic)
2. Critical sections, where defects can severely damage essential system capabilities	2. Sections of a type already reviewed several times by the team in similar past projects
3. Sections dealing with new environments	3. Sections that, if faulty, are not expected to affect functionality
4. Sections designed by new or inexperienced team members.	4. Reused design and code
	5. Repeated parts of the design and code

13.4.8 A comparison of review methods

For practitioners and analysts alike, a comparison of the three review methods discussed in this chapter may prove interesting. Table 13.4 presents this comparison.

13.5 Expert opinions

The last review method we will discuss is the use of expert opinions. Expert opinions, prepared by outside experts, support quality evaluation by introducing additional capabilities to the internal review staff, and thus reinforcing the organization's internal quality assurance activities. Outside experts transmit their expertise either by:

- Preparing an expert judgment about a document or a code section, or by
- Participating as a member of an internal design review, inspection, or walkthrough team.

An outside expert's judgment, as well as his participation as an external member of a review team, is most beneficial in the following situations:

- Insufficient in-house professional capabilities in a specialized area.
- Temporary lack of in-house professionals for review team participation due to intense workload pressures during periods when delaying could cause substantial delays in the project completion schedule.

Table 13.4 Comparison of the review methodologies

Properties	Formal design reviews	Inspections	Walkthroughs
Main direct objectives	1. Detect errors 2. Identify deviations from standards 3. Identify new risks 4. Approve the design document	1. Detect errors 2. Identify deviations from standards	Detect errors
Main indirect objectives	Knowledge exchange	1. Knowledge exchange 2. Support corrective actions	Knowledge exchange
Review leader	Chief software engineer or senior staff member	Trained moderator (peer)	Coordinator (peer, the project leader on occasion)
Participants	Top-level staff and customer representatives	Peers	Peers
Project leader participation	Yes	Yes	Yes; usually as the review's initiator
Specialized professionals in the team	—	1. Designer 2. Coder or implementer 3. Tester	1. Standards enforcer 2. Maintenance expert 3. User representative
Process of review			
1. Overview meeting	No	Yes	No
2. Participant preparations	Yes – thorough	Yes – thorough	Yes – brief
3. Review session	Yes	Yes	Yes
4. Follow-up of corrections	Yes	Yes	No

(continued)

245

Table 13.4 (*Continued*)

Properties	Formal design reviews	Inspections	Walkthroughs
Infrastructure			
1. Formal training of participants	No	Yes	No
2. Use of checklists	No	Yes	No
Error-related data collection	Not formally required	Formally required	Not formally required
Review documentation	Formal design review report	1. Inspection session findings report	Walkthrough session findings report
		2. Inspection session summary report	

- Indecisiveness caused by major disagreements among the organization's senior professionals.
- In small organizations, where the number of suitable candidates for a review team is insufficient.

Summary

1. **Direct and indirect objectives of the review methodologies**

   The direct objectives are:
   - To detect analysis and design errors.
   - To identify new risks expected to affect the completion of the project.
   - To locate deviations from software development instructions and procedures.
   - To identify deviations from templates and style procedures.
   - In formal reviews – to approve the analysis or design product, allowing the team to continue to the next development phase.

   The indirect objectives are:
   - To serve as an informal meeting place for the exchange of knowledge about software development.
   - To promote and support corrective action activities.
   - To identify deviations from standards, procedures, and work instructions.

2. **The contribution of outside experts to the performance of review tasks**

   An outside expert can support quality assessment efforts by evaluating a document or a code section, or by participating in an internal review team.

   Turning to outside experts is useful in situations when: in-house capabilities are insufficient in specialized areas, an insufficient number of available in-house suitable candidates are available, and so on.

3. **Comparison of objectives and participants of the three review methods**

   Three review methods were discussed: formal DRs, inspections, and walkthroughs. The direct objective common to all these methods is error detection. Other objectives, specific to formal design reviews, are the identification of new risks and the approval of design documents. The specific objective for inspections – identification of deviation from standards and support of corrective actions. The indirect objective shared by all review methods is the exchange of professional knowledge between participants.

   The project leader participates in the review teams of every method. However, while the other participants in the DR are superior, either professionally or administratively to the team leader and customer representatives, participants in the other review methods are all peers. Another major difference between the DR and the peer review methods is the inclusion of specialized professionals in the team: designers, coders or implementers, and testers in inspections; standards enforcers, maintenance experts, and user representatives in walkthroughs.

Selected bibliography

Aurum A., Petersson H., and Wohlin C. (2002) *State-of-the-art software inspections after 25 years, Software Testing, Verification and Reliability*, Vol. **12**, No. 3, pp. 133–154.

Ciolkowski M., Laitenberger O., and Biffi S. (2003) *Software reviews, the state of the practice, IEEE Software*, Vol. **20**, No. 6, pp. 46–51.

Dobbins J. H. (1998) Inspections as an up-front quality technique in Schulmeyer G. G. and McManus J. I., *Handbook of Software Engineering*, Prentice Hall PTR, Upper Saddle River, NJ, Vol. **3**, pp. 217–253.

Fagan M. E. (1976) *Design and code inspections to reduce errors in program development, IBM Syst. J.* Vol. **15**, No. 3, pp. 182–211.

Fagan M. E. (1986) *Advances in software inspections, IEEE Trans. Softw. Eng.*, Vol. **SE-12**, No. 7, pp. 744–751.

Hatton L. (2008) *Testing the value of checklists in code inspection, IEEE Software*, Vol. **25**, No. 4, pp. 82–88.

Horta H. (2014) Software defects: stay away from them. do inspections! *Proceedings of the 2014 9th International Conference on Quality of Information and Communications Technology (QUATIC)*, Guimaraes, Portugal, Sep. 2014, pp. 1–7.

Mishra D. and Mishra A. (2009) *Simplified software inspection process in compliance with international standards, Comput. Stand. Interfaces*, Vol. **31**, No. 4, pp. 763–771.

Nair T. R. G., Suma V., and Nair N. G. (2011) *Estimation of the characteristics of a software team for implementing an effective inspection process through inspection performance metric, Softw. Qual. Prof.*, Vol. **13**, No. 2, pp. 14–24.

O'Neill D. (2008) Inspections as an up-front quality technique in Schulmeyer G. G. (Ed.) *Handbook of software quality assurance*, 4th Edition, Artech House, Norwood, MA.

Parnas D. L. and Lawford M. (2003) *Inspection's role in software quality assurance, IEEE Softw.* Vol. **20**, No. 4, pp. 16–20.

Pressman R. J. and Maxim B. R. (2015) *Software Engineering – A Practitioner's Approach*, 8th Edition, McGraw-Hill International, London.

Sommerville I. (2015) *Software Engineering*, 10th Edition, Addison Wesley, Harlow, England.

Yourdon E. (1979) *Structured Walkthrough*, 2nd Edition, Prentice Hall International, London.

Review questions

13.1 There are five direct objectives and two indirect objectives attributed to the various review methods.

a. List the direct and indirect objectives of each review method.

b. For each objective, indicate the review technique or techniques that contribute(s) the most to achieve that objective.

13.2 One of the objectives of reviews is to identify deviations from templates and style procedures, and conventions.

- Explain the importance of enforcing templates and keeping to style procedures and conventions.

13.3 Some people claim that one of the justifications for a small design review team is the need to schedule the review session within a few days after the design product has been distributed to the team members.

   a. List additional reasons for preferring small DR teams, apart from the anticipated delays in convening a DR session composed of large teams.

   b. What reasons motivate attempts to schedule the review session as soon after distribution of the design reports to the team members as possible?

13.4 One can expect that in many cases, participants in an inspection session are able to suggest solutions for a detected defect, or at least point out possible directions for its solution. While it is clear that these suggestions are crucial for the development team, it is commonly recommended to avoid any discussion about solutions during the inspection session.

   a. List your arguments in favor of this recommendation.

   b. What other characteristics in the nature of cooperation between the moderator and the review team would you prefer to observe in a session?

13.5 It is quite natural to expect participation of the document's author (the designer) in a review of any type.

   a. What are the arguments in favor of his/her participation?

   b. What are the differences in the role played and existing status of the author in each of the review methods discussed?

13.6 The preparations made by the members of inspection teams are considered to be of greater depth and thoroughness when compared with the preparations for walkthroughs.

   a. What activities are included in such high levels of preparation?

   b. Do you think that inspection teams with 15 members can achieve similarly high levels of preparation?

13.7 Seven guidelines for successful design review are presented in Frame 13.4.

   a. It is often claimed that the seven guidelines dealing with the design review session are as applicable to inspections as they are to walkthrough sessions. Can you list these common golden guidelines and explain the reasons for their broad applicability?

   b. List situations where it is difficult for the moderator to keep up with the session's agenda.

c. The DR session has already lasted for 2 hours but a substantial part of the agenda has still not been discussed. Suggest reasons why a DR session should not be prolonged for over 2 hours.

Topics for discussion

13.1 A proposal for changing an inspection procedure involves adding a new reporting requirement as follows:

"At the end of the session or series of sessions, the inspection leader will submit a copy of the inspection session finding's report and a copy of the inspection session summary report to management."

a. Consider the proposal and list possible arguments for and against the change.

b. What would be your recommendation – to add the new reporting requirement or not? Explain your reasoning.

13.2 David Martin just finished his inspection coordinator course. After obtaining his first appointment, he plans to add his personal secretary to the inspection team for the purpose of serving as session scribe and producing the required reports. He assumes that her participation will free him of the coordination tasks and enable him to conduct the session successfully.

- Is it advisable to employ a secretary (a noninformation technology professional) as a scribe in an inspection session? List the pros and cons of adding such a nonprofessional to the inspection session..

13.3 Table 13.2 presents the results of Nair et al. for inspection efficiency. These results are characterized by their wide range, where the maximal design inspection efficiency is more than 12-fold the minimal efficiency. The author finds that team size and experience and project size are factors explaining the variety in results.

a. Could you suggest additional factors that may affect the inspection efficiency?

b. Could you rank the affecting factors, those you have suggested and those mentioned by the author, according to their impact on inspection efficiency?

13.4 Compare the various review techniques.

a. In which aspects are design reviews more formal than inspections?

b. In which aspects are inspections more formal than walkthroughs?

13.5 The chapter offers three different methodologies for the team review of design documents.

a. Which of the methodologies should a software development organization choose?

b. Can more than one method be chosen and applied for the same document? Alternatively, is it recommended to apply all three methods? List your arguments.

13.6 Despite the widely accepted importance and contribution of DRs to software project quality, there are situations where the development project leader or seniors in the developing organization are not interested in the affectivity of a DR.

  a. List situations where the organizers of a DR are not interested in its effectiveness.

  b. If you were chosen to participate in a review team, and not notified about the negative intentions of the organizers – how could you identify these intentions of the organizers?

Appendix 13.A: DR report form

DESIGN REVIEW REPORT

DR date: _____The report was prepared by: _____

Project name: _____

The reviewed document: _____Version:_____

The review team: _____

1. Summary of the discussions

#	Discussion subject	*Number* of action items

2. The action items

#	Action items to be performed	Responsible employee	Completion date	Approval of completion	
				Date	Signature

3. Decision regarding the design product

Full approval ☐
Partial approval ☐
Approval granted for continuation to next phase of following parts: ☐
Denial of approval
Comments:

The report was approved by:

Name of participant	Date	Signature	Name of participant	Date	Signature

Approval of successful completion of all action items
Comments:

Name: Signature: Date:

Appendix 13.B: Inspection session findings report form

INSPECTION SESSION FINDINGS REPORT

Session dates: _____ The report was prepared by: _____

Project name: _____

The inspected document: _____ Version: _____

The inspected document sections: _____

The inspection team: _____

_____

1. The error list

#	type	Error nature (W/M/E)	Error description	Error location	Error severity

2. Follow-up decisions

a	Follow up will be carried out by:
b	Re-inspection is recommended: Yes / No
c	

3 Comments

Prepared By:
Name: Signature: Date:

Appendix 13.C: Inspection session summary report

Goldenbug Ltd.

INSPECTION SESSION SUMMARY REPORT

Session date: ___17/5___

Project name: ___Oak Center___

The inspected document: ___Detailed Design___   Version: 3

The inspected document sections: _Ch. 5, Sec. 6.2 – 6.5___ Total:(A) _31 pages___ pages/k text lines

The inspection team: _Anita McMahon (inspection leader), John Woo, Ben Kinker___

---

1. Resources invested (hours *worked*)

#	Team member	Overview meeting	Preparation	Inspection session	Total (hours)	Comments
1	Inspection leader Anita	1	3	2.5	6.5	including report preparation
2	John	1	4	2	7	
3	Ben	1	4	2	7	
4						
5						
	Total	3	11	6.5	(B) 20.5	

2. Error summary   * W=Wrong. M-|Missing, E=Extra

Error severity	Error nature			Total Errors	Severity factor	Total errors (standardized)	Comments
	W	M	E*				
1 - critical	1			1	16	16	
2			2	2	8	16	
3	3			3	4	12	
4		2		2	2	4	
5 - minor	4	1	2	7	1	7	
Total	**8**	**3**	**4**	(C) 15		(D) 53	

3. Defect detection metrics

$$\text{Average defects per page} = C/A = \frac{15}{31} = 0.48$$

$$\text{Average defects per page (standardized)} = D/A = \frac{53}{31} = 1.71$$

$$\text{Defect detection efficiency (hours per defect)} = B/C = \frac{20.5}{15} = 1.37$$

$$\text{Standardized defect detection efficiency (hours per standardized defect)} = B/D = \frac{20.5}{53} = 0.39$$

Prepared by: ___Anita McMahon___ Signature: __Anita McMahon_ Date: 8/5_____

Chapter 14

Software Testing

14.1 Introduction

Software testing (or "testing") was the first software quality tool applied as "acceptance testing" to control the software product's quality before its delivery to, or installation at, the customer premises. At first, testing was confined to the final stage of development, after the entire software product had been completed. Later, as the importance of early detection of software defects penetrated as software quality assurance concepts, software development professionals were encouraged to extend testing to the partial in-process products of coding, which led to software module (unit) testing and integration testing. Common to all testing activities is their application through the running of code.

Some authors tend to broaden the scope of testing even further, and consider all quality assurance activities in the software life cycle as types of testing activities. In other words, these authors term all quality activities "tests" whether performed by running the software code or by examining documents.

In this book, we limit the scope of testing to those quality assurance activities performed by running the code. Quality activities performed by examining documents are termed "reviews."

The definition of software testing applied in this book focuses on the operative characteristics of testing as presented in the definition in Frame 14.1.

Frame 14.1: Software testing – definition

Source: IEEE Std. 829-2008 (IEEE, 2008)

Software testing – definition
An activity in which a **system or component** is **executed under specified conditions**, the results are observed or recorded and evaluation is made of some aspect of the system or component.

Software Quality: Concepts and Practice, First Edition. Daniel Galin.
© 2018 the IEEE Computer Society, Inc. Published 2018 by John Wiley & Sons, Inc.

The words and phrases stressed in the definition allow us to explain the key characteristics of software testing:

System or component – Testing may be performed on the entire software system (system test or acceptance test), on a component or module (unit test) or on the integration of several components (integration test).

Executed – Performed by running software on computer.

Under specified conditions – The tests will be performed applying approved test procedures, using test cases prepared and reviewed time in advance.

Software testing organization and performance

Software testing – unit testing, integration testing, and system acceptance testing – is organized and carried out by the development teams and the development departments. In some organizations, the acceptance testing is performed by specialized testing teams or by outsourced testing organizations.

The role of the SQA function in software testing

The role of the SQA function is supportive of the software acceptance testing organization (consulting basis), and is aimed at improving its efficiency and effectiveness. SQA function team members may participate in software acceptance testing, as part of the SQA activities to evaluate software products conformance.

Now that software testing has been defined, we can turn to a discussion of the objectives of software testing. These objectives are shown in Frame 14.2.

Frame 14.2: Software testing objectives

Software testing objectives
Direct objectives
• To identify and reveal as many errors as possible in the tested software.
• To bring the tested software to an acceptable level of quality, after correction of the identified errors and retesting.
• To perform the required tests efficiently and effectively, and within the budgetary and scheduling limitations.
• To establish with a degree of confidence that the software package is ready for delivery (or installment at customer premises).
Indirect objectives
To compile a record of software errors for use in software process improvement (by corrective and preventive actions – CAPA processes) and for managerial purposes.

It should be noted that the objective "to establish with a degree of confidence that the software package is ready for delivery" inherently contradicts the first direct objective mentioned, and may influence, or stated more accurately, bias the choice of tests and/or test cases or test results appraisal. Myers (1979), in his classic book, summarized the issue nicely: "If your goal is to show the absence of errors, you won't discover many. If your goal is to show the presence of errors, you will discover a large percentage of them."

The wording of the second objective reflects the fact that bug-free software is still a utopian aspiration. Therefore, we prefer the phrase "acceptable level of quality," meaning that a certain percentage of bugs tolerable to users will remain unidentified upon installation of the software. This percentage obviously varies according to the software package and developer.

The process approaches for the evaluation of software products guide software testing, as well as software reviews and other SQA activities: the verification, validation, and qualification approaches. The definitions of these approaches are presented in Frame 14.3.

Frame 14.3: The process approaches for the evaluation of software products

---

The process approaches for the evaluation of software products – the definitions

- **Verification** – A process for evaluating a software system or component product of a given development phase with the purpose of checking whether the examined item correctly and fully implemented the conditions and requirements presented at the beginning of the development phase.

- **Validation** – A process for evaluating a software system or component product of a given development phase with the purpose of checking whether the examined product correctly and fully implemented the relevant specified requirements.

- **Qualification** – A process for evaluating a software system or component product of a given development phase with the purpose of checking whether the examined product correctly and fully implemented the professional coding standards and style and structure, instructions, and procedures.

Verification examines the consistency of the coding products being developed with products developed in the previous phase. When doing so, the examiner follows the development process while assuming that all former development phases were completed correctly – whether as originally planned or after elimination of all discovered defects. This assumption causes the examiner to disregard deviations from a customer's original requirements that might have been introduced during the development process.

Validation represents customer interests by examining the extent that the coding product is compliant with the customer's original requirements. Thus, comprehensive code validation tends to improve customer satisfaction with the system.

Qualification focuses on operational aspects, where maintenance is the main issue. A software component that has been developed and documented according to professional standards, style and structure conventions, and procedures is expected to be much easier to maintain than one that offers "marvelous" coding improvisations, yet does not follow the accepted coding style procedures.

Testing planners are required to determine which of these approaches should be examined for each quality assurance activity. A combination of approaches is preferred in many, if not in most, SQA activities.

Three approaches toward the purpose of SQA activities are also applicable to software reviews, inspections, and walkthroughs of software products (reports, documents, code, etc.) throughout the software development process.

Software testing resources utilization

Software testing is undoubtedly the largest consumer of software quality assurance resources. Sommerville (2015) reports that about 40% of project costs are spent on testing (integration and system tests), while 14% of costs are dedicated to specifications including the analysis phase, 26% to the design phase, and 20% to the coding including unit testing. The quoted cost distribution fits the waterfall development process, while the cost portion of the testing phase does not change significantly and remains the largest of all software development methods.

Testing is not the only type of quality assurance tool applied to programming and system testing phases. Review processes, namely, inspections and walkthroughs, are applied to review program code listings. These review procedures, which are similar to those applied in the review of design documents, yield important results in identifying a great, and even major, part of code defects. Nevertheless, these tools usually do not replace software testing, which examines the functionality of a software product by running on a computer, in the form that the software will actually be used by the customer.

Additional material on testing can be found in numerous papers and books dealing with software testing. A small sampling of these sources are the books by Pressman and Maxim (2015), Sommerville (2015), Rubin and Chisnell (2008), and Perry (2006), to cite some major documents in this category. Several software engineering and SQA standards dedicate significant parts to software testing issues, to mention just three: IEEE (2014), ISO/IEC (2008), and ISO/IEC (1014).

The testing process is illustrated in Figure 14.1.

The testing process includes the following activities, presented in Sections 14.3–14.10:

- Determining software testing strategies
- Requirement-driven software testing

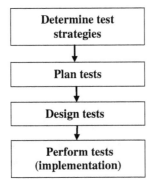

Figure 14.1 The software testing process

Planning the testing process:

- Designing the testing process
- Implementing the testing process
- Automated testing process
- Alpha and beta site testing programs
- Code review activities for the programming and testing phases

Before delving into the testing process details, let us examine the mini-case of the next section, Section 14.2, that may serve as an introduction to the next sections.

14.2 Joe decided to skip in-process testing – an introductory mini-case

Joe Brady, head of the development unit, was not satisfied with the tedious procedure of unit and integration testing conducted prior to the system tests. When looking into the resources utilized for the last five projects, he found that unit and integration tests had consumed more resources than the design and coding put together. What made him especially angry was that despite these early testing efforts, about 10% of the defects still "escaped," and were detected during the system tests. The new project, "S.F.G. Salaries," seemed an appropriate project to serve as a pilot to examine Joe's idea of a project without unit and integration testing.

The S.F.G. project was planned for 31 modules and 11 integrations, 7 of which were first-level integrations. The development team was instructed to skip the unit and integration tests. The design and coding took about 3 months, at that time a system test plan was prepared and almost 900 test cases were compiled. The first run of the system test yielded 310 failing test cases. It took 2 weeks to solve the first 100 defects. During the next 2 weeks, another 80 defects were removed. The main difficulty of locating the cause of the defect substantially reduced the rate of defect removals. The second month of correction yielded an additional 90 corrections. At this stage, Joe decided to run a second full-scale system test, which resulted in 45 failing test cases. While some of the unsolved defects disappeared, several new failing test cases were listed. Evaluating the results, Joe was concerned about the nearing delivery date, and applied for and received help from the other software development unit. Now, working in pairs, special efforts had been done to solve the remaining defects. A third full-scale system test carried out 4 months after the system tests had commenced revealed five failing test cases. Now, with the pressure of 2 months delay in delivery, Joe decided to install the package "as is," and to notify the customer about the remaining minor defects. He promised the customer to install a "defect free" version, once the correction process had been completed.

In the next team meeting, Joe stood up and declared: "My point has been proven quite enough. Thank you all for your efforts and patience in carrying out my experiment." He paused for few seconds and continued: "The failure in a relatively small project just proved the extent of potential disaster if my idea had been tried out on a larger project. Unit testing and integration testing should be carried out and improved, with the goal of zero defects during the system tests."

* * *

Joe's pilot testing procedure reflects discussions among followers of testing only the entire software package (frequently called "big bang" testing), and followers of partial testing of modules and integrations prior to system testing (frequently called "incremental testing"). This subject will be discussed later.

14.3 Software testing strategies

Software testing strategy deals with the steps to be carried out when performing testing, and the software testing approaches and procedures. The following strategic issues for testing will be discussed:

- Incremental testing versus "big bang" testing
- The order of performing incremental testing
- The testing concept – black box and white box testing
- Requirement-driven software testing

These software testing strategies will be discussed in the following sections.

14.3.1 Incremental testing versus "big bang" testing

There are two basic ways to test a software package:

- To test the software in its entirety, once the completed package is available; otherwise, "big bang testing."

- To test the software piecemeal, in modules, as they are completed (unit tests); then to test groups of tested modules integrated with newly completed modules (integration tests). This process continues until all the package modules have been tested. Once this phase is completed, the entire package is tested as a whole (system test). This testing strategy is usually termed "incremental testing."

"Big bang" versus incremental testing – compared

Unless the program is very small and simple, application of "big bang" testing strategies displays severe disadvantages:

- The rate of "big bang" error identification, as indicated by failing test cases, is relatively lower.
- Identification of the cause of an error in order to correct it becomes quite demanding when dealing with immense quantities of software. Moreover, when confronted with an entire software package, error correction is often an onerous task, requiring consideration of the possible effects of the correction on several modules at one and the same time.
- As a result of the vast resources invested in correcting errors, the effectiveness of this approach is relatively meager.
- These error correction difficulties obviously make estimating the required testing resources and schedule a rather fuzzy endeavor. This also implies that prospects of keeping on schedule and within budget are substantially reduced when applying the "big bang" testing strategy.

In contrast to "big bang" testing, "incremental testing" presents several advantages, the main ones being:

- Incremental testing is usually performed on relatively small software modules, as unit or integration tests. This makes it easier to identify higher percentages of errors when compared with testing the entire software package.
- Identification and correction of errors in unit and integration tests is much simpler and requires fewer resources because it is performed on a limited volume of software. In addition to preventing "migration" of defects to a later development stage, where their identification and correction requires significantly greater resources, it contributes to a higher total percentage of defect detection.
- The total resources invested in unit, integration tests, and system tests in incremental testing are lower than those invested in "big bang" testing system tests.

The following are the main disadvantages of incremental testing:

- The substantial amount of extra programming resources required for preparation for unit and integration testing. These extra resources are invested in the programming of stubs and drivers for the unit and integration tests (for details, see next section).

- The need to carry out numerous testing operations for the same program. (*Note*: Big bang testing requires only a single testing operation.)

To sum up, apart from cases of very small and simple software development projects, incremental testing should be highly preferred to "big bang" testing.

14.3.2   The order of performing incremental testing

Top-down and bottom-up incremental testing

Incremental testing is also performed according to two basic strategies: bottom-up and top-down. Both incremental testing strategies assume that the software package is constructed of a hierarchy of software modules. In top-down testing, the first module tested is the main module, the highest level module in the software structure; the last modules to be tested are the lowest level modules. In bottom-up testing, the order of testing is reversed: the lowest level modules are tested first, while the main module is tested last.

Figure 14.2 illustrates top-down and bottom-up testing of an identical software development project composed of 11 modules. In the upper part of Figure 14.2a, the software development process and its subsequent testing are carried out **bottom-up**, in four stages, as follows:

- Stage 1: Unit tests of modules 1–7.

- Stage 2: Integration test A of modules 1 and 2, developed and tested in stage 1, and integrated with module 8, developed in the current stage.

- Stage 3: Two separate integration tests, B, on modules 3, 4, 5, and 8, integrated with module 9, and C, for modules 6 and 7, integrated with module 10.

- Stage 4: System test is performed after B and C have been integrated with module 11, developed in the current stage.

In Figure 14.2b, software development and testing are carried out **top-down** in six stages. It should be apparent that the change of testing strategy introduces major changes into the test schedule. The testing will be performed as follows:

- Stage 1: Unit tests of module 11.

- Stage 2: Integration test A of module 11 integrated with modules 9 and 10, developed in the current stage.

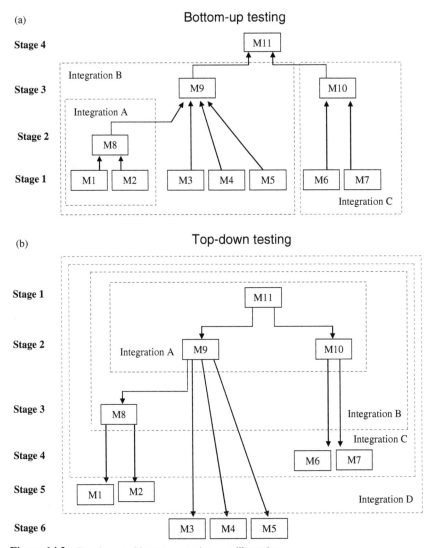

Figure 14.2 Top-down and bottom-up testing – an illustration

- Stage 3: Integration test B of A integrated with module 8, developed in the current stage.
- Stage 4: Integration test C of B integrated with modules 6 and 7, developed in the current stage.
- Stage 5: Integration test D of C integrated with modules 1 and 2, developed in the current stage.
- Stage 6: System test of D integrated with modules 3, 4, and 5, developed in the current stage.

The incremental test paths shown in Figure 14.1 represent only two of the many possible paths.

Other possible paths involve the clustering of modules into one testing stage. For example, for the top-down path of Figure 14.1b, one might cluster modules 16, 1, and 2, and/or modules 10, 6, and 7.

The main advantage of the top-down strategy is the early stage at which it is possible to demonstrate the program as a whole, a condition that supports early identification of analysis and design errors by the customer.

14.3.3 The testing concept – white box and black box testing

The issues of this section are the following:

a. The testing concept – black box and white box testing

b. White box testing realization

c. White box testing coverage

d. The advantages and disadvantages of white box testing

e. Black box testing realization

f. Equivalence classes for black box correctness tests

g. The Golden Splash Swimming Center – EC example

h. Advantages and disadvantages of black box testing

a. Black box and white box testing definitions

There is an ongoing debate over whether testing the functionality of software solely according to its outputs is sufficient to achieve an acceptable level of quality. Some claim that the internal structure of the software and the calculations (i.e., the underlying mathematical structure, also known as the software "mechanism") should be included for satisfactory testing. Based on these two opposing concepts or approaches to software quality, two testing classes have been developed:

- *Black box (functionality) testing* identifies bugs only according to software malfunctioning as they are revealed in its erroneous outputs. In cases that the outputs are found to be correct, black box testing disregards the internal path of calculations and processing is performed.
- *White box (structural) testing* examines internal calculation paths in order to identify bugs. Although the term "white" is meant to indicate its being a contrary alternative to black box testing, the method's other name, "glass box testing," better expresses its basic characteristic, that of investigating the correctness of code structure.

Table 14.1 presents white box and black box testing suitability to the various classes of tests. The classification of tests was done according to quality requirement factors (for details, see Chapter 2).

Table 14.1 White box and black box testing for the various classes of tests

Test classification according to requirements	White box testing	Black box testing
1.1 Correctness tests	+	+
1.2 User manuals tests		+
1.3 Availability (reaction time) tests		+
2. Reliability tests		+
3. Stress tests (load tests and durability tests)		+
4. Software system security tests		+
5.1 Training usability tests		+
5.2 Operational usability tests		+
6. Maintainability correctness tests	+	+
7. Flexibility tests		+
8. Testability tests		+
9. Portability tests		+
10. Reused software correctness tests	+	+
11.1 Software interoperability tests		+
11.2 Equipment interoperability tests		+

Examining Table 14.1 it is evident that correctness, maintainability, and reused software correctness tests could be performed either by white box testing, where data processing paths and calculations are examined, or by black box testing where only the program outputs will be checked. The other classes of tests are performed by black box testing.

Due to cost considerations, currently most of the testing carried out is black box testing.

When implemented, each concept approaches software testing differently, as we shall see in the next four sections.

b. White box testing realization

Realization of the white box testing concept requires verification of every program statement and comment. In order to perform *data processing and calculation correctness tests* (white box correctness test), every computational operation in the sequence of operations created by each test case (path) must be examined. This type of verification allows us to decide whether the processing operations and their sequences were programmed correctly for the path in question, but not for other paths.

Different paths in a software module are created by the choice in conditional statements, such as IF-THEN-ELSE or DO WHILE or DO UNTIL. Path testing is motivated by the aspiration to achieve complete coverage of a program by testing all its possible paths.

The next sections deal with white box issues:
• White box testing coverage (Section c)
• The advantages and disadvantages of white box testing (Section d)

c. White box testing coverage

The concept of white box testing is based on checking the data processing path for each test case, where the greater the number of paths checked, the larger the number of defects detected are. It immediately raises the question of coverage of the program's vast number of possible processing paths and the multitude of lines of code. Two alternative approaches have emerged:

- "Path coverage" – To plan our test to cover all possible paths, coverage is measured by the percentage of paths covered.
- "Line coverage" – To plan our tests to cover all program code lines, coverage is measured by the percentage of lines covered.

Path coverage. Hence, the "path coverage" metrics gauging a path's test completeness is defined as the percentage of the program paths executed during the test (activated by the test cases included in the testing procedure).

While the concept of path testing naturally flows from application of the white box testing concept, it is impractical in most cases because of the vast resources required for its performance. Just how costly these applications can be is illustrated in the following example.

Let us now calculate the number of possible paths created by a simple module containing 10 conditional statements, each allowing for only two options (e.g., IF-THEN-ALSO and DO WHILE). This simple module contains 1,024 different paths. In other words, in order to obtain full path coverage for this module (probably 25–50 lines of code), at least 1,024 test cases need to be prepared, one for each possible path. A straightforward calculation of the number of test cases required to test a software package that contains 100 modules of similar complexity, a total of 102,400 test cases, readily indicates the impracticality of the wide use of path testing. Thus, its application is directed mainly to high risk software modules, where the costs of failure resulting from software error fully warrant the costs of path testing.

This situation has encouraged the development of an alternative yet weaker coverage concept – line coverage. The line coverage concept requires considerably fewer test cases but, as expected, leaves most of the possible paths untested. The subject of line coverage is discussed next.

Line coverage. The line coverage concept requires that for full line coverage every line of code be executed at least once during the process of testing. The line coverage metrics for completeness of a line-testing (basic path testing) plan is defined as the percentage of lines actually executed – that is, covered – during the tests.

d. The advantages and disadvantages of white box testing

The main advantages of white box testing is (1) its direct statement-by-statement checking of code. It enables determination of software correctness as expressed in the processing paths, including whether the algorithms were correctly defined and coded. (2) It provides line coverage follow-up. (3) Its capability to test the quality of coding work.

The main disadvantages of white box testing are (1) the vast resources utilized (much more than those required for black box testing of the same software package), and (2) the inability to test software performance in terms of availability (response time), reliability, load durability, and other testing classes related to operation, revision, and transition factors.

The characteristics of white box testing limit its usage to cases of software modules of very high risk and very high cost of failure, where it is highly important to identify and fully correct as many of the software errors as possible.

e. Black box testing realization

Black box testing allows us to perform correctness tests and most other classes of tests, based on the processing outputs only. The success of black box testing relies only on the selection of the appropriate test cases that will uncover errors in the wide variety of program paths. While the effectiveness of black box testing relies on a wider variety of test cases, the efficiency of black box testing depends on the decrease in the number of test cases. There is a lengthy search for the optimal economic size of test cases sets.

The next sections will thus deal with the following black box issues:
• Equivalence classes for black box correctness tests (Section f).
• The Golden Splash Swimming Center – EC example (Section g).
• Advantages and disadvantages of black box testing (Section h).

For additional material on black box testing, I would mention Beizer (1995) as one of the major sources available.

f. Equivalence classes for black box correctness tests

Black box correctness tests are based on test cases. Improving the choice of test cases is an important goal of software testing, particularly of black box testing.

Equivalence class partitioning is a black box testing method aimed at increasing the efficiency of testing and, at the same time, improving coverage of potential error conditions.

There are two types of equivalence classes: input equivalence classes and output equivalence classes. An *input equivalence class* (IEC) is a set of input variable values that produce the same output results or that are processed identically. IEC boundaries are defined by a single numeric or alphabetic value, a group of numeric or alphabetic values, a range of values, and so on. An IEC that contains only valid values is defined as a "valid IEC," whereas an IEC that contains invalid input values is defined as an "invalid IEC." In cases where a program's input is provided by several variables, valid and invalid ECs should be defined for each variable. An *output equivalence class* (OEC) is an output result or an output function of an input variable values combination or is common to a set of input variable values combinations.

Test cases for valid ECS and invalid ECS

According to the equivalence class partitioning method, test cases are defined so that each valid ECs, invalid IECs, and OECs is included in at least one test case. The definition of test cases is done separately for valid and invalid IECs and for OECs.

Test cases for IECS

1. **Valid IECs.** In defining a test case for the valid IECs, we try to cover as many as possible "new" valid IECs (i.e., classes not included in any of the former test cases) in that same test case. Test cases are added as long as there are uncovered valid IECs. As a result of this process, the total number of required test cases to cover the valid IECs is equal to, and in most cases significantly below, the number of valid ECs.

2. **Boundary values for valid IECs.** According to the definition of input equivalence classes, one test case should be sufficient for each class. However, when equivalence classes cover a range of values (e.g., monthly income, apartment area), the tester has a special interest in testing border values for input IECs, when these are considered to be error prone. In these cases, preparation of three test cases – for mid-range, lower boundary, and upper boundary values – is recommended.

3. **Invalid IECs.** Note that in defining invalid ECs, we must assign one test case to each "new" invalid EC, as only one invalid EC can be included in a test case. A test case that includes more than one invalid EC may not enable the tester to distinguish between the program's separate reactions to each of the invalid ECs. Hence, the number of test cases required for the invalid ECs equals the number of invalid ECs.

4. **Test cases for OECs.** All OECs must be presented in the set of test cases. As some of the OECs are already covered by test cases prepared for the IECs, only those OECs not presented in the set of test cases already prepared for the IECs need a test case defined according to their OEC. One test case is prepared for each of these OECs.

Compared with the use of a random sample of test cases, equivalence classes save *testing resources because they eliminate duplication of test cases defined for each EC.* Importantly, as the equivalence class method is a black box method, equivalence class partitioning is based on software specification documentation, not on the code. Systematic constructing of equivalence classes for a program's input variables increases the coverage of the possible valid and error conditions of the input and output, thus improves the testing plan's effectiveness. Further improvement of testing effectiveness and efficiency is achieved by testing for the boundary values of IECs, a subject we shall elaborate on next.

g. The Golden Splash Swimming Center – EC example

The following example illustrates the definition of input equivalence classes (valid and invalid) and output equivalence classes, and the corresponding test case values. The software module in question calculates entrance ticket prices for the Golden Splash Swimming Center.

The center's ticket price depends on four variables: (1) day (weekday, weekend), (2) visitor's status (OT = one time, M = member), (3) entry hour (6.00–19.00, 19.01–24.00), and (4) visitor's age (up to 16, 16.01–60, 60.01–120).

The entrance ticket prices table is shown in Table 14.2.

The input equivalence classes, output equivalence classes, and corresponding test case values for the above example are presented in Tables 14.3–14.5.

A total of 25 IECs were defined for the ticket price module: 9 valid IECs, 10 valid boundary value IECs, and 6 invalid IECs.

A total of 12 OECs were defined for the outputs of the ticket price module.

The test cases that correspond to these IECs apply the representing values listed in Table 14.5. The test cases related to the OECs were selected from Table 14.3. The test cases for these IECs, including their boundary values, as well as the test cases related to the OECs, are presented in Table 14.4.

A total of 27 test cases cover all defined IECs and OECs:

- Three test cases for the valid IECs (for our example, a total of nine valid IECs were defined).
- six test cases for the boundary value IECs (in our example, boundary testing is applicable for only two of the four input variables).
- Six test cases for invalid IECs (for our example, a total of six invalid ECs were defined).
- 12 OECs. Only four OECs were presented in the IEC test cases, and accordingly, a set of eight test cases for the remaining OECs (OECs 3, 4, 5, 6, 7, 8, 9, and 11) was added to the list of test cases in Table 14.5.

Although the equivalence class method is mainly applied with correctness tests, it may be used for other operation factor testing classes, as well as for revision and transition factor testing classes.

h. Advantages and disadvantages of black box testing

The main advantages of black box testing are (1) the relatively lower resources required to perform black box testing compared with white box testing. (2) Further reduction of the black box testing resources is achieved by automatic testing. The application of automatic testing also contributes to shorter testing periods and to improved defect uncovering rates, mainly by the easier performance of regression tests. (3) The ability to perform almost all test classes, among them the

Table 14.2 The entrance ticket price table – the Golden Splash Swimming Center

The day	Mon, Tue, Wed, Thurs, Fri				Sat, Sun			
Visitor's status	OT	OT	M	M	OT	OT	M	M
Entry hour	6–19	19–24	6–19	19–24	6–19	19–24	6–19	19–24
Visitor's age				Ticket Prices – $				
0.0–16.00	4.00	4.00	4.00	4.00	6.00	6.00	6.00	6.00
16.01–60.00	10.00	8.00	7.00	6.00	15.00	12.00	10.00	8.00
60.01–120.0	5.00	5.00	5.00	5.00	7.00	7.00	7.00	7.00

Table 14.3 Input equivalence classes – the Golden Splash Swimming Center

The variable	Valid equivalence classes	Representing values		Invalid equivalence classes	Representing Values for the Invalid ECs
		Values for the valid ECs	Boundary values		
Day of the week	(1) Mon, Tue, Wed, Thurs, Fri (2) Sat, Sun	(1) Mon (2) Sat	None	Any alphanumeric value (not a day)	Mox
Visitor's status	(1) OT (2) M	(1) OT (2)M	None	Other than OT or M	88
Entry hour	(1) 6.00–19.00 (2)19.01–24.00	(1) 7.55, (2) 20.44	(1) 6.00, 19.00 (2) 19.01, 24.00	(1) Hours<6.00 (2) Any alphanumeric values (not time)	(1) 4.40 (2) & @
Visitor's age	(1) 0.0–16.0 (2) 16.1–60.0 (3) 60.1–120.0	(1) 8.4 (2) 42.7 (3) 65.0	(1) 0.0, 16.0 (2) 16.1, 60.0 (3) 60.1, 120.0	(1) Any alphanumeric value (not an age) (2) ages >120.0	(1) TTR (2) 150.1

Table 14.4 Output equivalence classes – the Golden Splash Swimming Center

Day	Mon, Tue, Wed, Thurs, Fri				Sat, Sun			
Visitor's status	OT	OT	M	M	OT	OT	M	M
Entry hour	6–19	19–24	6–19	19–24	6–19	19–24	6–19	19–24
Visitor's age				Ticket Prices – $				
0.0–16.00		OEC(1) = 4.00				OEC(2) = 6.00		
16.01–60.00	OEC(3) = 10.00	OEC(4) = 8.00	OEC(5) = 7.00	OEC(6) = 6.00	OEC(7) = 15.00	OEC(8) = 12.00	OEC(9) = 10.00	OEC(10) = 8.00
60.01–120.0		OEC(11) = 5.00				OEC(12) = 7.00		

Table 14.5 Test cases – the Golden Splash Swimming Center

Test case type	Test case no.	Day of the week	Visitor's status	Entry hour	Visitor's age	Test case results
Valid ECs Test cases	1	Mon	OT	7.55	8.4	$4.00
	2	Sat	M	20.44	42.7	$8.00
	3	Sat	M	22.44	65.0	$7.00
Test cases for valid	4	Sat	M	6.00	0.0	$6.00
border IECs	5	Sat	M	19.00	16.0	$6.00
	6	Sat	M	19.01	16.1	$8.00
	7	Sat	M	19.01	60.0	$8.00
	8	Sat	M	24.00	60.1	$7.00
	9	Sat	M	24.00	120.0	$7.00
Test cases for invalid	10	Mon	OT	7.55	8.4	Invalid day
IECs	11	Mon	88	7.55	8.4	Invalid visitor status
	12	Mon	OT	4.40	8.4	Invalid entry hour
	13	Mon	OT	fv	8.4	Invalid entry hour
	14	Mon	OT	7.55	TTR	Invalid visitor age
	15	Mon	OT	7.55	150.1	Invalid visitor age
Test cases for OECs	16	Tue	OT	11.40	55.8	$10.00
	17	Wed	OT	19.45	46.0	$8.00
	18	Thur	M	12.00	44.0	$7.00
	19	Fri	M	15.00	55.0	$6.00
	20	Sun	OT	17.04	33.6	$15.00
	21	Sat	OT	21.05	58.9	$12.00
	22	Sat	M	6.15	56.0	$10.00
	23	Tue	OT	7.15	77.0	$5.00

following test classes of availability (response time), reliability, load durability, and other testing classes related to operation, revision, and transition factors, not available with white box testing.

The main disadvantages of black box testing are (1) its inability to directly examine the software by checking the code statement-by-statement. Black box defect detection is indirect and based on the resulting outputs. (2) A coincidental aggregation of several errors can produce the correct response for a test case, and prevent error detection. (3) Absence of control of line coverage. In cases where black box testers wish to improve line coverage, there is no easy way to specify the parameters of the test cases required to improve coverage. Consequently, black box tests may not be conducted on a substantial proportion of code lines, which are not covered by a set of test cases. (4) Impossibility of testing the quality of coding and its adherence to the coding standards.

The characteristics of black box testing promote its use where applicable, while white box testing is preferred in cases of software products with a very high risk and very high cost of failure, where it is highly important to identify and fully correct as many of the software errors as possible.

14.4 Requirement-driven software testing

Chapter 2 presents McCall's classic model for the classification of software quality requirements. His model has been applied here to classify the tests classes to ensure full coverage of the respective requirements. This classification was used earlier in Table 14.1, for presenting the applicability of white box and black box testing to the various test classes. The requirements and their corresponding tests are shown in Table 14.6.

Table 14.6 Software quality requirements and test classification

Factor category	Quality requirement factor	Quality requirement subfactor	Test classification according to requirements
Operation	1. Correctness	1.1 Accuracy and completeness of outputs, accuracy and completeness of data	1.1 Correctness tests
		1.2 Accuracy and completeness of documentation	1.2 User manuals tests
		1.3 Availability (reaction time)	1.3 Availability (reaction time) tests
	2. Reliability		2. Reliability tests
	3. Efficiency		3. Stress tests (load and durability tests)
	4. Integrity		4. Software system security tests
	5. Usability	5.1 Training usability	5.1 Training usability tests
		5.2 Operational usability	5.2 Operational usability tests
Revision	6. Maintainability		6. Maintainability correctness tests
	7. Flexibility		7. Flexibility tests
	8. Testability		8. Testability tests
Transition	9. Portability		9. Portability tests
	10. Reusability		10. Reused software correctness tests
	11. Interoperability	11.1 Interoperability with other software	11.1 Software interoperability tests
		11.2 Interoperability with other equipment	11.2 Equipment interoperability tests

14.4.1 Operation factor testing classes

Operation factor testing classes include eight test classes for the following five operation factors categories:
Operation requirements factors:

• Correctness

• Reliability

• Efficiency

• Integrity

• Usability

a. Correctness tests

The correctness factor is covered by three test classes:
• Software correctness tests
• User manual tests
• Availability (reaction time) tests

These test classes are discussed, as follows:

1. Software correctness tests

Software correctness tests are aimed at verifying and validating the accuracy and completeness of the outputs produced by the software. These tests are carried out by black box and white box testing (discussed above).

2. User manual tests

User manuals are a tool prepared by the developer for the customer to guide the developer regarding proper implementation of the software functions. User manual errors disrupt the user operation and might even cause substantial damage in certain situations.

User manual tests are planned to reveal user manual defects by running test cases according to the manual's directions.

3. Availability tests

Availability is defined as the *reaction time* – the time needed to obtain the requested information or the time required for a firmware installed in computerized equipment to react. Availability is of the highest importance in online applications planned to serve a large population of users (i.e., Internet sites), and for real-time systems planned to handle high-frequency events. The failure of software systems or firmware software to meet availability requirements (i.e., retarded reaction time) can make the software system or equipment useless.

It is clear that the availability of real-time systems is affected by the system load. In other words, the higher the system load, the lower the availability (the longer the reaction time). Thus, a combined load and availability tests are needed where requirements for availability and load are defined for regular operation and for operation under maximal load. These combined availability–load tests are relatively difficult to conduct as it is required to carry out the tests under regular operation load, as well as under maximal load conditions as defined in the requirement specifications.

Carrying out the combined availability-load tests for systems planned to serve large user populations manually is impractical. Testing of this type is performed by computers that simulate the inputs of the software user population and enable measuring the resulting expected availability for any recorded load. For automatic availability and load tests, see Section 14.8.

b. Reliability tests

The software system reliability requirement deals with features that can be translated as events occurring over time, such as the average time between failures (e.g., no more than once in 500 hours), average time for recovery after system failure (e.g., no more than 15 minutes), or average down time per month (e.g., no more than 30 minutes per month). Reliability requirements are to be in effect during regular full-capacity operation of the system. It should be noted that in addition to the software factor, reliability tests also relate to the hardware, the operating system, and the data communication system effects.

Much like availability testing, reliability testing is especially difficult as it requires operating the full range of software applications conducted under regular and maximal workload conditions. To be practical, such tasks should be carried out only after computerized simulations have been run to obtain the required load values, and only once the system is completed. With respect to resources, the major constraint to performing tests of this type is the scope of resources required, which is vast, as testing may continue for hundreds of hours and a comprehensive test case file must be constructed. Shorter reliability tests may be achieved by simultaneously running more than one software system.

Bankmax software reliability tests – an example

Bankmax – a comprehensive custom-made software system – is developed for branch operations and bank management. The systems reliability requirements for a bank branch's reliability are as follows:

- Bankmax operation failure frequency – no more than once a year (on average)
- Recovery time after Bankmax software failure – no more than 15 minutes (on average)

As the reliability tests needed to be run on the complete software system, they were scheduled in parallel to the system tests – for a period of 3 months. The tests should be conducted for at least 3 years of branch operation in order to statistically prove that the system can cope with the maximal failure frequency requirement. The testers' problem is to work out how 3 years of branch operation may be compressed into the available testing period of only 3 months. We assume that system failures are random. Accordingly, if we run our reliability test for 24 hours daily, our testing day will be equal to several days of bank branch operation. Now let us find out what can be achieved during the 3-month testing period. The bank branch is open for 40 weekly hours; its annual hours of operation sum up to 2,080 hours (40×52). If we operate our reliability testing for 24 hours daily, our 3-month testing period will provide 2,160 testing hours ($24 \times 30 \times 3$), which can simulate a little more than a full year of bank branch operation. Now we have worked out that in order to perform 3 years of branch operation, it will be sufficient to carry out reliability tests for three independent branches for the planned testing period of 3 months.

Statistical reliability testing offers a much less expensive and speedier option to assess reliability on the basis of statistical models. Much literature is available on the subject, to mention just a few sources: Perry (2006), Mustafa et al. (2009), and Rubin and Chisnell (2008). However, despite its widespread use and practical benefits, statistical reliability tests have been subjected to criticism since their emergence. The main issue debated is the extent to which statistical models represent real-life software system operation.

c. Efficiency tests

The efficiency factor subsumes two main tests: (1) load test classes–load tests and (2) durability tests. It is possible to perform these tests only subsequent to software system completion. Durability tests, however, can generally be carried out only after the firmware or information system software has been installed and is ready for testing.

(1) Load tests

Load tests relate to the functional performance of the system under maximal operational load, that is, maximal transactions per minute, hits per minute to an Internet site and the like.

As explained above, as the load in real-time systems affects the system availability, where the higher the system load, the lower the availability, a combined load and availability tests are needed. The requirements for these combined tests define the availability and load for regular operation and for operation under maximal load.

As explained above, testing of this type is performed by computers that simulate the inputs of the software user population and enable measuring the resulting expected availability for any recorded load. For automatic availability and load tests, see Section 14.8.

It seems that a short example would be helpful.

The "Music in the Air" Example

"Music in the Air," a network of music stores, run a service on the Internet that registers requests for price quotations and orders.

On weekdays, the average rate of customer hits is 5 per minute for orders and 10 per minute for price quotations. The maximum loads recorded on Saturday afternoon are 10 per minute for orders and 25 per minute for price quotations.

The maximal load defined in the software specifications, which takes future growth into account, is 25 per minute for orders and 60 per minute for price quotation. As explained above, load and response time should be tested together. The response time required for regular time is 3 seconds and for maximal hit rate 30 seconds.

Tests will be begin with hardware of a lower capability and will gradually work up to hardware of higher capacities, till the test allocates the hardware with the appropriate capacity. This hardware system will enable coping with the availability requirements for the maximal load.

(2) Durability tests

Durability tests are carried out in physically extreme operating conditions such as high temperatures, humidity, and vibrations of high-speed driving along unpaved rural roads, as detailed in the durability specification requirements. Hence, these durability tests are typically required for real-time firmware integrated into systems such as weapon systems, long-distance transport vehicles, and meteorological equipment. Durability issues for firmware include firmware responses to climatic effects such as extreme hot and cold temperatures, dust, road bumps, and extreme operation failures resulting from sudden electrical failure, voltage "spikes" in the supply mains, sudden cutoffs in communications, and so on.

d. Integrity tests – software system security tests

Software security components of software systems are aimed at (1) preventing unauthorized access to the system or parts of it, (2) detection of unauthorized access and activities performed by penetration, and (3) recovery of damages caused by unauthorized penetration cases.

The following are the main security issues dealt with by these tests:

- Access control, where the usual requirement is for control of multilevel access (usually by a password mechanism). Of special importance here are the firewall systems that prevent unauthorized access to Internet sites
- Logging of transactions, system usage, access trials, and so on

The challenge of creating viruses and breaking into security systems has bred a special brand of delinquent, the hacker. Often very young, these enthusiasts find their ultimate pleasure first and foremost by breaking into complex secured computer systems, sometimes accompanied by system disruption, or planting of viruses that incapacitate others. Their success has been astounding in some cases (e.g., national banks, US military security systems, etc.), and embarrassing to the same extent. One "payoff" of their success is that it is no longer rare to find hackers invited to join tester teams, especially for software systems where security requirements are high.

e. Usability tests

Usability tests include training and operational usability tests.

(1) Training usability tests

When large numbers of users are involved in operating a system, training usability requirements are added to the testing agenda. The scope of training usability is defined by the resources needed to train a new employee; in other words, the number of training hours required for a new employee to achieve a defined level of acquaintance with the system or to reach a defined hourly production rate. The details of these, like any other tests, are based on system characteristics but, more importantly, on employee characteristics. The results of the tests should inspire a sophisticated plan of training courses and follow-up, as well as improved directions for software system training.

(2) Operational usability tests

The focus of this class of tests is the operator's productivity, that is, those aspects of the system that affect the performance regularly achieved by system operators. These tests are applied mainly for information systems that serve many users, and are of high importance in cases that the system can substantially affect the productivity of system users.

The implementation of this class of tests deals mainly with the productivity, quantitatively, and qualitatively.

Operational usability tests can be performed manually by means of time studies or by a computer program that collects the productivity data of the users. In addition to productivity data, these manual and computerized tests provide some insight into the reasons for (high or low) performance levels and initiate ideas for improvements. Accurate performance records can be achieved by automated follow-up software that records all user activities throughout shifts. Software packages of this type supply performance statistics and comparative figures for different variables, such as specific activity, time period, and industry.

Comprehensive discussions of usability testing issues and detailed examples can be found in Rubin and Chisnell (2008).

14.4.2   Revision factor testing classes

Easy revision of software is a fundamental factor assuring a software package's successful, long service and successful sales to larger user populations. Related to these features are the revision testing classes discussed in this section:

- Maintainability tests
- Flexibility tests
- Testability tests

a. **Maintainability correctness tests**

The importance of software maintenance and maintainability can never be overestimated; consider the fact that these functions consume the greatest part of the total design, programming, and testing resources invested in a software system throughout its life cycle. "It's not unusual for a software organization to expend as much as 60 to 70 percent of all resources on software maintenance" (Pressman and Maxim 2015, p. 797).

Regular software operation and maintenance begin once installation, running-in, and conversion have been successfully completed. Maintenance of the software system is needed throughout the regular operation period, which usually lasts for several years, until a new software of a new generation replaces it. Maintenance incorporates three types of services: (1) corrective – repairing software faults identified by the user and the developer during operation; (2) adaptive – using the existing software features with minor software adaptations to fulfill new customers' customization requirements; and (3) functionality improving (perfective) – adding new minor features to adapt the software package to market changes and improve software performance.

Maintainability correctness tests relate mainly to these maintenance issues:

- Testing the correctness of defect corrections
- Testing the correctness of adaptations performed
- Testing the correctness of changes and software additions performed for the new features added to the software package

b. **Flexibility tests**

Software system flexibility refers to the system's capabilities, based on its structural and programming characteristics. These factors significantly affect the ease to adapt the software to the variety of customer needs as well as to introduce minor changes required by customers and maintenance teams for the main purpose of enhancing system sales.

Flexibility tests are intended to test the software functionality in a variety of environments. These tests examine the software's functionality when applying parametric options to provide for the range of possible customers.

c. **Testability tests**

Testability requirements deal with the ease of testing the software system. Thus, testability here relates to the addition of special features in the program that help the testers in their work, such as the possibility to obtain intermediate results for certain check points and predefined log files. Although often overlooked, these special testing support features should be specified in the requirements document as integral to the functional software requirements.

Another objective of testability deals with diagnostic tool applications implemented for the analysis of the system performance and the report of any failure found. Some features of this kind are activated automatically when starting the software package or during regular operation, and report on conditions warranting an alarm arise. Other features of this type may be activated by the operator or maintenance technician. Testability is particularly crucial for support of control rooms of large operating systems (e.g., electricity plants) and for maintenance teams, especially with respect to diagnosis of failures. Maintenance support applications of this type may be activated either at the customer site and/ or at a remote help desk support center.

Testability tests will be carried out for the application of both types, as noted in the requirement specifications. The tests should relate mainly to aspects of correctness, documentation, and availability, as already discussed.

14.4.3 Transition factor testing classes

Software systems are required by transition requirements to be operative, with minor adaptations in different environments, In addition, they may be required to incorporate reused modules or to interface with other software packages or with other equipment's firmware. These required transition features are especially important for commercial software packages aimed at a wide range of customers. Hence, the following testing classes, discussed in this section, must be applied:

- Portability tests
- Reusability tests
- Interoperability tests:
  1. Software interfacing tests
  2. Equipment interfacing tests

a. Portability tests

Portability requirements specify the environments (or environmental conditions) in which the software system should be operable: the operating systems, hardware and communication equipment standards, among other variables. The portability test to be carried out will verify and validate these factors, as well as estimate the resources required for transferring a software system to a different environment.

b. Reusability tests

Software reusability is expected to substantially reduce project resources requirements and improve the quality of the new software systems. In doing so, reusability shortens the development period, which by itself benefits the software development organization.

Reusability relates to (1) parts of the software system based on the use of reused software, and (2) parts of the program (modules, integrations, and the like) that are to be developed for future reuse in other software development projects, whether already planned or not. These parts should be developed, packaged, and documented according to reused software library procedures.

Reusability requirements are of special importance for object-oriented software projects.

Reused correctness tests are devised to examine if these parts of the software system function as required.

c. Software interoperability tests

Software interoperability deals with the software capabilities of interfacing equipment and other software packages, to enable the joint operation as one complex computerized system. The requirements list delineates the specific equipment and/or software interfaces to be tested, as well as the applicable data transfer and interfacing standards. A growing share of commercial over-the-counter (COTS) software packages and custom-made software packages are now required to have interoperability capabilities, that is, to display the capacity to receive inputs from equipment firmware and/or other software systems and/or to send outputs to other firmware and software systems. These software capabilities are carried out under the rigid data transfer standards, international and global or industry-oriented interoperability standards, and tested accordingly.

Software interoperability tests examine whether the required interfaces with software packages and equipment were fulfilled.

14.5   Planning of the testing process

Planners should consider the following issues before initiating a specific test plan:

- Which sources should be used for test cases
- Who should perform the tests
- Where should the tests be performed

These three issues will be discussed in this section.

The last subject of this section will discuss test plan documentation, priorities (units 1 and 2), and the three lowest priorities (units 3, 4, and 7).

14.5.1 Which sources should be used for test cases

Test case data components

A test case is a documented set that includes (1) the data input/parameters of a test item, (2) the operating conditions required to run a test item, and (3) the expected results of running the test item. The tester is expected to run the program for the test item according to the test case documentation, and then compare the actual results with the expected results noted in the documents. If the obtained results completely agree with the expected results, no error is present, or at least has been identified. When some, or all, of the results do not agree with the expected results, a potential error is recognized. The equivalence class partitioning method, discussed in Section 14.3.3, is applied to achieve efficient and effective definition of the test cases files, as sets to be used for black box testing.

An example – Test cases for the basic annual municipal property tax on apartments.

The basic annual municipal property tax on apartments (before discounts to special groups of city dwellers) is based on the following parameters:

- S – The size of the apartment (in square yards)
- N – The number of persons living in the apartment
- A, B, or C – The suburb's socioeconomic classification

The annual Municipal Property Tax (MPT) is calculated as follows:

For class A suburbs	$MPT = (100 \times S)/(N + 8)$
For class B suburbs	$MPT = (80 \times S)/(N + 8)$
For class C suburbs	$MPT = (50 \times S)/(N + 8)$

Following are three test cases for the software module used to calculate the basic municipal property tax on apartments:

	Test case # 1	Test case # 2	Test case # 3
Size of apartment – (square yards)	250	180	98
Suburb class	A	B	C
No. of persons in the household	2	4	6
Expected result: Annual Municipal Property Tax (MPT)	**$2,500**	**$1,200**	**$350**

Application of the test case will produce one or more of the following types of expected results:

- Numerical
- Alphabetic (name, address, etc.)
- Error message. Standard output informing user about missing data, erroneous data, unmet conditions, and so on.

With real-time software and firmware, the expected results can be one or more of the following types:

- Numerical and/or alphabetic messages displayed on a monitor's screen or on the equipment display.
- Activation of equipment or initiation of a defined operation.
- Activation of an operation, a siren, warning lamps, and the like, as a reaction to identified threatening conditions.
- Error message. Standard output to inform the operator about missing data, erroneous data, and so on.

Implementation tip

It is highly important that the test case file includes items where the expected result is an error message, as well as nonstandard items and items displaying undesirable operation conditions, and so on. Only by testing the software for nonregular conditions can we be assured that it will remain under control should undesirable conditions arise. In such cases, the software is expected to activate predefined reactions, alarms, operator flags, and so on – all in ways appropriate to system and customer needs. See Section 6.7.7 for invalid equivalence classes.

Test case sources
There are two basic sources for test cases:
Random samples of real-life cases (sample cases)
Examples:

- A sample of urban households (to test new municipal tax information system)
- A sample of shipping bills (to test new billing software)
- A sample of control records (to test new software for control of manufacturing a plant production)
- A recorded sample of events that will be "run" as a test case (to test online applications for an Internet site, and for real-time applications).

Synthetic test cases, also called "simulated test cases" (synthetic cases).
This type of test case does not refer to an existing customer, shipment, or product prepared by the test case designers. These test cases are designed to

Table 14.7   Comparison of test data sources

	The type of test case source	
Implication	Random sample of cases	Synthetic test cases
Effort required to prepare a test case file	Less effort – especially when expected results are available and do not need to be calculated	High effort – the parameters of each test case must be determined, and expected results calculated.
Required size of test case	Relatively high – as most cases refer to simple situations that repeat themselves frequently. In order to obtain a sufficient number of nonstandard situations, a relatively large test case file would need to be compiled.	Relatively small – as it may be possible to avoid repetitions of any given combination of parameters
Efforts required to perform the software tests	High efforts (low efficiency) – as tests must be carried out for large test case files. The low efficiency stems from the repetitiveness of case conditions, especially for simple situations typical to most real-life case files.	Less efforts (high efficiency) – due to the relatively small test case file compiled in order to avoid repetitions.
Effectiveness –probability of error detection	Relatively low – unless the test case files are very large – due to the low percentage of uncommon combinations of parameters. No coverage of erroneous situations. Some ability to identify unexpected errors for unlisted situations.	Relatively high due to good coverage by design. Good coverage of erroneous situations by test case file design. Little possibility of identifying unexpected errors, as all test cases are designed according to predefined parameters.

cover all known software operation conditions, or at least those conditions that are expected to be in frequent use, or that belong to a high error probability class. For the equivalence class method, see Section 14.3.3f.

The implications of using each test case source are summarized, and a comparison between the random and synthetic cases is shown in Table 14.7.

In most cases, the preferred test case file should combine sample cases with synthetic cases. This is to overcome the disadvantages of a single source of test cases, and to increase efficiency of the testing process. In the case of combined test case files, test plans are often carried out in two stages: in the first stage, synthetic test cases are used. After correction of the detected errors, a random sample of test cases is used in the second stage.

The planners should consider which of the two main sources of test cases – (1) samples of real-life and (2) synthetic test cases – are most appropriate to their needs. Each component of the testing plan, dealing with unit, integration, or the system test, requires an individual decision about the respective test cases and their sources:

- Should a single source of test cases or both be used?
- How many test cases from each source are to be prepared?

Implementation tip

Substantial improvement in the efficiency of the random sampling of test cases is achieved by using a stratified sampling procedure, rather than a standard random sampling of the entire population. Stratified sampling allows us to break down the random sample into subpopulations of test cases, thereby reducing the proportion of the majority "regular" population tested, while increasing the sampling proportion of small populations and high potential error populations. This method application not only minimizes the number of repetitions but also improves the coverage of less frequent and rare conditions.

Example: Garden City's population of about 100,000 households is divided between the city itself (70%), suburb Orange (20%), suburb Lemon (7%), and suburb Apple (3%). The suburbs and the city differ substantially in the characteristics of their housing and socioeconomic status. Of the city dwellers, 5,000 enjoy tax reductions entailing 40 different types of discounts (disabled persons, very large families, low-income single parent families with more than six children, etc.). Originally, the standard 0.5% sample had been planned. This was later replaced by the following stratified random sample:

	Households N	Standard 0.5% sampling N	Stratified sampling N
Regular households	65,000	325	100
Households eligible for discounts	5,000	25	250
Suburb A	20,000	100	50
Suburb B	7,000	35	50
Suburb C	3,000	15	50
Total	100,000	500	500

Test cases for reused software. It is quite common for reused software to include many applications not required for the current software system, in addition to the required applications. In situations of this kind, planners should consider which reused software modules should be tested. Additional modules of the reused software will not be tested.

Automated test cases. The automated generation of test cases, an important challenge of software testing, is a subject of intensive research in recent years. Discussions on the subject are presented by Kruse and Luniak (2010) and Do et al. (2013).

14.5.2 Who should perform the tests

Who should perform the various tests is determined at the planning stage:

- Integration tests, and especially unit tests, are generally performed by the software development team. In some instances, it is the testing unit that performs the tests.
- System tests are usually performed by an independent testing team (internal testing team or external testing consultant team).
- In cases of large software systems, more than one testing team may be employed to carry out the system tests. The prerequisite decision to be made in such cases concerns the allocation of system tests between the internal and external testing teams.
- In projects performed according to the incremental delivery model and the Agile methodology models the testing is usually done by the development team.
- In small software development organizations, when a separate testing team does not exist, the following testing possibilities exist:
  - testing by the development team,
  - testing by another development team (each development team will serve as the testing team for projects developed by other teams), and
  - outsourcing of testing responsibilities.

14.5.3 Where should the tests be performed

Unit and integration testing are naturally carried out at the software developer's site. Location becomes an important issue only when system tests are concerned: Whether system tests should be performed at the developer's or customer's site (the "target site") is questioned. If the testing is to be performed by external testing consultants, a third option arises: the consultant's site. Main site selection considerations are the availability of the system's computerized environment, and the availability of testing resources to perform the tests. As a rule, the computerized environment at the customer's site differs from that at the developer's site, despite efforts to "simulate" the environment. In such situations, apprehension regarding the occurrence of unpredicted failures once the system is installed at the customer's site is reduced by performing the system tests at the customer's site. In such cases, the customer will usually perform acceptance tests.

An alternative testing site that has become common in recent years is to use cloud computing services. This option offers unlimited computing resources and creates the appropriate configuration environment required for the testing. These cloud services are especially attractive for a system's full-scale testing, and for tests that require a high volume of resources, such as availability and load automated testing. In many cases, performing tests that require a high volume of resources is not possible at the developer's or customer's site. In some cases, testing of these types is possible at the developer's or customer's site, but not without severe interruptions to the regular operation of customer's software systems. Publications that present the issues of testing using cloud services are Candea et al. (2010) and Incki et al. (2012).

Implementation tip

Once you consider terminating testing, whether on the basis of a mathematical model, the error seeding route, or the dual testing teams' route, validation of the accuracy of the results within the organization's testing environment is of highest importance.

Systematic follow-up activities are required for validation:

- *Data collection.* Collection of quality data on the errors detected in the project.
- Total number of code errors = errors detected in the testing process + errors detected by the customers and maintenance team during the first 6 or 12 months of regular software use.
- *Analysis of the error data.* The analysis will compare estimates supplied by the models with the real figures.
- *Comparative analysis of severity of errors.* Errors detected in the testing process are compared with errors detected by the customers and maintenance team during the first 6 or 12 months of regular software use.

14.5.4 Test planning documentation

The planning stage of the software system tests is commonly documented in a "software test plan" (STP). A template for the STP is presented in Frame 14.4.

14.6 Designing the testing process

The following are the products of the test design stage:

- Detailed design and procedures for each test.
- Test case database/file.

The testing design is carried out on the basis of the software test plan as documented by an STP. The test procedures and the test case database/file may be documented in a "software test procedure" document and "test case file" document, or in a single document called the "software test description" (STD). A template for the STD is presented in Frame 14.5.

14.7 Implementation of the testing process

This section deals with two subjects:

- The implementation process
- Documentation of the implementation results

Frame 14.4: The software test plan (STP) – template

Scope of the tests
<ul><li>The software package to be tested (name, version, and revision)</li><li>The documents that provide the basis for the planned tests (name and version of each document)</li></ul>**Testing environment**<ul><li>Testing sites</li><li>Required hardware and firmware configuration</li><li>Participating organizations</li><li>Manpower requirements</li><li>Preparation and training required of the test team</li></ul>**Tests details (for each test)**<ul><li>Test identification</li><li>Test objective</li><li>Cross-reference to the relevant design document and the requirement document</li><li>Test class</li><li>Test level (unit, integration, or system tests)</li><li>Test case requirements</li><li>Special requirements (e.g., measurements of response times, security requirements)</li><li>Data to be recorded</li></ul>**Test schedule (for each test or test group) including time estimates for:**<ul><li>Preparation</li><li>Testing</li><li>Error correction</li><li>Regression tests</li></ul>

14.7.1 The implementation process

Commonly, the testing implementation phase activities consist of a series of tests, corrections of detected errors, and retests (regression tests):

- **The tests** are carried out by running the test cases according to the test procedures. Documentation of the test procedures and the test case database/file comprise the "software test description" (STD), presented in Frame 14.5.

- **Correction of detected errors**, as carried out by the software developers, is a highly controlled process. Follow-up of the process is performed to ensure that all the errors listed in the STR have been corrected.

- **Retesting** (also termed "regression testing") is conducted to verify that errors detected in the previous test runs have been properly corrected, and that no new errors entered the system as a result of faulty corrections. It is quite common to find that the correction–regression testing sequence is repeated two to four times before satisfactory test results are achieved. Usually, it is advisable to retest according to the original test procedure.

Frame 14.5: Software test descriptions (STD) – template

Scope of the tests

- The software package to be tested (name, version, and revision)
- The documents providing the basis for the designed tests (name and version for each document)

Test environment (for each test)

- Test identification (the test details are documented in the STP)
- Detailed description of the operating system and hardware configuration and the required switch settings for the tests
- Instructions for software loading

Testing process

- Instructions for input, detailing every step of the input process
- Data to be recorded during the tests

Test cases (for each case)

- Test case identification details
- Input data and system settings
- Expected intermediate results (if applicable)
- Expected results (numerical, message, activation of equipment, etc.)

  Actions to be taken in case of program failure/cessation
  Procedures to be applied according to the test results summary

---

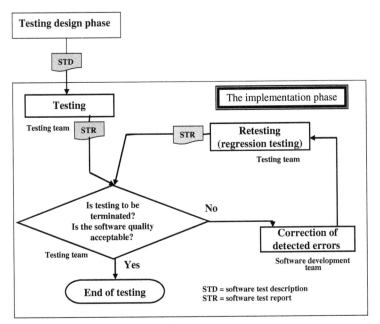

Figure 14.3 Implementation process activities

However, in many cases, especially in manual software testing, only a portion of the original test procedure is retested to save time and testing resources. The parts of the software system that are omitted are those where no errors were detected, or where all detected errors were properly corrected at a previous point. Partial reruns of the test procedure save resources and time, but involve the risk of not detecting new errors that were unintentionally introduced in the omitted parts during the erroneous correction of errors found in other parts of the software.

The implementation phase process is illustrated in Figure 14.3.

Symbolic execution for software testing in practice is discussed by Cadar et al. (2011).

14.7.2 Documentation of the implementation results

The results of the individual tests and retests are documented in a "software test report" (STR). A template for the STR is presented in Frame 14.6.

14.8 Automated testing

Test automation represents an additional step in the integration of computerized tools in the process of software development. These tools are utilized in the execution of the tests, as well as in the management and control of the testing process (testing results, error correction, and retesting). Test automation has increased the share of computer-aided software engineering (CASE) tools in the execution of software development projects.

Several factors have motivated the development of test automation tools. The main factors anticipated were cost savings, shortened test duration, the ability to perform test types impossible to perform manually, and improvements in test management and control processes.

Frame 14.6: Software test report (STR) – template

Test identification, site, schedule, and participation

- The tested software identification (name, version, and revision)
- The documents providing the basis for the tests (name and version for each document)
- Test site
- Initiation and concluding times for each testing session
- Test team members
- Other participants
- Hours invested in performing tests

Test environment

- Hardware and firmware configurations
- Preparations and training prior to testing

Test results

- Test identification
- Test case results (for each test case individually)
- Test case identification
- Tester identification
- Results: OK/failed.
- If failed: detailed description of results/problems.

Summary tables for total number of errors, their distribution, and types

- Summary of current tests
- Comparison with previous results (for regression test summaries)

Special events and tester proposals

- Special events and unpredicted responses of the software during testing
- Problems encountered during testing.
- Proposals for changes in the test environment, including test preparations
- Proposals for changes or corrections in test procedures and test case files

At this stage of development, the planning, design, and test case preparation of automated testing require substantial investment of professional manpower. It is the computerized test performance and the reporting that yield the main economic, quality, and timetable advantages of the process. Availability of the required professional manpower and the extent they are to be used represent the main factors to be considered before initiating automation of software tests.

14.8.1 Automated testing process versus manual testing

To better understand the issues, a comparison of automated and manual testing is presented in Table 14.8.

Table 14.8 A comparison of automated and manual testing by phase

| Testing process phases | Automated testing | | Manual testing | |
	Automated/ manual performance	Comments	Automated/ manual performance	Comments
Test planning	M	Preparing the test plan	M	Preparing the test plan
Test design	M	Preparing the test data base	M	Preparing the testing procedure
Preparing test cases	M	Preparing test cases and their recording into test case database	M	Preparing test cases
Performance of the tests	A	Computerized running of the tests	M	Performing the tests with testers
Regression tests	A	Computerized running of the tests	M	Performing the tests by testers
Preparing the tests log and test reports, including comparative reports	A	Computerized output	M	Prepared by the testers

Table 14.9   Automated versus manual testing – GUI testing experiment results

	Preparation time			Tester run Execution time		
		Time range			Time range	
	Average (hours)	Min (hours)	Max (hours)	Average (hours)	Min (hours)	Max (hours)
Automated testing	19.2	10.6	56.0	0.21	0.1	1.0
Manual testing	11.6	10.0	20.0	3.93	0.5	24.0

Quantitative comparison – empirical findings

Empirical comparative studies of manual versus automated testing are very rare. An interesting study was carried out by Dustin et al. (1999), who report the findings of a study initiated by the European Systems and Software Institute (ESSI). Graphical user interface (GUI) software was chosen to be tested. The study was composed of 10 comparative experiments, with parallel manual testing and automated testing performed in each experiment. A summary of the results is presented in Table 14.9.

The study results conform to qualitative evaluations, meaning that the average preparation time for automated testing is substantially more than that for manual testing of similar software system, with 65% more resources consumed on average, in preparation for the automated testing. Also, as anticipated, the time invested by testers to run execution time for manual testing is 18.7 times more than that for the automated testing on average. Based on these figures, the study's authors estimated N – the minimum number of test runs (the first test run and subsequent regression runs) that economically justify application of automated testing (the "breakeven point"). Assuming that the resources invested in regression tests, manual as well as automated, are similar to those invested in the first test run, N can be derived according to the following equation:

$$19.2 + 0.21 \times N = 11.6 + 3.93 \times N$$
$$N = 2.04$$

Based on this model, if the testing process requires one or more regression test runs, automated testing is to be preferred. In a short survey I conducted, I found that the common number of regression tests runs during the development stage was 4.

Some reservations, including those mentioned by Dustin et al. (1999), are evident:

- The breakeven point model ignores or considers negligible the heavy investments required for acquiring automated testing capabilities, namely, investments in purchasing the software package and training the operators of the automated testing professionals.
- Manual regression test runs, especially second, third, and later regression runs, are usually partial, therefore requiring only a portion of the resources consumed during the first test run.
- Automated test yields more accurate results than manual tests.

It should be emphasized that even when considering the above reservations, N would change to be $N = 4$ or more. The important qualitative advantages of automated testing would lead us to prefer it to manual testing in many cases. The fact that automated correctness tests are performed during the maintenance stage should also be considered.

Much additional research is needed to construct a comprehensive integrated model for the comparison, quantitative and qualitative, of the two testing approaches. The research efforts should be directed at collecting sufficient empirical data and at development models capable of quantifying a good portion of the qualitative advantages of automated testing.

Valuable sources for additional material on automated testing can be found in books and papers by Dustin et al. (2009) and Graham and Fewster (2013).

14.8.2 Types of automated testing

Numerous types of automated tests are available, many have become more or less routine. The more established automated tests are mainly those employed for testing tasks that require a high number of regression tests, and those performing test classes not feasible for manual testing such as availability and load testing. The main types of automated tests currently used are listed in Frame 14.7.

Frame 14.7: The main types of automated tests

The main types of automated tests
Correctness testing
• GUI tests
• Functional tests
Availability and load tests   Other tests
• Code auditing
• Coverage monitoring
• Integrity (security) testing

a. Automated correctness tests

(1) Graphical user interface (GUI) tests

The user interface is composed of a series of user actions performed to insert input data and system reactions/responses. The user inserts input items to a graphical interface with key strokes, mouse clicks, screen touches, and so on. The user expects changes in the graphical interface. The testing process is designed to validate that the system reactions/responses are correct.

The testing of automated graphical unit interfaces is based on the recording of user activities and the correct reactions/responses

The family of automated graphical user interface testing includes several variations related to the media used:

- Testing computer graphical input screens
- Testing website input pages
- Testing mobile computers and advanced phone screens inputs

Recent publications on the subject include Mariani et al. (2014).

(2) Functional tests

Automated functional tests often replace manual black box correctness tests. This type of test examines the calculations executed by the program and detects deviations from the required results. Prior to performing these tests, the test cases are recorded into the test case database. The tests are then carried out by executing the test cases through the test program. The test results documentation includes listings of the errors identified, in addition to a variety of summaries and statistics as demanded by the tester specifications.

After the corrections have been completed, retesting the whole program or parts of it (regression tests) is most usually required. Automated regression tests performed for the whole program verify that the error corrections have been performed satisfactorily and that the corrections have not unintentionally introduced new errors in other parts of the program. The regression tests themselves are performed with the existing test case database; hence, these tests can be executed with minimal effort or professional resources. An additional automated testing tool that supports functional tests, the output comparator, greatly supports the regression test stage. The automated comparison of outputs of successive tests, together with results from the functional testing tools, enables testers to prepare an improved analysis of the regression test results and to help developers discover the causes of errors detected in the tests. It is quite common for programs to require three or four regression tests before their quality level is considered satisfactory.

b. Automated availability and load tests

The history of software system development contains many sad chapters on systems that succeeded in correctness tests but severely failed – and caused enormous damage – once required to operate under standard full load. The damage in many cases was extremely serious because the failure occurred "unexpectedly," when the systems were supposed to start providing their regular software services. The most spectacular failures tend to take place in very large information systems that were planned to serve a large numbers of users at any one time, or in real-time firmware systems planned to handle a high volume of simultaneous events.

The maximal load environment must first be created for availability and load tests to be performed. The tests must be conducted when the system is under maximal user load, a condition that is, in most cases, impractical or impossible for manual testing. Therefore, the only way to carry out load tests for medium- and large-scale systems is by means of computerized simulations that can be programmed to closely simulate real load conditions.

The availability and load testing procedure

The environment required for availability and load test is created by a computer program that simulates scenarios of user behavior. For simulating these scenarios, virtual users and virtual events are generated and operated in a hardware and communication environment defined by the system planner. A virtual user or event emulates the behavior of a human user and real event. Its behavior is "constructed" by applying real outputs captured from real user applications that are then used as inputs for the simulation. The simulation then produces outputs similar to those captured from real-life users at the frequencies and with the user mix defined by the scenario. These outputs serve as inputs for the tested software. The tests are carried out by sending messages according to virtual events by virtual users to the tested software and receiving the messages sent by the tested software system.

The computerized monitoring of the automated availability and load tests is based on "answer" messages sent by the tested software system and its response times. It produces performance measurements of the software system in terms of response time, processing time, and other desired parameters. These are compared with the specified load performance requirements in order to evaluate how well the software system will perform when in daily use. Usually, a series of load tests is conducted with the load gradually increased to the specified maximal load and beyond. This step enables a more thorough study of system performance under regular and maximal loads. The computer-produced tables and graphs, based on the performance measurement information, allow the tester to decide what changes are to be introduced into each simulation for each test iteration. For example, the tester may wish to:

• Change the hardware, including the communication system, to increase or decrease its capacity to allow the software system to fulfill its performance requirements, in terms of response time, at each load level.

• Test new combinations of hardware and scenario components.

The tester will continue iterations till he finds the appropriate hardware and communication system configuration.

Example:

The "Tick Ticket" is a new Internet site designed to meet the following requirements:

• The site was planned to handle a regular load of 1,200 hits per hour, and should be able to handle up to a maximum of 3,000 hits per hour.
• Average response time required for the maximal load of 3,000 hits per hour.
• Average response time required for the regular load of 1,200 hits per hour – 3 seconds or less.
• Considering future expected growth of load, it was decided to define an average response time of 10 seconds or less for an extended load of 20% above the maximal load, namely, for 3,600 hits per hour.

The plan. The load tests were planned for the following series of hit frequencies (hits per hour): 300, 600, 900, 1,200, 1,500, 1,800, 2,100, 2,400, 2,700, 3,000, 3,300 and 3,600. An initial hardware configuration was defined, and is to be adapted according to the load test results

Implementation. Three series of load tests were run before the adequate hardware and communication software configuration were determined. After the first and second series of load tests, the hardware configuration was changed to increase the system capacity so as to achieve the required reaction times. The second configuration fulfilled the average reaction time requirement for the regular hit loads, but not for the extended maximal load. Therefore, capacity was further increased. In its final configuration, the software system could satisfactorily handle the requirement for loads 20% higher than the specified maximal load. See Table 14.10 for the average reaction times measured at each round of load testing.

c. **Other types of automated testing**

Three types of automated testing are presented:

• Automatic code auditing
• Automatic coverage monitoring
• Automatic integrity (security) testing

(1) **Automatic code auditing**

This test performs automated qualification testing. The computerized code auditor checks the compliance of the code to specified standards and procedures of coding. The auditor's report includes a list of deviations from the standards and a statistical summary of findings.

Table 14.10 Tick ticket load tests – measured reaction times

| | Average response time (seconds) | | |
| | Load tests – series | | |
Hit frequency (hits per hour)	I Hardware configuration I	II Hardware configuration II	III Hardware configuration III
300	2.2	1.8	1.5
600	2.5	1.9	1.5
900	3.0	2.0	1.5
1,200	3.8	2.3	1.6
1,500	5.0	2.8	1.8
1,800	7.0	3.5	2.2
2,100	10.0	4.5	2.8
2,400	15.0	6.5	3.7
2,700	22.0	10.5	4.8
3,000	32.0	16.0	6.3
3,300	55.0	25.0	7.8
3,600	95.0	38.5	9.5

A code auditor can verify the following:
- Does the code fulfill code structure instructions and procedures?
- Levels of loop nesting
- Levels of subroutine nesting
- Prohibited constructs, such as GOTO
- Does the coding style follow the coding style procedures?
- Naming conventions for variables, files, etc.
- Unreachable code lines of program or entire subroutines
- Do the internal program documentation and "help" support sections follow the coding style procedures?
- Comment format and size
- Comment location in the file
- Help index and presentation style

(2) Automatic coverage monitoring

Coverage monitors produce reports about the line coverage achieved when implementing a given test case file. The monitor's output includes the percentage of lines covered by the test cases, as well as listings of uncovered lines. These features make coverage monitoring a vital tool for white-box tests.

(3) Automatic integrity (security) testing

The vulnerability of software systems to activities of criminal bodies is of great concern to software system operators. The detection of software errors that cause the software vulnerability is a task recently being targeted by automated specialized testing tools, black box and white box tools. The white box tools generate test cases by creating random "mutations" from "well-formed program inputs" and examining the results. Promising results of vulnerability errors detection with a white box tool are described by Godefroid et al. (2007).

Another promising route for automatic vulnerability is based on black box testing tools. In a series of empirical vulnerability, tests of eight black box vulnerability tools are performed by Bau et al. (2010). It was found in this study that the vulnerability errors detection rate reached 60%, when the detection rate differs in the various vulnerability types.

Future development of this class of automated tools is expected to reach achievements that will place the automated vulnerability test as the major tool in integrity (security) testing level

(4) **Automatic test case generation**

Test case generation is probably the most labor intensive tasks in software testing that strongly affects the efficiency and effectiveness of the software testing process. Consequently, several research and development efforts are directed to automate the generation of test cases. A survey of these efforts and achievements is presented in Anand et al. (2013).

d. **Automation in test management and control**

Testing involves many participants occupied in actually carrying out the tests and correcting the detected errors. In addition, testing typically monitors performance of every item on long lists of test case files. This workload makes timetable follow-up important to management. Computerized test management supports these and other testing management goals. In general, computerized test management tools are planned to provide testers with reports, lists, and other types of information at levels of quality and availability higher than those provided by manual test management systems.

Automated test management software packages provide features applicable for manual testing together with automated testing and for automated tests alone. The inputs the testers key in, together with the software package capabilities, determine the application scope. Especially important in these cases is the package's interoperability with respect to the automated testing tools.

Frame 14.8 provides a concise summary of the features offered by automated test management software packages.

14.8.3 Advantages and disadvantages of automated tests

The first part of this section presents a comprehensive qualitative comparison of automated testing and manual testing, conducted by listing the advantages and

Frame 14.8: **Automated test management packages – main features**

Type of feature	Automated/manual testing
A. Test plans, test results, and correction follow-up	
Preparation of lists, tables, and visual presentations of test plans	A, M
List of test case	A, M
Listing of detected errors	A, M
Listing of correction schedule (performer, date of completion, etc.)	A, M
Listing of uncompleted corrections for follow-up	A, M
Error tracking: detection, correction, and regression tests	A, M
Preparing summary reports of testing and error correction follow-up	A, M
B. Test execution	
Execution of automated software tests	A
Automated listing of automated software test results	A
Automated listing of detected errors	A
C. Maintenance follow-up	
Follow-up of errors reported by users and their correction and retesting	A, M
Summary reports for maintenance correction services according to customer, software system applications, and so on	A, M

disadvantages of automated testing. A quantitative comparison, especially one based on empirical data, is sorely needed to support the qualitative comparison. The second part of the section deals with early quantitative findings that point to the economic advantages of using automated testing tools.

The following are the main advantages of automated tests:

- **Accuracy and completeness of performance**. Computerized testing guarantees – to the maximum degree possible – that all tests and test cases are being carried out completely and accurately. Manual testing suffers from periods of tester weariness or low concentration, traits that induce inaccurate keying in of test cases, omissions, and so on.

- **Accuracy of results log and summary reports**. Automated tests are programmed for accurate reporting of errors detected. In contrast, the testers who perform manual tests occasionally do not recognize errors, and may overlook others in their logs and summaries.

- **Comprehensiveness of information**. Naturally, once the test data – including test results – are stored in a database, queries and reports about the test and its results are incomparably more available by automated tests than by manual tests. The automated comprehensive reporting, besides supporting follow-up of testing and correction, and improving error information, enhances the input needed for preventive and corrective actions (see Chapter 16).

- **Lower manpower resources required for performing of tests**. Manual performance of testing, in comparison, is a major consumer of manpower resources.

- **Shorter duration of testing**. The duration of automated tests is usually far shorter than that of manual tests. In addition, automated tests can be carried out, uninterrupted, 24 hours a day, 7 days a week, in contrast to manual testing, which is difficult to be carried out by more than one testing team and in more than one shift a day.

- **Performance of complete regression tests**. Due to the shortage of time and manpower resources, manual regression tests tend only to be conducted on a relatively small portion of the software package. In contrast, the minimal time and manpower resources required to recycle the automated tests make it possible to completely rerun regression tests. This option substantially reduces the risk of not detecting errors introduced during previous round of corrections. An additional possibility to recycle automated tests exists for testing corrections and software changes performed in the maintenance stage.

- **Performance of test classes beyond the scope of manual testing**. Computerization enables the tester to perform, for example, availability and load tests, for medium- and large-scale systems. These tests are almost impossible to perform manually on systems that are not small.

The following are the main disadvantages of automated testing:

- *High investments required in package purchasing and training..* An organization that decides to implement automated testing must invest in software packages and in training staff to qualify for performing automated tests. Despite claims of the software package developers, although the amount of training varies per software package, it is still lengthy, and thus expensive.

- *High package development investment costs..* In cases where available automated testing packages do not fully suit the system's requirements, custom-made packages must be developed.

- *Extensive human resources required for test preparation..* The human resources required for preparing an automated test procedure are usually substantially higher than those required for preparing a manual procedure for the same software package.

- *Considerable testing areas left uncovered..* The variety of tools currently offered covers most prevailing programming areas/applications, and is readily available from software development companies specializing in automated testing tools. At present, automated software testing packages do not cover the entire variety of development tools and types of applications, and so manual tests are carried out in these cases.

The advantages and disadvantages of automated software testing are presented in Frame 14.9.

Frame 14.9: Automated software testing: advantages and disadvantages

Advantages	Disadvantages
1. Accuracy and completeness of performance	1. High investments required for package purchasing and training
2. Accuracy of results log and summary reports	2. High package development investment costs
3. Comprehensive information	3. Extensive manpower resources required for test preparation
4. Less manpower resources for test execution	4. Considerable testing areas left uncovered
5. Shorter testing periods	
6. Performance of complete regression tests	
7. Performance of test classes beyond scope of manual testing	

14.9 Alpha and beta site testing programs

The alpha and beta site tests are employed to enable comments related to the software quality from potential users of the package. These sites are additional tools, commonly used to identify software design and code errors in software packages in commercial over-the-counter sale (COTS). It is expected that unexpected combinations of inputs used by alpha and beta site participants will detect errors of types not expected to be revealed by testing plans. In a way, alpha and beta site tests replace the customer's acceptance test – a test that is impractical under the conditions of commercial software package development. However, an analysis of the characteristics of these tests leads one to conclude that in no case should they replace the formal software tests performed by the developer.

Alpha site tests

"Alpha site tests" are tests performed by potential users at the developer's site on a new software package. The customer, by applying the new software to the specific requirements of his organization, tends to examine the package from angles not expected by the testing team. The errors identified by alpha site tests are expected to include errors that only real users can reveal, and thus should be reported to the developer.

Beta site tests

Beta site tests are much more commonly applied than alpha site tests. The beta site test process can be described as follows: Once an advanced version of the software package is available, the developer offers it free-of-charge to one or more potential users. The users install the package in their sites (usually called the "beta site") with the understanding that they will inform the developer of all errors revealed during trials or regular usage. Participants in beta site testing are often users of previously released packages, sophisticated software professionals, and the like. As beta site tests are considered to be a valuable tool, some developers involve hundreds and even thousands of participants in the process.

The following are the main advantages of alpha and beta site tests:

- *Identification of unexpected errors.*. Users usually examine software in an entirely different way than developers do and, of course, apply the software in ways far different from those typically found in developer scenarios, such as unexpected combinations of inputs. Consequently, they reveal errors of a type that professional testers rarely identify.
- *A wider population in search of errors.*. The wide range of participants involved in beta site testing contribute a scope of software usage experience and potential for revealing hidden errors that go beyond those available at the developer's testing site.
- *Low costs.*. As participants are not paid for their participation or for error information they report, the only cost encountered is the cost of the package delivery to the customer.

The following are the main disadvantages of alpha and beta site tests:

- *A lack of systematic testing.* As participants in beta site tests are in no way obligated to prepare orderly reports, they tend to report scattered experience and leave applications, or segments of them, untouched.
- *Low-quality error reports.* Participants are not professional testers; hence, their error reports are often faulty (in some report no errors at all), and it is frequently impossible to reconstruct the *error* conditions.
- *Difficult to reproduce the test environment.* Beta site testing is usually performed in an uncontrolled testing environment, a fact that creates difficulties when attempting to identify the causes of the reported errors.

- *Much effort is required to examine reports.* A relatively high investment of time and human resources is needed when examining reports due to the frequent repetitions and low quality of reporting.

While alpha site testing enjoys the same advantages and displays the same disadvantages as beta site testing, alpha site tests are usually more difficult to organize than beta site tests, yet tend to be fruitful.

Implementation tip

Testers and developers should be especially cautious when applying beta site testing. Beta site testing of premature software may detect many software errors, but may also result in highly negative publicity among potential customers. In some cases, these negative impressions reach professional journals and cause substantial damage to a company's image.

We therefore recommend that alpha site testing be initiated first, and that beta site testing be delayed until alpha site tests have been completed, and their results analyzed.

14.10 Code review activities for the programming and testing phases

Two code review classes serve the programming and testing phases. These include:

- Reviews of code listings.
- Software qualification reviews

14.10.1 Reviews of code listings

Code reviews, namely, code inspections and walkthroughs, are performed on code listings of unit software and integration software and conducted prior to unit and integration tests. These code reviews successfully identify a significant part of the software errors.

Code reviews are also performed on software produced by the maintenance team during the operation phase.

14.10.2 Software qualification reviews

Software qualification reviews by code reviews is the preferred software quality assurance tool for checking adherence to programming and maintenance requirements. Software code and documentation that adhere to qualification requirements make it easier for the team leader to check the software, for the replacement programmer to comprehend the ready code and documents and to continue performing the tasks, and for the maintenance programmer to correct bugs and/or update or change the program upon request.

Software qualification reviews relate mainly to the following issues:

- Does the code or document fulfill the structure standards and development instructions and procedures, such as module size?
- Does the code style fulfill coding style procedures and instructions?
- Is the document (i.e., programmer manual) prepared according to approved documentation standards or template and provide complete documentation?
- Do the documentation and "help" sections fulfill coding style procedures?

Specialized software packages for code reviews (called code auditors) and document reviews (called automatic static analysis) can now perform a portion of the qualification tests by listing cases of nonconformity to coding standards, procedures, and work instructions. Other parts of the reviews continue to be the responsibility of trained personnel for their manual execution.

Summary

(1) Software testing objectives
One should distinguish between direct and indirect testing objectives.
The following are the direct objectives:

- To identify and reveal as many errors as possible in the tested software
- To bring the tested software to an acceptable quality level (after corrections)
- To perform the required testing in an efficient and effective way, within budget and scheduling limitations
- To establish with a degree of confidence that the software package is ready for delivery

The following is the indirect objective:

- To compile a record of software errors for use in software process improvement

(2) Software testing organization and performance
Software testing – unit testing, integration testing, and system acceptance testing – is organized and carried out by the development teams and the software development departments. In some organizations, the acceptance testing is performed by a specialized testing teams or by outsourced testing organizations.

The role of the SQA function in software testing

The role of the SQA function is supportive of the software acceptance testing organization (consulting basis), and is aimed at improving its efficiency and effectiveness. SQA function team members may participate in software acceptance testing, as part of the SQA activities to evaluate software product conformance.

(3) The process approaches for the evaluation of software products – the definitions

The three approaches are:

- **Verification** – A process for evaluating a software system or component product of a given development phase with the purpose of checking whether the examined product correctly and fully implemented the conditions and requirements presented at the beginning of the given phase.

- **Validation** – A process for evaluating a software system or component product of a given development phase with the purpose of checking whether the examined product correctly and fully implemented the relevant specified requirements.

- **Qualification** – A process for evaluating a software system or component product of a given development phase with the purpose of checking whether the examined product correctly and fully implemented the professional coding conventions, style and structure, instructions, and procedures.

(4) Big bang versus incremental testing

The two contrasting testing strategies are defined and compared

"Big bang testing": Tests the software as a whole, once the completed package is available.

"Incremental testing": Tests the software piecemeal – software modules as they are completed (unit tests), followed by groups of modules composed of tested modules integrated with newly completed modules (integration tests). Once the entire package is complete, it is tested as a whole (system test).

Unless the program is very small and simple, applying the "big bang" testing strategy presents severe disadvantages. In "big bang" testing, identification of errors in the entire software package is very difficult, and as a result, performing perfect correction of an error in this context is frequently laborious. In addition, estimates of the required testing resources and testing schedule tend to be rather fuzzy. In contrast, the incremental testing, as it is performed on relatively small software units, yields higher percentages of identified errors and facilitates their correction. Thus, usually incremental testing is more effective and more efficient. As a result, it is generally accepted that incremental testing should be preferred.

(5) The order of performing incremental testing

There are two possible order strategies for conducting incremental testing: bottom-up and top-down. In top-down testing, the first module tested is the main module, the highest level module in the software structure; the last modules to be tested are the lowest level modules. In bottom-up testing, the order of testing is reversed: the lowest level modules are tested first, with the main module tested last.

The main advantage of the top-down strategy is the early stage at which it is possible to demonstrate the program as a whole, a condition that supports early identification of analysis and design errors by the customer.

(6) Black box and white box testing

Black box testing identifies bugs only according to malfunctioning of the software as revealed from its outputs.

White box testing examines the internal paths of calculations in order to identify bugs.

The following are the main advantages of black box testing:

- Less testing resources are required compared with white box testing.
- The needed resources for black box testing may be further reduced by conducting automatic black box testing.
- The tester may carry out almost all test classes, some are not available with white box testing.

The following are the main disadvantages of black box testing:

- Inability to directly test software and identify errors.
- Lacks control of line coverage.
- Allows for identification of coincidental aggregation of several errors as correct.
- Lacks possibilities to test the quality of coding work.

The following are the main advantages of white box testing:

- Enables directly checking processing paths and algorithms.
- Provides line coverage follow-up that delivers lists of lines of code not yet been executed.
- Capable of testing the quality of coding work.

The following are the main disadvantages of white box testing:

- Requires vast resources, much more than those required for black box testing.
- Cannot perform important test classes: availability, reliability, stress, and so on.

(7) White box testing coverage

Two alternative approaches for white box coverage have emerged:

- "Path coverage" is defined as the percentage of possible paths covered by the test cases.
- "Line coverage" is defined as the percentage of executed lines of code examined during the tests.

In most cases, the conducting of full path coverage is impractical because of the scope of resources required for its implementation.

(8) Requirement-driven software testing

The software tests are classified by requirements, according to McCall's model, into three categories:

- Operation factor testing categories
- Revision factor testing categories
- Transition factor testing categories

Operation factor category includes the following test classes:

- Correctness tests: software correctness tests, user manuals tests, and availability (reaction time) tests
- Reliability tests
- Stress tests: load tests and durability tests
- Software system security tests
- Usability tests: training usability tests and operational usability tests factor

Revision factor testing classes include:

- Maintainability correctness tests
- Flexibility tests
- Testability tests

Transition factor testing classes include:

- Portability tests
- Reused software correctness tests
- Interoperability tests: equipment and software interfacing tests

(9) The process of tests planning

The planners consider the following issues for each test plan:

- Which sources should be used for test cases
- Who is to perform the tests
- Where should the tests be performed

Which sources should be used for test cases – A test case includes: (1) the data input/parameters of a test item, (2) the operating conditions required to run a test item, and (3) the expected results of running the test item.

There are two basic sources for test cases: (1) random samples of real-life cases, and (2) synthetic test cases.

The main advantages of samples of real life are as follows: (1) less efforts in preparing the test cases, especially where expected results are available and need not be calculated, and (2) some ability to identify unexpected errors for unlisted situations.

The main advantages of synthetic test cases are as follows: (1) less efforts to perform tests due to a relatively small test case file compiled to avoid repetitions, and (2) good coverage of erroneous situations by test case file design.

Who is to perform the tests – Unit and integration testing are generally performed by the software development team. System tests are, in many cases, performed by an independent testing team or by a testing consultant's off-shore team. In cases of large software system, more than one testing team can be employed to carry out the system tests.

Where should the tests be performed – Unit and integration testing is most naturally carried out at the software developer's site. System tests are performed at the developer's or customer's site (the "target site"). An alternative testing site, which has become common in recent years, is via the usage of cloud computing services. This option offers unlimited computing resources.

(10) Designing the tests

The following are the products of the test design stage:

• Detailed design and procedure for each test

• Test case database/file

(11) Implementation of the testing process

Frequently, the testing implementation phase activities consist of a series of tests, corrections of detected errors, and retests (regression tests). The software test report (STR) provides documentation of the tests performed. Five alternative routes for deciding test termination are available: (1) complete implementation of testing plans, (2) application of mathematical models, (3) according to fault injection results, (4) according to dual independent testing team results, and (5) termination after resources have depleted.

(12) Automated testing process versus manual testing

Automated testing includes the manual activities of planning and designing the tests and preparing the test cases. All the other activities, namely, performing the tests, including the regression tests, and reporting the test results, including comparative reports, are computerized, whereas in manual testing all activities are manual.

Quantitative comparisons based on empirical results show that a testing process requires one or more regression test runs in order for automated testing to be preferred.

(13) The main types of automated testing

The following are the main types of automated testing:

• **Correctness testing**

- GUI tests – The user's way to add input items to a graphical interface is by key strokes, mouse clicks, screen touches, and so on.

- Functional tests – This type of test examines the calculations executed by the program and detects deviations from the required results.
- **Availability and load tests** – The tests must be conducted when the system is under maximal user load, a condition that is impractical in most cases and impossible for manual testing. Conducting a series of availability and load tests for varying loads enables defining the appropriate hardware and communication configuration for a project.
- **Other automated testing types**
  - Code auditing – The code auditor checks the compliance of code with specified standards and procedures of coding. The auditor's report includes a list of deviations from the standards.
  - Automatic coverage monitoring – Coverage monitors produce reports about the line coverage achieved when implementing a given test case file.
  - Integrity (security) testing – The vulnerability of software systems to activities of criminal bodies is of great concern to software system operators. The detection of software errors that cause software vulnerability is a task recently being targeted by automated specialized testing tools

(14) Automation in test management and control

The following are the features offered by automated test management software packages:

- Documenting the planning and design of the tests
- Error tracking: detection, correction, and regression tests
- Preparing summary reports of testing, and error correction follow-up
- Execution of automated software tests
  - Automated listing of automated software test results and detected errors
  - Follow-up of errors reported by users, their correction, and retesting
- Summary reports for maintenance activities

(15) Discuss the advantages and disadvantages of automated computerized testing compared with manual testing

The following are the main advantages of automated tests:

- The accuracy and completeness of performance.
- Accuracy of results logs and summary reports.
- Ability to obtain substantially more comprehensive information.
- Performance requires less manpower resources.
- Shorter testing periods.
- Performance of complete regression tests.
- Performance of test classes beyond the reach of manual testing.

The following are the main disadvantages of automated tests:

• Substantial investments required in package purchasing and training.

• Substantial manpower resources for preparing the tests.

• The considerable testing areas not covered by automated testing.

(16) Beta site testing

Beta site testing is a method by which a selected group of users/customers receives an advanced version of the software to be installed in their sites, users report the errors they find in the process of their experiments with the program and its regular use.

The following are the main advantages of beta site testing:

• Identification of unexpected errors

• A wide scope coverage searching for errors

• Low costs

The following are the main disadvantages of beta site tests:

• Lack of systematic testing

• Error reports of low quality

• Difficulty to reproduce the test environment

• Substantial human effort required to examine participant reports

(17) Review Activities for the programming and testing phases

Several review classes serve the programming and testing phases. These include code reviews, documentation reviews, up-to-date reviews, and software qualification reviews. Code reviews, namely, code inspections and walk-throughs, are conducted for unit and integration software, prior to unit and integration tests. Review activities are the appropriate tools to assure the quality of the documents produced in the programming and testing phases. This type of requirement relates mainly to information processing. Reviewing up-to-date requires examining the operation procedures, and processes of handling the inputs to the software system. Software qualification reviews is the preferred software quality assurance tool for checking adherence to programming and maintenance requirements. Software code and documentation that adhere to qualification requirements make it easier for the team leader to check the software, for the replacement programmer to comprehend the code and documents and continue performing the tasks, and for the maintenance programmer to correct bugs and/or update or change the program upon request.

Selected bibliography

Anand S., Burke E. K., Chen T. Y., Clark J., Cohen M. B., Grieskamp W., Harman M., Harrold M. J., and McMinn P. (2013) *An orchestrated survey of methodologies for automated software test case generation, Journal of Systems and Software*, Vol. **86**, pp. 1978–2001.

Bau J., Bursztein E., Gupta D, and Mitchell J. (2010) State of the Art: automated black-box web application vulnerability testing, in *2010 Symposium on Security and Privacy (SP), Oakland, CA,* May 16–19, 2010, pp. 332–345.

Beizer B. (1995) *Black Box Testing – Techniques and Functional Testing of Software and Systems,* John Wiley and Sons, Inc., New York, NY.

Cadar C., Godefroid P., Khurshid S., Pasareanu C. S., Sen K., and Tillman N., and Visser W. (2011) Symbolic execution for software testing in practice – preliminary assessment, in *Proceedings of the International Conference on Software Engineering (ICSE'11),* pp. 1066–1071.

Candea G., Bucur S., and Zamfir C. (2010) Automated software testing as a service, in *Proceedings of the 1st ACM Symposium on Cloud Computing SoCC '10,* pp. 155–160.

Do T. B. N., Kitamura T., Nguyen V. T., Hatayama G., Sakuragi S., and Ohsaki H. (2013) Constructing test cases for n-wise testing from free-based test models, in *Proceedings of the Fourth Symposium on Information and Communication Technology (SoICT'13),* pp. 275–284.

Dustin E., Rashka J., and Paul J. (1999) *Automated Software Testing – Introduction, Management and Performance,* Addison-Wesley, Reading, MA.

Dustin E., Garrett T., and Gauf B. (2009) *Automated Software Testing,* Addison-Wesley Longman, Reading, MA.

Godefroid P., Levin M. Y., and Molnar D. (2007) Automated whitebox fuzz testing, *Technical Report MSR-TR-2007, Microsoft Research Redmond, WA,* May 2007, pp. 1–15.

Graham D. and Fewster M. (2013) *Experiences of Test Automation: Case Studies of Software Test Automation,* Addison Wesley Professional, Upper Saddle River, NZ.

IEEE . (2008) *IEEE Std. 829-2008 for Software and System Test Documentation,* The IEEE Computer Society, IEEE, New York.

IEEE . (2014) *IEEE Std. 730-2014 Software Quality Assurance,* The IEEE Computer Society, IEEE, New York.

ISO/IEC . (2008) *ISO/IEC/IEEE Std. 12207-2008 – Systems and Software Engineering – Software Life Cycle Processes,* International Organization for Standardization, Geneva, Switzerland.

ISO/IEC . (2014) *ISO/IEC 90003:2014 Software Engineering – Guidelines for the Application of TSO 9001: 2008 to Computer Software,* International Organization for Standardization (ISO), Geneva, Switzerland.

Incki K., An I., and Sozer H. (2012) A survey of software testing in the cloud, in *The 2012 IEEE Sixth International Conference on Software Security and Reliability Companion (SERE-C),* pp. 18–23.

Kruse P. M. and Luniak M. (2010) *Automated test case generation using classification trees, Software Quality Professional,* Vol. **13**, No. 1, pp. 4–12.

Mariani L., Pezze M., Riganelli O., and Santoro M. (2014) *Automated Testing of GUI-Based Applications,* pp. 1–28. doi 10.1.1002/stvr.1539.

Mustafa K. M., Al-Qutaish R. E., and Muhairat M. I. (2009) Classification of software testing tools based on the software testing methods, in *2009 Second International Conference on Computer and Electrical Engineering, Vol. 1, Dubai,* pp. 229–233.

Myers G. J. (1979) *Software Reliability: Principles and Practices,* John Wiley and Sons, Inc., Indianapolis, IN.

Nidhra S. and Dondeti J. (2012) *Black box and white box testing techniques – a literature review, International Journal of Embedded Systems and Applications,* Vol. **2**, No. 2, pp. 29–50.

Perry W. E. (2006) *Effective Methods for Software Testing: Includes Complete Guidelines, Checklists and Templates,* 3rd Edition, John Wiley and Sons, Inc., Indianapolis, IN.

Pressman R. S. and Maxim B. R. (2015) *Software Engineering: A Practitioner's Approach,* 8th Edition, McGraw-Hill International, London.

Rubin J. and Chisnell D. (2008) *Handbook of Usability Testing – How to Plan, Design and Conduct Effective Tests,* John Wiley and Sons, Inc., New York.

Sommerville I. (2015) *Software Engineering,* 10th Edition, Addison Wesley, Harlow, England.

Review questions

14.1 Quite a number of software industry professionals maintain that the main goal of software testing is "to prove that the software package is ready."
- Explain in your own words why this goal for software testing contradicts the first direct objective.

14.2 Explain in your own words why big bang testing is inferior to any method of incremental testing conducted for software packages that are not small.

14.3 Section 14.3.3c mentions the terms *path coverage* and *line coverage*.
- **a.** Explain in your own words what the terms mean and list the main differences between these coverage metrics.
- **b.** Explain why the implementation of path coverage is impractical in most test applications.

14.4 "Bengal Tours" is a city center travel agency that specializes in tours and vacations in Canada. The agency regularly employs 25 permanent employees. During the spring and summer, the agency employs an additional 20–25 temporary staff, mostly pensioners and students. The agency is considering purchasing the right to use the software system "Tourplanex," which supports planning for flight and vacation site vacancies and price information and expediting the orders and payments of customers for the services ordered. If purchased, the software will become the main working tool for the agency staff.
- **a.** Discuss the importance of the training usability and operational usability tests to be performed by the agency before it purchases "Tourplanex."
- **b.** Suggest to "Bengal Tours" management how they should apply training usability and operational usability tests to be performed on the program.

14.5 The student registration software package includes a student details form to provide information about a student's full name, birth date, address, phones, and so on. Now our focus is on the student's cellular phone number as listed in the student registration database.
- Explain the differences between the accuracy, completeness, and up-to-date quality requirements regarding the student's cellular phone number.
- Suggest quality requirements for the accuracy, completeness, and up-to-date of the student details regarding cellular phone numbers.
- The student registration department is considering replacing the student details form with a "computerized form," where the student keys-in his details. Besides saving the department's key-in resources, will this change also improve accuracy, completeness, and up-to-date of the student's cellular phone number data? Explain.
- The student is expected to stay in the university for at least 3 years. Are the quality of student cellular phone numbers expected to deteriorate throughout the years? What activities would you suggest in order to keep these date details within the quality requirements during all the students' studying years?

14.6 "Alpha phone" is a software package that includes the following among its features:

- It manages a household phone address book.
- It produces printouts of the phone book according to a variety of classifications.
- It analyses the monthly traffic of incoming and outgoing phone calls according to the classifications mentioned above.

   You are called to perform a documentation test of the very elegant "alpha phone" user manual.

- List at least five types of possible documentation errors in the manual.

14.7 "The MPT star" is a program for calculating the annual municipal property taxes, based on the neighborhood, the type of property (house, store, apartment, etc.), the size of the property, the discounts which 10% of the owners are entitled to (pensioners, low-income large families, single-parent families, etc.).

- Suggest a framework for stratified sampling test cases from the citizens file. List your assumptions about the population's distribution.

14.8 "In most cases, the test case file preferred should combine sample cases with synthetic cases, to overcome the disadvantages of a single source of test cases, and to increase the efficiency of the testing process" (in Section 14.5.1).

- Elaborate on how applying a mixed-source methodology overcomes the disadvantages of a single-source methodology.
- Elaborate on how applying a mixed-source methodology enhances testing efficiency. Provide a hypothetical example.

14.9 Software testing experts claim that applying a stratified sample of real-life test cases is more effective for identifying errors and more efficient than regular random sampling.

- If you agree, list your arguments.
- If you disagree, list your contradictory arguments.

14.10 Reviewing the advantages and disadvantages of automated software testing:

- Explain the main advantages and disadvantages of automated tests in your own words.
- Referring to your answer in (a) – suggest which project characteristics are most suitable for automated testing. List your assumptions.
- Referring to your answer in (a) – suggest which project characteristics are most unsuitable for automated testing. List your assumptions.

14.11 Mr. Aleppo, head of the software development department, claims that beta site tests should always be carried out as early as possible in the development process, as there are no disadvantages in this method.

- Are beta site tests really a "disadvantage free" method? If not, what are the main disadvantages and risks of beta site tests?
- List recommended guidelines that will minimize the risks and disadvantages in applying beta site tests as listed in (a).

Topics for discussion

14.1 "Police Star 1000 System" is the new prestigious software system for recording all the verbal communication (line telephone, cellular telephone, and wireless) nationwide to be instituted by the police force. One feature of the system is its ability to supply any voice record completed in the last 12 months within 15 minutes in 98% of the applications. The system is planned to be operative within 10 months.

- Discuss the importance of conducting comprehensive load tests for the system.
- Should the load test be required to combine availability and efficiency requirements? Explain.
- Suggest the recommended guidelines for planning these load tests.
- What basic data on police activities would you recommend to collect in order to plan the load test according to your recommended guidelines?
- Suggest availability and efficiency quality requirements for the "Police Star 1000 System." Discuss your answer.

14.2 "Super Saving Light" is a new software system to control street illumination and enhance its economy, developed for municipality maintenance departments. Among its functions are:

- Turning street lighting on and off according to a daily timetable, scheduled annually.
- Partial illumination (only one of each two lights will be activated) during the first and last 15 minutes of each illumination period activated by (1).
- Measurement of natural light conditions by special sensors to ascertain if natural lighting is insufficient (e.g., on cloudy days), leading to earlier commencement of street illumination and later conclusion of illumination. In these cases, only one of a trio of streetlights will be activated.
- Reduction of illumination time according to traffic density, monitored by a traffic sensor installed at every road section, will reduce illumination as follows: If traffic density is below 1 vehicle per minute, only half of the street lights in the road section will be activated; if traffic density is below 0.3 vehicles per minute, only one-third of the lights will be activated.

Mr. Jones, head of the testing team, claims that black box testing is insufficient and that white box tests are necessary for testing "Super Saving Light."

- Support Mr. Jones' claim with three software error examples based on the illumination rules described above. In the examples you choose, black box test results will be "OK," while white box testing of the same example will detect at least one error. For each example, explain why errors undetected by black box testing will be detected by white box testing.

14.3 Based on the "Super Saving Light" case described above:

- What input and output variables are required for defining test cases?
- Suggest three to five simple test cases having low potential to identify errors.
- Suggest three to five test cases that you believe contain serious potential for error.
- Suggest three to five test cases to deal with boundary value situations.

14.4 The Clean Fuel Ltd. is the owner of a chain of more than a hundred gas stations. The gas stations are operated by contractors. The monthly billing system includes the following table of basic monthly rent rates ($)

		The number of pumps		
		Up to 4	5–9	10 and more
The station's area	**Up to 10.00**	1,500	2.200	2,500
(thousands of	**10.01-20.00**	2,000	2,500	3,300
square feet)	**20.01-40.00**	2,400	2.700	4,000
	40.01 and more	2,800	3,000	4,500

a. Added rent for restaurant in the gas station:
   A restaurant – extra 100%.
b. Deductions according to the road level:
   National freeway – no reduction, Local, urban road – 20% deduction.

Required:
a. List the variables and equivalence classes according to the equivalence class partitioning method in the following table

No.	Variable name	Equivalence classes			
		1	2	3	4
1	_____	_____	_____	_____	_____
2	_____	_____	_____	_____	_____
2	_____	_____	_____	_____	_____
4	_____	_____	_____	_____	_____

b. List the IECs for the Clean Fuel's basic monthly rent rates in the following table

The Variable	Valid Equivalence Classes	Representing Values		Invalid Equivalence Classes	Representing Values for the Invalid ECs
		Values for the Valid ECs	Boundary Values		
____	____	____		____	____
____	____	____		____	____
____	____	____		____	____
____	____	____		____	____

c. List the OECs for the Clean Fuel's basic monthly rent rates in the following table

		The number of pumps										
		Up to 4				5–9				10 and more			
Restaurant		None		Exists		None		Exists		None		Exists	
Road level		NF	Loc	NF	Loc	NF	Loc	NF	Loc	NF	Loc	NF	Loc
Station's area	Up to 10.00	___	___	___	___	___	___	___	___	___	___	___	___
(thousands of	10.01–20.00	___	___	___	___	___	___	___	___	___	___	___	___
square feet)	20.01–40.00	___	___	___	___	___	___	___	___	___	___	___	___
	40.01 and more	___	___	___	___	___	___	___	___	___	___	___	___

NF = National freeway, Loc = Local road.

d. List the required test cases according to the equivalence class partitioning method in the following table

Test case type	Test case no.	Variable values in the test cases				Expected test case results
		Var. 1	Var. 2	Var. 3	Var. 4	
Valid IECs test cases	1	—	—	—	—	___
	2	—	—	—	—	___
	3	—	—	—	—	___
	4	—	—	—	—	___
Test cases for valid border IECs	5	—	—	—	—	___
	6	—	—	—	—	___
	7	—	—	—	—	___
	8	—	—	—	—	___
	9	—	—	—	—	___
	10	—	—	—	—	___
Test cases for invalid IECs	11	—	—	—	—	___
	12	—	—	—	—	___
	13	—	—	—	—	___
	13	—	—	—	—	___

Test cases for OECs	14	—	—	—	—	————
	15	—	—	—	—	————
	16	—	—	—	—	————
	17	—	—	—	—	————
	18	—	—	—	—	————
	19	—	—	—	—	————
	20	—	—	—	—	————

Note: The number of rows and columns in the answer form does not necessarily reflect the number of required test cases. In other words, your answer may not require filling out all the form rows.

Chapter 15

Assuring Software Quality Conformance for Operation Services

15.1 Introduction

The main part of the software life cycle is the operation phase, which usually lasts for 5–10 years, although cases of software being operational for 15 years, and even longer, are not rare. What makes one software package capable of reaching "old age" with satisfied users, while another package, serving an almost identical population, "perishes young?" The main factor responsible for a long-term service success is the quality of operation services, namely, the user support and maintenance services. Adding to the importance of software operation services is an investment aspect; with the resources invested in user support and maintenance services being equal to, or surpassing, those provided for the development of the software system itself. Estimates of the percentage of resources invested in operation phase services throughout its life cycle range from 50–75% of the total invested software system resources.

The main factor responsible for the long and successful service of a software system is the quality of user support and maintenance services.

User support services may be classified into two kinds:

- **User support services through the phone**. This kind of service frequently applies remote intervention in the user's computer to solve the problem.

- **Onsite user support service**. This kind of service is used only when support through the phone is inapplicable. Usually, this kind of service is provided in severe situations.

Software Quality: Concepts and Practice, First Edition. Daniel Galin.
© 2018 the IEEE Computer Society, Inc. Published 2018 by John Wiley & Sons, Inc.

In part of the users support calls, the solution requires corrective maintenance service.

Software maintenance services include the following three components, all are essential for successful maintenance:

- **Corrective maintenance** – user support services and software corrections
- **Adaptive maintenance** – adapts the software package to changes in new customer requirements, changing environmental conditions, and the like
- **Functionality improvement maintenance** – combines (1) **perfective maintenance** of new functions added to the software to enhance performance and (2) **preventive maintenance** – activities that improve software package reliability, enabling easier and more efficient maintainability

Generally, one may say that corrective maintenance ensures that current users can operate the system as specified, adaptive maintenance enables expanding the user population, while functionality improvement maintenance extends the software package's service period.

User support services characteristics

User support services (usually supplied through user support centers – USCs) are addressed by users to resolve all difficulties arising from software system usage. Software correction services are usually an integral part of this service. User difficulties may be caused by:

- Code failure (usually termed "software failure").
- A mistake/s or missing part/s in the user manual, help screen/s or other forms of documentation prepared for the user. In these cases, the support service can provide the user with the correct instructions (although corrections to the software documentation itself are not performed).
- Incomplete, vague, or imprecise documentation.
- User's insufficient knowledge of the software system or his/hers failure to use the documentation supplied. These situations do not indicate software system failures.

The first three causes are considered software system failures. An additional cause for the call is the user's inability to cope with the applications himself.

Thus, user requests for USC services are a mixture of requests for guidance in the usage of the software package, and requests for software failure corrections. In addition, the integration of user support services and software maintenance services is generally accomplished in close cooperation with the teams, and entails a great deal of information sharing.

The objectives of user support center's QA activities are presented in Frame 15.1

Frame 15.1: User support services' objectives

User support services objectives
• Ensure, with an accepted level of confidence, that the user support services comply with service norms defined by the software services department or in user contracts. • Ensure, with an accepted level of confidence, that user support services conform to scheduling and budgetary requirements. • Initiate and manage activities to improve the effectiveness and increase the efficiency of software maintenance activities. These activities improve the prospects of achieving user support services, while reducing costs.

Software maintenance services characteristics

Corrective maintenance services, as mentioned above, are usually initiated by users of the USC services. However, adaptive maintenance and perfective maintenance (functionality improvements) tend to be initiated in a different manner – by new customers (adaptive maintenance), and through planned development of new versions of the software package in accordance with the version policies of the organization (perfective maintenance).

Several estimates of the distribution of maintenance resources show the following average percentages for the various maintenance services:

Corrective maintenance	20%
Adaptive maintenance	20%
Functionality improvement maintenance	60%

The objectives of software maintenance QA activities are presented in Frame 15.2

Frame 15.2: Software maintenance services objectives

Software maintenance services objectives
• Ensure, with an accepted level of confidence, that the software maintenance activities conform to functional technical requirements. • Ensure, with an accepted level of confidence, that the software maintenance activities conform to scheduling and budgetary requirements. • Initiate and manage activities to improve the effectiveness and increase the efficiency of software maintenance activities. These activities improve the prospects of achieving functional and managerial requirements, while reducing costs.

Just as the nature of different software maintenance components varies substantially, so do the required quality assurance tools. In general, the perfective (functionality improvement) and adaptive tasks display the characteristics of a small or large software development project. This being the case, they basically share the same software quality assurance processes. However, QA processes employed for corrective maintenance tend to display some unique characteristics. It is important to remember that corrective maintenance activities are service activities and that unlike functionality improvement and adaptive tasks, they in many cases performed as part of user support services, and are as such under the close supervision of the user/customer. Management of corrective maintenance services focuses mainly on the availability of services and their quality (measured by time to solution, percentage of cases of correction failures, etc.), rather than on the budgetary and schedule controls typically applied when managing functionality improvements and adaptive maintenance tasks.

The subject of software operation services is addressed in software development and quality standards, to mention just two sources. IEEE Std. 730-2014 (IEEE, 2014) refers to software operation, and user support and maintenance services as software products (see Section 5.4). ISO/IEC Std. 90003-2014 (ISO, 2014) dedicates Sections 7.2.2.3 and 7.5.1.6 to operation and maintenance service quality. Additional information regarding the contribution of quality maintenance to competitiveness, and the relation between quality and maintenance achievements may be found in Stojanov et al. (2014), Al-Badareen et al. (2011), and Xiong et al. (2011). The aspects of collaboration and cooperation in software maintenance are discussed by Gupta (2012), Mohd Nor and Abdullah 2008), and Mohd Nor et al. (2010).

The chapter will pursue the following quality assurance issues as they relate to user support and software maintenance services:

- The foundations for high quality operation services
- Software Maintenance Maturity Model – a model for the operation phase
- Managerial processes of software operation quality assurance

A mini case presented in the next section introduces some of the software service issues during the operation period to be later discussed in the chapter.

15.2 HR Software's success – an introductory mini case

HR Software is a small software house specializing in human resource management. The company was founded 5 years ago, employs 40 software professionals, and has already performed several successful human resource management projects for small and medium-sized companies. Three years ago, the company began marketing HRMS1, a human resource management package for small and medium-sized companies. HRMS1 provided personnel file management and personnel salary processing. Even though the software package already has 350 customers who use its profitable HRMS1 support center, the product is considered only a "medium" success, mainly due to the high cancellation rate from customer service; 10–15 per month. The main reason for this rate was the provision of poor maintenance provided by the HRMS1 support center. Below are some typical complaints:

- "We had to call the support service three times till they finally successfully corrected a bug. It's already the third time that it has taken three times to successfully resolve a problem. We are left with no choice but to look for a different human resource software, one which provides actual support services . . ."

- "We purchased your HRMS1 just 9 months ago, after being verified that the support services would be able perform a small modification task required. All tests conducted following the modification performed by your support service failed, and we were left with inferior HR services. As a result, we needed to conduct a substantial number of unnecessary manual calculations. Consequently, we are now in search of an alternative HR software package."

- "This is the second month that we have been unable to prepare up-to-date accurate salary payments, as your support center does not seem to be capable of correcting the updating module, or instructing us to overcome the difficulty. We employ 2,200 staff members, and due to this unbearable situation, about 30% of them are currently either underpaid or overpaid. The HR software management must solve this situation with no additional delay."

Due to this substandard product experience, the management started to discuss a proposal by the development department for a new human resource management software package, HRMS2. The new software was to deal with data collection of employee attendance and incentive pay. The promoters of the proposal estimated a short development schedule with limited resources, as the proposal was based on experience from, and knowledge gained in, a comprehensive software project on the proposed subject completed just a few weeks earlier.

After a fairly long discussion, where opponents and supporters voiced their support and reservations, respectively, and deliberated over lessons learnt from the HRMS1 package, the proposed project was approved provided the following conditions were met:

- The development will be carried out under strict observance of the SQA software development procedures.
- Special attention will be paid to follow the project documentation guidelines.
- The project development team will not fade out or handover following development, but will instead function as a support center team for the maintenance of the HRMS2 software package.

- The HRMS2 will be able to handle a variety of attendance and wage incentive plans.
- The HRMS2 will include an interface with HRMS1, and will have interfacing capabilities with commonly used human resource software packages.
- The HRMS2 will be capable of serving companies with facilities located at several sites, while all collected data will be transmitted to a central database.

The project was executed without any noteworthy risk events, and provided comprehensive documentation and a high-quality user manual. Besides the functional and interfacing capabilities, the promotion campaign emphasized the super support center geared to immediately handle any service call by telephone or site visit within one working day. The promotion campaign offered special prices to HRMS1 customers, in addition to a substantial improvement of the support center services now available for the HRMS1 software too.

The first weeks of the promotion campaign were a time of tension for the marketing team, and especially for the development team. Finally, the manager's decision to approach five HRMS1 customers and propose they serve as beta sites for HRMS2, proved fruitful. The very positive feedback on HRMS2 led 150 HRMS1 customers to purchase HRMS2 within the first 6 months of the package sales. A very positive survey on HRMS2 by the computer expert of "HR Professional," a popular journal for human resource professionals, praised the functionality of the package, and especially noted the excellent support center. He interviewed several satisfied customers, who told him that all their requests for support were immediately answered in full. One of the interviewed HR managers told about an adaptation task completed within 4 hours. The marketing team noted that this journal article contributed tremendously to the sales of HRMS2. There were also those who claimed that the article contributed even more than the promotion campaign.

In a meeting called to sum up the first year of HRMS2 sales, it was reported that there were over 350 customers, and that most of them intend to join the support center service once their one-year warranty has terminated. More good news regarding the growth of sales, and a significantly reduced customer dropout rate were reported by the HRMS1 team. The wise marketing manager participating in the meeting announced he would recommend a special bonus for the HRMS2 maintenance team for their excellent work and very important contribution to the competitiveness of the company.

*   *   *

You may ask yourself:

- What are the possible reasons for the failing of the HRMS1 support center?
- What should have been done to change the situation, and establish outstanding software operation services?

15.3 The foundations of high-quality operation services

Three foundations of high quality operation services are discussed:

1. **Software package quality**. It goes without saying that the quality of the new software package is perhaps the single most important foundation underlying the quality of user support and maintenance services.

2. **Software release and software version policies**. Other critical foundations are the software releases and software version policies.

3. **Specific QA procedures for operation services**. The third foundation of software operation quality is the specific QA procedures, which the software development organization operates.

A discussion on these topics follows.

15.3.1 Foundation one – software product quality

The quality of the software product that is to be in operation clearly stems from the expertise and efforts of the development team, as well as the QA activities performed throughout the development process. If the quality of the product is poor, user support and maintenance services will be poor or ineffective, almost by definition. In other words, provision of a high-quality software product contributes to the effectiveness and efficiency of all types of user support and software maintenance services, and, namely, serves as a foundation for quality operation services.

15.3.2 Foundation two – software releases and version policies

The main "products" of perfective maintenance are new releases and new versions of software products. The management of software releases and version requires a policy to be defined regarding:

- The frequency of software version releases
- The model of version development

The frequency of software version releases – policy

The typical frequency is once a year, though twice a year and once in two years is also found. The perfective maintenance team may release one or more revisions between successive version releases. Software version releases include major changes and additions to the software system, while revision releases include minor changes and urgent software corrections.

The model of version development – policy

The maintenance team performs successive development or evolution (termed "perfective maintenance") during the years of service of a software system. The new version created during the service period should be undertaken according to a policy planned in advance by the system's developer. The choice of policy routes depends on the system characteristics, and the customer population, as well as the firm's intentions regarding the system's target market. Two fundamental software evolution models – the linear model and the tree model – are generally applied. We shall discuss these models next.

- **The linear evolution model**
  According to the linear model, only one unique software system version serves all customers at any given time. Each new version replaces the prior version. This model is the natural choice for software systems developed to serve a single organization. The model is also applied to popular software packages, which tend to be uniform in structure, and where the ability to meet a wide range of maintenance demands in a single version is a great advantage.

- **The tree evolution model**
  According to this model, several parallel versions of the software are developed to serve the different needs of different customers simultaneously throughout the system's life cycle. Tree models are typically applied in firmware configuration versions, where each branch serves a different product or product line.

Figure 15.1 presents two version models, a linear and a tree model. The version frequency for both models is once a year. The figure presents software versions (marked V1, V2, etc.) and some revision releases (marked Ra, Rb, etc.).

In Figure 15.1, the linear version model includes 4 versions over a period of 4 years. During the same 4-year period, the tree version model creates 16 versions released in 4 releases. The main difference being that at the end of the fourth year, the tree model needs to maintain 7 different software versions.

It is clear that the frequency of software version releases and models of version development are major issues for those COTS software packages planned to serve a large variety of customers. As mentioned above, models of version development from which the software developer may choose are the "linear" or "tree" models. When adopting a linear version policy, only one version is made available to an entire customer population. This version includes a profusion of applications that exhibit high redundancy, an attribute that enables the software to serve the needs of all customers. The software must be revised periodically, and once a new version is complete, it replaces the version currently used by an entire user population.

When adopting a tree version model, the software perfective maintenance team supports marketing efforts by developing a specialized, targeted version

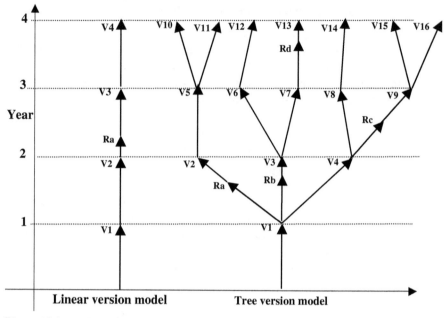

Figure 15.1   Comparison of linear and tree version models.

for groups of customers, or a major customer, upon request. A new version is inaugurated by adding special applications or omitting existing applications, in accordance with customer needs. The versions vary in complexity and level of application, for example, targeted industry-oriented applications. When this policy is adopted, the software package evolves after several years of service into a multiversion package. The package will resemble a tree, with several main branches and numerous secondary branches; each branch represents a version with specialized revisions. As opposed to the linear version model, software, maintenance, and management of tree version software is much more difficult and resource consuming. Considering these deficiencies, software development organizations try to apply a limited tree version model policy, allowing only a small number of software versions to be developed.

Example: After just a few years of application, *Inventory Perfect*, an inventory management package developed according to the tree policy, has evolved into a seven-version software package with the following main branches: Pharmacies, Electronics, Hospitals, Bookstores, Supermarkets, Garages (auto repairs), and Chemical Plants. Each of the branches includes four to five secondary branches that vary by their number of software modules, and level of implementation or specific customer-oriented applications. For instance, the version for bookstores has the following five secondary branches (versions): bookstore chains, "free" bookstores, advanced management bookstores; it also has special versions for the LP bookstore chain and for CUCB (City University Campus

Bookstores). The software maintenance team tends to a total of 30 different versions of the software package simultaneously, with each version revised periodically according to customer requests and the team's technical innovations.

The daily experience of the maintenance team, therefore, includes overcoming hardships, created by the version-structure of the package, that go beyond those related to the software itself:

- Faulty corrections caused by inadequate identification of the module-structure of the current version used by the specific customer.
- Faulty corrections caused by the incorrect replacement of a faulty module with a module of a different version that later proved to be unsuitable OR inappropriate to be integrated into the customer's package version.
- Efforts invested to convince customers to update their software package by adding newly developed modules or replacing current module versions with a new version. Some customers insisted on keeping their existing version of the package, adding to the number of versions to be maintained.

The Head of the Maintenance Team has often voiced his envy for his colleague, the Head of *Inventory Star*'s maintenance team, who insisted that the software package developed by his firm was to offer only one comprehensive version for all customers.

It is clear that if Inventory Perfect were to adopt a linear policy, the software would require substantially fewer maintenance efforts. In addition, as only one version needs to be maintained, it is much easier to maintain its quality level.

15.3.3 Foundation three – specific QA procedures for operation services

Specific procedures that regulate the performance of user support and maintenance services by the service teams include:

Specific procedures for user support services:

The phone procedure that directs the team in the following issues:

- The process of handling a user call
- User support call report
- Training requirements for USC team members

The onsite user support procedure directs the team in the following issues:

- Checkups to be performed before service
- The process of handling an onsite service call, including the documentation

- Criteria for escalating the call to a higher technical level when case is not successfully resolved
- Onsite user support call report
- Training and certification requirements for members of the onsite user support services team

USC services management procedure that directs the team in the following issues:

- Rules for handling incoming user calls, selection of the team member to handle the call, and guidelines for following the process
- Recording the users support timetable:
    For user service by phone: user call time, start of service, successful completion of service.
    For onsite user support service: user call time, registration as an onsite service, beginning of onsite service, successful completion of service.
- Procedure for handling USC customer complaints
    Procedure for follow-up and control of the services supplied by subcontractors. More about subcontracting may be found in Chapter 20.
- Preparing a periodic USC activity report

Software maintenance-specific procedures cover corrective and adaptive maintenance. No specific procedures are required for perfective maintenance projects as these can be served by software development procedures.

Corrective maintenance procedure that directs the team in the following issues:

- The process of handing a defect correction, including priorities of handling failure calls.
- Quality assurance processes for small-scale *patch repairs*. These *patch repair* tasks are characterized by a small number of coding line changes, which justify the use of a short correction process (a *"mini life cycle"*):
    - A short review process (mini review)
    - A short testing process (mini testing)
- Concise documentation of a patch repair. This documentation will ensure that relevant patch repairs are included in next revisions or version releases.
    The defect correction report
- Training requirements for corrective maintenance team members

Adaptive maintenance procedure that directs the team in the following issues:

- The process of handling adaptive maintenance request, including identifying the needs for an adapted software product and estimate of resources and schedule requirements for performing the request.

- The process of performing an adapting maintenance task
- Quality assurance processes for adaptive maintenance project: reviews, tests, and so on.
- Training and certification requirements for adaptive maintenance of team members.

15.4 Software maintenance maturity model – a model for the operation phase

The improvement of the quality of software maintenance processes is a common objective of managements of software operation. A managed process for improving software maintenance quality by the gradual implementation of maintenance QA processes is presented by April et al. (2005), April and Abran (2009), and Zarour et al. (2012). The process, named SMMM (Software Maintenance Maturity Model), is based on a six-level model that follows the principle, structure and practices of CMMI (see Appendix B, Section B.5). The software maintenance department that adopts the SMMM model gradually implements the QA processes, according to the model, achieves improved capability to perform software maintenance tasks. The gradually improved performance is also expected to gradually reduce maintenance failures.

Achievements of the improvement process are periodically assessed to assure the proper implementation of the SQA maintenance processes for each level of the SMMM model. Table 15.1 presents the SMMM levels and improvements required in each of the model levels.

15.5 Managerial processes of software operation quality assurance

The contribution of an organization's management to the quality of the various proposed operation services, namely, user support and maintenance services, begins in the early preparation stages of the service provision, and continues with performance follow-up. The following main processes are applied by the management:

- Software operation contract review
- Software operation plan
- Software operation progress control
- Software operation metrics
- Software operation services quality costs

Software operation services organization and performance

Software operation – user support and maintenance services – is organized and carried out by the software services development or another unit. In some

Table 15.1   The SMMM levels

SMMM level	Main implemented processes
0. Incomplete process	***No sense of software maintenance process (SMP)*** • No defined SMP is used • There is no knowledge or understanding of software maintenance activities that have been performed
1. Perform process	***Ad hoc software maintenance process*** • The organization is aware of the need to manage the SMP • Part of the teams begin implementing an SMP • There is no measurement of the SMP performance • The documentation of software maintenance activities is not adequate
2. Managed process	***Basic request-based software maintenance process*** • ASMP is defined and software maintenance activities documented locally (not generally) • Training and professional support are provided locally • Qualitative measurements of software maintenance activities are partly implemented
3. Established process	***State-of-the-art software maintenance process*** • Software maintenance practices are generally executed by trained staff • Basic performance metrics are implemented and collected data is analyzed • The required resources are assigned to SMP tasks and managed • Infrastructure services are available and used to support the SMPs
4. Predictable process	***The performance of software maintenance process is controlled, documented, and reviewed*** • Conformance to the SMPs is assessed • Records of software maintenance processes are reviewed and the SMPs are audited • Resources and infrastructure usage are planned, qualified controlled, and managed. • Main software maintenance activities are quantitatively measured, and deviating results analyzed in order to adjust and correct the causes
5. Optimizing process	***Innovations for improvements of the software maintenance process*** • Advanced techniques and technological improvements of processes are reviewed and implemented • Innovations of technologies are planned and their performance measured • Cost/benefit studies are performed, defect prevention is a main objective. Causes for failures and defects are studied.

Source: After April et al. (2005).

organizations, the services are performed by an external executer, usually an out-sourcing organization.

The role of the SQA function in software operation processes

The role of the SQA function is supportive regarding the organization of reviews and improving their efficiency and effectiveness. SQA function team members may participate in the organization's QA activities for evaluating software operation service's performance and their compliance with standards, and regulation instructions.

The next sections discuss the managerial processes of assuring the quality of software operation services. The discussion is from the standpoint of the supplier of software operation services.

15.5.1 Software operation contract review

Software operations are performed internally when the organization operates its software systems, and externally when an external software organization provides user support and software maintenance services according to a software operation contract. These external software operation contracts are developed for organizations for whom a custom-made package has been developed, and for COTS software package customers. Provision of software operations for custom-made software usually involves a proposal, and eventually a contract. The procedure of software operation's contract review very much resembles the processes of a software development project contract review. Thus, we will focus our discussion on cases of software operation services to COTS software customers. In cases such as these, the software operation services are usually provided to large populations of customers located in a particular country and, in many cases, also in additional countries.

Implementation tip

Software operation services for internal customers are often not contracted. In a typical situation, some services provided during the running-in period are continued, with no one bothering to determine the binding obligations related to their continuation. In such situations, dissatisfaction may be expected on both sides: Internal customers feel that they need to ask for favors instead of receiving the standard service they deserve, whereas development teams eventually experience requests to perform maintenance tasks as intrusions, once they have begun work on a different project.

To prevent these strains, an "internal service agreement" should be prepared. The services to be provided by the internal maintenance team to the internal customer should be clearly defined. By eliminating most of the misunderstandings related to these vital services, such an agreement may serve as the basis for satisfactory maintenance to internal customers.

When considering the operation services contract to be offered to the customers, a broad perspective should be embraced. More than anything else, decisions are required to be made in regard to the categories of services to be offered. These decisions depend on the number of customers served, and their locations. Therefore, before commencing to supply operation services to any of these customers, an adequate software operation contract that sets down the total range of operation service obligations according to the relevant conditions should be finalized.

The software operation contract review activities are based on the contract draft. The objective of the review is to examine the contract draft and to verify that all necessary elements of the contract have been correctly defined and documented, and to identify any missing, incomplete, or incorrect elements in the draft. Naturally, the objectives and implementation of software operation contract reviews follow the lines of preproject contract reviews (see Chapter 8). We shall next review the list of the major objectives of software operation contract reviews:

a. Review of customer requirements clarification
The following issues deserve special attention:
- The user support services to be provided: remote and on-site services, hours of service, response times, and so on.
- The size of the user population.
- The location of users, especially if at long distance and overseas sites.

b. Review of the alternative approaches to software operation provision
The following options deserve special consideration:
- Subcontracting of software operation services only for customers of specified areas, especially for overseas customers or for specific types of service.
- Performance of some services by the customer himself with support from external supplier teams in times of need.

c. **Review of the identified operation service risks**
Maintenance service risks relate to situations where failure to provide adequate services is anticipated. These risks include:
- Staff shortages, whether throughout the performance of the organization's services, in a specific maintenance support center or for a specific application.
- Inadequate qualifications or acquaintance of staff with part of the relevant software packages for performing user support services and/or corrective maintenance tasks.

d. **Review of the estimates of required resources**
The reviewed estimates include:
- The resources required for performing software operation tasks. Estimates should be examined based on the planned operation services defined in the contract draft, and the size of the customer population.

- The resources required for operating the planned user support centers.
- The cost estimates for performing the planned software corrective maintenance services including costs of subcontractor services.

e. **Review of the services to be provided by subcontractors and/or the customer**

This review refers to the definition of the services provided by each external participant, payments to subcontractors, quality assurance, and follow-up procedures to be applied.

f. **Review of the feasibility of the supplier's organization to perform the planned services**

The review will examine the availability of professional personnel with the required specialization that could (1) handle successfully the corrective maintenance tasks of failure repairs and the USC services, (2) perform adaptive maintenance tasks, mainly to serve new customers, and (3) perform functional improvement tasks, mainly for creating new versions according to the version policy of the organization. The review will consider the tasks planned to be performed by subcontractors and the customer himself.

15.5.2 Software operation plan

Software operation services plans are annual plans that direct the management regarding the required resources (personnel, equipment, offices, etc.) to perform all software operation services expected in the coming year. The software services operation contract will determine the resources required for operation services, while the version and frequency policies will affect the required resources for functional improvement maintenance. The plan should provide the framework within which the software operation services provision is organized for the coming year.

The plan includes the following bases:

a. **Estimate of the number of customers with contracted software operation services:**
- The number of customers currently receiving operation services for custom made projects and any expected changes in their number.
- The number and location of customers currently receiving COTS software operation services and any expected changes in their number.

b. **Estimate of the number of new COTS software customers and their software adaptation requirements**

c. **The number of COTS software package versions to be released in the coming year**

This number will be based on the policy regarding version models and the frequency of version releases.

d. The number of USC sites
- The current number of USC sites
- The change (increase/decrease) of USC sites due to the current/updated COTS software maintenance contract and other considerations.

e. The software operation unit organization
The software operations organization plan focuses on manpower requirements and the facilities to be operated in the coming year: the number of team members required for the coming year and their professional specialization. The total number of personnel and their allocation into operation services, adaptive and function improvement teams.
- The organization of the staff and teams located at various facilities. If services are to be provided from several facilities – the team requirement for each facility.
- The required qualifications of team members according to the software operation tasks, including familiarity with the said software package(s).
- Software operation tasks to be performed by subcontractors and the customers themselves.
- Organizational structure of the software operation teams, including names of team leaders.
- Definition of tasks (responsibility for customers, types of applications, etc.) for each team.

Implementation tip

When determining the software operations team and its organization, one should consider preparing for provision of services in peak demand. Support provided in peak situations may be based on the temporary utilization of development teams and other operation teams located at the same or other facilities. It should be emphasized that effective peak load support is based on preplanning, which also includes training. Software operation teams require regular training for these tasks; on the spot improvised solutions may prove to be harmful, rather than helpful.

---

f. The software operation services facilities
Software operation services facilities that make it possible to provide services include:
- The USCs with their installed hardware and communication equipment to provide user support and software correction services.
- The facilities that serve the modification and function improvement teams.
- The facility of the unit management and infrastructure services teams.

g. Identified software maintenance service risks
Software maintenance service risks relate to situations where failure to provide adequate software maintenance is anticipated. These risks include:
- Staff shortages, whether throughout the organization's operation services in a specific USC or for a specific application.

- Inadequate qualifications or lack of familiarity with part of the relevant software packages to perform user support services and/or corrective maintenance tasks.
- A lack of team members qualified to perform adaptive and functional improvement tasks – in case a customer places an order of significant size.

h. **The software operation services budget**
The annual budget of the software operation services, incomes and expenditures, is prepared according to the information provided in the above plan sections.

The components of the software operations plan are listed in Frame 15.3.

Frame 15.3: The components of the software operation plan

The components of software operation plan
a. **Estimate of the number of customers with contracted software operation services**
b. **Estimate of the number of new COTS software customers and their software adaptation requirements**
c. **The number of COTS software package versions to be released in the coming year**
d. **The number of USC sites**
e. **The software operation unit organization**
f. **The software operation services facilities**
g. **Identified software maintenance service risks**
h. **The software operation services budget**

15.5.3 Software operations progress control

Managerial SQA components are designed to improve control of software operation services by creating early alarms that signal reduced quality of service and increasing rates of service failures. While specialized managerial control QA tools are required for user support corrective maintenance services, the similarity between the software processes characterizing functionality improvement and adaptive maintenance and software development enables these processes to employ the same managerial tools (see Chapter 21).

The remainder of this section is dedicated to special managerial control tools, mainly those related to software correction and user support services. A great many of these tools rely on software operation quality metrics

Managerial performance controls of corrective maintenance services differ when applied to software development correction (failure repair) processes and to USC services. The managerial control tools yield, besides periodical performance information, alarms for management attention.

The following software operation information, mostly based on software quality metrics, serves managerial quality tools:

For software failure correction

- Decreased rate of remote failure repairs (low-cost repairs) versus increased rate of repairs at customer sites.
- Increased rate of on-site repairs at distant locations and overseas services.
- Increased percentage of failures, increased workload to meet repair schedule requirements.
- Increased rate of faulty repairs, and list of specific "model" cases of extreme failure situations.
- List of failure repair tasks not completed according to schedule requirements.
- Lower customer satisfaction from software failure correction performance based on customer satisfaction surveys.

For USC services

- General increased rates of requests for service, increase in requests for a specific software system part, and so on.
- Increased resource utilization in USC services.
- Increased rate of failures for provision of requested consulting services.
- List of specific "outstanding" faulty consulting or failure to provide required instructing service, including detailed information about these cases. In most cases, the managerial action will be to initiate training or replacement of USC staff members.
- Lower customer satisfaction in customer satisfaction surveys stemming from software failure correction performance.

In addition to the above managerial controls, based on periodic reporting, the periodic staff meetings, visits to the USCs, and examination of customer complaints serve as managerial progress control tools.

Implementation tip

Many bitter failures experienced with software operation contracts are due to the subcontracting of project parts. Failures often result from lack of control of the subcontractor's performance, not from the absence of software quality assurance clauses in the contract. The reasons for subcontracting, such as a shortage of software operation professionals at remotely located customer sites, may induce faulty control over the subcontractor's services. In other words, successful subcontracting requires adequate organization and procedures to implement proper control over performance of services.

15.5.4   Software maintenance quality metrics

Software operation quality metrics are used to identify trends in software operation services efficiency, effectiveness, and customer satisfaction, and as basic information for planning and budgeting. Changes in trends, negative as well as positive, besides being tools for managerial control on software operation services, provide the quantitative basis for managerial decision-making regarding:

- Estimation of resource requirements when preparing software operation plans for the next period.
- Comparison of methods of operation.
- Initiation of preventive and corrective actions.
- Estimation of resource requirements as a basis for proposals for new or modified maintenance services.

The SQA function usually initiates metrics and plans their implementation, while the software development department is responsible for the regular data collection and processing of the metrics.

For examples of quality metrics of software corrections and user support services – see Sections 21.4 and 21.5.

15.5.5   Cost of software operation services quality

The discussion of costs of software operations quality follows the approach of the discussion of cost of software quality (CoSQ) presented in Chapter 9. Accordingly, we present:

- Classic model of cost of software operation quality
- An extended model of cost of software operation quality

As in the former sections, we refer here to user support services and out of maintenance services, implemented only to corrective maintenance issues.

a. A classic model of cost of software operation quality

The model classifies quality costs into two general classes.

Costs of software operation control – relates to costs controlled by the software operation and includes the following subclasses:

- Prevention costs
- Appraisal costs

Costs of software operation failure of control – relates to costs of failures that occurred during the operation phase. The model further subdivides these costs into two subclasses.

- Internal failure costs
- External failure costs

In the next sections, the subclasses of the model are reviewed.

- **Cost of prevention:**
- Cost of instruction and training of software operation teams.
- Cost of preventative and corrective actions related to software operation processes.
- Cost of improving and updating software quality infrastructure related to software operation.
- Cost of carrying out contract reviews of software operation contract with customers.
- Cost of preparation and periodic updating of software operation plans.
- Cost of carrying out contract review of contracts with subcontractors for performing parts of software operation services.
- **Costs of appraisal:**
- Cost of review and testing of software failure corrections.
- Cost of internal audits of the implementation of software operation procedures and work instructions, that is, cost of USC service reviews carried out.
- Cost of external audits of software operation services.
- Cost of customer satisfaction surveys.
- Cost of periodic updating of software operation services plans.
- Cost of performing regular follow-up of performance of user support services.
- Cost of performing regular follow-up of performance of corrective maintenance services.
- Cost of performing regular follow-up of performance of external participants software operation services.
- **Cost of internal failure:**
- Cost of software failure corrections identified by the software operation team.
- Cost of review and testing of corrections of failures identified by the software operation team.
- *Internal managerial domino effect damages*: Damages to other company projects caused by failing management activities or decisions.
- **Cost of external failure:**
- Cost of software failure corrections identified by customer complaints.
- Cost of USC instruction services related to failures of the customer to understand the instruction manual and directions embedded in the software.
- Damages paid to customers in cases of severe delays in the completion of software failure repairs. Some of these are due to management's inability to recruit sufficiently professional team members.
- Insurance fees against customer claims in cases of severe delays in software failure correction.
- *External managerial domino effect damages*: Damages to other company projects caused by failing management activities or decisions.

b. An extended model of cost of software operation quality

Analysis of the software quality costs defined by the classic CoSQ model (in the Section (a) above) reveals that several costs with substantial magnitude are excluded. These costs are related to the management's invested efforts in software operation performance and to the costs caused by management failures.

The *extended cost of software quality model,* as proposed by the author of this book, extends the classic model to include management's "contribution" to the total cost of software quality. According to the extended CoSQ model, the costs of software quality (see Section 9.4) are divided into eight classes.

Following are types of software quality costs classified into the eight cost classes.

- **Cost of prevention:**
  - Cost of instruction and training of maintenance team.
  - Cost of preventative and corrective actions related to software operation processes.
  - Cost of improving and updating software quality infrastructure related to software operation services.
  - Cost of management reviews related to software operation services.

- **Costs of appraisal:**
  - Cost of review and testing of software failure corrections.
  - Cost of internal audits of the implementation of software operation procedures and work instructions, that is, cost of USC service reviews.
  - Cost of external audits of maintenance services.
  - Cost of ensuring the quality of services provided by external participants involved in supplying corrective maintenance.
  - Cost of software operation customer satisfaction surveys.

- **Cost of internal failure:**
  - Cost of software failure corrections identified by the software operation team.
  - Cost of review and testing of corrections of failures identified by the software operation team.

- **Cost of external failure:**
  - Cost of software failure corrections initiated by customer complaints.
  - Cost of USC instruction services-related failures of the customer to understand the instruction manual and directions embedded in the software.
  - Damages paid to customers in cases of severe delays in completion of software failure repairs.
  - Insurance fees against customer claims in cases of severe delays in software failure correction.

- **Management prevention costs:**
  - Cost of carrying out software operation contract reviews.

- Cost of preparation and periodic updating of software operation plans.
- Cost of carrying out contract review of contracts with subcontractors for performing parts of software operation services.

• **Management appraisal costs:**
   - Cost of periodic updating of software operation services plans.
   - Cost of performing regular follow-up of performance of user support services.
   - Cost of performing regular follow-up of performance of corrective maintenance services.
   - Cost of performing regular follow-up of performance of external participant's software operation services

• **Internal managerial failure costs:**
   - Unplanned costs for professional and other resources, resulting from underestimation of resources on which submitted proposals are based.
   - Additional staff costs paid to outsourcing companies, recruited under the pressure of last-minute situations.
   - *Internal managerial domino effect damages*: Damages to other company projects caused by failing management activities or decisions.

• **External managerial failure costs:**
   - Failed management activities or bad decisions.

Domino effect of software operation services failures

The domino effect is identified in cases of internal and external managerial failures (see Section 9.3.3). In such situations, an operation services failure in the original service causes failure in another operation service, and further causes a failure of operation services of another customer's services.

   Example. Several failures to complete repairs within the contract-assigned time were recorded for the correction services of package A during the month of April, mainly due to staff shortage. In order to support the package A team, the management shifted several maintenance team members from Package B maintenance team to package A team. This created severe difficulties for Package B team to maintain the high level of maintenance services previously held, till finally, in mid-August, these also failed. This negative domino effect continued in September with a substantial drop in sales of package A, due to the damaged reputation of package A's quality of maintenance. One could speculate whether the drop of package B's sales will be felt in October or November.

   In general, maintenance quality cost information, together with other managerial control information, is expected to assist management in making decisions regarding:

• Areas to focus on, and invest in, for the improvement of software operation services.

• Development of improved software versions, especially for COTS software packages that serve large populations of users.

Summary

1. **The components of software operation and the differences between them**

   Software operation services include user support and maintenance services.

   There are two kinds of user support services:

   • **User support service on the phone**. This kind of service frequently applies remote intervention on the user's computer to solve the problem.

   • **Onsite user support service**. This kind of service is only used when support on the phone is inapplicable. This kind of service is usually provided in severe situations.

   There are three components of software maintenance, with the following purposes:

   • **Corrective maintenance** of software corrections and user support services.

   • **Adaptive maintenance** adjusts the software package according to requirements of new customers and changing environmental conditions.

   • **Functionality improvement (perfective) maintenance** performs improvements to software functionality, performance, and reliability during the operation phase of the software system.

2. **The foundations of high-quality software operation services**

   Three factors are considered to be the foundations of high-quality software operation services: (a) the software package's quality, (b) the version release policies, and (3) the infrastructure services.

   It is clear according to the first foundation that software operation services quality may be guaranteed by implementing a quality software package. The version release policies, namely, the frequency of version release policy and the model of version development policy are the second foundation. The model of version development determines the number of versions to be updated every year, in other words, a number of software versions are maintained at the same time. Thus, these policies define, to a great extent, the workload on the software maintenance department. The infrastructure QA processes that serve the software operation services teams are the third foundation. The infrastructure tools include the following: (a) procedures and work instructions, (b) templates, checklists, and documentation control, (d) staff training and certification, (e) software improvements by corrective and preventive actions, and (f) configuration management.

3. Main managerial SQA components for software operation services
The following main tools are applied by the management:
- Software operations contract review
- Software operations plan
- Software operation progress control
- Software operation metrics
- Software operation services quality costs

The software operation contract review and software operation plan are dedicated to the appropriate preparation of operation activities, while both affect the quality of operation. The managerial operation progress control relies on regular periodic reporting, as well as staff meetings, visits to the USCs, and investigation of customer complaints. Software maintenance metrics and software maintenance quality costs provide additional supporting processes.

Selected bibliography

Al-Badareen A. B., Selamat M. H., Jabar M. A., Din J., and Turaev S. (2011) *The impact of software quality on maintenance process*, International Journal of Computers, Vol. **5**, No. 2, pp. 1–8.

April A. and Abran A. (2009) *A software maintenance maturity model (S3M): measurement practices at maturity levels 3 and 4*, Electronic Notes in Theoretical Computer Science, Vol **233**, pp. 73–87.

April A., Huffman Hayes J., Abran A., and Dumke R. (2005) *software maintenance maturity model (SMMM): the software maintenance process model*, Journal of Software Maintenance and Evolution: Research and Practice, Vol. **17**, No. 3, pp. 197–223.

Gupta A. (2012) *Practitioner-oriented collaborative and cooperative software maintenance*, International Journal of Computer Science: Theory, Technology and Applications, Vol. **1**, No. 2, pp. 18–31.

IEEE (2014) *IEEE Std. 730–2014 Software quality assurance*, The IEEE Computer Society, IEEE, New York.

ISO (2014) *ISO/IEC 90003:2014 Software Engineering – Guidelines for the Application of TSO 9001: 2008 to Computer Software*,International Organization for Standardization (ISO), Geneva, Switzerland.

Mohd Nor M. Z. and Abdullah R. (2008) A technical perspective of knowledge management in collaborative software maintenance environment, *Knowledge Management International Conference (KMIC)*, pp. 1–6.

Mohd Nor M. Z., Abdullah R., Azmi Murad M. A., and Selamat M. H. (2010) in Virtanen P. and Helsander N. (Eds.) *Managing knowledge in collaborative software maintenance environment*, InTech, pp. 73–92.

Stojanov Z., Hristoski I. H., Mitrevski P. J., and Brtka V. (2014) The role of effective software maintenance in increasing competitiveness of very small software companies, *SMEs Development and Innovation: Building Competitive Future of South-Eastern Europe conference, Ohrid, Macedonia*, October 2014, pp. 835–845.

Xiong C. J., Xie M., and Ng S.-H. (2011) *Optimal software maintenance policy considering unavailable time*, Journal of Software Maintenance and Evolution Research and Practice, Vol. **23**, No. 1, pp. 21–23.

Zarour M., Alarifi A., Abran A. and Desharnais J.-M. (2012) Evaluating the assessment method of the software maintenance maturity model. *3012 International Conference on Information Technology and e-Service (ICITeS), Sousse*. March 2012, pp. 1–6.

Review questions

15.1 Refer to the section on the foundations for high-quality operation services.

    a. Explain in your own words the importance of the first foundation.

    b. List and explain the importance of the various factors affecting the first foundation.

    c. Explain in your own words software operation services.

    d. Explain in your own words what the third foundation is and how it affects the quality of software operation services.

15.2 A company is anxious to sign a 3-year software operation contract for an ERP (Enterprise Resource Planning) software package for a multinational organization that employs 6,000 people in eight countries. The company has already acquired experience in the provision of software operation services for the ERP package. The multinational organization suggests paying a lump sum for user support, corrective and adaptive maintenance tasks, and a separate payment for functional improvements, based on the characteristics of each request. The pressure from the Sales Department to immediately sign the contract left little time to prepare a proposal, and practically no time for a contract review.

    a. What risks are entailed by neglecting to hold a contract review?

    b. What subjects would you most recommend for contract review in this case?

    c. If software operation services of a similar nature were requested by an internal customer (to serve employees of the same company), would you recommend carrying out a contract review? List your arguments.

15.3 Refer to the section on software operation services plans (Section 15.5.2).

    a. What are the basic elements of a software operation services plan? Explain the importance of each element in your own words.

    b. Who do you think should be responsible for preparing the plan? Who should approve it? List your reasons.

    c. What difficulties would you expect to arise when a plan has not been prepared?

15.4 It is claimed that higher standards are needed for the training and certification of maintenance team members than those needed for development team members.

    a. Do you agree or disagree with this claim? List your arguments.

    b. If you agree with the above, which component of software maintenance (corrective, adaptive, or functionality improvement) do you consider most suitable for the above claim?

15.5 Most software operation procedures require extensive documentation on the activities performed.

    a. List the main uses for the various types of software operations documentation.

    b. Explain the importance of the required documentation in your own words.

15.6 Refer to the section on managerial control of software operation services.

a. List the main issues dealt with by managerial software operation control.

b. Is there a need for meetings and audits after management has received satisfactory reporting from the software operation teams? What additional contributions to managerial control might be achieved with meetings and audits? List your arguments.

Topics for discussion

15.1 A lecturer in an SQA conference concluded his talk by recommending a software maintenance specialist participate in the quality assurance activities carried out during the development process.

a. Do you agree with the lecturer? What are the roles the SQA function staff should fulfill in these activities?

b. List your arguments for and against this suggestion.

c. Do you support "reverse" cooperation, where a development specialist participates in quality assurance activities related to the software operation conformance with contracts and standards?

d. List your arguments for and against this position.

15.2 Mr. Steve Barber, a software maintenance expert, was recruited to lead the team providing maintenance services for Hotelex, a hotel management software package, after the former team leader had resigned. The package had been on the market for 6 months and the team had already installed and maintained four different versions of Hotelex in seven hotels. The company is in the first stages of developing packages for sport clubs and community centers. The software maintenance team is expected to serve customers of all three packages.

During the team's monthly meeting, Barber mentioned that after a month in service, he found the foundations for maintaining Hotelex to be inadequate, and the cause of high software maintenance costs. While nothing could be done in relation to the software package's quality (the first maintenance foundation) at this point, he hoped to improve maintenance by employing the version release policies (the second foundation) within the next 3 months. In general, he declared that he would take action to ensure proper foundations for the two new software packages currently being developed.

a. Suggest which findings regarding the maintenance of Hotelex had brought Mr. Barber to his negative evaluation of the maintenance according to its second foundation.

b. Suggest which actions Barber might plan to assure proper foundations for the two new packages.

15.3 The suggested procedures for handling "patch repairs" includes "mini review" and "mini test" procedures and is suggested in Section 15.3.

a. Explain the importance of the "mini" procedures toward achieving adequate quality of software repairs.

   b. Compare the components designated for handling "patch repairs" with the components of the software development phase.

15.4 The weekly customer complaints piled on the desk of the Head of Software Operations included the following:

   a. A complaint repeated by several customers: The software maintenance technician, who was unable to solve the problem on site at the scheduled time, claimed that he was unaware that he was required to take the software programmers' manual with him at all times; and was therefore, unable to solve the problem on time.

   b. A complaint by the Operations Manager of a supermarket chain: The software maintenance team unsuccessfully tried to correct the software three times; as a result, several crucial functions could not be activated for 4 days.

   c. A customer's angry letter complaining about an unfair cost estimate for a requested minor improvement: Sixty man-days. He quoted the Head of the Software Functional Improvement Team, who said that the high estimate was the outcome of missing documentation and nonstandard coding of the original package.

Analyze each of the cases and then:

   a. Suggest the reasons for each of the software operations team's failures.

   b. Suggest the steps to be taken in each case to prevent the failures mentioned in (a).

15.5 At a recent SQA conference, a speaker mentioned the following costs as maintenance quality costs:

   a. High operating costs due to the unanticipated high frequency of overseas calls. It has been found that the overseas branches of a firm employ six times more employees than estimated by the software sales departments when preparing the maintenance plan.

   b. Damages to a Software Development Department due to increasing difficulties in sales, and higher rates of tender losses after two leading customers had decided not to renew their maintenance contracts, claiming inadequate quality of maintenance services.

   c. Increased penalties paid to customers during a two-month period in which the maintenance team was short of three team members.

   a. Can all costs in the three cases mentioned already be considered software operation quality costs according to the classic model of cost of software operation quality (see Section 15.5.5)? Analyze each of the cases separately. List your arguments.

   b. How would you classify each of the corrective maintenance quality costs described in the above cases according to the extended model of cost of software operation quality (see Section 15.5.5)? List your arguments.

Chapter 16

Software Product Quality Metrics

"You can't control what you can't measure."

Tom De Marco (1962)

This quote from Tom De Marco has become the motto for software quality experts trying to develop and apply quality metrics in the software industry.

16.1 What are software quality metrics? – an introduction

Software quality and other software engineers have formulated the main objectives for software quality metrics, presented in Frame 16.1:

Frame 16.1: Objectives of software quality metrics

Source: After ISO/IEC Std. 90003-2014 Sec. 8 (ISO/IEC 2014).

Objectives of software quality metrics:

- To assist management to monitor and control development and maintenance of software systems and their process improvements by:
- Observing the conformance of software product to functionality and other requirements, regulations, and conventions.
- Serving as a data source for process improvement by:
  - Identifying cases of low performance requiring improvement.
  - Demonstrating the achievements of process improvement proposals (corrective actions)

Software Quality: Concepts and Practice, First Edition. Daniel Galin.
© 2018 the IEEE Computer Society, Inc. Published 2018 by John Wiley & Sons, Inc.

The metrics are used for comparison of performance data with indicators that are quantitative values, such as:

• Defined software quality standards

• Quality targets set for organizations or individuals

• Previous year's quality achievements

• Previous project's quality achievements

• Average quality levels achieved by other teams applying the same development tools in similar development environments

• Average quality achievements of the organization

• Industry practices for meeting quality requirement

Comparison provides a practical basis for management's application of metrics and for SQA improvement in general.

The metrics' required characteristics

In order for the selected quality metrics to be applicable and successful, both favorable metrics characteristics and metrics implementation characteristics are required.

The metrics characteristics include being relevant, valid, reliable, comprehensive, and mutually exclusive.

The three metrics implementation characteristics are: being easy and simple, not requiring independent data collection, and immune to biased intervention by interested parties. Being easy and simple means that the regular data collection and processing involved in implementation are simple and require minimal resources. Being not requiring independent data collection means that there are possibilities to integrate the metrics data collection with other project data collection systems: employee attendance, wages, cost accounting, etc. In addition to its efficiency aspects, this requirement contributes to the coordination of all information systems serving the organization. Being immune to biased interventions by interested parties means that metric data collection is protected from any undesirable additions and deletions and changes. In other words, it is expected that in order to escape the expected results of the analysis of the metrics, it is expected that interested parties will try to change the data and, by doing so, improve their record. Such actions obviously cause the relevant metrics to be biased. Immunity (total or at least partial) is achieved mainly by a careful choice of metrics along with adequate procedures.

The required characteristics, as presented in Frame 16.2, must be satisfied.

Frame 16.2: Software quality metrics – required characteristics

Required characteristics	Explanation
Metrics characteristics	
• Relevant	Related to an attribute of substantial importance
• Valid	Measures the required attribute
• Reliable	Produces similar results when applied under similar conditions
• Comprehensive	Applicable to a large variety of implementations and situations
• Mutually exclusive	Does not measure attributes measured by other metrics
Metrics implementation characteristics	
• Easy and simple	The implementation of the metrics data collection is simple and performed with minimal resources
• Does not require independent data collection	Metrics data collection can be integrated with other project data collection systems: that is, employee attendance
• Immune to biased interventions by interested parties	The data collection and processing system is protected from unwanted changes; additions and deletions

Several books, book chapters, and numerous journals as well as conference papers have been dedicated to the subject of software quality metrics. A comprehensive discussion of software metrics is presented in books by Fenton and Bieman (2015) and Nicolette (2015), and in papers by Radjenovic et al. (2013), Kitchenham (2010), and Mordal et al. (2012) and Barkmann et al. (2009).

The IEEE and ISO/IEC offer software quality metrics criteria within their software engineering standards. In the ISO/IEC standards, we may also note that ISO/IEC Std. 90003:2014 (ISO/IEC, 2014) dedicates chapter 8 to the measurement, analysis, and improvement of software products. Section 6.3.7 of the ISO/IEC/IEEE Std. 12207-2008 (ISO/IEC/IEE, 2008) presents the measurement processes for project processes in a system life cycle. An ISO/IEC standard that should be mentioned is ISO/IEC Std. 15939:2007 (ISO/IEC, 2007), which is dedicated to measurement process.

A comprehensive presentation of software product metrics is provided by the four-part ISO/IEC Std. 9126 (ISO/IEC 2002–2004) (ISO/IEC, 2002). IEEE Std. 730-2014 (IEEE, 2014) discusses measure processes for product and process assurance activities.

The following sections discuss the following topics:

- Section 16.2: The implementation of software quality metrics
- Section 16.3: Product metrics and their classification

- Section 16.4: Software product size metrics
- Section 16.5: Software attribute metrics

16.2 Implementation of software quality metrics

The implementation of software quality metrics in an organization includes the following activities:

- Definition of software quality metrics – relevant and adequate for teams, departments, and so on.
- Regular application of the metrics (by units, project teams, etc.)
- Analysis of metrics data by the Corrective Action Board
- Taking action in response to metrics analysis results

16.2.1 Definition of software quality metrics

The definition of metrics involves a four-stage process:

1. Listing attributes to be measured: software quality, development team productivity, and so on.
2. Defining metrics that measure the required attributes and confirmation of their adequacy in complying with the requirements listed in Frame 16.2.
3. Determining comparative target values based on standards, previous year's performance, and so on. These values serve as indicators to whether the unit measured (a team, individual, or portion of a software package) complies with the characteristics demanded of a given attribute.
4. Determining the metrics application processes: (1) Reporting method, including reporting process and frequency of reporting. (2) Metrics data collection method.

The new metrics (updates, changes, and revised applications) will be constructed following analysis of the metrics data as well as developments in the organization and its environment.

16.2.2 Application of the metrics

The process of applying a metric or set of metrics is similar to the implementation of new procedures or methodologies. It involves:

- Assigning responsibility for reporting and metrics data collection.
- Instruction of the team regarding the new metrics.

- Follow-up includes: (1) Support for solving application problems and provision of supplementary information when needed. (2) Control of metrics reporting for completeness and accuracy.

Implementation tip

Many of the currently applied software quality metrics procedures and work instructions omit the third stage of the metrics definition process: setting target values (indicators). In other words, no target values for the metrics are to be found in the procedure or its appendices, in the accompanying work instructions, or in any other document. In most cases, this situation reflects a serious lack of commitment to using metrics in managerial control – the major reason for applying metrics in the first place. When application of metrics goes beyond lip service, target values should be set, even if updates of these values are expected soon after their first application.

An interesting global application of software quality metrics for comparison of national software industries is presented in the following example.

Example – Comparison of US, Japanese, and other software industries

Cusumano (1991) and Cusumano et al. (2003) makes use of two metrics in a comparison of the US, Japanese, and other countries software industries:

- Mean productivity. This metric is similar to the DevPL presented in Section 21.3.3.4.
- Failure density, based on measurements during the first 12 months following system delivery. This metric is similar to the DEDL presented in Section 21.3.1.

The results of Cusumano and Cusumano et al are presented in Table 16.1.

Examining Table 16.1 one may note: (a) The superiority of Japan in terms of productivity and failure density. (b) The failure density improvement of the United States during this decade. (c) The remarkable achievement of Japan in reducing its failure density to one tenth during this decade.

16.2.3 Analysis of metrics data by the Corrective Action Board

The Corrective Action Board (CAB) should perform analysis on the metrics' results, in order that the metrics data be a valuable part of the SQA process. Statistical tools may be used to identify any significant results. Analysis of these significant results is expected to lead to process improvements.

Table 16.1 Comparison of countries for two software quality metrics

Country		USA	Japan	India	Europe
Productivity – mean	2001/2	3,240	5,628	2,508	5,232
	1990	7,290	12,447	—	—
Failure density –	2001/2	0.400	0.020	0.225	0.263
median	1990	0.83	0.20	—	—

(i) Mean productivity is measured in lines of noncomment code per man-year. (ii) Failure density is measured in the number of failures in KLOC detected during the first year of regular use of a software package. (iii) The difference between the productivity of 1990 and 2001/2 do not indicate a decrease in average productivity during this period, but a difference in the programming language used in those years.

16.2.4 Taking action in response to metrics analysis results

The statistically analyzed metrics data provides opportunities for comparing a series of project metrics. These certainly include comparison of metric results against predefined indicators, as well as comparisons with former projects or team performance during different periods of time, and so on. Another important comparison relates to the effectiveness with which the metrics themselves fulfill their respective objectives. The following questions are just a sample of those that may be asked with respect to the metrics portion of the SQA process.

- Are there significant differences between the HD teams' quality of service?
- Do the metric results support the assumption that application of the new version of the development tool contributes significantly to software quality?
- Do the metric results support the assumption that reorganization has contributed significantly to a specific team's productivity?

The actions taken in response to metrics analysis as well as the developments in the organization and its environment are mainly initiated by the Corrective Action Board (CAB). The CAB actions are a result of analysis of metrics data accumulated from a variety of projects and/or development departments.

Examples of changes initiated include: (1) changes in comparative target values (indicators) of metrics; (2) changes in method of metrics data collection; and (3) replacement of a metrics, adding or dropping a metrics.

For a comprehensive discussion of the Corrective Action Board and its activities, see Chapter 19.

The software quality metrics implementation process is described in Figure 16.1.

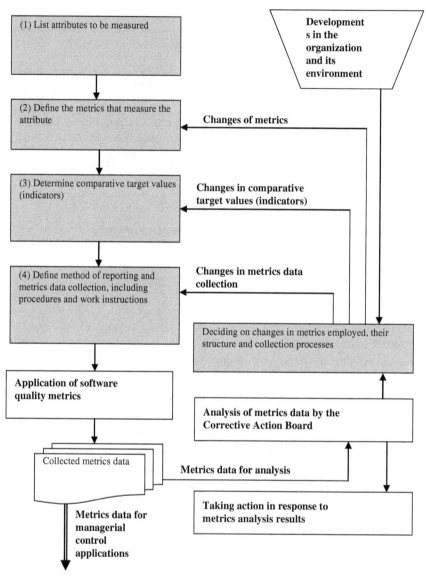

Figure 16.1   The implementation process of software quality metrics

16.3   Product metrics and their classification

SQA and software engineering professionals distinguished between software product metrics and software process metrics.

Software product metrics are a quantitative representation of software products or intermediate product's attributes, as experienced by the user when applying the software trying to adapt it or change it, such as size, effectiveness, productivity, and reliability.

Software process metrics are a quantitative representation of software processes, as experienced by developers and maintainers throughout the software life cycle, such as, prerelease defects, percent of modified code lines, and density of detected defects.

This chapter is dedicated to software product metrics.

Classification of software product metrics

The product metrics are classified into two classes:

1. Software product size metrics
2. Software attributes metrics

The software product size metrics and the software attribute metrics are discussed in the next two sections.

16.4   Software product size metrics

A measure of software product size is needed mainly: (a) to estimate the required development resources at the stage of preparing a proposal for a software project or planning and scheduling its process of development and (b) for use in other metrics when comparing the performance proportionally to the software project size, for example, in metrics of productivity, quality (defects rates), and so on.

Two approaches for software size metrics are offered:

a. KLOC (thousands off lines of code). This metric represents metrics based on the physical completed size of software, such as the number of lines of code or the number of software statements. While the application of this metric is very simple, once the software project is completed, its application during the early stages of development is very inaccurate. Estimates of the expected KLOC size of a planned project rely only on the personal experience of the evaluators, and the impression they form when examining the project specifications.

b. Function points (FPs). This metric represents the result of applying a measure from the group of functional size measurement (FSM) methods. These estimating methods are based on the functionality specified by the software project requirements. More specifically, the FSM concept requires counting items such as inputs and outputs of software systems, software transactions, and logical file systems derived directly from the requirement specifications where the level of complexity/difficulty is evaluated for each item, and an adequate factor is defined accordingly. A detailed function point calculation process and its implementation is presented in Appendix A.

The first to present an FSM method was Albrecht in 1979 (Albrecht, 1979). Several variations of the FSM method were publicized in the following decades. The ISO/IEC Std. 14143 standard, published in six parts during 1998–2007 (ISO/IEC, 1998), relates to these methods and determines rules for defining functional items to be included in an FSM method (see Czarnacka-Chrobot (2009)); standard classifies the implemented methods according to the area of application: business applications, real-time systems, scientific systems. Four of the FSM methods are certified according to this standard: IFPUG FPA, ark II FPA, COSMIC FFP, and NESMA FSM. As expected, there is a variance in the function point results among the different FSM methods. An example of such variation is presented by Efe et al. (2011) in a case study project. The number of function points calculated by three FSM methods for the same project were as follows: IFPUG FPA – 925, Mark II FPA – 1330, COSMIC FFP – 1060. The variation between the FSM methods leads to intensive research dedicated to conversion methods between the methods, a selection of research results are: Lavazza and Morasca (2011), Cuadrado-Gallego et al. (2010, 2008), and Abran et al. (2011).

At this stage, we are interested in the following applicability questions:

- What is the average number of programming logical statements per function point?
- What is the average productivity of a staff member in terms of the number of function points produced per month?

Answers for these questions are provided by Jones (2014), who found a gradual change in FP characteristics as a result of the progress in development tools through the last six decades. The changing FP productivity results for 1955–2015 are presented in Table 16.2.

Table 16.2   FP productivity characteristics 1955–2015

Year	Typical programming language	Logical statements per FP	FP per staff-month
1955	Basic, Assembler	320	3.5 FP
1965	Macro-Assembly	120	5 FP
1975	C	91	6 FP
1985	COBOL	58	7 FP
1995	Java	53	8 FP
2005	C#, MySQL	40	9.5 FP
2015 Estimate	RUP, TSP	27	12 FP

Source: After Jones (2014).

From Table 16.2, it is noteworthy that (a) the efficiency of programming languages grew 12 times during this period. In other words, coding the same application in 2015 required only 8.5% of the number of programming statements required in 1955. (b) Software engineering productivity grew 3.5-fold during the last six decades. In other words, in 1955 a staff-month produced a 3.5 FP project, while in 2015 a staff-month produced a 12 FP project.

FSM methods – advantages and disadvantages

Main advantages:

- The function point (FP) method estimates of development resources, based entirely on the software requirement specification, can be prepared at the preproject stage and can, therefore, support the management in its project proposal and preparation efforts. The method's reliability is relatively high.
- The FP evaluation of the volume of a development project can be "translated" into required development resources, once you specify the development tools or programming languages planned to be used (the FP method determines the tools productivity in terms of FP per staff months).

Main disadvantages:

- Estimates need to be based on detailed analysis of the software requirements specifications, which requires substantial work investments. It is to be compared with expert estimates based on personal past projects experience and professional and general understandings, which require just a few hours to prepare (and was in most cases not found to be very accurate).
- The implementation of the FP method involves counting distinct components, where the distinction of a component is not very clear in many cases. In addition, the implementer of the FP method is required to evaluate the level of complexity of each component, which is arguable in many cases, consequently, the FP result becomes subjective.
- To overcome or reduce the "subjectivity weakness," the entire process requires an experienced FP team to perform the process. As a result, the FP method cannot be implemented by a "regular" software engineer."
- A variety of FSM methods are offered, four of which are ISO/IEC-certified evaluation tools. The estimates produced by these tools vary substantially.
- Most successful applications and research results are related to data processing systems. Other areas of software systems require specialized adaptations. In other words, the function point method cannot be universally applied.

More about FSM methodology may be read in Gencel and Demirors (2008), Meli (2011), Lenarduzzi et al. (2015), Lenarduzzi and Taibi (2014), Alves de Oliviera and Noya (2013), Jones (2003), and Santillio (2006).

16.5 Software product attribute metrics

Source: After the three parts of ISO/IEC TR 9126.

A comprehensive presentation of software product metrics is presented in three parts of the ISO/IEC TR 9126 (ISO/IEC, [2003a, 2003b, 2003c]; ISO/IEC, 2004). The ISO/IEC technical reports relate to 10 attributes of software products, which are as follows:

- Software functionality
- Software reliability
- Software usability
- Software efficiency
- Software maintainability
- Software portability
- Software effectiveness
- Software productivity
- Software safety
- Software satisfaction

Examples of these metrics are presented in the following section.

16.5.1 Software functionality metrics

Functionality metrics relate to the following aspects: suitability, accuracy, interoperability, security, and functionality compliance. Four examples of functionality metrics are presented in Table 16.3. The first metric, FSS, relates to the

Table 16.3 Examples of functional (compliance) metrics.

Metric code	Metric name	Calculation formula
FSS	Functional specification stability	$\mathrm{FSS} = 1 - \dfrac{\mathrm{NFSC}}{\mathrm{NFSR}}$
FCI	Functional correct implementation	NFICI $\mathrm{FCI} = 1 - \mathrm{NFSR}$
AAL	Average accuracy level	NACUs $\mathrm{AAL} = \mathrm{TNCUs}$
IADn	Inaccuracy density	NIAC $\mathrm{IADn} = \mathrm{OT}$

NFSC: number of function specification changed, NFSR: number of function specification required, NFICI: number of functions incorrectly implemented, NACUs: number of accurate computations by users, TNCUs: total number of computations by users, NIAC: number of inaccuracy cases recorded over an observed period of time, OT: observation time.

tendency to change function specifications during the development process, when the fewer function specification changes, the lower the rate of software defects is likely to be. The second metric relates to the level of correctly implemented functions in the software product. The third metric relates to the user experience in computations accuracy. The last metric relates to the density of inaccuracy of computation cases, that is, five inaccuracy cases a day.

16.5.2 Software reliability metrics

User metrics distinguish between:

- Full reliability: when all software system functions perform properly – percentage of operation time.
- Vital reliability: when all vital functions function properly (but nonvital functions may fail) – percentage of operation time.
- Total unreliability: when all software system functions fail – percentage of operation time.

Where: Full reliability < Vital reliability < 1 - Total unreliability

For example, Full reliability = 0.92, Vital reliability = 0.94, and Total unreliability = 0.03.

The source for all availability metrics is user failure records. The latter specify the extent of damage (nonvital failures, vital failures, and total system failures) as well as duration (hours) for each failure.

Three software system reliability metrics are presented in Table 16.4.

Table 16.4 Software system reliability metrics

Code	Name	Calculation formula
FR	Full Reliability	$FR = \dfrac{NYSerH - NYFH}{NYSerH}$
VitR	Vital Reliability	$VitR = \dfrac{NYSerH - NYVitFH}{NYSerH}$
TUR	Total Unreliability	$TUR = \dfrac{NYTFH}{TYSerH}$

- TYSerH: number of hours per year that the software system is in service. For an office software system that is operating 50 hours per week for 52 weeks per year; NYSerH = 2,600 (50 × 52).

For a real-time software application that serves users 24 hours a day, NYSerH = 8,760 (365 × 24).

- NYFH: number of hours per year when at least one function failed (including total failure of the software system).
- NYVitFH: number of hours per year when at least one vital function failed (including total failure of the software system).
- NYTFH: number of hours per year of total system failures (all system functions failed).
- NYFH ≥ NYVitFH ≥ NYTFH.
- 1 – TUA ≥ VitA ≥ FA

Table 16.5   Examples of usability metrics

Metric code	Metric name	Calculation formula
EFL	Ease to learn function (hours)	$EFL = MTLUF$
MECT	Mean error (bug) correction time	$MECT = MTCC - MTSC$
PERUs	Percentage error recovery by user	$PERU = \dfrac{NCERUs}{TNEC}$
MC	Message clarity	$MC = \dfrac{NMCEx}{TNM}$

MTLUF: mean time for learning to use a function correctly (hours), MTCC: mean time till correction by technician is completed, MTSC: mean time till correction by technician is started, NCERUs: number of cases of error recovery by users, TNEC: total number of error cases, NMCEx: number of messages with clear explanation, TNM: total number of messages.

16.5.3   Software usability metrics

Usability metrics relate to the following aspects: understandability, learnability, operability, attractiveness, and usability compliance. Four examples of usability metrics are presented in Table 16.5. The first metric, EFL, relates to the time required by a user to learn a function using a help notice or a user guide. The second metric, MECI, refers to the time required to correct an error during the operation phase. The third metric, PERUs relates to errors detected during regular operation and to the capability of users to recover the error by themselves. The last metric, MC, relates to the cases where the user understands messages sent by the software system.

16.5.4   Software efficiency metrics

Efficiency metrics relate to the following aspects: behavior over time, resource utilization, and efficiency compliance. Four examples of efficiency metrics are presented in Table 16.6. The first metric, MRsT, relates to the performance of

Table 16.6   Examples of efficiency metrics

Metric code	Metric name	Calculation formula
MRsT	Mean response time (seconds)	MRsT
Throughput	Throughput (tasks per hour)	$Throughput = \dfrac{NTP}{OT}$
ThrComp	Throughput compliance	$ThrComp = \dfrac{NTPTP}{CTPTP}$
IOU	I/O utilization	$IOU = \dfrac{TIODOc}{STIOOp}$

NTP: number of tasks performed, OT: observation time (hours), NTPTP: number of tasks performed over a period of time, CTPTP: compliance tasks performed over a period of time, TIODOc: time I/O device occupied, STIOOp: specified time for I/O operation.

search tasks and is an important factor of the software efficiency. The second metric, throughput, is an important factor in services that include software usage, such as help desk services. The third metric, ThrComp, is based on the comparison of the actual throughput with that required in the contract. The last metric, IOU, measures the level of utilization of I/O equipment.

16.5.5 Software maintainability metrics

Maintainability metrics relate to the following aspects: analyzability, changeability, stability, testability, and maintainability compliance. Four examples of usability metrics are presented in Table 16.7. The first metric, DSCp, measures the level of support provided by the diagnostics function to resolve failure cases. The second metric, CSR, relates to the cases of change failure. The third metric, MFD, relates to the frequency of cases of modification failure.

16.5.6 Software portability metrics

Portability metrics relate to the following aspects: adaptability, installability, coexistence, replaceability, and portability compliance. Three examples of portability metrics are presented in Table 16.8. The first metric, TNFATest, measures the level of compliance to portability tasks. The second metric relates to the project of perfective maintenance (functionality improvement maintenance) and measures the successful acceptance of the improved functions. The last metric relates to the success of adapting a software system to a new organizational environment.

16.5.7 Software effectiveness metrics

Effectiveness metrics relate to a variety of implementation situations: corrections and changes of the original software product. Three examples of effectiveness

Table 16.7 Examples of maintainability metrics

Metric code	Metric name	Calculation formula
DSCp	Diagnostics support capability	$DSCp = \dfrac{NFMDF}{TNF}$
CSR	Change success ratio	$CSR = 1 - \dfrac{NCnF}{TNCn}$
MFR	Modification failure density	$MFD = \dfrac{NMF}{OT}$

NFMDF: number of failures discovered by usage of the diagnostic function, TNF: total number of failures, NCnF: number of change failures, TNCn: total number of changes, NMF: number of modification failures.

Table 16.8 Examples of portability metrics

Metric code	Metric name	Calculation formula
PorComp	Portability compliance	$PorComp = \dfrac{NCIFPComp}{TNF}$
PMAc	Perfective maintenance acceptability	$PMAc = \dfrac{NPMFAc}{TNPMF}$
AAcOE	Adaptability acceptance to organization's environment	$AAcOE = 1 - \dfrac{NFAFail}{TNFATest}$

NCIFPComp: number of correctly implemented functions in portability compliance, TNF: total number of functions, NPMFAc: number of perfective maintenance functions accepted, TNPMF: total number of perfective maintenance functions, CTPTP: compliance tasks performed over a period of time, NFAFail: number of functions that failed adaptability testing, TNFATest: total number of functions that underwent adaptability testing.

Table 16.9 Examples of effectiveness metrics

Metric code	Metric name	Calculation formula
TskEfc	Task effectiveness	$TskEfc = 1 - PTMICCom$
TSCR	Tasks successfully completed ratio	$TSCR = \dfrac{NTSC}{TNTAt}$
AAcOE	Adaptability acceptance to organization's environment	$AAcOE = 1 - \dfrac{NFAFail}{TNFATest}$

PTMICCom: proportion of missing tasks and incorrect components, NTSC: number of tasks successfully completed, TNTAt: total number of tasks attempted, NFAFail: number of functions that failed adaptability testing, TNFATest: total number of functions that underwent adaptability testing.

metrics are presented in Table 16.9. The first metric, TskEfc, measures the proportion of effective components versus missing or incorrect components. The second metric, TSCR, measures effectiveness by the proportion of tasks being completed successfully. The last metric is dedicated to measuring the success of the adaptation of a software system to a different environment.

16.5.8 Software productivity metrics

Productivity metrics relate to a variety of implementation situation allowing comparison between tasks and teams, and between time periods. Two examples of productivity metrics are presented in Table 16.10. The first metric, TskEfc, PP, presents figures for productivity in performing a task. The second metric, PC, allows calculating productivity changes when performing a given task.

Table 16.10 Examples of productivity metrics

Metric code	Metric name	Calculation formula
PP	Productivity proportion	$PP = \dfrac{MTPT}{MTT}$
PC	Productivity change	$PC = \dfrac{MTPTP2 - MTPTP1}{MTPTP1}$

MNPT: mean task productive time, MTT: mean task time, where MTT = MNPT + waiting time + error time + search time, MTPTP2: mean task performance time period 2, MTPTP1: mean task performance time period 1.

16.5.9 Software safety metrics

Software safety metrics relate to the user being injured as a result of software safety failure. The other metric deals with the prospects of suffering from a software corruption.

Safety metrics relate to a variety of implementation damage situations. Two examples of safety metrics are presented in Table 16.11. The first metric, USafL, relates to the user being injured as a result of software safety failure. The other metric deals with the prospects of suffering from a software corruption.

16.5.10 Software satisfaction metrics

Satisfaction metrics related to user satisfaction, where the level of satisfaction is measured by a questionnaire. Two examples of satisfaction metrics are presented in Table 16.12. Both matrices are based on user responses to satisfaction questionnaire.

Table 16.11 Examples of safety metrics

Metric code	Metric name	Calculation formula
USafL	User safety level	$USafL = \dfrac{NInjU}{1 - TNU}$
SWDL	Software corruption level	$SWDL = \dfrac{NOcSWC}{TNUSit}$

NInjU: number of injured users, TNU: total number of uses, NOcSWC: number of occurrences of software corruption, TNUSit: total number of usage situations.

Table 16.12   Examples of satisfaction metrics

Metric code	Metric name	Calculation formula
USatL	User satisfaction level	$\text{USatL} = \dfrac{\text{SURSQ}}{\text{TNRSQ}}$
USatC	User satisfaction change	$\text{USatC} = \dfrac{\text{USatLP2} - \text{USatLP1}}{\text{USatLP1}}$

SURSQ: sum of user responses to satisfaction questionnaire, TNRSQ: total number of user responses to satisfaction questionnaire, USatLP2: user satisfaction level period 2, USatLP2: user satisfaction level period 1.

Summary

1. **The objectives of software quality metrics**
   a. To support management control of software development projects and software maintenance in setting functionality, schedule, and budget performance targets.
   b. To observe the conformance of software product to functionality and other requirements, regulation, and convections.
   c. To serve as a data source for process improvement by:
      • Identifying cases of low performance that need improvement.
      • Demonstrate the achievements of process improvement proposals (corrective actions)

2. **The required characteristics for successful software quality metrics**
      Applicability of quality metrics is determined by the degree to which the following general and operative requirements are fulfilled:
   Metrics characteristics
      • Relevant – measures an attribute of considerable importance
      • Valid – measures the required attribute
      • Reliable – produces similar results when applied in similar conditions
      • Comprehensive – is applicable to a large variety of situations
      • Mutually exclusive – does not measure attributes that are measured by other metrics
   Metrics implementation characteristics
      • Easy and simple – implemented with minimal resources
      • Does not require independent data collection – metrics data collection is based on currently employed data collection systems
      • Immune to biased interventions by interested parties

3. **The process of defining a new software quality metric**
      The definition of a new metric involves a four-stage process:
   1. Definition of software quality metrics
   2. Application of the metrics

3. Analysis of metrics data by the Corrective Action Board

4. Taking action in response to metrics analysis results

4. **Software product metrics versus software process metrics**

   Software product metrics are a quantitative representation of a software product or intermediate product's attributes, as experienced by the user when applying the software to try to adapt or change features, such as size, effectiveness, productivity, and reliability.

   Software process metrics are a quantitative representation of software processes, as experienced by developers and maintainers throughout the software life cycle, such as, prerelease defects, percent of modified code lines, and density of detected defects.

5. **Classification of software product metrics**

   The product metrics are classified into two classes:

   1. Software product size metrics

   2. Software attributes metrics.

6. **Software product size metrics categories:**

   - KLOC
   - Function points

7. **The function point method process stages**

   Stage 1: Calculation of crude function points

   Stage 2: Calculating the relative complexity adjustment factor (RCAF)

   Stage 3: Calculate the number of function points (FP)

8. **Comparison of KLOC and function point measures for the size of software system**

   A significant number of the metrics presented here use one of two measures for software system size, which are compared according to the following criteria:

   - Dependency on the development tool, programming language, or programmer style. KLOC depends heavily on the development tool's characteristics and on the programmer's style. Alternatively, although the function point method does not depend on either of these factors, it does depend to some extent on the function point instruction manual used systems.
   - Professional experience required for implementation: Relatively little experience is required for counting KLOC, while relatively great experience is needed to evaluate function points.
   - Amount of professional work required: Relatively little work is required for KLOC; a relatively great deal of work is required to evaluate function points.
   - Subjective factors: Estimation of KLOC requires little subjective judgment, whereas the opposite is true for function points as subjective evaluations are required for determining the weight and relative complexity factors for each software system component.

Preproject estimates: Preproject estimates for KLOC are based only on the evaluator's experience, while function point estimates are based on facts, such as the number of inputs and outputs of the planned software as derived from the requirement specification documents

9. **Software attribute metrics types according to ISO/IEC Std. 9126**
   - Software functionality
   - Software reliability
   - Software usability
   - Software efficiency
   - Software maintainability
   - Software portability
   - Software effectiveness
   - Software productivity
   - Software safety
   - Software satisfaction

Selected bibliography

Abran A., Desharnais J. M., and Aziz F. (2011) Measurement convertibility – from function points to COSMIC FFP, in Rale D. and Abran A. (Eds.) *COSMIC Function Points Theory and Advanced Practices*, CRC Press, Boca Raton. FL, pp. 214–226.

Albrecht, A. J. (1979) Measuring application development productivity, in *Proceeding of the Joint SHARE/GUIDE/IBM Application Development Symposium*, October 1979, pp. 34–43.

Alves de Oliviera E. and Noya R. C. (2013) Using productivity measure and function points to improve the software development process, in *2013 International Conference on Software Engineering Research and Practice, Athens, Greece*.

Barkmann H., Linke R., and Lowe W. (2009) Quantitative evaluation of software quality metrics in open-source projects, in *Advanced Information Networking Workshops, WAINA'09*, Bradford, May 2009, pp. 1067–1072.

Cuadrado-Gallego J. J., Buglione L., Rejas–Muslera R. J., and Machado-Pinz F. (2008) IFPUG – COSMIC statistical conversion, in *Proceedings of 34th European Conference on Software Engineering and Advanced Applications*, Parma, Italy, pp. 427–432.

Cuadrado-Gallego J. J., Buglione L., Dominguz-Alda M. J., Femandez de Sevilla M., Gutierez de Mesa A., and Demirors O. (2010) An experimental study on the conversion between IFPUG and COSMIC functional size measurement unit, *Information and Software Technology*, Vol. 52, No. **3**, pp. 347–357.

Cusumano, M. A. (1991) *Japan's Software Factories – A Challenge to U.S. Management*, Oxford University Press, New York, NY.

Cusumano M. A., MacCormack A., Kemerer C. F., and Crandall B. (2003) Software development worldwide: the state of the practice, *IEEE Software*, Vol. 20, No. 5, pp. 28–34.

Czarnacka-Chrobot B. (2009) The ISO/IEC standards for the software processes and products measurement, in Fujita I.I. and Marik V., (Eds.) *New Trends in Software Methodologies: Tools and techniques*, IOS Press, pp. 187–200.

DeMarco T. (1978) "Structured analysis and system specification", Yourdon Press Prentice Hall PTR, upper Saddle River, NJ, USA

Efe P., Demirors O., and Gencel C. (2011) Mapping concepts of functional size measurement methods, in Rale D. and Abran A. (Eds.) *COSMIC Function Points: Theory and Advanced Practices*, CRC Press, Boca Raton, FL, pp. 57–71.

Fenton, N. E. and Bieman J. (2015) *Software Metrics: A Rigorous and Practical Approach*, 3rd Edition, CRC Press, Boca Raton, FL.

Gencel C. and Demirors O. (2008) Functional size measurement revisited, *ACM Transactions on Software Engineering and Methodology*, Vol. 17, No. 3, pp. 1–36.

IEEE (2014) *IEEE Std. 730–2014 Software quality assurance*, The IEEE Computer Society, IEEE, New York.

ISO/IEC (1998–2007) *ISO/IEC Std. 14143 Information Technology – Software Measurement – Functional Size Measurement*, in Parts 1–6, International Organization for Standardization, Geneva, Switzerland.

ISO/IEC (2002) *ISO/IEC TR 9120-1 Software Engineering – Product Quality – Part 1: Quality model*, in International Organization for Standardization (ISO), Geneva, Switzerland.

ISO/IEC (2003a) *ISO/IEC TR 9120-3 Software Engineering – Product Quality – Part 2: External Metrics*, in International Organization for Standardization (ISO), Geneva, Switzerland.

ISO/IEC (2003b) *ISO/IEC TR 9120-3 Software Engineering – Product Quality – Part 3: Internal Metrics*, in International Organization for Standardization (ISO), Geneva, Switzerland.

ISO/IEC (2003b) *ISO/IEC TR 9120-4 Software Engineering – Product Quality – Part 4 Quality In Use Metrics*, in International Organization for Standardization (ISO), Geneva, Switzerland.

ISO/TEC (2007) *TSO/IEC Std. 15939 Software and Systems Engineering – Measurement Process*, in International Organization for Standardization (ISO), Geneva, Switzerland.

ISO/IEC (2008) *ISO/IEC/IEEE Std. 12207-2008: Systems and Software Engineering – Software life cycle processes*, in ISO – International Organization for Standardization, Geneva, Switzerland.

ISO (2014) *ISO/IEC 90003:2014 Software Engineering – Guidelines for the Application of ISO 9001: 2008 to Computer Software*, in International Organization for Standardization (ISO), Geneva, Switzerland.

Jones C. (2003) Variations in software development practices, *IEEE Software*, Vol. 20, No. 6, pp. 22–27.

Jones C. (2014) *The Technical and Social History of Software Engineering*, Addison Wesley, Upper Saddle River, NJ.

Kitchenham B. (2010) What's up with software metrics? – a preliminary mapping study, *Journal of Systems and Software*, Vol. 83, No. 1, pp. 37–51.

Lavazza L. and Morasca S. (2011) Convertibility of function points into COSMIC function points: A study using piecewise linear regression, *Information and Software Technology*, Vol. 53, No. 8, pp. 874–884.

Lenarduzzi V. and Taibi D. (2014) Can functional size measures improve effort estimation in SCRUM?, in *The Ninth International Conference on Software Engineering Advances (ICSEA2014)*, Nice, France, pp. 73–178.

Lenarduzzi V., Lunesu I., Matta M., and Taibi D. (2015) Functional size measures and effort estimation in agile development: a replicated study, in *Proceedings of the International Conference on Agile Software Development, XP2015, Helsinki, Finland*, pp. 105–116.

Meli R. (2011) Simple function point: a new functional size measurement method compliant with IFPUG 4.x, in *Software Measurement European Forum 2011*, pp. 1–5.

Mordal K., Anquetil N., Laval J., Serebrenik A., Vasilescu B., and Ducasse S. (2012) Software quality metrics aggregation in industry, *Journal of Software: Evolution and Progress*, Vol. 25, No. 10, pp. 1117–1135.

Nicolette D. (2015) *Software Development Metrics*, Manning Publishing, Shelter Island, NY.

Radjenovic D., Hencko M., Torkar R., and Zivkovic A. (2013) Software fault prediction metrics: a systematic literature review, *Information and Software Technology*, Vol. 55, No. 8, pp. 1397–1418.

Santillo L. (2006) Function points usage in contracts – considerations and guidelines, in *Proceedings of the International Conference on Software Process and Product Measurement, MENSURA2006*, Cadiz, Spain, November, 2006, pp. 139–149.

Review questions

16.1 Three implementation metrics characteristics are listed in Frame 16.2.

- Explain in your own words the implementation metrics characteristics and their importance.

16.2 Five metrics characteristics are listed in Frame 16.2.

- Explain in your own words the metrics characteristics and their importance.

16.3 Table 16.3 presents a gradual improvement of function point productivity during 1955–2015.

a. Using the data in Table 16.3, what is the expected CLOC productivity change during these years?

b. Explain your result in (a)?

16.4 Table 16.4 presents two metrics for accuracy.

a. Explain the difference between these metrics.

b. Justify the separate metric categories.

16.5 An organization has decided to implement the metrics in Table 16.6.

a. What type of data collection are required?

b. How many days of data collection and how many people should be observed for the data collection.

c. Is there a requirement relating to the choice of days and staff to be observed?

16.6 At the end of his first year in office, the new manager of the sales department developed a new customer satisfaction questionnaire based on a 5-point scale to replace the old questionnaire that uses a 10-point scale.

The new manager plans to apply the USatC metrics in Table 16.12 to measure the changes in customer satisfaction during his year in office.

Might the planned application of the USatC produce valuable results? Explain your answer.

16.7 A planned human resource software system is estimated to require 5,000 logical statements of MYSQL code.

a. Estimate the number of function points required for the software system.

b. Estimate the number of months required for a team of three members to complete the software system.

16.8 Analysis of the requirement specifications for a tender for development of The Buyers Club CRM System has been publicized in a professional journal.

ABC Software Labs is considering participating in the tender. The team appointed to prepare the tender analyzed its requirement specifications and obtained the following results:

- Number of user inputs – 28

- Number of user outputs – 36
- Number of user online queries – 24
- Number of logical files – 8
- Number of external interfaces — 12

The team estimated that 50% of the components were simple, 25% average, and 25% complex.

The team also evaluated the project's complexity at an estimated RCAF = 57.

a. Compute the function points' estimate for the project.

b. Mr. Barnes, the chief programmer, estimated that 3,500 logical statements of C# code would be required for the project. Based on the result in (a), do you agree with his estimate?

Topics for discussion

16.1 Two versions for the measure of software system size – KLOC – are applied: one version counts every code line, while the other only counts the noncomment lines of code.

a. Discuss the advantages and disadvantages of each version. Refer to the validity of both versions.

b. Try to suggest an improved version that will comply with the arguments you mentioned in your answer to (a).

16.2 Money-Money, a software package for financial management of medium-to-small businesses developed by Penny–Penny Ltd., captured a substantial share of the market. The Money-Money help desk (HD) has gained a reputation for its high level of professional service to customers that use the software package. During the third and fourth quarters of 2016, the company invested substantial efforts in preparing an improved user manual. Distribution of the manual to customers was completed during December 2016.

The following table presents HD data summarizing the firm's HD activities for the first quarter of 2016 and 2017.

Data	Code	1st quarter 2016	1st quarter 2017
Number of customers	A	305	485
Total number of calls received during the quarter	B	2,114	2,231
Number of calls the HD failed to resolve	C	318	98
Satisfaction questionnaire – number of responses 1	D	5	10
– number of responses 2	E	10	15
– number of responses 3	F	20	40
– number of responses 4	G	40	30
– number of responses 5	H	25	5

a. Two software product metrics are presented in the table below. Can you develop a formula for calculating the second metrics, using the letters in the code column of the upper table?

No.	Metric code	Metric name	Calculation formula
1	TSCR	Tasks successfully completed ratio (Table 16.10)	$TSCR = \dfrac{NTSC}{TNTAt}$
2	USatL	User satisfaction level (Table 16.12)	$USatL = \dfrac{SURSQ}{TNRSQ}$

b. Compute the value of the quality metrics according to the data presented in the above for each quarter.

c. Can the investments made to improve the user manual be justified? List your arguments.

16.3 Mean response time metrics (see Table 16.7) are usually used to test the software product compliance with a contract requirement related to response time.

a. Prepare an implementation plan for implementing the metrics.

b. Justify times and location requirements regarding performance of the required data collection.

16.4 Two user support management software packages, Alpha and Beta, were examined. The accuracy metrics of Table 16.4 were chosen to be the basis for the decision about the software package to be adopted. A one month trial of both software packages yielded the following measures:

	Alpha	Beta
NACUs	1560	1870
TNCUs	1830	2070
NIAC	270	200
OT	320	180

a. Calculate the values of the two accuracy metrics for Alpha and Beta.

b. Based on the results of (a), what is your recommendation? List your arguments for the preferred software package.

16.5 Two human resource management software packages, HRM1 and HRM2, were being tested by two different departments in an organization. It was decided to base the choice between the two on usability characteristics (the first three metrics of Table 16.6).

The one-month trial of both software packages yielded the following measurements:

	HRM1	HRM2
MTLUF	32	28
MTCC	1.2	1.5
MTSC	0.5	0.5
NCERUs	34	26
TNEC	46	31

a. Calculate the values of the three usability metrics for HRM1 and HRM2.

b. Based on the results of (a), what is your recommendation? List the arguments for your preferred software package.

16.6 DSCp is a diagnostics support capability metric presented in Table 16.8.

a. Prepare an implementation plan for this metric according to the steps presented in Section 16.3.

b. Do you expect to encounter any difficulties in the data collection of this metric? If yes – how would you suggest dealing with these difficulties and collecting reliable data?

Appendix 16.A: FSM method implementation

16.A.1: The function point method

As an example of an FSM method, we present here the IFPUG version of the function point model. Estimation of project size is conducted in three stages as follows:

Stage 1: Calculation of crude function points
> The number of software system functional components is first identified followed by an evaluation of each component as "simple," "average," or "complex." At this point we are able to apply weighting factors according to the system components and complexity class. The sum of the weighted values for all the components of the software system is the CFP.
>
> The method relates to the following five types of software system components:
>
> **1.** User inputs – distinct input applications, not including inputs for online queries.
> **2.** User outputs – distinct output applications such as batch processed reports, lists, customer invoices, and error messages (not including online queries).
> **3.** User online queries – distinct online applications, where output may be in the form of a printout or screen display.
> **4.** Logical files – files that deal with a distinct type of data and that may be grouped in a database.
> **5.** External interfaces – computer-readable outputs or inputs transmitted through data communication on CD, diskette, and so on.
>
> The information needed at this stage is as follows:
>
> **1.** The number of user inputs, sorted into "simple," "average," and "complex" inputs.
> **2.** The number of user outputs, sorted into "simple," "average," and "complex" outputs.
> **3.** The number of user online queries, sorted into "simple," "average," and "complex" queries.
> **4.** Number of logical files – sorted into "simple," "average," and "complex" files.
> **5.** The number of external interfaces – sorted into "simple," "average," and "complex" interfaces.
>
> The function point method applies weight factors to each component according to its complexity; that is, for user outputs the factors are as follows: for simple outputs -4, for average outputs -5, and for complex outputs -6. The factors vary for the software system components and the complexity class. The factors have been determined according to extensive field studies. A specialized form for implementation of stage 1 is shown in Table 16.A.1.
> Stage 1 can assist in computation of the CFP.

Table 16.A.1 Stage 1: Crude function points (CFP) calculation form

Software system component									Total CFP
	Simple			Average			Complex		
	Count	Factor	Points	Count	Factor	Points	Count	Factor	Points	
	A	B	$C = A \times B$	D	E	$F = D \times E$	G	H	$I = G \times H$	$J = C + F + I$
User inputs	—	3	—	—	4	—	—	6	—	
User outputs	—	4	—	—	5	—	—	7	—	
User online queries	—	3	—	—	4	—	—	6	—	
Logical files	—	7	—	—	10	—	—	15	—	
External interfaces	—	5	—	—	7	—	—	10	—	
Total CFP										

Stage 2: Calculating the relative complexity adjustment factor (RCAF)

The Relative Complexity Adjustment Factor (RCAF) summarizes the complexity characteristics of the software system as a whole. The implementer of the function point method is asked to assign grades (0–5) to each of the 14 subjects that substantially affect the required development efforts. Accordingly, the RCAF results range from 0 to maximum 70. The specialized form for stage 2 calculation of RCAF presents these 14 subjects and supports the calculation shown further. The list of subjects is presented in the RCAF calculation form; see Table 16.A.2.

Stage 3: Calculate the number of function points (FP)

The function point value for a given software system is computed according to the results of stages 1 and 2, by applying the following formula:

$$FP = CFP \times [0.65 + 0.01 \times RCAF)$$

16.A.2: An example – The Attend-Master software system

Attend-Master is a basic employee attendance system that is planned to serve small-to-medium-sized businesses employing 10–100 employees. The system is planned to have interfaces to the company's other software packages: Human-Master, which serves human resource units and Wage-Master, which serves the wages units. Attend-Master is planned to produce several reports and online queries. The scheme of the planned software system is found in the data flow diagram (DFD) shown in Figure 16.A.1.

Table 16.A.2   Stage 2: Relative complexity adjustment factor (RCAF) – calculation form

No.	Subject	The grade
1	Requirement for reliable backup and recovery	0 1 2 3 4 5
2	Requirement for data communication	0 1 2 3 4 5
3	Extent of distributed processing	0 1 2 3 4 5
4	Performance requirements	0 1 2 3 4 5
5	Expected operational environment	0 1 2 3 4 5
6	Extent of online data entries	0 1 2 3 4 5
7	Extent of multiscreen or multioperation online data input	0 1 2 3 4 5
8	Extent of online updating of master files	0 1 2 3 4 5
9	Extent of complex inputs, outputs, online queries and files	0 1 2 3 4 5
10	Extent of complex data processing	0 1 2 3 4 5
11	Extent that currently developed code can be designed for reuse	0 1 2 3 4 5
12	Extent of conversion and installation included in the design	0 1 2 3 4 5
13	Extent of multiple installations in an organization and variety of customer organizations	0 1 2 3 4 5
14	Extent of change and focus on ease of use	0 1 2 3 4 5
	Total = RCAF	

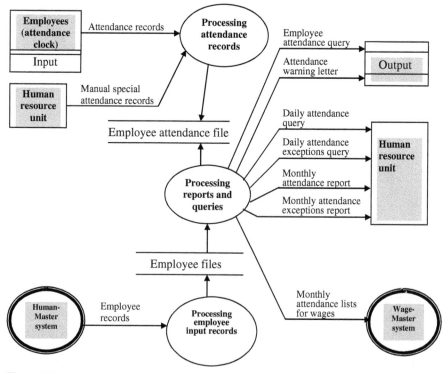

Figure 16.A.1   The Attend-Master Data flow diagram

Table 16.A.3 Attend-Master crude function points (CFP) – calculation form

Software system component	Simple Count A	Simple Factor B	Simple Points C = A × B	Average Count D	Average Factor E	Average Points F = D × E	Complex Count G	Complex Factor H	Complex Points I = G × H	Total CFP J = C + F + I
User inputs	1	3	3	—	4	—	1	6	6	9
User outputs	—	4	—	2	5	10	1	7	7	17
User online queries	1	3	3	1	4	4	1	6	6	13
Logical files	1	7	7	—	10	—	1	15	15	22
External interfaces	—	5	—	—	7	—	2	10	20	20
Total CFP										81

Let us now compute the function point value for the proposed Attend-Master software system.

Stage 1: Calculation of crude function points

Analysis of the software system as presented in the DFD summarizes the number of the various components:

- Number of user inputs – 2
- Number of user outputs – 3
- Number of user online queries – 3
- Number of logical files – 2
- Number of external interfaces – 2

The degree of complexity (simple, average, or complex) was evaluated for each component (see Table 16.A.3), after which CFP calculations were performed.

Stage 2: Calculating the relative complexity factor

The evaluation of the complexity characteristics of Attend-Master and calculation of the Relative Complexity Adjustment Factor (RCAF) are presented in Table 16.A.4.

Stage 3: Calculate the number of function points (FP)

After stages 1 and 2 were completed, the calculation was performed as follows:

$$FP = CFP \times [0.65 + 0.01 \times RCAF) = 81 \times (0.65 + 0.01 \times 41) = 85.86$$

Table 16.A.4   Attend-Master RCAF – calculation form

No.	The affecting subjects	The grade
1	Requirement for reliable backup and recovery	0 1 2 3 4 ⑤
2	Requirement for data communication	⓪ 1 2 3 4 5
3	Extent of distributed processing	⓪ 1 2 3 4 5
4	Performance requirements	0 1 2 3 4 ⑤
5	Expected operational environment	⓪ 1 2 3 4 5
6	Extent of online data entries	0 1 2 3 ④ 5
7	Extent of multi-screen or multi-operation online data input	0 1 ② 3 4 5
8	Extent of online updating of master files	0 1 ② 3 4 5
9	Extent of complex inputs, outputs, online queries, and files	0 1 2 3 ④ 5
10	Extent of complex data processing	0 1 2 3 ④ 5
11	Extent that the currently developed code be designed for reuse	0 1 2 ③ 4 5
12	Extent of conversion and installation included in the design	0 1 ② 3 4 5
13	Extent of multiple installations in an organization and variety of customer organizations	0 1 2 3 4 ⑤
14	Extent of change and the focus on ease of use	0 1 2 3 4 ⑤
	Total = RCAF	41

Chapter 17

Procedures and Work Instructions

17.1 Introduction – the need for procedures and work instructions

- "Why should we use SQA procedures and work instructions?"
- "Wouldn't it be better if every professional relied on his own experience and performed the task the best way he knows?"
- "What are the organizational benefits of forcing me to perform a task exclusively in the way specified by the company?"

Questions like these are frequently voiced by staff in most organizations. The answers uncover the challenge to be met by procedures and work instructions: Application of the organization's accumulated know-how, experience, and expertise.

SQA procedures and work instructions aim at:

- Performance of tasks, processes, or activities in the most effective and efficient way without deviating from quality requirements.
- Effective and efficient communication between the different teams involved in the development and maintenance of software systems. Uniformity in performance, achieved by conformity with procedures and work instructions, reduces misunderstandings that lead to software errors.
- Simplified coordination between tasks and activities performed by the various bodies of the organization. Better coordination translates into fewer errors.

This chapter will discuss the following topics:

- Procedures and work instructions and their conceptual hierarchy (Section 17.3)
- Procedures and procedure manuals (Section 17.4)
- Work instructions (Section 17.5)

Software Quality: Concepts and Practice, First Edition. Daniel Galin.
© 2018 the IEEE Computer Society, Inc. Published 2018 by John Wiley & Sons, Inc.

• Procedures and work instructions: preparation, implementation and updating (Section 17.6)

Section 17.2 is a mini case that illustrates the importance of procedures and their possible contribution.

17.2 Superbox pays $9000 in damages due to failing support center – a mini case

A damage of $9,000 was paid by Lion Software to Superbox, a chain of 80 supermarkets, for failure to repair a software problem. The failure totally paralyzed Superbox's sales and inventory systems for 96 hours, many beyond the 36 hours contracted-maximal time allowed for the complete repair of software failures. The damages paid were actually just a fraction of the losses caused by the total shut down of the sales during these 4 days. Superbox announced that damages paid, although calculated according to the maintenance contract damages clause, are not satisfactory, and that its lawyer is preparing a legal claim on the basis of Lion Software's negligence to provide an appropriate software correction service.

The story behind this event is as follows. A major software failure, completely halting the software processing of sales and inventory systems, was reported at the Lion Users support center on Saturday about midday. Jack Fox, on duty at the time, tried for about 3 hours to perform remote correction of the failure, but with no success. Hence, he scheduled Ben Tracy, a new member of the maintenance team, to arrive at Superbox headquarters on Monday morning and handle the software problem. After a one and a half hour drive from Lion Software headquarters, Ben arrived at Superbox headquarters shortly before midday. He spent the afternoon hours examining the documentation available on site, and performed a number of unsuccessful attempts to locate the faulty software module. He left Superbox office in the afternoon, promising to return early the next morning, which he did. Ben spent the next day trying out various routes to correct the failure, but again with no success. By Tuesday afternoon, the Superbox operations manager approached the head of the Lion Software maintenance department for help. He received calming words of encouragement, and promises that system recovery is just around the corner. Shortly after this, the head of the Lion Software maintenance department called Ben and asked for explanations. Ben, in his defense, claimed that he is just an hour or two away from fixing the problem. However, by the end of Tuesday, no solution had been achieved. On Wednesday, Ben arrived at Superbox head offices – much earlier than the previous day – and full of new ideas to solve the problem. While Ben continued his efforts, Superbox's general manager tried desperately to locate the general manager of Lion Software, who was "out of office." When they finally managed to talk, a heated discussion took place, with Superbox's general manager demanding the immediate replacement of Ben Fox with a senior software maintenance team to enable solving the already very costly problem with no delay. In response, a team of three very experience technicians were sent to

Superbox offices early Wednesday afternoon. The software problem was finally solved in the late evening hours. Thursday morning was spent recovering the software system, and finally by Thursday midday, everybody sighed with relief as the software system was again fully functioning.

A week later, all relevant management and staff members were called for a discussion on management's conclusions of the Superbox event. The general manager opened the meeting, "As things are, it is clear that the damages paid to Superbox are just a small part of the expected damage to our company. The severe damage to our reputation is going to be costly." He then started to discuss his conclusions. "I found that after five years of operation, our company has no procedures relating to the handling of service calls at our user support center, and no follow-up and reporting procedures for technicians working at customer sites. The guidelines according to which the user support center will operate from now on will be as follows:

- The technician receiving the service call must first try to resolve the problem remotely.
- An inexperienced technician may join the repair work at a customer site – only as an integral part of his training.
- When no remote solution may be found, only an experienced technician is to be sent to the site, and only after thorough efforts to remotely handle the failure have been invested.
- In cases of priority customers, such as Superbox, a team of two experienced technicians will be sent to resolve the software problem at the customer's site.
- In cases of priority customers, correction work will continue thru Sunday, given the customer provides necessary arrangements for the correction team.

The procedure for a technician visiting a customer site:

- Before leaving for the customer site, the technician will be notified of the senior technician, with whom he must consult regarding his difficulties to resolve the software problem
- The technician will report to the user support center once every three hours about the progress in his failure repair work.

Follow-up activities will be as follows:

- The follow-up and control of technicians at customer sites must be ongoing at all times.
- In cases when a solution has not been found within 8 hours following the customer's call, a senior technician will be sent to join the technician on site.
- In cases when a solution has not been found within 24 hours, the head of the maintenance team must be notified about the situation. The head of the maintenance team will, from this moment on, direct efforts required to solve the problem."

The general manager left no time for discussion, and appointed a team of three to prepare a draft within 2 weeks of the required procedures.

17.3 Procedures and work instructions and their conceptual hierarchy

A *procedure* is "a particular way of accomplishing something or of acting" (Webster's New College Dictionary). In other words, procedures, as transmitted in documents, are detailed activities or processes to be performed, according to a given method, for the purpose of accomplishing a task. The procedures adopted by an organization are considered to be binding for the organization employees, meaning that each employee is to perform his or her tasks according to the steps appearing in the relevant procedure document, often bearing the name of the designated task. Procedures also tend to be universal within an organization, meaning that they are applied whenever the task is performed, irrespective of the person performing the task, or the organizational context.

Work instructions are used mainly in cases when a uniform method of performing the task throughout the organization is crucial to its success. As a result, work instructions are specific to a team or department; they supplement procedures by providing explicit details that are suitable solely to the needs of one team, department, or unit.

The software quality assurance procedures and work instructions of special interest to us are those that affect the quality of a software product, software maintenance, or project management.

Professionally developed and maintained SQA procedures conform to an organization's quality policy, and also tend to conform to international or national SQA standards. An important point to bear in mind, when preparing the procedures, is that procedural conformity with an SQA standard supports certification of the organization's SQA system (see Part V). ISO/IEC 90003:2014 standard (ISO/IEC 2014) is one of the main certification standards that guide the preparation of procedures.

Figure 17.1 presents a conceptual hierarchy frequently used to govern development of procedures and work instructions.

17.4 Procedures and procedure manuals

Procedures

Procedures supply all the details needed to carry out a task according to the prescribed method for fulfilling the task's function. These details may be regarded as a response to five issues, known as the *Five Ws,* listed in Frame 17.1.

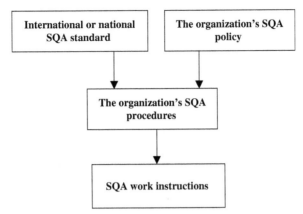

Figure 17.1 A conceptual hierarchy for development of procedures and work instructions.

Frame 17.1: The Five Ws: issues resolved by procedures

- What activities should be performed?
- How should the activity be performed?
- When should the activity be performed?
- Where should the activity be performed?
- Who should perform the activity?

Standardization – the application of a fixed format and structure – is the principle applied to all SQA procedures. A typical example of a fixed table of contents that may be used for all the procedures in an organization is presented in Frame 17.2.

Frame 17.2: The fixed table of contents for procedures

1. Introduction*
2. Purpose
3. Terms and abbreviations*
4. Applicable documents
5. Method
6. Quality records and documentation
7. Reporting and follow up*
8. Responsibility for implementation*
9. List of appendices*

Appendices*

*Sections included only if applicable

Although they are not mandatory features, appendices are commonly used to present reporting forms and documentation related to the activities included in a procedure. Other appendices provide tables and lists that support the selection of the appropriate sequence of activities among the options, if any, defined by the procedure.

ISO (2001) discusses issues of procedure preparation, including a table of contents for the procedures.

Appendix 17.A presents an example of a procedure prepared according to the table of contents shown in Frame 17.2. Special attention should be directed to the section on the method of the procedure prepared in a table format. The main advantage of a table format compared to textual descriptions is the clarity of the presentation of responsibilities and the activity's documentation requirements. Another benefit of the table format is its completeness of definition, where the employee responsible to perform the task and the approving person is defined for each activity, as well as the required documentation and reporting. The annex to this sample procedure presents the form to be used when preparing a design review report.

Implementation tip

Constructing/Choosing appendices

Documentation and report forms, especially tables or lists of conditions that determine alternative sequences of activities, and tables that define limits of authority, tend to change frequently in response to external developments or internal modifications of a product or task. Most changes of this kind do not reflect any inherent modification of the procedure. Appendices that provide these details simply provide an effective way to introduce changes without interfering with the procedure itself. It should be emphasized that although there are no changes in the body of the procedure, a new version of the procedure should be issued when appendices are added or updated.

The procedures manual

A collection of a company's SQA procedures is usually referred to as an *SQA procedures manual*. The contents of an organization's procedures manual vary according to:

- The types of software development and maintenance activities carried out by the organization.
- The range of activities belonging to each activity type.
- The range of customers (e.g., internal/customers of custom-made software/COTS software customers) and suppliers (e.g., self-development

and maintenance/subcontractors/suppliers of COTS software and reused software modules).

- The conceptions governing the choice of method applied by the organization to achieve the desired SQA objectives.

The procedures manual reflects the SQA level implemented by the organization. Organizations seeking a higher quality assurance level usually achieve it by adopting a national or international quality assurance standard. An organization that adopts a quality standard has to adapt its procedures to the standard's requirements, where the standard defines "what has to be performed" and the relevant organization's procedure determines "how this requirement is to be fulfilled." In other words, each of the standard requirements has a corresponding, relevant quality assurance standard.

The ISO/IEC 90003 standard is probably one of the most suitable international standards to serve as a model for adoption as a basis for a high-level SQA system and development of the required quality procedures manual. The SQA requirements topics, as expressed by the 2014 version of the standard (ISO/IEC 90003:2014), serve as procedure subjects to be adopted by organizations. The standard's requirement topics are best presented by the standard's table of contents (Chapters 4–7) shown in Table B.1 (Appendix B).

Frame 17.3: SQA work instructions subjects – examples

Departmental work instructions

- Audit process for new software development subcontractors (supplier candidates)
- Priorities for handling corrective maintenance tasks
- Annual evaluation of software development subcontractors
- On the job instructions and follow-up for new team members
- Design documentation templates and their application
- Objective C (or other code languages) programming instructions

Project management work instructions

- Coordination and cooperation with customer
- Weekly progress reporting by team leaders
- Special design report templates and their application in the project
- Follow-up of beta site reporting
- Monthly progress reporting to the customer
- Coordination of installation and customer's team instruction

17.5 Work instructions

As already mentioned, work instructions deal with the application of procedures, adapted to the requirements of a specific project team, customer, or other relevant party. While general methodology is defined in a procedure, the precise details that allow its application to a specific project or unit are often laid out in a work procedure. Work instructions should never contradict their parent procedure, although several instructions may be associated with another procedure. This means that one may add, change, or cancel work instructions without altering the respective procedure.

Examples of work instructions, summarized by their titles, are found in Frame 17.3.

17.6 Procedures and work instructions: preparation, implementation, and updating

An "active" SQA procedures manual conceals numerous and often ongoing activities that guarantee the procedures' continued applicability: preparation of the procedures, their implementation, and regular updating. These ongoing activities performed by SQA team members, together with members of the teams and managers of the organizational units involved, ensure that the procedures are properly adapted to technology-related changes – as well as changes to clientele and competition.

17.6.1 Preparation of new procedures

The initial steps taken to develop a new SQA procedures manual should deal with the conceptual and organizational framework that determines the following:

- The "menu" of the proposed procedures manual.
- The persons responsible for the preparation, updating, and approval of procedures.
- The structure of a procedure.
- The methods in which a current procedure is chosen to be updated.
- The methods in which procedures and their updating are published and communicated to the relevant users.

This framework is usually also formulated as a procedure (frequently called *the procedure of procedures*). The subsequent steps will, naturally, deal with specific procedures.

Procedure manual preparation by a consultant. An outside expert may be assigned the responsibility of preparing one or more procedures, or even the complete manual. The main advantages of employing a consultant are the added value of his or her expertise and experience in other organizations, a reduced burden on the organization's senior professionals, as well as a shortened task completion timetable. The main disadvantage experienced with consultants is a reduced applicability due to the consultant's insufficient acquaintance with the organization's unique characteristics.

The process of preparing procedures is:

a. **Appointment of an *ad hoc* committee**: The *ad hoc* committee is comprised of professionals working in the units involved, SQA unit members, and experts in the respective topics to be dealt with.

b. **Assessment of the existing process**. The assessment will be based on an observation of the process, documents review, study of quality problems, and client complaints. The findings will be summarized in a report.

c. **Preparation of a procedure draft**. The committee will prepare the proposed draft.

d. **Review of the proposed draft**. The draft should be reviewed by the leaders of the teams responsible to implement the procedure, the managers of the unit/department, and other persons involved in the procedure.

Implementation tip

The importance of the procedure review. In many cases, due to time pressure and other reasons, developers of procedures tend to omit the draft review phase, or to conduct it in a hasty manner, leaving almost no time for reviewer comments. This almost always results in: (a) lower quality of the proposed procedure, specifically displaying a lack in adaptations required for the relevant unit. (b) More substantial difficulties in implementing the procedures, as persons who participated in the process of preparing the procedure, by raising comments, tend to cooperate in the implementation of the procedure, while persons that have not been given the chance to participate tend to oppose it.

---

e. **Preparation of the final draft for approval**. A satisfactory final draft will be prepared by the committee, based on the comments and suggestions.

f. **Approval of the proposed procedure by the authorized person(s)**. It should be noted that the approval is not automatic, and in a number of cases, the senior employee, serving as the authorizing person, initiates further changes according to his/her comments.

17.6.2 Implementation of new or revised procedures

Approval of a new or revised procedure says little about the ease of that procedure's implementation, which is a separate and often difficult issue. A successful implementation of procedures usually requires performing all the following activities:

a. **Distribution of the procedure material** in a printed form, intranet site, and so on to ensure availability to team members and all persons involved in software development and maintenance. While substantial resources are invested in the communication and publicizing of the procedures, these are not enough to ensure full or even nearly full conformity.

b. **Supporting/coaching the users** in implementation by providing explanations and solving user difficulties in performing the required processes. Support should continue for as long as is required for users to fully implement the new procedure.

c. **Follow-up of implementation** in order to identify users, who do not perform correctly the new procedure, and instruct them as needed.

17.6.3 Updating procedures

The motivation to update existing procedures is based, among other reasons, on the following:

External changes

• Technological changes in development tools, hardware, communication equipment, and so on
• Changes in legal requirements
• Changes in the organization's areas of activity

Proposals for process improvements

• User proposals for improvement
• Analysis of failures as well as successes
• Proposals for improvements initiated by internal audit reports
• Learning from the experience of other organizations
• Experiences of the SQA team

Procedural reasons

• Termination of a version lifetime, after which an update review is mandatory as defined by the procedure itself.

Implementation tip
A procedure (as well as a work instruction) that has not been updated for a considerable period (e.g., three years) will, in most cases, be inadequate, and in the worst cases, obsolete; that is, no longer needed or, simply disregarded. Both situations justify a review of the procedure and its implementation environment. A periodic review of "neglected" (i.e., unused) procedures can generally remedy this situation by initiating updating or removal of the procedures from the manual.

Once the need to update a procedure has been recognized, a process, similar to that applied when preparing new procedures, can be put into operation: An *ad hoc* team is convened to prepare an updated version. The assessment of the existing process, preparation of an updated procedure draft, review of the proposed updated procedure draft, and preparation of the final updated draft, is followed by authorization and implementation activities. This implies that updating should be viewed as an integral stage to software quality assurance, and as important as preparing new procedures.

Summary

1. **The contribution of procedures to software quality assurance**
    SQA procedures, when developed and maintained properly, are assumed to reflect the most adequate method known to date for the performance of design and maintenance activities. SQA procedures that are up-to-date and fully implemented by developers and maintenance teams ensure conformity of their activities to the software's quality requirements and performance of the associated activities in an efficient and effective way. At the same time, uniform development and maintenance enables easier and more effective professional reviews together with better communication with maintenance teams. It likewise facilitates cooperation and coordination between all bodies, internal and external, involved in the project. No less important is the reduction in errors made possible by uniformity.

2. **The difference between procedures and work instructions**
    Procedures define the activities performed in order to achieve given tasks, where performance is universal to the entire organization. Work instructions are complementary tools, used to define local variations in the application of procedures by specific teams and/or departments. Work instructions, however, detailed and targeted, cannot contradict the organization's procedures.

3. The activities involved in maintaining an organization's procedures manual

Activities involved include activities for preparing new procedures, updating existing procedures, and implementing new and updated procedures and are as follows:

- Initiation of a new procedure or updating of an existing procedure
- Appointment of an *ad hoc* committee
- Assessment of the existing process
- Preparation of a procedure draft
- Review of the proposed draft
- Preparation of the final draft for approval
- Approval of the proposed procedure by the authorized person(s)

These efforts involve the organization's SQA team members, in addition to members of *ad hoc* committees gathered to prepare a new or update an existing procedure. Additional contributors to new and updated procedures are team members, managers and others, who review the proposed procedures through their comments and suggestions.

Participants in the implementation process include unit leaders and SQA trustees.

Selected bibliography

ISO   (2014) *ISO/IEC 90003:2014 Software Engineering – Guidelines for the Application of TSO 9001: 2008 to Computer Software*, International Organization for Standardization (ISO), Geneva, Switzerland.

ISO   (2001) *ISO/TR 10013:2001 Guidelines for Quality Management System Documentation*, International Organization for Standardization (ISO), Geneva, Switzerland.

Review questions

17.1 Figure 17.1 presents a conceptual hierarchy for the development of SQA procedures and work instructions.

 a. Describe each of the components in the diagram in your own words.

 b. Explain the meaning of each of the hierarchical relationships defined in the diagram in your own words.

17.2 List the benefits of implementing an SQA procedures manual in an organization.

17.3 The table of contents suggested in Frame 17.2 includes an optional section, "Terms and Abbreviations."

 a. Do you recommend including terms like software program, printed output, configuration management, or ATM in this section? List your arguments.

 b. What criteria should be applied when including a term or abbreviation? List your reasoning.

17.4 Some software quality experts claim that a standard procedures manual with no changes or adaptations can serve 90% of the organization.

- Do you agree with this statement? List your arguments.

Topics for discussion

17.1 "The Software Lions" recently completed compilation of their SQA procedures manual. The following are the "purpose" and "method" sections taken from the "Certification of professional employees" procedure.

---

2. Purpose

2.1. To determine the professional positions that require certification and the respective updating of processes.

2.2. To define the process by which a candidate is certified.

5. Method

5.1. Candidates for a position that requires certification, whether new or long-term employees, must successfully pass the relevant certification examination before starting the role.

5.2. The content and format of the certification examinations will be prepared by the Quality Assurance Unit after consultation with the Chief Software Engineer. The certification examinations will be approved by the General Manager of the company.

5.3. A list of Examiners will be determined for every position that requires certification.

5.4. A candidate for a position that requires certification will be directed to one of the listed Examiners.

5.5. The Examiner will report the results of the certification examinations to the Quality Assurance Unit. The candidate will be able to appeal the results. In special circumstances, the candidate can be reexamined.

5.6. The department that is interested in a candidate's appointment will be informed about the certification examination results.

5.7. The Quality Assurance Unit will update the content and format of the certification examinations in response to organizational changes and information technology developments.

5.8. Management will receive a summary report of the certification examinations and their results.

---

a. Read the sections of the proposed procedure carefully and list your comments while referring to any defects and shortcomings (usually incomplete sections).

b. For each item listed in (a), suggest an appropriate change, addition or deletion, in order to correct the detected defects or shortcomings.

17.2 "Wild solutions" is a medium-sized software house, employing about 250 employees. The new SQA manager has decided to prepare several new procedures to replace the company's very old and outdated procedures. You are asked to join him in his efforts and prepare a draft for the procedure entitled "Progress control of software development projects."

The procedure should deal with the following subjects:

1. Preparation of a timetable, manpower resources usage plan, and budget.
2. Progress reporting for those parts of the project carried out by the company.
3. Progress reporting for those parts of the project carried out by subcontractors, partners, and the customer(s).
4. Control process for progress reporting.
5. Updating of the timetable, manpower resources usage plan, and budget.
6. Responses to deviations from the project development plan (risks, timetable, manpower resources, and budget) in parts carried out by the company.
7. Responses to deviations from the project development plan (risks, timetable, manpower resources, and budget) in parts carried out by subcontractors.
8. Responses to deviations from the project development plan (risks, timetable, manpower resources, and budget) in parts carried out by partners or customers.

a. Sketch what you imagine to be the company's organizational chart. The chart may be used for your procedure draft.
b. Prepare a draft of the "Progress control of software development projects" procedure. The procedure should cover all eight subjects listed above. Add appendices if required.
c. List your assumptions regarding the procedure.

17.3 As an SQA unit member, you are required to prepare the first draft of a new procedure.

a. Suggest sources of information that may be used to prepare the draft.
b. Mark the sources mentioned in your answer to (a) that are essential for a good draft.

17.4 It is recommended that the new and updated procedures be prepared by an *ad hoc* committee rather than by an expert member of the SQA unit or a consultant.

a. List the expected advantages of the "*ad hoc* committee" option in preparing new and updated procedures. Does reliance on a company "expert" option have any advantages?
b. List the expected advantages of the "*ad hoc* committee" option to be realized in the implementation stage.

Appendix 17.A: Design review procedure

Bla-Bla Software Industries Ltd.	SQA procedures
SQA Procedure 8-09: Design reviews	**Revision 6 (May 8, 2016)**

1. Introduction

Design reviews are carried out throughout software development projects according to the project's quality plan, as defined in Procedure 8-02.

2. Purpose

To define the method for carrying out design reviews in software development projects.

3. Scope

The procedure will apply to all software development projects, excluding minor projects carried out according to Procedure 8-17.

4. Applicable documents

Procedure 8-02: Project quality plan for software development projects.
Procedure 8-17: Minor software development projects.

5. Method

No.	Step	Activity	Responsibility: performer/approval	Documentation	Notes
5.1	Preparation of design documents	Preparation of a complete draft of the design documents	Perf: Project leader. Approval: Not required.	Drafts of design documents	
5.2	Coordination of DR meeting	(1) Define the list of participants.	Perf: Project leader. Approval: Development dept. manager	List of participants.	(1) See project quality plan for preliminary list of participants.
		(2) Coordination of DR meeting	Perf: DR team leader. Approval: Not required.	DR invitation letters to DR team members	(2) See contract for customer participation.
		(3) Distribution of documents to DR team members.	Perf: DR team leader. Approval: Not required		(3) Distribution of documents in printed or electronic format at least 48 hours before DR meeting.
5.3	DR meeting	Agenda: – Presentation (concise) – DR team comments and discussion – Definition of action items (AI)	Perf: DR team members. Approval: Not required.	DR minutes	See DR report template in procedure Annex.

Bla-Bla Software Industries Ltd.	SQA procedures
SQA Procedure 8-09: Design reviews	**Revision 8 (May 8, 2016)**

5. Method (*Continued*)

No.	Step	Activity	Responsibility: performer/approval	Documentation	Notes
		– Designation of AI schedule and person responsible for execution. – Designation of DR member responsible for corrections follow-up – DR team decision about continuation of development work.			
5.4	DR report	(1) Preparation of DR report.	Perf: DR team leader. Approval: DR team members.	DR report	The report should be completed and signed within 48 hours of the meeting.
		(2) Distribution of the report to the participants, as well as the chief software engineer, development dept. manager, head of quality assurance unit.	Perf: DR team leader. Approval: Not required		
5.5	Implementation of DR decisions	(1) Implementation of required corrections included in AIs list.	Perf: Project team. Approval: Project leader.	Corrected design documents	
		(2) Examination of corrections and approval by DR team member.	Perf: DR team member. Approval: Not required	(1) Approval of each correction. (2) Approval of completion of all corrections	

Prepared by: Dave Towers	QA engineer	Date: April 3, 2016	Signed: *Dave Towers*
Approved by: Barry Hotter	Head, QA unit	Date: May 2, 2016	Signed: *Barry Hotter*

Bla-Bla Software Industries Ltd.	SQA procedures
SQA Procedure 8-09: Design reviews	**Revision 8 (May 8, 2016)**

Annex: DR report form

DR report

Date of the DR: _____ Project title: _____

Participants: _____

_____

DR type: _____

Documents reviewed

Document title	Version and Revision

Action items (AIs)

No.	Description of AI	Responsibility	Scheduled Completion	Approval of Completion	
				Completion Date	Signed

Decisions: ( ) Approved

( ) Approval conditional upon completion of all AIs.

( ) Corrected document should be submitted for repeated review.

The repeated DR will be on _____.

( ) Other: _____

_____

DR team member responsible for follow up: _____

Signed: _____ _____ _____ _____ _____

Name : _____ _____ _____ _____ _____

Date : _____ _____ _____ _____ _____

DR leader   Member   Member   Member   Member

Part IV

Process Assurance Activities for Conformance

This part of the book is dedicated to the process quality assurance activities of the SQA function, and includes six chapters:

- Chapter 18 deals with SQA activities aimed at evaluating the conformance of software processes and related documentation for contract requirements and relevant regulations and conventions.

The following five chapters describe services related to process assurance activities:

- Chapter 19 is dedicated to process improvements and the services of corrective and preventive actions.
- Chapter 20 is dedicated to activities applied for assuring the quality of software processes to be performed by subcontractors and other external participants.
- Chapter 21 is dedicated to process quality measurement techniques.
- Chapter 22 is dedicated to the software change control process.
- Chapter 23 is dedicated to issues relating to the assessment of staff skills and knowledge, and conducting training and certification of staff members.

Software Quality: Concepts and Practice, First Edition. Daniel Galin.
© 2018 the IEEE Computer Society, Inc. Published 2018 by John Wiley & Sons, Inc.

Chapter 18

Evaluation of Processes and Development Environment for Conformance

18.1 Introduction

One may assure software product quality by evaluating the conformance of the software product to requirements and correcting the identified nonconformities. An alternative way to ensure software product quality is by evaluating the implementation of appropriate processes throughout the software life cycle, and in this way, totally or almost totally, preventing the creation of nonconformities. Perhaps, the combined implementation is the preferred way to assure the process and also the product.

This chapter is dedicated to activities performed to evaluate process assurance and development environment for conformance to requirements, standards, regulations, and conventions.

The process requirement definition is presented in Frame 18.1.

Frame 18.1: Process requirement definition

Source: IEEE Std. 730–2014 (IEEE, 2014)

Process requirement definition
"Process requirements specify the processes the project will use to produce the project outcomes. Process requirements may include specific processes mandated to be in place, specific tasks the project or organization is mandated to perform, and the manner in which specific tasks are to be performed. Process requirements are derived from, and are a response to, stakeholder requirements."

Software Quality: Concepts and Practice, First Edition. Daniel Galin.
© 2018 the IEEE Computer Society, Inc. Published 2018 by John Wiley & Sons, Inc.

The scope of process assurance activities include all phases of the software life cycle.

The software life cycle includes the following phases (according to ISO/IEC/IEEE Std. 12207-2008):

- Software requirement analysis
- Software architectural design
- Software detailed design
- Software implementation/construction
- Software integration
- Software qualification testing
- Software installation
- Software acceptance support service (during running in of the software system)
- Software operation
- Software maintenance
- Software disposal

The SQA function performs process evaluations using project reports, and by participating in SQA processes performed by the project teams.

The next sections present the following topics of evaluation:

- The evaluation of life cycle processes and plans for conformance.
- The evaluation of the required environment for conformance.
- The evaluation of processes for conformance of subcontractors and other external participants.
- The evaluation of software process by measurements.
- The assessment of staff skills and knowledge.

This chapter is based on IEEE Std. 730–2014.

18.2 The evaluation of life cycle processes and plans for conformance

The objective

The objective of the SQA function is to evaluate the planned project processes and processes being performed for their conformance with the project requirements, regulations, and conventions. The evaluation should yield a list of nonconformities to be corrected by the project team.

The evaluation process

The evaluation process to be performed by the SQA function includes the following activities:

1. Identify the life cycle processes required by the contract requirements, regulations, and conventions.

    Examples of possible processes requirements:
    - C# programming language
    - RUP unified modeling language (UML)
    - Database-driven website PHP and MySQL
    - Agile methodology
    - Cloud application and data storage

2. Review planned life cycle processes for their conformance to the relevant established process requirements.

3. Audit processes being performed for their conformance to the relevant established process requirements. The audit should yield lists of nonconformities:
    - Planned life cycle processes that do not conform to contract requirements.
    - Processes performed that do not conform to contract requirements.
    - Planned and performed life cycle processes that do not conform to regulations and conventions.

18.3 The evaluation of the required environment for conformance

The objective

The objective of the SQA function is to evaluate the degree of conformance of the software engineering development tools and testing environment required by the contract, regulations, and conventions. An outcome of the evaluation should be a list of nonconformities.

The software engineering environment provides assistance to the programmer through a work station equipped with compilers, program database systems, an interactive debugger, and other development tools.

The test environment enables performing efficient testing by local computing when adequate capacity exists or with cloud computing technology. The testing environment may support test management, test failure analysis, automatic test execution, and more.

The evaluation process

The evaluation of software development and test environments include the following activities:

1. Evaluate the software development environment planned to be used, and that which is actually used, by the project team for conformance to contract requirements and conventions.

2. Evaluate the software and application libraries and software development tools used by the project team for conformance to contract requirements and planned libraries.

3. Evaluate the test environment for conformance to contract requirements and planned environment.

All evaluation activities are followed by lists of nonconformities to be corrected.

18.4   The evaluation of subcontractor processes for conformance

Subcontracting organizations have become a major participant in software projects, especially in large-scale projects. The participation of subcontractors raises severe quality assurance problems, these specific software quality assurance issues are discussed in this section.

The objective

The objective of the SQA function is to evaluate the degree of conformance of software processes performed by subcontractors to the processes required by the acquirer and stated in the project contract.

The evaluation process

The evaluation process to be performed by the SQA function includes the following:

1. Identifying the project parts to be performed by subcontractors and the contracted project processes included in these parts.

2. Verifying that processes of the subcontractor project plans conform to the list identified earlier.

3. Evaluating the processes of the subcontractor software development for conformance to the list of software processes allocated to be performed to enable correction of nonconformities.

For more about assuring the quality of software processes performed by subcontractors and other external software project participants – see Chapter 20.

18.5 The evaluation of software process by measurements

Quantitative criteria of software processes provided by software process metrics are a very important tool for the evaluation of software processes. The application of software process metrics is a requirement in software engineering, software quality assurance standards, and in an organization's procedures.

Objective

Develop and implement software process metrics for evaluating software process quality to measure the degree with which they fulfill the requirements.

The required processes

Software process measurements to be performed by the SQA function include the following activities:

1. Defining a set of process metrics, where each metric enables to determine whether the process conforms to the requirements, standards, and procedures.
   Examples of process metrics are shown in Table 18.1:

Table 18.1 Examples of process metrics

Metrics code	Metrics name	Calculation formula
PRLV	Percent of revised code lines in a version	$PRLV = \dfrac{NRL \times 100}{KLOC}$
PASCO	Percent of approved software change requests	$PASCO = \dfrac{NSCO \times 100}{NSCR}$
LOHDS	Level of help desk skills and knowledge	$LOHDS = \dfrac{NHDCNH}{TNHDC}$

Where:
- NRL =_The number of revised (code) lines.
- KLOC: The size of the software product, as measured in thousands of code lines.
- NSCO: The number of software change orders.
- NSCR: The number of software change requests.
- NHDCNH: The number of help desk calls for which the HD staff needed assistance from another staff member.
- TNHDC: The total number of help desk (user support center) calls.

2. Implementation of the metrics that result in a list of gaps between the results of measurements and the expected quality result. Development of software or hardware improvements to close the gaps.

3. Reapply the measurements and determine the effectiveness of the improvements.

4. Activities 3 and 4 may be repeated till measurement results are satisfactory.

More about software metrics and specifically about process measurements for the evaluation of software process conformance may be found in Chapter 21.

18.6   The assessment of staff skills and knowledge

The objective

The objective of the SQA function is to evaluate the skills, knowledge, competency, and abilities of the project assigned staff and determine the degree with which they fulfill the project professional requirements and attend training, as required by staff members.

The assessment process

The assessment process should be performed at an early stage, before the assigned staff begins its work. The assessment process to be performed by the SQA function includes the following activities:

1. Defining skills, education, and other professional qualifications required for all project staff.

2. The assigned staff are identified and evaluated in respect to their professional qualifications to perform the project. The assessment yields a list of skill and knowledge gaps and training required per person.

3. Prepare an education and training plan to close any qualification gaps. List assigned staff members that will not be able to complete their training plan in time for the planned project task. These staff members should be replaced.

4. Assessment of new staff members joining the team.

5. Professional training activities are evaluated and documented.

For more about staff training requirements and certification processes – see Chapter 23.

Summary

The types of software process evaluation activities

The types are:

1. Evaluation of life cycle processes and plans for conformance.
2. Evaluation of the required environment for conformance.
3. Evaluation of subcontractor processes for conformance.

1. **The evaluation process of the required environment for conformance**

   The evaluation process to be performed by the SQA function includes the following:

   1. Evaluate the software development environment to be used by the project team for conformance to contract requirements and conventions.
   2. Evaluate the software and application libraries used by the project team for conformance to contract requirements and planned libraries.
   3. Evaluate the test environment for conformance to contract requirements and the planned environment.

2. **The objective of evaluation of subcontractors processes**

   The objective of the SQA function is to evaluate the degree of conformance of software processes performed by subcontractors to the processes required by the acquirer and stated in the project contract.

3. **The process of software process evaluation by measurements**

   Software process measurements to be performed by the SQA function includes the following activities:

   1. Defining a set of process metrics, where each metric enables to determine whether a process conforms to the requirements, standards, or procedures.
   2. Implementation of the metrics that result in a list of gaps between the results of measurements and the expected quality result.
   3. Reapply the measurements after performing improvements and determine the effectiveness of the improvements.
   4. Activities 3 and 4 may be repeated till measurement results are satisfactory.

Selected bibliography

IEEE (2014) *IEEE Std. 730–2014 Software Quality Assurance*, The IEEE Computer Society, IEEE, New York.

Review questions

18.1 Three types of evaluation of software project processes conformance are presented in Frame 18.1.

    a. Explain in your own words the purpose of each type of evaluation.

    b. Explain the differences between the different types of evaluations.

18.2 The evaluation of the conformance of life cycle processes and plans for conformance to the contract yields three lists of nonconformities (see Section 18.2).

    a. List in your own words the contents of each of the lists.

    b. Explain the differences between the lists, and also the importance of each list.

18.3 An SQA function team leader decided not to evaluate the test environment for a software project and save the evaluation efforts.

    a. Can you suggest any undesired situations resulting from this decision?

    b. Explain the damages expected from each of the situations mentioned in your answer to (a).

18.4 The organization operates a user support service for its major software systems.

    a. Suggest three process metrics for the user support services.

    b. Suggest desired levels for the results of the suggested metrics that will conform to the requirements.

18.5 Overloaded with SQA tasks, the team leader decided to postpone the evaluation of staff skills and knowledge planned to be performed about a month after work on the project has started.

    a. What are the expected undesired results of this decision?

    b. Can you suggest situations where the undesired results of this decision are minimal?

Topics for discussion

18.1 Some professionals claim that the evaluation of project products and processes are sufficient and that there is no justification for evaluation of project plans.

    a. Do you agree with this claim?

    b. List your arguments for your reply to (a).

18.2 The evaluation of the required environment for conformance is discussed in Section 18.3.

    a. Some SQA professionals claim that evaluation of software processes and products are sufficient and that there is no need to invest efforts in evaluation of the software engineering and testing environment. Do you agree with these professionals?

    b. Provide your argument for your answer to (a).

18.3 The organization has developed a list of authorized subcontractors, which is regularly updated according to a subcontractor performance report issued by the project leader.

The SQA function head claims that there is no need to evaluate the conformance of authorized subcontractors.

a. Do you agree with the SQA function head?

b. List your arguments for your reply to (a).

c. Suggest situations you would recommend not to evaluate the conformance of an authorized subcontractor.

18.4 A procedure carried out by an SQA function requires performing an evaluation of staff skills and knowledge once before submitting a large-scale proposal, and a second time after signing the project contract – as part of the activities required to prepare the project plan.

a. Do you support the above procedure?

b. List the advantages and disadvantages of the above procedure compared with performing evaluation of staff skills and knowledge before the work on the project begins.

18.5 Describe the cooperation that is required between the SQA function and the project team for performing the evaluation of staff skills and knowledge.

Chapter 19

Improvement Processes – Corrective and Preventive Actions

Continual improvement requirement

"The organization shall continually improve the effectiveness of the quality management system through the use of the quality policy, quality objectives, audit results, analysis of data, corrective and preventing actions and movement review".

ISO/IEC Std. 90003-2014 Sec. 8.5.1

Continual improvement, in other words, ongoing improvement of overall performance, is also a basic principle of software quality assurance. The issues involved in successful implementation of this principle by corrective and preventive actions (CAPA) are discussed in this chapter.

19.1 The "3S" development team – revisited – an introductory mini case

The project for Apollo Ltd. (discussed in Chapter 23) that was completed by Team 7 has now been operative for about 7 months. With its previous experience in mind, the development department's manager decided that the causes of the team's difficulties should be analyzed, and while all conclusions reached should be implemented by Team 7, some should be implemented department wide.

Participants at the meeting organized by the department manager included Team 7's team leader, head of the SQA unit, and head of the human Resources Department. The objective of the meeting was defined by the participants: "To detect systematic causes for the improper performance of Team 7, and to devise

Software Quality: Concepts and Practice, First Edition. Daniel Galin.
© 2018 the IEEE Computer Society, Inc. Published 2018 by John Wiley & Sons, Inc.

measures to prevent their recurrence." Amongst topics raised were the cancellation of the Athena application generator training, and the unsuccessful recruitment of a replacement programmer. In addition to some personal conclusions, the participants recommended that the following actions be taken:

a. The training procedure should be updated to include the following clause "In cases when team members are not able to undergo required training prior to the introduction of new applications, a special consultant or mentor should be appointed to support the team members."

b. The appendix of the job certification procedure should be changed to include programmers in the list of positions requiring certification.

c. The recruitment procedure should be changed to include the following "A mentor should be appointed for a minimum period of three months for new department employees, and for two months for employees in new positions. Modification of the mentoring period be subject to approval by the department manager."

d. All the department's teams will begin to use Focus Version 6.1 within the next 3 months. This action item was based on a comparison of the performance of the Focus Version 6.1 application generator (used by Team 7 for integrations B, C, D, E, and G), to that of Focus Version 5.1 (used for integrations A and F).

Before closing the meeting, one of the participants commented that the subject of their meeting should have been handled long ago by the CAB (Corrective Action Board). The CAB is the committee responsible for reviewing such incidents and for initiating corrective and preventive actions in cases similar to the Apollo Ltd. project. The other participants agreed. The head of the SQA unit then stood up and said "The firm's CAB committee has been inactive for about a year now ever since the resignation and departure from '3S' of its last head. Shortly after his leaving, another two members of the committee resigned. Since then, we have negotiated with several senior staff to replace the vacant positions, but with no success, I hope that the current candidate to head the CAB committee will finally agree and thus "revive" the committee's activities." After a short pause he added "I must inform you that, to the best of my knowledge, the CAB's activities have never been internally audited. The company procedures do not explicitly require this." As a result, the participants added two additional action items to their list of recommendations:

e. "Reactivate" the CAB committee by, first of all, finding a proper candidate to head the CAB, and fulfill the committee's membership, and renew its paralyzed activities.

f. Prepare a new appendix to the internal quality auditing procedure to deal with CAB activities.

The above six recommendations are examples of activities that are not intended to deal with the immediate correction of detected defects, but to eliminate the causes of those defects throughout software development departments. The systematic activities that implement organization-wide improvements of effectiveness and operational efficiency fall under the heading of *corrective and preventive actions* (CAPA).

19.2 Introduction

Promoting continuous improvement of effectiveness and efficiency is one of the important objectives of SQA. The corrective and preventive actions (CAPA) process has become one of the main tools used to achieve this objective. The improvements initiated by the CAB who implements the CAPA process are characterized by improved software quality together with improved productivity. Improved productivity is expected to result from the improved development process and reduced correction time resulting from reduced software faults.

The CAPA process is the subject of this chapter. The last section presents illustrations of its implementation.

The importance of CAPA in any SQA system is emphasized by CMMI Guidelines, and the ISO/IEC 90003:2014 (ISO, 2014) standard, which dedicates its Sec. 8.5 to the subject. The standard requires that the organization aims to continually improve its software quality, and states that one of the main ways to achieve this is by implementing CAPA. Furthermore, the standard provides definitions, and defines the process of correcting and preventing software faults. IEEE Std. 730–2014 (IEEE, 2014) presents in Sec. 4.7 a process of process improvement that includes the activities of data collection, analysis of the data, resolution of identified problems, implementation of corrective and preventive actions, and follow-up of improvement results – with an emphasis on costs reduction. ISO/IEC/IEEE Std. 12207-2008 (ISO/IEC, 2008) focuses in its Sec. 7.2.8 on software problem resolution processes.

Support for CAPA data storage, as well as sorting, information retrieval, and other data processing activities is provided by specialized software packages such as ABCI Consultants (2015) and R. M. Baldwin Inc. (2005).

Corrective and preventive actions – definitions

Frame 19.1 presents the ISO/IEC 90003:2014 standard's most inclusive definitions of corrective and preventive actions with respect to software development and maintenance.

It should be emphasized that the analytic distinction between corrective and preventive actions is somewhat artificial, as can be seen by the analogous elements in their definitions. This means that certain items of information may support both corrective and preventive actions. Furthermore, it should be remembered that the two aspects of CAPA create, in practice, a joint response; and therefore, they will be treated as one in the remainder of this chapter.

Frame 19.1: Corrective and preventive actions – definitions

Source: ISO/IEC Std. 90003:2014

Corrective actions

A regularly applied feedback organizational process that initiates and performs actions to eliminate causes of nonconformities (software faults).

Preventive actions

A regularly applied feedback organizational process that initiates and performs actions to prevent the occurrence of potential nonconformities (software faults).

It is noteworthy that a major part of the changes in the training and certification practices, dealt with in Chapter 23, are initiated by the CAPA process

19.3   The corrective and preventive actions process

Successful operation of a CAPA process includes the following activities, as presented in Frame 19.2.

Frame 19.2: The corrective and preventive actions process

Source: According to IEEE Std. 730 and ISO/IEC Std. 90003-2014

The corrective and preventive actions process

• Information collection
• Analysis of information
• Development of solutions and improved methods
• Implementation of improved methods
• Follow-up of CAPA activities – implementation and outcome

The process is regularly fed by the flow of information from a variety of sources. In order to estimate its success, a closed-feedback loop is applied to control the flow of information, implementation of resulting changes in practices and procedures, and measurement of the outcomes.

A schematic overview of the CAPA process is shown in Figure 19.1. Each of its stages will be discussed in a separate subsection of this chapter.

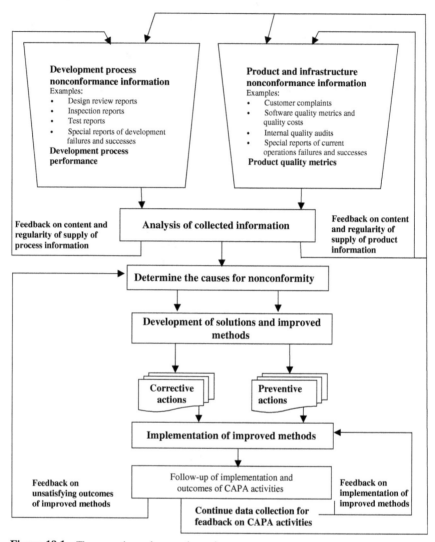

Figure 19.1 The corrective and preventive action process

19.3.1 Information collection

The variety of information sources, internal and external, that serve the CAPA process is quite remarkable. Following this internal/external dichotomy, the four main internal sources of information are the (1) Software development process, (2) Software maintenance, (3) SQA infrastructure, and (4) Software quality management procedures. External sources of information are mainly customer application statistics and customer complaints. The classification of information sources is presented in Frame 19.3.

Frame 19.3: Sources of information for corrective and preventive actions

Sources of information for corrective and preventive actions

Internal information sources

Software development process

- Software risk management reports
- Design review reports
- Inspection reports
- Walkthrough reports
- Expert opinion reports
- Test reviews
- Special reports on development failures and successes
- Proposals suggested by staff members

Software maintenance

- Customer application statistics
- Software change requests initiated by customer applications
- Software change requests initiated by maintenance staff
- Special reports on maintenance failures and successes
- Proposals suggested by staff members

SQA infrastructure type of sources

- Internal quality audit reports
- External quality audit reports
- Performance follow-up of trained and certified staff
- Proposals suggested by staff members

Software quality management procedures type of sources

- Project progress reports
- Software quality metrics reports
- Software quality cost reports
- Proposals suggested by staff members

External information sources

- Customer complaints
- Customer service statistics
- Customer-suggested proposals

An alternative classification of information sources, as shown in Figure 19.1, distinguishes between the development process-related and product infrastructure-related (including managerial and maintenance) sources of information.

Implementation tip

The initiation of inquiries into major project failures is almost instinctive. The conclusions reached by these inquiries affect a project's immediate environment; in many cases they also contribute to improved practices and procedures through the application of CAPA.

Success stories, however, are rarely investigated. Although the staff immediately responsible for the success is usually rewarded, the likelihood of applying a CAPA analysis is low. Such a process can yield meaningful information regarding which aspects of the process led to the project's success, as well as identify activities that could benefit from further improvement.

19.3.2 Analysis of collected information

Regular operation of the CAPA process is expected to create a massive flow of documents related to a wide range of information sources.

Analysis involves:

- Screening the information and identifying repeated cases of nonconformities. Documents received from the various sources of information are reviewed by professionals in order to identify repeated nonconforming cases; with potential opportunities for CAPA. This stage includes a comparison of documents of the same type received from a number of units as well as a comparison of documents of different types related to the same case.

- Analysis of potential improvements
    Efforts are directed to determine:
    - Expected types and levels of damage resulting from the identified nonconformities (fault).
    - Estimates reading the extent of potential organization-wide faults of each type. This information is needed to estimate the total damage expected and to determine the priority of each fault case.

Two opposing requirements affect responses at this stage – comprehensive analysis of masses of information conflicts with the need for a swift reaction to faults. Resolution of this conflict lies in organization and methods. A team of professionals assigned to deal with incoming information should be created forthwith and without delay. This team will set priorities for resolving identified faults, with low-priority cases that have been delayed, or not be handled at all.

Implementation tip

The staff responsible for information analysis is expected to face mounds of documents, making it unfeasible for all the documents to be screened. One approach to reducing this load is to only report those cases that the units believe are amenable to initiation of a CAPA process. This approach can induce a situation of "no fault" reporting through use of the "of no importance" excuse. Another approach is to ask the units to indicate the priority of each case in their reports. This information will induce the CAPA team to deal with the high-priority items first. A third approach is to sample the fault documents. Application of random sampling to each type of information and document can reduce the load to a manageable level and increase the probability of identifying the most important cases. Sampling can also be used in combination with the second approach, where it is applied to low- and medium-priority cases.

A combination of the second and third approach is preferable in most instances.

19.3.3 Determine the causes of nonconformities

The CAPA team identifies the causes for faults. In cases when expertise support is needed, this type of support is usually found in the development and maintenance teams. The following are the typical causes:

- Noncompliance with work instructions and procedures
- Insufficient technical knowledge
- Extreme time and/or budget pressures mainly due to unrealistic estimates
- Lack of experience with new development tools

19.3.4 Development of solutions

Prior to investing efforts to solve the nonconformities, it is required to consider the needs to develop a solution. Items considered include the total damage expected and the issue regarding the temporary, or not, nature of the nonconformity events. At a later stage, the expected costs of the solution may also be considered for "no solution development justified."

Solutions to identified causes of recurrent software systems faults are required to:

- Eliminate recurrence of the types of faults detected
- Contribute to improved efficiency by enabling higher productivity and shorter schedules

Several courses for solutions are commonly taken:

- Updating relevant procedures. Changes may refer to a spectrum of procedures, from those related to specific stages of software development or maintenance (e.g., changes in style of software comments, changes in contract review procedure in clauses dealing with proposals for small projects) to procedures of a general nature (e.g., changes in employee recruitment procedures, changes of the maximum and minimal number of participants in a formal design review).

- Changes in practices, including updating of relevant work instructions (if exist).

- Replacement of development tools and shifting to a development tool that is more effective and less prone to the detected faults.

- Improvement of reporting methods, including changes in report content, frequency of reporting, and reporting tasks. This course is expected to improve prospects for identifying software system faults and for their earlier detection, both resulting in substantial reductions in damages.

- Improvement in the operation of SQA infrastructure tools, that is, initiatives for training, retraining or updating staff, improving the performance of the CAB.

It is worth noting that:

a. In many cases, the recommended solutions combine several action items, from one or several courses.

b. Changing and updating of procedures and work instructions needs to be discussed and approved by the bodies assigned to their development and maintenance.

Returning to our example, the "3S" (Section 19.1) case displays six instances for CAPA implementation:

- Updating of existing procedure (recommendations (a), (b), (c), and (f)).

- Replacement of development tools of low efficiency and effectiveness by better tools (recommendation (d)).

- Improvement in the operation of SQA infrastructure tools (recommendation (e)).

Example A: High percentage of severe defects

Analysis of software quality metrics for the "Peak Performance Software Ltd." The development department identified a high proportion of high-severity software defects in the projects completed by two of its six teams. It was also found that the resources these teams required to correct the defects were substantially higher in comparison to the time required by other teams to correct defects of a similar nature.

The analysis was based on documented information relating to past projects as well as current projects of the two teams, in addition to projects performed by the four "healthy" teams. Further investigation revealed that most of the severe faults of these two teams were found in modules characterized by the presence of algorithms of medium to high complexity. Inquiries related to the SQA tools applied by all the teams revealed a meaningful difference in the number of applications inspected, especially in the analysis and design stages: while the "healthy" teams treated inspection as a more-or-less standard procedure for more complicated modules, the other teams used inspections rather sparingly. The recommended CAPA solution was to introduce definitions of the module types requiring inspection within the inspection work instructions.

The following example illustrates how a CAPA process can produce unexpected findings and recommendations.

Example B: Increase in help desk calls that require service at the customer's site

The "Perfect Programming Company" regularly operates two help desk teams to support users of its two most popular software products; Team 1 specializes on point of sale (POS) packages, Team 2 on accountancy packages. The help desk unit's management devised a number of new quality metrics to support control of the teams' effectiveness and efficiency. These new metrics emphasized control of services performed at the customer site, due to their high cost, and kept track of two variables (metrics), namely, percentage of customer site visits and average technician time per site visit. The fourth quarterly metrics reports for the two help desk teams are shown in Table 19.1.

The fourth quarter report set off a warning signal among company management. Whereas Team 2 showed stability in its performance, a dangerous change in Team 1's performance was observed. Management was very concerned by the substantial increase in the percentage of customer site visits and average technician time per site visit. A corrective and preventive action team (CAPA team) headed by an SQA unit staff member was appointed. The CAPA team held three

Table 19.1 Help desk quarterly report – IV quarter

The HD team	Quality metrics	I Quarter	II Quarter	III Quarter	**IV Quarter**
Team 1	Number of packages installed	2,105	2,166	2,200	**2,223**
POS packages	% of customer site *visits*	8.5	8.7	12.8	**19.9**
	Average technician time per site *visit* (hours)	2.8	2.6	3.3	**3.8**
Team 2	Number of packages installed	987	1,011	1,011	**1,189**
Accountancy	% of customer site *visits*	10.5	10.1	10.4	**10.2**
packages	Average technician time per site *visits* (hours)	2.9	2.7	2.8	**2.8**

long meetings devoted to interviewing the help desk team leaders, reviewing a sample of their customer site visit report and examining their detailed monthly statistical report. The team also observed the help desk teams at work for one afternoon.

The CAPA team discovered that while the previous year was rather low key for Team 2, who displayed some regression in their efficiency, it had been a year of major change in the operations of Team 1. During the first and second quarters, the team had invested substantial efforts to improve the user interface of the POS package and had added several helpful error messages. In addition, a revised user manual has been issued. All these improvements were included in the new Version 6.4 that replaced Version 6.3 of the POS packages that had served the company for the last 20 months. Version 6.4 had been installed by most users during the third quarter.

Analysis of the quarterly operations statistics and metrics revealed that the currently used quarterly reports were misleading. Unexpectedly, after applying an improved statistics and metrics reporting, shown in Table 19.2, it soon became obvious that in the last two quarters, Team 1 had actually achieved a substantial reduction of total help desk efforts, as measured in hours of help desk service per customer per quarter. The improved user interface and user manual caused a dramatic decrease in the number of user calls. Evidently, it was a result of the new friendlier and more proficient version of the packages. The increase in average time spent at a customer site visit was due to the higher percentage of services now given to new customers. The CAPA team based its conclusions on the revised, extended quarterly report, presented in Table 19.2. Application of the revised help desk quarterly report for Team 2 figures revealed a constant decrease in the efficiency and effectiveness of the team's HD services.

It should be noted that according to the HD procedure, each customer call is first served trying to solve the problem through the phone and internet communication (remote service). Only if this trial fails, a technician is sent to solve the problem on the site (on the site service).

Two corrective actions were proposed by the CAPA team: (1) To replace the currently used quarterly report with a more comprehensive one, based on the lines of Table 19.2. (2) An inquiry into the practices implemented by Team 2 was suggested to achieve a substantial improvement in the team's performance.

19.3.5   Implementation of improved methods

Implementation of CAPA solutions and improved methods relies on proper instructions, and often training, but most of all on the cooperation of the relevant units and individuals. Therefore, successful implementation requires targeted staff members be convinced of the appropriateness of the proposed solution. Without cooperation, the contribution of a CAPA can be undermined.

Table 19.2 Revised help desk quarterly report – IV quarter

The HD team	Quality metrics	I Quarter	II Quarter	III Quarter	**IV Quarter**
Team 1	Number of packages installed	2,105	2,166	2,200	**2,223**
POS packages	Total number of customer calls	1,454	1,433	872	**512**
	Number of phone service calls	1,330	1,308	755	**410**
	Average technician time per phone	0.21	0.22	0.18	**0.15**
	service call (hours)	124	125	117	**102**
	Number of customer site calls	8.5	8.7	12.8	**19.9**
	% of customer site calls	2.8	2.6	3.3	**3.8**
	Average technician time per	0.310	0.295	0.247	**0.209**
	customer site call (hours)				
	Average HD hours per customer per quarter (hours)				
Team 2	No of packages installed	987	1,001	1,011	**1,089**
Accountancy	Total number of customer calls	585	604	615	**698**
packages	Number of phone service calls	524	543	551	**627**
	Average technician time per phone	0.28	0.29	0.31	**0.30**
	service call (hours)	61	61	64	**71**
	Number of customer site calls	10.5	10.1	10.4	**10.2**
	% of customer site calls	2.9	2.7	2.8	**2.8**
	Average technician time per	0.345	0.339	0.366	**0.375**
	customer site call (hours)				
	Average HD hours per customer per quarter (hours)				

19.3.6 Follow-up of CAPA activities – implementation and outcome

Three main follow-up tasks are necessary to properly implement a corrective and preventive action process in any organization:

- Follow-up of the flow of development and maintenance CAPA records from the various sources of information. This type of follow-up reveals unreported cases as well as cases with low-quality reports, where important details are missing or inaccurate. This type of follow-up is conducted mainly through analysis of *long-term* activity information, while feedback is generated to the CAPA information sources.
- Follow-up of implementation. The object of this activity is to indicate whether the designated actions – training activities, replacement of development tools, procedural changes (after approval), and so on – have been performed. Adequate feedback is delivered to those bodies responsible for implementation of the corrective and preventive actions.

- Follow-up of outcome. Follow-up of the improved methods' actual outcome, as observed by project teams and organizational units, enables assessing the degree to which corrective or preventive actions have achieved the expected results. Feedback on the outcome is delivered to the improved methods' developers. In cases of low performance, formulation of a revised or a new corrective or preventive action is needed; a task undertaken by the CAPA team.

Clearly, regular follow-up activities that promptly examine incoming information and initiate adequate flows of feedback are an essential link in the CAPA chain of activities.

19.4   Organization for preventive and corrective actions

Proper performance of CAPA activities depends on the existence of a permanent core organizational unit as well as many *ad hoc* team members. The nucleus, generally known as the CAB committee, although it may have different names in different organizations, promotes the CAPA cause within the organization. Its tasks include:

- Collecting CAPA records from the various sources.
- Screening the collected information.
- Nominating *ad hoc* CAPA teams to tend to given subjects. CAB committee members may head some of the teams.
- Promoting implementation of CAPA in units, projects, and so on.
- Following up information collection, data analysis, progress made by *ad hoc* teams, implementation as well as outcome of improved CAPA methods.

Members of the SQA unit, top-level professionals, and development and maintenance department managers are natural candidates for membership in a CAB committee.

A complementary group of potential participants, from the regular staff, join CAPA efforts as members of *ad hoc* CAPA teams; they regularly focus on:

- Analysis of the CAPA information related to the team's topic
- Initiation of additional observations and inquiries
- Identification of fault causes
- Development of solutions and relevant corrective and preventive actions
- Preparation of proposed implementation revisions
- Analysis of the CAPA implementation outcome and CAPA revision, if necessary

Most members of the CAPA *ad hoc* team are department members, experienced in the subject matter. In cases when localized knowledge is inadequate, other internal or sometimes external experts are asked to join the team.

Summary

1. **The difference between defect correction and corrective and preventive actions.**
   Defect correction is a limited activity directed toward the immediate solution of the defects detected in a project or a software system.
   Corrective and preventive actions are wider in scope; their aim is to initiate and guide performance of organization-wide actions to eliminate the causes of known or potential faults.

2. **The main types of internal sources for CAPA process.**
   There are four main information source types that support and feed the CAPA process:
   1. Software development process
   2. Software maintenance
   3. SQA procedures
   4. Software quality management procedures

3. **The main approaches for introduction of CAPA.**
   Five approaches are commonly used:
   - Updating relevant procedures.
   - Changing software development or maintenance practices and updating work instructions.
   - Changing current software development tools to more effective tools that are less prone to faults.
   - Improving reporting methods by revising task content and reporting frequency. This approach aims to detect faults earlier and thus reduce damages.
   - Initiating training, retraining, and updating of staff.

4. **The main CAPA follow-up tasks.**
   Three main follow-up tasks necessary for successful CAPA process:
   - Follow-up of the flow of development and maintenance CAPA records: Enables cases of no reporting and cases with inadequate reports.
   - Implementation follow-up: Determines whether CAPA solutions have been performed as required.
   - Outcome follow-up: Ascertains the degree to which a CAPA has achieved the expected results.

5. **The participants in the CAPA process and their contribution to its successful implementation.**

The CAPA process is carried out by the joint efforts of a permanent CAPA body together with *ad hoc* team participants. The permanent CAPA body, commonly called the CAB committee, activates the CAPA process by screening information, appointing members of targeted *ad hoc* CAPA teams, promoting implementation, and following up the process. The *ad hoc* CAPA team's task is to analyze information about a given topic in addition to developing solutions and a CAPA implementation process. The team members are expected to implement the CAPA and use CAB-provided assistance, if needed. Most members of *ad hoc* CAPA teams are department staff members experienced in the subject matter.

Selected bibliography

ABCI Consultants (2015) *QMSCAOPA Software for ISO 9001 Quality Management Systems*, Software package.

R. M. Baldwin Inc . (2005) *CAPA Facilitator Professional – Corrective Action, Preventive Action Software*, Software package.

IEEE (2014) *IEEE Std. 730–2014 Software Quality Assurance*, The IEEE Computer Society, IEEE, New York.

ISO/IEC (2008) *ISO/IEC/IEEE Std. 12207-2008 – Systems and Software Engineering – Software Life Cycle Processes*, International Organization for Standardization, Geneva, Switzerland.

ISO (2014) *ISO/IEC 90003:2014 Software Engineering – Guidelines for the Application of TSO 9001: 2008 to Computer Software*, International Organization for Standardization (ISO), Geneva, Switzerland.

Review questions

19.1 Analysis of the cases discussed in Section 19.3 involves identifying the causes of the defects, but also determining the types and levels of damage expected from an identified fault followed by preparation of estimates of damages related to the organization-wide distribution of the respective defects and damages.

    a. Some SQA professionals believe that analysis of the case should be limited to identifying the causes of the defects. Do you agree?

    b. List your arguments.

19.2 Improved reporting methods are discussed (in Section 19.3.4) as possible solutions for an identified defect, though no change of performance practices is recommended in the associated CAPA.

    a. Some SQA professionals believe that a CAPA has no place for changes in reporting methods. Do you agree? List your arguments.

    b. If you do not agree, list possible contributions a CAPA can make based on changed reporting methods

19.3 Section 19.3.6 lists three main tasks of CAPA follow-up.

  a. List the three tasks.

  b. Explain in your own words the importance of the follow-up tasks to the success of the process.

19.4 Section 19.3.3 lists the following typical causes for defects that should be treated by CAPA: (1) noncompliance with work instructions and procedures, (2) insufficient technical knowledge, (3) extreme time and/or budget pressures mainly due to unrealistic estimates, and (4) lack of experience with new development tools.

  Section 19.3.4 presents five possible approaches to the solution of the above five causes.

  Examine the feasibility of applying each of the five approaches to each typical cause of defects.

Topics for discussion

19.1 Frame 19.2 lists four different types of internal CAPA information sources.

  a. Considering the multitude of internal CAPA information sources, are external information sources necessary?

  b. If you believe that external information sources are required, list your arguments and explain their special contribution to the CAPA process.

19.2 "Statement Software Ltd." is a software house that specializes in development of custom-made billing systems for the manufacturing industry. A common "Statement Software" contract offers the customer 12 months of guarantee services. The company's help desk (HD) supplies solutions to customer calls by phone or at the customer's site. The last quarter's performance report indicates a decline in service quality, a trend that also characterizes the previous two quarters. This trend was identified by the following four help desk quality metrics:

- Percentage of recurrent calls: the percentage of customer site calls that required a recurrent call to deal with a defect supposedly solved by the prior call.
- Average reaction time to customer site calls (working days).
- Average hours invested in customer site calls, including travel time.
- Customer satisfaction computed from a quarterly customer satisfaction questionnaire, using a 0–10 scale.

The SQA metrics	I Quarter	II Quarter	III Quarter	IV Quarter
Percentage of recurrent calls	12	13	19	21
Average reaction time to customer site calls (days)	0.7	0.8	1.7	1.8
Average hours for customer site calls	4.7	4.9	3.3	3.1
Customer satisfaction	8.3	8.4	6.7	6.5

The *ad hoc* CAPA team appointed to deal with the subject decided that each member should prepare a separate list of possible causes for the decline in the quality of HD services, prior to analysis of the collected information and complementary observations.

a. Can you list possible causes for the recorded phenomenon?

b. Indicate possible solutions for each of the causes proposed in (a).

19.3 The head of the *ad hoc* CAPA team became quite angry and offended when it was discovered that the team's recommendations regarding two procedures, sent to the Procedures Committee five months ago, had not yet been approved; he subsequently forwarded his protest to the Procedures Committee. In reply to the angry letter, the Procedures Committee head mentioned that the committee has already dedicated two of its meetings to the subject, and hoped to finalize the issue in their next meeting.

a. Is it reasonable for a Procedures Committee to require such a lengthy period of time to approve a recommended CAPA?

b. Suggest reasons where such delays might be justified.

c. Suggest changes to the route taken by the head of the CAPA committee and the Procedures Committee that could have improved the process in this, and similar, situation.

19.4 The head of the CAB committee suggested adding three new members, and voiced his belief that the extended CAB committee would be able to handle all the tasks currently carried out by *ad hoc* teams. He believes that this proposed change will substantially reduce the difficulties experienced by the *ad hoc* teams.

a. Do you support this proposal? List your arguments.

b. If you disagree, discuss the advantages of *ad hoc* teams.

Chapter 20

Software Process Assurance Activities for External Participants

20.1 Introduction

The partners of a software development project – traditionally the party interested in the software system (the "acquirer") and the organization that undertakes to carry out the development contract (the "supplier") – are very often not the only participants in a development project. This is especially true for large-scale projects, which frequently include external participants. The four external participant types are classified into two main groups: external performers and readymade software suppliers.

External performers include:

a. **Subcontractors** (a general term for "off-shoring" and "outsourcing") who undertake to carry out parts of a project – small or large – according to project conditions and requirements.

b. **The customer, as a participant in performing the project**. It is quite common for customers to perform parts of a project; apply special expertise, respond to commercial or other security needs, keep internal software development staff occupied, prevent future maintenance problems, and so forth. Hence, the inevitability of this situation has become a standard element of many software development projects and contractual relations.

Readymade software suppliers include:

a. **COTS software and reused software modules** provided by specialized suppliers. The benefits of integrating these ready components are

Software Quality: Concepts and Practice, First Edition. Daniel Galin.

obvious, and range from timetable and cost reductions to quality. One might expect these ready-for-use elements be of higher quality, as these components have already been tested and corrected by developers, as well as corrected according to faults identified by previous customers. The characteristics of COTS software and quality problems involved in their usage are discussed by Basili and Boehm (2001).

b. Open source software available through specialized sites. These specialized sites offer a huge variety of software packages and modules. One such site offers over 150,000 open software items (Obrenovic and Gasevic, 2007). The contact with the developers of open source software is partial and rare, while similarly, the available documentation of OSS is also usually partial.

The external participants and readymade software suppliers involved in a software development project contribute to the project, but are not contractors, nor are they the contractors' partners. Their contribution to the project is structured through agreements of subcontractors and suppliers of COTS software with the contractor, and through those clauses of the project contract that state which parts of the project will be performed by the customer. In most cases, no bonding contract related to the application of open source software exists. The larger and more complex the project, the greater the likelihood that external participants and readymade software will be required, and the larger the proportion of work to be transmitted or parceled out. The motivation for turning to external participants and readymade software rests on several considerations, ranging from economic to technical and to personnel-related interests, and reflects a growing trend in the allocation of work involved in completing complex projects.

The typical contracting structure of projects is presented in Figure 20.1.

The responsibility for quality of software processes performed by external participants. The project manager and the software development are responsible for the performance of quality assurance activities that will ensure that the processes carried out by subcontractors and other external participants conform to the project requirements.

The role of the SQA function in assuring the quality of external participants' software products. SQA function supports the project manager by consultation regarding the planning of quality processes related to the contract with external participants and the follow-up of the processes of the contract implementation. The SQA function team members may participate in part of the project team quality assurance activities as part of their efforts to evaluate the conformance of the software products of the external participants with the project requirements.

The ISO/IEC Std. 90003:2014 (ISO/IEC, 2014) states detailed requirements related to external participants under the general classification "purchases,"

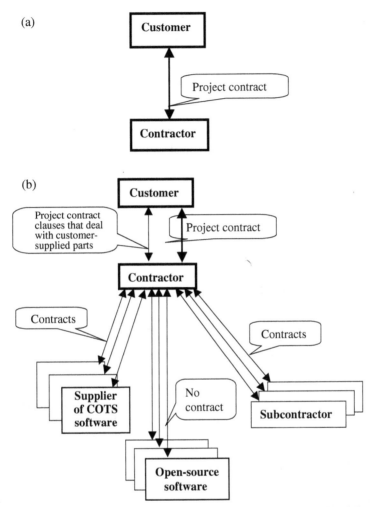

Figure 20.1 Software development projects: a typical contracting structure. (a) "Simple" contracting project (no external participants). (b) "Compound" contracting project (with external participants).

considering subcontractors, outsourcers, COTS, and open source software suppliers. The detailed requirements included in the standard deal with the purchasing process, beginning with selection of the supplier of purchased software product and ending with verification of purchased product. IEEE Std. 730–2014 (IEEE, 2014) dedicates Sec. 5.5.3 to evaluation of subcontractor processes for conformance. ISO/IEC/IEEE Std. 12207-2008 (ISO/IEC/IEEE, 2008) includes a brief requirement related to subcontractors in Sec. 7.2.3.3.3.3.

The ensuring of the quality of external participants' contributions, and the use of readymade software is widely discussed in software quality assurance literature. A few examples are Basili and Boehm (2001), Obrenovic and Gasevic (2007), Li et al. (2009), Maki-Asiala and Matinlassi (2006), Suleiman (2008), and Musa and Alkhateeb (2013).

The next sections are dedicated to the following subjects:

- Benefits and risks of introducing external performers
- Benefits and risks of using readymade software
- QA activities for assuring external performers' process quality
- QA activities for assuring quality of readymade software

Section 20.2 presents the case of a large-scale project involved in sizable participation of external participants.

20.2 The Pharmax tender – a mini case

"Pharmax," a tender issued by RedAid Health Insurance, presented a real challenge for HealthSoft, a software house that specialized in hospital and pharmacy software. A main section of the tender was an integrative nationwide system for handling the fees charged by pharmacies for prescription supplied to RedAid's insured persons. RedAid's insured persons are entitled to receive medications at authorized pharmacies, paying just 10% of the price as a participation fee. Accordingly, the pharmacies submit RedAid a monthly account for the medications supplied to RedAid insured persons. RedAid checks the pharmacies' accounts, and calculates the sums to be paid to them. The Pharmax software system tender included the following subsystems and units:

Subsystems	Units (modules)
1. Physician prescription subsystem	1.1 Unit that inserts barcodes to prescriptions printed by the physician. Barcoded fields include: physician's and insured person's identifications, catalog numbers and quantities of medications, and date and prescription number.
2. Pharmacy prescription processing subsystem	2.1 Unit that reads the prescription data and checks it.
	2.2 Unit that authorizes validity of the physicians and RedAid insured persons through online checks at RedAid's updated database; unauthorized prescriptions are rejected.
	2.3 Processing of prescription and printing pharmacy invoice for RedAid's insured person.

3. Pharmacy monthly processing subsystem	3.1 Unit that processes the prescriptions into monthly reports that include a detailed prescription log and a summary monthly account.
	3.2 Unit that transmits the pharmacies' monthly reports to RedAid MIS via the Internet.
4. RedAid monthly processing subsystem	4.1 Unit that receives and checks the pharmacies' monthly reports.
	4.2 Unit that performs computerized fraud reports according to specialized algorithms based on past records of physicians and RedAid insured persons.
	4.3 Unit that calculates the sums to be credited to the pharmacies' bank accounts, and processes reports to be sent to the pharmacies.
	4.4 Unit that processes RedAid's managerial monthly reports.

The customer's Management Information System (MIS) Department was to develop the home office modules of subsystem 4 based on existing software. In addition, the MIS Department was to purchase and install the hardware and communication equipment according to the contractor's specifications, see to the computerized interfacing agreements required with RedAid's authorized pharmacies, and instruct RedAid personnel on the new system's operation. The system was to be a high-integrity system, and secured with a high-reliability requisite for all components. The system was to become fully operative no later than 13 months after contract signing, with the contractor fully responsible for the quality and timely completion of all system parts.

Already at the beginning of the RedAid tender proposal preparations, the HealthSoft tender team realized that they would need professional support from companies that specialize in software security and data communication. The size of the anticipated programming load led the team to decide that a subcontractor would be able to carry out 30–40% of the programming load. Cape-Code, a very small software house located in a nearby suburb, was chosen as the programming subcontractor on the basis of the lowest price proposed. Some "breathing space" when preparing the proposal was obtained, when the team discovered that the new enhanced Version 5 of Medals Software's product of the widely used Medalux package, a laboratory accounting software program, included important relevant modules. The relevant modules were for the online external authorization of patient credit, and for the preparation of monthly laboratory accounts for organizational customers, such as RedAid, and they suited the tender requirements. Medalux's developers had stressed the wide variety of their package's interfacing capabilities, which were thought to be suited to almost any requirements. The possible integration of Medalux's version 5 into the proposed software would solve one of the remaining difficulties hampering completion of the tender proposal, and enable substantial reduction of development costs. Finally, HealthSoft signed agreements with all its potential external participants – Lions Securities, Comcom, and Cape-Code, subcontractors for security, communication, and programming, respectively – who together framed the project responsibilities for financial issues, as well as coordination between the various participating organizations.

The day HealthSoft was announced winner of the tender was one of satisfaction and joy for the company. Within a few days, all the project teams were working at full speed, with monthly coordination meetings conducted regularly. The subcontractors reported satisfactory progress in accordance with the project schedule.

The first warning signs appeared in the ninth meeting. Comcom, the communication subcontractor, reported that some of RedAid's major pharmacy chains had refused to supply the information needed for planning the communication equipment to be installed on their premises, as they had not reached an agreement with RedAid on the issue. Meanwhile, and as expected, Lion Securities, the security subcontractor, was facing similar difficulties. Both subcontractors declared that even if full cooperation was achieved within the following week, a month's delay in completion of the project was inevitable. During this entire period, Cape-Code people continued to express their satisfaction with the progress of the development tasks they had undertaken.

The next coordination meeting was a special meeting, called just 2 weeks after the previous one, to discuss the severe delays now evident in Cape-Code's schedule. The delays had been discovered by a HealthSoft team when they had tried to coordinate a planned integration test. At this late stage, HealthSoft had found out that Cape-Code had subcontracted its development task to another small software house. It became clear that the previous calming reports had not been based on actual information; but were fabrications intended to satisfy HealthSoft people (and ensure regular payments by RedAid to Cape-Code).

Integration tests for the Cape-Code modules began 10 weeks behind schedule. During the tests, many faults, of all kinds – many more than anticipated – were identified, while the correction time required exceeded the original plan. It was around this time that the team assigned to integrate the Medalux Version 5 software into the system realized that not all new modules in the enhanced version were operative, particularly the online external authorization of patients' credit status. In addition, the interfacing trials with other system modules failed. Medal Software assigned a special team to complete development of the missing module parts, and perform the necessary corrections. Though the software house's efforts were evident, successful completion of the software integration tests was accomplished almost 20 weeks behind schedule.

The system test started 19 weeks behind schedule, with the same severity of quality problems observed at the integration phase. Finally, and about 5 months late, it became possible to install the hardware and software equipment at RedAid's main offices, and at the authorized pharmacies.

The three-week conversion phase of the project that was started 23 weeks behind schedule was, surprisingly, a great success, and no major faults discovered. All faults that were revealed were immediately repaired. However, the implementation phase was a colossal failure: Only one third of the staff listed for training actually participated in the instruction courses, and the majority of those who participated displayed insufficient preliminary knowledge of the new systems. Success with pharmacy personnel was even lower. Only 8 weeks later could regular operation of the system begin, but with only about quarter of RedAid's pharmacies integrated into the new system.

The project, a frustrating one for all involved parties, ended with a series of court claims. RedAid sued HealthSoft, and HealthSoft sued RedAid, Cape-Code, and Medal Software, the developers of the Medalux software package. Lion Securities and Comcom decided not to sue HealthSoft – despite extra costs incurred – due to RedAid's lack of cooperation, and the subsequent obstacles tolerated during its efforts to bring the performance of their parts in the project on par with requirements – in lieu of its expectations for continued cooperation with HealthSoft on future projects. The trials lasted for years. The only consolation was that the new software, once in operation, was a great success, with many of RedAid management admitting that the system worked well beyond expectations.

You may ask yourself:

- Could the final gratifying results have been achieved without the "mess" experienced during the course of the project?
- Was the HealthSoft process for selecting subcontractors satisfactory?
- Were the HealthSoft contracts that included the follow-up procedures of progress of external participants adequate?
- Was the method of purchasing COTS software appropriate?
- Was the method of controlling the implementation of the customer's contribution to the project adequate?
- Was HealthSoft's control of its external participants adequate?

Whatever your responses to the specific questions, we can readily claim that had HealthSoft properly implemented SQA activities, problems such as those described above could have been avoided. Prevention of such issues is the main subject of this chapter.

20.3 Benefits and risks of introducing external performers

The main benefits and risks to project quality associated with introducing external participants within the framework of a project are:

The main benefits

For the contractor:

1. **Budget reductions** are achieved by lower prices offered by subcontractors, who specialize on the subject, and or the development tool. In some cases, a tender among subcontractors leads to even lower quotations.

2. **Remedy of professional staff shortages** achieved by participation of a subcontractor, who employs professionalism of the required kind.

3. **Shorter project schedule.** The participation of a subcontractor, or shifting part of the development tasks to the customer's MIS department, enables performing more development tasks at the same time.

4. **Acquisition of expertise in specialized areas** is achieved by choosing an external participant with the required expertise.

For the customer (as external participant):

1. **Protecting the customer's commercial secrets.** The development of sensitive tasks by a subcontractor inevitably exposes the subcontractor's team to the customer's sensitive information. The risk that sensitive, commercial, and technological information will be revealed to other customers of the subcontractor or other nonauthorized persons always exists. By performing the sensitive tasks, the customer reduces these risks.

2. **Provision of employment to internal software development department.** Participation in a software development project, in most cases, a large-scale project, creates an opportunity for enriching the customer's MIS teams' professional know-how, as well as an employment possibility for any staff not fully occupied.

3. **Acquisition of project know-how for self-supplied maintenance.**

4. Customer software development teams participating in the development project are expected to be better prepared to operate the system, and to possess the necessary know-how for maintaining the system software.

5. **Project cost reductions.**

The main risks

1. **Delays in completion of the project**. In those cases where external participants are late in completing their parts of the software system, the project as a whole is delayed. In many cases, control over the subcontractor's and customer's software development obligations is loose. This creates a situation that causes tardy recognition of delays, and leaves no

time for activities necessary to cope with lateness and limits its impact on the project.

2. **Low quality of project parts developed by external participants**. Quality problems can be classified as (a) defects: a higher than expected number of defects, often of greater than expected severity; (b) non-standard coding and documentation: violations of style and structure instructions and procedures (supposedly stipulated in any contract). Low-quality and nonstandard software are expected to cause difficulties in the testing phase, and later in the maintenance phase.

3. **Communication problems with subcontractors.** Language and cultural barriers cause communication difficulties that result in coordination, cooperation, and project control difficulties. These difficulties are more severe when working with overseas subcontractors.

4. **Loss of control over project parts**. Whether intentional or not, the control of software development by external bodies may involve interrupted communication with external participant's teams for several weeks, a situation that prevents assessment of the project's progress. As a result, alerts about development difficulties, staff shortages, and other problems are likely to reach the contractor belatedly.

5. **Future maintenance difficulties**. The fact that several organizations take part in the software development creates two possible difficult maintenance situations: (a) One of the organization, most probably the contractor, is responsible for maintenance of the whole project. The contractor may then be faced with nonstandard coding and incomplete documentation supplied by external participants. (b) Maintenance services are supplied by more than one organization, possibly the contractor and subcontractors, and occasionally the customer's software development department. Each of these bodies takes limited responsibility, a situation that may require the customer to search among the different bodies involved to find the one responsible for a specific software failure, once discovered. Damages of software failures are expected to grow in "multimaintainer" situations.

6. **Termination of work on contracted activities due to the subcontractor going out of business.** Cases of subcontractors terminating their work are usually surprising, involved with difficulties recruiting replacement teams, and difficulties of the replacement team to continue the work due to insufficient documentation and the inability to collect missing information from the subcontractor's team.

The associated benefits and risks of introducing external participants in a project are summarized in Frame 20.1.

Frame 20.1: Introduction of external participants: Benefits and risks

Benefits

For the contractor:

1. Budget reductions
2. Remedy of professional staff shortages
3. Shorter project schedule
4. Acquisition of expertise in specialized areas

For the customer (as external participant):

1. Protecting the customer's commercial secrets
2. Provision of employment to internal software development departments
3. Acquisition of project know-how for self-supplied maintenance
4. Project cost reductions

Risks

For the contractor and the customer:

1. Delayed project completion
2. Low quality of parts supplied by external participants.
3. Language and cultural barriers cause communication problems, resulting in coordination and cooperation difficulties
4. Loss of control over development of specific project parts
5. Increased probability of difficulties in maintaining parts supplied by external participants
6. Termination of work on contracted activities due to the subcontractor going out of business

20.4 Benefits and risks of using readymade software

The main benefits and risks for the contractor associated with using readymade software, namely, COTS software and open source software, are:

The main benefits

1. **Budget reductions** are achieved by the lower costs associated with using readymade software. These costs are much lower than those associated with the development of the required software.

2. **Remedy of professional staff shortages** is achieved by using readymade software. Though the use of readymade software requires investing efforts in selecting the preferred software, and integrating it in the project, it does reduce a substantial part of the team's workload.

3. **Shorter project schedule.** The use of readymade software reduces the number of development tasks, and enables performing the rest of the development within a shorter schedule.

The main risks

1. **Difficulties integrating readymade software**. In many cases, difficulties integrating readymade software into the software project arise. These

difficulties are made worse when appropriate documentation does not exist, and support services are not available.

Implementation tip
Purchasing a software package or module (COTS software) for integration into a newly developed software system usually entails substantial savings of development resources, including budgeted funds. This is especially true when the relevant software has been tested and currently serves a substantial population of users. In some cases, the contractor is persuaded to purchase a new, supposedly advanced version of an accepted software package, soon to be on the market and thought to be better suited to project requirements. However, it is not uncommon to discover, just a week or two later, that the version's release is (unexpectedly) delayed – repeatedly. A more thorough investigation into the status of the new version, including requests for information from users, may also reveal that vital parts – for instance, development of equipment and software interfaces or an advanced application – have been shifted to a later stage.

2. **Difficulties in correcting faults revealed in readymade software**. The lack of knowledge of the software design and, in a great part of the cases also a lack in documentation, cause severe difficulties in handling software faults. Support services for fault correction are available only for a small part of the readymade software packages and modules. Substantial difficulties exist in the self-correction of faults appearing in COTS software sold without the source code.

3. **Future maintenance difficulties**. The maintenance of readymade software by the organization that purchased it also includes the difficulties already mentioned. These difficulties are eased in cases when support services are offered by the developer of the readymade software and software user communities.

The associated benefits and risks of readymade software in a project are summarized in Frame 20.2

Frame 20.2: Using readymade software: Benefits and risks

Benefits	Risks
1. Budget reductions	**1.** Difficulties integrating readymade software
2. Remedy for professional staff shortages	
	2. Difficulties in correcting faults revealed in readymade software
3. Shorter project schedule	
	3. Future maintenance difficulties

20.5 QA activities for assuring external performers' process quality

We can expect external participants to operate their own SQA systems as they include the tools necessary for achieving acceptable quality levels for their own software products and services. The tools mentioned here are those that contractors can apply vis-à-vis their external participants. For this purpose, the issues of quality and schedule are the most important, and are addressed further.

The main SQA tools to be applied before and during incorporation of external participants in a software development project are listed in Frame 20.3.

Frame 20.3: QA activities applied to subcontractor's participation in a software development project

QA activities applied to subcontractor's participation in a software development project
• Reviewing the requirements document and subcontractor contract • Evaluation of selection process regarding external\performers • Review of the external performer's project plans and development processes • Establishment of project coordination and joint control committee • Participation in external participants' design reviews and software testing • Formulation of external performers' procedures • Certification of external performer's team leaders and members • Regular follow-up of progress reports of external performers' development activities

20.5.1 Reviewing the requirements document and subcontractor contract

Requirement documents provide the formal basis for the contracts signed between the contractor and subcontractors, as well as for the contract clauses dealing with customer obligations to carry out parts of the project. Hence, review of the requirement documents to be presented to external participants is expected to assure their correctness and completeness. The contracts proposed to the subcontractors require reviews as well. The principles guiding this contract review are adjusted to the different roles of the contractor, in this case – the customer.

In general, the requirements documents presented by contractors to external participants should be correlated with the customer requirements. The main issues to be dealt with in a requirements document are presented in Table 20.1.

Table 20.1 Requirements list presented to external participants

Requirements type	The requirements subject
Software functionality	1. Functional requirements (related to the customer requirements) 2. Interfaces between the external participant's part and other parts of the project 3. Performance, availability, usability and reliability (related to the customer requirements) 4. Required maintenance services
Formal and staff	1. Required qualifications of team leaders and members, including certification where applicable 2. Establishment of coordination and a joint control committee, including procedures for handling complaints and problems 3. List of software development documents to be delivered by external participant 4. Criteria for completion of external participant's part 5. Financial arrangements, including conditions for bonuses and penalties 6. Subcontractor authorization requirement
SQA	1. Requirements regarding the contractor's participation in the external participant's design reviews 2. Requirements regarding the contractor's participation in the external participant's software testing

---

Implementation tip

One of the main surprises encountered by contractors is the revelation that the sub-contractor – without any authorization or prior consent – has subcontracted his task to another company. Whatever the reason or justification for this step, it leads to the contractor losing control over project quality and schedule, with subsequent delays and noncompliance with quality requirements.

Contract clauses dealing with these issues are often inadequate to prevent such behavior. Improved prospects for eliminating such phenomena can only be achieved by combining stringent contractual clauses with strict implementation control.

20.5.2 Evaluation of selection process regarding external\performers

While it is clear that cases of customer's software development participation in projects is difficult and sometimes impossible to limit or prevent, a good degree of choice is available with respect to the subcontractors' participants. Any selection of external participants requires collection of information about the candidates themselves, products they have developed and team qualification, and also evaluation of this information.

Sources of information

The main sources of information that support this selection are:

- Contractor information about subcontractors based on previous experience with their services
- Audit summaries from subcontractor's quality assurance system
- Survey of opinions regarding subcontractors from outside sources

These information sources are described as follows:

a. **Use of contractor's internal information about subcontractors.** A subcontractor's file that records past performance is the main source of information for the contractor. Such an information system is based on cumulative experience with previous tasks performed by the subcontractor. Implementation of this tool requires systematic reporting that is based on SQA procedures prepared by the departments involved:
   - Teams or committees that evaluate subcontractors' proposals.
   - User representatives and coordination committee members responsible for project follow up.
   - Other users who have identified software faults or gained experience with the supplier's products and maintenance service.

Implementation tip

Two issues impinging on the adequacy of a "Suppliers File" should be considered:

1. Individuals evaluating a proposal prefer receiving full documentation on the organization's past experience with a prospective subcontractor/supplier, together with information gathered in the past from various outside sources. Yet, these same individuals are likely to neglect preparing records related to their own experience with an external participant.
2. Difficulties often result from unstructured reporting to the Suppliers File. If the information is not properly structured, evaluation and comparison of suppliers become taxing, if not impossible.

The answer to these difficulties frequently lies in procedures applied, and forms used. Procedures that define who should report what and in which situations can limit the reporting burden. A structured reporting form, supported by unstructured descriptions, can be helpful in addressing both issues.

---

b. **Auditing the supplier's quality system**. Auditing the supplier's SQA system is often encouraged by the subcontractors themselves, in an effort to promote acceptance of their proposals. In some cases, such an audit is part of the tender requirements. The auditors should verify that the audited features are relevant to the project in its content, magnitude, and complexity. Another issue to be considered is the demonstration project and team, which are usually chosen by the subcontractor. The preferred route is, of course, for the auditors to randomly choose the project and team from a relevant list.

c. **Opinions of other users of the subcontractor's performance**. Opinions can be gathered from other organizations with experience from the subcontractor's services in the past, from professional organizations that certified the subcontractor as qualified to specialize in the field, and from firms that have had professional dealings with the potential subcontractor. The purpose of this step is also to ascertain reliability among other variables that may affect contractual relations.

Evaluation and comparison of potential subcontractors should be based on the information collected, and carried out according to procedures designed for this purpose. Among the factors included in the procedure are the designation of the evaluation committee or responsible manager, and the process of evaluation, including the method for defining the relative importance attached to each item along with the information source.

20.5.3 Review of the external performer's project plans and development processes

A review of an external performer's project plan, development processes and procedures is performed by the contractor to ensure conformance with the subcontractor's contract. The requirement for this review is part of the contract itself.

20.5.4 Establishment of project coordination and joint control committee

The scope of the committee's activities and responsibilities vary in relation to the part the external participant plays in the project. Substantial coordination, monitoring, and evaluation of progress are essential when external participants carry out major parts of a project.

The committee's main activities related to external participants are:

- Confirming project schedule and milestones related to external participants' tasks.

- Performing follow-up according to progress reports submitted to the committee by external participants.
- Early identification of difficulties arising in the progress of external participants.
- Holding meetings with team leaders and others in the field in severe situations.
- Making decisions regarding ways to resolve problems identified in design reviews and software tests for external participants tasks.

The goal of follow-up and coordination of a subcontractor's performance may also be accomplished by alternative ways. The contractor could appoint a manager to perform these tasks. In general, the method of coordination, and its extent, should suit the size and complexity of a subcontractor's tasks.

Application of the specific SQA procedure that regulates follow-up and coordination of external participants' activities can be of great benefit.

20.5.5 Participation in external performers' design reviews and software testing

The extent to which contractor participation is required in subcontractors' design reviews and software testing depends on the nature of the project parts provided by the external participants. When the contractor participates, we can expect him or her to function as a full member of the review and testing management team. Participation in design reviews and software testing should include all stages of the development process: design reviews, (of planning and tests design), reviews of the test results, and follow-up meetings for corrections and regression testing. Additional review activities refer to software development documents that summarize phases of the project (deliverable documents). To sum up, the nature of participation in the development process is sufficiently comprehensive to enable the contractor's representative to intervene, if necessary, to obtain assurance that the quality and schedule requirements are fulfilled.

20.5.6 Formulation of external performers' procedures

The procedures would support the contractor in handling the relationship with external performers and regulate SQA activities within the context of contractual relations with external performers. The main objectives of specialized procedures are:

- Selection of subcontractors based on auditing the subcontractor's software development and QA capabilities
- Contract requirements contents with subcontractors

- Review of the external performer's project plans and development processes
- Review arrangements of subcontractor's performance
- Coordination arrangements with subcontractors
- Formulation of external performers' procedures
- Certification requirements from external performers

20.5.7 Certification of external performers' team leaders and other staff

Requirements for qualification and certification of the external participants' team leaders and other staff, especially subcontractors' staff, are intended to ensure an acceptable level of professional work as required by the project or the customer. This requirement is not to be belittled, for the quality of staff is the heart of any contractual relationship. The SQA activities required here are:

- Qualification and certification of staff is listed as a contractual requirement.
- Implementation of these clauses is to be confirmed by the contractor at outset of the work.
- Changes and replacement of the respective team members are to be approved by the contractor.
- Periodic review of implementation of the mentioned three clauses by the contractor.

Implementation tip

Subcontractors, when under pressure due to other projects or other activities, frequently try to replace qualified and professional certified team members needed elsewhere with staff that is not fully qualified and/or lacking certification. "Partial" violations – with the team leader or team member allocating his time, without approval, on more than one project – are also common. The control activities mentioned should deter the subcontractor from changing staff midproject in this manner, and help the contractor quickly identify violations, should they occur.

20.5.8 Regular follow-up of progress reports of external performers' development activities

When external participants share the project workload, the main objectives of the progress reports prepared for the coordination and joint progress control committee are:

- Regular follow-up of the project schedule
- Regular follow-up of the risks identified in the project work

a. **Follow-up of the project schedule**. This report focuses on activities that are behind schedule, and milestones expected to be reached later than scheduled. The report describes the actions taken to minimize delays and suggests further actions and changes in plans to be approved by the committee.

b. **Follow-up of the risks identified in the project work**. The report describes the current status of risks identified in previous reports, such as shortage of professionals with special expertise, shortage of equipment, difficulties in developing a module. For risks still unsolved, the report should discuss possible remedial actions. The new risks identified in the period covered by the report, as well as actions to be taken and their prospects, should also be mentioned.

Two other issues to be covered in progress reports are:

- Follow-up of resource utilization
- Follow-up of the project budget

In most cases when subcontractors perform their parts as fixed-price tasks, these issues seem to be of importance mainly to the external participants. However, it is clear that an unfavorable situation regarding these two issues can affect project quality, an event that makes them of immediate concern to the contractor.

20.6 QA activities for assuring quality of readymade software

We can expect developers of COTS software and open-source software to operate their own SQA systems. These include the tools necessary for achieving acceptable quality levels for their software products. In addition, previous users of these software products are expected to have identified defects already corrected by the providers of these software products. Consequently, the quality of readymade software is considered to be relatively high. However, it is clear that readymade software is not defect free, and that defect density varies.

The tools mentioned here may be applied by the user of readymade software to ensure the quality of these software products.

The subject of quality assurance of COTS software and open source software is the subject of many papers, these include: Li et al. (2009), Maki-Asiala and Matinlassi (2006), Carvallo and Franch (2006), Obrenovic and Gasevic (2007), Suleiman (2008), Malhotra et al. (2010), Musa and AlKhateeb (2013,) and the classic Basili and Boehm (2001). Perry (2006) dedicates a chapter of his book (Chapter 18) to the topic of testing COTS and contracted software.

The main SQA tools to be applied before and during incorporation of readymade software are listed in Frame 20.4.

Frame 20.4: SQA tools applied to usage of readymade software in a software development project

SQA tools applied to usage of readymade software in a software development project

• Requirements document reviews
• Performing appropriate selection process
  - The system requirements
  - The readymade software product characteristics
  - The provider's characteristics
  - Estimates of efforts required for readymade component's integration
• Requirement changes to adapt to readymade software features
• Peer reviews and testing readymade package or component
• Knowledge management of components integrated in the software system
• Preparing specialized procedures

20.6.1 Requirements document reviews

Requirements documents provide the basis for the choice between alternative COTS and open-source software packages and components.

For a list of the main issues to be dealt with in a requirements document, see Table 20.1.

20.6.2 Performing appropriate selection process

A vast variety of COTS and open source software items are available to software developers. Web-based search engines are the most common tool for finding potential software packages and components to fit the system's requirements. The main kinds of information to be considered in the selection process are:

- The system requirements
- The readymade software product characteristics
- The vendor's characteristics
- Estimates of efforts required for the readymade component's integration

The different types of information are described below:

a. **The system requirements.** The degree the software package or component fulfils the requirements is a major consideration in the decision to adopt a readymade software candidate. The ISO/IEC 9126 standard focuses on requirements that belong to functionality, reliability, usability, efficiency, maintainability, and portability factors.

b. The readymade software product characteristics
- **Source code availability**. For part of the COTS software, no source code is supplied, this increases the dependency on the COTS software provider for performing corrections of identified defects.
- **The quality of the software product documentation.** The readability, accuracy, and completeness of the component documentation supplied by the provider.
- **The software product (component of package) quality.** Understandability, its compatibility with industrial standards of coding and documentation, and its maturity in terms of the number of clients it has already served (the possibility that its defects have already been identified and corrected).

c. The provider characteristics
- **Provider's reputation** based on experience with provider's software products, recommendations from other clients, and provider's maturity, in terms of number of years and clients the provider has already served.
- **Availability of support by COTS and open source providers.** Support provided by providers for software structure and defect correction is evaluated by its comprehensiveness, quality, and response time.
- **Support of COTS and open-source software community**. Support for user and developer communities relates to provision of information regarding the features and quality of the component or package, and assistance in defect correction.

d. Estimates of efforts required for readymade components' integration. These efforts are affected by the software understanding ability, as well as the extent of conformance of the system's environment and the component's environment/technology.

Implementation tip

The timing of the selection process is important. Early selection, even during the requirement phase, has proved to yield better selection results, due to the wider search of possible component and package candidates. Late selection usually means only a partial search for sources of readymade components, a collection of partial information on the components and providers, and a quick and hasty evaluation process of comparisons. A result of late selection is the expected selection of an inferior component or software package.

A risk that early selection faces is the release of a new version of the selected component or package during the software development process. This requires a reselection process, though efforts required of this second process are significantly lower than those required for the early selection process. Even when considering the possibility of the need for a reselection process – an early selection should be preferred.

20.6.3   Requirement changes to adapt to readymade software features

In many cases, readymade software does not offer certain required features. In most cases, a provider upgrade of the readymade software is not possible. No upgrading is the case when the COTS software source code is absent. In such situations, especially when the missing feature relates to a minor requirement, one should consider changing the relevant requirement. The developer negotiates with the client regarding requirement changes.

20.6.4   Testing readymade package or component

It is expected that readymade components be of as high a quality, at least as that of the in-house components. Static peer review testing (code inspections and walkthroughs) of readymade software are not possible in most cases. However, dynamic testing (by a computer running the software) are frequently used prior to the final decision regarding the preferred software product. In some cases, applying the prototyping procedure for verifying component's functionalities, as well to discover defects, was found to be applicable.

20.6.5   Knowledge management of components integrated in the software system

The developer's company is responsible to manage the knowledge about components supplied by the provider and other external sources. In addition to saving information that becomes available during integration and usage. In other words, to capture knowledge not included in the documentation by the provider and others, including defects.

20.6.6   Preparing specialized procedures

The specialized procedures that regulate SQA activities within the context of the use of COTS and open source software have already been mentioned in this chapter. These special procedures are usually adaptations of procedures applied in projects that the organization has carried out.

It should be noted that developers tend to use informal processes for selecting readymade components and packages. Time-to-market considerations and relying on in-house expertise and on the provider's advice are the justifications mentioned by integrators of the development teams.

Summary

1. **The difference between contractors and external participants**. Software development contractors are organizations or groups of

organizations contracted by a customer to develop a software system with a project contract. External participants are parties that participate in the development process and perform small to large parts of the work, according to a contract with the contractor, but are not parties to the project's contract.

2. **The types of external participants and readymade software and the benefits they provide to the contractor.**

    The external participants can be categorized into two main groups: external performers and readymade software suppliers.

    The external supplies are:

    • Subcontractors
    • The customer, as an active participant in performing parts of the project
      The readymade software suppliers are:
    • Suppliers of COTS software and software components
    • Open source software available through Internet sites

    The main benefits to the contractor of using external participants are:

    a. **Budget savings** achieved when subcontractors offer prices below those incurred by performing the project internally, and by the use of COTS and reused software.

    b. **Overcoming shortages of professional staff** by transferring parts of the project to be carried out to firms employing staff with relevant skills.

    c. **Potentially shorter project schedules** achieved by purchasing COTS software and reused software rather than developing the software.

    d. **Expertise acquired in areas that need specialization** through the participation of owners – the subcontractor or the customer's development department – of that expertise.

    The main benefits to the contractor from using readymade software are:

    a. **Budget reductions** are achieved as the cost of the purchased software or open-source software, and its integration in the software developed are much lower than the development costs.

    b. **Remedy of professional staff shortages** as it reduces required efforts from the development team.

    c. **Shorter project schedule** as parts of, or whole development tasks may be performed at the same time.

3. **The risks for the contractor associated with working with external performers and readymade software**

    The main risks for the contractor from using external performers are:

    a. **Delays in completion of project parts** due to the competing interests of external participants, who are only partially committed to keeping to schedule. Even the customer – as supplier of his own project – might prefer another project and delay completion of his own part.

b. **Low quality of project parts** caused by insufficient capabilities, attempts to save resources, or other factors.

c. **Future maintenance difficulties** due to low quality or nonstandard software and/or incomplete or poor documentation of parts carried out by external participants.

d. **Loss of control over parts of the project** instigated by periods of cut off communication, whether intentionally or inadvertently initiated.

The main risks to the contractor from using readymade software are:

a. **Difficulties in integration of readymade software**. In many cases, difficulties arise in the integration of the readymade software into the software project. These difficulties are worse when no appropriate documentation exists, and no support services are available.

b. **Difficulties in correcting faults revealed in readymade software**. The lack of software design knowledge and, in a great number of cases, also a lack in documentation, causes severe difficulties in handling software faults.

c. **Future maintenance difficulties**. Due to the lack of knowledge and documentation of the software, maintenance of readymade software by the purchasing organization is not without difficulties. In some cases, support from the software providers and user communities' eases the situation.

4. **QA activities appropriate for use with external performers**

   a. **Reviewing the requirements document and subcontractor contract** ensures a correct and complete list of the requirements related to software functionality, to formal and staff aspects of the project, and to SQA issues.

   b. **Reviewing the requirements document and subcontractor contract.** An appropriate selection process requires collecting and analyzing information about the external participants.

   c. Review of the external performer's project plans and development processes.

   d. Establishment of project coordination and joint control committee. One of the committee's main tasks is to identify and resolve quality and schedule problems. Early alerts and cooperation can reduce, and even eliminate, these risks.

   e. **Participation in external participants' design reviews and software testing** provides an excellent opportunity to examine the real quality of an external participant's work, and to introduce corrections when necessary.

    f. Formulation of external performers' procedures is part of a contractor's SQA infrastructure. These procedures are expected to cover all aspects of work with external participants.

    g. Certification of the external participant's team leaders and other staff, as part of their contract with the contractor.

    h. Regular progress reports of external participants' development activities are prepared mainly in order to identify risks to the schedule.

5. The QA activities appropriate for use with readymade software
    a. Requirements document reviews
    b. Performing appropriate selection process

The main types of information to be considered in the selection process are:
- The system's requirements
- The readymade software product characteristics
- The provider's characteristics
- Estimates of efforts required for the readymade component's integration

    c. Requirement changes needed to adapt to readymade software features. Performing such changes are especially suitable when the required changes are minor.

    d. Peer reviews for, and testing of, readymade packages or components to be performed before purchase or after integration.

    e. Knowledge management of components integrated in the software system. Developer procedures are to capture knowledge not included in the documentation by the provider or others, including defects.

    f. Preparing specialized procedures to handle selection and integration of readymade software packages and components.

Selected bibliography

Basili V. R. and Boehm B. (2001) *COTS – based systems top 10 list, Computer,* Vol. **34**, No. 5, pp. 91–93.

Carvallo J. P. and Franch X. (2006) Extending the ISO/IEC 9126-1 quality model with non-technical factors for COTS components selection, *The 4th ICSE International Workshop of Software Quality,* pp. 9–14.

IEEE (2014) *IEEE Std. 730–2014 Software Quality Assurance,* The IEEE Computer Society, IEEE, New York.

ISO/IEC/IEEE (2008) *ISO/IEC/IEEE Std. 12207-2008 – Systems and Software Engineering – Software Life Cycle Processes,* International Organization for Standardization (ISO), Geneva, Switzerland.

ISO/IEC (2014) *ISO/IEC Std.90003:2014 Software Engineering – Guidelines for the Application of TSO 9001: 2008 to Computer Software,* International Organization for Standardization (ISO), Geneva, Switzerland.

Li J., Conradi R., Slyngstad O. P. N., Bunse C., Torchiano M., and Maurizio M. (2009) *Development with off-the-shelf components: 10 facts, IEEE Software*, Vol. **20**, No. 2, pp. 80–87.

Maki-Asiala P. and Matinlassi M. (2006) Quality assurance of open source components integrator point of view, *Computer Software and Applications Conference, Chicago, IL*, September 2006, pp. 189–194.

Malhotra R., Kaur A., and Singh Y. (2010) *Empirical validation of object-oriented metrics to predict fault proneness using open source software, Software Quality Professional*, Vol. **13**, No. 1, pp. 29–41.

Musa K. and Alkhateeb J. (2013) *Quality model based on COTS quality attributes, International Journal of Software Engineering & Applications*, Vol. **4**, No. 1, pp. 1–8.

Obrenovic Z. and Gasevic D. (2007) *Open source software: all you do is put it together, IEEE Software*, Vol. **24**, No. 5, pp. 86–95.

Perry W. E. (2006) *Effective Methods for Software Testing: Includes Complete Guidelines, Checklists and Templates*, 3rd Edition, Wiley Publishing, Indianapolis, IN.

Suleiman B. (2008) Commercial-off-the-shelf software development framework, *ASWEC 2008 Australian Conference on Software Engineering, Perth, WA, Australia*, March 2008, pp. 690–695.

Review questions

20.1 The customer as a developer of parts of a project is listed as one of the two types of external participants.

- Compared to subcontractors and suppliers of COTS software, the customer as a developer-supplier causes the contractor special difficulties before and during implementation of the project. List the special difficulties and explain their possible effects on the project.

20.2 External participants introduce four main risks into the project quality.

- List the main risks and explain in your own words the implications of each one.

20.3 Employing external participants provides the contractor with four major benefits with respect to carrying out a project.

- List the main benefits to a contractor and explain in your own words the implications of each one.

20.4 The customer enjoys four principle benefits from the employment of external participants when carrying out a project.

- List the main benefits to the customer and explain in your own words the implications of each one.

20.5 Employing readymade components and packages provides the contractor with major benefits, but involves risks with respect to carrying out a project.

- **a.** List the main benefits to a contractor and explain in your own words the implications of each one.
- **b.** List the main risks to a contractor and explain in your own words the implications of each one.

20.6 Qualifications and certification requirements for team leaders and team members are included in many subcontracting contracts.

a. Can you suggest examples of project team functions and list a number of relevant qualification and certification requirements?

b. What do contractors expect to gain from qualification and certification requirements?

20.7 For contractors, project adherence to schedule and discovery of hitherto unknown project risks are the main areas of interest in progress reports.

- Explain in your own words what actions are to be taken and what information items are to be required to ensure that progress reports comply with these two demands.

20.8 Performing a software development project of significant size almost always involves employing external participants and using readymade software

a. List the QA activities appropriate for use when external participants are involved in a project.

b. Add short statements regarding the risks involved with projects, including external participants and the QA activities that can help to eliminate or reduce these risks.

c. List the QA activities appropriate when using readymade software

d. Add short statements regarding the risks involved with using readymade software and the QA activities that can help to eliminate or reduce these risks.

Topics for discussion

20.1 Refer to the Pharmax tender mini case.

a. List the errors made by HealthSoft in the proposal preparation stage.

b. List the errors committed by HealthSoft during performance of the project.

c. Suggest SQA activities that could have prevented the above errors.

20.2 A nationwide furniture store chain has issued a tender for the development of its new generation software system; integrating advanced data communication systems, online applications, and a new feature – an Internet site – to display the chain products.

The chain received several proposals, two of which were selected for the last stage of the tender. Both contenders were well-established software houses, experienced in large-scale projects with sound professional reputations. Both proposals adequately addressed the tender schedule and other organizational demands, as well as the software specification requirements. The difference in price between the proposals was negligible.

Proposal A: The "in-house proposal," based entirely on in-house development, proposed integrating various company teams. The company declared that substantial parts of the project would be based on reused software modules from the company's software library.

Proposal B: The "big coalition proposal" was based on six external participants, half of them suppliers of reused software, while the remaining subcontractors were leading specialists in their fields of expertise.

You have been appointed to present your recommendations for the final choice between the closing proposals.

a. Which of the two final proposals would you recommend?

b. List your arguments for and against your preferred proposal.

c. Given that the cost of the nonpreferred proposal (not recommended in (a)) is 10% lower than the preferred proposal, would you consider changing your recommendation? List your arguments for this decision.

20.3 There are three sources of information reviewed in the process of selecting external participants.

a. List each source of information and explain in your own words the contribution of each one.

b. Why is it important to use all three types of sources?

c. What are the difficulties involved in employing each of the information types of sources?

20.4 Some professionals claim that in cases when the contract specifies reviews of deliverables, and acceptance tests of project parts carried out by external participants, the contractor has no justification to participate in design reviews and software tests.

a. Do you agree with these professionals? List your arguments.

b. Do you agree with others who suggest that there *is no need* to carry out acceptance tests in cases when comprehensive participation in design reviews and software tests has been executed? List your arguments.

Chapter 21

Software Process Quality Metrics

21.1 Software process metrics – an introduction

Software quality metrics are quantitative measures of the attributes of a software system as a product and also in its development and operative processes. Measures are based on relevant collected data related to these attributes. Fundamental tools are employed to assist management in three basic areas: setting targets for the software development and maintenance performance, evaluating the degree of achievement of the targets of development and maintenance tasks, and ensuring the detection of changes in those attributes.

Introductory issues on the objectives of software quality metrics, required characteristics of software quality metrics, and the implementation process of software quality metrics are presented in Chapter 18.

SQA and software engineering professional use to distinguish between software process metrics and software product metrics.

Software process metrics are a quantitative representation of software processes, as encountered by developers and maintainers throughout the software life cycle, such as prerelease defects, percent of modified code lines, and density of detected defects.

Software product metrics are a quantitative representation of attributes of software products or intermediate products, encountered by the user when applying software in efforts to adapt or change the product. Attributes changed include effectiveness, productivity, and reliability. Chapter 16 is dedicated to the topic of software product metrics.

This chapter is dedicated to software process metrics.

Classification of software process metrics

The software process metrics are classified into four classes:

1. Software development process quality metrics
2. Software operation process quality metrics
3. Software maintenance process quality metrics
4. Management process quality metrics

Software development process metrics include the following:

- Software development process quality metrics
- Software development by readymade suitability metrics
- Software development process effectiveness, efficiency, and productivity metrics
- Software development process rework metrics

Software operation process quality metrics include the following:

- Software operation process quality metrics
- Software operation process effectiveness, efficiency, and productivity metrics

Software maintenance process metrics include the following:

- Software maintenance process workload metrics
- Software maintenance process quality metrics
- Software maintenance process effectiveness, efficiency, and productivity metrics

Management process metrics include the following:

- Software development process management metrics
- Software reuse process metrics

Several books, book chapters, and numerous journals as well as conference papers have been dedicated to the subject of software quality metrics. A comprehensive discussion of software metrics is presented in books by Fenton and Bieman (2015) and Nicolette (2015), and in papers by Radjenovic et al. (2013), Kitchenham (2010), and Mordal et al. (2012).

Object-oriented (OO) software quality metrics.

The characteristics of OO design and coding methodology, namely, classes, methods, coupling, cohesion, inheritance, and so on, require adaptations as well as new quality metrics specialized in measuring OO software projects. Proposals of OO metrics and evaluation proposed OO metrics are discussed by a multitude of papers, to mention but a few: Darcy and Kemerer (2005), Aggarwal et al. (2007), Cheikhi et al. (2014), Ani et al. (2015), and Ferreira et al. (2012).

IEEE and ISO/IEC offer software quality metrics criteria within their software engineering standards. In the ISO/IEC standard, we may again note that ISO/IEC 90003:2014 (ISO/IEC, 2014) dedicates Chapter 8 to measurement, analysis, and improvement processes. ISO/IEC/IEEE Std. 12207-2008 (ISO/IEC/IEEE, 2008) presents the measurement processes for project in a system life cycle in Section 6.3.7. An ISO/IEC standard that is worthwhile mentioning is ISO/IEC Std. 15939:2007 (ISO/IEC, 2007), which is dedicated to measurement processes.

The chapter's next sections discuss the following topics:

- Section 21.3 – Software development process metrics
- Section 21.4 – Software operation process metrics
- Section 21.5 – Software maintenance process metrics
- Section 21.6 – Management process metrics
- Section 21.7 is dedicated to a discussion on the limitations of software metrics

The following section presents a mini case that illustrates the implementation uses of process software metrics.

21.2   North against South – who'll win this time round? – a mini case

John Kaine, the new manager of Norman Computing, was surprised to find out that the two software development departments, located at the south and north wings of the company building, employ entirely different methodology and development tools. His discovery led him to understand that this situation should be amended as soon as possible, to ensure that all the company's software development activities be conducted according to the same methodology and development tools. In a meeting initiated by Mr. Kaine to try to find the preferred methodology and development tools for the company, a loud discussion took place between the participants, with each claiming their department's technology and tools to be substantially superior to the others. Mr. Kaine cut the discussion short with his decision – a test project will be performed in each of the departments, and the company's methodology and development tools will be defined according to the results.

A week later, the test project was decided: The north wing department will perform the Oak project, a customer club for a major hardware shop, while the south wing department, the Tower project, will perform a customer service for a large sport center. Both projects were very similar in size (35.1 and 34.8 function points, respectively), and had a similar complexity level. The projects were scheduled to begin the following month with an expected duration of 6 months. It was further agreed that the achievements of both development teams will be compared according to the three metrics presented in Table 21.1.

Table 21.1   The comparison metrics

No.	Metrics code	Metrics name	Calculation formula
1	DevPF	Development Productivity by Function Points	$DevPF = \dfrac{DevH}{NFP}$
2	DEF	Development Error Density by Function Points	$DEF = \dfrac{NDE}{NFP}$
3	DERE	Development Error Removal Effectiveness	$DERE = \dfrac{NDE}{NDE + NFHY}$

DevH, total working hours invested in the development of the software system; NFP, the number of function points; NDE, number of development errors; NFHY, the number of all software failures detected during the first-half a year of regular operation.

The Tower and Oak projects began on time, with both teams keen to prove the superiority of their methodology and development tools. The teams completed their work about 2 weeks before schedule and the software packages were installed successfully a few weeks later. The data collected during the development period and the first half a year of customer regular use are listed in the following table.

Data item	Tower project	Oak Project
DevH	537	581
NFP	35.1	34.8
NDE	123	107
NHYF	14	17

The following table presents the metrics defined for comparing the Tower and Oak projects:

Metric	Tower project	Oak Project
DevPF	15.30	16.90
DEF	3.50	3.07
DERE	0.90	0.86

Mr. Kaine opened the comparison summary meeting with a sigh. "I am really sorry. The results of the test projects were a real disappointment, as no decisive superiority of one of the wing's tools was proved. While the Tower project yielded better results in development productivity and development error removal effectiveness, the results of the Oak project for development error density were better." He left no time for questions and continued: "The heads of the software development departments are requested to meet and discuss which methodologies and development tools of those employed by the two departments should be preferred, and eventually become the Norman Computing official tools. I wish you fair and professional discussions, and will expect your results within ten days."

21.3   Software development process metrics

This section presents the following examples of metrics:

- Software development process quality metrics
- Software development by readymade suitability metrics
- Software development process effectiveness, efficiency, and productivity metrics
- Software development rework metrics

21.3.1   Software development process quality metrics

Software development process quality metrics may be classified into two groups:

- Development error severity metrics
- Development error density metrics

A discussion of the above two classes is as follows.

a. Development error severity metrics

Metrics belonging to this group are used to detect adverse situations of increasing numbers of severe errors. Thus, the average severity of errors is calculated by weighting errors according to their severity.

Errors number measures. Two error measures are used for calculating the average severity metrics: (a) The number of errors counted that include requirement specification errors, design errors, and coding errors. (b) The weighted number of errors. The weighted number of errors considers the severity of the errors.

A common method applied to arrive at these measures is by classification of the detected errors into severity classes, followed by defining a severity weight for each class. The weighted error measure is calculated by summing up multiples of the number of errors found in each severity class by the adequate severity weight. A commonly used five-level severity classification for design errors that applies also to the other phases of software development is presented in Table 13.1.

Example 1 demonstrates the calculation of the weighted number of development errors (WNDE).

Example 1

The development error summary for the department's Atlantis project indicted the following:

Low severity errors: 42; medium severity errors: 17; high severity errors: 11.

Three classes of error severity and their relative weights were defined:

Error severity class	Relative weight
Low severity	1
Medium severity	3
High severity	9

The calculation of NDE (number of development errors, relates to the total number detected throughout the development process) and WNDE (weighted number of development errors) is presented in Table 21.2.

Error severity metrics for the entire development process and the development process phases are presented in Table 21.3.

b. Development error density

The counted number of errors and a measure for the project size are used to calculate the error density.

Software size measures. Two software project size measures are used:

a. KLOC (thousand lines of code). The estimated KLOC measure is to be used during the development process, and replaced by the real measure once the programming phase is completed.

b. NFP (the number of function points). The number of function point estimates should be replaced by more accurate ones as the project progresses.

The subject of software project size is discussed in Section 16.4.

Table 21.2 Calculation of NDE and WNDE – an example

Error severity class	Calculation of NDE Number of errors	Calculation of WNDE	
		Relative weight	Weighted errors
a	b	c	$D = b \times c$
Low severity	42	1	42
Medium severity	17	3	51
High severity	11	9	99
Total	70	–	192
NDE	70	–	–
WNDE	–	–	192

Table 21.3 Development error severity metrics

Metrics code	Metrics name	Calculation formula
ADES	Average Development Errors Severity (for the entire development process)	$ADES = \dfrac{WNDE}{NDE}$
ARES	Average Requirement Specifications Errors Severity	$ARES = \dfrac{WNRE}{NRE}$
ADSES	Average Design Errors Severity	$ADSES = \dfrac{WNDSE}{NDSE}$
ACES	Average Coding Errors Severity	$ACES = \dfrac{WNCE}{NCE}$

NDE, number of development errors; NRE, number of requirement specification errors; NDSE, number of design errors; NCE, number of coding errors; WNDE, weighted number of development errors; WNRE, weighted number of requirement specification errors; WNDSE, weighted number of design errors; WNCE, weighted number of coding errors.

Table 21.4 Error density metrics – for the development process

Metrics code	Metrics name	Calculation formula
DEDL	Development Error Density by KLOC	$DEDL = \dfrac{NDE}{KLOC}$
DEDF	Development Error Density by Function Points	$DEDF = \dfrac{NDE}{NFP}$
WDEDL	Weighted Development Error Density by KLOC	$WDEDL = DEDL \times ADES$
WDEDF	Weighted Development Error Density by Function Point	$WDEDF = DEDF \times ADES$

KLOC, the size of the software product, as measured by thousands of code lines; NFP, the size of the software product, as measured by the number of function points.

As error average severity and error density metrics alone provide two partial and different descriptions of the error situation, only a combination of both metrics (the weighted density metrics) can present a full picture of the error situation.

Table 21.4 displays four error density metrics dedicated to the development process as a whole.

Example 2

This example follows example 1 and demonstrates implications of their usage.

A software development department applies two alternative metrics for the calculation of development error density: DEDL and WDEDL. The size of the

Table 21.5   Metrics calculations for the Atlantis project

Measures and metrics	Metrics formulae	Metrics calculation	Metrics result
DEDL	$DEDL = \dfrac{NDE}{KLOC}$	$\dfrac{70}{40}$	1.75
WDEDL	$WDEDL = DEDL \times ADES$	1.75×2.74	4.8

project is 40 KLOC. According to the Atlantis project in example 1: $NDE = 70$ and $WNDE = 190$. ADES may now be calculated as $192/70 = 2.74$

The unit determined the following indicators as unacceptable software quality achievements of the development team:

$$DEL > 2 \text{ and } WDEL > 4$$

1. **Calculation of the two metrics according to example 1** follows in Table 21.3.

   The conclusions reached by applying the two metrics are contradicting. While the DEDL metrics do not indicate unacceptable team quality achievements, the WDEDL metrics do. The contradicting results call for management intervention (Table 21.5).

2. **Error density for phases of the development process**

   The study of the origin of software errors is of importance in planning the SQA components to be applied. We refer to three development phases: the requirement specification analysis, design, and coding (programming). The number of errors detected in these phases are NSE, NDSE, and NCE, and the weighted number of errors are WNSE, WNDSE, and WNCE, where

   $$NDE = NSE + NDSE + NCE \text{ and}$$
   $$WNDE = WNSE + WNDSE + WNCE.$$

   The error density for these development phases is shown in Table 21.6.

The error density metrics by function points for the development phases may be calculated similarly to those shown in Table 21.6.

It should be noted that as the number of detected errors grows as the project progresses, the error density of the development phases grows. In other words, requirement specification errors detected in the design phase add to those detected in the requirement specification phase, causing an increase of the specification error density metrics. Accordingly, if somebody quotes a design error density metric, it should be clarified at which development phase the metrics were calculated.

Table 21.6   Development error density for development phases

Metrics code	Metrics name	Calculation formula
REDL	Requirement Specification Error Density by KLOC	$REDL = \dfrac{NRE}{KLOC}$
DSEDL	Design Error Density by KLOC	$DSEDL = \dfrac{NDSE}{KLOC}$
CEDL	Coding Error Density by KLOC	$CEDL = \dfrac{NCE}{KLOC}$
WREDL	Weighted Requirement Specification Error Density by KLOC	$WREDL = REDL \times ARES$
WDSEDL	Weighted Design Error Density by KLOC	$WDSEDL = DSEDL \times ADSES$
WCEDL	Weighted Coding Error Density by KLOC	$WCEDL = CEDL \times ACES$

21.3.2   Software development by readymade suitability metrics

Metrics for measuring the quality of readymade software components

Software products of recent years include a growing number of ready-made components: COTS software components, complete packages, and open-source software components. Venkatesan and Krishnamoorthy (2009) suggest a metrics suite for measuring the quality of readymade software components. They distinguish between functional and nonfunctional metrics, where the functional metrics include complexity, accuracy, suitability, and accuracy metrics, and the nonfunctional metrics include usability, maintainability, reusability, and performance metrics. The metrics suite for readymade software components are shown in Figure 21.1.

Venkatesan and Krishnamoorthy (2009), Barkmann et al. (2009), and Aloysius and Maheswaran (2015) present a comprehensive set of software metrics that measure the functionality of the components in the entire software system. A great part of the applied metrics is generally used in software measuring.

Preliminary metrics specific to the readymade software are the suitability metrics, which measure the degree of fulfillment of software requirements and extra functionalities provided by a candidate component. These metrics can support choosing the best component out of candidate components. Refinement of these metrics is achieved by using weighted metrics. Combined suitability metrics are created using weigh factors to represent the relative values of conforming functionalities and the extra functionalities.

The suitability metrics are presented in Table 21.7.

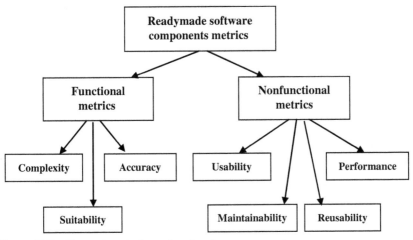

Figure 21.1 The metrics suite for readymade software components

Table 21.7 Suitability metrics for readymade components

Metrics code	Metrics name	Calculation formula
FunSC	Functionality Suitability of a Component	$FunSC = \dfrac{NRFunC}{NRFun}$
WFunSC	Weighted Functionality Suitability of a Component	$WFunSC = \dfrac{WNRFunC}{WNRFun}$
ExFunC	Extra Functionality of a Component	$ExFunC = \dfrac{NExFunC}{NRFun}$
WExFunC	Weighted Extra Functionality of a Component	$ExWFunSC = \dfrac{WNRFunC}{WNRFun}$
CFunSC	Combined Functionality Suitability of a Component	$CFunSC = C1 \times WFunSC + C2 \times ExWFunC$
CWFunSC	Combined Weighted Functionality Suitability of a Component	$CWFunSC = k1 \times FunSC + k2 \times ExFunC$

NRFunC, number of required functionalities provided by the component; NRFun, number of required functionalities (relevant to the component); WNRFunC, weighted number of required functionalities provided by the component; WNRFun, weighted number of required functionalities (relevant to the component); NExFunC, number of extra functionalities provided by the component; WNExFunC, weighted number of extra functionalities provided by the component.

The subject of integrating readymade software components in a software product is discussed in Chapter 20.

21.3.3 Software development process effectiveness, efficiency, and productivity metrics

This section deals with three subjects related to error removal productivity during the development process:

- The effectiveness of the employed error removal processes in terms of the percentages of errors removed
- The efficiency of error removal processes in terms of manpower resources to be invested to remove an error
- The productivity of development processes in terms of manpower resources to be invested relative to software product size

a. Error removal effectiveness

Software developers are interested in measuring the total effectiveness of all the error detection tools applied throughout the development process. In other words, the proportion of software errors not detected in spite of all efforts invested in error removal. For this purpose, errors detected during a project's regular operation need to be collected in addition to development process errors. For practical reasons, we limit the observations of regular operation errors to a period of 6 or 12 months. Thus metrics combine the error records of the development stage with the failure records compiled during the first year (or any defined period) of regular operation.

Five error removal effectiveness metrics of the development process and its phases are presented in Table 21.8.

Weighted removal effectiveness metrics for the development phases may be defined similarly to those of the development phase presented in Table 21.5.

b. Error removal efficiency

When discussing the efficiency of error removal efforts, we relate to the whole development process as well as to the efficiency of the review and coding activities. The efficiency of error removals relates to the number of errors detected, and the resources invested in detection. The review error removals refer to errors in inspection, walkthrough, and design review activities, whereas testing error removals refer to errors in unit, integration, and software system test activities. Table 21.9 presents the error removal metrics:

c. Software process productivity metrics

This group of metrics includes metrics that deal with the project's human resource productivity

Table 21.8 Error removal effectiveness metrics

Metrics code	Metrics name	Calculation formula
DERE	Development Error Removal Effectiveness	$DERE = \dfrac{NDE}{NDE + NYF}$
WDERE	Weighted Development Error Removal Effectiveness	$WDERE = \dfrac{WNDE}{WNDE + WNYF}$
RERE	Requirement Specification Error Removal Effectiveness	$RERE = \dfrac{NRE}{NRE + RYF}$
DSERE	Design Error Removal Effectiveness	$DSERE = \dfrac{NDSE}{NDSE + DSYF}$
CERE	Coding Error Removal Effectiveness	$CERE = \dfrac{NCE}{NCE + CYF}$

NYF, number of all software failures detected during the first year of regular operation; WNDE, weighted number of development errors; WNYF, weighted number of software failures detected during the first year of regular operation; RYF, number of requirement specification failures detected during the first year of regular operation; DSYF, number of design failures detected during the first year of regular operation; CYF, number of coding failures detected during the first year of regular operation.
Here, $NYF = RYF + DSYF + CYF$.

Table 21.9 Error removal efficiency metrics

Metrics code	Metrics name	Calculation formula
DevERE	Development Error Removal Efficiency	$DevERE = \dfrac{DevQH}{NDE}$
RERE	Review Error Removal Efficiency	$RERE = \dfrac{RevH}{NRE}$
TERE	Testing Error Removal Efficiency	$TERE = \dfrac{TesH}{NTE}$

DevQH, development hours invested in quality assurance activities (actual); RevH, review hours (actual); TesH, testing hours (actual); where $DevQH = RevH + TesH$.
NDE, number of development errors; NRE, number of errors detected in review activities; NTE, number of errors detected in testing activities, where $NDE = NRE + NTE$.

Two development process productivity metrics, direct and indirect, are presented in Table 21.10.

21.3.4 Software development rework metrics

An alternative metric to measure the quality of the development performance is to refer to the resources invested in the rework. This may be done by referring to

Table 21.10   Development process productivity metrics

Metrics code	Metrics name	Calculation formula
DevPL	Development Productivity by KLOC	$DevPL = \dfrac{DevH}{KLOC}$
DevPF	Development Productivity by Function Points	$DevPF = \dfrac{DevH}{NFP}$

DevH, total number of working hours invested in the development of the software system.

Table 21.11   Software development rework metrics

Metrics code	Metrics name	Calculation formula
PDRw	Percentage of Development Rework	$PDRw = \dfrac{DRwH \times 100}{DevH}$
PDSRw	Percentage of Design Rework	$PDSRw = \dfrac{DSRwH \times 100}{DevH}$
PCRw	Percentage of Coding Rework	$PCRw = \dfrac{CRwH \times 100}{DevH}$

DRwH, development team hours invested in rework; DSRwH, team hours invested in design rework; CRwH, team hours invested in coding rework; DevH, total number of working hours invested in the development of the software system.

the development process as a whole, or to phases of the process. The following metrics relate to rework percentages and are presented in Table 21.11.

21.4 Software operation process metrics

Operation of the user support center (help desk) services relates to software support to internal or external customers, who bought and installed software packages or COTS software. User support center (USC) services include instructing customers regarding the method of application of the software, solution of customer implementation problems, and correction of software failures.

The demand for these services depends to a great extent on the following:

- The size of the user population of software packages or COTS software sold.
- The quality of the software package, especially the quality of its user manual and the user's interface as experienced by the online software use instruction. The higher the quality, the lower the rates of customer calls.

This section deals with the following topics:

- Software operation process workload
- Software operation process quality metrics
- Software operation process effectiveness, efficiency, and productivity metrics

Table 21.12   USC calls – workload metrics

Code	Name	Calculation formula
AFUCH	Average frequency of USC calls per hour	$\text{AFUCH} = \dfrac{\text{NUYC}}{\text{NUSHY}}$
UDL	USC Call Density by KLOC	$\text{UDL} = \dfrac{\text{NUYC}}{\text{KUS} \times \text{KLOC}}$
UDF	USC Call Density by Function Point	$\text{UDF} = \dfrac{\text{NUYC}}{\text{KUS} \times \text{NFP}}$

NUYC, the number of USC calls during a year of service; KUS, thousands of users; NUSHY, the number of USC service hours a year.

21.4.1   Software operation process workload

The operation process workload is observed according to (a) frequency and its (b) density proportional to the operated software package size and the number of users. The USC calls workload metrics are presented in Table 21.12.

21.4.2   Software operation process quality metrics

The quality of USC, to great extent, defines the quality of software operation services. The USC services quality may be evaluated according to three aspects: the waiting time for USC service, the average service time, and the percentage of users waiting above target time and the percentage of user's service time above target time.

Three metrics were defined accordingly, and presented in Table 21.13.

An example for the application of the USC quality metrics is as follows: The USC services for an inventory management software package are required to comply with the following requirements:

- Average waiting time for USC service will be below 2 minutes per call.
- Percentage of USC calls served within 5 minutes will exceed 95%.

Productivity metrics

a. USC effectiveness metrics

The effectiveness of USC services is measured by the success rate in solving the user's problem in the first call.

b. USC efficiency metrics

A prevalent metric of USC services efficiency refers to the average resources invested in responding to a customer's USC call.

Table 21.13 USC quality metrics

Metrics code	Metrics name	Calculation formula
AUWT	Average Waiting Time for USC Service	$AUWT = \dfrac{TUWT}{NUOT}$
PDWTET	Percentage of USC Calls Exceeding Target Waiting Time	$PUWTET = \dfrac{NUYCET}{NUYC}$
PUSFC	Percentage of USC Calls Exceeding Target Service Time	$PUSFC = \dfrac{NUYCFC}{NUYC}$

TUWT, total users waiting time for USC service; NUOT, the number of USC calls during the observation time; NUYCET, the number of calls per year exceeding USC target waiting time; NUYCFC, the number of calls per year when USC achieved first call resolution (FCR); NUYC, the number of USC calls per year.

Table 21.14 USC effectiveness, efficiency, and productivity metrics

Metrics code	Metrics name	Calculation formula
PUSFC	Percentage of USC Problems Solved in the First Call	$PUSFC = \dfrac{NUYCFC}{NUYC}$
UE	USC Efficiency	$UE = \dfrac{UYH}{NUYC}$
UPL	USC Productivity by KLOC	$UPL = \dfrac{UYH}{KUS \times KLOC}$
UPF	USC Productivity by Function Point	$UPF \dfrac{UYH}{KUS \times NFP}$

UYH, total annual working hours invested by the HD servicing the software system.

c. USC productivity metrics

USC productivity is considered to be proportional to the size of the user population and the size of the software package (being supported).

Four process metrics are presented in Table 21.14.

21.5 Software maintenance process metrics

Software maintenance activities include:

- *Corrective maintenance* – Correction of software failures detected during regular operation of the software.
- *Adaptive maintenance* – Adaptation of existing software to new customers or new requirements.

- *Functional improvement maintenance* – Addition of new functions to the existing software; improvement of reliability; and so on.

In the metrics presented here, we limit our discussion to those dealing with corrective maintenance.

Software maintenance process metrics include the following groups:

- Software maintenance process workload metrics
- Software maintenance process quality metrics
- Software maintenance process effectiveness, efficiency, and productivity metrics

21.5.1 Software maintenance process workload

The maintenance process workload is observed according to three attributes.

a. Failure frequency

Failure frequency reflects the daily workload of the corrective maintenance team.

b. Failure severity

The failure severity measured relates either to the disturbance and damage caused to the customer (represents the customer's point of view) or to the resources required to resolve the failure (represents interests of the maintenance team). Metrics from this group detect adverse situations with increasing severity of software failures in the maintained software system. Results may trigger retesting of all or parts of the software system. The metric presented here can be used for both aspects of severity, that is, to apply weights that refer to the severity of the disturbance and damage experienced by the customer, or to the extent of resources required by the maintainer to correct the failure.

The ASFS metrics refer to the severity of software failures detected during the period of 1 year. To implement the ASFS metric, the severity should be evaluated for each failure. The metrics are presented in Table 21.14

c. Software system failure density

Software system failure density during the regular operation phase depends not only on the complexity of the software but also on the effectiveness of the error removal activities during the development phase (see Section 21.3.2b). It should be noted that changes and additions performed during the operation phase are a significant source for software errors that have to be treated by the corrective maintenance team.

The presented software system failure density metrics in Table 21.15 relate to the number of failures. The size of the maintenance tasks is measured by the

Table 21.15 failure cases workload metrics

Code	Name	Calculation formula
AFMCD	Average frequency of failures (maintenance cases) per day	$AFMCD = \dfrac{NYF}{NMSDY}$
ASFS	Average Software Failure Severity	$ASFS = \dfrac{WNYF}{NYF}$
SFDL	Software System Failure Density per KLOC	$SFDL = \dfrac{NYF}{KLOC}$
SFDF	Software System Failures per Function Point	$SFDF = \dfrac{NYF}{NFP}$

NUYC, the number of failures during a year of service; NMSDY, number of maintenance service days per year; NYF, number of software failures detected during a year of maintenance service; WNYF, weighted number of software failures per year detected with their severity evaluated; KLOC, thousands lines of code; NFP, number of function points.

total number of code lines of the maintained software as well as by the function point evaluation. The sources of data for these metrics are software maintenance reports.

21.5.2 Software maintenance process quality metrics

The method proposed here for the evaluation of software maintenance process quality is to refer to two failure situations: maintenance time failure and maintenance total repair failure. In other words, maintenance services can fail either by being unable to complete the failure correction within the specified time, or by failing to correct the problem, when no time limit for repair is specified. Failure metrics for the two situations are as follows:

Maintenance time failure metrics – MTimF

Software service agreements define a maximum time duration for the maintenance repair to be completed, that is, repair should be completed no later than 12 hours after the customer's failure notice has been received. Maintenance time failure is a repair that failed to be completed on time.

Maintenance total repair failure metric – MRepF

A repair failure that could not be repaired despite repeated trials and unlimited invested resources.

The two maintenance quality failure metrics are presented in Table 21.16.

Table 21.16 Maintenance quality failure metrics

Metrics code	Metrics name	Calculation formula
MaiTimF	Maintenance Time Failure Proportion	$MaiTimF = \dfrac{NTimYF}{NYF}$
MaiTRepF	Maintenance Total Repair Failure Proportion	$MaiTRepF = \dfrac{NTRepYF}{NYF}$

NTimYF, number of failure repairs not completed on time per year; NTRepYF, number of maintenance total repair failures per year.

21.5.3 Software maintenance process effectiveness, efficiency, and productivity metrics

This group of metrics includes the following metrics:

a. **Maintenance effectiveness metrics**

The metrics refer to the repair success. In other words, a successful repair is one that does not require a recall where the first correction failed.

b. **Maintenance efficiency metrics**

The metrics refer to the average amount of resources invested in resolving a failure. One prevalent metric is presented in Table 21.16.

c. **Maintenance productivity metrics**

Maintenance productivity is considered to be proportional to the size of the maintenance task, measured by KLOC or number of function points. Accordingly, two metrics are presented in Table 21.17.

Table 21.17 Software corrective maintenance effectiveness, efficiency, and productivity metrics

Metrics code	Metrics name	Calculation formula
CMaiEff	Corrective Maintenance Effectiveness	$CMaiEff = \dfrac{NYFCFT}{NYF}$
CMaiE	Corrective Maintenance Efficiency	$CMaiE = \dfrac{CMaiYH}{NYF}$
CMaiPL	Corrective Maintenance Productivity by KLOC	$CMaiPL = \dfrac{CMaiYH}{KLOC}$
CMaiPF	Corrective Maintenance Productivity by Function Point	$FCMPF = \dfrac{CMaiYH}{NFP}$

CMaiYH, total annual working hours invested in the corrective maintenance of the software system; NYFCFT, number of yearly failures corrected by the first time.

21.6 Management process metrics

This class of software process metrics includes the following:

- Software development process management metrics
- Software reuse process metrics

21.6.1 Software development project progress management metrics

Three attributes describe the project progress for managerial control of software development projects:

- Schedule keeping
- Resource usage compliance
- Budget keeping

Software process metrics were developed for these three attributes. The metrics presented here may be applied at any time during the performance period of the project.

a. Project schedule keeping metrics

Schedule keeping metrics relate to schedule keeping during the development process. The metrics offered here are based on records of schedule keeping for project milestones. Two approaches may be used for these metrics: (a) percentage of project milestones completed on schedule, or earlier out of the total number of milestones completed, and (b) the average time delay calculated for the completion of all milestones, or milestones during a specified phase.

b. Project resource usage compliance metrics

One of the important tools of SQA is the monitoring of resource usage. The metrics measure the human resource usage compliance with the planned human resources of the project plan. The metrics may be implemented during the development process by referring only to the planned and actual human resource usage of the completed development activities. Our resource usage metrics refer only to human resources, which are the main resource investment in software development projects.

c. Project budget-keeping metrics

Project budget-keeping metrics relate to all types of resources, and thus it is complementary to the project resource usage compliance metrics. The source for project-planned budget is the project plan. It should be noted that part of the cases of not complying with budget proves to be cases of unrealistic project budget.

Table 21.18   Software development project progress management metrics

Metrics code	Metrics name	Calculation formula
PMSK	Percentage of Milestone Schedule Keeping	$PMSK = \dfrac{MSOT}{NMS}$
DMSK	Average Delay of Milestone Schedule Keeping	$DMSK = \dfrac{TMSCD}{NMS}$
HRUE	Human Resource Usage Efficiency	$HRUE = \dfrac{DevH}{PDevH}$
BKE	Budget-Keeping Efficiency	$BKE = \dfrac{CCAct}{PCCAct}$

MSOT, Milestones completed on time; NMS, Total number of milestones; TMSCD, total milestone completion delays (days, weeks, etc.) for all milestones; DevH, working hours actually invested in the completed development activities; PDevH, planned working hours to be invested in the completed development activities; CCAct, actual costs of the completed development activities; PCCAct, planned costs of the completed development activities.

The metrics for the three attributes are presented in Table 21.18.

To calculate the DMSK measure, delays reported for all relevant milestones are summed up. Milestones completed on time or before schedule are considered "0" delays.

Some professionals refer to completion of milestones before schedule as "minus" delays, to balance milestones accounted for delays. In these cases, the value of the DMSK may be lower than the value obtained according to the metric originally suggested.

The PMSK and DMSK metrics are based on data for all relevant milestones scheduled and completed in the project plan. Therefore, these metrics can be applied throughout development and need not wait for the project's completion.

21.6.2   Software reuse process metrics

Reuse practices are used for software code and software documentation. The metrics may reveal the success level of the management policy for promoting reuse in the organization. Software reuse substantially affects productivity and efficiency of software development processes. The software reuse process metrics are presented in Table 21.19.

21.7   Limitations of software metrics

Application of quality metrics is strewn with obstacles. These can be grouped as follows:

- Budget constraints in allocating the necessary resources (manpower, funds, etc.) for the development of a quality metrics system and its regular application.

Table 21.19 Software reuse process metrics

Metrics code	Metrics name	Calculation formula
CRe	Code Reuse Rate	$CRe = \dfrac{ReKLOC}{KLOC}$
DocRe	Documentation Reuse Rate	$DocRe = \dfrac{ReDoc}{NDoc}$

ReKLOC, number of thousands of reused lines of code; ReDoc number of reused pages of documentation; NDoc number of pages of documentation.

- Human factors, especially opposition of employees to the evaluation of their activities.
- Uncertainty regarding the data's validity, rooted in partial and biased reporting.

These difficulties are fairly universal and, as such, apply to software quality metrics, too. However, additional obstacles that are uniquely related to the software industry may appear. These obstacles are discussed in this section.

The unique obstacles in the application of software quality metrics – comparing performances for managerial use – are rooted in the attributes measured. As a result, most commonly used metrics suffer from low validity and limited comprehensiveness. Examples of the software measures that exhibit these severe weaknesses are:

- Parameters used in development process metrics: KLOC, NDE, and NCE.
- Parameters used in product HD and corrective maintenance metrics: KLOC, NHYC, and NYF.

The main factors affecting development process parameters, especially their magnitude, are:

a. *Programming style*: strongly affects software volume, where "wasteful" coding may double the volume of produced code (KLOC).

b. *Documentation comments volume*: volume of documentation comments included in the code: affects volume of the code. The volume of comments is usually determined by the programming style (KLOC).

c. *Software complexity*: Complex modules require much more development time (per line of code) in comparison to simple modules. Complex modules also suffer from more defects than simple modules of similar size (KLOC, NDE, and NCE).

d. *Percentage of reused code*: The higher the percentage of reused code incorporated into the software developed, the greater the volume of code that may be produced per day, and the lower the number of defects detected in reviews, testing, and regular use (NDE, NCE).

e. *Design review quality*: Professionalism and thoroughness of design reviews and software testing: affects the number of defects detected (NCE).

f. *Reporting style of review results*: Reporting style of the review and testing results: some teams produce concise reports that present the findings in a small number of items (small NDE and NCE), while others produce comprehensive reports, showing the same findings for a large number of items (large NDE and NCE).

The main factors affecting the magnitude of the product HD and corrective maintenance parameters are:

a. *Quality of installed software*: The quality of the installed software and its documentation is determined by the quality of the development team as well as that of the review and testing teams. The lower the quality of the maintained software, the greater the anticipated software failures identified and subsequent maintenance efforts (NYF, NHYC).

b. *Programming style and volume of documentation comments*: Programming style and volume of comments included in the code defined in the development stage both strongly impact the volume of software to be maintained, where wasteful coding and documentation may double the volume of code to be maintained (KLOC).

c. *Software complexity*: Complex modules require investment of many more maintenance resources per line of code than do simple modules, and suffer from more defects left undetected during the development stage (NYF, NHYC).

d. *Percentage of reused code*: The higher the percentage of reused code, the lower the number of defects detected in regular use, as well as the fewer required corrective maintenance and HD efforts (NYF, NHYC).

e. *Number of installations*: The size of the user population and level of applications in use affects the number of HD calls, as well as the number of defects detected by users during regular use (NHYC, NYF).

By impacting the magnitude of the parameters, these factors distort the software process and software product quality metrics on which they are based. The inevitable result is that a major portion of the metrics that we have discussed does not reflect the real productivity and quality achievements of development or maintenance teams in what may be the majority of situations. As a result, the possibility to compare the performance achievements becomes very limited. While a comparison of projects performed by the same team is less affected by the obstacles mentioned above, comparison between different departments becomes problematic. In other words, many of the metric applications reviewed here are characterized by limited validity and comprehensiveness.

Examples of practices used to resolve some of the mentioned difficulties are by counting coding lines without comments, adding a factor to counted lines of comments (i.e., 0.5), adding a factor to reused software lines (i.e. 0.2) and using weighting factors to reflect severity of failures or complexity of software tasks.

Substantial research efforts are needed in order to develop metrics appropriate for the software industry. The function point method, discussed in Section 23.4, is an example of a successful methodological development aimed at replacing the problematic KLOC metric.

Discussion of the difficulties in applying software quality metrics, especially for decision-making in the context of software development, was presented by Rifkin (2001), McQuaid and Dekkers (2004), Texel (2015a, 2015b), and Cross (2004).

Summary

1. **The categories of software process metrics**

   A two-level system of categories is used here. The first level distinguishes between four categories:
   1. Software development process quality metrics
   2. Software operation process quality metrics
   3. Software maintenance process quality metrics
   4. Management process quality metrics

   The second level of metrics classes includes:
   - Software operation process quality metrics
   - Software operation process quality metrics
   - Software operation process effectiveness, efficiency, and productivity metrics

   Software maintenance process metrics include the following:
   - Software maintenance process workload metrics
   - Software maintenance process quality metrics
   - Software maintenance process effectiveness, efficiency, and productivity metrics

   Management process metrics include the following:
   - Software development process management metrics
   - Software reuse process metrics

2. **Count metrics versus weighted metrics**

   A common way to compare quality of software development or operation services is by comparing the number of events or errors. A familiar reaction will raise the question – Are the errors comparable? The weighted metric is a good way of reaching an improved solution that combines the count and severity of events in one metric.

3. **Metrics for measuring the quality of readymade software components**

   Suitability metrics are a tool for determining and comparing preferences of COTS software components. It is expected that the COTS or open-source software component will not only own part of the functionalities required but also own some extra functionalities not specifically required (but that still may prove useful). Combined suitability metrics are created using weight factors to represent the relative values of conforming functionalities and the extra functionalities.

4. **Software reuse process metrics as management process metrics**

Reuse practices are used for software code and software documentation. The metrics are designed to reveal the success level of the management policy of promoting reuse in the organization. Software reuse substantially affects productivity and efficiency of software development processes.

5. **Difficulties characterizing some software quality metrics**

A unique difficulty faced by users of software quality metrics is rooted in the measures (parameters) that comprise many of the software quality metrics. As a result, a large proportion of software metrics, including most of the commonly used ones, suffer from low validity and limited comprehensiveness. Examples of metrics that exhibit severe weaknesses are:

- Software development metrics that are based on measures such as KLOC, NDE, and NCE.
- Product maintenance metrics that are based on measures such as KLOC, NHYC, and NYF.

For example, the KLOC measure is affected by the programming style, volume of documentation comments included in the code, and the complexity of the software. NYF is affected by the quality of the installed software and its documentation as well as the percentage of reused code, among the other factors affecting maintenance.

Selected bibliography

Aggarwal K. K., Singh Y., Kaur A., and Malhotra R. (2007) Software design metrics for object-oriented software, *Journal of Object Technology*, Vol. 6, No. 1, pp. 121–138.

Aloysius A. and Maheswaran K. (2015) A review on component based software metrics, *International Journal Fuzzy Mathematical Archive*, Vol. 7, No. 2, pp. 185–194.

Ani Z. C., Basri S. and Sarlan A. (2015) Validating reusability of software projects using object-oriented design metrics, in *Information Science and Applications, Part 7*, Springer, Berlin, pp. 845–850.

Barkmann H., Linke R., and Lowe W. (2009) *Quantitative evaluation of software quality metrics in open-source projects*, Advanced Information Networking Workshops, WAINA'09, Bradford, May 2009, pp. 1067–1072.

Cheikhi L., Al-Qutaish R. A., Idri A., and Sallami A. (2014) Chidamber and Kemerer object-oriented measures: analysis of their design from a metrology perspective, *International Journal of Software Engineering and its Applications*, Vol. 8, No. 2, pp. 359–374.

Cross P. (2004) The uses and abuses of software metrics, *Software Quality Professionl*, Vol. 6, No. 2, pp. 4–16.

Darcy D. P. and Kemerer C. F. (2005) OO metrics in practice, *IEEE Software*, Vol. 22 No. 1, pp. 17–19.

Fenton, N. E. and Bieman J. (2015) *Software Metrics: A Rigorous and Practical Approach*, 3rd Edition, CRC Press, Boca Raton, FL.

Ferreira K. A. M., Bigonha M. A. S., Bigonha R. S., Mendes L. F. O., and Almeida H. C. (2012) Identifying thresholds for object-oriented software metrics, *Journal of Systems and Software*, Vol. 85, No. 2, pp. 244–257.

ISO/IEC (2014) *ISO/IEC 90003:2014 Software Engineering – Guidelines for the Application of ISO 9001: 2008 to Computer Software*, International Organization for Standardization (ISO), Geneva, Switzerland.

ISO/IEC (2007) *ISO/IEC Std. 15939 Software and Systems Engineering – Measurement Process*, International Organization for Standardization (ISO), Geneva, Switzerland.

ISO/IEC/IEEE (2008) *ISO/IEC/IEEE Std. 12207-2008 – Systems and Software Engineering – Software Life Cycle Processes*, International Organization for Standardization (ISO), Geneva, Switzerland.

Kitchenham B. (2010) What's up with software metrics? A preliminary mapping study, *Journal of Systems and Software*, Vol. 83, No. 1, pp. 37–51.

McQuaid P. A. and Dekkers C. A. Steer clear of hazards on the road to software measurement success, *Software Quality Professional*, Vol. 6, No. 2, pp. 27–33.

Mordal K., Anquetil N., Laval J., Serebrenik A., Vasilescu B., and Ducasse S. (2012) Software quality metrics aggregation in industry, *Journal of Software: Evolution and Progress*, Vol. 25, No. 10, pp. 1117–1135.

Nicolette D. (2015) *Software Development Metrics*, Manning Publishing, Shelter Island, NY.

Radjenovic D., Hencko M., Torkar R., and Zivkovic A. (2013) Software fault prediction metrics: a systematic literature review, *Information and Software Technology*, Vol. 55, No. 8, pp. 1397–1418.

Rifkin S. (2001) What makes measuring software so hard? *IEEE Software*, Vol. 18 (3), pp. 41–45.

Texel P. P. (2015a) Exploring government contractor experiences assessing and reporting software development status, Doctoral dissertation,Faculty of Management, Walden University.

Texel P. P. (2015b) *Measuring software development status: Do we really know where we are?* in Southeastcon 2015 Conference, Fort Lauderdale, FL, pp. 1–6.

Venkatesan V. P. and Krishnamoorthy M. (2009) A metrics suite for measuring software components, *Journal of Convergence Information Technology*, Vol. 4, No. 2, pp. 138–153.

Review questions

21.1 Table 21.6 defines the following two code error density metrics: CEDL and WCEDL.

    a. Compare CEDL and WCEDL including references to their managerial application characteristics as well as their validity.

    b. Which of the above metrics would you prefer? List your arguments.

21.2 Table 21.10 defines the following two development productivity metrics: DevPL and DevPF

    a. Compare DevPL and DevPF including references to their managerial implementation characteristics as well as to their validity.

    b. Which of the above metrics – DevPL or DevPF – would you prefer in this case? List your arguments.

21.3 Section 21.4 and Section 21.5 list metrics for USC and corrective maintenance services.

  a. Explain the difference between these services.

  b. Justify the separate metric categories and actions (based on their differences).

21.4 Table 21.15 defines two maintenance failure density metrics – SFDL and SFDF.

  a. Evaluate each of the above metrics as to the degree they fulfill the requirements for a software quality metric as listed in Frame 23.2.

  b. Indicate the expected direction of distortion for each of the metrics.

21.5 USC services are vital for successful regular use of a software system.

  a. Suggest situations where the USC service is a failure.

  b. What metrics can be applied for the failure situations mentioned in (a)?

21.6 Section 21.6 describes several measures used to construct the software development management metrics presented in this section.

  • Based on the listed measures, suggest a new schedule metrics and a new process productivity metrics.

21.7 Section 21.4 and Section 21.5 describe several measures used to construct the USC and corrective maintenance metrics presented in this section.

  • Based on the listed measures, suggest two new USC call density metrics and two new software system reliability metrics.

21.8 Choose one of the corrective maintenance quality metrics described in Section 21.4 that includes NYF as one of its measures.

  a. Examine the five factors affecting the maintenance measures listed in Section 21.7 and indicate in which direction the metrics you have chosen might be biased by each one, and indicate how this bias affects the metric's validity.

  b. Examine the above factors and indicate how each of them may limit the comprehensiveness of the metrics you have chosen.

Topics for discussion

21.1 Two versions for the measure of software system size – KLOC – are applied: one version counts every code line, while the other only counts the noncomment lines of code.

  a. Discuss the advantages and disadvantages of each version. Refer to the validity of both versions.

  b. Try to suggest an improved version that will comply with the arguments you mentioned in your answer to (a).

21.2 The selection of quality metrics presented in Tables 21.3 and 21.4 includes several error severity, error density, and weighted error metrics.

    a. Explain the importance of error severity and error density metrics, and illustrate with examples why the use of only one of the metrics does not provide the full picture of the software error situation.

    b. Explain the contribution of the weighted error density metrics to the improvement of the evaluation of the error situation. Use the examples of (a) to support your arguments.

21.3 Examine the metrics described in Tables 21.3 and 21.4.

    a. Analyze the measures (parameters) that comprise the respective metrics and decide whether they are objective or subjective, where objective measures are based on reliable counts, and subjective measures are partly or totally determined through professional evaluation.

    b. Compare the attributes of objective and subjective measures.

    c. List the advantages and disadvantages of the two types of measures.

21.4 The two software development department teams have recently completed their projects. Both applied the same development tool and similar programming style.

    The following measures (see Table 21.3) were supplied:

	Team A	Team B
NCE	154	91
NDE	223	206

    a. What additional data would you require to determine which of the teams achieved results with the better quality?

    b. After examining the metrics, what differences in software quality conception held by the team leaders may be concluded from the results?

21.5 Choose one of the process metrics described in Table 21.6 that includes KLOC as one of the constituent measures.

    a. Examine the six factors listed in Section 21.7 affecting KLOC (as a measure of the software development task) and indicate for each one the direction in which there might be a bias to the metrics you have chosen. Explain how each bias could affect metric validity.

    b. Examine the above factors and indicate the way in which each of them may limit the comprehensiveness of the metrics you have chosen.

21.6 Comparison of the number of errors detected during the development process for the recently completed project with the team's previous project revealed the following:

	Recent project	Former project
Total number of errors detected	188	346

a. What additional data would you require to determine whether real progress in software quality has been achieved (as claimed by the team leader)?

b. Which software quality metrics would you use to examine the team leader's claim?

Chapter 22

Software Change Control Processes

22.1 Introduction

The software development process is inevitably characterized by a constant flow of change requests from customers and sometimes other parties involved in the software project. Carrying out a change during the software development process involves investing additional resources; their quantity varies according to the nature of the request, and the development stage of the project. The need to cope with software changes throughout the software life cycle is one of the more important and onerous tasks of the software development and maintenance teams. Moreover, performing changes usually under time constraints is one of the processes more susceptible to software errors.

The process of examining change requests; selecting which should be rejected and which approved, along with scheduling of the implementation of approved changes is the software change control (SCC) process. The SCC function in the development organization performs the following tasks:

a. Examination of requested or suggested changes.

b. Approval of implementation of only those changes which are worthy and necessary, while all remaining are rejected.

c. Scheduling of the implementation of each of the approved changes.

d. Follow-up of the approved changes.

Following change control processes correctly throughout the software life cycle is key to the effective and efficient performance of software development and maintenance.

The importance of SCC is stressed in Section 5.3 of the IEEE Std. 730-2014 (IEEE 2014) and Section 7.3 of the ISO/IEC Std. 90003:2014 (ISO/IEC 2014). Change control issues are likewise discussed in software engineering books,

Software Quality: Concepts and Practice, First Edition. Daniel Galin.
© 2018 the IEEE Computer Society, Inc. Published 2018 by John Wiley & Sons, Inc.

such as Pressman and Maxim (2015). Also worth mentioning is Reifer (2012), a book specializing in the diverse issues of software change management, while various aspects are also discussed in Wang et al. (2008).

The next sections discuss the following:

- The process of handling an SCR
  - Submission of software change requests
  - Examination of SCRs by the SCC committees
  - Approval to carry out requested changes by the SCC committee
  - Follow-up of software change processes by the SCC committee
- The SCC function in the organization
- The role of SQ when following the SCC process

Before turning to study the above topics, let us observe a mini case in Section 22.2 presenting the potential damage from careless running of the software change control process.

22.2 How a well-planned project lost over half a million dollars – a mini case

The quarterly management review meeting opened with the usual progress report on project performance and maintenance team accomplishments. But the main subject that morning was the city taxes project, which had lost over half a million dollars.

Patrick, head of software development, was the first to speak. "The project was to yield a profit of half a million. We invested a great deal of time and effort planning and budgeting our proposal, and our most experienced project managers conducted the contract review. Staffing of the teams went smoothly, no other difficulties were encountered, and the project even progressed according to schedule – for the first 4 months that is. In fact, we were actually one week ahead of schedule, and even started discussing the possibility of receiving the 2% bonus for early completion . . ."

Patrick continued: "During the next 3 months, progress slowed down, and by the end of the seventh month, the project was about two weeks behind schedule. During this time, resources invested increased to 15% more than the original project estimates. Consequently, the number of staff was also increased in efforts to reduce, and finally eliminate, the project delay. Unfortunately, this costly action reaped no success. It was at this stage that we realized that the reasons for the project delay were rooted in the software change control joint committee's decisions. After examining the committee's decisions, we noted that 97% of the software change requests (SCRs) were placed by the customer; 94% of these were approved, and software change orders (SCOs) were issued accordingly. The committee, in addition to granting approval, had to define charges for performing these changes, and approve project completion delays according to schedule delay estimations. The committee showed remarkable 'generosity'; and below are some painful facts affirming this:

- 34 change requests were approved with no charge and no estimated schedule delay. In total, about 250 working days were invested in completing these 34 SCOs.

- The committee approved a schedule delay of only one week for design and coding resources needed for each of the two major SCRs; this was obviously insufficient.

A typical, and especially outrageous, example was the committee's handling of an SCR requesting to entirely change tax reduction rules relating to various populations of deprived and low income city residents, such as unemployed citizens, students and low-income pensioners. Additional changes were also requested to tax reduction rules related to poor neighborhoods. This important SCR, despite the fact that it should have been approved, was only placed at a stage when almost all coding for the current reduction rules had been completed."

At this point, he turned to the audience and asked, "What extra resources do you think the committee should have approved for the design and coding efforts needed for performing this SCR? How many weeks delay in schedule would you deem to have been appropriate?" He continued, without actually waiting for anyone to say anything. "The committee, as expected, approved the SCR, but, would you believe it, they decided to grant the extra resource of 10 working days, with no expected delay to the schedule."

At this stage, the general manager who was heading the meeting stopped Patrick and asked, "What could be the explanation for the 'generosity' of the committee?"

Patrick answered immediately, "I thoroughly searched the committee documentation regarding the SCC discussions, and to my surprise only a few records included estimates of the resources needed to perform the approved SCOs. Still, I believe that George and Norman, both company members of the committee, were greatly influenced by the interest shown by management in this first project for the new city management. Everyone stressed the great potential, and so it was understood that the client's satisfaction was of utmost importance. The committee members grossly exaggerated, and in no way did they take into account the accumulated burden they put on the development teams."

At this point, one of the meeting participants asked: "Why didn't the committee approve the so obviously necessary schedule delays?"

Patrick let out a sigh, "The committee's decisions were motivated by the developers' promises to install the final project after testing before the beginning of the new fiscal year, and for the system to be fully implemented at the beginning of the new year."

A short discussion followed before the general manager summarized the meeting:

a. The SCC committee's first consideration should be: Is the immediate implementation of the SCR really necessary, should it be delayed to the second version of the software project, or not handled at all?

b. The SCC committee should perform its duties, including decision-making, in a more professional way, and base their decisions, among other considerations, on estimates of (1) additional required development resources and (2) additional project time needed to implement the requested change. All these estimates should be fully documented.

c. Performance of the SCC committee should be audited.

22.3 The process of handling an SCR

The process of handling an SCR

- Submission of software change requests
- Examination of the SCR by the SCC committee
- Approval to carry out requested changes by the SCC committee
- Follow-up of software change processes by the SCC committee

22.3.1 Submission of software change requests

From the very beginning of the software development process till later on, sometimes years later in the operational stage of a software system, SCRs continue to flow. These SCR initiatives (also termed as change requests (CRs) and engineering change request (ECRs)) may relate to one or more of the following:

- A need to correct a software error.
- A need to adapt the software to changes in the operations of a customer's business or organization missions.
- A need to adapt the software to a new customer's needs.
- A need to adapt the software to changes in general business and market changes.
- A proposal to update and improve the software product, to achieve higher customer satisfaction (in custom-made projects) or to affect the marketability of the software (in COTS software).
- A need to adapt the software to budget and schedule constraints.

Initiatives to submit SCRs in the software development stage are mainly proposed by the customer and the developer. In the software operational stage, it is the maintenance teams and customers (COTS software customers and custom-made software customers) who initiate.

A typical SCR template is shown in Frame 22.1

Frame 22.1: Software change request (SCR) document – a template

Change principles

- The initiator
- The date the SCR was presented
- The character of the change
- The goals
- The expected contribution to the project/system
- The urgency to complete

Change details

- Description of the proposed change
- A list of the software configuration items (SCIs) to be changed
- Expected effect on other SCIs
- Expected effect on interfaces with other software and hardware systems
- Expected delays in development schedules and expected interruption to customer software services.

Change schedule and resources estimates

- Schedule for implementation
- Estimated required professional resources
- Other resources required
- Estimated total cost of requested change

22.3.2   Examination of SCR

The SCC committee performs an examination of each SCR by professionals. The SCR evaluation report refers to the various aspect of the request, and serves as a basis for the SCC committee's decision

22.3.3   Approval to carry out requested changes

The factors affecting the decision whether to implement a proposed change include:

- Expected contribution of the proposed change
- Urgency and preference of the change.

- Effect of the proposed change on project schedule, level of service, and so on.
- Estimated required professional resources and cost of performing change.
- Estimated delays in project schedule and completion time, resulting from the change implementation.

Decisions regarding each SCR are made by the SCC committee after examining the SCR. In part of the cases, decisions are made by a specialized change control team appointed by the SCC committee.

The SCC committee may approve, delay, or deny the request for immediate implementation. For each SCR approved for immediate implementation, a SCO is issued. In some organizations, these orders are called change orders (CO) or engineering change orders (ECO). The SCO provides the change details, its costs and schedule, which may differ from the original estimates, as the SCC committee exercised its discretion on the related issues of the SCR.

22.3.4 Follow-up of software change processes

The SCC committee follows-up implementation of the SCQs regarding conformance to the project schedule, successful completion of change activities, and the actual resources utilized for the SCO.

Experience gained in follow-up activities provides the SCC committee with improved know-how on what to base its future decisions.

22.4 The SCC function in the organization

The responsibility for implementation of the above SCC tasks in software development and maintenance organizations is usually assigned to professional committee appointed by the management. Additional *ad hoc* members include the project manager, the customer representative, and experts for specific subjects. This committee is commonly called the software change control authority (SCCA) or the software change control board (SCCB), and also frequently known as the change control authority (CCA) or change control board (CCB). In some cases, the SCC function is performed by the software configuration management board (SCMB), who appoints an SCC committee.

The operation of SCC activities is supported by SCC procedures defining the process of SCR submission, and the activities of the SCC committee.

During the software development phase, when the development is carried out according to a contract, the main considerations of the SCCA committee are the cost of changes and schedule delays. During the operational phase, the SCCA decisions, typical to maintenance, are the continuity of regular service, in addition to cost of changes. In organizations developing COTS software, it is expected that decisions regarding SCRs are strongly affected by merchantability considerations.

22.5   Software quality assurance activities related to software change control

The SCC committee, whose decisions might have a strong effect on the quality of the development and maintenance processes, as well as the development product, clearly needs to oversee software quality assurance activities, including:

- Review of change control procedures
- Initiation of changes and improvement revisions of SCC procedures
- Review of the SCC committee's performance: compliance with procedures, completeness of SCR examinations by the committee, and delays in decision making by the committee.
- Review of SCC decisions regarding approvals and rejections, approved additional resources, project completion delays and more
- Auditing of the implementation of SCOs; on schedule and implementation processes of the approved changes

Summary

1. **The components of the SCR**
   The components are:
   Change principles, including the goals of the change, its expected contribution, and the urgency of the change.
   Change details, including descriptions of the required change, a list of software configuration items to be changed or impacted by the proposed change, and expected delays in development schedules and customer service interruptions.
   Change schedule and resources estimates, including implementation schedules and resources, and cost estimates.
2. **The main tasks of software change control**
   The main tasks of software change control committee can be listed as follows:
   - To examine software change requests (SCRs)
   - To approve SCR and issue SCOs
   - To follow-up and control requested changes
   - Quality assurance of software changes

3. **The SCC function in the organization**

   The responsibility for the SCC tasks is assigned to a professional SCC committee assigned by the management. In some cases, the committee is called a change control board (SCCB), or a change control authority (SCCA). Project managers and customer representatives serve as *ad hoc* members of the committee, and are assigned according to the specific subject. Performance of SCC activities is supported by SCC procedures, which define the SCR submission process, and activities of the SCC committee.

4. **The SQA unit reviews and audits the SCC procedures and activities:**
   - Review of change control procedures.
   - Initiation of changes and improvement revisions of SCC procedures.
   - Reviews of the SCC committee's performance.
   - Reviews of SCC decisions regarding approvals and rejections.
   - Auditing of the SCO implementation.

Selected bibliography

IEEE (2014) *TEEE Std. 730-2014 IEEE Standard for Software Quality Assurance Processes*, IEEE, Piscataway, NJ.

ISO/IEC (2014) *ISO/IEC 90003:2014 Software Engineering – Guidelines for the Application of ISO 9001: 2008 to Computer Software*, International Organization for Standardization (ISO), Geneva, Switzerland.

Pressman R. J. and Maxim B. R. (2015) *Software Engineering – A Practitioner's Approach*, 8th Edition, European adaptation, McGraw-Hill International, London.

Reifer D. J. (2012) *Software Change Management: Case Studies and Practical Advice (Developer Best Practices)*, Microsoft Press, Redmond, Washington.

Wang E. T. G., Ju P-H., Jiang J. J., and Klein G. (2008) The effect of change control and management review on software flexibility and project performance, *Information and Management*, Vol. 85, pp. 438–442.

Review questions

22.1 An SCR relating to changes in only two of the software source SCIs has been approved. However, the software test plan prepared by the Testing Unit included nine of the system's software source SCIs.

- Explain in your own words why it may not be sufficient only to test the two SCIs specified in the SCR after they were changed.

22.2 The SCC committee assigns the task of examination of an SCR to one of the committee members.

a. Why is there a need to examine the submitted SCR?

b. List types of expected examination findings that need to be corrected

22.3 The SQA unit periodic review of the activities of the organization's |SCCA identified many shortcomings in the committee's activities and decisions.

a. List at least four different types of shortcomings.

b. Suggest ways to prevent succession of each of the shortcomings mentioned in (a).

Topics for discussion

22.1 A developer's success to complete a project, while successfully fulfilling the project requirements and being on schedule depends, to a great extent, on compliance to SCC procedures.

a. While referring to the software change control tasks, explain in your own words the risks incurred with software quality by only partially complying with SCC procedures.

b. It is widely accepted that by performing a full SCR process, the risks of failing to complete a software development project on schedule are substantially reduced. Explain

22.2 Two SCRs have been placed before the CCB for a decision. Some of their characteristics are:

SCR-1:

- Expected to contribute substantially to the sales of the company's leading software package.
- Essence of the change: introduction of new software functions.
- Changes in two software SCIs are required.
- Other SCIs expected to be affected by the requested change – none.
- Estimate of required professional resources – 40 man-days.
- Estimated timetable for implementation – 2 months.

SCR-2

- Expected to save substantial help desk resources, due to the improved user interface.
- Essence of the change: improvement of the user interface to make it easier and more user-friendly.
- Changes in 11 software SCIs are required.
- Other SCIs expected to be affected by the requested change – 8.
- Estimate of required professional resources – 15 man-days.
- Estimated timetable for implementation – 2 months.

a. Can you determine which of the requests deserve the higher priority? What are your supporting arguments?

b. If you find it difficult to determine the priorities, what additional information do you require to prioritize the SCRs?

22.3 The software maintenance department provides services to 215 customers who use one or more of the company's three popular software packages. From time to time, a maintenance team discovers that the software version installed in a customer's site includes unrecorded changes that were not requested by an SCR, nor approved as part of an SCO.

    f. Who do you believe inserted the unrecorded changes and under what conditions could this have occurred?

    g. What effect could this event have on maintenance performance, and what is the expected influence on software quality from the perspective of the customer?

    h. What measures could be taken to make sure that no such unauthorized changes occur?

Chapter 23

Staff Skills and Knowledge – Training and Certification

23.1 Introduction

Successful team performance is based on the staff possessing adequate skills and knowledge. Accordingly, skill and knowledge requirements are discussed with every team candidate. The organization's skill and knowledge requirements may differ from specific projects. Project-specific requirements may be included in the project contract requirements.

It goes without saying that keeping staff abreast of the latest professional advancements available is the key to achieving quality in development and maintenance. Moreover, it is generally accepted that regular professional training, retraining, and updating are mandatory, if the gap between required and current professional knowledge is to be maintained as narrow as possible.

Position certification (hereinafter "certification") is conducted for staff members assigned to key positions, and is a way of achieving conformance of a candidate's skill and knowledge to a specific position's skill and knowledge requirements. It may be conducted for software development and maintenance positions. Certification may be considered as another complementary tool for ensuring suitable professional skill and knowledge of team members. Position certification of staff should not, however, be confused with professional certification awarded by the American Society for Quality (ASQ), IEEE Computer Society, in addition to other types of professional certification granted by commercial organizations such as Microsoft or Red Hat.

The importance of professional training as a vital component of any SQA system is emphasized in ISO/IEC 90003-2014 (ISO, 2014) (Section 6.2.2), as well as the CMM Guidelines.

The case where staff skill and knowledge assessment for a project and the plan for determining the needed staff training are discussed by IEEE Std. 730-2014 (IEEE, 2014) (Sec. 5.5.6). Training program for software quality managers,

---

Software Quality: Concepts and Practice, First Edition. Daniel Galin.
© 2018 the IEEE Computer Society, Inc. Published 2018 by John Wiley & Sons, Inc.

activities, and evaluation methods of quality programs are discussed by Baker and Fisher (2008).

The training and certification objectives and activities are dealt with in Sections 23.3–23.7.

Section 23.2 illustrates potential damages to a project when no staff knowledge and skills assessment have been performed, and subsequently no training or certification were required.

23.2   Surprises for the "3S" development team – an introductory mini case

Team 7 of "3S - Sahara Software Specialists" started its new project for Apollo Ltd. 3 weeks late due to delays in the completion of a previous project. Severely pressured for time, the team leader decided to cancel the scheduled 5-day training course on the new Athena application generator to be used for subsystem F – as required by contract. He believed that the concise Athena manuals supplied by the customer would be an adequate substitute for the course. This decision, however, proved to be very costly. The two team members responsible for subsystem F found it very difficult to operate a generator they had never used. In addition to 3 days spent receiving expert advice, they needed to spend a total of 25 working days over the scheduled number of days to complete development of the subsystem. At this point, the project was already 2 weeks behind schedule, yet the team still hoped that they would be able to close the gap over the 18 weeks left to complete the package, prior to the system tests. Then, within the space of 2 weeks, two of the team's six programmers suddenly resigned and left. As no in-house programmers were available to be shifted, management contacted an employment agency with a request to find replacements as quickly as possible. The team leader was relieved as the urgently needed programmers were located and temporarily recruited within a few days. Under immense pressure, the team leader decided to undergo the regular recruitment procedure that required certifying new programmers and conducting certification courses, when necessary. The newly recruited employees were immediately sent to the programmer stations. Both new team members were experienced programmers, and almost never troubled the other team members with requests for assistance or instruction. This arrangement seemed to suit the situation wonderfully as it did not interfere with the intensive efforts the team was exerting to complete the project with minimal delay.

Considering the project's unexpected difficulties – the Athena application problems and two programmers resigning – the team felt very lucky when they managed to complete the programming stage by November 11, only 11 days behind schedule.

The team's troubles began in earnest with the issuance of the test report 3 weeks later. Together with a long list of minor defects, the report mentioned numerous severe faults in units A2, A6, A7, A9, and A11 of subsystems A and F5, and F7 of subsystem F. Although correction of the faults detected in units F5 and F7 required only 5 days' programmer time, correcting the faults found in the other units proved to be a whole different story. All five units of subsystem A were programmed by John Abrams, one of the temporary programmers recruited by the agency. The two team members who were directed to repair the units were confronted with unexpected difficulties: In addition to severe programming errors and what appeared to be a total lack of understanding in regards to the relevant design documents, the coding did not comply with any of the company coding procedures or work instructions. When describing the situation, the temporary workers jokingly stated that they felt more like archaeologists than programmers. Later, they concluded that John Abrams's professional qualifications were far below those claimed in his letters of recommendation. After investing several days attempting to correct the errors, four out of the five units had to be recoded, as all efforts to repair the existing code were to no avail. Altogether, 6 exhausting weeks were spent verifying the units were operative.

At this point, 7 weeks behind schedule, the team leader concluded that the "super saving strategy" applied to the "super recruitment procedure shortcut" as well as to the recruiter training, instruction, and follow-up, had proven to be quite costly.

23.3   The objectives of training

The objectives of software development staff training are listed in Frame 23.1 and those of the SQA function team are listed in Frame 23.2.

Frame 23.1:   The objectives of software development staff training

The objectives of software development staff training
• To develop the knowledge and skills required by new staff to perform software development tasks, including those related to quality assurance at an adequate level of efficiency and effectiveness. Such training facilitates the integration of new team members.   • To bring up to date the knowledge and skills of the existing staff in response to developments in the organization and technology, and to ensure efficient and effective performance of updated requirements of project tasks.

The mentioned objectives conform to the general goals of software quality assurance by inspiring management to persistently nurture the level of knowledge and skills of the organization's staff and improve its efficiency and effectiveness. The objectives of the SQA function team training are presented in Frame 23.2.

Frame 23.2: The objectives of the SQA function team training

The objectives of the SQA function team training
• To develop the knowledge and skills related to SQA methodology, and the procedures and standards adopted by the organization required by new SQA function team members to perform their tasks at an adequate level of efficiency and effectiveness. Such training facilitates integration of new team members in the SQA function. • To bring up to date the knowledge and skills of the existing staff in response to developments in the organization and SQA methodology, and to ensure efficient and effective performance of updated requirements of tasks.

23.4 The staff training process for software development

The operation of successful training demands that the following activities be regularly performed:

- Audit needs for professional training and updating needs for filling any knowledge gaps for the software development staff.
- Plan training and upskill programs for the software development staff.
- Conduct training programs for the software development staff.
- Perform follow-up on training activities and new knowledge acquired by trainees.

All these activities converge into an integrated process in which feedback from past activities, and information about professional developments, stimulate a cycle of continuous training and adaptation to changing software engineering and quality assurance requirements.

Comprehensive follow-up of the outcomes of current programs, as well as keeping track of developments in the profession are required to make sure that programs are performed and are adequately up-to-date.

The role of the SQA function is supportive regarding the skill and knowledge required from software development staff, especially related to quality assurance topics.

The training process for software development staff is displayed in Figure 23.1.

A detailed discussion of each of these activities is presented in the next sections.

23.4.1 Determine training and updating needs for software development positions

Most organizations set education and professional training requirements for each of the software development and maintenance positions. Staff members who

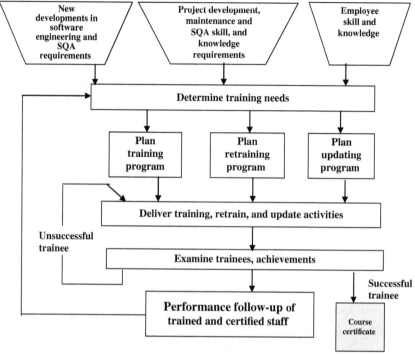

Figure 23.1 The software development staff training process.

fulfill these requirements still need additional "local" or "internal" knowledge and skills, related to specific development and maintenance procedures. This specialized knowledge can be grouped into two categories:

- Knowledge and skills related to software engineering topics, such as software development tools, programming language version, and CASE tool version, applied by the specific organization or unit.

- Knowledge of quality assurance topics, such as the procedures pertaining to the various development and maintenance activities, assigned to be performed by the individual in a specific position.

Training and updating needs are determined by a comparison of the staff's current knowledge with the updated knowledge requirements. The type of training is adapted to the needs of three distinct groups of staff:

- Training: for new employees, according to their designated assignment.
- Retraining: for employees assigned to new positions or new assignments.
- Updating: for staff members as demanded by their position.

The need to train new employees and retrain and update staff should be assessed regularly to facilitate planning of the required programs.

The guide for software engineering body of knowledge – SWEBOK (Bourque and Fairley, 2014) can serve as a source for determining general software engineering knowledge and skill requirements.

23.4.2 Plan training and updating programs

Practically speaking, two basic programs should be devised for software development staff – one for software engineering topics and one for SQA topics.

The planning of training, retraining, and updating activities refers to the program contents, the number of participants, and the form of training. Of special importance is the choice of the form of training: traditional training course, workshops, computer-based training, web-based training, self-study, mentor supervision, and on-the-job training.

Planning training programs for software engineering topics

The timing and number of participants of many training and retraining activities cannot be determined in advance, as new personnel is recruited and veteran staff shifted – often after relatively short notice. Thus, the training and retraining activities, being of an *ad hoc* nature and varying number of trainees, should be planned accordingly and employ the adequate form of training. Irrespective of whether the programs are carried out in-house or by an outsourcing organization, high-level staff, such as the chief software engineer, usually participates in their preparation.

Implementation tip

Unless the software development organization is rather large, it is often the case that only one or a small number of new staff needs to be trained or retrained. Moreover, as new employees may be recruited to a variety of different positions, the training program may need to be highly differentiated. When the same training program applies to all the recruited employees, the training is frequently inappropriate for carrying out specific tasks, and will have subsequent negative implications on the trainees' performance in their new role. The appropriate solution for these circumstances is to prepare personal training options and to employ a variety of training such as computer-based training, self–training, on-the-job training, and so on.

Planning update programs for software engineering topics

Updating activities can be scheduled well ahead, to be performed once in a period, for example, once every 3 months. The audience of these updating activities is known, and the program contents closed up to the date of the training.

Planning update programs for SQA topics

Updating programs for SQA topics are carried out for new employees as well as for the more senior staff members. Typical SQA updating programs are carried out once a year or once every 6 months, depending on the pace of change. The topics to be discussed include new and updated SQA procedures, analysis of software quality failures, quality success stories, and so on. The SQA unit or the unit designated to be responsible for SQA issues in the organization usually prepares these training and updating programs.

23.4.3   Perform training programs for software development staff

The training team is responsible for performing the training. Retraining and updating programs need to cover *ad hoc* requirements of newly recruited and repositioned employees. These activities include registering the candidates and taking care of all the logistics. Only those who completed successfully the examinations will be eligible to join the software development and maintenance teams.

23.4.4   Perform follow-up of training activities and trainees

Managers and software professionals often express doubts about the effectiveness of training in general, or regarding specific activities. They question whether the substantial resources and efforts invested in training are really worthwhile. To assuage these doubts and for additional considerations, systematic follow-up is necessary:

- To provide information to verify whether all training program activities were conducted and about the participation of enlisted participants.
- To provide feedback indicating whether the training efforts were justified in terms of improved productivity and quality of trainee performance.
- To identify ineffective and unsuccessful training activities in order to ensure continuous improvement of training activities.

Analysis of the data accumulated following a training course or an individual training session provides the information necessary to revise programs by guiding the modification: addition and deletion of identified activities and materials.

The follow-up information sources include:

- Performance data, collected regularly and processes into metrics – such as errors and productivity metrics, corrective maintenance statistics and resources invested – prepared by the respective units. For a discussion of software quality metrics in general and the specific issue of performance metrics – see Chapters 16 and 21.

- Questionnaires completed by the trainees, their superiors, customers, and others.
- Information regarding outstanding achievements, as well as failures.
- Specialized review of software products (documents and code) prepared by trained employees.

The Corrective Action Board (CAB), based on the follow-up subsequent to training and other sources of information, may initiate training programs improvements. For more about process improvements and corrective and preventive actions in the context of training and other issues, see Chapter 19.

23.5 The training process for the SQA function team

Conducting successful training for the SQA function team requires the following activities to be regularly performed:

- Determine needs for professional training and needs for filling any knowledge gaps for the SQA function team.
- Plan training and upskill programs for the SQA function team.
- Conduct training programs for the SQA function team.
- Perform follow-up on training activities and new knowledge acquired by trainees.

Comprehensive follow-up of the outcomes of current programs, as well as keeping track of developments in the profession are required to make sure that programs are performed and are adequately up-to-date.

The training process for the SQA function team is very similar to the process displayed in Figure 23.1.

23.5.1 Determine training and updating needs for software development positions

SQA functions position require skill and knowledge of the following three categories:

Most organizations set education and professional training requirements for each of the software development and maintenance positions. Staff members who fulfill these requirements still need additional "local" or "internal" knowledge and skills, related to specific development and maintenance procedures. This specialized knowledge can be grouped into the following categories:

- Professional SQA education
- Knowledge and skills related to SQA local procedures and conventions

- Knowledge of skills in implementation of SQA and software engineering standards adopted by the organization

Training and updating needs are determined by a comparison of the staff's current knowledge with the updated knowledge requirements. The type of training is adapted to the needs of three distinct groups of staff:

- Training: For new SQA function team candidates, according to their designated assignment
- Retraining: For employees assigned to new SQA positions
- Bringing up to date: SQA team members

In small SQA teams, a common list of requirements is a useful resource to expedite team replacements and team enforcements when the need is great.

The certified software quality engineer (CSQE) body of knowledge (ASQ, 2016) can serve as a source for determining general software quality engineering knowledge and skill requirements. A book by Linda Westfall (Westfall, 2010) provides explanations on topics from the former edition of the CSQE BOK (the 2008 edition).

23.5.2 Plan training and upskilling programs for SQA function positions

The planning of training, retraining, and updating activities refers to the program contents, the number of participants, and the form of training. Of special importance is the choice of the form of training: traditional training course, workshops, computer-based training, web-based training, self-study, mentoring, and on-the-job training.

Planning update programs

Updating activities can be scheduled well ahead, to be performed once in a period, for example, once every 3 months. The audience of these updating activities is known, and the program contents closed up to the date of the training.

23.5.3 Conduct the training programs for software development staff

The training team is responsible for performing the training. Updating programs need to cover advancements of SQA methodologies and standards. In many cases the training and updating will be delivered by external training centers.

23.5.4 Perform follow-up of training activities and trainees

The head of the SQA function is required to follow up on the outcomes of the training efforts:

- To verify whether all training program activities were conducted and about the participation of enlisted participants.
- To provide feedback indicating whether the training efforts were justified in terms of improved effectiveness and quality of trainee performance.
- To identify ineffective and unsuccessful training activities in order to ensure continuous improvement of training activities.

The CAB, based on the follow-up subsequent to training and other sources of information, may initiate training programs improvements.

23.6 The objectives of certification

The objectives of certification are listed in Frame 23.3

Frame 23.3: The objectives of certification

The objectives of certification
• To determine which of the key positions of software development and maintenance requires certification. • To ensure that candidates for key software development and maintenance positions are adequately qualified.

The above objectives conform to the general goals of software quality assurance by inspiring management to persistently nurture the level of knowledge and skills displayed by staff, and improve its efficiency and effectiveness.

23.7 The certification process

The successful operation of development and maintenance processes is supported in most cases by position certification of the key positions involved in performing these processes. The following activities are required for the certification process:

- Define positions requiring certification
- Plan certification programs for the selected positions
- Deliver certification programs
- Perform certification follow-up

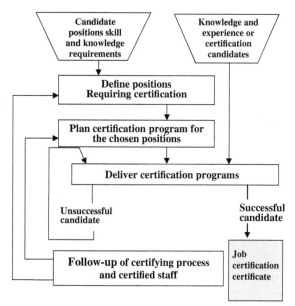

Figure 23.2   The certification process.

Certification activities are aimed at filling any knowledge gaps and sometimes upskilling qualified staff. Comprehensive follow-up of the outcome of current programs as well as keeping track of developments in the relevant field/s are required to make sure that programs are adequately up-to-date.

The organization performs the certification process, while the SQA function supports the process by providing consultation on the various activities of the process.

The issues of certification programs for project management, and especially the need for such programs, are discussed by Catanio et al. (2013) and McHugh and Mairead (2008).

A detailed discussion of each of these activities is presented in the next sections.

The certification process is displayed in Figure 23.2.

23.7.1   Defining the positions requiring certification

It is commonly accepted that assignment of personnel to key positions in software development and maintenance requires extreme care. One of the procedures used to improve the suitability of candidates is certification. Examples of positions frequently requiring certification are software development team leaders, software testing team leaders, software maintenance technicians, and internal quality auditors. The last two positions are particularly sensitive because the related tasks are usually performed by one staff member, acting alone, and subject to little close control or support by superiors.

A certification committee (or designated senior staff member) defines the list of positions that require certification and whether the certification will be effective permanently or for a limited period. Considering the volatility of the profession, this list should be revised periodically. Periodical review and modification of certification requirements, ensures that staff members possess up-to-date knowledge and skills according to the current certification requirements.

The list of positions that require certification naturally varies by firm or organization. Some use certification sparingly while others apply tool on a large scale, even to standard programmers.

23.7.2 Planning certification programs for the selected positions

Certification is aimed at providing a framework for the thorough investigation of a candidate's qualifications and a demonstration of his/her professional knowledge and skills. Details of the certification programs are unique to the organization; they reflect its special characteristics, areas of specialization, software development, maintenance tools, customers, and so on.

Every detail of the certification program for every position requires approval, as defined in the certification procedure.

Typical certification requirements

A typical certification process entails meeting some, or even all, of the following requirements:

- Professional education: Academic or technical degrees and in some cases certification by a professional organization or by a leading commercial software producer. A program of importance are professional certification programs for software quality professionals (CSQA and CSQE) delivered by the ASQ (see Carver, 2012 and Westfall, 2010). All these programs are based on a comprehensive "Body of Knowledge". The Microsoft professional certification (MCP) was found to be a contributor to performance (Kabia et al., 2013). Another example of a certification program by a commercial company is Red Hat (Jang, 2007).
- Participation in internal training courses.
- Professional experience in the organization (may partially or completely be replaced by experience in other organizations).
- Assessment of achievements and abilities as noted in periodical performance appraisals (for internal candidates).
- Evaluation by a candidate's direct superior (often by completion of a special questionnaire).
- Demonstration of knowledge and skills by means of a test or project.
- Mentor supervision for a specified period of time.

The main requirements of a certification program are shown in Frame 23.4.

Frame 23.4: The main requirements of a certification program

The main requirements of a certification program

- Professional education
- Internal training courses
- Professional experience in the current organization and other organizations
- Evaluation of the candidate's achievements and ability as found in periodic performance assessments
- Evaluation by the candidate's direct superior
- Demonstration of knowledge and skills by means of a test or a project
- Mentor's supervision for a specified period

Functions of the certification committee

The person or committee members responsible for certification are usually senior software development and maintenance staff.

The responsibilities of the certifying body include:

- To perform certification activities for individual applicants or for a unit and to grant certification to those who qualify.
- To follow-up certification activities (such as mentoring) carried out by others.
- To follow-up the success of the certification process in terms of the candidate job performance.
- To update certification requirements in response to developments in the organization as well as the profession.
- To revise the list of positions requiring certification.

Implementation tip

An additional task to be performed by those responsible for certification is the active search for qualified personnel, who may be encouraged to become certification committee members. These persons could serve as testers in certification test, mentors, or instructors.

Example

Certification requirements at SKF Advanced Software

SKF Advanced Software is a medium-sized software house. The firm's certification requirements document for a programming team leader is presented in Frame 23.5.

Frame 23.5: SKF Advanced Software – Position Certification Requirement (Example)

SKF Advanced Software
Position Certification Requirements

Position 11.3 – Programmer team leader
Version 5 Valid as from 10.1.2018

Certification requirements

- Professional education: Two options: (a) BA or BSc in software engineering or equivalent degree. (b) Technician or equivalent degree in software engineering granted by a recognized school.
- Internal training courses: Two required courses: (1) Project management – 5-day course. (2) Advanced project management – 5-day course.
- Professional experience in the organization: For candidates holding a technician's degree – 3 years' experience as a programmer in SKF. For candidates holding an academic degree – 2 years' experience as a programmer in SKF. For candidates with over 5 years' experience as a programmer or programming team leader in another organization – double the respective period of experience in SKF.
- Periodic performance appraisal. The average score of each of the last two semi-annual performance appraisals will not fall below 3.8 (out of a maximum of 5).
- Targeted evaluation by direct superior. The score of each of the eight items in the questionnaire will be no less than 3 (out of 5), with an average score of at least 3.8 for all items.
- Demonstration of knowledge and skills by means of a test or project: 8-hour programming skill test according to a specially selected software design document. Minimum grade: 80.
- Mentor supervision for a designated period. Mentor supervision and on-the-job instruction by a senior programming team leader for a period of 6 months.

Responsibility for certification

- **Overall responsibility: Chief software engineer**
- Responsibility for skill demonstration test: Manager of relevant software development or software maintenance department (preparation of candidate's test/task and its evaluation).
- Responsibility for carrying out certification process: Head of the training and certification unit.

Approved by C. Haley
Position: Chief Software Engineer
Date of approval: September 17, 2017

23.7.3   Delivery of certification programs

Application for certification, whether individual or presented by units of the organization, will be handled by the certification team. The team will perform the following:

a. Examine the documents presented by the candidates and define the candidate certification process.

b. Coordinate and schedule the individual certification activities for the candidates: software engineering, software quality assurance, and management skills (within the framework of certification requirements). The method used to carry out certification varies accordingly. Courses may be conducted in-house by the organization's training and certification unit, or externally, either by vocational or academic institutions that prepare programs attuned to the organization's requirements, or by an individual computer-based training or other forms of training.

c. Verify that the candidate undergoes the required certification activities.

d. Evaluate the candidate success in the certification activities.

e. Present the candidate's achievements in the various certification activities to the certification committee for approval or disapproval of their qualifications for the position.

23.7.4   Follow-up of certification process and results

Managers and software professionals often express doubts about the effectiveness of certification in general, or in regard to one of the associated activities. They question whether the substantial resources and efforts invested in certification are really worthwhile. To relieve these doubts, systematic follow-up is necessary to provide feedback to the professional units. Such feedback indicates whether the certification efforts were justified, while also serves to ensure continuous improvement of certification activities. The information provided by follow-up relates to:

• Records of the performance of the participants in the program for all certification programs conducted.

• Information about special cases of certification activities that proved to be either highly successful, or clearly unsuccessful, in improving staff performance.

• Information about proven cases of failures of certified staff that point to clearly inadequate certification requirements.

Analysis of the data accumulated following a certification activity provides the information necessary to revise programs by guiding the modification, addition, and deletion of identified activities and materials. Meaningful follow-up of certification requires performance information collected prior, as well as subsequent, to certification. In regard to certification follow-up, comparisons of the performance of noncertified with those of certified staff is impossible, as noncertified staff are not expected to hold positions that require certification. Instead, it is possible to base the follow-up on performance comparisons of certified staff whose achievements in the certification process were high, with certified staff whose achievements were substantially lower. Given these constraints, the units responsible for training and certification should perform follow-up regularly using instruments such as:

- Collection of regular performance metrics – such as errors and productivity statistics, corrective maintenance statistics and resources invested – prepared by the respective units. For a discussion of software quality metrics in general and the specific issue of performance metrics – see Chapter 21.
- Questionnaires completed by certified staff members, their superiors, customers, and others.
- Analysis of outstanding achievements as well as failures.
- Specialized review of software products (documents and code) prepared by certified and trained employees.

The CAB, based on follow-up subsequent to certification and other sources of information, may initiate changes to the certification process activities subsequent to analysis of the cases presented to it. For more about corrective and preventive actions in the context of certification and other issues, see Chapter 19.

Summary

1. **The main objectives of training software development staff**
   - To develop the knowledge and skills needed by new employees and to update the knowledge and skills of veteran employees so as to assure efficient and effective task performance.
   - To update the knowledge and skills of existing staff in response to developments in the organization and technology, and to ensure efficient and effective performance of updated requirements of project tasks.
2. **Discuss what is needed to prepare training and updating program for software development staff**

   The three activities to be performed prior to planning a program:
   - **Determine the knowledge requirements for each software development position**

     Determine knowledge and skills related to software engineering and quality assurance topics, including professional education, and internal procedures and conventions.

- **Determine training and professional updating needs of software development staff**

  These needs are ascertained through comparisons of the staff's knowledge and skills with the state of the art. These should be specified for three populations:
  - New employees (training)
  - Employees assigned to new position (retraining)
  - Other staff (professional updating)

    Training and updating needs should also be determined by performance requirements, based on feedback transmitted by the organization's various units.

- **Plan training and updating programs for software development staff**

  These programs will respond to the following issues:
  - The use of in-house training teams and facilities or outsourcing
  - The timing of the training and updating activities (whenever possible)
  - The use of e-learning programs

3. **The training process for the SQA function team**

   Successful training of the SQA function team requires performing the following activities:
   - Determine needs for professional training and needs for filling any knowledge gaps for the SQA function team.
   - Plan training and upskill programs for the SQA function team.
   - Conduct training programs for the SQA function team.
   - Perform follow-up on training activities and new knowledge acquired by trainees.

4. **The main components of a certification program**

   A certification program defines position requirements and responsibilities for carrying out the program and its revision.

   Certification requirements may include some or even all of the following components, depending on their relevance to the task or position:

   Certification responsibilities include:
   - Response to requests made by applications or the organization
   - Conduct of follow-up
   - Revision of certification requirements according to technological developments
   - Revision of the list of positions requiring certification

5. **Explain the objectives of follow-up of trained and certified staff performance and main sources of the follow-up data**

   Follow-up is meant to provide the information necessary to initiate revisions of the training and certification programs based on performance data.

Sources for performance data include:

- Regular performance metrics – such as errors and productivity statistics – prepared by the individual units.
- Questionnaires completed by trainees, their superiors, and others.
- Analysis of outstanding achievements as well as failures.
- Specialized review of software products (documents and code) produced by certified and trained employees.

Selected bibliography

ASQ (2016) The 2016 certified software quality engineer (CEQE) body of knowledge.

Baker E. R. and Fisher M. J. (2008) Training for quality managers, in Schulmeyer G. G. (Ed.) *Handbook of Software Quality Assurance*, 4th Edition, Artech House, Norwood, MA, pp. 111–119.

Bourque P. and Fairley R. E. Eds. (2014) *Guide to the Software Engineering Body of Knowledge, Version 3.0*, The IEEE Computer Society, New York, NY.

Carver D. (2012) *Certified Software Quality Analyst (CSQA)*, ASQ Quality Press, Milwaukee, WI.

Catanio J. T., Armstrong G., and Tucker J. (2013) The effects of project management certifications on the triple constant. *Information Technology Project Management*, Vol. 4, No. 4, pp. 1–13.

IEEE (2014) *IEEE Std. 730-2014 Software Quality Assurance*, The IEEE Computer Society, IEEE, New York, NY.

ISO (2014) *ISO/IEC 90003:2014 Software Engineering – Guidelines for the Application of ISO 9001: 2008 to Computer Software*, International Organization for Standardization (ISO), Geneva, Switzerland.

Jang M. (2007) *RHCSA/RHCE Red Hat Linux Certification Study Guide*, McGraw Hill, New York, NY.

Kabia M., Oni O., and Booher L. (2013) Information technology certification as a predictor of job performance, *Journal of Leadership and Organizational Effectiveness*, Vol. 1, No. 1, pp. 15–32.

McHugh O. and Mairead H. (2008) Project managers – do they need to be certified? in Barry, C. et al. Eds, *Information Systems Development: Challenges in Practice, Theory, and Education*, vol. 2, pp. 195–208.

Westfall L. (2010) *The ASQ Certified Software Quality Engineer Handbook*, Quality Press, Milwaukee, WI.

Review questions

23.1 It has been claimed that training and certification objectives of software development staff conform to objectives of SQA activities (see Section 1.1 of Chapter 1).

- Review each of the SQA objectives and explain in your own words how they conform to the relevant training and certification objectives.

23.2 The main tasks of training software development staff are classified into training and updating.

- Discuss the main differentiating characteristics between the two types of tasks.

23.3 One of the training methods mentioned in Section 23.5.2 is "on-the-job training."

- Discuss the advantages and disadvantages of the "on-the-job training" compared with participation in a course.

23.4 Consider the certification requirement "mentor supervision."

a. Explain in your own words the unique contribution of supervision to the success of the certification process.

b. Can you suggest certification requirements that can be replaced, wholly or partially, by a mentor's supervision? List your arguments.

23.5 The Certification Committee of SKF Advanced Software has decided to extend the list of positions requiring certification. The following positions were added:

- C# programmer
- Automated testing planner
- Tester team leader
- Prepare a proposal for a position certification document for one of the above positions (see Frame 23.4).

Topics for discussion

23.1 Refer to the "3S" development team mini case.

a. List the decisions made by the team leader that led to the problematic situation.

b. Can you suggest procedures that could have eliminated or reduced the risk of arriving at a situation similar to that found in "3S"? Explain, in a few sentences, how each of your proposed procedures may contribute to eliminating these risks.

23.2 In the last few years, many human resource management departments and staff training units have invested substantial resources in computer-aided training.

a. Discuss the advantages of computer-aided training and retraining.

b. Discuss the advantages of computer-aided training for professional updating.

c. Discuss the disadvantages of computer-aided training for professional training, retraining, and updating.

d. Suggest ways to overcome the above disadvantages.

23.3 New Ventures Bank (NVB) operates 87 branches throughout the state. The Software Development and Maintenance Department employs a professional staff of 350. Lately, the bank's General Manager, who has often expressed his dissatisfaction with the performance of NVB's certification processes, took away responsibility for the staff certification from the manager of the Software Development Department. A day later, he assigned the responsibility to Raphael Jones, the very successful Finance Department Head.

a. Do you expect the new choice to be successful? List arguments for each view.

b. Some senior staff members of the Development Department suggested that Victor McFaden, a senior software development consultant, well-experienced with the certification process, serve as head of the new Certification Committee to be established. Do you agree with this recommendation? List your arguments and compare this appointment to that of Mr. Jones.

23.4 The managers of a software development department have decided that all training and certification programs will only be delivered by members of the department staff. They explained that the decision is based on the importance of a "local color" in a training and certification activity, and stressed that economic considerations did not play a role in the decision.

    a. Discuss the appropriateness of the decision.

    b. Suggest ways for improving the decision.

23.5 Follow-up of the certification process, discussed in Section 23.7.4, rests on four different sources of information. An SQA expert claims that the quantitative information provided by performance metrics is sufficient, and that collecting additional information is unnecessary, and may very well prove to be a waste of resources.

    a. Do you agree with the claim? List your arguments for and against.

    b. If you disagree, discuss the unique contribution of each source of information to a successful feedback process.

Part V

Additional Tools and Methods Supporting Software Quality

This part of the book presents three additional tools and methods that support development teams in their efforts to assure the quality of their software processes and software products:

- Chapter 24 presents two simple tools, templates and checklists, that in addition to time savings, improve the quality of reports including their structures by supporting the report preparation and reviewing stages.
- Chapter 25 is dedicated to configuration management systems, their tasks, implementation processes, and the related software quality assurance activities.
- Chapter 26 is dedicated to CASE Tools, computerized software development tools that support the software developer and maintenance, their classification and contributions to the efficiency, effectiveness, and quality of the processes.

Software Quality: Concepts and Practice, First Edition. Daniel Galin.
© 2018 the IEEE Computer Society, Inc. Published 2018 by John Wiley & Sons, Inc.

Chapter 24

Templates and Checklists

24.1 Introduction

The task of preparing a report is always time-consuming, and despite investing time and thought into the process, you may often find yourself troubled with deliberations about the completeness and structure of the result, the "product." An improvised solution to these structure and completeness difficulties is to scan old reports in order to apply their table of contents to the current report. Furthermore, you may find out that you need past reports on which to base your arguments. Unfortunately, only half of these may be available, and it is most often that the most important ones are missing. Once you finish your report, you may wish to look at the questions asked in last year's report's discussion. Again, frustration, the management clerks could not find the minutes of that meeting.

Software development and maintenance processes involve the production and use of a multitude of documents. Two simple SQA tools, templates and checklists, could support the preparation of documents. In addition to time savings, these tools improve the quality of reports including their structures (contributed by templates), and also provide better preparation for debate on reports by improving them according to checklists, and by preparing responses to the checklist topics.

The contribution of templates and checklists and the organizational framework for implementing these SQA tools are the topics discussed in the sections of this chapter:

- Section 24.2 presents the templates.
- Section 24.3 presents the checklists.

24.2 Templates

In nonsoftware areas of work, a *template* is "a gauge, pattern or mould (as a thin plate or board) used as a guide to the form of a piece being made" (Webster's

---

Software Quality: Concepts and Practice, First Edition. Daniel Galin.
© 2018 the IEEE Computer Society, Inc. Published 2018 by John Wiley & Sons, Inc.

New College Dictionary). When applied to software engineering, the term "template" refers to a format (especially tables of contents) created by units or organizations, to be applied when compiling a report or other types of documents. Application of templates may be obligatory for some documents and elective for others; in some cases, only part of a template (e.g., specific chapters or general structure) is demanded.

Three examples of templates are presented in the following frames in Chapter 14:

- Frame 14.4: The software test plan (STP)
- Frame 14.5: Software test description (STD)
- Frame 14.6: Software test report (STR)

An additional two examples of templates appear in Chapters 22 and 25:

- Frame 22.1: Software change request (SCR)
- Frame 25.5: Documentation of software configuration release

The next sections deal with the contribution of templates to software quality and the efforts required for producing, maintaining, and implementing templates.

The contribution of templates to software quality

The usage of templates is quite advantageous to development teams and to review teams.

For development teams, template use:

- **Facilitates the process of preparing documents** by saving the time and energy required to create the document's structure. Most organizations allow templates to be copied from an SQA public file, or downloaded from the organization's Intranet files, which even saves keying in the table of contents to a new document.

- **Means that documents prepared by developers are more complete** as all the subjects to be included in the document have already been defined and repeatedly reviewed by numerous professionals over the course of the template's use. Common errors, such as the overlooking of a topic, are less likely to occur.

- **Provides for easier integration of new team members** through familiarity. The document's standard structure, prepared according to templates that may be known to the new member from previous work in another of the organization's units or teams, makes finding information much easier. It also smooths ongoing document preparation in cases where parts of the document have been prepared by another team member, who may or may not have left.

For DR committee members, template use:

- **Facilitates review of documents** by eliminating the need to study a document's structure and confirm its completeness – if the document is based on the appropriate template. It also simplifies reviewing the completed document as its structure is standard and reviewers are familiar with its expected contents (chapters, sections, and appendices). As a result of this consistency, the review is expected to be more thorough yet less time-consuming.

For software maintenance teams, template use:

- **Enables easier location of the information** required for performing maintenance tasks.

The summary of the contribution of templates to software quality is presented in Frame 24.1.

Frame 24.1: The contribution of templates to software quality

The contribution of templates to software quality
For development teams:
• Facilitates the process of preparing documents
• Means that documents prepared by developers are more complete
• Provides for easier integration of new team members
For DR committee members:
• Facilitates review of documents
For software maintenance teams:
• Enables easier location of the information

24.3 The organizational framework for implementing templates

Organizations tend to save their internal resources, which often means using successfully employed reports as models for company-wide reports, or even employing a whole report as is. Thus, if Mr Brown's or Mr Johnson's reports have acquired a reputation as comprehensive and highly professional, their tables of contents may be used as base templates by their colleagues. One disadvantage of this situation is that often not everyone who can benefit from these basis templates is aware of their existence. Another disadvantage is that further improvement of the templates, accomplished through their review by professional teams, may be thwarted.

The SQA unit is usually responsible for preparing professional templates for the more common types of reports and documents required by the organization's staff. Developing the general infrastructure for using templates, the subject of this section, is an integral part of the unit's tasks.

24.3.1 Preparation of new templates

Development of a template infrastructure naturally centers on the work of a group of professionals devoted to the task. This group (or committee) should include senior staff who represent the various software development lines, the department's chief software engineer, and SQA unit members. Informal developers of "template services" should likewise be encouraged to join the group.

One of the group's first tasks is to compile a target list of templates to be developed and common structure parts for all template types, or for most of them. Once the list is accepted, priorities must be set. Higher priority should be given to templates of the most commonly prepared documents, as well as to "informal" templates already in use, as it is estimated that only minimal efforts will be required for their completion and authorization. Subcommittees are then assigned the task of preparing the first drafts. The subcommittee may use examples of existing templates to facilitate and improve the process of preparing a template draft.

The most common information sources used in preparing a template are listed in Frame 24.2.

Frame 24.2: Common information sources for template

Common information sources for template
• Informal templates already in use in the organization
• Template examples found in professional publications
• Templates used by similar organizations

An SQA unit member can be anticipated to undertake the task of leading the group, but a template "freak," who is also a member of the committee, may just as readily be chosen for the job. Irrespective of who the group's head is, he or she must see to the distribution of template drafts among members, the organization of meetings, and the follow-up of progress made by template preparation subcommittees. Distribution of template drafts among team leaders for their comments can yield important improvements and at the same time promote future use of the template.

24.3.2 Application of templates

Several fundamental decisions are involved in the implementation of new or updated templates:

- What channels should be used for promoting the templates?
- How should the templates be made available to the organization's internal "consumers"?
- Which templates should be compulsory and how can their application be enforced?

All internal means of communication may be used for promoting templates internally, within the organization: leaflets, e-mails, SQA intranet, as well as short presentations at meetings.

One of the most efficient methods of making templates available to the organization is the internal net (intranet), to be preferred to any paper-based route. Distribution through the internal net ensures users use the latest revision of the template needed and also saves keying in (required for paper-based templates) the document's table of contents.

Directions regarding compulsory use of specific templates are generally found in the organization's procedures or work instructions. The chief software engineer or other senior staff member is usually authorized to determine the list of compulsory templates appropriate for the selected procedure, although we can expect the template group to submit its own recommended list.

A common "tool" for enforcing the use of templates is the DR committee that can demand restructuring reviewed documents to comply with relevant templates.

24.3.3 Updating templates

The decision to update an existing template may be considered a reactive measure stemming from any of the following:

- User proposals and suggestions
- Changes in the organization's areas of activity
- Proposals initiated by design reviews and inspection teams based on their review of documents prepared according to the templates
- Analysis of failures as well as successes
- Experience from other organizations
- SQA team initiatives

The process of updating templates is quite similar to that of template preparation.

24.4 Checklists

The checklist used by software developers refers to the list of topics, usually a comprehensive one, especially constructed for each type of document. Checklists are used:

- By developers prior to completing a document to ensure that all required topics have been included and discussed properly
- By developers prior to performing an activity (e.g., installing a software package at the customer site) and to ensure the completeness of preparations
- By DR committee members for verifying that a document complies with content topics requirements
- By DR committee members to verify the correct order of topics in the review sessions discussions

Usually, a checklist tends to be considered an optional infrastructure tool, depending mainly on the list's professional attributes, user acquaintance with the list, and availability.

Figure 24.1 presents an example of a checklist for design reviews of requirement specification documents. The presented checklist serves for documenting the findings of the checks performed, where the checker can mark whether the document complies with the topic's issue or not and list necessary comments.

Two additional examples of checklists can be found in Chapter 8:

- Appendix 8.A: Proposal draft reviews – subjects checklist
- Appendix 8.B: Contract draft review – subjects checklist

Several examples of comprehensive and detailed checklists may be found in a book by Perry (2006). The important contribution of checklists is discussed by Houston (2004).

Next, we deal with the contribution of checklists to software quality and the efforts required for their implementation: establishing, maintaining, and applying the lists.

The contribution of checklists to software quality

Like templates, checklists provide many benefits to development teams, committee members, and software maintenance teams and contribute to document and performance quality.

The advantages to development teams:

- **Help developers carry out self-checks of documents or software code** prior to formal design reviews, inspections, or testing. Checklists are

Goldenbug Ltd.

DR checklist for requirement specification report

Project name: ___ _____

The reviewed document: _____Version:__ _____

Item No.	Subject	Yes	No	N.A.	
1	**The document**				
1.1	Prepared according to configuration management requirements.				
1.2	Structure conforms to relevant template.				
1.3	Reviewed document is complete.				
1.4	Proper references to former documents, standards, etc.				
2	**Specifying the requirements**				
2.1	Required functions were properly defined and clearly and fully phrased.				
2.2	Design inputs conform to required outputs.				
2.3	Software requirement specifications conform to product requirements.				
2.4	Required interfaces with external software packages and computerized equipment are fully defined and clearly phrased.				
2.5	GUI interfaces are fully defined and clearly phrased.				
2.6	Performance requirements – response time, input flow capacity, storage capacity – are correctly defined and fully and clearly phrased.				
2.7	All error situations and required system reactions are correctly defined and fully and clearly phrased.				
2.8	Data interfaces with other existing or planned software packages or product components are correctly defined and fully and clearly phrased.				
2.9	Procedures to test specified requirements are fulfilled, correctly and fully defined, and clearly phrased.				
3	**Project feasibility**				
3.1	Are the specified requirements feasible considering the project's resources, budget, and timetable?				
3.2	Are the specified performance requirements (see 2.6) feasible considering the constraints imposed by other system components and external systems interfaced with the system?				

Comments:

Signed: Name:_____ Date:_____ Signature: _____

Figure 24.1 DR checklist for requirement specification reports

expected to help the developer discover incomplete sections as well as detect overlooked parts. Checklists are also expected to contribute to the quality of documents or software code submitted for review, as the quality issues to be surveyed by the review team are already listed in the checklist.

- **Assist developers in their preparations for tasks** such as installation of software at customer sites, performance of quality audits at subcontractors' sites, or signing of contracts with suppliers of reused software modules. Checklists are expected to help developers become better equipped for task performance.

The advantages to review teams:

- **Ensure completeness of document reviews by review team members** as all relevant review topics appear on the list.
- **Facilitate improved efficiency of review sessions** as the subjects and their order of discussion are defined and well known in advance.

The summary of the contribution of checklists to software quality is presented in Frame 24.3.

Frame 24.3: The contribution of checklists to software quality

The contribution of checklists to software quality
The advantages to development teams:
• **Help developers carry out self-checks of documents or software code**
• **Assist developers in their preparations for tasks**
The advantages to review teams:
• **Ensure completeness of document reviews by review team members**
• **Facilitate improved efficiency of review sessions**

24.5 The organizational framework for implementing checklists

Although highly recommended, the use of checklists remains in most organizations as discretionary. Checklist preparation and updating, and the promotion of their use, are usually assigned to the SQA unit. A "checklist group," headed by an SQA unit member, can undertake the task of maintaining a collection of updated lists. The participation of additional staff interested in promoting the use of checklists in the group is also voluntary; in some cases, however, the assistance of an SQA consultant is recommended. In the remainder of this section, we describe the processes required to maintain a checklist infrastructure: preparation of new checklists, updating, and promoting their use.

24.5.1 Preparation of new checklists

One of the first tasks awaiting the "checklist group" is the compilation of a list of checklists targeted for development, followed by the definition of a common format for all the checklists released by the group.

The first checklists approved by the group are usually based on informal checklists already in use by a number of development team members and reviewers. In most cases, a few changes and adaptations of these checklists are sufficient to satisfy the format and contents defined by the group. Preparation of new checklists, as well as the improvement of informal checklists, is supported by the information sources listed in Frame 24.4.

Frame 24.4: Common sources of checklist

Common sources of checklist
• Informal checklists already in use in the organization. • Checklist examples found in books and other professional publications. • Checklists used by similar organizations.

The process of preparing a new checklist is similar to the one for a template.

24.5.2 Updating checklists

Like templates and procedures, initiatives to update an existing checklist generally flow from the following sources:

- User proposals and suggestions
- Changes in technology, areas of activity, and clientele
- Proposals initiated by inspection teams in design and document reviews
- Analysis of failures as well as successes
- Experience from other organizations
- SQA team initiatives

The process of updating checklists is quite similar to their preparation.

24.5.3 Promotion of checklist use

As the use of checklists is rarely mandatory, promoting their use is based on their circulating and guaranteed availability. Staff interested in promoting the use of checklists and internal channels of communication can be used for publicizing the checklists: through leaflets, e-mail, SQA intranet, as well as professional meetings. The internal net remains, however, the preferred and most efficient method for making checklists available to the organization's internal "consumers."

Summary

1. **The main contribution of templates to software quality assurance**
   The main contributions are:
   - The use of templates facilitates the process of preparing a document by saving the efforts required for planning the document structure.
   - Documents submitted for review are complete, thus common errors of overlooked topics are eliminated.
   - Documents submitted for review are complete. As a result, review teams can direct their efforts to examining the document and to further improving the final product.
   - Document reviews are facilitated as their structure is standard and well known among the reviewers. Freed of structural concerns, reviewers can focus on issues relating to the document content.

2. **The main contributions of checklists to software quality assurance**
   The main contributions are:
   - Checklists support document quality as all relevant topics may be self-checked according to the checklist and quality issues to be reviewed are already listed.
   - Checklists support the developer's preparation for tasks such as installing software or/and verifying subcontractor's performance.
   - Checklists **ensure completeness of document reviews by review team members** as all relevant review topics appear on the list.
   - Management of review sessions becomes less problematic when topics and their order of priority are defined and well known. An efficient session is expected to carry out a thorough analysis of comments by reviewers.

3. **The activities involved in maintaining templates and checklists**
   The activities involved in maintaining state-of-the-art compilations of templates and checklist collections include preparation, implementation, and updating.
   The preparation and updating of both types of SQA tools are the work of groups of interested staff, including those who have already

proposed informal templates and checklists to their colleagues. Leadership of the group is usually an SQA unit obligation. The group members decide on target lists of templates and checklists, which they later try to complete. Drafts are prepared by the group members and reviewed by other group members and others. Team members, SQA unit members, and others, especially those in the relevant field, can readily initiate updating efforts. Updates are effected to improve current releases on the basis of team and external experience, and to cope with organizational changes, altered consumer tastes, failure analysis results, and so on. The implementation of templates and checklist is successful when the majority of users or relevant internal consumers apply them regularly. Successful application is based on both promotion activities and availability. Promotion is based on advertising, especially on internal communication networks, while easy access is usually achieved through the internal net. In many organizations, use of some or all templates is compulsory in situations that demand adequate procedures and/or work instructions.

Selected bibliography

Houston D. (2004) The value of a good checklist, *Software Quality Professional*, Vol. 6, No. 2, pp. 17–26.
Perry W. (2006) *Effective Methods for Software Testing*, 3rd Edition, John Wiley & Sons Inc, New York, NY.

Review questions

24.1 Explain the advantages of templates in your own words.

24.2 The SQA unit has prepared a list of eight new additional templates awaiting preparation.

    a. Whom would you recommend to participate in an *ad hoc* committee for preparing the templates?

    b. The head of the SQA unit is considering hiring an SQA consultant to join the committee. Is this advisable? List your arguments.

    c. If you agree with the unit head, what tasks would you prefer the consultant attend to? List your arguments.

24.3 The organizational framework for implementing templates deals with updating procedures.

    a. Explain in your own words the sources for initiatives for procedure updating.

    b. Explain the process of updating procedures.

24.4 Explain the advantages of using checklists in your own words.

24.5 Relate to new checklists and their updates.

   a. What are possible sources for preparing a new template?

   b. Evaluate the advantages and disadvantages of each possible template source.

Topics for discussion

24.1 Mr John Bogart, head of the SQA unit, has decided that henceforth it will be mandatory for all developers to apply the templates included in a well-known *Templates Manual for the SQA Professional*. A procedure has been prepared to enforce adherence to the templates. The manager of the software development department has been asked to approve the procedure.

   a. Would you recommend that the manager approve the procedure? List your arguments.

   b. If your recommendation is against approving the procedure, suggest how the department's informal templates, if deemed more suitable than the *Manual*'s templates, may be adopted.

24.2 Tommy, a software development team leader, tends to delete standard (i.e., template) sections and chapters that are not applicable from the tables of contents of the documents he compiles. He claims that by doing this the documents "look nicer."

   a. Do you agree with this method of adapting templates to current application?

   b. What are the disadvantages of "template editing" by the team leader? What do you recommend doing in cases of inapplicable template chapters or sections?

24.3 An SQA professional claims that the availability of design review checklists makes the DR redundant.

   a. Do you agree with this claim? List your arguments.

   b. Compare the expected situation in the following two DR sessions: first session, when designers do not use a checklist, and second session, when designers make use of a DR document checklist.

24.4 Tom Haley, a software development team leader, prepared new work instructions. The head of the SQA function claimed that as these instructions do not comply with the relevant procedure, changes should be made to verify that they do. Tom Haley responded saying that there is no need to adapt the instructions to the procedure.

   a. Do you agree with Tom Haley? If yes, list your arguments.

   b. If you disagree with Tom Haley, what are the expected damages of such non-compliance between work instructions and relevant procedures?

24.5 It is suggested that the revised edition of the *Templates and Checklists Procedure* includes the following section: "If a template or checklist has not been updated or changed for a period of 36 months – a team should be nominated to check these templates and checklists and recommend any required changes and updates. The

SQA unit is responsible for performing the needed review at least semi-annually. A committee, nominated by the head of the Software Development Department, should submit its recommended changes and updates not later than six months after their nomination."

a. Is the proposed procedure for updating templates and checklists justified or a waste of time?

b. Suggest situations where templates and checklists, accepted as proper and highly professional when released, need to be changed.

24.6 It is recommended that an *ad hoc* committee (or group), rather than an expert member of the SQA unit or a consultant, prepares a new and updated checklist file.

- List the expected advantages and disadvantages of the committee/group option for performing this task.

Chapter 25

Configuration Management

25.1 Introduction

The need to cope with software versions throughout the software life cycle is one of the more important tasks of software development and maintenance teams. The software quality support function to perform this task is software configuration management (SCM). Operation of software configuration control throughout the software life cycle is key to the effective and efficient performance of successful software development and maintenance.

In many organizations, the function of software change control, as discussed in Chapter 22, is integrated into the configuration management function.

All the SCM processes of software version storage release and recovery of stored information are based on the use of identified configuration items.

The SQA activities related to SCM include overseeing the SCM activities performed by the software development organization and supporting them professionally.

SCM is sometimes referred to simply as configuration management (CM). Its definition along with its objectives are presented in Frame 25.1.

The importance of SCM to support software development and maintenance processes is stressed in the ISO/IEC/IEEE Std. 12207-2008 Section 7.2.2 (ISO, 2008), ISO/IEC Std.90003:2014 Section 7.5.3.2 (ISO, 2014), and also in the CMM Guidelines (Leon (2015) and Aiello and Sachs (2010)). These are just two of the books dedicated to the CM subject. Chapters dedicated to CM are likewise found in software engineering texts such as Pressman and Maxim (2015). Various aspects of configuration management are discussed in papers, a sample of these include Kogel (2008), Lapouchnian et al. (2007), Sarma (2008), Fauzi (2010), Buchmann et al. (2013) Alidoosti (2015), and Estublier et al. (2005).

Frame 25.1: Definition and tasks of software configuration management

Software configuration management – definition

A quality support function for software development and maintenance processes responsible for applying (computerized and noncomputerized) technical tools and administrative procedures that enable completion of the tasks required to identify, store, and maintain availability and accuracy of the information related to all aspects of the components of a software system and their versions.

The tasks of configuration management

- Systematic storage of identified versions of software configuration items and other approved items.
- Release of SCI and software configuration versions.
- Provision of information services based on recovery of stored data.
- Verification of compliance to CM procedures.
- Control software change (in cases the SCMA is responsible for the change control task)

The next sections deal with the following:
The storage tasks of SCM

- The configuration items
- Release of software configuration items
- Documentation of software configuration versions
- Configuration management planning
- Provision of CM information services
- Computerized tools for performing configuration management tasks
- The CM function in the organization
- Software quality assurance activities related to CM

25.2 Software configuration items

Storage, release, and recovery of software items to support a reliable software configuration process require the use of software configuration items, software configuration item versions, and software configuration versions. Definitions of these software items are presented in Frame 25.2.

A unit of software code or a document is defined as an SCI if assumed that it may be needed for further development of the software system and/or its maintenance. In other words, the main criterion governing a noncode item's classification as an SCI, and its inclusion in a software configuration version, is its potential contribution to the software development and maintenance process.

Frame 25.2: Software configuration items – definitions

Software configuration item (SCI) or configuration item (CI)

An approved unit of software code, a document or piece of hardware that is designed for configuration management and treated as a distinct entity in the software configuration management process.

SCI version

The approved state of an SCI at any given point of time during the development or maintenance process.

Software configuration version

An approved selected set of documented SCIs that **constitute** a software system or document at a given point of time. Activities related to a software configuration version are controlled by *software configuration management* procedures. The software configuration versions are released according to the cited procedures.

A software configuration is composed of as many SCIs as the developers assume will be needed in the future, with each SCI approved, identified, and registered. The SCIs aggregated in each software configuration version naturally correspond to the software components and software definitions reviewed earlier in the book. The SCIs are generally placed into the following four classes:

- Design documents
- Software code
- Data files including files of test cases and test scripts
- Software development tools

A list of common types of SCIs is presented in Frame 25.3.

Table 25.1 lists the SCI contents of two software configuration versions. The software package, whose software configuration versions are shown, includes 11 SCIs: 5 reports, 3 code modules, a test cases file, a compiler, and a software user manual. It should be noted that for part of the SCIs, the same SCI version is used in both software configuration versions, that is, Ver. 1 of SRD is included in both software configuration versions.

Frame 25.3: Common types of software configuration items

Design documents:

- Software development plan (SDP)
- System requirements document
- Software requirements document (SRD)
- Interface design specifications
- Preliminary design document (PDD)
- Critical design document (CDD)
- Database description
- Software test plan (STP)
- Software test procedure (STPR)
- Software test report (STR)
- Software user manuals
- Software maintenance manuals
- Software installation plan (SIP)
- Software maintenance requests (including problem reports)
- Software change requests (SCRs) and software change orders (SCOs)
- Version description document (VDD)

Software code:

- Source code
- Object code
- Prototype software

Data files:

- Test cases and test scripts
- Parameters, codes, and so on

Software development tools (the versions applied in the development and maintenance stages):

- Compilers and debuggers
- Application generators
- CASE tools

Table 25.1   Software configuration versions and the included SCI versions

SCI	Software configuration Version 6.0 SCI version in the SC version	Software configuration Version 7.0 SCI version in the SC version
SRD	Ver. 1	Ver. 1
CDD	Ver. 3	Ver. 4
STP	Ver. 3	Ver. 4
SIP	Ver. 2	Ver. 2
VDD	Ver. 6	Ver. 7
Code Module 1	Ver. 3	Ver. 5
Code Module 2	Ver. 8	Ver. 8
Code Module 3	Ver. 2	Ver. 2
Test cases file	Ver. 3	Ver. 4
CL compiler	Ver. 5	Ver. 7
Software user manual	Ver. 6	Ver. 7

25.3   Release of software configuration versions

The need to release a new software configuration version usually stems from one or more of the following conditions:

- Defective SCIs identified in former version/s
- Special features requested by new customers
- Team initiatives to introduce SCI improvements
- New features initiated to manage market changes, and also the desire to improve the software product marketability

A discussion of the following issues, all of which are part of the process of software configuration version release, is presented in the remainder of this section:

- Software configuration evolution models
- Software configuration management plans (SCMPs)
- Documentation of software configuration versions

25.3.1   Types of software configuration releases

Baseline versions, intermediate versions, and revisions are considered to be the three main types of configuration releases.

Baseline software configuration releases (baseline releases)

Baseline releases are planned ahead, while their content and schedules are defined in the SCMP.

The first baseline configuration version is defined at an advanced stage of the development process following the review, testing, and approval of all development items. The next baseline releases are expected to be released according to the SCMP, at the end of the software development stage, following an organizational change, or the likes.

Baseline configuration versions are defined for design documents, test plans, source code, and so on.

Intermediate software version releases (intermediate release)

When problems requiring immediate attention arise – such as the need to correct defects identified in an important SCI, or perform immediate adaptations required by legal changes – an intermediate version of the software is often prepared.

Usually, intermediate versions only serve a portion of a firm's customers, and for a limited period until replaced by a new baseline configuration version. Naturally, we can expect that these intermediate versions will not receive the attention and efforts typically devoted to the release of new baseline versions. An intermediate software configuration version release can thus serve as a "pilot" or springboard to the next baseline version.

Revision software releases (revision release)

Revision releases introduce minor changes and corrections to a given software baseline release. In some cases, several successive revisions are released before a new baseline configuration version is released.

COTS software configuration version releases

COTS software packages present typical software configuration versions. These are planned versions usually released once or twice a year. These releases are designed to achieve improved marketability by presenting substantial software improvements and new features in each new release.

Numeration conventions for identification of SCI and software configuration versions

A numeration convention applied for software configuration versions: baseline configuration versions are numbered 1.0, 2.0, 3.0, 4.0, and so on, and intermediate and revisions versions are numbered 1,1, 2.5, 3.1, 3.2, 4.1, 4.2, and so on. Each software configuration version is composed of SCIs, each of which is identified by its own version and revision numbers.

The numeration conventions can likewise be used to identify firmware to be embedded in a variety of product lines and models, but these may require special adaptations.

25.3.2   Software configuration version evolution models

The organization's policy of version evolution defines the number of software configuration versions that will follow any given software configuration version. According to the linear evolution model, only one new software configuration version will replace the former "old" software configuration version. However, according to the tree evolution model, one or more new software configuration versions will replace former software configuration version. The version evolution models and their advantages and disadvantages are discussed in Chapter 15, and an illustration of linear and tree model "history" can be viewed in Figure 15.1.

Tables 25.2 and 25.3 list seven software configuration versions and their configuration item versions for software packages that adopt the linear evolution model and the tree evolution model, respectively. In both examples, decimal numeration is implemented with the configuration version type – baseline, intermediate, or revision releases, clearly marked.

Table 25.2 presents the SCI contents of seven configuration versions of an accounting software system that adopts the linear evolution model throughout its development and operational stages.

Table 25.2 presents seven software configuration versions released over a period of more than 3 years 6 months. The baseline versions were released once a year, in the middle of January. In addition, two revision versions and an intermediate version were released during this period. Note that software configuration version1.0 is a *design baseline software configuration* version, and as such it only includes two SCIs, both of which are design configuration item versions. Note also that software module SM-4 was only added to the software package for the baseline software configuration version release 4.0.

Version release 2.1 is a revision released with only three of its SCIs changed from the baseline software configuration version 2.0: DD-1, DD-2, and SM-3. Baseline configuration version 4.0 introduces the new software module, SM-4, which was released in response to a new accounting regulation. Version 6.03 of the commercial CASE tool, applied for the development and maintenance, was replaced with the more advanced version 7.0, while the baseline configuration for this release is version 3.0 of our software system.

Table 25.3 presents the SCI contents of the 10 software configuration versions of a system developed for printer firmware, where separate versions were developed for the standard printer, fast black printer, and printer-fax. Further development of the product line resulted in two separate configuration versions, one for the fast black ink printer and one for the printer-fax. In this case, the first baseline software configuration version was defined at the end of the development stage.

Table 25.2 Configuration versions of an accounting software package – a linear evolution model policy

SCI name	1.0	2.0	2.1	2.2	3.0	4.0	4.1
	BI	BI	Re	In	BI	BI	Re
	Jan. 1, 2014	Jan. 1, 2015	Aug 7, 2015	May 1, 2015	Jan. 1, 2016	Jan 1, 2017	Sep 9, 2017
Design document DD-1	1.0	1.0	1.3	1.3	2.0	2.0	2.4
Design document DD-2	1.0	2.0	2.2	2.3	3.0	3.0	3.1
Software module SM-1	–	1.0	1.0	1.1	2.0	2.0	2.2
Software module SM-2	–	1.0	1.0	1.5	2.0	2.0	2.0
Software module SM-3	–	1.0	1.3	1.4	2.0	3.0	3.3
Software module SM-4	–	–	–	–	–	1.0	1.0
Test case file TC	–	1.0	1.0	1.0	1.0	1.0	1.3
User manual UM	–	–	–	–	1.0	2.0	2.2
CASE tool CA	–	6.03	6.03	6.03	7.0	7.0	7.0

BI = Baseline, Re = Revision, In = Intermediate.

Table 25.3 Configuration versions of printer firmware products – tree evolution model

	Standard printer			Fast black printer				Printer-fax		
	a1.0	a2.0	a2.1	a1.0	b1.1	b2.0	b3.0	a1.0	c1.1	c2.0
	Bl	Bl	In	Bl	In	Bl	Bl	Bl	In	Bl
	Jan 1, 2015	Jan 1, 2016	Aug 8, 2016	Jun 1, 2015	Sep 3, 2015	Jan 1, 2016	Jan 1, 2017	Jan 1, 2016	Feb 4, 2016	Jan 1, 2017
Design document DD-1	1.0	2.0	2.0	1.0	11.4	12.0	13.0	2.0	21.3	22.0
Design document DD-2	1.0	2.0	2.1	1.0	11.2	12.0	12.0	2.0	21.3	22.0
Design document DD-3	–	–	–	–	–	–	–	–	21.1	22.0
Design document DD-4	–	–	–	–	–	11.0	11.0	–	–	–
Software module SM-1	1.0	2.0	2.3	1.0	1.0	11.0	11.0	2.0	21.4	22.0
Software module SM-2	1.0	1.0	1.4	1.0	11.4	12.0	13.0	1.0	1.0	21.0
Software module SM-3	–	–	–	–	–	–	–	–	21.2	22.0
Software module SM-4	–	–	–	–	–	11.0	11.0	–	–	--
Test case file TC	1.0	2.0	2.0	1.0	11.4	12.0	13.0	2.0	2.0	2.0
User manual UM	1.0	1.0	1.1	1.0	11.1	12.0	12.0	1.0	21.1	22.0
Development tool DT	1.5	2.3	2.3	1.5	2.3	2.3	2.5	2.3	2.3	2.5

Bl = Baseline, Re = Revision, In = Intermediate.

Table 25.3 illustrates the evolution of software configurations in the development and maintenance stages according to the tree model. Three parallel firmware configuration versions evolved so as to serve three product lines: standard printers, fast black printer, and printer-fax. The table displays two version partitions:

First: The baseline version a1.0, common to the standard printer and the fast black printer firmware, is partitioned into a standard printer baseline version a2.0 and fast black ink printer b2.0, an intermediate version b2.1.

Second: The standard printer baseline version a2.0, common to the standard printer and the printer-fax, is partitioned into a standard printer intermediate a2.1and printer-fax intermediate version c1.1.

Table 25.3 also displays the SCIs common to the firmware of more than one product. In addition, the table displays unique SCIs included in the firmware of only one product: DD-4 and SM-4 are unique to the fast black printer, while DD-3 and SM-3 are unique to the printer-fax. In other words, several improvement features were added to the fast black printer and to the printer-fax in a later version. For instance, a new feature based on software module SM-4 was added to the fast black printer in ver. b2.0 released on January 1, 2016, and another new feature, based on software module SM-3, was added to the printer-fax revision c1.1 on February 4, 2016.

25.4 Documentation of software configuration versions

Within the framework of software configuration management, the project manager must verify that all documentation tasks are properly performed. Two of the main types of tasks to be completed are:

- Documentation of SCI versions
- Documentation of software configuration releases (versions and revisions)

The information items required for documentation of an SCI version are listed in Frame 25.4.

Frame 25.4: Documentation of SCI version – a template

Identification of an SCI version

- SCI version number
- Name(s) of software engineer(s) who implemented the change
- Date when the new version was completed and approved

Changes in the new SCI version

- Former SCI version number
- Short description of the introduced change/s
- List of other SCIs that had to be changed as a result of the current changes
- List of SCOs included in the new version
- List of software problem reports resolved by the new version
- Operational and other implications of the changes introduced in the new version

---

The documentation for a new SCI version may be submitted as a document or as part of the code (i.e., as "release notes" in the code listing).

Documentation of software configuration releases, often referred to as a VDD, is presented in Frame 25.5.

Frame 25.5: Software configuration release documentation – version description document (VDD) template

---

Identification of configuration version and its installed sites

- Release version and revision number
- Date of the new version's release
- List of installations where the release was entered (site, date, name of technician that installed the version) – if applicable

Configuration of the released version

- List of SCIs in the released version, including identification of each SCI version.
- List of hardware configuration items required for operating the specified version, including specification of each hardware configuration item.
- List of interfacing software systems (including version) and hardware systems (including model).
- Installation instructions for the new release.

Changes in the new version

Previous software configuration version

- List of SCIs that have been changed, new SCIs, introduced for the first time, and deleted SCIs.
- Short description of introduced changes.
- Operational and other implications of changes introduced in the new release.

Further development issues

- List of software system problems that have not been solved in the new version.
- List of SCRs and proposals for development of the software system, for which implementation of development was delayed.

25.5   Configuration management planning

The main objectives of configuration management planning are:

- To plan the schedule and contents of baseline and other software configuration version releases.
- To prepare estimates of the resources required to carry out the plan.
- To enable to follow-up the progress of activities involved in software version releases.

Configuration management plans (CMPs) are required during the development stage, as well as the operation (maintenance) stage. Accordingly, a CMP usually includes:

- An overview of the software development project or existing operating software system.
- A list of scheduled baseline version releases.
- A list of scheduled software configuration version intermediate releases.
- A list of SCIs (documents, code, etc.) planned to be included in each planned version.
- A table identifying the correlation between software development project plans and maintenance plans with scheduled releases of new SCIs or SCI versions.
- Estimates of the human resources and budget needed to perform the CMP.

SCMP for the development stage

The SCMP sets the baseline versions release dates based on the project plan; these usually coincide with the conclusion of one or more of the following two events: the design stage and the system test stage. As these annual plans represent the software development activities planned up to the time when the SCMP is prepared, they will inevitably require updates during the year. Contracts for new development projects, as well as project cancellations will make it necessary to periodically update the SCMP.

The project manager is usually the person responsible to carry out these SCM planning tasks in accordance with the SCM procedures.

External participants in the project are required to comply with the SCMP, or to suggest an alternative appropriate for their part of the project – contingent on acceptance by the project manager.

SCMP for the operational (maintenance) stage

During the operational (maintenance) stage, further releases of software configuration versions are required in order to introduce improved software versions. These new versions are released following the accumulation of SCI changes during regular customer use and their subsequent incorporation, or following software error corrections made soon after their identification and resolution.

SCM planning is of special importance for COTS software developers. The SCMPs generally schedule periodic releases for new baseline configuration software versions. These are usually annual, semiannual, or according to the anticipated number of accumulated changes in SCIs. Intermediate software configuration releases are occasionally released, to correct severe software errors or to add features needed to cope with legal or urgent change requirements. The periodic planned baseline releases include corrected and improved versions, as well as new SCIs – each of which include the adaptations and/or improvements initiated by the company. Only SCIs for which changes have been completed and approved by the targeted release date can be included in the new baseline software configuration version.

25.6 Provision of SCM information services

Requests for information frequently raised by software developers:

- "Which SCI MM4 version should I continue coding?"
- "What changes have been introduced in the new version 6.0 of the software?"
- "Who was involved in the development of the new SCI GK11version 1/0?"

Requests for information frequently raised by maintenance teams:

- "Who can provide me with an accurate copy of last year's version 4.1 of the TMY software system?"
- "What version of the design document correlates to the software version we are currently adapting to the new customer requirements?"
- "What version of the software system is installed at ABC Industries?"
- "What changes have been introduced in the version currently installed at the ABC Industries site?"
- "Where can I find the full list of customers that use version 6.8 of our software?"
- "Can we be sure that the version installed at Top Com Ltd. does not include undocumented changes (and changes that have not been approved)?"

These and many similar questions reflect the essentiality of a service that provides accurate and reliable information regarding parts of, or whole, software products for developers and maintenance teams. This service ensures the reliable availability of approved versions of SCIs and software configuration versions, and is of critical importance, considering the constant changes every active software information system undergoes every year. SCM is the information service required to provide this service to professionals – mainly developers, maintenance teams, and customer representatives.

The information provided may be classified into information related to software change control and information dealing with SCI and software configuration versions.

Information services about SCIs and software configuration versions:

- Accurate copies of SCI versions (code SCIs, document SCIs, etc.) and entire software configuration versions.
- Full reports of changes introduced between successive releases (versions and/or revisions) of code SCIs, as well as between successive releases of other types of SCIs.
- Lists of version history for CMIs and software configuration versions.
- Copies of SCI version documentation and software configuration VDDs.
- Detailed version and revision history for SCIs and software configurations versions for any specific SCI or software system product.
- Information about current versions installed at a given site.
- List of sites where a given software configuration version is installed.

Provision of the above information services is practically impossible for manual SCM systems. Only a computerized service may be expected to cope with this task effectively and reliably. For more about this subject, see Section 25.7.

25.7 Computerized tools for performing configuration management tasks

Computerized CM tools have been on the market for many years. These tools differ in their level of comprehensiveness, structure model of their repository, flexibility of application, and ease of use. More comprehensive tools can supply most or almost all of the CM information services listed in Section 25.6.

It is expected that a computerized tool for storage and recovery of data will be able to comply with the required high level of accuracy and completeness of storage and recovery of information, and with the required level of availability (measured by the response time from request for information to its provision).

The computerized SCM tools also operate the mechanisms coordinating the work on SCI changes and prevent damages to software items from teams simultaneously introducing changes in the same SCI. Current-enhanced tools are characterized by easier input capacities, coordination of SCM support teams operating in different development environments, including geographically distributed teams, and provision of an expanded variety of reporting options.

Additional benefits from a computerized SCM system is the high security level it is able to provide:

- Secures the code version and documentation file versions by protecting them from any unintentional damages: changes, deletions, and other damages.

- Activates backup procedures required to secure SCM repository storage.
- Prevents unauthorized bodies from copying, damaging, or deleting SCIs or software configuration versions stored in the SCM repository.

A comparative analysis of two leading computerized tools for configuration management is presented by Akukary (2013).

25.8   The software configuration management function in the organization

The software configuration management function is performed by a specialized unit, the SCO unit, supported by technical professionals of the organization. The SCM unit, in some places called the SCM Authority (SCMA), implements the SCM procedures and oversees their compliance by the software development and maintenance teams.

According to the ISO/IEC/Std. 12207-2008 (ISO, 2008), the processes required to be performed by the SCM unit supported by the organization technical professionals include:

1. To prepare a software configuration plan. The plan should be coordinated with software configuration plans of the various ongoing development projects and operating systems.

2. To control the identification of SCIs to be stored in the SCM repository. The identification of the stored SCIs should be according to a scheme defined in the SCM procedures.

3. In cases when SCC is performed by the SCM to control software changes and verify their full documentation according to the requirements detailed in the SCC chapter of the SCM procedure, the SCC documentation should include the SCR, SCR evaluation report, SCC committee decision, verification results for changed SCI, and release details of modified SCI. The change documentation should provide an audit trail to all documents of the change as well to the persons involved.

4. To produce, on request, a detailed status of each stored SCI, including full history of changes, versions, and releases. Preparation of software release code and documentation is carried out by the software development or maintenance teams.

5. To prepare an evaluation report regarding the quality of the SCM operation, including completeness of the stored SCIs.

6. To release and deliver software products and their documentation as required by developers and maintenance teams, while storing master copies of each SCI for the software product lifetime; providing security and safety measures for the repository items.

25.9 Software quality assurance activities related to SCM

The SQA authority performs tasks to assure that the activities and products of SCM comply with the standards and procedures requirements. These are mainly a variety of SCM processes audits performed by the SCMA:

- Prepare audit plans adapted to the characteristics of the projects to be audited.
- Coordinate audits with all involved parties.
- Verify that the SCM processes conform to the relevant procedures and standards.
- Document audit findings – compliance and noncompliance with the required standards and procedures.
- Report findings to supplier and purchasing bodies.
- Support the problem resolution process.

The SQA audit activities cover all the SCM processes, namely, the preparation of SQA plans, control of SCI identification, control of the implementation of SCC procedures (in cases when the SCS function is integrated in the SCM function), production of status reports for SCIs, evaluation of the performance quality of the SCM, and release and delivery of software products and their documentation.

The SQA audit activities related to SCM are presented in Frame 25.6.

Frame 25.6: SQA audit subject for SCM processes

1. **Preparation of software configuration plan**
2. **Control of SCI identification**
3. **Control of software changes** (in cases that SCC is performed by the SCM)
4. **Production, on request, of a detailed status of each stored SCI**
5. **Preparation of an SCM performance evaluation report for release of SCI and software configuration versions**

All respective tasks are defined in CM procedures. SCM audits performed by the SQA unit may be supported by:

- Metrics of SCM performance
- Statistics of SCM performance
- Examining samples of SCM documentation
- Discussions with SCM authority persons and others

Following is a list of typical metrics and statistics of SCM performance used for SCM audits of the various tasks:

1. **Preparing software configuration plan:**
   - Percentage of SCMP items not complying with the procedure and standards (sample results).
   - Percentage of software project plans not complying with the procedure and standards (sample results).
   - Number of SCMP items recorded in the last year.

2. **Control the identification of SCIs:**
   - Percentage of cases where the SCIs identification is incomplete or not compliant with the procedures (sample results).
   - Percentage of cases where the software configuration version identification is incomplete or not compliant with the procedures (sample results).
   - Number of SCIs and software configuration versions stored in the last year.

3. **Control of software changes** (in cases when SCC is performed by the SCM)**:**
   - Total numbers of SCRs submitted to the SCCA in the last year.
   - Percentage of unapproved SCRs relating to development or operation (maintenance activities).
   - Percentage of submitted SCR documents found incomplete or not compliant with the procedure (sample result).
   - Percentage of SCOs not carried out according to requirement instructions or not completed on schedule (sample result).

4. **Production, on request, a detailed status of each stored SCI:**
   - Percentage of cases of SCI versions, where change history is incomplete (sample results).
   - Percentage of software configuration version release history that is incomplete or not fully compliant with the relevant procedures (sample results).

5. **Preparing an SCM performance evaluation report:**
   - Percentage of incomplete or incorrect identification of software configuration versions (sample results).
   - Percentage of cases of missing software configuration version records.

6. **SCI and software configuration versions release:**
   - Percentage of cases of failure to release complete SCI or software configuration version information according to requests (sample results).
   - Number of cases the SCM failed to provide the requested information during the last year.
   - Percentage of cases where production of software configuration version records is not performed immediately.

SQA audits may be combined with software development department audits and documentation control audits relating to issues performed by the project development teams.

Summary

1. **The tasks of software configuration management**

   Software configuration management tasks are classified into the following groups:
   - Storage of identified SCI and software configuration versions
   - Release of SCI and software configuration versions
   - Provision of SCM information services
   - Verification of compliance to SCM procedures
   - Control software change (in cases the SCMA is responsible for the change control task)

2. **Definition of software configuration version**

   An approved selected set of documented SCIs, that **constitute** a software system or document at a given point of time, where the activities related to a software configuration version are controlled by *software configuration management* procedures. The software configuration versions are released according to the cited procedures.

3. **The difference between baseline, intermediate, revision releases**

   Baseline releases: Baseline releases are planned ahead and their content and schedule are defined in the SCMP.

   The first baseline configuration version is defined at an advanced stage of the development process following review, testing, and approval of all development items. The next baseline releases are expected to be released according to the SCMP, at the end of a software development stage, following an organizational change, and so on.

   Baseline configuration versions are defined for design documents, test plans, source code, and so on.

   Intermediate releases: When problems that require immediate attention arise – such as the need to correct defects identified in an important SCI, or perform immediate adaptations required by legal changes, an intermediate version of the software is often prepared.

   Revision releases: Revision releases introduce minor changes and corrections to a given software baseline release. In some cases, several successive revisions are released before a new baseline configuration version is released.

4. **COTS software configuration version release**

   COTS software packages present typical software configuration versions planned to be released once or twice a year. These releases are designed to achieve improved marketability by presenting substantial software improvements and new features in each new release.

5. The objectives of configuration management plans

The main objectives of configuration management planning are:

- To plan the schedule and contents of baseline and other software configuration version releases
- To prepare estimates of the resources required to carry out the plan
- To enable to follow-up the progress of activities involved in software version releases

6. The information services of SCM

Information services about SCIs and software configuration versions include:

- Accurate copies of SCI versions (code SCIs, document SCIs, etc.) and entire software configuration versions.
- Full reports of change history of code SCIs, as well of software configuration versions.
- Copies of SCI version documentation and software configuration VDDs.
- Information about current versions installed at a given site.
- List of sites where a given software configuration version is installed.

7. Security applications that the computerized SCM system provide

Additional benefits from a computerized SCM system is the high security level it is able to provide:

- Secures the code version and documentation files versions by protecting them from any unintentional damages: changes, deletions, and other damages.
- Activates back-up procedures required to secure SCM repository storage.
- Prevents unauthorized bodies from copying, damaging, or deleting SCIs or software configuration versions stored in the SCM repository.

8. The SCM tasks performed by the organization

According to ISO/IEC/Std. 12207-2008 (ISO, 2008), the processes required to be performed by the SCM unit include:

1. To prepare a software configuration plan.
2. To control the identification of SCIs to be stored in the SCM repository.
3. To control software changes and their full documentation in cases when SCC is performed by the SCM.
4. To produce, on request, a detailed status of each stored SCI, including full change history of versions and releases.
5. To prepare an evaluation report regarding the quality of the SCM operation in terms of completeness of the stored SCIs.
6. To release and deliver software products and their documentation as required by developers and maintenance teams.

9. **Software Quality assurance activities related to SCM**

The SQA unit tasks to assure that the activities of SCM comply with standards and procedures are performed mainly by audits:

* Preparing audit plans adapted to the characteristics of the projects to be audited.
* Coordinating audits with all involved parties.
* Examining the SCM processes conformance with the relevant procedures and standards.
* Documenting audits findings – compliance and noncompliance with the required standards and procedures.
* Reporting the findings to the supplier and acquirer bodies.
* Supporting the problem resolution process.

Selected bibliography

Aiello R. and Sachs L. (2010) *Configuration Management Best Practices: Practical Methods that Work in the Real World*, Addison-Wesley, Upper Saddle River, NJ.

Akukary A. M. (2013) Configuration management: a comparative analysis of CVS and SVN, *International Journal of ICT and Management*, Vol. 1, No. 1, pp. 157–162.

Alidoosti R., Moaven S., and Habibi J. (2015) Service oriented configuration management of software architecture, *International Journal for Network Security and Its Applications*, Vol. 7, No. 1, pp. 29–43.

Buchmann T., Dotor A., and Westfechtel B. (2013) MOD2-SCM: A model-driven product line for software configuration management systems, *Information and Software Technology*, Vol. 55, No. 3, pp. 530–650.

Estublier J., Leblang D., van der Hoek A., Ntnu R. C., Clemm G., Tichy W., and Wiborg-Weber D. (2005) Impact of software engineering research on the practice of software configuration management, *ACM Transaction on Software Engineering and Methodology*, Vol. 14, No. 4, pp. 1–48.

Fauzi S. S. M. (2010) Software configuration management in global software development: a systematic map, *17th Asia Pacific Software Engineering Conference, Sydney, NSW, Australia*, pp. 404–403.

ISO/IEC/IEEE (2008) *ISO/IEC/IEEE 12207-2008 Systems and Software Engineering – Software Life Cycle Processes*, International Organization for Standardization (ISO), Geneva, Switzerland.

ISO (2014) *ISO/IEC 90003:2014 Software Engineering – Guidelines for the Application of ISO 9001: 2008 to Computer Software*, International Organization for Standardization (ISO), Geneva, Switzerland.

Kogel M. (2008) Towards software configuration management for unified models, *Proceedings of the 2008 International Workshop on Comparison and Versioning of Software Models (CVSM'08)*, pp. 19–24.

Lapouchnian A., Yu Y., and Mylopoulos J. (2007) *Requirements-Driven Design and Configuration Management of Business Processes*, Proceedings of 5th International Conference on Business Process Management, LNCS, vol. 4714, Springer, Berlin, Germany, pp. 246–261.

Leon A. (2015) *Software Configuration Management Handbook*, 3rd Edition, Artech House, Boston, Mass.

Pressman R. J. and Maxim B. R. (2015) *Software Engineering – A Practitioner's Approach*, 8th Edition (European adaptation), McGraw-Hill International, London.

Sarma A., Redmiles D., and van der Hoek A. (2008) Empirical evidence of the benefits of workspace awareness in software configuration management, in *Proceedings of the 16 ACM SIGSOFT International Symposium of Foundations of Software Engineering*, pp. 113–132.

Review questions

25.1 One of the tasks of an SCM is to supply information about sites where a given software configuration version is installed (Section 25.6).

- Explain potential uses of this type of information and its contribution to software quality.

25.2 Design documents or source code files are identified and stored as SCIs (see Frame 25.3) for obvious reasons: Further development of the software system or its correction cannot take place without accurate copies of these items.

     Explain in your own words why the following should be identified and stored as SCIs:

a. Test cases

b. Compiler

c. Software installation plans

d. Software change requests files

25.3 It is mentioned that a version history of a software system configuration includes baseline, intermediate, and revision version releases.

a. Explain in your own words the function of each type of release.

b. Explain in your own words the particular importance of baseline versions.

25.4 Frame 25.6 is a template that lists the information items necessary for software configuration version documentation (VDD).

- List possible uses for each of the information items mentioned in the template.

25.5 The SQA unit is expected to spend a significant part of its resources carrying out software configuration audits.

a. List the main SQA audit tasks.

b. Explain the contributions of each task to software quality.

Topics for discussion

25.1 The success of an SCM authority depends to a great extent on compliance to SCM procedures.

a. Referring to the release of new versions of the software system, explain in your own words the risks incurred to software quality by partial compliance to SCM procedures.

b. What tools are available for verification of compliance to SCM procedures?

25.2 "Audit trails" are basic requirements of proper SCM documentation. In order for a document to comply with audit trail requirements, the documentation has to provide information enabling identification of the source for each event and/or item recorded.

This information enables future location of the source according to the document reference, name of programmer who coded the software unit, and so forth.

  a. List at least two audit trails required within the framework of SCM and show how the required audit trail information may become available.

  b. Explain how the audit trails you described in (a) contributes to software quality.

25.3 Software houses that develop and maintain COTS software packages to serve large customer populations are recommended to adopt the line evolution model for their packages rather than the tree evolution model.

  a. Describe the principles of line and the tree evolution models, and the environments in which they are used.

  b. Do you agree with the above recommendation? List your arguments – pros and cons.

  c. What consequences for the structure and size of the COTS software packages would you follow when adopting this recommendation?

  d. What are the consequences of this recommendation from the user's perspective?

25.4 The software maintenance department provides services to 215 customers who use one or more of the company's three popular software packages. From time to time, a maintenance team discovers that the software version installed in a customer's site includes unrecorded changes that were not requested by an SCR, nor approved as part of an SCO.

  a. Who do you believe inserted the unrecorded changes and under what conditions could this have occurred?

  b. What effect could this event have on maintenance performance, and what is the expected influence on software quality from the perspective of the customer?

  c. What measures could be taken to make sure that no such unauthorized changes occur?

25.5 The VDD document (see Frame 25.5) includes a list of unsolved problems pertaining to a released software version.

  • Discuss the justification for including this type of information in a VDD.

25.6 Most SCM systems are operated nowadays by specialized software packages.

  • Explain the special features offered effectively and efficiently only by computerized configuration management software packages and explain their contribution to software quality.

  a. Discuss the appropriateness of the decision.

  b. Suggest ways for improving the decision.

Chapter 26

CASE Tools and IDEs – Impact on Software Quality

26.1 What is a CASE tool?

An increasing variety of specialized computerized tools (actually software packages) have been made available to software engineering departments since the early 1990s.

The purpose of these tools is to make the work of development and maintenance teams more efficient and effective, collectively named CASE (computeraided software engineering) tools.

Frame 26.1 contains the basic definition of a CASE tool.

Frame 26.1: CASE tools – definition

CASE tools – definition
CASE tools: Computerized software development tools that support the software developer and maintenance staff by increasing the efficiency and effectiveness of the processes, and reducing the resources required and reducing defects generated when supporting the performance of one or more phases of the software life cycle.

CASE tools contribute substantially to the economy of software project development and maintenance. In addition, from an SQA point of view, these tools also improve project quality.

The contribution of CASE tools to the software process is presented in Frame 26.2.

Software Quality: Concepts and Practice, First Edition. Daniel Galin.
© 2018 the IEEE Computer Society, Inc. Published 2018 by John Wiley & Sons, Inc.

Frame 26.2: The contribution of CASE tools to the software project

The contribution of CASE tools to the software project
• Substantial savings in software development resources
• Shorter time to market
• Reduced generation of defects
• Increased automatic identification of defects and their correction during development
• Greater reuse due to increased standardization of software components and programs and improved search of potential COTS components and software
• Substantial savings in maintenance teams' resources
• Improved project scheduling and control of project performance

In light of their characteristics, CASE tools serve as a source to ease the amount of effort expended on the development of increasingly complex and large software systems.

The following sections will deal with the below subjects:

- The classic CASE tool
- IDE CASE tools
- Real CASE tools

The generality of the definition of CASE enables compilers, interactive debugging systems, configuration management systems, and automated testing systems to be considered as CASE tools. The CASE tools may be classified into three groups:

- **The first group** includes the well-established computerized software development support tools (such as interactive debuggers, compilers, configuration management services, and project progress control systems). These tools can readily be considered *classic* CASE tools.

- **The second group** includes CASE tools based on the integration of several classic CASE tools into a common work environment, providing a substantial improvement on the efficiency and effectiveness of software development, and also known as *IDE* CASE tools.

- **The third group** includes new tools that support the developer during several consecutive project development phases, and are referred to as *real* CASE tools. When referring to *real* CASE tools, it is customary to distinguish between *upper* CASE tools that support the analysis and design phases, *lower* CASE tools that support the coding and testing phases (where "upper" and "lower" refer to the location of these phases in the Waterfall Model – Annex D, Sec. D.1.1), and *integrated* CASE tools that support the analysis, design, and coding phases.

26.2 The classic CASE tool

The main types of classic CASE tools deal with the following areas:

- Code editing
- Configuration management
- Automatic documentation
- Software project management

Some software quality assurance publications include word processing and spreadsheet programs.

26.2.1 Code editing

Compiling, interpreting, or applying interactive code debugging based on examination of the code for language consistency. Accordingly, special compilers and interpreters need to be developed for each version of programming language or development tool.

26.2.2 Configuration management

Basic software configuration management (SCM) tools separately store each of the products of the software development process, including software versions created by maintenance teams. Besides storage tasks, the important service provided by configuration management is the retrieval of stored files according to the needs of the development and maintenance teams.

Advanced configuration management is achieved by the repository methodology, where all products of the development (and maintenance) processes are integrated and stored under a uniform structure (metadata model). The project information accumulates in the repository as development proceeds, and is updated as changes are initiated during the development phases and maintenance stage. The repository of the previous development phase serves as a basis for the next phase. The computerized configuration management of the repository guarantees the information's consistency and integrity, and its compliance with project methodology as well as its standardization according to style and structure procedures and work instructions. Many CASE tools are based on the use of the repository data. Some lower CASE and integrated CASE tools can automatically generate code based entirely on the design information stored in the repository. Reverse engineering (reengineering) tools are also based on the use of repository information.

Figure 26.1 presents a comparison of CASE tools in the development process: basic SCM-supported process versus repository-supported process.

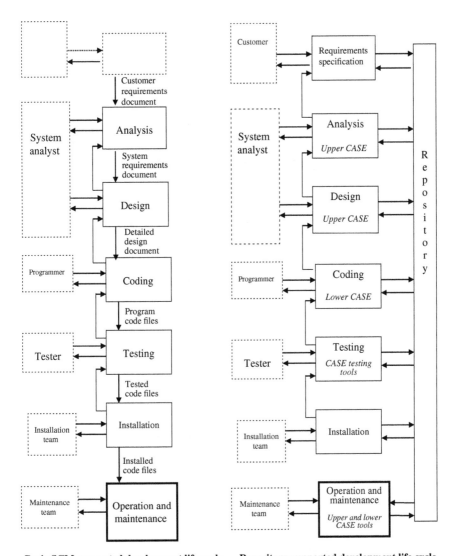

Basic SCM-supported development life cycle   **Repository-supported development life cycle**

Figure 26.1   Basic SCM-supported versus repository-supported development life cycle

26.2.3 Automatic documentation

The documentation is expected to support the software development process as a basis for team work, maintenance for error correction and software changes, and also contract–legal issues. While it is commonly accepted that comprehensive documentation is an important part of software development and maintenance, the fact that programmers dislike documentation tasks is well known. Thus, automated documentation becomes especially important and, when based on the project repository, is provided by various automated tools.

The substantial reduction in documentation is a major part of agile methodologies, mainly to save developing resources and achieve shorter "time to market." An important study by Cozzetti et al. (2005) tried to realize the need for documentation by maintenance staff. The survey found that while, on the one hand, the maintenance staff intensively used certain types of documentation, on the other hand, many other types of commonly available documentation were hardly used. The types of documentation found to be most used for structured analysis projects were unit source code, system and acceptance test plans, requirement lists and descriptions, logical and physical data models, component specifications, implementation plans, and data dictionary. More than half of the types of documentation were scarcely ever used, even if available to the staff.

Considering the survey results, and the typical state of affairs when documentation is only poor, partial, not updated, or even nonexisting, a rational conclusion for development and maintenance departments would be to reduce the variety of documentation, and to ensure quality for the essentially required documentation types.

26.2.4   Software project management

Software project management tools support the planning of project schedule and resources required. The tools enable progress control of software development projects, serving the different levels of participants in software development projects: departments, units project teams, and individuals in development teams.

For more on project management, see Appendix C.

26.3   IDE CASE tools

An integrated development environment (IDE) is a software program that creates an advanced computing environment enabling the programmer to easily employ several software development tools, that is, code editor, interpreter, debugger, and compiler, in the same work environment. Practically, the IDE enables the programmer to use a variety of development tools while applying the same user interface (in the same work environment). This capability facilitates a significant improvement for the programmer's functionality in regard to productivity and effectiveness.

An example of IDE features, JCreator – a Java IDE, is presented in Frame 26.3.

Frame 26.3: IDE features example – JCreator, Java IDE

IDE features example – JCreator, Java IDE
• Project management templates • Code completion • Debugger interface • Editor and syntax highlighting • Wizard for walk-through assistance • Customizable user interface • Tabbed documents with dockable windows and toolbars

IDEs have already been in use for more than three decades. The IDEs have become more and more comprehensive over the years, and today serve a growing population of software developers. The popular IDEs regularly release new versions that typically increase the variety of integrated software development tools and improve the existing development tools and their user interface. Part of the IDEs support the object-oriented software development methodology. The last decade has provided IDE support developments for mobile applications. IDEs differ in their user interface type, the computing platform they run on, and the programming languages they support.

Classification of IDEs can be made according to several IDE attributes:

a. **Type of user interface**, textual or graphical/visual. An example of a textual IDE is Turbo Pascal. Most modern IDEs are graphical; some of the most popular ones are Visual Studio, Eclipse, and NetBeans.

b. **Computing platform**. Part of the IDEs were developed for one computing platform, while others are applicable to more than one computing platform. Common computing platforms include UNIX, Linux, Microsoft Windows, and OS. An example of a multicomputing platform is the Judo IDE that runs on Windows, Mac OS, and Linux.

c. **Language support**. Part of the IDEs support one programming language, while others support more than one. Examples of IDEs supporting one language are JCreator that supports Java, WingWare that supports the Python programming language, and Zend Studio that supports PHP. Examples of IDEs supporting multilanguages are Eclipse supporting C, C++, PHP, Java and more, and Geany supporting C, Java, HTML, Pascal and more. Language plugins are installed in many IDEs to add new programming languages to the IDE. Eclipse IDE uses plugins for C++, Ada, Python, PHP, and other programming languages.

d. **Cost**. Many IDEs are free of charge, while some are charged according to a variety of plans.

A multitude of articles are dedicated to IDE applications, evaluating their performance and contribution to software development: Kerrigan et al. (2007), Muslu et al. (2012), Bragdon et al. (2010), Murphy et al. (2006), Chafle et al. (2007), Sentilles et al. (2008), and Leino and Wustholz (2014), to name but a few.

26.4   Real CASE tools

Real CASE tools contribute to a variety of software development and maintenance processes. In this section, examples of the following areas are provided:

- Analysis and design tools
- Coding tools
- Automated testing tools
- Detection of defect and their correction
- Advanced automatic documentation tools
- Reengineering tools

26.4.1   Analysis and design tools

Generating design and diagramming

CASE tools of this group create design diagrams based on requirement text and diagrams. Other tools create design diagrams according to requirement specifications.

26.4.2   Coding tools

Automatic code generation

Code generation tools transform design records into prototypes or application software compatible with a given software development language (or development tool/s).

Refactoring

Refactoring CASE tools perform a process of rewriting program source code automatically without changing its functionality or behavior. The improvements include eliminating redundancies, improving data structures, changing inefficient processes, as well as correcting cases of noncompliance with coding rules and instructions. The refactoring process is applied by software developers. Refactoring tools are of various sophistication levels and perform anywhere from part of the refactoring steps to the whole process. Two of the many publications dedicated to refactoring tools are Murphy-Hill and Black (2008) and Drienyovszky et al. (2010).

Software components reuse

To enable utilizing software reuse tools for integration of reused components in a new software, the reused component requires customization so that it may be suited in terms of size and programming language. Other tools of this group deal with fitting components of object-oriented software to new software products. Examples of papers that present these issues are Rosello et al. (2007) and Biggerstaff (2001).

26.4.3 Automated testing tools

Automated testing includes the manual activities of planning and designing the tests, and preparing the test cases. All other activities, namely, performing the tests, including the regression tests, and reporting the test results, including comparative reports, are computerized; in manual testing, where all activities are manual, quantitative comparisons based on empirical results show that a testing process requires one or more regression tests run for automated testing to be preferred.

The following are the main types of automated testing:

a. Correctness testing
  - GUI tests
  - Functional tests

b. Availability and load tests

c. Other automated testing types
  - Code auditing
  - Automatic coverage monitoring
  - Integrity (security) testing

Additional contributions of automation are in the test management and control.

The following are the features offered by automated management software testing:

- Documenting the planning and design of the tests
- Error tracking: detection, correction, and regression tests
- Preparing summary reports of testing, and error correction follow-up
- Execution of automated software tests
- Automated listing of automated software test results and detected errors
- Follow-up of errors reported by users, their correction, and retesting
- Summary reports for maintenance activities

A detailed discussion of automated testing is presented in Section 14.8.

26.4.4   Detection of defect and their correction

Automatic repair of software defects

Classic CASE tools provide us with comprehensive tools for the detection of defects – debuggers and compilers. The challenge of developing real CASE tool to automatically identify defects and repair them is adopted by several groups of CASE tools developers. These tools implement a variety of approaches. A summary of the achievements of these efforts is presented in several papers from 2014 to 2015 (Durieux et al., 2015; Mechtaev et al., 2015; Pei et al., 2014; Smith et al., 2015).

Encouraging results were presented for AutoFix (Pei et al., 2011, 2015). In a 2015 experiment, AutoFix successfully fixed 42% of the software faults (86 out of 204 faults), where in most cases (51 out of 86 cases) the quality of the fix was comparable to a fix performed by a programmer. The remainder of the fixes were all correct but their quality was lower, when evaluated for readability and simplicity. A great part of the unfixed faults were found to be design faults. The computer processing was quite "heavy," with an average processing time of almost 20 minutes per fix. The AutoFix procedure is based on the following steps: (1) Preparing simple base statements on the system requirements (termed "contracts"). This step is manual and performed by the programmer. The rest of the steps are performed automatically. (2) Processing the contracts to create a set of test cases. (3) Performing analysis of the tested software with static and dynamic methods analysis (methods for identifying faults and producing a collection of suggested fixes). Through applying the prepared set of test cases, the suggested fixes are tested. (4) Ranking the suggested fixes according to defined heuristics, and locating the fix with the higher quality. Higher successful repair rate of 60 and 57% are reported for two other automated fixing tools by Smith et al. (2015). However, these promising results, as well as other experimental results, were obtained only for the type of software types for which the tool was developed.

Less promising results were presented by Mechtaev et al. (2015) when comparing two fault repair tools, DirectFix versus SemFix. The rate of correct fixes by DirectFix and SemFix were 53 and 17%, respectively. The rate of fixes that failed by DirectFix and SemFix were 31 and 51%, respectively. The more successful results of DirectFix are probably achieved with a more comprehensive tool, as shown by the average computer resource used before fix: about 3.5 minutes for DirectFix compared with 9 seconds for SemFix.

Quite disappointing results were reported by Durieux et al. (2015) when implementing three fault repair tools together. The three tools together fixed only 41 out of 224 faults (18%) with 59 patches; however, only 8 patches were undoubtedly correct.

Further analysis of 42 of the produced fixes showed that most of them are incorrect (26 out of 42–62%). The computer resources consumed in this experiment reached an average of 1 hour per fault fixed.

26.4.5 Advanced automatic documentation tools

Automatic documentation of program changes

Documenting software changes due to bug correction or function improvement is usually a burden to the heavily loaded maintenance teams. The result in many cases is incomplete and inaccurate documentation. A real CASE tool performs this task and creates an automatic generation of human-readable documentation. The documentation, based on the comparison of old and new software versions, includes identification of the location of the software change and description of the effect of the change on behavior of the program, including the conditions under which the behavior changes and what the new behavior is. The automatic documentation of changes leaves the information on "why it was changed" for manual documentation. Experimental application of documenting 10,000 changes in an entire repository took about 3 hours. For additional information, see Buse and Weimar (2010).

26.4.6 Reengineering tools

Reverse engineering

Reverse engineering is a group of technologies that focus on knowledge of higher abstraction level extracted from available software products. Reverse engineering processes are capable of deriving procedural design representation, data and program structure out of available source code, high-level programming code, and website code. These outcomes of a reverse engineering process are invaluable in cases of well-established software systems that have undergone a series of changes over the years, and have no up-to-date accurate and complete documentation of the requirement, design, data structure, and so on. Available CASE tools are based on a variety of algorithms and processes, and provide different levels abstraction and completeness as well as differences in effectiveness and efficiency. Development efforts invested in these CASE tools generate more advanced tools every year. Reverse engineering processes include processes targeted to the retrieval of data structures, data bases details, and so on. Another types of processes deal with the extraction of procedural and functional aspects of a software system, especially to support the understanding of its modules performance, security procedures, interoperability, customizability features, and so on. A comprehensive survey of reverse engineering tools is presented by Kienle and Muller (2010).

Restructuring

Restructuring CASE tools transform old "legacy" software systems that have been "patched" with many corrections and changes. The process of restructuring includes code and data restructuring. Code structuring generates a new code without changing the functionality of the software, and improves its quality by improving its maintainability and understandability, as well as usability. Data restructuring includes the redesign and modification of data structures and databases, data names standardization, elimination of aliases, and correction of noncompliance with coding standards and instructions. The results are improved efficiency of data base services and improved understandability and maintainability of data structures and databases. Improved restructuring data may transform an old programming language into a new (modern) programming language, or replace old data structures with new ones.

Automatic extraction of nonfunctional requirements in available documentation

Requirement specification for a software system, especially for information processing systems, includes, in addition to functional requirements, many nonfunctional requirements, which the developer and maintainer have to fulfill. Examples for these nonfunctional requirements are security requirements (i.e., username and password and rules for their usage), legal requirements (i.e., reporting formats, frequency, and dates), and privacy requirements (i.e., rules for publication, mailing lists). Maintenance teams are typically in need of lists of nonfunctional requirements, when applying corrections or functional improving changes, to ensure coping with those requirements. Several CASE tools perform extraction of nonfunctional requirements out of natural language documents, such as requirement specifications, requests for proposals, agreements, and install manuals and user manuals. These tools implement specialized algorithms and produce lists of the located nonfunctional requirements in human-readable documents. One of these tools is described by Slankas and Williams (2013).

Frame 26.4 presents a summary of the real CASE examples mentioned in Section 26.4.

26.5   The contribution of CASE tools to software quality

CASE tools contribute to software product quality by fulfilling the functional and nonfunctional requirements, improving the productivity and schedules of software development processes and reducing the number of errors in the delivered software product. In order to evaluate the contribution of CASE tools to reduce or eliminate software errors anticipated by each of the nine causes of software errors listed in Section 2.3, classic and real CASE tools are included in our evaluation.

Table 26.1 lists the contribution of CASE tools to software quality. When examining the table, we find that the contribution of CASE tools is either by eliminating or reducing errors generated by a given cause, or by identifying or correcting software errors created by a specific cause. The contribution of CASE tools varies from small to very large for some error causes, while no contribution may be found for other error causes.

Frame 26.4: Examples of real CASE – a summary

Area of real CASE application	Examples of CASE tools
1. Analysis and design tools	**Generating design and diagramming** create design based on requirements text and diagrams and design diagrams according to requirements.
2. Coding tools	**a. Automatic code generation** generates code based on design records
	b. Refactoring performs rewriting of source code without changing the functionality and behavior of the software
	c. Software components reuse performs fitting of the size and programming language of reused components to new software.
3. Automated testing tools	Automatically performs correctness testing, availability, and load tests and other types of testing. Additional tools contribute to planning and control of software testing.
4. Detection of defect and their correction	**Automatic repair of software defects** automatically performs identification of defects and repairs them.
5. Advanced automatic documentation tools	**Automatic documentation of program changes** creates automatically generated human-readable documentation of software changes due to error corrections and functional improvement software changes.
6. Reengineering tools	**a. Reverse engineering and restructuring** performs knowledge extracting from available artifact, such as extracting design information out of source code.
	b. Restructuring transforms old software into new structured code, without changing the functionality or behavior of the software.
	c. Automatic extraction of nonfunctional requirements in available documentation performs search for nonfunctional requirements in various documentation such as manuals, requests for proposals.

Table 26.1 The contribution of CASE tools to software quality

	Extent and manner of contribution to quality	
Cause of software errors	Classic CASE tools	Real CASE tools
1. Faulty requirements definition	No contribution	**Small contribution** • Reverse engineering • Automatic extraction of non-functional requirements in available documentation
2. Client-developer communication failures	No contribution	No contribution
3. Deliberate deviations from software requirements	No contribution	**Large contribution** • Generating design and diagramming
4. Logical design errors	No contribution	**Small contribution** • Automatic code generation • Reverse engineering
5. Coding errors	**Very large contribution** • Code editing • Configuration management	**Very large contribution** • Refactoring • Software components reuse
6. Noncompliance with coding and documentation instructions	**Large contribution** • Code editing	**Very large contribution** • Automatic code generation • Refactoring • Reverse engineering
7. Shortcomings in the testing process	No contribution	**Large contribution** • Automated testing tools • Automatic repair of software defects
8. Procedural errors	**Large contribution** • Configuration management	No contribution
9. Documentation errors	**Very large contribution** • Automated documentation	**Large contribution** • Automatic documentation of program changes

Summary

1. **The contribution of CASE tools to software development**

    Major contributions of CASE tools to software development may be seen in the improvement in the developer's productivity, and in the shortening of the development period. Even more impressive is the contribution to productivity and quality of software maintenance. Another highly valuable contribution is software reuse, supported by complete, updated documentation and maximum standardization. Last but not least, the contribution to software quality attained through the substantial reduction of errors is also very important.

2. **The difference between classic and real CASE tools and some examples**

    Classic CASE tools are long-established computerized tools that support developers (and maintenance teams), that is, compilers, interpreters, and configuration managers. *Real* CASE tools are "newer" tools, that is, automated design tools based on repository data and automated software testing.

3. **Integrated development environment (IDE)**

    An integrated development environment (IDE) is a software program that creates an advanced computing environment enabling the programmer to easily employ several software development tools. Practically, the IDE enables the programmer to use a variety of development tools while applying the same user interface. This capability facilitates a significant improvement on the programmer's functionality in regard to productivity and effectiveness.

4. **The contributions of CASE tools to the management of software development and maintenance**

    The main CASE tools that contribute to the management of software projects are project scheduling and software metrics tools. Software scheduling tools are aimed at the planning and follow-up of projects. Software metrics tools measure the performance of software development and maintenance teams automatically, showing improvement (or decline) of a team's performance and compliance to performance standards.

5. **CASE tools with a very large contribution to quality**

    Classic CASE tools with a very large contribution are:
    - Code editing
    - Configuration management
    - Automated documentation
        Real CASE tools with a very large contribution are:
    - Refactoring
    - Software components reuse
    - Automatic code generation
    - Reverse engineering

Selected bibliography

Biggerstaff T. J. (2001) *A characterization of generator and component reuse technologies, in* Proceedings of the 3rd International Conference on Generative and Component-Based Software Engineering, Eifurt, Germany, September 2001, pp. 1–9.

Bragdon A., Reiss S. P., Zeleznik R., Karumuri S., Cheung W., Kaplan J., Coleman C., Adeputra F., and LaViola J. J. (2010) *Code Bubbles: rethinking the user interface paradigm of integrated development environments, in* IEEE Proceedings of the 32nd ACM/IEEE Conference on Software Engineering, Cape Town, South Africa, May 2010.

Buse R. P. L. and Weimar W. R. (2010) *Automatically documenting program changes, in* ASE '10 Proceedings of the IEEE/ACM International Conference on Automated Software Engineering, pp. 33–42.

Chafle G., Das G., Dasgupta K., Kumar A., Mittal S., Mukherjea S., and Srivastava B. (2007) An integrated development environment for web services composition, *IEEE International Conference on Web Services (ICWS)*, **2007**, pp. 839–847.

Cozzetti S., de Souza B., Anquetil N., and de Oliveira K. M. (2005) *A study of the documentation essential to software maintenance, in* Proceedings of SIGDOC 05, the 23rd Annual International Conference on Design of Communication Documentation & Designing for Pervasive Information, pp. 68–75.

Drienyovszky D., Horpacsi D., and Thompson S. (2010) *Quickchecking refactoring tools, in* Proceedings of the 9th ACM SIGPLAN Workshop on Erlang, pp. 75–80.

Durieux T., Martinez M., Monperrus M., Sommerard R. and Xuan J. (2015) Automated repair of real bugs: an experience report on the Defects4J dataset, CoRR.abs/1505.07002.2015.

Kerrigan M., Mocan A., Tanler M. and Fensel D. (2007) The web service modeling toolkit – an integrated development environment for semantic web services. (System Description), European Semantic Web Conference (ESWC2007), Inbruck, Austria, pp. 1–8.

Kienle H. M. and Muller H. A. (2010) The tools perspective on software reverse engineering requirements, construction and evaluation, *Advances in Computers*, Vol. 79, pp. 189–290.

Leino K. R. M. and Wustholz V. (2014) The Dafny integrated development environment, *Electronic Proceedings in Theoretical Computer Science (EPTCS)*, Vol. 149, pp. 3–15.

Mechtaev S., Yi J., and Roychoudhury A. (2015) *DirectFix: Looking for simple program repair, in* Proceedings of the 37th International Conference on Software Engineering (ICSE 15), Florence, Italy, May 2015.

Murphy G. C., Kersten M., and Findlater L. (2006) How are Java software developers using the Eclipse IDE? *IEEE Software*, Vol. 23, No. 4, pp. 76–83.

Murphy-Hill E. and Black A. P. (2008) Refactoring tools: fitness for purpose, *IEEE Software*, Vol. 25, No. 5, pp. 38–44.

Muslu K., Brun Y., Holmes R., Ernst M. D., and Notkin D. (2012) Speculative analysis of integrated development environment recommendations, in *Proceedings of the ACM International Conference on Object Oriented Programming System Languages and Applications, Tucson, AZ, October 2012*, pp. 669–682.

Pei Y., Furia C. A., Nordio M., Wei Y., Meyer B., and Zeller A., (2014) Automated fixing of programs with contracts, *IEEE Transaction on Software Engineering*, Vol. 40, No. 5, pp. 427–449.

Pei Y., Wei Y., Furia C. A., Nordio M., and Meyer B. (2011) *Cod-based automated program fixing, in* Proceedings of the 26th IEEE/ACM International Conference on Automated Software Engineering, pp. 1–22.

Rosello E. G., Lado M. J., Mendez A. J., Dacosta J. G., and Cota M. P. (2007) A component framework for reusing a proprietary computer-aided engineering environment, *Advances in Engineering Software*, Vol. 38, No. 4, pp. 256–266.

Sentilles S., Pettersson P., Crnkovic I., and Hakansson J. (2008) *Save-IDE: an integrated development environment for building component-based embedded systems, in* IEEE/ICM 23rd International Conference on Automated Software Engineering, pp. 1–2.

Slankas J. and Williams L. (2013) *Automated extraction of non-functional requirements in available documentation, in* 2013 1st International Workshop on Natural Language Analysis in Software Engineering, San Francisco, CA, May, pp. 9–16.

Smith E. K., Barr E. T., Goues C. Le. and Brun V. (2015) *Is the cure worse than the disease? Overfitting in automated program repair, in* Proceedings of the 2015 10th Joint Meeting on Foundations of Software Engineering, pp. 532–543.

Review questions

26.1 Explain in your own words the expected benefits for software system developers and software maintenance teams of using CASE tools.

26.2 "Advanced configuration management is achieved by the repository methodology, where all the products of the development (and maintenance) processes are integrated and stored under uniform structure ('metadata model')."

a. Define "repository" in your own words.

b. List the functions a repository fulfils and explain their impact on software development productivity.

c. List the functions a repository serves and explain their impact on software quality.

26.3 Software development and functional improvement maintenance are said to have much in common.

a. Discuss their similarities regarding quality assurance and the application of CASE tools. List and explain which CASE tools, if any, can be applied in the same way to both functions.

b. Discuss the special quality assurance problems typical to functional improvement maintenance, and how CASE tools may be applied to the correction process.

26.4 Explain in your own words the expected benefits for software developers and software maintenance teams of using IDEs tools.

The contribution of CASE tools to the quality of project management and quality metrics are questionable.

a. Describe the quality aspects of classic CASE tools for project management and those for quality metrics.

b. Discuss the contributions real CASE tools can make to the quality of project management, and the way in which they actually improve quality.

Topics for discussion

26.1 It has been claimed that "the availability of full and updated documentation provided by an integrated CASE system is of higher value for a maintenance team than for a development team."

a. Discuss the above statement with respect to the team's productivity.

b. Discuss the above statement with respect to the quality of the work performed by the teams.

26.2 The *Shureshure/Ashure* Insurance Company has just marked completion of a reengineering project that generated a new version of its main legacy software system. The budget for the reengineered alternative was 30% below the budget estimated for development of a similar but new software system. The reengineered version, which includes several additions and changes, was developed by applying a fourth-generation lower CASE tool that replaced the third-generation language of the legacy system. The project, planned to take 6 months, was completed 1 week earlier than scheduled.

The company's monthly magazine dedicated two pages to a report on the event. In its description of the company's satisfaction from the project, the following statements were made:

- The management expressed their full satisfaction from the project's budget and their admiration for the team's punctuality.

- The leaders of the quality assurance and software maintenance teams declared that the new software version is a real success. It can be maintained more easily and with fewer failures when compared with the former legacy system.

- The only staff disappointed with the system were the managers of the Operations and Local Branch Departments. They claimed that the users they represent are highly dissatisfied with the new version.

a. Why was the software maintenance team leader satisfied with the system? Try to list his arguments.

b. Why was the software quality assurance team leader satisfied with the system? Try to list his arguments.

c. Can you suggest why users were dissatisfied from the reengineered version?

26.3 It is claimed that IDEs contribute to the quality of software products.

a. Do you agree? List your arguments?

b. Could you provide some examples of software development situation that illustrate software IDEs contribute to the quality of software?

Part VI

Appendices

The appendices in this book present basic software quality and software engineering topics that are very much related to SQA.

The use of standard is a vital part of engineering as software and software quality engineering and project management.

The first two appendices examine software engineering, software development management, and SQA standards:

- Software development and quality assurance process standards (Appendix A).

- Quality management standards and models (Appendix B).

- Appendix C is dedicated to project progress control. The main issues discussed are control of risk management activities, project schedule control, project resource control, and project budget control.

- Appendix D focuses on the various software development models in current use, with emphasis on the way that quality assurance activities are integrated into the development process.

Software Quality: Concepts and Practice, First Edition. Daniel Galin.
© 2018 the IEEE Computer Society, Inc. Published 2018 by John Wiley & Sons, Inc.

Appendix A

Software Development and Quality Assurance Process Standards

A.1 Introduction – standards and their use

One can easily imagine professionals asking themselves questions like: "Should SQA standards be implemented in our organization and software projects? Wouldn't it be preferable to apply our experience and professional knowledge and employ the procedures and methodologies that best suit our organization?"

Despite the legitimacy of pondering on such issues, it is widely accepted that the benefits gained from standardization are far beyond those reaped from professional independence.

To introduce the subject, let us refer to the following issues:

- The benefits of using standards
- The organizations involved in standards development
- The classification of standards

A.1.1 The benefits of using standards

The main benefits gained by the use of standards (benefits that are not expected in organizations who embrace a high level of professional independence) are listed in the Frame A.1:

Software Quality: Concepts and Practice, First Edition. Daniel Galin.
© 2018 the IEEE Computer Society, Inc. Published 2018 by John Wiley & Sons, Inc.

Frame A.1: The benefits of using standards

- The ability to apply for software projects and department's software development and maintenance of the state-of-the-art methodologies and procedures of the highest professional level.

- Better mutual understanding and coordination among development teams, and especially between development and maintenance teams.

- Better cooperation between the software developer and external participants in the project.

- Better understanding and cooperation between software suppliers and customers/ acquirers, based on the adoption of known development, maintenance, and quality assurance standards.

These advantages, together with the growing complexity and scope of software projects, have prompted a wider application of standards in the industry.

A.1.2 The organizations involved in standards development

Development of SQA standards has been undertaken by several national and international standards institutes; professional and industry-oriented organizations that invest substantial resources in the development and updating of standards projects.

The following institutes and organizations are among the most prominent developers of SQA and software engineering standards, and have gained international reputation and standing in this area:

- IEEE (Institute of Electrical and Electronics Engineers) Computer Society
- ISO (International Organization for Standardization)
- ANSI (American National Standards Institute)
- IEC (International Electrotechnical Commission)
- EIA (Electronic Industries Alliance)

The last two decades saw rapid development in international SQA standards. This was expressed through increasing comprehensive coverage of related topics, which also led to a greater understanding of the standards and the need for them. Also, currently a great part of the efforts in development of new and updating standards is carried out as "joint ventures" of two or more of these major organizations, a trend that promotes internationalization of standards. Examples of such "joint ventures" are the standards issued by the IEEE/ANSI, the ISO/IEC, and the IEEE/ISO. Examples of "mergers" of three institutes are:

- ISO/IEC/IEEE 90003-2014 (ISO, 2014) – Software engineering – Guidelines for the application of ISO 9001:2008 to computer software

- ISO/IEC/IEEE 15504:2012 – Information technology – Process assessment
- ISO/IEC/IEEE 12207:2008 – Systems and software engineering – Software life cycle processes

Another parallel and growing trend is the adoption of international standards as national standards by national standards institutes. This trend further supports internationalization.

The above developments inaugurated a trend toward the application of software industry standards worldwide.

A.1.3 Classification of SQA standards

Software development and quality assurance standards can be classified into two main classes:

- **Process standards.** Standards of this class focus on methodologies for carrying out software development and maintenance projects, and assure their quality, that is, on "how" a software project is to be implemented. These standards define: steps to be taken, design documentation requirements, the contents of design documents, design reviews and review issues, software testing to be performed, testing topics, and so forth. Naturally, due to their characteristics, many standards in this class can serve as software engineering and SQA textbooks versa.

- **Management standards.** Standards of this class focus on the organization's software development and SQA management infrastructure and requirements, while leaving the choice of methods and tools to the organization. By complying with quality management standards, organizations can steadily assure that their software products achieve an acceptable level of quality. Some current software development tenders require participants to be certified with one of the quality management standards.

The characteristics of the two classes of standards are summarized in Table A.1.

As could be anticipated, standards vary in their scope; from comprehensive standards that cover all (or almost all) aspects to specialized standards that deal with one specific area or issue. The ISO/IEC/IEEE Std.90003 Standard and ISO/IEC/IEEE Std. 12207 and IEEE Std. 730 Standard are examples of comprehensive standards that cover all aspects of software quality management and the software development life cycle, respectively. Examples of specialized standards of both classes may be found in IEEE software engineering standards, such as the IEEE 1012 Standard for software quality assurance verification.

Table A.1 Classes of standards – comparison

Characteristics	Process standards	Management standards
The target unit	A software development and/or maintenance project **team**	**Management** of software development and/or maintenance and the specific **SQA units**.
The main focus	Methodologies for carrying out software development and maintenance projects	Organization of SQA systems, infrastructure, and requirements
Standard's objective	"How" to perform	"What" to achieve
Standard's goal	Assuring the quality of a specific software project.	Assuring supplier's software quality and assessing its software process *capability*
Examples	IEEE 730 Standard ISO/IEC/IEEE12207 Standard IEEE 1012 Standard	ISO/IEC/IEEE 90003 Standard SEI CMMI ISO/IEC 15504 Standard

The next two chapters discuss some of the most commonly used software quality assurance standards from each of the two classes.

- Appendix A is dedicated to software development and quality assurance process standards.
- Appendix B is dedicated to software development management standards.

A review of systems engineering standards is presented by Guey-Shin et al. (2008).

This chapter deals with the following standards:

- IEEE Std. 730: Standard for software quality assurance
- ISO/IEC/IEEE Std. 12207: Establishing common framework for processes
- IEEE Std. 1012: On verification and validation

A.2 IEEE Std. 730-2014 Standard for software quality assurance

The IEEE Std. 730-2014 (IEEE, 2014) presents requirements that cover all aspects of software quality assurance; initiation, planning, control, and execution for the full life cycle of a software project.

A.2.1 IEEE Std. 730 concepts

The concepts expressed in this standard deal with six basic issues:

1. **Applicability of the standard** – The standard applies to software projects of all sizes and types; whether new, enhanced, or being actively maintained.

2. **Users of standard** – The standard serves all participants in a software life cycle of software and system products, suppliers, developers, operation and maintenance staff, project managers, and SQA staff.

3. **Levels of standard's task implementation** – The standard specifies three classes of implementation:

   Requirement – the user of the standard must conform with this task (shall tasks).

   Recommendations – the user is recommended to implement these tasks (should tasks).

   Might tasks – optional requirements to be considered by the user (may tasks).

4. **Achieving compliance to the standard** – An organization achieves compliance to the standard by performing the standard requirements (shall tasks).

5. **Alignment with software development standard** – The standard is aligned with ISO/IEC/IEEE Std. 12207-2008 (ISO/IEC/IEEE, 2008) and ISO/IEC/IEEE Std. 15289-2011.

6. **Standard adaptability by tailoring** – The SQA unit may adapt the standard to the specific characteristics of the development or maintenance project. A process of tailoring may take place and omit part of the standards requirements. Tailoring is limited to tasks mentioned in Sections 5.4 and 5.5 of the standard.

A.2.2 IEEE Std. 730-2014 – structure

The first four clauses of the standard deal with:

- Overview
- Normative references
- Definitions, acronyms, and abbreviations
- Key concepts of software quality assurance

The main part of the standard (Clause 5), describing the SQA processes, activities, and tasks, is grouped into three major areas:

- SQA process implementation activities
- Product assurance activities
- Process assurance activities

The standard includes 12 appendices, of which I will mention six:

- Appendix C: Guidance to creating a software quality assurance plan (SQMP). The appendix, holding 36 pages reflects the great importance attached to preparing an SQAP by the IEEE Std. 730).
- Appendix E: Applying IEEE Std. 730:2014 to specific industries.
- Appendix F: SQA's relationships to agile development methods.
- Appendix H: Validating software tools.

- Appendix J: Examples of corrective actions, preventive actions, and root cause analysis processes
- Appendix L: Bibliography of this standard.

A.2.3 IEEE Std. 730-2014 – contents

A total of 16 activities comprise the SQA process. The list of SQA activities is presented in Frame A.2.

Frame A.2: IEEE Std. 730-3014 SQA activities

Source: IEEE Std. 730-3014

SQA activity title
SQA process implementation activities
• Establish the SQA processes
• Coordinate with related software processes
• Document SQA planning
• Execute the SQA plan
• Manage SQA record
• Evaluate organizational independence and objectivity
Product assurance activities
• Evaluate plans for conformance to contracts, standards, and regulations
• Evaluate product for conformance to established requirements
• Evaluate product for acceptability
• Evaluate product lifecycle support for conformance
• Measure products
Process assurance activities
• Evaluate life cycle processes and plans for conformance
• Evaluate environment for conformance
• Evaluate subcontractors for conformance
• Measure processes
• Assess staff skills and knowledge

The standard provides comprehensive description for each of the activities.

Description of activity

The description of each activity of the standard has a fixed format that includes:

- The text of ISO/IEC/IEEE Std. 12207:2008 relevant to the activity, presenting the conformance of the IEEE Std. 750-2014 with Std. 12207.
- Purpose of the activity.

- Outcomes: Specific results of the successful implementation of the activity, such as documentation, a change of project constraint. The number of activity outcomes varies between 3 and 8.
- Tasks: Specific actions required to achieve the purpose of the activity. The activity tasks include required (shall), recommended (should), and might (may) tasks. The number of activity tasks varies between 2 and 13.

An example of an activity description is presented in Frame A.3.

Frame A.3: IEEE Std. 730-2014 activity description – an example

Source: IEEE Std. 730-2014 Section 5.5.3

Activity: Evaluate environment conformance

This subclause addresses the following ISO/IEC/IEEE 12207:2008 subclause:

7.2.3.3.3.2 It shall be assured that the internal software engineering practices, development environment, test environment, and libraries comply with the contract.

Purpose

Determine whether software engineering environment (SEE) and software test environment (STE) conform to project process and plans.

Outcomes

This activity shall produce the following outcomes:

- Software engineering environments are consistent with project plans.
- Software test environments are consistent with project plans.
- Nonconformances are raised when software engineering environment do not conform to project plans.
- Nonconformances are raised when software test environment do not conform to project plans.

Tasks

To accomplish this activity, the SQA function shall perform the following tasks:

1. Review the software engineering environment used by the project team to determine whether they conform to the contract.
2. Review the software engineering libraries used by the project team to determine whether they conform to the contract.
3. Review the software test environment used by the project team to determine whether they conform to the contract.

A.3 ISO/IEC Std. 12207-2008: system and software engineering – software life cycle processes

ISO/IEC/IEEE Std. 12207-2008 (ISO/IEC, 2008) provides a framework that incorporates the entire spectrum of software life cycle processes.

The objectives of the 12207-2008 Standard can be summarized thus:

- To establish an internationally recognized model of common software life cycle processes that can be referenced by the software industry worldwide to facilitate communication among acquirers, suppliers, and other stakeholders.

- To serve all participants in a software life cycle: acquirers of software and system products, suppliers, developers, operation and maintenance staff, managers, SQA staff, and product users.

- To promote understanding among business parties by applying commonly recognized processes, activities, and tasks.

A discussion of the various aspects of implementing the standard is the subject of a considerable number of papers. I will mention several. The implementation of the standard to small and medium enterprises (SME) is presented by Laporte et al. (2006) and Laporte et al. (2008). The issues of application of the standard for open-source software is discussed by Krishnamurthy and O'Connor (2013). Clarke et al. (2012) and Clarke and O'Connor (2010) present the aspects of software process improvement (SPI) activities included in the standard. The subject of product management and reuse are discussed by Stallinger and Neumann (2012).

The following sections present the standard's concepts and contents.

A.3.1. 12207 Standard: concepts

The concepts expressed in this standard deal with 10 basic issues:

1. **Applicability to every participant in the software life cycle.** The standard applies to all participants in the software life cycle: buyers, suppliers, developers, operators, and maintenance professionals. It provides separate definitions of processes, activities, and tasks for each role.

2. **Adaptability of the standard.** Organizations are encouraged to tailor the standard to their needs by omitting irrelevant or unsuitable elements. The remaining processes, activities, and tasks thus become the standard for that particular project. Tailoring the standard allows it to be applicable to a large variety of software projects: large, highly complex as well as small, simple projects, stand-alone projects, and projects that

represent parts within extensive systems. Also, tailoring supports the applicability of the standard to fit all parties, whether external customers (within customer–supplier relationships) or internal customers (developed for other departments within the organization).

3. **Flexibility and responsiveness to technological changes.** The standard instructs its users "how to" perform activities, but does not specify "exactly how to" perform the activities", that is, it leaves room for users to choose their own life cycle model, development tools, software metrics, project milestones, and documentation standards. Despite this freedom, the standard's highly detailed tasks, as well as required level of conformance to its principles, are firmly imposed. Benefits of the "how to" approach include a reduction of the user's dependence on a specific technology, a feature that introduces flexibility and enhances responsiveness to changes in information technology (software and hardware).

4. **Relationship between software and systems.** The standard establishes a strong link between a system and its software, where software is an integral part of the total system. It is implemented by the strong relationship with the 15288 system life cycle processes international standard.

5. **Applicability to software products and services.** The standard applies to software products and software services.

6. **Nature of evaluation task.** The standard requires evaluating entities and their objectives through defined criteria.

7. **Absence of organizational structure requirements.** The standard does not imply a certain organizational structure. The processes of the standard may serve a wide range of organizations, large or small, where each organization may select an appropriate set of processes and activities.

8. **Evaluation, verification, and validation.** The standard requires that the performer of a life cycle task evaluates the product of the task. An additional evaluation will be provided by verification and validation conducted by the buyer, the supplier, or another participator.

9. **Life cycle models and stages.** The standard allows a range of life cycle models comprised of sequences of stages that may overlap and iterate, as appropriate for the project characteristics. Each stage is defined a purpose and an outcome.

10. **Absence of certification requirements.** The standard does not require certification of the developer organization; a fact that supports its worldwide acceptance. It should be noted that the international standard 90003, which does require certification, is closely coordinated with the international standard 12207.

A.3.2   12207 Standard: contents

The main body of the 12207-2008 Standard is dedicated to a description of the processes, activities, and tasks of the software life cycle:

The software life cycle architecture outlined in the 12207-2012 Standard is structured as a five-level tree composed of:

1. **Process classes:** System context processes and software-specific processes. Each process class includes 3–4 process categories.

2. **Process categories:** A total of seven categories are defined. Each process category includes 2–11 processes.

3. **Processes:** A total of 43 processes are defined for the 7 process categories.

4. **Activities**

5. **Tasks**

The three upper levels of the standard's process architecture, namely, the process classes, the process categories, and their integral processes, are illustrated in a fishbone diagram in Figure A.1.

The standard provides comprehensive definitions of the tasks comprising each activity. Comprehensiveness is realized in the number of tasks assigned to each activity and the level of detail characterizing the descriptions. An example of the tasks of an activity is presented in Frame A.4.

Frame A.4: Standard 12207 activity's tasks description – an example

Source: ISO/IEC Std. 12207-2008

Activity: Contract agreement (Standard section 6.1.1.3.4)

The activity consists of the following three tasks:

1. The acquirer may involve other parties, including potential suppliers or any necessary third parties (such as regulators), before contract award, in determining the acquirer's requirements for tailoring of this international Standard for the project. In making this determination, the acquirer shall consider the effect of the tailoring requirements upon the supplier's organizationally adopted processes. The acquirer shall include or reference the tailoring requirements in the contract.

2. The acquirer shall then prepare and negotiate a contract with the supplier that addresses the acquisition requirements, including the cost and schedule, of the software product or service to be delivered. The contract shall address proprietary, usage, ownership, warranty, and licensing rights associated with the reusable off-the-shelf software products.

3. Once the contract is underway, the acquirer shall control changes to the contract through negotiation with the supplier as part of a change contract mechanism. Changes to the contract shall be investigated for impact on project plans, costs, benefits, quality, and schedule.

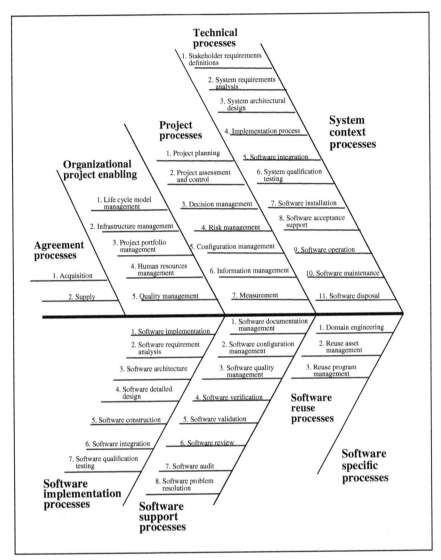

Figure A.1   ISO/IEC Std. 12207-2008 – a fishbone diagram

The standard includes nine annexes. Three of these are dedicated to the following issues:

- Annex A – Discusses the various aspects of the tailoring process.
- Annex B – Process reference model for assessment purposes, presents conformance of the 12207 standard with the 15404-2 international standard: information technology – process attribute – number 2: performance management.

- Annex D – ISO/IEC 12207 and ISO/IEC 15288 process alignment presents the relationships between the processes of both these standards.

A.4 IEEE Std. 1012-2012 systems and software verification and validation

A.4.1 Introduction

The IEEE Std.1012-2012 (IEEE, 2012) is a process that defines all SQA activities throughout the entire software life cycle as V&V activities. The standard requires the application of V&V activities for system, software, and hardware processes as well as for managerial and administrative processes. As such, it became a comprehensive broad standard, and includes hundreds of SQA activities and tasks to be performed during the software life cycle. The IEEE Std. 1012 deals with the processes applied to determine whether a software product conforms to its requirements specifications (verification) and whether it satisfies the objectives of its intended use (validation).

The current standard version, IEEE Std. 1012-2012, is the fourth version, first issued in 1986. The following standard versions were issued in 1998 and 2004.

The IEEE Std. 1012 presented in this section was chosen as an example of the collection of IEEE typical software engineering standards, dedicated to a wide variety of software engineering topics. Each of the IEEE typical standards deals with a specific phase of the software cycle, a methodology or process in the software life cycle process. The standards are updated once every 5–10 years, when the updating process by technical committees is completed.

Typical examples are presented in Table A.2.

In addition to typical software engineering standards, the IEEE develops and adopts several international comprehensive standards that deal with the entire software life cycle or the whole range of managerial activities throughout the entire software life cycle. A great part of these standards is developed in cooperation with other standard institutes or adopted from these institutes, that is, ISO/IEC/IEEE Std. 12207 and ISO/IEC/IEEE Std. 90003.

The objectives of the IEEE Std. 1012 are:

- To help developers introduce quality into the software system during the software life cycle.
- To establish a common framework for V&V activities and tasks for software life cycle processes.
- To define V&V processes to provide an objective assessment of the product and processes to demonstrate whether these are correct, complete, accurate and consistent, and also conform with relevant requirements and satisfy their intended use and user needs.

Table A.2   Examples to IEEE typical standards

Standard code	Standard name
IEEE Std. 610.12-1990	Glossary of Software Engineering Terminology
IEEE Std. 828-2012	Configuration Management – Systems and Software Engineering
IEEE Std. 829-2008	Software Test Documentation
IEEE Std. 982.1-2005	IEEE Dictionary of Measures to Produce Reliable Software
IEEE Std. 1012-2012	Software Verification And Validation
IEEE Std. 1016-2009	IEEE Recommended Process for Software Design Descriptions
IEEE Std. 1028-2008	Software Reviews
IEEE Std. 1061-1998	Software Quality Metrics Methodology
IEEE Std. 1175.4-2008	CASE tools Interconnections Reference Model for Specifying System Behavior
IEEE Std. 1233-1998	Guide for Developing System Requirement Specifications
IEEE Std. 1420.1b-1999	Information Technology - Software Reuse, Data Model for Reuse Library Interoperability: Intellectual Property

A.4.2   IEEE Std. 1012-2012 concepts

The concepts expressed in IEEE 1012-2012 address six basic issues:

1. **Broad definition of V&V activities**
   Broad definition of V&V activities enables the standard to embrace all SQA activities performed throughout the software life cycle, relating to management, systems, software, and hardware.

2. **Integrity levels** system performance
   "Major" – A function that affects important system performance.
   "Moderate" – A function that affects system performance; however, availability of an alternative method of operation enables the system to overcome the associated difficulties.
   "Low" – A function that affects system performance only by inconveniencing the user.
   The standard requires that integrity levels be assigned to components as early as the software V&V plan (SVVP) is prepared.

3. **Minimum V&V tasks**
   The standard defines the minimum tasks required for each integrity level, and includes tables of optional task selection for each integrity level.

4. **Detailed criteria for V&V tasks**
   The standard includes criteria for each V&V task, including minimum criteria for correctness, consistency, completeness, accuracy,

readability, and testability. The V&V task descriptions include a list of required inputs and outputs.

5. **Intensity and rigor applied to V&V tasks**

According to the standard, the intensity and rigor applied to the V&V tasks vary according to the integrity level, the higher the integrity level, the higher the required intensity and rigor applied to the V&V task.

6. **Detailed criteria for V&V tasks**

The V&V task descriptions include a list of required inputs and outputs. They also include specific quantitative criteria for each V&V task, including minimum criteria for correctness, consistency, completeness, accuracy, readability and testability.

7. **Compliance and compatibility to international standards**

The IEEE Std. 1012-2012 standard defines the V&V processes to conform to the international life cycle standards ISO/IEC/IEEE Std. 12207-2008 and ISO/IEC/IEEE Std. 15388-2008, as well as to the entire group of IEEE typical software engineering standards.

A.4.3 IEEE Std. 1012-2012 contents

a. **Processes, activities, and tasks**

The main body of IEEE 1012-2012 is dedicated to a description of the processes, activities, and tasks of the software life cycle.

The software life cycle architecture presented in the standard is structured as a three-level tree composed of:
- Processes
- Activities
- Tasks

The processes covered by the standard are classified as:
1. Common processes
2. System processes
3. Software processes
4. Hardware processes

The description of each process includes the requisite 1–6 activities, while 3–10 tasks are assigned to each activity. The common processes include verification and validation activities of management, acquisition, supply planning, project planning, and configuration planning. The verification and validation activities for systems, software, and hardware relate to the entire variety of software systems development, including concept definition, requirements analysis, design, implementation, transition, regular operation, maintenance efforts, and finally disposal of used systems.

The task descriptions provided by the standard are very detailed and include task details and required inputs and outputs. An example of a task description is shown in Frame A.5.

Frame A.5: IEEE Std. 1012 task description – an example

Source: IEEE Std. 1012:2012

Process: Common V&V activities
Activity 7.3: Supply planning V&V
Task (2): Contract verification

Task description	Required input	Required output
Verify the following characteristics of the contract: 1. System requirements (from RFP or tender and contract) satisfy and are consistent with user needs. 2. Procedures are documented for managing requirement changes and for identifying management hierarchy to manage problems. 3. Procedures for interface and cooperation among the parties are documented, including ownership, warranty, copyright, and confidentiality. 4. Acceptance criteria and procedures are documented in accordance with requirement.	1. V&V Plan (VVP) 2. RFP of tender 3. Contract 4. Supplier development plans and schedules	1. Task(s) reports 2. Contract verification 3. Updated VVP 4. Anomaly report(s)

The standard defines four integrity levels, where the higher the integrity level, the greater the number of tasks assigned to the pertinent activity. Accordingly, the standard presents tables as follows:

- Minimum V&V – task assigned to each integrity level
- Optimal V&V – technical suggested applications in implementation process

b. Reporting, administrative, and documentation requirements

The next chapter of the standard is dedicated to reporting, administrative and documentation requirements and includes lists of required reports.

c. Outline of the V&V plan (VVP)

A detailed outline of the V&V plan is presented in the following discussion.

The comprehensive scope of the required VVP is well demonstrated by its outline (template). For the VVP to conform to the standard's

Table A.3   IEEE Std.1012-2012's V&V plan outline (template)

1	**Purpose**
2	**Referenced Documents**
3	**Definitions**
4	V&V Overview
	4.1 Organization
	4.2 Master Schedule
	4.3 Integrity Level Scheme
	4.4 Resources Summary
	4.5 Responsibilities
	4.6 Tools, Techniques, and Methods
5	**V&V Overview**
	5.1 Common V&V processes, activities and tasks
	5.2 System V&V processes, activities and tasks
	5.3 Software V&V processes, activities and tasks
	5.4 Hardware V&V processes, activities and tasks
6	**V&V reporting requirements**
	6.1 Test reports
	6.2 Anomaly reports
	6.3 V&V final reports
	6.4 Special studies report (optional)
	6.5 Other reports (optional)
7	**Administrative requirements**
	7.1 Anomaly resolution and reporting
	7.2 Task iteration policy
	7.3 Deviation policy
	7.4 Control procedures
	7.5 Standards, practices and conventions
8	**V&V test documentation requirements**

Source: IEEE Std. 1012:2012

requirements, planners have to thoroughly understand the software system and ascertain the professional, administrative, and resource issues implicit in the V&V project as planned. Table A.3 presents the outline for the VVP document as required by the IEEE Std.1012.

For each section and subsection of the VVP outline, the IEEE 1012 supplements provide detailed definitions of the requisite contents.

The standard includes 10 informative annexes that present a great variety of subjects. Five of the annexes are dedicated to the following topics:

Annex D: V&V of reuse software

Annex E: V&V measures. Included are V&V measures for evaluating anomaly density, effectiveness, and efficiency

Annex I: V&V of system, software, and hardware integration

Annex J: Hazard, security, and risk analysis

Summary

1. **The concepts underlying IEEE Std. 730-2014**
   a. **Applicability of the standard**
      The standard applies to software projects of all sizes and types; whether new, enhanced, or being actively maintained.
   b. **Users of standard**
      The standard serves all participants in a software life cycle: acquirers of software and system products, suppliers, developers, operation and maintenance staff, project managers, and SQA staff.
   c. **Levels of standard's task implementation**
      The standard specifies three classes of implementation:
      Requirement – the user of the standard must conform with these tasks (shall tasks).
      Recommendations – the user is recommended to implement these tasks (should tasks).
      Might tasks – optional requirements to be considered by the user (may tasks).
   d. **Achieving compliance to the standard**
      An organization achieves conformance compliance to the standard by performing the standard requirements (shall tasks).
   e. **Alignment with software development standard**
      The standard is aligned with ISO/IEC/IEEE Std. 12207-2008 and ISO/IEC/IEEE Std. 15289-2011.
   f. **Standard adaptability by tailoring**
      The SQA unit may adapt the standard to the specific characteristics of the development or maintenance project by a process of limited tailoring.

2. **The content of the IEEE Std. 730-2014**
   The standard defines 16 activities to be performed by the SQA unit. These activities are divided into three areas:
   - SQA process implementation activities – processes to be implemented by the SQA unit/team.
   - Product assurance activities – evaluation activities for products of software development projects.
   - Process assurance activities – activities of evaluation of processes employed by software development project teams comply with the standard.

3. **The concepts underlying IEEE/EIA Std. 12207-2008**
   a. **Applicability and adaptability of the standard**
      The standard is applicable to all participants in the software life cycle for projects that vary in size and complexity. Much of its broad applicability is due to tailoring within the limits allowed to users.

b. Flexibility and responsiveness to technological changes

The standard instructs "how to do" and not "exactly how to do" a project; hence, users can choose their life cycle model, development tools, software metrics, project milestones, and product and documentation standards. As a consequence, this approach contributes to reduced dependency on specific technologies, coupled with increased responsiveness to technological change.

c. Software links with its system

The standard establishes strong links between the software and the system of which it is a part in each phase of the life cycle. The standard is implemented with a strong relationship with the ISO/IEC 15288 system's life cycle international standard.

d. Nature of evaluation tasks

The standard requires that an evaluation of entities (process, activity, report, etc.) with the associated objectives be conducted against their defined criteria. An additional evaluation will be provided by verification and validation conducted by the buyer, the supplier, or others.

e. Life cycle models and stages

The standard allows a range of life cycle models comprised of a sequence of stages that may overlap and iterate, as appropriate for the project characteristics, where each stage is defined by objective and outcome.

f. Absence of certification of developer organizations

The standard does not require certification of the developer organization.

4. The concepts underlying of IEEE Std. 1012.

a. A broad definition of V&V activities

The standard provides a broad review of the V&V activities to be performed throughout the software life cycle. These include: reviews, tests, evaluations, risk analyses, hazard analyses, retirement assessments, and so on.

b. Software integrity levels and adapted V&V requirements

The standard identifies four integrity levels – high, major, moderate, and low – according to the criticality of the software function, module, or unit. Graded requirements are attuned to the integrity level. The standard requires that integrity levels be assigned to components as early as the SVVP.

c. Minimum V&V tasks

The standard defines the minimum tasks required for each integrity level, and includes tables of optional task selection for each integrity level.

d. Detailed criteria for V&V tasks

The V&V task descriptions include a list of required inputs and outputs. They also include specific quantitative criteria for each V&V task, including minimum criteria for correctness, consistency, completeness, accuracy, readability, and testability. The V&V task descriptions include a list of required inputs and outputs.

e. Detailed criteria for V&V tasks

The V&V task descriptions include a list of required inputs and outputs. It also includes specific quantitative criteria for each V&V task, including minimum criteria for correctness, consistency, completeness, accuracy, readability, and testability. The V&V task descriptions include a list of required inputs and outputs.

f. Compliance and compatibility to international standards

The IEEE Std. 1012-2012 defines the V&V processes to conform to the international life cycle standards; ISO/IEC/IEEE Std. 12207-2008 and ISO/IEC/IEEE Std. 15388-2008 as well as the entire group of IEEE topical software engineering standards.

g. Recognition of special characteristics of V&V of reusable software

The difficulties of performing V&V activities for reusable software are recognized, and possible directions for performing V&V activities are shown.

5. Explain the essence of the SVVP as required by IEEE Std.1012.

The SVVP is designed to thoroughly delineate a plan for V&V activities that will include all aspects of their performance, including the schedule, resources, responsibilities, tools, and techniques to be used. In addition, the SVVP documents administrative directions concerning anomaly resolution procedures, task iteration and deviation policies, performance control procedures, and the standard practices and conventions that have to be applied. Special instructions are given for documentation.

Selected bibliography

Clarke P. and O'Connor R. V. (2010) *Harnessing ISO/IEC 12207 to Examine the Extent of SPI Activity in an Organization*, Proceedings of the 17th Conference on European Systems, Software and Services Process Improvement, CCIS, Vol. 99, Springer, Berlin, Germany, pp. 25–36.

Clarke P., O'Connor R. V., and Yilmaz M. (2012) *A Hierarchy of SPI Activities for Software SMEs: Results from ISO/IEC 12207-Based SPI Assessments*, Proceedings of the 12th International Conference on Software Process and Capability Conference (SPICE'12), CCIS Vol. 290, Springer, Berlin, Germany, pp. 62–74.

Guey-Shin C., Horng-Linn P., and Jer-Nan J. (2008) A review of systems engineering standards and processes, *Journal of Biomechanics Engineering*, Vol. 1, No. 1, pp. 71–85.

IEEE (2012) *IEEE Std. 1012–2012 - IEEE Standard for System and Software Verification and Validation*, The IEEE Computer Society, IEEE, New York, NY.

IEEE (2014) *IEEE Std. 730–2014 Software Quality Assurance*, The IEEE Computer Society, IEEE, New York.

ISO/IEC/IEEE (2008) *ISO/IEC/IEEE Std. 12207-2008 – Systems and Software Engineering - Software Life Cycle Processes*, ISO – International Organization for Standardization, Geneva, Switzerland.

ISO (2014) *ISO/IEC 90003:2014 Software Engineering – Guidelines for the Application of TSO 9001: 2008 to Computer Software*, International Organization for Standardization (ISO), Geneva, Switzerland.

Krishnamurthy A. and O'Connor R. V. (2013) *Using ISO/IEC 12207 to Analyze Open Source Software Development Processes: An e-Learning Case Study*, Proceedings of the 13th International Conference on Software Process Improvement and Capability Determination (SPICE 2013), CCIS Vol. 349, Springer, Berlin, Germany, pp. 1–12.

Laporte C. Y., April A., and Renault A. (2006) Applying ISO/IEC software engineering standards in small settings: historical perspectives and initial achievements, in *Proceedings of SPICE 2006 Conference*, Luxembourg, May 2006, pp. 1–5.

Laporte C. Y., Alexandre S., and O'Connor R. V. (2008) A software engineering lifecycle standard for very small enterprises, *Software Process Improvement. Communications in Computer and Information Science*, Vol. 16, No. 2, pp. 129–141.

Stallinger F. and Neumann R. (2012) *Extending ISO/IEC 12207 with Software Product Management: A Process Reference Model Proposal, Communications in Computer and Information Science*, Vol. 290, Springer, Berlin, Germany, pp. 93–106.

Review questions

A.1 Two classes of standards dealing with software development and quality assurance are discussed in the book: process standards and management standards.

- Explain the difference between these two classes.

A.2 The IEEE Std.730-2014 presents six concepts.

- Explain these concepts in your own words.

A.3 The IEEE Std.730-2014 divides its activities into three areas.

- Explain the difference between the SQA process implementation activities and the product and process assurance activities, regarding methods of implementation and relationships with the software development project teams.

A.4 ISO/IEC/IEEE Std.12207-2008 is considered an international standard.

  a. Explain, in your own words, why this status is warranted.

  b. Explain the importance of international standards.

A.5 The initiators of Std. 12207 were highly interested in the broad applicability of the standard.

- Name concept topics contributing to its broad applicability, and explain the way these topics contribute to the applicability.

A.6 Consider the purpose of the IEEE Std.1012-2012.

- Explain, in your own words, the purpose of the standard.

A.7 The 2012 version of the IEEE Std. 1012 incorporates system and software V&V activities.

- Explain the contribution of both system and software V&A activities in the same standard.

Topics for discussion

A.1 One of the concepts of IEEE Std. 730-2014 is its alignment with ISO/IEC/IEEE Std. 12207-2008 and ISO/IEC/IEEE Std. 15289-2011.

    a. How does the alignment contribute to an SQA unit's activities?

    b. How does the alignment contribute to software product quality?

A.2 IEEE Std. 730-2014 assigns a special activity and an annex to SQA planning.

- What is the special importance of the SQA planning?

A.3 The annual SQA plan is usually required to be revised several times a year.

    a. List events that warrant revising the annual SQA plan.

    b. What are some possible results of failing to revise the SQA plan following an event or events listed in your above answer.

A.4 The 10 concepts at the foundation of the ISO/IEC/IEEE Std. 12207-2008 are listed in Section A.3.2.

- Examine the concepts and determine which of these contributes most to the standard's wide applicability. Explain your choice.

A.5 IEEE/EIA Std. 12207-2008 sets three levels of tasks: requirements, recommendations, and permissible tasks. These represent levels of conformance to the standard's requirements.

    a. Explain, in your own words, the significance of each level.

    b. Discuss the contribution made by the clear definition of these levels.

A.6 IEEE Std.1012-2012 dedicates a special appendix to V&V of reusable software.

    a. List the kind of software that is considered to be "reusable."

    b. Explain the special characteristics of "reusable software" in relation to V&V activities.

    c. List what you consider to be options for overcoming the difficulties inherent in performing V&V for reusable software.

A.7 Some senior system analysts claim that as a result of their experience, the VVP required in the IEEE Std. 1012-2012 is simply a "waste of time," and that a development (project) plan should suffice.

    a. Do you agree with this claim?

    b. List the arguments backing your position. Base them on a comparison of the contents of the two document templates (a VVP and a project plan).

A.8 The IEEE Std. 1012 includes the notion "level of integrity."

    a. Address the contribution of the "level of integrity" to the effectiveness of the standard's prescribed V&V activities.

    b. How does the notion "level of integrity" influence the standard's applicability?

Appendix B

Software Quality Management Standards and Models

B.1   ABC Software Ltd – an unnecessary loss – a mini-case

2015 was ABC Software's worst year since being founded in 1985. The company lost almost $2.1 million, sales dropped 35%, and it had to let go of 145 out of its 390 personnel.

ABC Software specializes in the development of custom-made information systems for governments and government agencies. Only a very small part of the company's activities was directed toward the development of COTS software packages. By 2013, the company's annual sales reached over $65 million.

"A clear case of negligence caused unnecessary losses and severe damage to the company's reputation – that will need at least 5 years to recover," Sam Baron, the company's deputy manager operations and quality, explained.

"It all began in 2005, when management realized that in order to further grow the company business, it would need to become ISO 90003 certified. It took us about a year to get organized with a full set of procedures and written work instructions, and to train our staff in implementing the procedures. National Standard Institute experts reviewed our procedures and performed a comprehensive audit to verify staff compliance with our procedures. A few days after the audit, we received the much anticipated ISO 90003 standard certification document, which I proudly presented at the following management and board meeting, and to which the participants expressed their appreciation. The original framed certification document is still hanging in the board meeting room. In the following years, the ISO 90003 certification proved very helpful in winning government tenders."

Software Quality: Concepts and Practice, First Edition. Daniel Galin.
© 2018 the IEEE Computer Society, Inc. Published 2018 by John Wiley & Sons, Inc.

"It sounds like you made a very good decision, and that the organization performed exceptionally well to adapt to the needed changes for the certification. So what went wrong?" We asked Baron.

"I believe that the cause of our current trouble is rooted in one line of the certification document – a line stating that the certification is valid for one year only, a line which was overlooked by management. In other words, the National Standards Institute (NSI) needs to re-audit the organization every year to verify continued conformance to procedures and work instructions." Baron then suggested that the head of the SQA unit explain the events that took place from that time till December 2015.

The head of the SQA unit started to recap the chain of events. "The audits conducted by the National Standard Institute (NSI) annual certification in the following years had high evaluation scores – well, at least at the beginning. But gradually the audit scores became less and less positive and the number of 'topics for required attention' quickly grew. Nevertheless, a renewed certification was granted to ABC Software each year. In December 2014, a change came about and the audit ended with a warning; unless a substantial improvement of in the company's SQA performance is evident by in the next audit, the ISO 90003 certification will be cancelled." He paused for a minute, and the following questions were raised.

"What caused the decline of your SQA system?" "What changed in the company?"

The SQA manager picked up where he had left off, "During the last few years management has been putting a great deal of pressure on the software development department to make substantial resource savings and stick to the schedules. These directives forced the project staff to skip reviews and cut tests plans. And all this happened despite my repeated requests to follow procedures in order to avoid any negative outcomes. Actually, several of these projects failed the system tests, and two projects were even rejected in acceptance tests performed by customers. The worst situation evolved closely after February 2015, when ABC Software won the Treasury project, the company's largest ever project. The win was achieved mainly due to proposing the lowest price and the shortest schedule. It took just a few weeks for the project manager to realize that the proposed project budget and schedule were unrealistic. From this moment on, the Treasury project team came under immense pressure to cope with the meager budget and tight schedule. Round about this time, the December 2015 ISO 90003 audit took place. As unfortunately expected, during their review of the Treasury project, the auditors found a handful of nonconformance issues, some examples are:

- The contract review was only partly performed, and worse, there was no sign of discussions on its findings, nor for changing the proposal accordingly.

- The design review of the design document listed 23 action items. None of which were implemented.

- No corrective or preventive actions were initiated during 2015, and no minutes of meeting of the CAB were found for this period.
- Half of the planned unit tests were not performed, while no record was found for the defects correction process, including the testing of the corrected software, for the remaining unit tests.
- The joint customer–supplier committee required the procedure to take place once in 2 weeks but was conducted every 4–6 weeks.

A total of 43 audit team findings, all of them negative, led to the inevitable result of the certification being cancelled, and management requests for a reaudit were denied. The NSI also denied a request to hold the next planned audit earlier when the company may present corrected SQA behavior and gain back its ISO 90003 certificating. The next NSI audit was scheduled for December 2016.

"The full impact of losing the certification was felt just a few weeks later," the head of the SQA unit continued, "When the management found out that the company could not participate in about two thirds of the tenders; those requiring the participants hold valid ISO 90003 certification. Following this discovery, a decision was made to submit the remaining tenders with minimal profit margins, in order to improve winning prospects." By May 2016, when most of the work on the Treasury project had been completed, it became clear to the company that no tasks at all could be allocated to a great many of the company professionals. This led to 145 staff members being let go.

The company expects an annual loss of over $2 million by the end of 2016. It is widely agreed among company management and employees alike that the major, if not the only, cause for this loss was the revoked certification.

"The lesson was learned, but not before paying high 'tuition fees.' Management was now committed to regain the certification, and invested efforts to promote SQA activities, and instruct members of staff to strictly conform to procedure requirements. In addition, a special consultant was hired to perform internal audits."

Jerry concluded his speech, "I hope that the coming NSI audit will note the significant change, created by the joint efforts of the SQA unit and professional staff, and restore our ISO 90003 certification."

We did not react to the ABC Software's sad "story," but only wish the deputy operations and quality manager, head of the SQA unit, and the company itself success in remembering the lessons learnt, and the substantial contribution of professional certification, but especially in never losing sight of the vast damages that could be caused by the loss of certification.

B.2 The scope of quality management standards

Quality management standards and methodologies focus on the software quality assurance system – its organization, infrastructure, and requirements performance – yet leave the choice of the methods and tools to be used in the hands of the organization. In other words, these standards focus on the "what" of SQA and not on the "how." Compliance to quality management standards supports the organization's steady efforts to assure an acceptable quality level for its software products. The application of these standards is directed mainly as an assessment tool, but also as a certification tool. The standards of both routes, ISO/IEC 90003 and ISO/IEC 15504, are international standards and have also been adopted by the Institute of Electrical and Electronic Engineering (IEEE) and as national standards in many countries.

Standards for the software industry, belonging to the certification class – mainly ISO 90003, structure the SQA certification procedures applied to software developing organizations. Some standards and methodologies for the software industry of the assessment class, such as the Capability Maturity Model Integrated (CMMI) and ISO/IEC 15504, serve mainly for self-assessment of the organization's SQA achievements as guidance to the development of its SQA system.

Certification standards vary from assessment standards by content and emphasis.

The following are the aims of certification standards:

- To enable a software development organization to demonstrate consistent ability to ensure that its software products or maintenance services comply with acceptable quality requirements. This is achieved through certification granted by an external body.

- To serve as an agreed-upon basis for customer and supplier evaluation of the supplier's quality management system. This may be accomplished with a quality audit of the supplier's quality management system conducted by the customer. The audit will be based on the certification standard's requirements.

- To support the software development organization's efforts to improve quality management system performance and enhance customer satisfaction through compliance with the standard's requirements.

One indication of the importance of certification standards is the current trend in software development tenders, which requires certification of participants according to at least one of the dominant quality management standards.

The following are the aims of assessment standards:

- To serve software development and maintenance organizations as a tool for self-assessment of their ability to carry out software development projects.

- To serve as a tool for improvement of development and maintenance processes. The standard indicates directions for process improvements.

- To help purchasing organizations determine the capabilities of potential suppliers.
- To guide training of assessor by delineating qualifications and training program curricula.

To sum up, while the certification standards emphasis is external – to support the supplier–customer relationships – the emphasis of the assessment standards is internal and focuses on the improvement of the software process.

Comparison and evaluation of maturity process models for process improvement are the subject of several papers. A selection of these includes Helgesson et al. (2011), Salviano and Figueiredo (2006), and Bella et al. (2008).

The next section of the chapter presents the software process improvement aspects of quality management standards and their methodologies. Following this, the next three sections, Sections B.4–B.6, are dedicated to the scope of three major certification and assessment standards. These are followed by Section B.7 that presents two additional software quality management methodologies: TickIt and Bootstrap.

B.3 Software quality management standards as SPI standards

The concept of software process improvement (SPI) seeking to achieve process improvement throughout the software life cycle corresponds well to the SQA principle of continuous improvement. SPI, much like software quality management, promotes:

a. Software development organizations to focus more on improving the effectiveness and efficiency of the development process.

b. Software development organizations to assess their professional level of performance (termed also "maturity").

c. Use of quantitative and qualitative indicators to measure the level of improvement of software development processes of an organization.

One of the major approaches for managements to implement process improvement is by the adoption of appropriate quality management standards that support SPI.

These standards may be classified into two classes:

- *Certifying standards.* An example of this class of standards, ISO/IEC 90003, is discussed in this chapter.
- *Assessment standards.* CMMI, P-CMM, and ISO/IEC 15504, discussed in this chapter, are all examples of standards belonging to this class.

B.4 ISO/IEC 90003

The ISO/IEC 90003 international standard was developed for the application of the ISO 9001 standard to computer software. In other words, ISO/IEC 90003 presents implementation of the general methodology of quality management of ISO 9001 standards, which deals with product development, product production, and product services and maintenance, for the special case of software development and maintenance. Both ISO 9001 and ISO/IEC 90003 are separately reviewed and updated once every 5–8 years. The current ISO/IEC 90003:2014 international standard (ISO/IEC, 2014) is an application of ISO 9001:2008 to computer software.

The ISO/IEC 90003 international standard is planned to serve the entire population of software development and maintenance organizations by adopting a policy of comprehensiveness and standard redundancy. These features facilitate achieving universality that allows the ISO/IEC 90003 to fit the immense variety of organizations belonging to the software industry, and be especially suitable to serve as a tool for assessing and certifying organizations of the software industry.

There is a growing worldwide interest in ISO/IEC 9001 certification from organizations in many industries, including ISO/IEC 90003 in the worldwide software industry. Many national standard institutes, including the IEEE, have adopted the ISO/IEC 90003 standard.

One indication of the importance of these standards is the current trend in software development tenders requiring certification of participants according to at least one of the leading quality management standards.

In Section B.4.1, the principles underlying the 9001 and 90003 standards are reviewed. The contents of the current version of the standard are discussed in the following section, and the certification process according to ISO/IEC 90003 is the subject of the third section, Section B.4.3.

B.4.1 Guiding principles of ISO 9001 and ISO/IEC 90003 standards

Eight principles guide the ISO 9001 and ISO/IEC 90003 standards as follows:

1. Customer focus

   Organizations depend on their customers and therefore should understand current and future customer needs.

2. Leadership

   Leaders establish the organization's vision. They should create and maintain an environment in which people can become fully involved in achieving the organization's objectives in the designated route.

3. Involvement of people

People are the essence of an organization; their full involvement, at all levels of the organization, enables their abilities to be applied for the organization's benefit.

4. Process approach

A desired result is achieved more efficiently when activities and resources are managed as a process.

5. System approach to management

Identifying, understanding, and managing processes, if viewed as a system, contributes to the organization's effectiveness and efficiency.

6. Continual improvement

Ongoing improvement of overall performance should be high on the organization's agenda.

7. Factual approach to decision-making

Effective decisions are based on the analysis of information.

8. Mutually supportive supplier relationships

An organization and its suppliers are interdependent; a mutually supportive relationship enhances the ability of both to create added value.

B.4.2 ISO/IEC 90003: 2014 standard's content

The current standard edition of ISO/IEC 90003-2014 (ISO/IEC, 2014) presents the standard's requirement that is classified into the following five groups:

- Quality management system
- Management responsibilities
- Resource management
- Product realization
- Management, analysis, and improvement

Each of the requirement groups is further classified into requirement areas. The standard includes a total of 22 requirement areas.

Each of the requirement areas is further subdivided into several specific requirements.

Each of the specific requirements is followed by guidelines.

This standard structure provides detailed guidelines to the standard user. However, the standard presents detailed requirements listing "what" has to be done, but not "how" it should be performed.

The requirement groups and their requirement areas are presented in Table B.1. A typical example of the detailing level of the guidelines for a specific requirement is shown in Frame B.1.

Frame B.1: An example of ISO/IEC 90003 detailed requirements – maintenance requirements

Source: ISO/IEC 90003-2012

Guidelines for: Requirement area: Customer-related processes

Specific requirement: Review of requirements related to the product.
Guidelines subject: Risks (Standard Sec. 7.2.2.2)

The following risks may be included when reviewing requirements related to the product:

1. Criticality, safety, and security issues

2. Capabilities and experience of the organization or its suppliers

3. Reliability of estimates of the resources and the duration required for each activity

4. Significant difficulties between the times required to deliver product or service, and the times determined from plans through the optimization of cost and quality goals

5. Significant geographical dispersion of the organization, customers, users, and suppliers

6. High technical novelty including novel methods, tools, technologies, and supplied software

7. Low quality or availability of supplied software and tools

8. Low precision, accuracy, and stability of the definition of the customer requirements and external interfaces

---

B.4.3   Certification process according to ISO/IEC 90003

The ISO/IEC 90003 certification process verifies that an organization's software development and maintenance processes fully comply with the standard's requirements.

The certification service is organized by the International Organization for Standardization (ISO) through a worldwide network of certification services that are authorized by means of *accreditation bodies* and *certification bodies*. Each accreditation body is licensed by ISO to authorize other professional organizations as certification bodies. Certification bodies, whose number may vary by country, perform the actual certification audits and certify the organizations that qualify.

Obtaining certification. Organizations wishing to obtain ISO/IEC 90003 certification are required to complete the following:

- Develop the organization's SQA system
- Implement the organization's SQA system
- Undergo successfully the certification audits

Table B.1 ISO/IEC 90003–TOC – requirement areas and their classification

Requirement groups	Requirement areas
4. Quality management system	4.1 General requirements
	4.2 Documentation requirements
5. Management responsibilities	5.1 Management commitments
	5.2 Customer focus
	5.3 Quality policy
	5.4 Planning
	5.5 Responsibility, authority, and communication
	5.6 Management review
6. Resource management	6.1 Provision of resources
	6.2 Human resources
	6.3 Infrastructure
	6.4 Work environment
7. Product realization	7.1 Planning of product realization
	7.2 Customer-related processes
	7.3 Design and development
	7.4 Purchasing
	7.5 Production and service provision
	7.6 Control of monitoring and measuring devices
8. Measurement, analysis, and improvement	8.1 General
	8.2 Monitoring and measurement
	8.3 Control of nonconforming products
	8.4 Analysis of data
	8.5 Improvement

Source: ISO/IEC Std. 90003-2014.

Fulfillment of these requirements demands thorough planning of the structures and resources necessary to perform the activities culminating in certification.

Retaining certification. Once the organization has obtained the ISO/IEC certification, efforts should be invested to retain the organization's certification. The organization has to undergo successfully the periodical certification audits.

This process may vary somewhat from one organization to another, depending on the characteristics of the organization's design and maintenance activities as well as the certification bodies. The certification processes for obtaining and retaining certification are discussed in greater detail in the rest of this section and illustrated in Figure B.1.

The process for obtaining the certification includes the following activities:

a. Planning the process leading to certification

b. Development of the organization's SQA system and its procedures

(a) *Organization's first certification*   *The certifying organization*

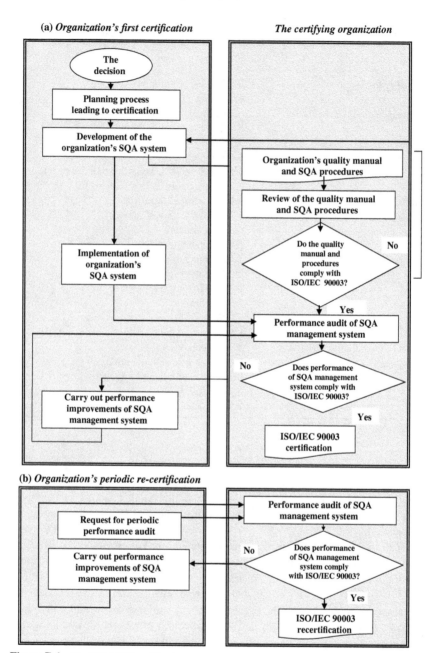

(b) *Organization's periodic re-certification*

Figure B.1   The ISO 90003 certification process

c. Implementation of the organization's SQA system

d. Undergoing the certification audits
   The process for retaining the certification includes the following activities:

e. Procedures for retaining ISO certification

a. **Planning the process leading to certification**
   Once management has made its decision to obtain ISO 90003 certification for its software development and maintenance activities, an action plan is needed.
   An internal survey of the current SQA system and how it is implemented is a good place to begin. The survey should supply information about:
   - Gaps between currently employed SQA and required procedures: missing procedures in addition to inadequate procedures.
   - Gaps between staff know-how and knowledge required regarding SQA procedures and SQA tools.
   - Gaps regarding documentation of development as well as maintenance activities.
   - Gaps/imparity regarding software configuration system capabilities and implementation.
   - Gaps regarding managerial practices demanded for project progress control.
   - Gaps regarding SQA unit organization and its capabilities.
   After completing the above analysis, the plan for obtaining certification can be constructed. It should include:
   - A list of activities to be performed, including schedules.
   - Estimates of resources required to carry out each activity.
   - Organizational resources: (a) Internal participants – SQA unit staff (including staff to be recruited) and senior software engineers; (b) SQA consultants.

b. **Development of the organization's SQA system and its procedures**
   Before proceeding, the organization's SQA management system should be developed to a level adequate to meet ISO/IEC 90003 requirements. These efforts should include:
   - Development of a quality manual and a comprehensive set of SQA procedures
   - Development of additional SQA infrastructure:
     - Staff training and instruction programs, including staff certification programs
     - Preventive and corrective actions procedures, including the CAB committee
     - Configuration management services, including a software change control management unit

    – Documentation and quality record controls
- Development of a project progress control system

c. **Implementation of the organization's SQA system**

Once the components of the SQA management system conform to certification requirements, efforts are shifted toward implementing the system. These efforts include setting up a staff instruction program and support services appropriate for the task of solving problems that may arise when implementing SQA tools. These arrangements are targeted especially at team leaders and unit managers, who are expected to follow up and support the implementation efforts made by their units.

Throughout this stage, internal quality audits are carried out to verify the success of implementation and to identify units and SQA issues that require additional attention. The internal quality audit findings will enable determining whether the organization has reached a satisfactory level of implementation.

d. **Undergoing the certification audits**

The certification audits are carried out in two stages:

a. *Review of the quality manual and SQA procedures developed by the organization.* The review ascertains completeness and accuracy. In cases of noncompliance with standards, the organization is obligated to complete the corrections prior to advancing to the second stage of certification.

b. *Verification audits of compliance with the requirements defined by the organization in its quality manual and SQA procedures.* The main questions to be answered are:
- Has the staffs been adequately instructed on SQA topics and does it display a satisfactory level of knowledge?
- Have the relevant procedures – project plans, design reviews, progress reports, and so on – been properly and fully implemented by the development teams?
- Have documentation requirements been fully observed?

The main sources of information for certification audits are: (a) interviews with members of the audited unit and (b) review of documents such as project plans, design documents and test plans and procedures, and design review records. In order to ensure reliable results and avoid biased conclusions, audits are based on a random selection of projects and/or teams.

e. **Procedures for retaining ISO/IEC certification**

Periodic recertification audits, usually carried out once or twice a year, are performed to verify continued compliance with ISO/IEC 90003 requirements. During these audits, the organization has to demonstrate continuing development of its SQA management system, which is indicated in quality and productivity performance improvements, regular updates of procedures to reflect technological changes, as well as process improvement.

B.5 Capability maturity CMMI models – assessment methodology

Carnegie Mellon University's Software Engineering Institute (SEI) took the initial steps toward development of what is termed as a *capability maturity model* (CMM) in 1986, when it released the first brief description of the maturity process framework. The initial version of the CMM was released in 1992, mainly to receive feedback from the software community. The first version for public use was released in 1993 and was dedicated to the assessment of software development processes (Paulk et al., 1995). The current integrated CMMI methodology includes software development, software service, and acquisition models, integrated into the CMMI (CMMI Product Team, 2010a, 2010b, 2010c).

Another maturity model, P-CMM (People-CMM), was developed by the SEI team similarly to other maturity models, and dedicated to the process improvement of human resources management.

Several CMMI methodology implementation issues are presented by Ramanujan and Kesh (2004), Diaz et al. (2009), Trujillo et al. (2011), and Alyahya et al. (2012). The applicability of capability models for small software organizations is examined by Suominen and Makinen (2014).

B.5.1 The principles of CMMI

CMM assessment is based on the following concepts and principles:

- Application of elaborate management methods based on quantitative approaches increases the organization's capability to control the quality and improve the productivity of the software development process.
- The vehicle for enhancement of software development is composed of the five-level capability maturity model. The integrated models for software development, software services, and acquisition enable an organization to evaluate its achievements and determine the efforts needed to reach the next capability level by locating the process areas requiring improvement.
- Process areas are generic; they define the "what" – not the "how." This approach enables the model to be applied to a wide range of implementation organizations as:
  - It allows using any life cycle model.
  - It allows using any design methodology, software development tool, and programming language.
  - It does not specify any particular documentation standard.

B.5.2   The CMMI structure and processes areas

The three CMMI models share the same conceptual framework. The CMMI models, like the original CMM model, are composed of the following five levels:

- Capability maturity level 1: Initial
- Capability maturity level 2: Managed
- Capability maturity level 3: Defined
- Capability maturity level 4: Quantitatively managed
- Capability maturity level 5: Optimizing

Each of the CMMI models includes almost the same number of process areas (PAs): CMMI model for software development – 22 PAs, CMMI model for services – 23 PAs, and CMMI model for acquisition – 22 PAs. The organization is required to successfully perform a set of PAs in order to be awarded a higher maturity level.

The CMMI models share a great part of their PAs as follows:

- CMMI model for software development shares 14 PAs with CMMI model for services share
- CMMI model for software development shares 16 PAs with CMMI model for acquisition
- CMMI model for services shares 14 PAs with CMMI model for acquisition

Thirteen of the PAs are common to the three CMMI models.

The CMMI model for software development and its process areas (PAs) are presented in Figure B.2.

The CMMI assessment standards provide detailed guidance for the performance of each PA. This guidance includes:

- Purpose statement of the PA
- Specific goals for each PA
- Specific practices for each specific goal
- Examples of information sources, categories of practices, criteria, situations, selection considerations, and so on
- Examples of work products and subpractices for each specific practice

In addition, the CMMI assessment standards define generic goals for each PA, where

- Purpose statement of the PA is defined
- Generic goals are defined for each PA
- Generic practices are defined for each generic goal

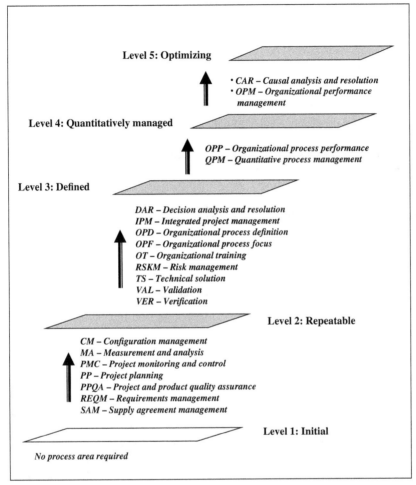

Figure B.2   The CMMI model for software development – model levels and process areas (PAs). (After Paulk et al., 1995.)

- Subpractices and generic practice elaborations and additions are provided for each generic practice

B.5.3 CMMI appraisal process

CMMI standards do not have a certification process, but enable the professional appraisal of the quality management achievement of the organization. The appraisal could be performed as a self-assessment or by an external assessor. The appraisal results determine the organization's capability level or its capability achievement profile.

The following are the main justifications for performing an appraisal:

- To determine the quality management performance achievements compared with CMMI requirements, in order to identify areas that need improvement.
- To present to customers the organization's capability level as a supplier of software development and services.
- To meet capability level requirement by customers.

CMMI methodology stresses the importance of the assessor's qualifications. A certified assessor is required to be SEI-trained and to be certified by the institute.

B.5.4   CMM implementation experience

In our discussion of CMMI implementation experience, we refer to:

- Performance improvements
- Time required for the transition from one CMMI level to the next

Performance improvements

Implementation of a CMMI program by an organization is a costly investment. Managers often wonder what the expected benefits of this investment are. A response to this request, based on quantitative measurements by 19 organizations, is provided by Galin and Avrahami (2006). It was found that "climbing" to a higher capability level (i.e., from CMM level 2 to CMM level 3) is followed by the following average performance improvements in Table B.2.

Even when considering the fact that the resulting benefits are somewhat biased, being based on CMM success stories, the benefits are still remarkable.

Table B.2   Performance improvement by transition to the next CMM level

Performance criterion	Average performance improvement (%)
Reduction of error density	48
Increase of productivity	52
Decrease of percentage of rework	39
Reduction of project cycle time	38
Increase of schedule fidelity	45
Increase of error detection effectiveness	63

Source: Galin and Avrahami (2006).

Table B.3   Time required to progress to the next
CMM capability level

Capability level transition	Mean time (months)
Level 1 to level 2	24
Level 2 to level 3	21.5
Level 3 to level 4	33
Level 4 to level 5	18

Expected CMMI transition time

A report by Gartner Group Inc., a leading consulting company on information technology management, summarizes the firm's accumulated experience regarding the time required for progress from one capability level to the next (Gartner Group, 2001). The average time required for progress from one CMM capability level to the next is a measure of the efforts required for achievements in a CMMI project. As such, this information is of great interest to managers considering implementation of a CMMI project in their organization. These results for CMM projects are shown in Table B.3.

The results for performance improvement and time required for transition from one capability level to the next are based on studies of CMM project experience. No similar studies were found for CMMI projects. We expect that similar results will also be achieved in CMMI applications.

B.5.5   The People CMM model

The People-CMM (P-CMM) methodology (Curtis et al., 2009a) is an important complementary part to the CMMI methodology as it guides management of the human resources, whom are occupied with the development of the software systems and the provision of software services. In other words, implementing P-CMM increases the organizational capability to perform CMMI process areas and reach higher CMMI capability levels. The P-CMM process areas deal with HR management, skill and knowledge development, quantified managerial control of HR, and improvement of HR management practices.

The P-CMM model is a "traditional" 5-capability level model, dedicated to the HR-specific process areas. The P-CMM model levels and their process areas are presented in Figure B.3.

Several papers discuss the issues of People-CMM and the experience of its implementation in organizations: Gama et al. (2011) and Colomo-Palacios et al. (2010), to name but a few. A comprehensive discussion of the P-CMM methodology, possible uses of the model and experience gained by implementation of the model, can be found in a book by Curtis et al. (2009b).

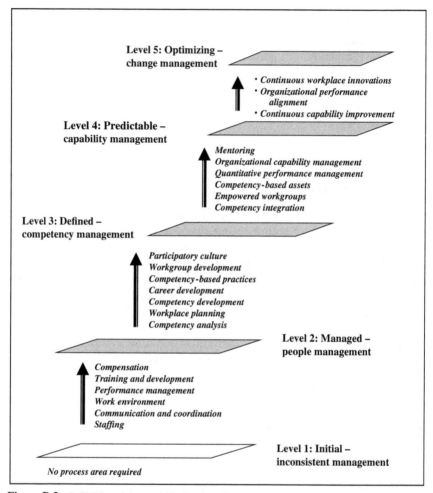

Figure B.3   P-CMM model – capability levels and process areas

B.6   The SPICE project and the ISO/IEC 15504 software process assessment standard

The success of CMM created parallel development of several software process assessment methodologies. The most important of these was a joint initiative by ISO and IEC, the SPICE (Software Process Improvement for Capability Determination) Project, established in 1993 by developing an international standard of software process assessment methodology.

The SPICE Project released its Version 1.0 report in 1995, which became the basis for the development of the TR (technical report) version of the ISO/IEC 15504 standard released in 1998.

The next stage in the development of the ISO/IEC 15504 standard will be its release as an international standard. An ISO/IEC working group has been assigned the responsibility of developing the standard and publishing its revisions. Each revision draft is examined and edited by the national standard institute members of ISO and IEC before being finally approved. Another route taken to identify features demanding revision was the conduct of a major three-phase trial within the framework of the SPICE Project.

The current ISO/IEC standard is composed of eight parts, four of which are technical specifications (TSs). The eight standard parts are dedicated to the following subjects:

- Part 2: Performing an assessment (ISO/IEC, 2003)
- Part 3: Guidance on performing an assessment (ISO/IEC, 2004a)
- Part 4: Guidance on use of process improvement and process capability determination (ISO/IEC, 2004b)
- Part 5: An exemplar process assessment process model (ISO/IEC, 2012a)
- Part 6: An exemplar system life cycle process assessment model (TS) (ISO/IEC, 2013)
- Part 8: An exemplar process assessment process model for IT service management (TS) (ISO/IEC, 2012b).
- Part 9: Target process profiles (TS) (ISO/IEC, 2011a).
- Part 10: Safety extension (TS) (ISO/IEC, 2011b)

Former parts 1 and 7 of the 15504 standard were replaced by a new standard: ISO/IEC 33001: Concepts and terminology.

This first replacement is part of the entire ISO/IEC 15504 set of standards being replaced by a new set of ISO/IEC 33000 series of standards as follows:

- ISO/IEC 33001: 2015 Information technology – Process assessment – Concepts and terminology (ISO/IEC, 2015a).
- ISO/IEC 33002: 2015 Information technology – Process assessment – Requirement for performing process assessment (ISO/IEC, 2015b).
- ISO/IEC 33003: 2015 Information technology – Process assessment – Requirement for process measurement framework (ISO/IEC, 2015c).
- ISO/IEC 33004: 2015 Information technology – Process assessment – Process reference, process assessment, and maturity models (ISO/IEC, 2015d).
- ISO/IEC 33014: 2015 Information technology – Process assessment – Guide for process improvement (ISO/IEC, 2015e).
- ISO/IEC 33063: 2015 Information technology – Process assessment – Process measurement framework for assessment of process capability.

B.6.1 Principles behind ISO/IEC 15504 assessment model

The initiators of the SPICE project and the ISO/IEC standard have defined the following guiding principles for the new assessment model:

- Harmonize the many existing "independent" assessment methodologies by providing a comprehensive framework model (instructing the users in "what" has to be accomplished rather than on "how" it has to be done).
- Be universal to serve all or almost all categories of software suppliers and customers as well as software categories.
- Be highly professional.
- Be worldwide accepted. Aim at reaching international acceptance to emerge as a real-world standard. Becoming a world standard is expected to save supplier resources by eliminating the need to perform several different capability assessments simultaneously in response to different customer requirements. The standard allows conformity of its process model with existing assessment models.

Comparative studies have already proved high conformity of the ISO/IEC 15504 standard with the CMM model and Bootstrap model.

B.6.2 Structure of the ISO/IEC 15504 assessment model

The 15504 process assessment model is a two-dimensional model:

- The capability dimension
- The process dimension

The capability dimension

The capability dimension model is composed of six levels of capability, where level 0 is the lowest and level 5 the highest. The model defines process attributes (PAs) that have to be attained to achieve each capability level. Process attributes are generic, defining "what," not "how,"

The model is composed of:

- Capability levels and process attribute requirements (PAs) for each level

- Indicators for each PA, which are used as a basis for collecting the objective evidence that enables an assessor to assign ratings
- Achievement grades scale for process attributes
- Accumulative achievement requirements for each capability level

Capability levels and process attribute requirements

Level 0: Incomplete process
   No process attributes are expected. There is no (or only little) implementation of any planned or identified process.

Level 1: Performed process
   PA1: **Process performance** includes identifying processes and their inputs and outputs.

Level 2: Managed process
   PA2: **Performance management** – Processes performed according to procedures, their progress is controlled.

   PA3: **Work product management** – Work products are controlled and documented, their compliance is verified.

Level 3: Established process
   PA4: **Process definition** – The organization applies well-defined processes throughout. Processes tailored to any specific project originate in standard processes.

   PA5: **Process deployment** – The organization controls use of project resources: human resources, infrastructure resources, and so on.

Level 4: Predictable process
   PA6: **Process measurement** – Performance measurement supports achievement of project goals.

   PA7: **Process control** – The organization controls processes by collection of data on performance and product measures, analysis and implementation of needed corrections of process performance to achieve process goals.

Level 5: Optimizing process
   PA8: **Process innovation** – The organization initiates and controls processes and managerial systems to improve its effectiveness and efficiency for achievement of its business goals and assures continuous improvement of processes and management.

   PA9: **Process optimization** – The organization persistently monitors the changes implemented through quantitative measurement to achieve optimization.

   An example of indicators for a process attribute is presented in Frame B.2.

   The capability dimension model and the process attributes required for each level are illustrated in Figure B.4.

Frame B.2: Indicator for process control attributes – an example
Source: ISO/IEC Std. 15504-2

Level 4: Predictable process.

PA7: Process control attribute.
Indicators:

a. Suitable analysis and control techniques determined and applied where applicable
b. Control limits of variation are established for normal process performance
c. Measurement data are analyzed for special cases of variation
d. Corrective actions are taken to address special causes of variation
e. Control limits are reestablished (as necessary) following corrective action

---

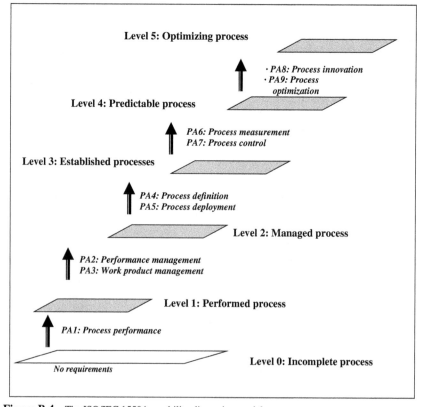

Figure B.4   The ISO/IEC 15504 capability dimension model

The process dimension

The 15504 process dimension fully adopts the process reference model of the 12207 standard presented in Figure A.1. The process dimension model is composed of more than 40 processes. (The number of processes varies slightly for the different versions of the 12207 standard.) The processes are classified into seven categories:

System life cycle category group:

- AGR: Agreement process
- ORG: Organization project-enabling processes
- PRO: Project processes
- ENG: Technical processes

Software life cycle category group:

- DEV: Software development processes
- SUP: Software support processes
- REU: Software reuse processes

The relationship between the capability dimension and the process dimension is defined by the standard in a table that indicates relevant PAs for each process. According to the table, a process could be relevant for one to four PAs. The two-dimensional process assessment model and the relationships between the dimensions are presented in Figure B.5.

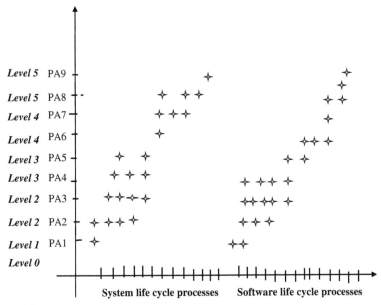

Figure B.5 The 15504 two-dimensional process assessment model

B.6.3   The ISO/IEC 15504 appraisal process

The standard allows performing the appraisal as a self-assessment or independent assessment. In both cases, the standard presents strict requirements regarding the qualifications of assessors:

a. Have adequate education, training, and experience on the relevant processes.

b. Have access to the guidance documentation on how to perform the relevant assessment activities.

c. Have the competence to use the tools to support the appraisal that are provided by the standard

The assessment result ratings for each PA are summarized by grades. A PA may be graded with one of the following four grades according to its evaluation:

- Fully achieved (F) for ratings in the range of 86–100%.
- Largely achieved (L) for ratings in the range of 51–85%
- Partially achieved (P) for ratings in the range of 16–50%
- Not achieved (N) for ratings in the range of 0–15%

The ISO/IEC 15504 model likewise determines the achievements required for each of the relevant process areas. An organization's SQA system capability maturity would be evaluated to a certain capability maturity level if (1) all level PAs are fully or largely achieved, and (2) all PAs of lower capability maturity levels are fully achieved. For example, an organization is evaluated as capability maturity level 3 if all PAs of level 3 are rated fully or largely achieved and all level 2 and level 1 PAs are fully achieved.

B.6.4   The SPICE project

The SPICE project operates the professional working groups that created the ISO/IEC 15504 standard in the mid-1990s and continue to conduct work to develop the standard.

Once the standard became public, the SPICE project management planned a large-scale trial of the ISO/IEC 15504 technical report version to facilitate its transformation into an effective standard. The trials had three goals:

- To validate the model's conformity with current standards
- To verify its usability in determining whether software satisfies user requirements
- To gain experience in applying the model

The three phases of the trial were carried out during 1995–2000. A database was built of data collected during full-scale assessments performed in organizational environments. Each volunteer organization agreed to carry out at least one full-scale assessment. Special efforts were invested to create a diversified database, including participants from every continent and a variety of software specializations. During these trials, more than 200 full-scale assessments were carried out with several technical reports that summarized the SPICE trials empirical experience published in the late 1990s. The analysis of the collected empirical data served as a major basis for the full version of the ISO/IEC international standard parts that were published during 2003–2006.

The SPICE project working group continued to develop and update the standard in the following years. Other activities within the SPICE project are the SPICE annual conferences dedicated to software development assessment research and experience with the application of the 15504 standard and other software development assessment models.

A new direction in the development of the SPICE project was the adaptation to individual domains by development of SPICE PRM, PAM, and OMM models. Another development was the automotive industry, with the 2005 release of the automotive SPICE standard.

Detailed descriptions of the history of the SPICE project can be found in Rout et al. (2007), Salviano et al. (2012), and Mesquida et al. (2014).

B.7 Additional software quality management standards

Several software quality management methodologies were developed in parallel to ISO/IEC 90003, CMMI, and ISO/IEC 15504 standards. TickIT and Bootstrap methodologies will be presented in this section.

TickIT

TickIT was launched in the late 1980s by the British software industry in cooperation with the British Department for Trade and Industry to promote development of a methodology for adapting ISO 9001 to the characteristics of the software industry known as *the TickIT initiative*. Currently, with the TickIT Plus methodology and TickIt standards, it provides a variety of consulting, auditing, and certification services, mainly to the British IT industry.

At the time of its launching, ISO 9001 had already been successfully applied in the manufacturing industry; however, no significant methodology for its application to the special characteristics of the software industry was yet available. In the years to follow, the TickIT initiative, together with efforts invested in the development of ISO/IEC 90003, achieved this goal.

TickIT activities include:

- Publication of the TickIt standards of software quality management and capability assessment.
- Publication of the *TickIT Guide* and other publications that support the software industry efforts to spread ISO 9001 and ISO/IEC 90003 certification. The current guide, which includes references to ISO/IEC 12207 and ISO/IEC 15504 and other TSO/IEC standards, is distributed to all TickIT customers.
- Performance of audit-based assessments of software quality systems and consultation to organizations on improvement of software development and maintenance processes in addition to their management.
- Conduct ISO/IEC 90003 and TickIT Plus in addition to certification audits and assessment audits. TickIT auditors who conduct audit-based assessments and certification audits are registered by the International Register of Certificated Auditors (IRCA).
- Provide consulting and training services.

The Bootstrap

The Bootstrap Institute, a nonprofit organization that operates in Europe as part of the European Strategic Program for Research in Information Technology (ESPRIT) in cooperation with the European Software Institute (ESI), offers another route for professional SQA support to organizations based on its Bootstrap methodology.

The Bootstrap Institute provides various types of support to its licensed members:

1. Access to the Bootstrap methodology for assessment and improvement of software development processes. The Institute constantly updates and improves its methodology.
2. Training and accreditation of assessors.
3. Access to the Bootstrap database.

The Bootstrap methodology measures the maturity of an organization and its projects on the basis of quality attributes grouped into three classes: process, organization, and technology. A five-grade scale is applied to each of the quality attributes separately. The methodology facilitates detailed assessment of the software development process by evaluating its achievements with respect to each attribute, and indicates the improvements required in the software development process and projects. The assessment options include:

- Evaluation of the current position of the software quality assurance system as a basis for improvement initiation.

- Evaluation of level of achievements according to the Capability Maturity Model Integrated (CMMI) models.
- Evaluation of achievements according to ISO 15504 (the SPICE project).
- ISO 90003 gap assessment to support preparations for a certification audit.

Training and accreditation of assessors. Bootstrap trains three levels of registered assessors, namely, trained assessor, assessor, and lead assessor. A person can become a registered lead assessor, having overall responsibility for planning and performing a Bootstrap assessment, only after successfully performing as a trained and then registered assessor. In order to become a trained assessor, a person has to successfully complete a basic assessor training program, after which she or he can participate in Bootstrap assessments. Trained assessors who have demonstrated knowledge in performance of assessments and have been recommended by a registered lead assessor may qualify as a registered assessor. Registered assessors are likewise required to demonstrate knowledge and competence in carrying out higher level assessments in addition to participation in a lead assessors training course. Only then they can apply for acceptance as lead assessors.

The Bootstrap database contains the findings of Bootstrap assessments conducted for its member organizations. Although the sources of the data are kept anonymous, the assessment results are classified according to the type of organization, country, type of product or service, market, and development effort. Members can obtain the following information:

- Members own assessments – retrieved from the database
- Aggregate assessments results from comparable organizations
- Data for surveys and research of software development to improve development processes and product quality

Summary

1. **The aims of certification standards**
   - Enable a software development organization to demonstrate consistent ability to perform software development and or maintenance services that comply with quality requirements.
   - Serve as an agreed-upon basis for customer and supplier evaluation of the supplier's quality management system.
   - Support the software development organization's efforts to improve quality management system performance and enhance customer satisfaction.

2. The aims of capability assessment standards

- Serve software development and maintenance organizations as a tool for self-assessment of their capability level to carry out software development projects.
- Serve as a tool for improvement of development and maintenance processes. The standard indicates directions for process improvements.
- Help purchasing organizations determine the capabilities of potential suppliers.
- Guide training of assessor by delineating qualifications and training program curricula.

3. Ways by which continuous improvement principle of SPIs are achieved

- Serve software development and maintenance organizations as a tool for self-assessment of their ability to carry out software development projects.
- Serve as a tool for improvement of development and maintenance processes. The standard indicates directions for process improvements.
- Help purchasing organizations determine the capabilities of potential suppliers.
- Guide training of assessor by delineating qualifications and training program curricula.

4. Description of the general principles underlying quality management according to ISO/IEC 90003

- Customer focus – understanding a customer's current and future needs.
- Leadership exercised in the creation and maintenance of a positive internal environment in order to achieve the organization's objectives.
- Involvement of people at all levels to further organizational goals.
- Process approach – activities and related resources are perceived and managed as a process.
- Systems approach to management – managing processes as a system.
- Continual improvement of the organization's overall performance.
- Factual approach to decision-making – decisions are based on the analysis of data and information.
- Mutually beneficial supplier relationships – emphasis on coordination and cooperation.

5. Description of the ISO/IEC 90003 certification process

To acquire ISO/IEC 90003 certification, organizations must carry out the following:

- Plan the organization's activities for gaining certification.
- Development the organization's SQA system, including procedures.

- Obtain approval of procedures by the certifying organization.
- Implement the organization's SQA system.
- Undergoing certification audits of actual performance of the SQA system.
  To retain the ISO/IEC certification, the organization
- must undergo certification audits of actual performance of the SQA system;
- is required to improve its performance in cases of low audits results to a level that complies with the standard requirements.
- undergo recurrent certification audits.

6. **Description of the principles embodied in the CMM**
   - Application of highly elaborated software quality management methods increases the organization's capability to control quality and improve software process productivity.
   - Application of the five levels of the capability maturity model enables the organization to evaluate its achievements and determine which additional efforts are needed to reach the next capability level.
   - Process areas are generic, with the model defining "what" and leaving the "how" to the implementing organizations, that is, the choice of life cycle model, design methodology, software development tool, programming language, and documentation standard.

7. **Description of the principles that guided the developers of ISO/IEC 15504**
   - Harmonization of independent assessment methodologies by providing a conceptual framework based on "what," not "how."
   - Universality of applicability to all or almost all categories of software suppliers and customer organizations as well as software categories.
   - Professionalism.
   - Worldwide acceptance.

Selected bibliography

Alyahya M., Ahmad R., and Lee S. P. (2012) Impact of CMMI-based process maturity levels of effort, productivity and diseconomy of scale, *The International Arab Journal of Information Technology*, Vol. 9, No. 4, pp. 352–360.

Bella F., Hormann K., and Vanamali B. (2008) *From CMMI to SPICE – experiences on how to survive a SPICE assessment having already implemented CMMI, in* The 9th International Conference on Product-Focused Software Process Improvement, pp. 133–142.

CMMI Product Team (2010a) CMMI for Acquisition, CMMI-ACQ, V1.3. Technical report CMU/SEI-2010-TR-032 ESC-TR 201-032, Carnegie Mellon University, Software Engineering Institute, Pittsburgh, PA.

CMMI Product Team (2010b) CMMI for Development, CMMI-ACQ, V1.3. Technical report CMU/SEI-2010-TR-033 DEV-TR 2010-033, Carnegie Mellon University, Software Engineering Institute, Pittsburgh, PA.

CMMI Product Team (2010c) CMMI for Services CMMI-SER, V1.3. Technical report CMU/SEI-2010-TR-034 ESC-TR 2010-034, Carnegie Mellon University, Software Engineering Institute, Pittsburgh, PA.

Colomo-Palacios R., Tovar-Caro E., Garcia-Crespo A., and Gomez-Berbis J. M. (2010) Identifying technical competences of IT professionals: the case of software engineers, *International Journal of Human Capital and Information Technology*, Vol. 1, No. 1, pp. 31–41.

Curtis B., Hefley W. E., and Miller S. A. (2009a) People Capability Maturity Model (P-CMM) Version 2.0, 2nd Edition. Technical report CMR/SEI-2009TR-003 ESC-TR-2009-003, Carnegie Mellon University, Software Engineering Institute, Pittsburgh, PA.

Curtis B., Hefley W. E., and Miller S. A. (2009b) *People CMM – A Framework for Human Capital Management*, 2nd Edition, Pearson Education, Boston, MA.

Diaz J., Garbajosa J., and Calco-Manzano J. A. (2009) Mapping CMMI level 2 to scrum practices: an experience report, *Communications of Computer Information Systems*, Vol. 42, No. 2, pp. 93–104.

Galin D. and Avrahami M. (2006) Are CMM program investments beneficial? Analyzing past studies, *IEEE Software*, Vol. 23, No. 6, pp. 81–87.

Gama N., da Silva R. N., and da Silva M. M. (2011) Using People-CMM for diminishing resistance to ITIL, *International Journal of Human Capital and Information Technology Professionals*, Vol. 2, No. 3, pp. 29–43.

Gartner Group (2001) *Describing the Capacity Maturity Model*, Measure, Special Edition 2001, Gartner Inc., http//www.gartner.com/measurements.

Helgesson Y. Y. L., Host M., and Weyns K. (2011) A review of methods for evaluation of maturity models for process improvement, *Journal of Software: Evolution and Process*, Vol. 24, No. 4, pp. 436–454.

ISO/IEC (2003) *ISO/IEC 15504-2:2003 Software Engineering – Process Assessment – Part 2 – Performing an Assessment*, International Organization for Standardization (ISO), Geneva.

ISO/IEC (2004a) *ISO/IEC 15504-3:2004 Information Technology – Process Assessment – Part 3 – Guidance on Performing an Assessment*, International Organization for Standardization (ISO), Geneva.

ISO/IEC (2004b) *ISO/IEC 15504-4:2004 Information Technology – Process Assessment – Part 4 – Guidance on Use for Process Improvement and Process Capability Determination*, International Organization for Standardization (ISO), Geneva.

ISO/IEC (2011a) *ISO/IEC TS 15504-9:2011 Information Technology – Process Assessment – Part 9 – Target process Profiles*, International Organization for Standardization (ISO), Geneva.

ISO/IEC (2011b) *ISO/IEC TS 15504-10:2011 Information Technology – Process Assessment – Part 10 – Safety Extension*, International Organization for Standardization (ISO), Geneva.

ISO/IEC (2012a) *ISO/IEC 15504-5:2012 Information Technology – Process Assessment – Part 5 – An Exemplar Software Life Cycle Process Assessment Model*, International Organization for Standardization (ISO), Geneva.

ISO/IEC (2012b) *ISO/IEC TS 15504-8:2012 Information Technology – Process Assessment – Part 8 – An Exemplar Process Assessment Model for IT Service Management*, International Organization for Standardization (ISO), Geneva.

ISO/IEC (2013) *ISO/IEC TS 15504-6:2013 Information Technology – Process Assessment – Part 6 – An Exemplar System Life Cycle Process Assessment Model*, International Organization for Standardization (ISO), Geneva.

ISO/IEC (2014) *ISO/IEC 90003:2014 – Software Engineering – Guidelines for the Application of ISO 9001:2008 to Computer Software*, International Organization for Standardization (ISO), Geneva.

ISO/IEC (2015a) *ISO/IEC 33001:2015 Information Technology – Process Assessment – Concepts and Terminology*, International Organization for Standardization (ISO), Geneva.

ISO/IEC (2015b) *ISO/IEC 33002: 2015 Information Technology – Process Assessment – Requirement for Performing Process Assessment*, International Organization for Standardization (ISO), Geneva.

ISO/IEC (2015c) *ISO/IEC 33003: 2015 Information Technology – Process Assessment – Requirement for Process Measurement Frameworks*, International Organization for Standardization (ISO), Geneva.

ISO/IEC (2015d) *ISO/IEC 33004: 2015 Information Technology – Process Assessment – Requirements for Process Reference, Process Assessment and Maturity Models*, International Organization for Standardization (ISO), Geneva.

ISO/IEC (2015e) *ISO/IEC 33014: 2015 Information Technology – Process Assessment – Guide for Process Improvement*, International Organization for Standardization (ISO), Geneva.

Mesquida A. L., Mas A., Lepnets M., and Renault A. (2014) *Development of the project management SPICE (PMSPICE) framework, in* Proceedings of the 14th International Conference, SPICE 2014, Vilnius, LT, November, pp. 60–71.

Paulk M. C., Weber C. V., Curtis B., and Chrissis M. B. (1955) *Capability Maturity Model: Guidelines for Improving the Software Process*, Addison-Wesley, Reading, MA.

Ramanujan S. and Kesh S. (204) Comparison of knowledge management and CMM/CMMI implementation, *Journal of the American Academy of Business, Cambridge*, Vol. 4, No. 1–2, pp. 271–277.

Rout T. P., El Emam K., Fusani M., Goldenson D. and Jung H-W. (2007) SPICE in retrospect: developing a standard for process assessment, *Journal of Systems and Software*, Vol. 80, pp. 1483–1493.

Salviano C. F., Alves A., Stefanuto G. N., Maintinguer S. T., Mattos C. V., Zeitoum C. and Reuss G. (2012) *Developing a process assessment model for technological and business competencies on software development, in* The 8th International Conference on the Quality of Information and Communication Technology, pp. 125–130.

Salviano C. F. and Figueiredo A. M. C. M. (2006) *Unified basic concepts for process capability models, in* Proceedings of the 20th International Conference on Software Engineering and Knowledge Engineering, SEKE'06, San Francisco, CA, July, pp. 173–178.

Suominen M. and Makinen T. (2014) On the applicability of capability models for small software organizations: does the use of standard processes lead to a better achievement of business goals? *Software Quality Journal*, Vol. 22, No. 4, pp. 579–591.

Trujillo M. M., Oktaba H., Pino F., and Orozo M. J. (2011) Applying agile and lean practices in an software development project into a CMMI organization, in Calvano D. et al. (Eds.) *PROFES 2011 LNCS 6759*, Springer, Heidelberg, Germany, pp. 17–29.

Review questions

B.1 Section B.2 presents classes of software quality management standards.

  a. Explain the differences between the two classes.

  b. Compare the scope of the two classes and discuss the differences with respect to the goals of software quality assurance.

B.2 The evolution and diversification of the CMM methodology have produced several specialized CMM products. At a certain point, SEI moved toward creation of integrated CMMI models.

  a. Explain the reasons for this move.

  b. List arguments for and against integration.

B.3 The SPICE project performed a comprehensive trial with the early versions of the ISO/IEC 15504 standard.

- Explain in your own words the contribution of the trial to development of the standard.

B.4 One of the main activities of the Bootstrap Institute is training and accreditation of assessors.
- Discuss the special role of assessors in implementation of the Bootstrap methodology.

Topics for discussion

B.1 ISO/IEC 90003 serves as a certification standard for interested software development organizations throughout the world.

a. The ISO and the IEC are neither capable nor interested in carrying out certification audits. How do standards organizations ensure the performance of audits conducted with the same method and requiring the same level of achievement in the same subjects for organizations worldwide?

b. Describe in your own words the certification for an organization.

c. Explain the unique importance of each stage of a certification audit.

B.2 Organizations are usually interested to retain their ISO/IEC 90003 certification.

a. Describe in your own words the recertification process of an organization.

b. Describe situations when an organization does not retain its certification.

B.3 CMMI models are composed of almost identical capability maturity models. The models include 24 process areas.

a. Explain the differences between the CMMI models process areas in relation to the respective subject matter.

b. Indicate which of the capability levels present the most differences among the models.

c. Can you characterize the observed differences among the models?

B.4 Section B.5.4 describes the CMM implementation experience.

a. Discuss in your own words the experience presented in the section.

b. What additional information could be helpful for organizations considering the adoption of the CMMI methodology in their decision making?

Appendix C

Project Progress Control

C.1 Introduction

Months of project delay and budget overruns exceeding 10 and sometimes up to 30 and more percent over project estimations, typical of too many software development projects, are "red flags" for software project management. Unfortunately, these events are usually coupled with the low quality of software projects – a natural reaction of the developers to schedule and budget issues. This chapter is dedicated to methods and procedures that ensure timely performance in a software project, verifying schedule and budget keeping.

These events, which are mainly failures of management itself, are caused by situations such as:

- Overly or even blindly optimistic scheduling and budgeting
- Unprofessional software risk management presented in tardy or inappropriate reactions to software risks.
- Belated identification of schedule and budget difficulties and/or underestimation of their extent.

Situations of the first type can be prevented by performing contract reviews and preparing quality and project planning tools. Project progress control is expected to prevent situations of the second and third types.

While design reviews, inspections, and software tests focus on a project's quality and technical functional aspects, project progress control deals mainly with the managerial aspects, namely, scheduling, human and other resource management, and budget and risk management.

The aim of software project progress control is defined in Frame C.1.

Software Quality: Concepts and Practice, First Edition. Daniel Galin.
© 2018 the IEEE Computer Society, Inc. Published 2018 by John Wiley & Sons, Inc.

Frame C.1: The aim of software project progress control

> The aim of project progress control is to provide a thorough follow-up of a project's implementation, enabling the timely detection of schedule, resource, and budget deviations from project plan. Accurate information about a project's status enables the management to take action to resolve schedule, resource, budget, and risk issues. Project plans may be adjusted when appropriate.

The first understanding from examining the definition is the importance of a professional thorough project plan. The prompt follow-up of the project plan, which reveals project development is the basis for taking correction action, leads the project back to the original route. The project progress control process is presented in Figure C.1.

The components of project progress control are discussed in the next section. Special attention is given to difficulties and solutions for controlling distributors and globally distributed software development projects in Section C.4. The difficulties entailed with controlling external participants and internal projects are discussed in Section C.5. The implementation of project progress control processes is the subject of Section C.6, while Section C.7 is dedicated to computer-aided project progress control.

Management control over maintenance contracts is discussed in Chapter 15 Several software maintenance activities, especially perfective maintenance, include tasks that are similar to software development tasks. Hence, progress

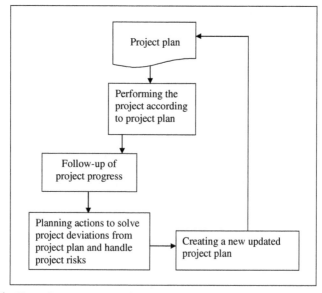

Figure C.1   The project progress control process

control of these tasks can be performed applying the progress control components discussed in this chapter.

The place of project progress control is attested to in SQA general software life cycle standards of ISO/IEC and IEEE software, just to mention ISO/IEC/IEEE International standard 12207:2008 (ISO (2008), which dedicates Section 6.2 to project management processes.

C.2 Finally, a successful project – a mini case

Chemsoft was a medium-sized software company specializing in the chemical industry. The company had well-earned its bad reputation, as most of its projects were behind schedule and almost always over budget. Last year's "record" included 14 projects (out of the 19 completed) with late schedules, and to top it off, a total of $115,000 was paid out in late completion penalties for 11 of the projects.

Dave, the manager of the project operation department was very proud of the new "project progress control procedure," and decided to apply it for the first time on the OPC, Oils Processing Control project. The project duration was determined as 21 weeks, with about a third of the development work to be carried out by MSPR, as a subcontractor. According to the procedure, the first PPC (project progress control) meeting was to be set for the week before work was scheduled to start on the OPC project. Let us examine some of the minutes of the PPC meetings.

Minutes of the first meeting

Participants: Dave, Brian, the project leader, and Kevin, the MSPR team leader.

Brian: Presented ver.1 of the project plan – completion schedule – 22 weeks, human resources – 385 staff-days, purchase budget – $5,200, mainly for sensors for chemical processes. Subcontractor budget – $78,000. Risks: (1) We are not yet sure about the suitability of the BBX Industry sensors, and they may need to be replaced by another brand. (2) The consulting company cannot commit its availability. And have not signed the contract yet.

Kevin: The OPC team will be ready to begin on time.

Dave: The OPC project is to be a model project for schedule and budget keeping.

Decided: According to the procedure, PPC meetings will take place every two weeks on a Monday.

Minutes of the third meeting (beginning of the fifth week)

Brian: There is a week's delay in activities 8 and 11. Staff days invested – 34, planned – 34. Presented a revised activities plan (Ver. 2) that will bring the project back to the original completion schedule within 4 weeks. Risk manage-ment: (1) A satisfactory contract was signed with the consulting company. (2) Laboratory tests proved that the BBX Industries sensors are not suitable: We examined sensors of three alternative brands.

Kevin: The OPC team is on schedule.

Minutes of the fifth meeting

Brian: The new project plan has successfully been followed during the last 4 weeks and the project is now back on schedule. Staff days invested – 77, planned – 75. Risk management: One of the alternative sensor brands was found suitable. The testing of the other alternative brands is expected to be completed next week.

Kevin: Informs about a 3 week delay in the start of system tests. Accord-ingly, a delay of 3 weeks is now expected in the delivery of MSPR share in the OPC project. He said he would take actions to reduce the schedule delay.

Dave: Expresses dissatisfaction regarding the late delay notice from the sub-contractor and mentioned the penalty section of the contract.

Decided: (1) MSPR will submit within a week a plan for extensive testing and error corrections to reduce the delay to a maximum of 1 week. (2) Dave will discuss the situation with Gail, head of the MSPR software department.

Minutes of the eighth meeting

Brian: Presented a new version of the activities plan with 1 week's delay in the scheduled completion, based on the assumption of the 2-weeks delay in the deliv-ery of MSPR share. He expects that an additional 4–5 staff-days on top of the previous plan will be needed to carry out this "crash" plan. Regarding the current status, his project parts are on schedule, but, due to the ver.2 changes, he had to employ a new team member causing staff days spent to grow to 246, planned 242. Risk management: After testing the three alternative brands, it was decided to choose alternative C, which fully fulfils all the requirements and also means a reduction of $920 to the purchasing budget.

Kevin: The MSPR team is progressing according to the extensive plan. A 2-week delay in the team's completion schedule is expected.

Dave: Supports Brian's "crash" plan.

Decided: To approve Brian's "crash" plan.

Minutes of the eleventh meeting

Brian: Integration tests of the MSPR share began as scheduled (2 weeks delay from the original schedule) and while no surprises were encountered, tests will be completed on schedule. System tests were completed successfully, including the prompt correction of identified errors. All sensors and other equipment, required for installation of the system, have already been delivered. The installation work and running-in of the system begins today, as scheduled, to be concluded at the end of the twenty-second week of the project. Staff days spent up to last week – 354, planned 348.

Kevin: Satisfied with the results of the MSPR integration tests that showed the quality of their project parts, and suggests considering the project delay penalties.

Dave: We should also consider that the expected 1 week delay in project completion, as well as the need for Brian's team to spend extra resources, were caused by MSPR's delay.

Decided: To communicate Kevin's request to Chemsoft's deputy for software development with no recommendations.

Minutes of the twelfth meeting – took place after project completion

Brian: Really satisfied with the expected completion date – only 1 week delay. Staff days invested – 391, compared to 385 planned. Considering the pressure caused by the MSPR delays, efforts invested in reducing the overall project delay are a minimal price to pay.

Dave: Believes the PPC meetings and project management were performed strictly accordingly to the PPC procedure, and that this contributed substantially to the success of the project. The readiness of Brian to replan the project, and the team's ability to cope with ver.2 and ver.3 changes should be commended. Considering the difficulties encountered, 1 week delay in the scheduled completion, and a "slip" of 7 staff-days; less than 2% of the planned resources, may be considered a real success. The main lesson learned is that there is an urgent need to update the subcontractor follow-up procedure to verify the close follow-up and early detection of development and potential delays.

C.3 The components of project progress control

Project progress control has one immediate objective: early detection of irregular events. Detection promotes the timely initiation of problem-solving responses. The accumulated information on progress control, as well as successes and extreme failures, also serves a long-term objective: initiation of corrective actions.

The main components of project progress control are:

- Control of risk management activities
- Project schedule control
- Project resource control
- Project budget control

Control of risk management activities refers to the software development risk items identified in the project plan, some of which are already listed in the contract review (proposal draft review – see Appendix 8.A) document, together with other risk items identified throughout the project's progress. The software development team copes with software risk items by applying systematic risk management activities. Control of the progress of risk management begins with the preparation of periodic assessments about the state of software risk items, and the expected outcomes of the risk management activities performed in their wake. Based on these reports, in the more extreme cases, project managers are expected to intervene and help arrive at a solution. More about software project risks and software risk management can be found in Chapter 7 and its Appendix 7.A.

Project schedule control deals with the project's compliance with its approved and contracted schedules. Follow-up is based mainly on milestones, which are set (in part) to facilitate identification of delays in completing planned activities. Milestones set in contracts, especially dates for the delivery of specified software products to the customer, or completion of a development activity generally receive special emphasis. Although some delay can be anticipated, management will focus its control activities on critical delays, those that may substantially affect the final completion of the project. Much of the information needed for management project progress control is transmitted by means of milestone reports and other periodic reports. In response to this information, management may intervene by allocating additional resources or even renegotiating the schedule with the customer.

Project resource control focuses on professional human resources but it can deal with other assets as well. For real-time software systems and firmware, software development and testing facility resources typically demand the tightest control. Here as well, management's control is based on periodic reports of resource use that compare actual to scheduled utilization because, it should be stressed, the true extent of deviations in resource use can be assessed only from the viewpoint of the project's progress. In other words, a project displaying what appears to be only slight deviations in resource utilization, when considering the resources scheduled used up to a specific point of time (e.g., 5%), may actually experience severe cumulative deviations (e.g., 25%), if severe delays in its progress are suffered.

Another aspect of resource control is internal composition or allocation. For example, management may find that no deviations have taken place in total man-months allocated to system analysts. However, review of itemized expenditures may disclose that instead of the 25% of man-months originally allocated to senior system analysts, 50% was actually spent, a step that may eventually undermine the planned budget. Although project budget controls also reveal deviations of this type, they do so at a much later stage of the project, a fact that impedes introduction of remedial actions.

If the deviations are justified, management can intervene by increasing the resources allocated; alternatively, management can shift resources by reorganizing the project teams, revising the project's plan, and so forth.

Project budget control is based on the comparison of actual with scheduled expenditures. As in resource control, a more accurate picture of budget deviations requires that the associated delays in completion of activities be taken into consideration. The main budget items demanding control are:

- Human resources
- Development and testing facilities
- Purchase of COTS software
- Purchase of hardware
- Payments to subcontractors

Again, like resource control, budget control is based on milestones and the periodic reports that facilitate early identification of budget overruns. In cases of deviations by internal bodies, the menu of optional interventions is similar to that applied in project resource control. In deviations by external participants, legal and other measures may also be applied.

Budget control is obviously of the highest priority to management because of its direct effect on project profitability. Managers, therefore, tend to neglect other components of project progress control, especially if they are under serious constraints imposed by monitoring staff. Neglecting other components related to project progress control naturally reduces the effect of control in general. This is regrettable because if applied correctly and in a timely manner, these other progress control tools can reveal unresolved software risk items, delays in completion of activities and excessive use of resources, at a much earlier stage in the project life cycle. This means that reliance solely on budget control activities may be more costly in the long run than application of the full spate of project progress control activities because implementation of effective solutions to problems may be delayed.

C.4 Progress control of distributed and globally distributed software development projects

The growing size of software projects, the availability of geographically distant and offshore professionals, and above all the potential lower costs cause growing parts of software projects to be carried out as distributed and global projects. Cusumano (2008), Jimenez et al. (2009), and Colomo-Palacios et al. (2014), among others, discuss the special nature of managing these projects and the ways to succeed in doing so.

The difficulties of distributed software development (DSD) and global software development (GSD) projects include communication and coordination difficulties, and in GSD projects, culture differences and insufficient facility of the English language also.

Success factors for controlling the progress of DSD and GDS projects offered by the mentioned authors include:

- Application of incremental development methodology (used by Agile projects) or iterative development methodology.
- Planning frequent incremental deliveries (2–4 weeks frequency).
- Employing prototyping to achieve higher user participation in the development process.
- Despite the expected flow of change requests, typical to projects of the incremental development process, it is recommended to plan ahead all the project's increments, and schedule the deliveries.

Of special importance for successful controlling of the progress of DSD and GDS projects are the following (which will naturally contribute to success of "regular" software projects):

- Close communication with the customer.
- Communication with the distributed developers.

C.5   Progress control of internal projects and external participants

Project progress control is initiated in order to provide management with a comprehensive view of all the software development activities carried out in an organization, and thus increases the probability of the project being completed as scheduled. Nevertheless, in most organizations, project control provides, for different reasons, a limited view of the progress of internal software development and an even more limited view of the progress made by external participants. Control over internal projects and external participants tends to be somewhat flawed, as I will describe.

Internal projects, such as those undertaken for other departments or projects dealing with software packages for the general software market exclude, by definition, the option of external customers. These projects thus tend to be assigned a lower management priority. The inadequate attention awarded is often accompanied by inappropriate or lax follow-up on the part of the internal customer. Similar tendencies are observed in the earlier preproject stage, in carrying out contract reviews and preparation development plans (see Sections 20.7 and 21.5.2). Typically, this situation results in tardy identification of adverse delays and severe budget overruns, with the ensuing limited correction of the problems encountered. The inevitable solution to this situation is the imposition of the full range of project progress controls to internal projects as well.

It is expected that internal project with loose development contractor none at all, will also result in lower quality of software products.. The SQA function is required to tend with these risks by tight review and follow-up activities.

External participants include subcontractors, suppliers of COTS software, open-source software, and reused software modules and, in some cases, the customer himself. The more sizeable and complex the project, the greater the likelihood that external participants will be required, and the larger the portion of work allocated to them. Management turns to external participants for a number of reasons, ranging from economic to technical to personnel-related interests; this has become a growing trend in project contracting and subcontracting. Moreover, the agreements entered into by the participants in a project have become so intricate that communication and coordination have become problematic for the project team as well as for management. In response, more significant efforts are called for in order to achieve acceptable levels of control. Hence, project progress control of external participants must focus mainly on the project's schedule and the risks identified in planned project activities.

The performance of the SQA tasks of review and follow-up of quality issues of external participants are much more difficult than those of the developer software project teams. These situations result from coordination and cooperation difficulties typical to external participants. Thus, coordination and cooperation contract requirements as well as appropriate choice of external participants are way to overcome those difficulties.

For a comprehensive discussion of the subject of assuring quality in projects with external participants, see Chapter 20.

C.6 Implementation of project progress control

Project progress control is usually based on procedures that determine:

- The allocation of responsibility for performance of the process control tasks that are appropriate for the project's characteristics, including size:
  - The person or management unit responsible for executing progress control tasks.
  - The frequency of reporting required from each of the project's units and administrative level.
  - The situations requiring project leaders to report immediately to management.
  - The situations requiring lower management to report immediately to upper management.
- Management audits of project progress deal mainly with: (1) how well progress reports are transmitted by project leaders and by lower to upper level managers and (2) the specific management control activities to be initiated.

In large software development organizations, project progress control may be conducted on several managerial levels, such as, software department management, software division management, and top management. Though each level is expected to define its own project progress control regime, one that reflects the parameters considered adequate for assessing the project's progress from that particular location, coordination among the various levels is mandatory for progress control to be effective.

The entire reporting chain transmits information culled from the lowest managerial level – the project leader's periodic progress report – which summarizes the status of project risks, project schedule, and resource utilization, which is, the first three components of progress control. The project leader bases his or her progress report on information gathered from team leaders. An example of a project leader's project progress report is presented in Figure C.2.

C.7 Computerized tools for software progress control

Computerized tools for software progress control include:

- Programs for the planning and control of schedule and resource usage
- Project progress metrics and progress tracking charts

C.7.1 Computerized programs for planning and control of schedule and resource usage

Computerized tools for software project progress control are a clear necessity given the increasing size and complexity of projects as well as the growing distribution and global distribution of projects on one hand, and the solutions they bring with them on the other. The comprehensive project management tools that have been available on the market for many years can serve most of the control components of software projects quite effectively and efficiently. The majority of these general-purpose packages apply PERT/CPM analysis so that the resulting reports take the interactions between activities and the criticality of each activity into account. These packages are usually readily adaptable to specific cases due to the great variety of options that they offer. An important aspect for evaluating these software tools is the ability to communicate with the development teams and other stakeholders involved with inputs and outputs, especially in size, of distributed and globally distributed projects.

The choice of the appropriate computerized tool is of utmost importance. The size of the project, the project complexity, and organizational complexity (e.g., performance by external participants and distributed project) should be considered when choosing progress control software package. Especially, small project should beware of adopting a package for large-scale project, which will require excess reporting and updating processes.

Typical services that computerized tools can provide are all based on project plans inputs reporting:

Project leader's progress report   **For the period:** _____

The project:_____

1. Status of software risks

No.	Risk item	Activities involved	Other projects involved	Solved	Current risk severity	Comments
1						
2						
3						
4						
5						
6						

Risk severity: 1- Solution expected within 1 month. 2- Solution expected within 3 months. 3- Solution expected within 6 months. 4- Solution directions are available, good success prospects. 5- All trials failed, no possible solution has been identified.

2. Status of resource usage

No.	Activity	Hours worked				% of activity completed	Comments
		Planned	Used prior to the report period	Invested during the report period	Total invested		
1							
2							
3							
4							
5							
6							
7							
8							
9							
10							

3. Project completion estimates   (Mark the most probable estimate.)

Human resources	Completed with less than planned	No additional resources required	10% Excess	20% Excess	30% Excess	40% Excess	50% Excess or more
Schedule	Completed before planned date	Completed on time	2 weeks delay	1 month delay	2 months delay	4 months delay	6 months delay and more

Comments:

Signed: Name:_____ Date: _____ Signature:_____

Figure C.2   Project leader's progress report – an example

Control of risk management activities

- Lists of software risk items by category and their planned solution dates
- Lists of exceptions of software risk items – overrun risk solution dates, project activity schedule expected according to the risk management status.

Project schedule control

- Activities and milestones scheduling presented by Gantt, PERT, and CERT or other methods, according to progress reports and applied correction measures – for teams, development units, and so on.
- Updated schedules according to expected schedules in case change requests are approved.
- Classified lists of delayed activities.
- Classified lists of delays of critical activities that, if not corrected, can affect the project's completion date.
- Updated activity schedules generated according to progress reports and correction measures applied – for teams, development units, and so on.
- Classified lists of delayed milestones.

Project resource control

- Project human resources allocation plan according to activities schedule – for activities and software modules, teams, development units, designated time periods, and so on.
- Project resource utilization according to human skill – by period or accumulated – as specified above.
- Project resource utilization exceptions, compared to the original project plan – by period or accumulated – as specified above.
- Updated resource allocation plans generated according to progress reports and correction measures applied, as well as expected, in case change requests are approved.

Project budget control

- Project budget plans – by activity and software module – for teams, development units, designated time periods, and so on.
- Project budget utilization reports – by period or accumulated – as specified above.
- Project budget utilization deviations (as compared with the original project plan) – by period or accumulated – as specified above.

- Updated budget plans generated according to progress reports and correction measures applied and approved change requests.

Several commercial software project management software packages are offered to managers; probably the most popular is MS Project by Microsoft. Discussion of the capabilities of computerized software management tools and their comparison are presented by Cicibas et al. (2010), Alba and Chicano et al (2007), Gholami and Murugesan (2011), and others.

C.7.2 Project progress metrics and progress tracking charts

Project process metrics and progress tracking charts present numerically and graphically the actual project progress relative to the planned, with regard to schedule, resource and budget usage. This information serves managements in the control the progress of projects.

Project progress metrics provide momentary information about the status of the project with regard to schedule keeping, human resource usage, and budget spent up to the time of observation. This topic of "management process metrics" is discussed and illustrated by metrics in an example presented in Section 21.6.

The project process metrics, when plotted according to the project time, create a graph showing project performance deviations from the planned schedule over time. Two classic project progress tracking charts are the burn down chart and the earned value management (EVM) chart – both have been widely used for decades

The burn down chart presents the work left to be performed (backlog) compared to the planned work left, both are presented versus time.

An illustration of the burn down chart for a 10-week project is shown in Figure C.3.

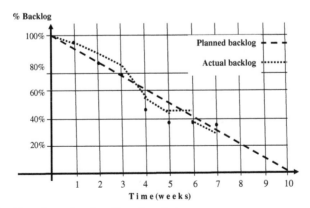

Figure C.3   A burn down chart for a 10-week project

As shown in Figure C.2, at the beginning of the first week the planned backlog is equal to the actual backlog, simply because the work has not yet started. The planned backlog by the end of the tenth week is 0%, while the actual backlog might deviate from the planned backlog. The chart presents the achievements of the project team for the first 7 weeks. At the end of the first week, the planned backlog is 90%, while the actual backlog is 94%. The chart presents the negative status of the project, which is behind planned performance, this lasts for the first 3 weeks of the project. However, the next 2 weeks, weeks 4 and 5, are very productive weeks for the project team and result in the project catching up to the planned backlog.

An earned value management chart presents project performance, in terms of schedule keeping and expenditures during the project schedule. Three attributes of project progress are tracked for any point of time in the project:

PV – The planned cumulative cost (budget) of the project activities planned to be completed up to the time of observation.

EV – The budgeted cost of the activities that were actually completed till the time of observation.

AC – The actual project costs spent till the time of observation.

An illustration of an earned value management chart for a $100,000 10-week project is shown in Figure C.4.

As shown in Figure C.3, at the beginning of the first week, the planned value (PV) is 0%, equal to the actual costs (AC) and the earned value (EV), simply because the work has not yet started. The PV by the end of the tenth week is $100,000, as the work is completed. EV reaches $100,000 at the end of the ninth week, showing early completion by one week, while AC are $90,000 at the end of the ninth week, which means savings of $10,000 by the diligent team. When checking the project status at the end of the third week, we find that the PV and

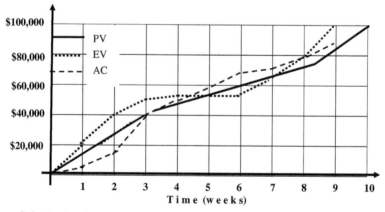

Figure C.4   An earned value management chart for a $100,000, 10 weeks project

CW are equal, $40,000; however, the EV reached $50,000 showing the team is highly skilled. Observing the status at the end of the eighth week, we find that EV is equal to AC, $80,000, much above the PV, which was only $70,000. Moreover, when observing the team's charted performance, we find that in the first 4 weeks, the EV is above the PV, in other words the performance of the team surpassed the project plans.

There is a variety of versions of the burn down and EVM charts, to enable their adaption to the charts, type of projects, and nature of the organization.

Summary

1. **The components of management's control of project progress**

    There are four main components of project progress control. Management is expected to intervene and contribute to arriving at solutions in extreme cases.

    a. **Control of risk management activities** refers to actions taken with respect to software risk items identified in the project plan, as well as to risk items identified later, during the project's progress. In practice, the software development team attempts to solve risk situations by applying systematic risk management activities. Management controls these efforts through review of periodic reports and evaluation of progress information.

    b. **Project schedule control** deals with compliance with the project's approved and contractual schedules. Follow-up is based on updated schedules for activities and milestones, which enable identification of delays in completion of planned activities. Special emphasis is given to customer-demanded milestones, as noted in the contract. Management tends to focus control on those critical delays that threaten to substantially delay project completion dates.

    c. **Project resource control** focuses on professional human resources, and also deals with software development and testing facilities, typically required by real-time software systems and firmware. Management exercises control on the basis of periodic reports of resources used.

    d. **Project budget control** is based on the comparison of actual to scheduled costs. The main budget items to be controlled are:

    * Human resources
    * Development and testing facilities
    * Purchase of COTS software
    * Purchase of hardware
    * Payments to subcontractors

    Budget control requires input transmitted by periodic reports related to activities and milestone. These reports enable early identification of budget overruns that affect project profitability. The other components of process control are expected to identify deviant situations earlier than budget control is capable of doing.

2. **The implementation issues associated with project progress control**
   - Initiation of project progress control requires the following to be defined for each project:
     - Person or management unit responsible for progress control.
     - Frequency of progress reports required from the various project management levels.
     - Situations where project leaders are required to report immediately to management.
     - Situations where lower level management is required to report immediately to upper level management.
   - Management audits of project progress deal with how well reporting by project leaders and other managers as well as management project control activities are functioning.

3. **Project progress metrics and progress tracking charts** Project process metrics and progress tracking charts, presented numerically and graphically, show the actual project progress relative to that planned, regarding schedule, resource and budget usage. This information serves management to control the progress of projects.

   Project progress metrics provide the momentary information about the status of the project up to the time of observation, with regards to schedule keeping, human resource usage, and budget spent.

   Two classic project progress tracking charts are the burn down chart and the EVM chart, which have been widely used for decades. The burn down chart presents graphically the work left to be performed (backlog) compared to the work planned to be left at this stage; both are presented versus time. The earned value management chart presents project performance, in terms of schedule keeping and resources spent.

Selected bibliography

Alba E. and Chicano J. F. (2007) *Software project management with GAs, Information Science*, Vol. **177**, No. 1, pp. 2380–2401.

Colomo-Palacios R., Casado-Lumbreras C., Soto-Acosta P., Garcia-Penalvo F. J., and Tovar E. (2014) *Project managers in global software development teams: a study of the effects on productivity and performance, Software Quality Journal*, Vol. **22**, No. 1, pp. 3–19.

Cicibas H., Unal O., and Demir K. A. (2010) A comparison of project management software tools (PMST), in *Proceedings of the 9th International Conference on Software Engineering Research and Practice*, Las Vegas, USA, pp. 1–6.

Cusumano M. A. (2008) *Managing software development in globally distributed teams, Communications of the ACM –Alternate Reality Gaming*, Vol. **51**, No. 2, pp. 15–17.

Gholami B. and Murugesan S. (2011) *Global IT project management using Web 2.0, International Journal of Information Technology Project Management*, Vol. **2**, No. 3, pp. 30–52.

ISO (2008) *ISO/IEC 12207:2008 Systems and Software Engineering – Software Life Cycle Processes*, International Organization for Standardization, Geneva.

Jimenez, M., Piattini M., and Vizcaino A. (2009) *Challenges and improvements in distributed software development: a systematic review, Advances in Software Engineering*, Vol. **20009**, No. 1, pp. 1–14.

Review questions

C.1 The introduction of the chapter presents three situations that can cause managerial failure in the control of a software development project.

    a. What measures could management have taken to prevent each of these adverse situations?

    b. Which of these adverse situations could have been detected by auditing adherence to the project progress control procedures?

C.2 In April, the project progress control system identified an *expected* delay of months to the project's delivery date (originally planned for October).

    a. List your proposed interventions in this situation, including the assumptions underlying each proposal.

    b. Would you alter your proposals if the project were an internal project for development of a computer game software package scheduled for the pre-Christmas market?

C.3 A project progress control process has been planned to involve two levels: (1) Management of the Development Department, which regularly operates six to eight software development teams and (2) Management of the Software Development Division, which covers three software development departments.

    Consider the case of a standard 1-year software development project.

    a. Inform the project leader of your suggestions for the proper progress reporting frequencies and conditions for immediate reporting to department management.

    b. Inform the Department Manager of your suggestions for the proper progress reporting frequencies and conditions for immediate reporting to division management.

    c. What type of progress-related information would you recommend be reported to division management?

C.4 A project plan includes 100 tasks; each budgeted for 4–6 designer or programmer days. The head of the SQA team claims that the burn in chart could be applied when the number of uncompleted tasks is used instead of the actual backlog, and the planned number of uncompleted tasks instead of the planned backlog.

    a. Do you agree with the head of the SQA team's claim? List your arguments.

    b. Is there expected to be a difference in the accuracy of the charted results when these are based on the backlog compared to the number of uncompleted tasks

Topics for discussion

C.1 The "Golden Bridge" software development project was scheduled to be completed in about 12 months. Two to six team members were planned to work on the project at the same time. Project progress control was based on a monthly report that would refer to each of the 32 activities to be performed and to the components (1) risk item management, (2) schedule, and (3) human resource utilization.

The first three monthly progress reports submitted to management did not indicate any deviation from the plan. The fourth progress report presented an unresolved risk item that was listed in the project plan, a substantial overrun in human resource utilization (overtime, etc.), as well as a month's delay in the expected completion dates for some of the activities.

a. Can you suggest possible reasons for the relatively late detection of the deviations from the project plan?

b. For each of the above three components, describe the measures that could have prevented the deviations and their adverse effects.

C.2 Consider the "Golden Bridge" software development project discussed in Topics for Discussion C.1.

- Suggest some interventions that management could have introduced to compensate for the project's failures, including the assumptions behind each intervention.

C.3 Some managers claim they must use both the burn down and the EVM charts as they are complementary to each other.

a. Do you agree with this claim? List your arguments.

b. If you agree, explain the importance of relying on both charts for project follow-up.

Appendix D

From SDLC to Agile – Processes and Quality Assurance Activities

This chapter is dedicated to the various software development models in current use. This chapter defines the models and the way that quality assurance activities are integrated into the development process. Furthermore, the way the customer's team is involved in the quality assurance process is also discussed. By deciding which models are to be applied, the project leader determines how the project will be carried out.

The SQA function professionals need to be familiar with the various software engineering models in order to be able to fulfill tasks such as preparing a quality plan that is properly integrated into the project plan, providing development teams with professional support to perform quality assurance activities, and following up on the performance of these activities.

Seven models of the software development process are discussed in this chapter:

- Classical software development models
  - The software development life cycle (SDLC) model
  - The prototyping model
  - The spiral model
- The object-oriented methodology
- The incremental delivery model
- The staged models
- The Agile methodology models

The models presented here are not merely alternatives, but could also represent a complementary ways of software development, or refer to different development contexts. Additional material on software development processes can be

Software Quality: Concepts and Practice, First Edition. Daniel Galin.
© 2018 the IEEE Computer Society, Inc. Published 2018 by John Wiley & Sons, Inc.

found in numerous papers and books dealing with software testing. A small sampling of book sources are the books by Pressman and Maxim (2015) and Sommerville (2015).

D.1 The classical software development models

The following three classical models are discussed:

- The SDLC model
- The prototyping model
- The spiral model

D.1.1 The software development life cycle model

The software development life cycle model is the classic model (still applicable today). The model displays the major building blocks of the entire development process, which is defined as a linear sequence. In the initial phases of the software development process, requirement, definition, analysis, and design documents are prepared, with the first version of the computer program presented for evaluation only at a relatively late stage of the process. The SDLC model may serve as a framework within which the other models may be presented.

The most common illustration of the SDLC model is the waterfall model, shown in Figure D.1.

The model shown in Figure D.1 presents a seven-phase process. At the end of each phase, the outputs are examined and evaluated through formal and informal quality assurance activities performed by the developer and, in many cases, by the customer as well. These quality assurance activities are aimed at detecting errors in the phase outcomes. Possible outcomes of the formal review include:

- Approval of the phase outputs, and progression to the next phase (indicated in the waterfall model by an arrow directed to the beginning of the next development phase).

- Demands to correct, redo, or change parts of the last phase; in these cases, earlier phases need to be repeated (indicated in the waterfall model by an arrow directing back to the beginning of the previous phase). In some cases, a correction related to earlier phases is required (as indicated by a thin arrow pointing upward).

A description of the software development phases and the related or associated SQA activities is as follows:

- **Requirements definition**. The customers must define requirements for the software system to be developed. In many cases, the software system is part of a larger system. Thus, some of the requirements are related to

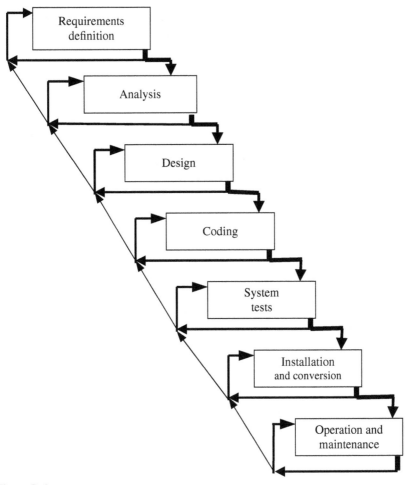

Figure D.1 The waterfall model

interfaces with other parts of the expanded system. These requirements are essential to ensure the interoperability of the developed software system.

Quality assurance activities that follow the requirement specifying phase: FDR of the requirement specification document.

- **Analysis**. The main effort in this phase is to analyze the requirements' implications in order to form the initial definition of the software system. SQA activities of peer reviews and expert opinions are applied throughout this phase.

Quality assurance activities that follow the analysis phase: FDR and informal review activities of the software analysis report. For more about reviews, see Chapter 13.

- **Design.** This phase involves a detailed definition of the outputs, inputs, and processing procedures, including data structures and databases, software structure, and so on.

  Quality assurance activities that follow the design phase: similar to those of the analysis phase.

- **Coding.** In this phase, the design is translated into code. The coding phase integrates SQA activities in the process.

  Quality assurance activities of the coding phase: The quality assurance activities include unit code inspection and unit tests related to units of the software product, and integration tests related to the integration of the software product units.

- **System tests.** This phase is dedicated entirely to quality assurance activities, namely, to those tests that assess the software system as a whole. These tests are performed once the coding phase is completed. The main goal of system testing is to uncover as many software errors as possible, so as to achieve an acceptable level of software quality once corrections have been completed. System tests are carried out by the software development team or by the developer's testing unit or by an external organization that specializes in software testing. Software testing is performed before the software is supplied to the customer. In many cases, the customer performs independent software system tests (acceptance tests) to ensure that the developer has fulfilled all commitments, and that no software failures are anticipated. It is quite common for a customer to ask the developer to perform joint system tests, a procedure that saves time and resources, otherwise required for separate system tests and acceptance tests.

- **Installation and conversion.** When the software system quality has been approved, the system is installed in the customer premises in order to start servicing. The first period of new installed software system serves as a run-in period, while special attention is paid to examine its performance and to verify that it is according to specifications. If the new software system is to replace an existing system, a software conversion process is combined within the running-in process.

  Quality assurance activities that follow the installation and conversion phase: FDR and informal reviews of installation and conversion plans.

- **Regular operation and maintenance.** Regular software operation commences once installation, running-in, and conversion have been successfully completed. Maintenance of the software system is needed throughout the operation period, which usually lasts for several years, until it is replaced by new software of a new generation. Maintenance incorporates three types of services: (1) corrective – repairing software faults identified by the user and the developer during operation; (2) adaptive – using the existing software features to fulfill new requirements; and (3) functionality improving (perfective) – adding new minor features to improve software performance.

Quality assurance activities that follow the operation and maintenance phase: Follow-up of the user support centers (USCs) and maintenance services.

Table D.1 summarizes the SDLC quality assurance activities.

The number of phases tends to vary according to the characteristics of the project. In complex, large-scale models, some phases are split, causing the number of phases to grow to eight, nine, or more. In smaller projects, some phases may be merged, reducing the number of phases to five, six, and even four.

The main deficiency of the SDLC model, in relation to software quality, is the lateness of the phase (coding phase), in which the developer may obtain valuable

Table D.1 The SDLC quality assurance activities

Development phase	Quality assurance activity	The performers	SQA function activities
1. Requirement definition	FDR	The development team	Provision of professional support for the development team and follow-up of activity performance
2. Analysis	FDR	The developer[a], and in many cases, the customer participates	
3. Design	Informal reviews	Colleagues of the development team	
	FDR	The developer[a], and in many cases, the customer participates	
4. Coding	Code inspection	Development team colleagues	
	Unit tests	The development team	
	Integration tests	The development team	
5. System tests	Final software tests	The development team, and the developer's[a] testing unit or an external testing organization. In many cases, the customer representatives participate.	
6. Installation and conversion	FDR	The developer[a], and in many cases, the customer participates	
7. Regular operation and maintenance	Follow-up of USC and maintenance services	The software operation team and the developer's[a] managers	

[a]The developer = the software development organization.

user feedback regarding the adequacy of the developed software product. The products of the first three phases are written reports only made available to software developers. Thus, as mentioned above, it is only the coding phase products, namely, working programs, that are suitable for user examination and review.

The classic waterfall model was suggested by Royce (1970), and later presented in its commonly known form by Boehm (1981). The processes and activities of the life cycle of software development and maintenance are defined in the IEEE/12207 (IEEE, 2008) and other international standards.

D.1.2   The prototyping model

The prototyping methodology is an iterative one, where in each iteration a prototype software is developed. In the first iteration, only part of the specified requirements is implemented, and in each of the next iterations the new prototype implements an additional part of the requirements. Each prototype is examined and evaluated by the customer and the user's team. Their demands for corrections, changes, and additions related to the current prototype are to be considered by the developer in the next integration prototype. These iterations will continue till all the requirements are fulfilled.

A typical application of the prototyping methodology is shown in Figure D.2.

The process of prototyping could be best illustrated with an example.

The store management example

A store is interested in a store management information system to process sales, inventory, suppliers, and customer data. The information system developer has suggested to employ the prototyping methodology, in which the store manager and two of the senior staff participate in the evaluation and examination of the prototypes (the products of each software development iteration). The contents of each development cycle (iteration) are shown in Table D.2.

The prototyping methodology excels in enabling customer and user participation in the examination and evaluation of the evolving software product in its early stage of development. This is in contrast to the SDLC methodology that allows receiving user and customer feedback only at a very late phase of the software development stage.

Practitioners and software researchers realized the great efficiency of prototyping, and estimated a 50% savings in development resources, as well as substantial improvements to the project schedule. While these savings were widely accepted professionally, no actual evidence has ever been produced. This is due to the fact that no customer would be willing to order a project to be developed twice; once by prototyping and then by SDLC methodology, in order to compare the methodologies. Such wishful evidence came from the academy, when a comparative research enabled the same project to be developed by four student teams

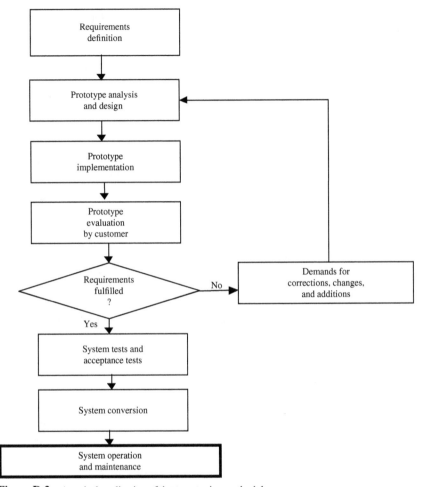

Figure D.2 A typical application of the prototyping methodology

using SDLC and three student teams using prototyping (Boehm et al., 1984). The statistically significant results derived from the research were as follows:

- The prototyping projects consumed 45% less resources than the SDLC project.
- The prototyping projects produced 40% less code.
- The prototyping projects produced 63% less documentation.
- The prototyping projects were rated somewhat lower on functionality and robustness.
- The prototyping projects were rated higher on ease of use and ease of learning.

Table D.2   Developer and user evaluation collaboration in a prototyping development process

Iteration no.	New contents of prototype prepared by developer for current iteration	Contents corrected and changed by developer per iteration	Corrections and changes requested by the user evaluation team per iteration
1	Sales invoice, item price database, and daily sales report	No corrected contents available	Corrections and changes of iteration 1 requested by the evaluation team
2	Discount options, sales promotion options	Corrections related to iteration 1	Corrections and changes of iteration 2 requested by the evaluation team
3	Inventory management (sales and supply recorded), daily order list according to inventory level	Corrections related to iteration 2	Corrections and changes of iteration 3 requested by the evaluation team
4	Customer sales and suppliers reports and monthly store reports	Corrections related to iteration 3	Corrections and changes of iteration 4 requested by the evaluation team
5	Customer club options	Corrections related to iteration 4	Corrections and changes of iteration 1 requested by the evaluation team
6	All specified requirements have been fulfilled. No new contents	Corrections related to iteration 5	No requests for corrections exist. The completed information system will progress to system tests

The prototyping methodology has been found to be especially successful for small and medium projects. It is also applicable for developing parts of large-scale projects. Prototyping may be applied in combination with other methodologies or as a "stand-alone" methodology. In other words, the extent of prototyping can vary from replacing one SDLC (or other methodology) in part of a project to the complete prototyping of an entire software system.

There are a variety of typical situations when prototyping is used:

- Projects with vaguely defined specifications, where feedback from users on prototypes serves to explore the requirements. In many of these cases, the sole interest in the prototyping process is to accurately define the system requirements produced throughout the process. Thus, the produced prototyping software is a "throwaway" software and not put to service.

- Software systems planned for short service and for a limited population of users, that is, research management, temporary usage as a pilot software system.

- Projects for regular use, characterized by low complexity and a limited population of users.

The main advantages and deficiencies of prototyping over the complete SDLC benefit from the intense involvement of users and customers in the software development process. Such involvement facilitates a better understanding of the system and a lower probability of the system failing. However, the intensive participation of customers and users in the development process limits the developer's freedom to introduce innovative changes into the system.

The main advantages and deficiencies of prototyping over the SDLC methodology are summarized in Frame D.1.

Frame D.1: Prototyping versus SDLC methodology – advantages and disadvantages

Prototyping versus SDLC methodology — advantages and disadvantages

Advantages of prototyping:

* Shorter development process
* Substantial savings of development resources (man-days)
* Better fit to customer requirements and reduced risk of project failure
* Better system usability

Disadvantages of prototyping:

* Diminished flexibility and adaptability to changes and modifications
* Reduced preparation for unexpected instances of failure
* Implementation depends on availability of adequate customer representatives to participate in prototyping process

The quality assurance activities for prototyping are summarized in Table D.3.

D.1.3 The spiral model

The spiral model provides an iterative methodology for ensuring performance is effective at each of the SDLC model phases. It involves integrating customer comments and change requirements, risk analysis and resolution, and software system planning and engineering activities at each of the SDLC model phases. One or more iterations of the spiral model may be required to complete each of the project's SDLC phases. Thus, the spiral model offers an improved methodology for overseeing large and more complex development projects displaying higher prospects of failure. The associated engineering phases may be performed according to the SDLC, prototyping, or additional software development models.

The advanced spiral model, the Win-Win Spiral model (Boehm, 1998), enhances an earlier version of the Spiral model (Boehm, 1988). The advanced

Table D.3 The prototyping quality assurance activities

Development phase	Quality assurance activity	The performers	SQA function activities
1. Requirement definition	Self-review	Development team	Provision of professional support for the development team and follow-up of activity performance
2. [a] Analysis and design iteration	Self-review	Development team	
3. [a] Prototype implementation (coding) iteration	Self-testing	Development team	
4. [a] Prototype evaluation iteration	Prototype testing	Customer representatives team	
5. System tests	Final software tests	The development team, and in many cases, the customer representatives participate	
6. Installation and conversion	FDR	The developer[b], and in many cases, the customer representatives participate	
7. Regular operation and maintenance	Follow-up of USC and maintenance services	The software operation team and the developer's[b] managers	

[a]Phases 2–4 are repeated for each iteration.
[b]The developer = the software development department.

model places extra emphasis on communication and feedback between the customer and the developer. The model earned its name as by using this process, the customer "wins" in the form of improved chances to receive the system that most satisfies his needs, and the developer "wins" in the form of improved chances to stay within the budget and complete the project by the agreed-upon date. This is achieved by increasing the emphasis on customer participation in iterative engineering activities and by periodical risk analysis and resolution activity.

Accordingly, in the advanced spiral model shown in Figure D.3, the following six activities are carried out in each iteration:

- Customer's specification of requirements, comments, and change demands
- Developer's planning activities
- Developer's risk analysis and resolutions
- Developer's design activities
- Developer's construction activities pertaining to, that is, coding, testing, installation, and release
- Customer's evaluation

Table D.4 presents the advanced spiral model quality assurance activities.

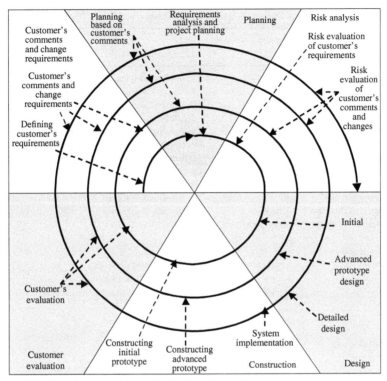

Figure D.3   The advanced spiral model – the Win-Win model

D.2   The object-oriented model

D.2.1   The object-oriented method

The object-oriented model differs from the former models as it is based on a collection of independent units (termed "classes"), each dedicated to a physical or other entity saving its related data and software functions (termed "methods"). A class contains all the items of the type (termed "objects"). For instance, class "client address" will include the addresses of each of the clients. Methods related to "client address" may include adding an object for a new client, updating client's address, answering a query "what is the address of a client whose ID is X," and so on. These independent classes are "self-sufficient" classes and are said to be "encapsulated." Boundary classes are dedicated to interfaces with other software systems, to production of outputs (printouts, computer displays, etc.), and input tools. It is the collaboration among these entities that enables achieving all the system's specified requirements. The performance of a certain goal, that is,

Table D.4   The advanced spiral model quality assurance activities

Development phase	Quality assurance activity	The performers	SQA function activities
1. [a] Requirement analysis and project planning	Self-review	The development team	Provision of professional support for the development team and follow-up of activity performance
2. [a] Risk analysis	FDR	The software development department	
3. [a] Prototype design iteration	Self-review	The development team	
	Informal reviews	Development team colleagues	
4. [a] Prototype implementation (coding) iteration	Code inspection	Development team colleagues	
	Prototype testing	The development team	
5. [a] Project evaluation	Unit tests	The development team	
6. [a] Customer comments and change requirements	Integration tests	The development team	
7. System tests	Final software tests	The development team, and the developer's testing unit or an external testing organization. In many cases, the customer representatives participates	
8. Installation and conversion	FDR	The developer[b], and in many cases, the customer representatives participate	
9. Regular operation and maintenance	Follow-up of USC and maintenance services	The operation team and the developer's managers	

[a]Phases 1–6 are repeated for each iteration.

[b]The developer = the software development department.

creating a report, requires the collaboration of the relevant classes. In order to perform a goal by a group of classes, each of the group classes performs part of the processing tasks required, and transmits data (via "messages") to other member classes till the goal is achieved.

The use of classes, each dedicated to an entity, such as "client's address," "client's payments," "inventory item," and so on, creates possibilities for reuse of classes in additional software systems developed by object-oriented methodology. Thus, object-oriented methodology excels through its intensive reuse of software components compared with other methodologies. In other words, it is characterized by its easy integration of existing library items of software classes (called also components) into newly developed software systems. A software component library serves this purpose by supplying software components for reuse.

D.2.2 The object-oriented software development process

The development process and its quality assurance activities are adapted to the class structure, which differs substantially from forms of software.

Analysis. In the analysis phase of the object-oriented development process, the definition of classes needed to perform the specified requirements and the goals required for implementations of the requirements are performed.

The software quality assurance activities of object-oriented projects are quite unique. The design reviews (DRs) of the analysis phase examine the object-oriented analysis (OOA) model, the class model planned to achieve all the software development goals (stemming from the specified requirements).

Design. In the design phase that follows, the design of the classes is refined, and the details processed for achieving each of the software system goals are defined. The design phase is followed by acquisition of suitable components from the reusable software library, when available. "Regular" development is otherwise carried out. Copies of newly developed software components are then "stocked" in the software library for future reuse. It is expected that the growing software component stocks in the reusable software library will enable the substantial and increasing reuse of software.

The DRs of the design phase examine the refined object-oriented design (OOD) model that includes the connectivity planning and detailed class structure design, related to the classes' data and methods.

Coding. The coding phase follows the class structure design, where coding tasks include programming the class methods and the required communication messages network.

Testing. The testing phase includes class testing, integration testing, and system tests, all adapted to the class structure of the software system. Class testing is equivalent to unit testing, where the data and methods of the encapsulated class are tested. Integration testing is performed to clusters of classes, where in the next step additional classes are integrated and tested – this continues till all classes have been included in the integration tests. System tests encompass the entire software system, with the task of screening out the remaining errors. Black box testing may be employed throughout the various levels of object-oriented testing.

The remaining life cycle phases are similar to those of the SDLC model.

The object-oriented model is shown in Figure D.4.

D.2.3 Advantages of the object-oriented methodology

The advantages of the object-oriented methodology over other methodologies stem from its class structure.

a. There are greater possibilities for software reuse, which leads to the following advantages in the following areas:

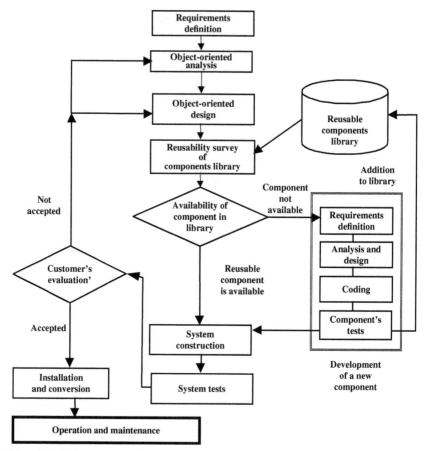

Figure D.4   The object-oriented model

- Cost-efficiency – The cost of integrating a reusable software component is much lower than developing a new component.
- Improved quality – Used software components are expected to contain considerably fewer defects than newly developed software components due to the detection of faults by former users.
- Shorter development time – The integration of reusable software components reduces pressures pertaining to project schedule.

b. It is possible to assign relatively small tasks to be developed by a team member.

c. It is easier to carry out large-scale projects, due to the division into classes.

d. The design and analysis, as well as programming of software systems, are easier and reach higher quality levels.

   e. Easier maintenance, easier to locate faulty software, and easier to intro-
      duce software changes.

   f. The minor defined tasks result in easier cooperation and coordination with
      team members, and thus easier project management.

The advantages of the object-oriented methodology compared with other methodologies are summarized in Frame D.2.

Frame D.2: **The advantages of object-oriented methodology**

The advantages of object-oriented methodology:

(Compared to other technologies)

1. Easier software reuse, based on local or commercial class libraries. Software reuse
    contributes to lower project costs

2. Easier distribution of development tasks among team numbers

3. Easier to cope with software development of large-scale projects with high
    complexity

4. Easier to perform and easier to achieve high quality of analysis design and pro-
    gramming (for the non-reused parts of the software product)

5. Easier maintenance

6. Easier to manage software projects

The quality assurance activities of the object-oriented development process are presented in Table D.5.

D.3 The incremental delivery model

The incremental software development models share the concept of delivery of software projects in parts (increments) with the Agile models. According to this concept, each increment implements only part of the specified require-ments of the software system. The "size" of the increment varies according to the group of goals selected to be implemented in the increment. Imple-mentation of each increment will include the following phases: analysis, design, coding, system testing, installment, conversion, and run-in and main-tenance. Each increment is integrated with the accumulation of earlier incre-ments (creating a new version of the developing software product). A schematic description of the staged incremental delivery model is presented in Figure D.5.

    The reasons for clients and developers to prefer incremental delivery rather than to wait for the complete software product vary:

Table D.5   The quality assurance activities of the object-oriented development process

Development phase	Quality assurance activity	The performers	SQA function activities
1. Requirement definition	FDR	Development team	Provision of professional support for the development team and follow-up of activity performance
2. Object-oriented analysis	FDR	The developer[a], and in many cases, the customer participates	
3. Object-oriented design	Informal reviews	Colleagues of the development team	
	FDR	The developer[a], and in many cases, the customer representatives participate	
4. Reusability survey of component library	Self-review	The development team	
5. System construction (coding)	Code inspection	Development team colleagues	
	Unit tests	The development team	
	Integration tests	The development team	
6. System tests	Final software tests	The development team, and the developer's[a] testing unit or an external testing organization. Frequently, the customer representatives participate	
7. Installation and conversion	FDR	The developer[a], and in many cases, the customer participates	
8. Regular operation and maintenance	Follow-up of USC and maintenance services	The software operation team and the developer's[a] managers	

[a]The developer = the software development department

- The customer wishes to satisfy the urgent and highest priority goals of the project at the earliest possible schedule, and to gain substantial value from the project at the earliest possible time. The second increment will include goals of the second priority, and so on.
- The developer implements the goals that are defined more clearly in the first increment. The developer will use the first increment to explore the requirements of the next increment, and so on.
- The incremental delivery is based on limited goals implemented in each increment and reduces the risk of project failure, as each increment is required to handle a much lower number of less risks.

The incremental delivery concept is one of the main concepts of the Agile methodologies.

The quality assurance activities of the incremental development process are presented in Table D.6.

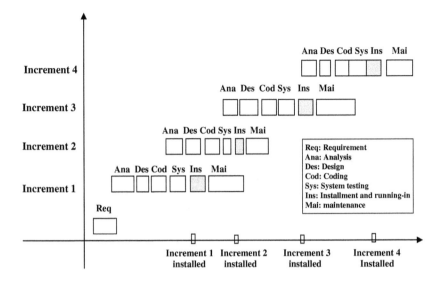

Project schedule

Figure D.5 The staged-incremental delivery software development model

Table D.6 The quality assurance activities of the incremental development process

Development phase	Quality assurance activity	The performers	SQA function activities
1. Requirement analysis	Team's self-review	The development team	Professional support to the development team and follow-up of performance
2. [a] Design iteration	Team's self-review	The development team	
3. [a] Analysis iteration	Team's self-review	The development team	
4. [a] Coding iteration	Code inspection	Development team colleagues	
	Unit test	The development team	
	Iteration integration tests	The development team	
5. [a] Iteration system tests	Iteration software tests	The development team. In some cases, the customer representatives participate	
6. [a] Installation and conversion	Self-review	The developer, and in many cases, the customer representatives participate	
7. [a] Regular operation and maintenance	Follow-up of USC and maintenance services	The software operation team and the developer's[b] managers	

[a]Phases 2–7 are repeated for each iteration.

[b]The developer = the software development department.

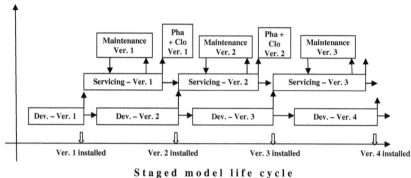

Figure D.6   The staged model life cycle

D.4   The staged model

The staged model is an evolutionary model. It is applied to the development process of software products for both commercial and company usage. The software starts off as basic software and gradually becomes more sophisticated and comprehensive through a series of software versions.

The model describes the process where a software version is in use and maintained for a period of time. During this period, the maintenance team performs corrections of errors identified by users and carries out adaptations and minor changes and additions to perfect the software according to user requests, and the development team completes the next, more advanced software version. In time, after a successful period of servicing, the software version phases out, and finally closes down. The current software version should be replaced by the next more advanced version. The new version usually includes new functionalities, changes according to environmental developments, and current user requirements. Figure D.6 presents the staged model life cycle.

The quality assurance activities in staged model life cycle are presented in Table D.7.

D.5   The Agile methodology models

The growing cost of software development, long supply schedules, and difficulty to introduce requested changes during the development process all lead to lower customer satisfaction. Several software development methodologies offered radical changes to traditional software development processes in order to create new effective and efficient ways for software development to cope with the above deficiencies of traditional methodologies. All these new methodologies have much in common, which was what led, on February 2001, to the forming of an alliance of

Table D.7 The quality assurance activities in a staged model life cycle

Development phase	Quality assurance activity	The performers	SQA function activities
1. Requirement analysis	Team's self-review	The development team	Professional support to the development team and follow-up of performance
2. [a] Design version	Team's self-review	The development team	
3. [a] Analysis version	Team's self-review	The development team	
4. [a] Coding version	Code inspection	Development team colleagues	
	Unit test	The development team	
	Iteration integration tests	The development team	
5. [a] Version system tests	Iteration software tests	The development team. In some cases, the customer representatives participate	
6. [a] Version installation and conversion	Self-review	The development team	
7. [a] Regular version service	Follow-up of USC services	The software operation team and the developer's[b] management	
8. [a] Version maintenance	Follow-up of maintenance services	The software operation team and the developer's[b] managers	
9. [a] Version phases out and closes down	Follow-up of phase out process	The software operation team and the developer's[b] managers	

[a]Phases 2–9 are repeated for each version.
[b]The developer = the software development department.

the developers of these methodologies – "the Agile Alliance." The purpose of the alliance was to promote these methodologies.

D.5.1 The Agility principles

The radicalism of the new methodologies is well expressed by the Agile Alliance members in their values:

- Individuals and interactions over processes and tools
- Working software over comprehensive documentation
- Customer collaboration over contract negotiation
- Responding to change over following a plan

The Agile Alliance published the Agile Manifesto that presented the 12 Agile principles.

The Agility principles (Agile, 2003) are shown in Frame D.3.

Frame D.3: The Agility principles

The Agility principles

1. Our highest priority is to satisfy the customer through early and continuous delivery of valuable software.

2. Welcome changing requirements, even late in development. Agile processes harness change for the customer's competitive advantage.

3. Deliver working software frequently, from a couple of weeks to a couple of months, with a preference to the shorter timescale.

4. Business people and developers must work together daily throughout the project.

5. Build projects around motivated individuals. Give them the environment and support they need, and trust them to get the job done.

6. The most efficient and effective method of conveying information to and within a development team is face-to-face conversation.

7. Working software is the primary measure of progress.

8. Agile processes promote sustainable development. The sponsors, developers, and users should be able to maintain a constant pace indefinitely.

9. Continuous attention to technical excellence and good design enhances agility.

10. Simplicity – the art of maximizing the amount of work not done – is essential.

11. The best architectures, requirements, and designs emerge from self-organizing teams.

12. At regular intervals, the team reflects on how to become more effective, then tunes and adjusts its behavior accordingly.

The software development methodologies that share the Agility principles include the following:

- Agile modeling
- SCRUM
- Extreme programming (XP)
- Crystal
- Feature-driven development (FDD)
- Dynamic system development method (DSDM)
- Kanban
- Lean software development
- Rapid application development (RAD)

Besides sharing the Agile principles (see Frame D.3), each of these Agile methodologies has specific distinguishing features related to the rules of behavior regarding commitment to schedule, acceptance, handling of change requests, and so on.

D.5.2 Typical Agile software development process

The typical software development process, as realized according to Agile methodologies, includes the following activities:

- Project requirements are only vaguely defined, in most cases in the form of "user stories."
- Estimates of budget and schedule are prepared by the developer based on the list of "user stories." Naturally, these estimates are very general.
- The customer arranges the "user stories" into increment groups according to customer priority, where the first increment group is of the highest priority. In other words, the early increments create higher values for the customer or include urgent functionality. Each increment will be designed within a short schedule with a duration of no longer than several weeks.
- The development process is performed by small teams, usually made up of pairs of development professionals.
- The development process includes analysis and design phases with limited documentation.
- The developers are not bound to software development standards or work instructions.
- The quality assurance task is performed by mutual examination of development products by the development team. In other words, design, analysis, or coding performed by a team member is reviewed or tested by his partner in the development team. The practice of development and quality assurance tasks being performed within the team makes them "self-sufficient," and places the heavy burden of software quality almost entirely upon them.
- Customers will actively participate throughout the development process by responding to developer queries, examining development issues raised by the developers, and so on on a daily basis.
- The released software increment is gradually added to the required software product. However, throughout the development process additional "user stories" initiated by the customer are included. This causes the final software product to grow by an each additional requirement or "user story."
- The teams keep daily stand-up meetings to update and synchronize the development efforts.

- Periodical team meetings are dedicated to the retrospect examination of the team methods for ongoing improvements to the team's development work.

Team members participating in Agile projects are expected to own key traits, as shown in Frame D.4.

Frame D.4: Expected key traits of Agile project team members

Expected key traits of Agile project team member
- Competent
- Highly motivated
- Collaborative within the team (pair) and the project team
- Able to make professional decisions
- Able to handle fuzzy requirements
- Able to cope with frequent requirement changes
- Able to share trust and respect with the team partner

D.5.3   Quality assurance in Agile software development projects

Quality assurance activities are incorporated in each iteration. There may be 10 iterations or more, with each iteration delivering a relatively small software increment – a product of a few weeks of development effort. The following quality assurance activities are included in each iteration:

- Review of analysis results, together performed by team members and customer representatives throughout the analysis.
- Review of design results, together performed by team members and customer representatives throughout the design.
- Most Agile methodologies adopt the test-driven development, where unit tests are planned before programming. This method supports the quality of testing. Code reviews and unit testing are together performed by team members and customer representatives.
- Testing the integration of the current delivered code increment with former software increments is performed by the development team.

Quality assurance of Agile projects has major advantages and disadvantages over that of SDLC projects:

- SQA activities are performed on software increments, where each increment relates only to a small number of requirements and to just a few weeks of development efforts. Thus, the increment to be delivered creates much less of a quality challenge than the SDLC SQA activities examining entire projects.

- The customer's close collaboration (daily) and involvement with the development team provides continuous follow-up and valuable input throughout the entire project life cycle. Participation of the customer in the SDLC development process is limited to joint follow-up committees and examining and commenting on the finished products of the software development process (various analysis and design documents, etc.).
- These two advantages counter-affect the deficiency of only the development team performing quality assurance activities – with no support from independent reviewers or testers.

The quality assurance activities of an Agile project are presented in Table D.8.

A comparative analysis of quality assurance practices in Agile projects versus SDLC projects is presented by Huo et al. (2004). Empirical studies of Agile software development processes are presented by Dyba and Dingsoyr (2013).

Table D.8 Quality assurance activities of an Agile project

Development phase	Quality assurance activity	The performers	SQA function activities
1. Requirement analysis	Self-review	The development pair	Provision of professional support for the development team and follow-up of activity performance
2. [a] Design increment	Review	The developing pair and customer representatives	
3. [a] Analysis increment	Team's self-review	The developing pair and customer representatives	
4. [a] Coding increment	Code review and unit test	The developing pair and customer representatives	
5. [a] Integration of increment with former software increments	Software tests	The development pair	
6. [a] Increment installation and conversion	Team's self-review	The development pair	
7. [a] Regular service and maintenance	Follow-up of USC services	The software operation team and the developer's[b] managers	

[a]Phases 2–6 are repeated for each increment.

[b]The developer = the software development department.

D.5.4 The Agile experience

Efforts needed to introduce Agile methodologies into an organization employing conventional methodology vary. Some organizations reported the change to be easy and required just 1 week of instruction, while others report that a long process of training and follow-up support was required. It was reported that more qualified and experienced teams experienced an easier adoption of Agile methodologies (mainly regarding the XP method). The last decade's experience has shown difficulties in employing Agile methodologies in large-scale projects, and in large and complex organizations. Despite difficulties moving over to Agile methodologies, there is a constantly growing number of organizations that adopt these methodologies.

Obstacles to introducing Agile methodologies in organizations employing traditional development methods are discussed by Gandomani et al. (2013). Implementing Agile methods challenges the team members themselves; it changes their personal relations and status by the need to work in small teams – usually in pairs, and to collaborate with, and trust their new teams. A major challenge for managers is the new organizational structure that reduces their ability to control and manage, and introduces the need to manage through collaboration. Another managerial difficulty arises from the very limited documentation, typical to Agile projects, where a great part of the project's know-how is left in the developer's mind. This creates severe difficulties when replacing team members. Another personal difficulty results from the participation of customers in the development team, and sharing with them the decision-making processes of the project. Difficulties were reported when attempting to employ Agile methodologies in large-scale projects and in large and complex organizations. The change in process from traditional SDLC methods to the Agile incremental delivery method is a major challenge that involves changes in strategies, tools, and techniques.

The Agile literature, as well as Agile promoters, claims that there exist substantial gains to Agile projects when compared with "conventional" software development projects. These claims are supported by empirical comparative research, though still scarce. These findings could be considered as indications rather than "solid" evidence, due to their limitability. These benefits refer mainly to the following areas of interest: project management, productivity, software quality, and job satisfaction (of development teams).

The main management issues considered in the comparative studies were the project progress control and communication with the customers. Managers of Agile projects had better control of the development process, fulfillment of requirements, and an easier introduction of changes. These studies found Agile projects to have better, more effective communication with the customers, which led to the management's higher satisfaction of its customer relationships. In relation to human resource management, greater difficulties were found in Agile projects regarding team member replacement.

Productivity comparative studies were few, all of them showed a substantial increase of productivity (40% and more), where productivity was measured by lines of code per hour. In most of the studies, the quality of the Agile software products was found to be higher regarding internal quality as well as external quality measured by errors identified by the customer. In other comparative studies, no quality differences were found. A comparative study of defects in Scrum and "conventional" projects show similar defect density and similar defect profiles in both projects. However, the Agile project achieved more efficient defect removal processes and provided a higher quality of delivered software. The results for job satisfaction were not conclusive, and only in part of the studies the Agile teams were found to enjoy higher job satisfaction.

It should be noted that in most of the comparative studies, the most important requirement to enable comparing between Agile and "conventional" teams, namely, the controlling of a team's level of expertise, was not exercised. In other words, in most of the studies, team members were not assigned randomly, and as a result Agile teams were of higher expertise and higher abilities. This situation leads us to attach a lower value to the findings.

D.5.5. Agile methodologies' limitations

The limitations of the Agile methodologies stem from their very basic principles:

  a. The high qualifications (see Frame D.3) required from Agile team members limit the number of participants in Agile teams.
  b. The practice of performing all software quality assurance activities within the team encourages the team to try to do the best to produce a high-quality product. However, the practice of mutual development and then relying on mutual reviews and testing within the team might lead to the misidentification of errors and lack the external reviewer's and tester's independent ability to identify errors. Thus, despite the team's efforts, a high-quality product is not always ensured.
  c. It is expected that the very limited documentation, where a substantial part of the project's know-how is not documented, will cause substantial difficulties in cases when team members leave the team.
  d. The very limited documentation is expected to cause difficulties performing maintenance tasks.
  e. Another difficulty in maintaining the products results from the permitted free use of tools and procedures by Agile team members, rather than keeping to standards and instructions for documentation of analysis, design, and programming (typical to some of the Agile methods).

Summary

1. The classic software development models

Three classic models of software development processes are discussed in this chapter:

- The SDLC model
- The prototyping model
- The spiral model

The classic SDLC model is a linear sequential model composed of several phases, beginning with requirements definition and concluding with regular system operation and maintenance.

At the end of each phase, outputs are reviewed and evaluated by the developer, as well as the customer in many cases. The outcomes range from approval of the phase results and continuation to the next phase, to demands to correct, redo, or alter parts of the respective phase.

The waterfall model can be viewed as the basic framework for the other models, which may be considered complementary, which represents different perspectives of the process, or as diverse development process.

According to the prototyping methodology, users of the developed system are required to comment on versions of the software prototypes prepared by the developers. The developers thereafter correct the prototype and incorporate additional parts into the system. This process is repeated till the software system is completed or till the prototyping goal is achieved.

The main advantages of the prototyping over the SDLC model for small-to-medium projects are the shorter development processes, substantial savings in development resources, better fit to customer requirements, reduced risk of project failure, and facilitated usability of the new system.

The advanced spiral model provides an improved methodology for larger and more complex projects. This improvement is achieved by introducing and emphasizing elements of risk analysis and customer participation in the development process. Each of the model's iterations includes planning, risk analysis and resolution, engineering, and customer evaluation and comments.

The advantages of the object-oriented process stem from its class structure: intensive software reuse possibilities (cost savings, shorter development schedule, and lower error rates), easier software development and maintenance, easier quality assurance, and easier development of large-scale projects.

2. The object-oriented methodology

The object-oriented methodology is based on a collection of independent units (termed "classes"), each dedicated to a physical or other entity and saving its related data and software functions (termed "methods").

These independent classes are "self-sufficient" and are said to be "encapsulated." The collaboration among these entities, by applying a message network, enables achieving all system's specified requirements. The object-oriented model encourages intensive reuse of software components. According to this model, the development process begins with a sequence of object-oriented analysis and design activities. The design phase is followed by acquisition of reusable software components together with "regular" development of the unavailable software components. The SQA activities are adapted to the class structure of object-oriented software development.

3. **The incremental delivery model**

According to the incremental delivery model, software products are delivered to the customer in increments, rather than as an entire software product. Each increment implements only part of the specified requirements of the software system. The advantages of incremental delivery relate to clients and developers. Customers are able to satisfy urgent and highest priority project goals at the earliest possible schedule, and to gain substantial value of the project at an earlier stage. For the developer, the development in increments makes development easier and reduces the risk of project failure. The common approach of these methodologies was more individual interactions throughout the process.

4. **The staged model**

The staged model is an evolutionary model dedicated to the development process of a software product that begins as basic software and gradually becomes more sophisticated and comprehensive through a series of software versions.

5. **The Agile methodology models**

The growing cost of software development, long supply schedules, and the difficulty of introducing requirement changes all lead to lower customer satisfaction. Several software development methodologies offered radical changes to the traditional software development process in order to confront these challenges. The common approach of these methodologies is the Agility concept: more individual interactions throughout the project over processes, priority to working software over documentation, customer collaboration over contract negotiations, and responding to change requests over following a plan. The main Agility principles are as follows: incremental delivery to satisfy customers, allowing requirement changes throughout the project, customer joins the development team on a daily basis, the importance of motivated team members, the importance of face-to-face conversation, the importance of achieving working software, and the continuous attention to development excellence and improvement of methods and behavior.

Quality assurance activities incorporated in each iteration. Agile quality assurance activities are performed together by team members and customer representatives throughout the development process. SQA activities are conducted on software increments. Each increment relates to a small number of requirements, and together with the customer's contribution, these activities are easier to perform and ensure a higher quality of products.

The move from the "traditional" development method to Agile development methodologies is a radical change for team members and managers. Despite difficulties, many organizations already implement Agile methodologies in their organizations and more organizations are moving to Agility each year.

6. **The participants in quality assurance activities**

A great variety of participants perform quality assurance activities in the software life cycle of the various development models and methodologies:

- The developing team
- The developer (footnote a in tables), and in many cases, the customer representatives also participate.
- Development team colleagues
- The software development department
- The developer's testing unit
- The developer's (footnote a in tables) managers
- Customer representative teams
- An external testing organization
- The software operation team

Selected bibliography

Agile Alliance (2003) The Agility Principles, The Agile Alliance homepage, agilealliance.org/home.

Boehm B. W. (1981) *Software Engineering Economics*, Prentice Hall, Upper Saddle River, NJ, Ch. 4.

Boehm B. W. (1988) *A spiral model of software development and enhancement, Computer*, Vol. **21**, No. 5, pp. 61–72.

Boehm B. W. (1998) *Using the win-win spiral model: a case study, Computer*, Vol. **31**, No. 7, pp. 33–44.

Boehm, B. W., Gray T. E., and Seewaldt T. (1984) *Prototyping versus specifying: a multiproject experiment, IEEE Transactions on Software Engineering*, Vol. **SE-10**, No. 3, pp. 290–303.

Dyba T. and Dingsoyr T. (2013) *Empirical studies of Agile software development: a systematic review, Information and Software Technology*, Vol. **50**, No. 9–10, pp. 839–859.

Gandomani T. J., Zulzalil H. A., Ghani A. A. A., Sulan A. B., and Nafchi M. Z. (2013) *Obstacles in moving to agile software development methods: at a glance, Journal of Computer Science*, Vol. **9**, No. 5, pp. 620–625.

Huo M., Verner J., Zhu L., and Babar M. A. (2004) *Software quality and agile methods, in* The Annual International Computer Software and Applications Conference (COMPSAc4), pp. 520–525.

IEEE (2008) *IEEE/ISO/IEC Std. 12207:2008 – Systems and Software Engineering – Software Life Cycle Processes*, The Institute of Electrical and Electronics Engineers, New York, NY.

Pressman R. J. and Maxim B. R. (2015) *Software Engineering – A Practitioner's Approach*, 8th Edition, European adaptation, McGraw-Hill International, London.
Royce W. W. (1971) Mapping the development of large scale systems concepts and techniques, in *Proceedings of IEEE WESCON*, August 1970.
Sommerville I. (2015) *Software Engineering*, 10th Edition, Addison Wesley, Harlow, England.

Review questions

D.1 In reference to the SDLC model:

    a. What are the seven basic phases of the development process suggested by the model?

    b. Suggest situations where the number of process phases should be reduced.

    c. Suggest situations where the number of process phases should be increased.

D.2 With respect to the prototyping methodology:

    a. List the conditions necessary for the prototyping model to be applied.

    b. Can you suggest an imaginary project ideally suited for the prototyping methodology?

    c. Can you suggest an imaginary project that is obviously unsuitable for the prototyping methodology?

D.3 With respect to the prototyping methodology:

    a. List the participants in quality assurance activities

    b. Explain the special contribution of each participation group to quality

D.4 The prototyping development process is used in a variety of project environments.

    a. List the advantages prototyping may bring to projects, with the prototype serving as a "throw away" project.

    b. List the advantages of a prototyping project for an active organization when a full-scale software project is expected to be completed in only 12 months.

    c. An agricultural experimental site is expected to follow a new experiment to investigate the effects of irrigation, fertilizers, and shading variations on the crops of several kinds of vegetables. Most measurements should be automatic. The research team comprises eight researchers. The research is planned to start within 2 months and to last for 3 years. Explain why the prototyping development process would be the most suitable?

D.5 Comparing the SDLC and prototyping methodologies.

    a. List the advantages of the prototyping compared with the SDLC methodology for the development of small-to-medium projects.

    b. Explain why the advantages of prototyping cannot be realized for large software systems.

    c. In which ways can prototyping support the development of large-scale projects?

D.6 Referring to the advanced spiral model:

   a. Describe the six activities to be repeated in each iteration of the development process. Explain why the six designated activities are to be repeated in each iteration of the development process.

   b. The advanced spiral model received from its author a second title, "The Win-Win Model." Can you explain this additional title?

D.7 Object-oriented software is based on the class structure.

   a. Explain how the class structure promotes software reuse.

   b. Imagine a software system for managing a large store, which was developed according to the object-oriented model. Can you suggest five classes of the software system with high reuse potential?

   c. Referring to the above-mentioned classes, could you suggest two software systems belonging to different areas that could reuse the particular class for each of the above-mentioned classes?

D.8 A software house is to perform two projects: internal development of a commercial software package, and a custom-made project for long-term customers. The staged model is applied for the development of the commercial software package, while an incremental delivery model is employed for the development of the custom-made project.

   a. Do you support the decision to employ the staged model for the commercial software package?

   b. Do you support the decision to employ the incremental delivery, rather than the SDLC model, for the development of the custom-made project?

D.9 The prototyping model, incremental delivery model, and Agile models employ iterative processes.

   a. Explain the differences in the part iteration in these three development models.

   b. Compare the customer representative's task in each of the three development models.

Topics for discussion

D.1 A software development firm is planning a new and very large-scale airport luggage control project. The system is to control the luggage transfer from the terminal to the planes, from the planes to the terminal's luggage release system, and from plane to plane (for transit passengers). The airport requires the highest reliability for the system, and wishes to initiate several new applications that have yet to be implemented in any other airport.

   a. Two professional consultants recommend using the object-oriented model, but differ regarding their choice of method – Agile versus "traditional" method. What would you suggest as the recommended method? What are your arguments?

   b. Estimate the risk involved in the project. Does it justify the use of the spiral model?

D.2 The software development department employs almost 100 analyzers, designers, and programmers. The department's manager plans to move the department's professional staff from the traditional development methods to an Agile development methodology within the next year. His deputy claims that only half of the teams are suited to be moved to Agile development methods, while the rest should continue to employ the traditional methods.

   a. What are the arguments the department's manager could present?

   b. What are the arguments the deputy could present to support only partial transition to the Agile development method?

D.3 HRS Ltd. is a software house that specializes in human resource management packages sold mainly to small- and medium-sized organizations. Its recruitment management software packages are already very popular.

   a. Which methodology should be applied by HRS? List your arguments.

   b. The company wishes to penetrate the area of custom-made human resource management software systems for large organizations such as banks and government agencies. Which methodology or combination of methodologies would best fit its new needs?

D.4 Software reuse has become an important factor in the software development industry.

   a. Explain the advantages of software reuse.

   b. How can a software development firm get organized to efficiently reuse software?

   c. What similar trends can you identify in manufacturing industries (automobiles, home appliances, etc.)?

D.5 The Agile models and the incremental delivery model adopt the incremental delivery concept.

   a. Explain the differences between these two models.

   b. The head of an Agile development team has decided to double the increment size and deliver software every 8, instead of 4, weeks, claiming an important 50% savings on integration tests. Do you support the team head's decision considering its effect on the team performance and the customer satisfaction?

D.6 Refer to the quality assurance efforts invested in quality assurance activities of the SDLC model and the incremental development process.

   a. Compare the efforts invested in the quality assurance activities of these software development processes.

   b. Explain the reasons for these differences.

   c. Discuss the advantages of the incremental development process.

Author Index

Software Quality: Concepts and Practice, First Edition. Daniel Galin.
© 2018 the IEEE Computer Society, Inc. Published 2018 by John Wiley & Sons, Inc.

Subject Index